Research methodology

HANDBOOK OF
COLLABORATIVE
MANAGEMENT
RESEARCH

HANDBOOK OF COLLABORATIVE MANAGEMENT RESEARCH

A. B. (Rami) Shani
California Polytechnic State University and
FENIX Centre for Innovations in Management

Susan Albers Mohrman
University of Southern California

William A. Pasmore
Oliver Wyman Delta Consulting

Bengt Stymne
Stockholm School of Economics and
Pôle Cindyniques (Sophia Antipolis) Mines Paris

Niclas Adler
Jönköping International Business School and
FENIX Centre for Innovations in Management

SAGE Publications
Los Angeles • London • New Delhi • Singapore

For information:

Sage Publications, Inc.
2455 Teller Road
Thousand Oaks, California 91320
E-mail: order@sagepub.com

Sage Publications Ltd.
1 Oliver's Yard
55 City Road
London EC1Y 1SP
United Kingdom

Sage Publications India Pvt. Ltd.
B 1/I 1 Mohan Cooperative Industrial Area
Mathura Road, New Delhi 110 044
India

Sage Publications Asia-Pacific Pte. Ltd.
33 Pekin Street #02-01
Far East Square
Singapore 048763

Printed in the United States of America

Library of Congress Cataloging-in-Publication Data

Handbook of collaborative management research/editors, A. B. Shani . . . [et al.].
    p. cm.
Includes bibliographical references and indexes.
ISBN 978-1-4129-2624-9 (cloth)
    1. Management—Research—Handbooks, manuals, etc. 2. Research teams—Handbooks, manuals, etc. I. Shani, Abraham B.

HD30.4.H348 2008
658.4'034—dc22   2007011266

This book is printed on acid-free paper.

07   08   09   10   11   10   9   8   7   6   5   4   3   2   1

Acquisitions Editor:	Al Bruckner
Editorial Assistant:	MaryAnn Vail
Production Editor:	Diane S. Foster
Copy Editor:	Halim Dunsky
Typesetter:	C&M Digitals (P) Ltd.
Proofreader:	Scott Oney
Indexer:	Molly Hall
Cover Designer:	Bryan Fishman
Marketing Manager:	Nichole M. Angress

Contents

Preface

If Kurt Lewin was correct that the best way to understand something is to change it, then we ought to have a lot of opportunities to develop new understandings in our 21st-century world, with more on the way. The rate of change and the criticality of developing new knowledge about management and organization have never been greater. The development of a global economy has radically transformed the practice of managing organizations, is introducing change that challenges the viability of long-standing social and governmental practices, and is threatening the global and local ecologies that make possible life and society as we know them. Surely this amount of change brings all kinds of requirements and opportunities to develop greater understanding. And yet, the field of management studies is not adequately responding to the challenges and opportunities that are being presented. Practice is moving far faster than traditional academic approaches to research. Even when scientific breakthroughs occur, their dissemination through publications and executive education programs is painfully slow and not likely to be recognized by the vast majority of managers of organizations and systems. We believe that obtaining superior knowledge about how organizations and systems can be helped to achieve their immediate goals while at the same time advancing the practice of managing complex systems should be of key concern to scientists, managers, policy makers, and citizens.

This *Handbook* reflects our desire as an editorial team to bring attention to a mode of research that tightly links practice and theory development, generating knowledge that builds on established theory and empirical knowledge of the academy but is tightly coupled with the actions that organizations take in real time as they develop solutions. We are advocating a truly combinatorial knowledge-production process—putting knowledge into context, and acknowledging that true advances in understanding, particularly if they are to be more than esoteric academic exercises, require that the knowledge from many fields of the academy and of practice need to be combined if we are to understand and deal with the complexity of the systems that need to change in today's world.

The original idea for this *Handbook* dates back to a 2004 symposium on collaborative research at the annual conference of the Academy of Management. It centered on the insights from a recently published book titled *Collaborative Research in Organizations: Foundations for Learning, Change, and Theoretical Development* (Adler, Shani, & Styhre, 2004). The book captured the insights from five years of ambitious and innovative collaborative research endeavors, most of which were conducted within the context of a long-standing tradition of boundary spanning between management researchers and companies in Sweden. The dialogue with the audience at the symposium triggered the realization that many more academics and practitioners around the globe have been involved in an emerging research paradigm that we label "collaborative management research."

Collaboration is not a new approach to research. Indeed, many of the early advances in management and organizational sciences came from academics who were working very closely with companies that were beginning to rationalize their production and administrative practices (Taylor and scientific management, Mayo and the human relations model, and Trist and Emery and the sociotechnical systems school, for example). These studies involved managers, organization members, and researchers who were investigating issues of mutual interest and resulted in changes in practice at the participating companies and widespread dissemination of the frameworks that resulted. More broadly, it can be argued that over the years, the field of organization development has incorporated collaborative research methods into the diagnostic phase of many of its methodologies.

Research institutes have been set up to house collaborative research, and all of the editors have been associated with such centers. For example, noting that practice was leading theory, and that academic studies were in danger of becoming irrelevant, Edward Lawler in 1979 established the Center for Effective Organizations (CEO) at the University of Southern California for the express purpose of setting up collaborative research relationships. In their foundational book *Doing Research That Is Useful for Theory and Practice* (Lawler, Mohrman, Mohrman, Cummings, & Ledford, 1985), Lawler and the other researchers at CEO argue that the greatest progress in the organizational sciences will occur when researchers bring strong theoretical and empirical perspectives to bear on the problems that companies are actually facing. They also advocate that the research be collaborative, with academics and

practitioners working together with the joint goals of testing and advancing theory while contributing to and studying the changes that companies make to address complex problems. The FENIX Centre in Sweden was established in 1997 and had a similar mission. Its goals were to create a transdisciplinary program of research in management, to intensify collaboration between managers and researchers throughout the research process, to advance theory by linking research and action, to develop new collaborative research methodologies, to deliver scientific training to managers, and to more broadly influence the course of management research in universities. The organizational behavior department at Case Western Reserve University was founded in 1964 by Herb Shepard and became known for its action research and later appreciative inquiry methodologies, which encouraged students and faculty to work closely with organizations and systems in formulating research, theory, and action. Many other centers have been founded in universities and institutes around the world to address complex management problems, in some cases with a purposefully collaborative approach.

We are impressed with the growing influence of research programs that are addressing critical organizational and societal problems and at the same time furthering organizational theory and developing new research methodologies. For example, the collaborative work at Harvard of Wheelwright and Clark about new product development and of Cohen, Gibson, and Mankin at CEO about virtual teams have introduced frameworks that are in use in companies around the world. In England, academics such as Andrew Pettigrew and Paul Bate are applying the knowledge of the organizational sciences to transform the National Health Services and, in the process, engaging in many different research collaborations. Researchers at Case Western Reserve, FENIX, and many other academic institutions are engaging deeply with practitioners to understand, define, and learn how to achieve environmental sustainability. It is safe to say that the kinds of problems that these scholars are dealing with can be neither understood theoretically nor solved without combining theory and practice.

Today, more and more voices in the academic literature are calling for a shift in the way research is conducted. "Contemporary writings in the natural, social, and management sciences indicate some fundamental changes in the social production of knowledge" (Pettigrew, 2004). These changes center on who is involved in the knowledge production process, the types of available knowledge, new settings for data collection, and new opportunities for knowledge dissemination and use. The emerging changes in the nature of knowledge production rest on broad theoretical and empirical arguments that are anchored in the coevolutionary process between science and society (Gibbons et al., 1994; Hatchuel & Glise, 2004). These changes are being contested and debated in the natural, social, and managerial sciences. The historical model of research, in which the experimenter completely controls the variables that affect experimental outcomes, is still the dominant paradigm. Against this paradigm, researchers in the social sciences have learned that there can be no best way in which to frame, produce, disseminate, and use knowledge (Pettigrew, 2004). Moreover, we have begun to recognize that the methodologies and technologies that exist at a certain point in time are inadequate for addressing all the problems that are experienced at that moment, not to mention challenges that will appear in the future. The current millennium's social science concerns are increasingly focused on phenomena that are caused by complex interactions among variables that are not easily controlled by an experimenter. In these situations, it is recognized that methodologies will be required take into account such factors as human beliefs, aspirations, and whims. We believe that collaborative approaches to management research are an integral part of the emerging paradigms of research.

We (the editors) began our journey with the basic belief that broader and deeper collaboration between academic researchers, managers of organizations, union leaders (when they are a part of the system), management consultants, and other stakeholders can yield significant benefits to all parties involved. Researchers would have access to organizations to discover and test new theories and hypotheses, thereby advancing knowledge and using it to enhance undergraduate, graduate, and executive education. Managers would learn much more about how organizations function and new approaches to managing complex systems, thereby improving their individual and organizational performance. Managers, union leaders, and other stakeholders would learn how to enhance partnerships, and management consultants would gain access to new management knowledge and models that could become the basis for their practices—a key way that such knowledge becomes widely disseminated. Our discovery is that collaborative management research is even more powerful than we initially envisioned.

What we did not realize at the time we began this effort was how much we would learn about collaborative management research from our colleagues who have contributed manuscripts to this volume and how much we would learn from one another as editors. In essence, our collective efforts have begun to build a global collaborative research community that is framing the field of study, describing its evolution, illuminating its scientific discovery mechanisms, and shaping its present and future direction. The 30 chapters in this *Handbook* were written by 82 authors, conducting collaborative management research in

13 countries, involving a wide variety of organizations and systems, in diverse industries and regions. Researchers involved in these studies came from 20 different universities and eight different research, training, or consulting institutions. The rich and diverse set of projects reviewed here, seen through the lenses of a multidisciplinary group of researchers, led to the discovery that our contributors have very different ideas about what constitutes collaborative management research. Nevertheless, all share a common belief in the merit of collaborative management research as a scientific discovery process that generates knowledge relevant to both science and practice.

We have had internal debates about the wisdom of calling this collaborative *management* research. Some of us were focused on for-profit organizations, while others were concerned about broader community, regional, and global issues. In some of these larger, more complex systems, it would be difficult to identify who the "manager" of the system is; and yet, the processes that shape how these systems operate can be influenced and therefore, to some extent, "managed." We decided to use the term *management* to refer to intentional efforts to influence a system (any system) toward its purposes and goals. Actors of all kinds, individuals and groups, aspire to *influence* the behavior or performance of a given organization, and thus are engaged in managing the system, even if they are not officially designated as "managers."

Researchers are actors who aspire to *understand* and explain these same systems. Collaborative management research looks upon knowledge creation as a joint undertaking between researchers and managers. The basic premise is that scientific discourse is likely to benefit from the perspective of those applying management theories, and that managerial practice will benefit from more systematic research regarding which methods produce improvements in the operation of complex systems.

As this *Handbook* will demonstrate, collaborative management research requires skills and methodologies that may be new to the traditional researcher. Creating productive collaborative research partnerships that produce mutual benefits for scientists and practitioners requires that a great deal of effort be put into the relationship between the parties, the formulation of research plans and methods, and the interpretation, application, and diffusion of results. As it turns out, these things are more easily said than done. Despite these hurdles, we believe that collaborative management research provides perhaps the most promising new approach to advancing knowledge of how to make organizations and systems more effective in an increasingly competitive and chaotic (some would say dangerous) world.

Existing research methods have not provided the needed knowledge, and while there is no guarantee that collaborative management research will do so either, it is our hope that this new collection of methodologies will advance our ability to make the contributions to knowledge and practice that are so badly needed. We consider the development of sound approaches to collaborative research to be a work in progress. Toward that end, this *Handbook* offers both theoretical contributions and empirically based findings about the ways in which collaborative management research can be designed and managed. Our contributors provide guidance concerning a variety of ways to build boundary-spanning knowledge-creation processes through new types of partnerships, and they offer empirical results that were obtained through interventions in organizations and complex systems. From working with individuals to groups to organizations and regions, our contributors have demonstrated the usefulness of collaborative management research methods in a wide variety of settings.

This *Handbook* is a stimulus for continued dialogue, rather than a complete description of the methodology. Our wish is that students of management and organization studies, academics, managers, union leaders, consultants, policy makers, and change agents will find it to be a valuable resource for research, learning, reflection, and practice. Our purpose will have been achieved if the dialogue begun here continues and collaborative research approaches evolve and become much more common, thus stimulating further application of these methods to organizational and global issues.

REFERENCES

Adler, N., Shani, A. B. (Rami), & Styhre, A. (2004). *Collaborative research in organizations: Foundations for learning, change, and theoretical development.* Thousand Oaks, CA: Sage.

Gibbons, M., Limoges, L., Nowotny, H., Schwartman, S., Scott, P., & Trow, M. (1994). *The new production of knowledge: The dynamics of science and research in contemporary societies.* London: Sage.

Hatchuel, A., & Glise, H. (2004). Rebuilding management. In N. Adler, A. B. (Rami) Shani, & A. Styhre (Eds.), *Collaborative research in organizations: Foundations for learning, change, and theoretical development* (pp. 5–22). Thousand Oaks, CA: Sage.

Lawler, E., Mohrman, A. M., Mohrman, S. A., Cummings, T., & Ledford, G. (Eds.). (1985). *Doing research that is useful for theory and practice.* San Francisco: Jossey-Bass.

Pettigrew, A. M. (2004). Some challenges of collaborative research. In N. Adler, A. B. (Rami) Shani, & A. Styhre (Eds.), *Collaborative research in organizations: Foundations for learning, change, and theoretical development* (pp. xv–xviii). Thousand Oaks, CA: Sage.

Dedications and Acknowledgments

All knowledge builds on the pillars that have been established by those who came before. We dedicate this book to many sage individuals whose work helped shape us and our deep concern with collaborative research. We clearly cannot name all those whose work was instrumental in the shaping of our views and professional aspirations, but we will name a few in honor of the many.

- Kurt Lewin, for his pioneering work in action research.
- Herbert Simon, for introducing and evolving the notion of the sciences of the artificial.
- Eric Rhenman, whose work helped shape the Scandinavian School of Management and its collaborative management research approach.
- Einar Thorsrud, who, with Fred Emery, Eric Trist, and other Tavistock researchers, initiated collaboration between researchers, unions, and industry in the democratization of working life.
- Yvonna Lincoln and Egon Guba, who helped us understand just how collaborative research can and should be, and made it clear that while there is a place for objective and detached research in the sciences, there is just as important a place for inquiry that involves collaboration.

We also acknowledge and thank institutions where we have been privileged to carry out our work and test our ideas. In many cases, the very existence of these institutions was the work of one or more visionary individuals. Heartfelt thanks go to the following:

- The Department of Organizational Behavior in the Weatherhead School of Management at Case Western Reserve University, for the faculty's willingness to support innovative approaches to research and intense collaboration with organizations as a way of helping people learn how complex systems really work. It has provided a remarkable environment for ongoing stimulating discussions about scientific inquiry and learning in and around the workplace.
- The Stockholm School of Economics (SSE), which has always engaged with Swedish industry. Under the leadership of Per Jonas Eliaeson, the school entered a long-lasting relationship with the Chalmers University of Technology by establishing IMIT (the Institute for Management of Innovation and Technology), with the expressed aim of carrying out collaborative research with industry and researchers in both management and engineering.
- Flemming Norrgren and Horst Hart, who, despite many challenges, have protected, developed, and established the collaborative management research agenda in Sweden through the Gothenburg Centre for Work Sciences, the Centre for Organizational Renewal (CORE), and the FENIX Centre for Innovations in Management.
- The Center for Effective Organizations (CEO) at the University of Southern California and its founder, Edward Lawler, who bucked the U.S. trend toward purely positivistic research and set up an institution dedicated to collaborative research in pursuit of advances in theory and practice.

- The Center for Management Studies, CGS at l'Écoles des Mines de Paris under the leadership of Armand Hatchuel, for their continuous innovative and inspiring work to push the boundaries of collaborative management research.
- Mercer Delta Consulting for continuing to value research as a part of consulting.
- The Management Group at Orfalea College of Business, CalPoly, who provided the support and inspiration in searching for ways to bring management practice into academic programs and in the continuous search for the integration of theory and practice via the "learning by doing" philosophical orientation.

We are also grateful to Hilary Bradbury and Peter Reason, who have established a journal and edited handbooks that build a community of practice in the area of action research. Similarly, the establishment of *Human Relations* by the Tavistock institute, and Dick Woodman's leadership and dedication first as coeditor of the long-standing series *Research on Organizational Change and Development* and more recently as editor of the *Journal of Applied Behavioral Science,* have played a large role in providing publishing outlets for this work, and thus in making it possible for it to be carried out by academics.

We also thank the many, many companies with which we have been privileged to work. There are far too many to list, but rest assured that we understand that collaborative research can only occur if there are individuals in companies willing to pioneer this approach, and interested in finding out what companies and academics can do together to make work and society better for all.

We have been blessed with incredible colleagues, only some of whom are represented among the authors in this volume. There are far too many to list, but you know who you are. Having collaborated, we carry around a bit of each other as we proceed through life.

We are grateful that our work and lives have intersected.

Books are clearly not produced without collaboration with our very critical colleagues who help behind the scenes and make everything go so much more smoothly than it would if only academics were involved. Special recognition goes to

- Anita Söderberg-Carlsson, at SSE, for managing the project and the manuscript, and for dealing with the numerous contingencies that are bound to happen in a project containing 82 authors and 30 contributions.
- Arienne McCracken, at CEO, for managing our Web site, which turned out to be a dynamic and well-used communication device for authors and editors.
- Kelly Olsson for her contribution as a linguistic editor. In this undertaking, comprising contributions of scholars from many countries, Kelly Olsson has done a much-appreciated job by ensuring that the authors' ideas will be readily discerned.

Our Sage editor (pun intended), Al Bruckner, has been tremendously important to this project, first by encouraging us to edit a handbook on this topic, and then by arguing persuasively for getting it out in a timely fashion. We are grateful to him for both contributions, as well as for his many substantive ideas and suggestions.

We are grateful to our authors, who delivered multiple drafts of contributions in support of our concern for the coherence of the book and our desire for the readers of this book to benefit from the rich experience and knowledge of each. Thank you to these many busy people for the timely and responsive turnaround of these contributions.

And finally, we acknowledge each other. In this process we have learned—about the topic of the book, collaborative management research; about collaboration across cultures, continents, time zones, institutional bases, and life stages; and about ourselves and the limitations of our own assumptions. During this project, our team members have experienced births and deaths, and countless other transitions and traumas that are part of life. We are grateful to our families, who have borne the extra strain with us. We feel enriched by having worked together on this project for the past two years—and we, too, will happily carry a bit of each other with us as we proceed to our next opportunities and challenges.

List of Tables

List of Figures

Part I

FRAMING THE ISSUES

OVERCOMING THE SEPARATION

Management research and management practice have become too far separated from each other. Collaborative research between management science and management practice can bring these areas closer together and make them mutually reinforcing. The focus of this handbook is on how collaborative management research can be accomplished and its potential yields. The first chapter in the framing section of the book, "The Promise of Collaborative Management Research," provides some points of departure by discussing the meaning of the three concepts *collaborative*, *management*, and *research*. In addition, that chapter contains an orientation to the other parts and the individual chapters in this *Handbook*.

In addition to the first chapter, Part I consists of the four chapters listed at the top of Table I.1. They present four high-level visions for collaborative research, what each requires of the management researcher, how each can be carried out, and what payoffs can be claimed for the scientist and for the practitioner.

All four chapters assume that management science has a relevancy problem. As is explained in the chapter by Werr and Greiner, academic management research has become too self-referential. The relevance criteria are set and controlled by members of the community of management researchers itself, including the editors of the scientific journals in management and the senior professors that review doctoral dissertations. Formal aspects of traditional research, such as following a certain research protocol or using formalized language, are given great attention by members of the academic community. In the absence of a relevance criterion situated outside the community of management researchers, subdisciplines can create their own criteria of relevance, which in turn leads to a fractionalization of the field. Adopting *relevance for management practice* as a criterion would make the problem of self-referencing controls less serious. Werr and Greiner suggest a number of actions that could strengthen the importance of relevance for practice as a criterion for management research, such as requiring that a section for management implications be included in articles published in scientific management journals.

Table I.1   Four Approaches to Collaboration Between Management Research and Practice

	David & Hatchuel, From Actionable Knowledge to Universal Theory in Management Research	Tenkasi & Hay, Following the Second Legacy of Aristotle: The Scholar-Practitioner as an Epistemic Technician	Bartunek, Insider/Outsider Team Research	Werr & Greiner, Collaboration and the Production of Management Knowledge
Form of collaboration	Contract defining scientific aims. Longterm empirical studies.	Scholar-practitioner carries out a consultancy project.	A team of insiders collaborates with, outside researcher to publish, accounts that give, a better public understanding of the setting.	Establishment of a collaborative, knowledge-creating triad of practitioners, consultants, and researcher.
Essential researcher skills	Theoretical thinking. Skills in field research.	Consultancy skills. Good command of existing theories.	Skills of team building, trust creation, and handling conflicts with insiders.	Conventional researcher skills that in fact could provide value to managers and consultants.
Payoff for management science	Discovery of new management models.	Feeling for what is relevant in practice. Possibility of applying models.	More and richer data that can be used for comparative studies.	Access to research site. Possibility of testing hypotheses. Access to consultants' broad experience.
Payoff for practice	A new model for dealing with changing business conditions. Better understanding of the way the organization operates.	Better-grounded consulation.	Better-grounded understanding of the setting. Feeling of confidence.	Ensuring quality of management knowledge. New understanding and inspiration.

As Tenkasi and Hay point out, the split between science and practice can be traced back to Aristotle. *Episteme*, pure science, is to be regarded as a kind of knowledge that is more valuable than practical knowledge, which is influenced by the limited experience of the practical man and by politics. However, Tenkasi and Hay point out that Aristotle also had a second vision of what constitutes valuable knowledge. That knowledge is *phronesis*, wisdom, which is grounded on a complex of *empeiria* (experience), *techne* (practice), and *episteme* (theory). The program of collaborative research can be seen as a fulfillment of Aristotle's second conception of useful knowledge. It is personified in the scholar-practitioner, a management researcher who is also an accomplished consultant. Tenkasi and Hay studied eleven researchers in this role. It is interesting to note that in all these cases but one, the services provided by the scholar-practitioner were contracted for as "consultation," and no preliminary agreement about conducting research was made.

FORMS OF COLLABORATIVE RESEARCH

Of the four chapters, David and Hatchuel's is closest to Aristotle's first vision of knowledge. The authors see the discovery of new management models as the most valuable knowledge that management research could produce. The discovery or invention of a new model requires close interaction with a pioneering organization. The authors emphasize that it is essential that the contract between the researchers and their partners in collaboration specify that the project aims at the discovery of a new model. In David and Hatchuel's view, a requirement for the implementation of the model does not have to be included in the contract. The practitioners have to draw their own conclusions from the discoveries of the joint research project and act upon them.

The other three chapters in Part I are more in the tradition of Aristotle's second vision, which involves a blending of theory, methodology, and practical wisdom. Bartunek's chapter describes an approach she and others call an *insider/outsider research team*. A research team including both members of the focal organization and outside researchers is formed. The task is usually to gain an understanding of how the organization functions and the sources of problems it may be experiencing. The outsiders are often able to provide a more detached view than the insiders of what is going on; they can help in designing the research process and draw parallels to other research in similar situations. The insiders can provide rich data on their own organization as well as interpretations of unfolding events.

Werr and Greiner's chapter compares the relationship between management researchers and practice with that of consultants and practice. They conclude that both consultants and management researchers have strong and weak sides in relation to practice. The weak sides of each could be compensated for by the other party's strong sides. The authors therefore suggest a metamodel for collaborative research based on a triad consisting of researchers, consultants, and practitioners.

ESSENTIAL RESEARCHER SKILLS

The different chapters of Part I emphasize different skills that are required for researchers engaging in each type of collaboration discussed. David and Hatchuel's researchers need skills in theoretical thinking and model creation. They also need the skill of interpreting detailed empirical work in terms of theoretical constructs. In this interpretation process they can of course be greatly helped by their collaborators from practice.

Since scholar-practitioners act as consultants, they need the social skills required of a consultant in addition to their research skills. Tenkasi and Hay devote a large part of their chapter to describing how skillfully scholar-practitioners they studied used theory as an instrument in their consulting. These individuals used management theories for framing, that is, for deciding the character of the client's problem. They also used theories for influencing and legitimating the suggestions that they wanted to promote. Still another use of theories by the scholar-practitioners was in sense making in discussions during which consultants and practitioners jointly tried to understand what they had learned.

Bartunek's insider/outsider research approach puts special focus on the skills needed to handle the intergroup dynamics and tensions that sometimes make collaboration between researchers and practitioners very difficult. Although Werr and Greiner talk less about specific skills required for collaborative research, they show how traditional research skills such as analytical capability, knowledge of theory, and understanding different methodologies could be very useful when combined with consultants' skills in joint projects.

PAYOFFS FOR SCIENCE

Collaborative management research holds the potential to enhance the payoffs for science as well as for practice. Beginning with the benefits to practice, Werr and Greiner cite research results that indicate that academics who spend more time in organizations report greater personal learning and a higher frequency of citations for their publications (Rynes, McNatt, & Bretz, 1999). They also find that academics' involvement in organizations increases the likelihood that their findings will be implemented by practitioners.

David and Hatchuel talk about the discovery or invention of new actionable theories in the form of management models. A management model consists of a theoretical-philosophical explanation of how organizational systems function and a set of instruments and methods that should be used to influence the outcomes of activities within the system. It is a prescription for collective action. To the extent that science advances as its models become more robust and more widely applicable, collaborative management research benefits science by offering a way to develop and test theories in a more direct and timely fashion.

All the chapters in Part I emphasize that collaboration will provide the researcher with more information about, and understanding of, practice. This understanding will facilitate the formulation of research problems that are better grounded in, and more relevant for, practice. In addition, due to the close relationships that evolve between academics and practitioners in collaborative research, scientists are likely to have access to otherwise inaccessible aspects of organizational life. Finally, as the chapters in this volume demonstrate, collaborative management research is contributing new methodologies for the collection of data that could be useful in other fields of inquiry.

PAYOFFS FOR PRACTICE

The chapters in the framing part of the book provide many arguments for why collaborative research creates value for practice. David and Hatchuel present a compelling chain of reasoning. They start with an observation that can be made by anyone familiar with business and industrial history. The observation is that new, actionable management models have triggered revolutions in business and industrial practice and contributed to increased efficiency and effectiveness. Some of these new management models have been discovered or diffused by management scientists such as Frederick Taylor, who originated *scientific management*, Elton Mayo, who spread the *human relations* approach, and Alfred Chandler, who described the *divisional form of organization*. Other important actionable management models such as *just-in-time inventory* have been invented by industry, sometimes assisted by consultants. Still others seem to have emerged over long periods of time, such as the *assembly line,* which was first put into practice in the Arsenal of Venice in the 15th and 16th centuries. Even if management scientists were not directly involved in the invention and discovery of these models, they have helped to improve them by adding to their theoretical underpinnings and their associated instrumentation and methodological apparatus. The second step in David and Hatchuel's reasoning is that the invention and early discovery of new management models requires a close, long-term collaboration between a firm and a research team. Discovery of a new management model is a bit like discovering America or making an egg stand on its top: it looks simple when you see the result, but arriving there may involve considerable accurate observation, logical reasoning, planned experimentation, trial and error, and creative thinking.

Not all management research will be pathbreaking, but the chapters in this first part of the book point to some advantages that even more mundane collaborative research can contribute to practice. One is that the involvement of researchers in the study of organizational issues may provide alternative perspectives on the problems and new solutions for consideration. Another is that collaborative research methods like the insider/outsider model may help to educate members of the system in how the system actually operates, allowing them to create more effective approaches to accomplishing objectives of interest. A third benefit derives from the researchers' analytical skills, which may help practitioners draw more insightful conclusions about causes of events or the likely consequences of different lines of action. A fourth benefit is that scientists can bring the latest thinking in the literature to managers, so that they can choose whether or not to adopt practices that have worked for others.

PAYOFFS FOR THE READER

The chapters in Part I help to set the stage for what follows in this *Handbook*. By defining the field, examining the roles of the parties involved in collaborative management research, and discussing its strengths and benefits, these thoughtful chapters will prepare the reader to get the most out of those that follow. Scientists should find many ideas in Part I that stimulate invention, call for further research, or pose challenges to conducting collaborative research efforts. Practitioners should catch glimpses of how their partnership in collaborative research efforts could benefit their organizations and of what makes for productive and satisfying relationships with scientists. Although this approach to studying and improving organizations is still evolving, the chapters in Part I make it clear that a great deal of thought has gone into this approach already and that we are poised to reap the benefits of the work done by those who have led the way.

REFERENCE

Rynes, S. L., McNatt, B. D., & Bretz, R. D. (1999). Academic research inside organizations: Inputs, processes, and outcomes. *Personal Psychology, 52*(4), 869–899.

CHAPTER 1

The Promise of Collaborative Management Research

WILLIAM A. PASMORE

BENGT STYMNE

A. B. (RAMI) SHANI

SUSAN ALBERS MOHRMAN

NICLAS ADLER

As editors of the *Handbook of Collaborative Management Research,* we began this project with a firm belief based on our experience that broader and deeper collaboration between managers of organizations and academic researchers could yield significant benefits for both parties. Managers would learn much more about how organizations function and new approaches to managing complex systems, thereby improving their individual and organizational performance. Researchers would have access to organizations to discover and test new theories and hypotheses, thereby advancing knowledge and using it to enhance undergraduate, graduate, and executive education. What we didn't realize at the time was how much we would learn about collaborative management research from each other and from our colleagues who have contributed chapters to this volume. As we began work on the editorial statement and guidelines for the book, we quickly realized that we held different ideas of what collaborative management research entailed.

As we tried to define what we meant by management and collaboration, we disagreed on some basic points. Did management include both profit and nonprofit organizations? Did it include the "management" of systems that weren't even formal organizations, such as regional economies? Did it address issues that "managers" as discrete individual actors could influence, or did it address "management" issues that groups of people shared some collective responsibility for, even if they didn't view themselves as managers? And what did we mean by "collaboration"? How intense, extended, and personal did the relationship need to be before it qualified as collaborative? Did the sharing of decisions about research objectives, methods, and conclusions need to be determined equally by both parties, or was it enough for organizations to simply open their doors to academics? What exactly differentiated an in-depth case study from something that we would consider legitimate collaborative management research?

We were all involved in some way with an ongoing program between universities and organizations in Sweden (the FENIX Centre) in which major corporations sent individuals to be trained as organizational researchers as they worked with faculty to undertake research projects in their own organizations. The projects were conducted within the context of a long Scandinavian tradition of boundary-spanning collaboration between management researchers and companies. The logic behind the program is that by training managers to be researchers while undertaking different forms of collaborative research projects, the gap between academia and organizations can be bridged. Certainly, the founders of the program believed that managerial researchers would choose topics of great relevance to their companies and that companies in turn would find the results of their research compelling. Recently, in a book titled *Collaborative Research in Organizations: Foundations for Learning, Change, and Theoretical Development*, the FENIX community captured the learning from its first five years of leading and participating in some very ambitious and innovative collaborative research endeavors (Adler, Shani, & Styhre, 2004).

The FENIX Centre will be represented in the work of several authors in this volume, so we won't go into more detail about it at the moment. The point is simply that the program created a mindset for us about what collaborative management research is, and set implicit standards against which we initially assessed other efforts.

When we began receiving manuscripts from our contributing authors covering the theory and practice of collaborative management research, we were confronted by a much broader view of what collaborative management research currently entails. We were forced to question our narrow view and opened ourselves up to the possibility that the project would be much more informative and challenging than we first imagined. We also recalibrated our assessment of progress in the field. Despite the best efforts of many of the contributors to this volume and their managerial collaborators, the practice of collaborative management research is neither well defined nor widely practiced. We see this as natural for an emergent and promising research approach. There are intriguing possibilities for the development of future modes of collaboration as we build upon the knowledge accumulated to date. The challenge involved is to continue to develop the research approach, its epistemological foundation, its research methods, and its institutional anchoring in scientific journals and textbooks. That a study is "collaborative research" is not a justification for its claims to scientific and practical relevance if it is poorly conducted. Poorly conducted studies may further erode the trust and confidence that managers have in academics to contribute relevant and timely insights in return for the support that managers provide for research.

There are important issues here. We are of the firm belief that more collaborative research can help to improve the relevance of two fields that are the targets of much criticism. *Management* and its practitioners are criticized in the public debate and in scholarly writings for acting irrationally based on unfounded beliefs and imitation (Pfeffer & Sutton, 2006). *Management science* and the researchers it engages are criticized for producing knowledge of little or no relevance for management practice (Ghoshal, 2005; Hoffman, 2004). We are convinced that there are ample opportunities for improvement of this situation. Management, based on better knowledge and appreciation of the specific contexts in which it acts, could contribute to socially more useful goods and less waste of resources. Management research, based on a better appreciation of management practice and the challenges it faces, could contribute to better-grounded actions and more relevant theories.

The argument for collaborative management research, at a basic level, is that by bringing management and researchers closer together, the rate of progress in understanding and addressing issues such as innovation, growth, change, organizational effectiveness, and economic development will be faster than if either managers or researchers approach these topics separately. Managers are continuously acting out models of good management but are not always aware of where the models came from, how they were developed, whether they are robust, or whether they fit the current circumstances. Management scientists are continuously building new models while keenly observing what is going on in the world of business. If the two groups join forces they will have the components necessary for faster and more relevant knowledge creation: model building, testing out models, observing consequences, and analyses of cause and effect. Closed groups and systems do not easily change or innovate. Left on their own, managers might continue to develop local solutions to organizational issues that do not draw upon the vast shared knowledge that exists, in an uncoordinated fashion and without the benefit of the latest thinking on the topic. The result would be to reinvent the wheel, misdirect or suboptimize the application of organizational resources, and ultimately achieve slower progress. On the other hand, left to their own devices, researchers could frame questions with no practical significance, draw erroneous conclusions from data, or suggest remedies that are entirely impractical. In theory at least, bringing together managers with practical experience and urgent needs with academics who are in touch with accumulated wisdom and possess the capacity for research-driven innovation should be a win-win situation for both, as well as for society at large.

This is not a new thought. In one of the chapters in this volume (Chapter 3), Tenkasi and Hay draw upon Socrates for guidance that is extremely relevant to the conduct of collaborative research today. As several of our other authors note, efforts at collaborative management research in the early part of the 20th century produced innovations ranging from time and motion studies (Taylor, 1911) to high performance work systems (Trist & Bamforth, 1951) to human relations at work (Roethlisberger & Dickson, 1939). These efforts were not formulated with an explicit intention of undertaking collaborative research; they were simply natural evolutions of existing collaborative relationships that led to groundbreaking projects with benefits to both the organizations involved and the field of management more broadly. It is only now as we look back on these efforts that we can see in each how perfectly the context for collaboration was created, even though it seemed so effortless that it was given almost no attention at the time.

In the intervening decades, collaborative management research has continued, as evidenced by many of the chapters in this volume. At the same time, the academic field of management research has grown and developed, using a mix of research methodologies that are more or less collaborative. By sheer volume and influence within academic circles, less-collaborative research has become the dominant mode, leading to current concerns that management research and thinking have become too theoretical and of less interest to managers (Huff, 2000). It is as if a large part of the field has lost touch with its roots, its audience, or perhaps both. Several of our authors note that the criteria for success in the fields of management and management research have diverged, with short-term profitability issues dominating the minds of managers, while publishing articles in the proper journals (whether or not they deal with issues important to managers) is the primary goal for academics (e.g., Werr & Greiner, Chapter 5; Roth, Chapter 17). As a result, it is the exception rather than the rule today that conditions optimal for conducting collaborative management research develop spontaneously. Instead, much is required on the part of both parties to justify the expenditures involved, defend against critics who hold other measures of performance to be more important, and overcome the many forces that impede or limit the dissemination of knowledge (see Pasmore, Woodman, & Simmons, Chapter 27, and other chapters in this volume).

Management science and research have undoubtedly made contributions that have had a profound impact on management practice. Academics have been instrumental in developing accounting practices that form the skeleton upon which the rest of the economic system is constructed. Operations research has contributed to the organization of production and logistics, applied psychology to methods of marketing, and advanced mathematical modeling has been instrumental for the emergence of an integrated global financial system. However, as research in a certain area of management matures into a scientific subdiscipline, the gap between practice and research widens. The result today is that astonishingly little cross-fertilization takes place between the universes of management

practice and management research. Management research has become more of a closed system that is governed by relevance criteria developed internally based on idealized images of the natural sciences. Demonstrated practical usefulness is not required for research publication, and research aiming at improving the effectiveness of a particular organization may even be frowned upon by those who believe research should remain detached from those who are studied. In some of the contributions here, such as those of Roth (Chapter 17) and Knights, Alferoff, Starkey, and Tiratsoo (Chapter 19), the debate has been raised to an institutional level as universities struggle with the tensions raised by the acceptance of corporate-funded research that threatens to hijack research agendas. Incidentally, the natural sciences struggle with the same issues concerning corporate funding, but the point is still the same: Any type of relationship between those studied and the researchers involved raises the question of whether scientists can remain completely objective.

The value of objective research to the management science community is obvious. The goal of management science is to explain how managed systems function, which requires sorting out popular myths or cultural beliefs from actual underlying causes of events or outcomes. The value of objective research to managers might not be as clear initially but is just as important in the end. Management practice has always been based on past experience, trial and error, and what is "acceptable practice" inside an organization or system. Management is often based on idealized images of leadership, imitations of others, and the adoption of management fads. If "accepted practice" is in fact based on incorrect assumptions or beliefs, this can create inefficiency, malfunctioning, or even the demise of organizations over time. The result is waste in the larger economic system and unnecessary human suffering in social systems. Management action anchored in more careful and realistic appreciation of the situation and context of the managed system can bring more success at less cost. Management research that fulfills the criterion of practical relevance will have greater possibilities to make a difference for practice, that is, will in fact contribute to better management and higher goal fulfillment of organizations and other managed social and economic systems.

We are convinced that collaborative research spanning management science and management practice can be beneficial to both parties. Management action can be guided by tested models, systematic evaluation of present practices, and analyses of relevant information. Management research can discover, develop, and validate better models based on careful observation of the consequences of management actions. Together, practicing managers and management researchers can engage in joint reflection that clarifies the actual situation, the prior experience that might be applicable, the indicators and dimensions that would be relevant and useful to apply when evaluating progress, and the broader knowledge that could be applied to achieve greater success. Preliminary studies and experiments could be designed and carried out to obtain more information on key uncertainties before decisions are made, resources committed, and final approaches launched. Information about the consequences of actions can be gathered and interpreted through joint efforts and give inspiration for new management strategies and scientific explanations.

To advance our understanding of management, we need to conduct research that is more insightful, influential, and immediately applicable. For this, in turn, we need greater collaboration between management and researchers, which is not always easy to achieve. The promise of collaborative management research is that it will produce more powerful and applicable solutions to some of our most pressing organizational and societal issues. Whether or not we are capable of undertaking efforts of sufficient magnitude to fulfill the promise remains to be seen.

Despite the potential benefits of collaboration, the contributions in this volume attest to the difficulty associated with creating and maintaining collaborative relationships that support significant, sustainable research leading to transformations in organizational performance and meaningful additions to the body of scholarly knowledge. The challenges of collaborative management research only intensify as we increase the scope of concern from understanding single organizations to understanding complex networks of organizations and even societies. As more players with vested interests enter the equation and the stakes become higher, achieving progress becomes more difficult. Improving productivity in a single organization is difficult, but achieving better outcomes for a region, segment of society, or entire industry is a daunting task.

A pessimist might argue that the most important issues facing the world today are the least amenable to collaborative resolution. We take a view that is both more optimistic and pragmatic. Optimistically, we believe that, given time and continued effort, the field of collaborative management research will overcome current obstacles in order to make a greater contribution to management at the individual, organizational, and societal levels. Pragmatically, we would argue that many of our most vexing challenges can only be resolved by research that is truly collaborative, because collaboration is required to both understand and change the dynamics underlying complex systems. In this introductory chapter, we discuss the importance of collaborative management research, define the scope of our endeavor, and preview some of the exciting ideas readers will find between the covers of this book.

FRAMING THE ISSUES

The first section of the book helps us understand the nature of collaborative management research. From our perspective, we believe it is important to understand what it is that we are addressing here and, just as important, what we are not. The phrase "collaborative management research" is not universally understood or applied in a uniform fashion by managers and academic researchers. If we deconstruct the phrase, we gain insights into a field of endeavor that is only beginning to come into sharper focus.

Collaborative

By *collaborative* we intend to signify research efforts that include the active involvement of managers and researchers in the framing of the research agenda, the selection and pursuit of methods, and the development of implications for action. Our definition of *collaborative* does not impose the requirement of an equal partnership in each of these activities, although we understand that a more equal partnership would be ideal (see Lincoln & Guba, 1985, and Reason, 1988, for a discussion of the benefits of collaborative inquiry). At the heart of this endeavor is "collective inquiry," which is the joint pursuit of answers to questions of mutual interest through dialogue, experimentation, the review of knowledge, or other means. To be more precise, management engages in collective inquiry in order to get a better understanding of a certain issue or phenomenon by means of input of scientifically valid knowledge from researchers. Similarly, scientists engage in collective inquiry in order to get a better understanding

of a certain issue or phenomenon by means of knowledge regarding practice from managers. If two parties don't share a fundamental interest in learning, there can be no collective inquiry and no collaborative research. We should note here that the parties may be motivated by different aspirations. Managers may desire quick fixes to pressing organizational problems while researchers care more about generalizable solutions to widespread issues. Still, if there is a coming together of interests to learn about some phenomenon occurring in the organization, collective inquiry may be not only possible but also the best means for achieving the aspirations of both.

Collaborative research goes beyond collective inquiry because inquiry itself does not require collection and analysis of external data in addition to data that the interlocutors possess in their heads or close at hand. A well-performed professional medical consultation is an illustration of what a collective inquiry could be. The patient tells the M.D. how his ailment developed and his symptoms and feelings, while the doctor gives a recommendation to the patient based on what she hears, based on her former experience and what she has read. The patient may walk away from the meeting with new insights into his troubles and how he could deal with them. The doctor may be left with not only payment but also an insight that could lead to testing new insights about how to treat other patients. A powerful example of collective inquiry in the context of management is Chris Argyris's method of engaging managers in a conversation that helps them understand how their single-loop reasoning chains them and how double-loop learning can permit them to find creative new ways of acting (see Werr & Greiner, Chapter 5, and Argyris & Schön, 1982).

We think of *collective inquiry* as the core activity that takes place in the study of a single organization or system, as managers and management researchers seek to understand the naturally occurring or intentionally induced effects of different organizational arrangements on behavior and performance. As scientists like Argyris and Freud have shown, the inquiry process can itself generate scientifically useful data that result in radical reorientations of practice, methodology, and theory. The collective inquiry process may often be extended into a process of collaborative research. There are two reasons for such an extension. One is to avoid the cognitive traps of reflexivity and superstitious learning stemming from groupthink and the confusion of causes and effects that easily take place in a closed system. A second is to be able to benefit from the experience of others and the greater variability of larger systems. *Collaborative research* concerns the dual and intermingled processes that are going on as an organization is undergoing development by adopting new structures and processes while researchers attempt to provide knowledge, which is not readily accessible in the organization, from scientific sources or by gathering and analyzing observations.

The scholarly knowledge can be about the process through which organizations undergo inquiry and development or it can be about content: the frameworks, solutions, and features that lead to a system being more effective in accomplishing its goals and fulfilling the aspirations of its stakeholders—and the boundary conditions, which are requisite features of such approaches. More about this when we discuss what we mean by "research."

Different degrees of collaboration are possible, and we see examples of this throughout this volume. At one extreme, collaboration may be limited to access to an organization for data collection, with minimal interest on the part of the manager in framing the questions, methods, and conclusions of the research. Certainly, there is some threshold below which collaboration is no longer genuine, and

we should at that point cease to describe the effort as collaborative research. At the other extreme is collaborative research that seeks not only to produce knowledge but also to fundamentally transform a system via the research process. In these efforts, collaboration is a necessity and occurs broadly, deeply, and almost continuously over the course of the project. In between these two extremes are instances of selective collaboration, in which only a few members of management are deeply engaged in collaborative inquiry activities around a narrow topic, usually without there being a strong agenda to transform the entire organization in fundamental ways.

Collaborative management research is therefore defined as *an emergent and systematic inquiry process,* embedded in an agreed-upon *partnership* between actors with an interest in influencing a certain system of action and researchers interested in understanding and explaining such systems. The collaborative research process integrates scientific knowledge, methods, and values with practical knowledge, ways of working, and values. One aim for the new knowledge generated through the collaborative process is that it should be actionable for those who in practice intend to influence the system. Another aim is that the researchers should be able to claim that it is scientifically relevant and useful for the development of their field.

The collaborative research process is difficult to master because values and aims of science and practice are often experienced as antagonistic. A balance must nonetheless be struck between dependence and independence of the actors, between the quest for generalizable patterns and the development of specific applications, between time-consuming analysis and quick fixes, between conceptual reasoning and concrete problem solving, and between the emphatic advocacy of insiders and the disinterested inquiry of outsiders. Collaborative research requires the formation of a "community of inquiry" through a partnership among individuals with varying priorities and goals.

As ideas are tested and applied, collaboration doesn't stop, but the parties involved may be augmented by others with an interest in the outcomes of the research. This is true not only in the economic and management sciences but to a high degree in the engineering area, where research and practical applications are often closely integrated. As is illustrated by Walshok and Stymne (Chapter 15), the ongoing dialogue between scientific research, industry, and other interested parties increases the chances for significant breakthroughs. We share this view and hope that this volume adds additional voice to the argument that research conducted with the involvement if others, even if more difficult to control in an experimental sense, holds tremendous potential for the advancement and application of knowledge.

Management

While one would think that the definition of *management* is obvious, our most vociferous debates have been about the legitimate scope of our work with regard to this term. Indeed, at least one invited author declined to participate because he associated the term *management* in the title of the book with capitalism and all its ills, rather than holding a broader interpretation of the term that could include the management of not-for-profits and even political or economic systems. Rather than settle the debate by narrowing ourselves to a definition of management as "what MBAs do," or accepting a broad definition of management as "any process that involves organizing a system," we elected to leave the issue open and allow our authors to help us define the field of inquiry through their submissions. The result, as one might expect, was that we were pulled toward a somewhat broader definition of management than we had in mind at the outset.

Management can be carried out by an individual or a team, or even by groups of people who are not formally managers—for example, by representatives of various stakeholder groups. An example is provided in the contribution by Apel, Heikensten, and Jansson, Chapter 18 in this volume, which discusses how several central banks attempted to influence one country's entire economy by managing its monetary policy. *Management* therefore can be thought of as a noun: an individual or collective group of actors who aspire to influence the behavior or performance of a system. *Management (or managing)* also can be a verb: the practice of those actors. In this sense, *management* signifies an art or practice, that is, what managers tacitly or explicitly know and believe about how to go about managing an organization or complex system.

As evidenced by the contributions here, collaborative management researchers are not in strict alignment about the *subjects* of their inquiry. To some, like Boyatzis, Howard, Rapisarda, and Taylor (Chapter 11), the focus is on improving the capabilities of the individual manager. To others, like Kolodny and Halpern (Chapter 13), the concern is with improving the performance of an organization; and for some, like Tandon and Farrell (Chapter 14), the reference is to a class of organizations and their influence on society as a whole.

Nor are we in complete alignment regarding the *objects* of our research. Stebbins and Valenzuela (Chapter 23) discuss research in a single organizational setting, and Mohrman, Mohrman, Cohen, and Winby (Chapter 24) describe related studies in multiple organizations. Coghlan and Coughlan (Chapter 21) and Huzzard and Gregory (Chapter 16) focus on organizational networks; Walshok and Stymne (Chapter 15) and Tandon and Farrell (Chapter 14) address regions; while Roth (Chapter 17) and the ARC Research Team (Chapter 22) examine research networks.

We can easily imagine a two-dimensional matrix in which we study the actions of different types of managerial actors (individual, organizational, systemic) in different settings (a single organization, networks of organizations, systems, regions, or communities); but those two dimensions would be too simplistic to cover the diversity of research we see in practice. We would need to add at least one more dimension that addresses the *aspect* of management studied: specific managerial actions, systems of management processes affecting organizational culture or performance, or coordinating mechanisms among networks of organizations.

So, the question of what management is and how one should approach its study is open to debate and experimentation. Even when we try to simplify things by studying management in a single organizational system, we are confronted by the complexity of modern organizations. There are multiple levels of managers in a system, and rarely are they aligned in their views or actions up and down the chain of command or across the enterprise. There are formal and informal leaders who vary in their level of participation and influence in shaping decisions depending upon the issue under consideration. Individual leaders join and leave the organization, and even systems of management change over time, sometimes gradually and occasionally in dramatic ways. Interventions are not uniformly undertaken or adopted, nor are they carried out uniformly across the organization as planned. Local adaptation to different cultures or customer groups can create variations in management methods across units and cause centrally initiated strategies to be rejected or adapted beyond recognition. Even in a single unit close to headquarters, interviews of a random sample of managers will reveal different philosophies and beliefs about what effective management entails. Despite the application of highly collaborative research methods described in some of the contributions here, understanding what is really going on and what management actions or systems of management processes are really responsible for causing variations in performance is extremely difficult.

The promise of collaborative management research is that through multiple studies, the accumulation of knowledge over time about different aspects of management and across different types of systems will help clarify when and how managerial actions can make a difference. Continued attempts to learn from experience, apply knowledge in the form of new innovations, and thereby confirm or disconfirm assumptions will result in the gradual accumulation of wisdom that can be captured by scientists and applied by new generations of managers. Although individual studies may not be appreciated or even come to the attention of more than a few managers, the accumulation of knowledge over time can produce changes in widely held paradigms that are interesting and well-publicized, and that may eventually influence how management is taught and practiced (Kuhn, 1962).

Research

This brings us to the last of the terms to be defined. What is it that we mean by research? When does a casual conversation between a research scientist and a manager suddenly become a moment of collective inquiry leading to fascinating insights that challenge established management science and justify serious rethinking of corporate policies? How rigorous do data collection methods need to be to qualify as legitimate research, as opposed to being biased reflections on a momentary event by well-intended but unsophisticated partners in a collaborative research alliance? These are important questions that, as editors, we found ourselves unable to answer with precision.

For many centuries, the purpose of conducting research has been to enable us to better understand the world about us, and through that understanding, improve the quality and sustainability of our lives and endeavors. In the physical sciences, research has relentlessly pursued ways to expand our knowledge about the characteristics and functioning of the tiniest processes and particles as well as of the universe as a whole. Long ago, we abandoned the view of a classical Newtonian ordered universe. New hypotheses are constantly being suggested, methods for testing them are being developed, and theories that experiments do not contradict are provisionally retained.

Management science and many of its books on research methodology try to live up to an image of physical science that even physical science does not entertain. In reality, the story of highly controlled experimental laboratory research is a lot messier than is often portrayed. In order to carefully eliminate the influence of other variables, experiments are conducted in ways that remove the influence of significant factors that operate in the real world. This can make transfer of knowledge from the laboratory to the outside world difficult.

As Kaplan (1964) has pointed out, methodology books deal mainly with the logic of verification that results when observations are collected in the correct manner. The social sciences use reliability and validity as the criteria for objectivity. However, trustworthy observation by itself does not really move science forward. The main mover is discovery. The logic of discovery builds on intuition, serendipities, chance encounters, and power games and depends on whom you collaborate with. The logic of discovery is almost never described in methodology textbooks. It is time that management science take the logic of discovery seriously (see also David & Hatchuel, Chapter 2).

As we move into the human realm, research conditions become more difficult to control. In medical research, for example,

variation in the previous condition of patients undergoing a particular treatment or operation can greatly influence the outcomes observed from a given medical intervention. So may a variety of other factors, such as age, metabolism, genetics, race, gender, and sensitivity to dosage levels. The "error" introduced into research studies by these types of human variations is unavoidable. To minimize risks to patients, research methods in the medical sciences have evolved over the years to include early studies done in other species, followed by preliminary studies on small samples of carefully selected human patients, and finally larger clinical trials. Despite these efforts, variations in treatments of specific individuals still produce a range of results, some of which are not predictable and can be quite serious. The benefits of medical advancement for the many outweigh the risks to the few, but these risks are carefully monitored by government bodies and professional groups who make certain that researchers pay strict attention to accepted research practices.

As we turn our attention to research in the social sciences having to do with individual human behavior, the behavior of groups, and ultimately the actions of organizations and systems, we find that the challenge of remaining "rigorously scientific" becomes even more difficult (Gergen, 1982). The ability to "control" extraneous factors affecting behavior in natural settings is limited, making it more difficult to draw cause-effect conclusions between specific variables of interest. The problems that interest us the most aren't amenable to laboratory experiments to begin with; if we are concerned with the impact of different work systems on productivity, for example, we find it difficult or impossible to bring an entire organization into the laboratory where we can control everything that takes place. Instead, we might design pilot plants that operate on different principles than traditional plants and assume the differences in results we observe are due to design features rather than exogenous variables like the quality of the people working in the plant or the use of improved technical controls. As noted by Stymne (2006), collaborative management research often must rely on testing a model in practice rather than conducting controlled experiments:

> Another reason for experiments not being used in management science is that the natural science experiment tries to control the impact of the result of all factors other than the experimental treatment. A firm is an ongoing activity and there is no way to control everything in it or around it. However, the manager and the researcher can together establish a model of how the manager's world hangs together. The outcome of the action under study can be evaluated against the model, and conclusions can be drawn about both the impact of actions and the appropriateness of the model. In natural science, rats are often used in experiments but, even if rats are intelligent animals, our means of communication with them are quite limited. In contrast, conceiving action in firms as quasi-experiments makes it possible to use the managers' intelligence and insights as partial substitutes for laboratory controls. A whole chain of interpretation and translation processes has to take place before the responses from the rat can be used for a drug that can help an ill person. Contrary to rats, managers have the ability to interpret the consequences of their action and incorporate that interpretation in their articulated model of future action. (p. 267)

Added to the difficulty of achieving control in social science research is the problem of overcoming reflexivity, or the impact of the scientist's methods of observation on what he or she is observing. A study of motivational factors that affect performance, for example, could falsely conclude that higher pay is associated with greater output, when in fact simply the effects of being observed by others (the so-called "Hawthorne effect") could have something to do with the results. Although it has long been recognized that this is not entirely possible (Mitroff, 1974), the natural science researcher is supposed to remain detached from and be able to observe the objects under study using tools, such as a telescope, that don't influence the behavior of those objects. The social science researcher, and especially the collaborative management researcher, cannot remain detached from the people under study. The act of observing, intervening in, or collaborating with managers of systems to conduct research changes those systems in ways that are impossible to fully comprehend and, furthermore, vary from organization to organization or system to system. Each collaborative management researcher, in seeking to add practical value through his or her work with the system, will recommend courses of action that are intended to influence the outcomes observed in a positive fashion. As they interpret what they observe, these researchers will not be able to completely detach themselves from their theories and biases, which makes objective assessment of outcomes difficult. Third parties can be brought in as objective observers to mitigate this effect, but the influence of the researcher on the behavior of those under study can never be isolated completely, leaving open the question of just how generalizable the findings may be.

As we conduct research designed to understand organizations and even more complex human systems, we are struck by the pervasiveness of the conundrum of reflexivity in systems that are essentially artifacts—creations of their designers and participants (Simon, 2001). Social orders are socially constructed in practice (e.g., Berger & Luckmann, 1966; Bourdieu, 1990). We design our organizations over and over in the course of making sense of what is happening as we carry out the work of management and the transformation work of the firm (Weick & Quinn, 1999), and as various individual and collective actors pursue their purposes. Giddens (1993) addresses this as the "duality of structure," which refers to the notion that social order or institutional properties of the social system are created by human action and in turn serve to shape human action. Thus the various participants in any collaboration, in pursuing their goals for the collaboration, cannot help but change the phenomena that are being studied, because that is the very nature of organizing.

Finally, we should note that collaborative management research struggles with the question of ethics just as do other scientific undertakings. Medical researchers must decide on when it is "safe" to bring a drug to market, trading off the greater degrees of certainty that come with larger clinical trials against the knowledge that patients will die (and profits be delayed, a counter-ethical pressure of the corporate sponsorship of research) if the drug is not made available as quickly as possible. In collaborative management research, scientists must decide whether to offer their help to make an intervention in an organization succeed or to let the course of events unfold naturally, even if that would mean the organization under study would be more likely to fail. The former is more in keeping with the spirit of true collaboration, while the latter is more in line with scientific doctrine and the pursuit of "objective truth." If, in following his or her collaborative instincts, the scientist becomes so involved in the intervention at a personal level that the results reported could never be repeated in another setting, what is the value of this study to society? On the other hand, if scientists stand by and watch managers fail in high-risk organizational change programs, what would be the incentive for managers to collaborate?

Despite these many challenges, the pressing nature of problems confronting our organizations, systems, and societies forces us to carry on in our search for better management solutions. As in other sciences, the "truths" that we can expect to find in one organization or one study will be neither universal nor constant. Generalizability is therefore not a very powerful criterion of scientific value in management sciences. It is a vain hope to understand how people behave in organizational settings in general, but it may be more fruitful to investigate how people act in different types of organizational settings and under different conditions. Over time, we can build on what we learn across organizations and systems to build a more nuanced, deeper, and broader understanding of the phenomenon of organizational behavior.

We are interested not only in data that describe things as they are, but in understanding why things are that way. Collaborative management research respects the contextual character of management knowledge. It also respects the fact that organizational and other managed systems are artifacts designed in social processes. Investigating specific systems by including their designers therefore makes good sense. Collaborative research is certainly not the only way to generate trustworthy and useful knowledge in management science, but it has many advantages as a complement to other approaches, by which we can continue to add to the body of knowledge concerning the effectiveness of management behaviors, systems, and approaches.

There are management researchers who study important questions related to the appropriateness of different strategies or leadership systems without ever setting foot in an organization. Simply by studying records, we can learn a great deal about classes of organizations that have thrived while others have perished, or about the success of leaders with different levels of preparation for their jobs. There are other researchers who generate important insights by running managers through simulations and observing their reactions to various types of scenarios or inputs. Still others use surveys as their preferred method to gather data from large numbers of people across different organizations and geographies, in the hope that through an analysis of the relationships among the variables measured, they can arrive at tentative conclusions about what kinds of attitudes or self-described behaviors are associated with different kinds of outcomes, such as absenteeism, turnover, acceptance of change, or the quality of decision making. We applaud all of these researchers and support the need for a multimethod approach to inquiry in the field, because we recognize that in the complex, interconnected, ever-changing world that is our reality, no single approach can ever proclaim that it has led us to an absolute truth. By no means are we making a case that all management research must be collaborative; but we do insist for our purposes here that collaborative management research must involve research.

At the most fundamental level, what all forms of research share is the desire to understand something of importance through the use of means that limit the likelihood that we will reach false conclusions. The world is full of people with opinions about things, whether they are speaking about diets, weight-loss plans, management techniques, or ways to bring about world peace. What researchers aspire to add to the discussion of these topics is "objective data," or, rather, to express beliefs justified by earlier research, by observations gathered through rigorous methods, and arrived at by a better application of formalized logic than one would casually use in forming an opinion about something based on one's personal experience or informal conversations with others.

This brings us back to the questions at the beginning of this section. How can we tell when someone is casually formulating an opinion as opposed to conducting "research"?

There are no hard-and-fast answers to this question. The social sciences have never agreed to impose finite standards upon those who claim to be conducting research. Professional peers, including professors or editors of journals and books (like ourselves), make decisions about the quality of work that deserves to be published or receive credit. Publishers of books make decisions about what they believe will sell, or whether scientific work meets the standards by which they feel their reputations will be protected. But these standards are not published anywhere, and they vary from institution to institution and person to person. When someone publishes a popular book on management with little or no objective research behind it, scientists bemoan how easily managers can be duped into accepting a point of view that is based on a case study or two and largely represents the author's unscientific opinion. Yet there are case studies in this volume that, while carefully done and thoughtful in nature, would be hard to distinguish from the cases used in those best-selling popular books, at least from a methodological perspective. One thing that does help us maintain a certain level of rigor in management research is that we expect our work to be reviewed by our professional peers. This is not always the case among popular authors. Aside from this important caveat, the definition of what constitutes an "acceptable" level of rigor in management research must be formulated with an open mind toward research methods that are different from those in use in the physical or medical sciences.

Over the past hundred years, many approaches have been employed to study the effects of different organizational arrangements, leadership behaviors, and management systems. These methods have varied from detached observation to "controlled" experiments to surveys to active intervention. All of these constitute approaches to research that, if done well, can be valid, even if not perfect.

Some methods of research are better at answering certain types of questions than others. Surveys, for example, are more useful for gathering reactions of large numbers of people to a specific managerial practice than conducting hundreds of controlled experiments. Controlled experiments, on the other hand, allow researchers to do a better job of isolating the effects of different leadership styles on the quality of decisions reached in a small group. No one way of conducting research can possibly hope to answer the full range of questions that we must ask ourselves if we are going to continue to advance the ability of managers and organizations to tackle the important issues that confront our workplaces, economies, and societies today. Therefore, it should not surprise us that the contributors to this volume employ a wide range of research methods in conducting collaborative management research, as they work together closely with their counterparts to learn about different types of phenomena. It is therefore less important to define research here in terms of specific methods than in terms of the effort that is made to achieve rigor in guarding against false conclusions.

We have had debates among us as editors in regard to the level of rigor that is required for a contribution to be considered a valid piece of collaborative management research. If we brought our many contributors into the debate, it would be even more difficult to settle. It has been our experience throughout our careers in the field that the tension between observing organizations in their natural state and applying scientific rigor to "control" the impact of extraneous variables on outcomes of interest is always present. It is never satisfying to simply say, "We know good research when we see it," because we recognize that our standards and those of others will vary. Yet due to the inherent limitations in the study of human systems, we also realize that there can be no absolute standards that everyone can apply across the board to judge the goodness of different research efforts. We are forced to acknowledge that our definition of research is not as precise as any of us would like it to be, and that for now we will have to trust our judgment to determine when an author has paid "sufficient attention" to eliminating the likelihood of drawing false conclusions by applying scientific methods to their work.

Collaborative Management Research

If we bring together our views of collaboration, management, and research, we arrive at a statement of the focus for this volume. *Collaborative management research* is an effort by two or more parties, at least one of whom is a member of an organization or system under study and at least one of whom is an external researcher, to work together in learning about how the behavior of managers, management methods, or organizational arrangements affect outcomes in the system or systems under study, using methods that are scientifically based and intended to reduce the likelihood of drawing false conclusions from the data collected, with the intent of both improving performance of the system and adding to the broader body of knowledge in the field of management.

RELATED SCHOOLS OF THOUGHT

Collaborative management research, as advanced in this *Handbook*, shares common views of the philosophy of science with other schools of thought that have emerged in the social sciences over the past decade, all of which involve some form of collaboration between researchers and those being studied. Proponents of these methods have raised similar questions concerning the ontological and epistemological foundations of collaborative research and have contrasted collaborative research with scientific methods associated with positivistic philosophy (e.g., Susman & Evered, 1978; Reason & Torbert, 2001).

To the extent possible, it is important for us to distinguish collaborative management research from these other forms of collaborative research, such as action research or participatory research, in order to make the unique added contribution of this volume clear. While it would be redundant here to retrace in detail the comparative discussions of eight different collaborative research methods offered by Shani, David, and Wilson (2004) and the dozen reviewed by Coghlan and Brannick (2005), it is probably of value to remind readers of some of the conclusions drawn from these efforts.

First, it is important to note what all these approaches have in common. All of the emerging collaborative orientations attempt, in one way or another, to combine some features of both "inquiry from the outside" and "inquiry from the inside" (e.g., Evered & Louis, 1981). They also share the value that "knowledge production" and "action" are not set apart as two separate processes. Finally, as our basic definition of collaborative research indicates, all share the approach that some kind of research team composed of actors from within and outside the organization is created to work together and learn using methods that are scientifically based.

What makes collaborative management research unique and different is that it is interested specifically in understanding the influence in organizations and other complex systems of behaviors, actions, and purposeful designs that are intended to manage the system toward intended outcomes. In contrast, action research has historically addressed a much wider scope of social science issues, beginning with Lewin's classic studies on the impact of participation on the adoption of new behaviors in small group settings. Action science and developmental action inquiry (Argyris, 1980; Argyris, Putnam, & Smith, 1985; Argyris & Schön, 1989;

Torbert, 1976, 1999) are primarily concerned with the cognitive processes of individuals' theories-in-use, which are described in terms of Model 1 (strategies of control, self-protection, defensiveness, and covering up embarrassment) and Model 2 (strategies eliciting valid information, free choice, and commitment). Participatory research (Brown, 1990; Tandon, 1989; Whyte, 1991) has been associated with engaging members of complex systems to bring about changes in society and has been less concerned with the functioning of single organizations. Each of these schools, and others not covered here, has its disciples and detractors.

What collaborative management research seeks to add to these emerging approaches is the value that could be gained when practitioners and researchers engage in a joint undertaking where each partner takes some responsibility also for the other partners' learning and knowledge. The reason for this mutual sharing of responsibility is not only altruistic but also pragmatic. The practitioner will gain if the researcher succeeds in formulating an innovative management model that will give an advantage over competitors. The researcher will gain if the practitioner tries out some of the advice given and if scientifically interesting observations of the process can be made. We suggest a change in the perspective on the task of management. It implies less of a focus on the characteristics and behavior of individual leaders but emphasizes the mechanisms for the creation of a useful knowledge base for managerial action. We hope that the principles and examples of practitioner-researcher collaboration and interaction offered in this *Handbook* will provide epistemological justification and useful methodological advice as well as inspiration for engaging in collaborative research.

We now turn to an overview of the *Handbook*. We will provide a high-level overview here and rely on the sections and the chapters to speak for themselves.

SECTIONS OF THE HANDBOOK: A PREVIEW

Framing the Issues

The first section is intended to provide multiple viewpoints on the issues we have outlined above. Following our discussion, Albert David and Armand Hatchuel (Chapter 2) address the challenges inherent when knowledge is generated from collaborative efforts in the interplay between aspects that are immediately actionable and those that contribute more broadly to universal theories of management. Their chapter proposes a framework for understanding the issues involved in moving back and forth between actionable knowledge and universal theory. Using the dimensions of discovery versus validation and theoretical versus applied, they distinguish among four types of contributions that collaborative management research can make: (1) the discovery of new theory, (2) the invention of new models for application in practice, (3) capturing new knowledge from practice, and (4) improving upon known theory and practice.

Next, Tenkasi and Hay (Chapter 3) transport us back in time to remind us of Aristotle's support for integrating theory and practice. By studying 11 instances of collaborative management research, they discovered six unique strategies used by scholars and practitioners for interrelating theory and practice: framing, influencing and legitimizing, sense making, demonstrating, turns, and scaffolding. The authors describe each of these methods in detail using examples, and then they discuss overall implications from their analysis for the design of collaborative management research efforts.

Bartunek (Chapter 4) takes us on a journey through the realm of "insider/outsider research." Using examples, Bartunek demonstrates how the roles of insider/outsider researchers are shaped throughout the steps that take place in most efforts of this kind.

She notes that the roles are socially constructed and much more malleable than one might imagine, with the boundaries for both academics and practitioners stretching toward one another. What's more, Bartunek points out that insider/outsider relationships are not without conflict and other complications that make the creation and maintenance of a collaborative relationship challenging. Again using examples from actual efforts, Bartunek reveals these issues in compelling fashion before offering some guidelines on how to create more effective insider/outsider relationships.

Werr and Greiner, in the next contribution (Chapter 5), explore the dynamics that often limit collaboration in research among managers, academics, and consultants. They view all three as producers of management knowledge and ask what they can learn from each other. Werr and Greiner suggest that there is a strong potential for collaboration within the triad manager-researcher-consultant but also acknowledge the institutional forces that make such collaboration difficult and discuss how these forces may be overcome. The authors use interviews with three noted academics who have built important contributions to management knowledge through their consulting activities— Edgar Schein, Chris Argyris, and Edward Lawler—to illustrate the mechanisms that can be employed to reduce the tensions academics and consultants experience when collaborating in the production of more valid and useful knowledge.

Based on this set of framing chapters, it's clear that the topic of collaborative management research is more interesting and challenging than we might have imagined at the outset of this journey. The sections that follow make the journey all the more worthwhile.

Mechanisms and Processes

The next section of the book introduces us to a variety of approaches to the conduct of collaborative management research. McGuire, Palus, and Torbert (Chapter 6) offer us the theory of developmental action inquiry, along with the notions of engaging in 1st-, 2nd-, and 3rd-person research/practice, single-, double-, and triple-loop learning, and an interweaving of collaborative research and collaborative practice. In contrast to modern science—which offers a model of 3rd-person research "on" "subjects" for scientific publication alone rather than for their own development and enlightenment—developmental action inquiry is a model of research that requires a high voluntary commitment and collaboration by participants. The authors identify a specific sequence of action-logics through which any human system can (but may not) transform. McGuire, Palus, and Torbert illustrate how developmental action inquiry is applied through a longitudinal case study of individual, interpersonal, team, and organizational transformations. They conclude that the special challenge of developmental action inquiry is that it cannot be routinized. Its highly collaborative and introspective nature requires that the general theory be understood but that specific approaches be developed when engaging each unique individual or system.

In their second contribution to this volume, Hatchuel and David (Chapter 7) note that in the first hundred years of management research, many of the main revolutions in management have come from innovative firms and not from academic research. To enhance the potential for academia to contribute to future breakthroughs, Hatchuel and David ask us to consider intervention research in management, or IRM. Using Renault and other examples of the application of IRM techniques, the authors help us understand the conditions that are necessary for effective industry-academic collaboration. Hatchuel and David outline some critical principles that IRM researchers must

follow, as well as the importance of distinguishing between espoused management practices and management practices in use.

Docherty and Shani, in the next contribution (Chapter 8), outline the processes through which collaborative management research can help organizations become more capable of learning. In order to make collaborative research more than an event, Docherty and Shani argue, collaborators should focus on the design of more permanent mechanisms for organizational learning as a part of collaborative management research efforts. Just as there are many types of organizational designs, there are also many ways to design and manage organizational learning mechanisms. These mechanisms can be cognitive, structural, or procedural in nature, or some combination of the three. The authors argue that collaborative researchers should shoulder the responsibility of facilitating the design of learning mechanisms that are an integral part of the scientific discovery process and learning. Using a collaborative research project with Skandia Corporation, the nature and tapestry of the learning mechanisms used is illustrated and the role that they play in the collaborative management research project is discussed.

Holmstrand, Härnsten, and Löwstedt (Chapter 9) describe an additional enhancement to collaborative research methods, that of the research circle approach. Underlying this approach is a deep conviction, long held among the Swedish people who gave birth to it, that for knowledge to have maximum benefit, the processes for creating it must be democratic. The research circle is described as a forum where organized knowledge construction takes place and knowledge development in cooperation with all participants is established. The circle starts its work from a multifaceted problem that allows the participants involved to work collectively on its resolution. As one might imagine, the dynamics of bringing together people of widely differing backgrounds and research capabilities to generate knowledge regarding a problem can be challenging. They conclude that despite its challenges, use of the research circle method allows the generation of knowledge that could not be obtained through more traditional research methods.

The final chapter in this section, by Mirvis (Chapter 10), examines three different forums in which collaborative management research took place. Each forum involved multiple companies with their distinct as well as common interests and multiple researchers with different agendas. The work concerns how research and practice interests are defined, combined, and realized in a collaborative, interorganizational relationship. Mirvis compares the examples in order to provide insights into why the participants chose to collaborate in learning, how the forums were structured to produce knowledge, and what the outcomes of the forums were for the people and organizations involved. Of particular interest is how learning occurs between academics and practitioners through processes of knowledge transfer, translation, and transformation. Mirvis concludes that academics should understand their goals before joining a particular forum, since not all are well suited to the generation of traditional scientific knowledge.

Collectively, the contributions in the "mechanisms" section of the book help us understand that collaborative management research is an evolving field and that we are learning from our experiences as we continue to invent new ways to do this work. While there are certainly identifiable themes, such as the democratization of knowledge and the focus on higher level awareness of the processes and structures that we are using to learn, there can be no rigid epistemology of collaborative management research at this time. The chapters in this section suggest that each participant brings different knowledge about practice, about the scientific discovery process, and about what might work. The chapters also illustrate the diverse approaches, mechanisms, and processes that have emerged in the field and the need to investigate alternative approaches for those interested in pursuing collaborative management research.

Exemplars: Cases and Projects

Perhaps the best way for us to advance the state of knowledge in the field of collaborative management research is through its continued application. In this section, a wide variety of efforts are discussed that provide interesting insights into the current state of the art. Boyatzis, Howard, Rapisarda, and Taylor (Chapter 11) lead off with a discussion of collaborative research at the level of the individual manager. After reviewing the literature concerning the effectiveness of managerial coaching interventions, they note that coaching is most effective when it involves the formulation of a joint plan for inquiry. Using an evocative story of one manager going through a personal transformation during coaching, Boyatzis et al. conclude that coaching is collaborative, contagious, and mutually transforming; when done well, the coach learns as much as the manager.

In the next contribution, Olascoaga and Kur (Chapter 12) explore the application of a method they call "dynamic strategic alignment" in a Mexican manufacturing company. The approach included the collection of data through surveys and interviews; the data was shared with various groups of people throughout the organization in order to better align people's efforts with the changes that were occurring in the firm. Working closely with representatives of the organization, the actual approach for the collaborative research changed almost continuously as conditions changed and new insights emerged. While the authors were able to measure important results from this effort in terms of goal alignment in the organization, they concluded that in the long run the learning they and the organization gained about managing change through collaborative research was ultimately much more valuable.

Kolodny and Halpern (Chapter 13) review the broad global evolution of sociotechnical systems practice as well as specific Canadian cases to demonstrate that the tradition of collaboration and knowledge sharing has been a part of the field of sociotechnical systems since its inception. The authors provide a primer on the field for those who might not be familiar with its rich history and use recent applications as evidence that the concern with collaborative research among managers, academics, and practitioners has not faded over time. The authors do note that many of the early founders of the field were associated with institutes rather than universities, and raise the question of whether the increased distance between academics and industry may be partially to blame for the comparatively slow evolution of new forms of collaborative management research.

Tandon and Farrell (Chapter 14) examine a group of Indian nongovernmental organizations dealing with the role of women in society. As the authors note, women's marginalization, exclusion, and deprivation are pervasive in many societies around the world due to a wide variety of cultural and religious practices and taboos. A group of Indian nongovernmental organizations was dedicated to changing the role of women in society, beginning with a review of the role of women in their own organizations. Using collaborative research methods, what the organizations learned about themselves was not always easy for them to accept, yet the knowledge proved to be transformational. Building collaborative and learning-process-oriented inquiry processes on the theme of gender mainstreaming made it possible for organizational teams to discover their own reality of structures and practices that were gender-fair or unfair. Interpretation of data by the teams themselves made it possible for the analysis to be owned by the organizations, thereby enhancing possibilities for fundamental changes to happen.

Walshok and Stymne (Chapter 15) discuss how the collaboration between science and research can be organized on the regional level in order to result in commercially highly successful product innovations and important scientific progress. The examples they cite are fetched from engineering and life sciences and intended to demonstrate the fertility of collaboration between practice and scientific fields not limited to management research. By describing the region as a playing field for the game of collaborative research, they point out that science-practice collaboration not only is an issue for specific projects but can be successfully institutionalized in supraorganizational systems.

Huzzard and Gregory (Chapter 16) discuss the use of collaborative research methods in a trade union setting. Most industrial relations scholars have tended to focus on levels of analysis of a rather macro nature, seeking to describe trends and explain structural relationships rather than seeking to intervene at a more local level. This study adopted collaborative methods to study a number of important issues of concern to both labor and management.

The authors show how single-site cases generated knowledge outputs that were fed by collaborative researchers into a broader network spanning some eight countries all with different institutional contexts and industrial relations legacies. Dialogue and experiences from the latter, in turn, generated refined knowledge outputs that were then taken back to the single-site settings. The collaborative researchers were able to establish learning forums and provide training that enabled labor and management to invent rather than simply negotiate new solutions to issues of shared concern.

Next, George Roth (Chapter 17) examines the rich history of company-sponsored research conducted with MIT. As the representative of the university in a key research program sponsored by Ford, Roth was able both to gain insights from his experience and to experiment with different methods of improving the collaboration between academics and managers. Roth is also able to stand back from his individual program to examine issues that industry-sponsored research presents to both companies and universities. While several of the insights that Roth gained from his own experience can be applied to improve these relationships, it is clear from his discussion that collaborative management research raises issues that can never be easily or fully resolved.

Providing a very novel perspective in this volume, Apel, Heikensten, and Jansson (Chapter 18) discuss how academic research has influenced monetary policy and economic development in Sweden. More specifically, after addressing the history of monetary reform policies in Sweden, the authors examine the forms of interplay between researchers and practitioners that have facilitated the application of research findings in the practical domain. The authors identify three such forms: informal interaction, formal collaboration, and internalization. The authors end their contribution with the inclusion of an interview with Professor Lars Svensson, Princeton University, who has combined a central role in the academic research on inflation-targeting policy with close contacts with monetary policy's practical side. His voice lends credibility to the viewpoint expressed in the chapter and provides yet another perspective on the importance of collaboration between academics and managers of complex systems.

Knights, Alferoff, Starkey, and Tiratsoo (Chapter 19), along the same lines as the

contribution by Roth, investigated multiple instances of university-industry voluntary collaborative networks in the UK. Drawing on their own experience in one such network, the authors conclude that despite their popularity and benefits, maintaining industry-academic networks is painstakingly troublesome, because a diverse range of practical problems besets their continuity. As new economic forces threaten the viability of government-sponsored university research, the authors call for careful consideration of the value of voluntary collaborative management research networks among faculty and administrators who have tended to view such networks with a good deal of skepticism in the past.

Bammer (Chapter 20), writing with the Goolabri Group in Australia, describes the first stage of a process to promote the trading of information between disciplines and practice areas aimed at overcoming the ignorance and uncertainty that arises from a lack of sharing across disciplinary boundaries. Drawing upon their own experiences, they describe the evolution of what they call the integration and implementation sciences, which are intended to help tackle complex problems by focusing on crosscutting theory and methods to aid integration of knowledge from different disciplines and from practice, as well as the implementation of research knowledge in practice. While integration and implementation science holds out much hope, there are interesting challenges in its application that remain to be fully addressed.

The Multiple Voices in Collaborative Research

The "voices" section is intended to bring the subject of collaborative management research to life through the eyes of those who have lived the experience from multiple perspectives. While in other chapters some authors included the voices of the participants, in this section we specifically asked the authors to capture and share the various voices of participants. As you will read in the first four chapters of this section the authors captured and shared the voices in varying ways, ranging from formal interviews to including quotes from other papers where the participants had described their experience or their learning.

In the first contribution in this section, Coghlan and Coughlan (Chapter 21) describe a complex example of industry-academic collaboration in a European Union-funded effort to improve supply chain performance. The focus of the collaboration between the three industrial partners in three different countries, researchers from four universities in different nations, and two IT companies from two different countries was the discovery of models and learning mechanisms to improve supply chain performance. Together, these parties set out on a three-year collaborative learning improvement journey that involved overcoming organizational and cultural borders in several projects. Although the results of the projects were mixed, the voices of the managers involved offer an interesting perspective on the work and demonstrate the underlying value of collaborative management research in complex networks.

The next contribution, by the ARC Research Team (Chapter 22), is an inquiry into the nature of building a partnership between a college and its surrounding community in Israel. The Action Research Center (ARC) was initiated by the college and community for the purpose of learning together, initiating projects to stimulate mutual development, and generating new knowledge. The voices heard in this story are those of the authors of five different papers that were eventually combined to compose the account that appears in this volume. The insights gained through this very interesting form of collaboration have relevance for anyone who is interested in spanning the gulf between the ivory tower and the "real world." As in other

contributions to this volume, many of the insights pertain to the deep challenges involved in maintaining a common agenda as critical decisions about the focus of the partnership and the efforts of its primary champions are debated.

Stebbins and Valenzuela (Chapter 23) discuss a collaborative research effort within the Pharmaceutical Operations department of Kaiser Permanente. At the outset, a group was formed as a microcosm of the pharmacy organization to create a new capability centered on democratic dialogue. Representative pharmacists, clerks, warehouse personnel, supervisors, and other pharmacy employees were to tackle problems not solved by the hierarchy. Two of our editors, Rami Shani and Susan Mohrman, interviewed the authors to learn more about the insights they had gained from watching the collaborative forum they had created develop and evolve over a period of 30 years. We know of very few collaborative research efforts with as long and rich a history as this. Obviously, those who are interested in creating sustainable relationships rather than short-term projects should pay careful attention to the description offered here.

Mohrman, Mohrman, Cohen, and Winby (Chapter 24) describe a program of collaborative research investigating the design of team-based organizations within the new-product development environment in nine divisions of Hewlett-Packard (HP). This study was an intersection of the knowledge-generating work of three communities of practice: researchers at the Center for Effective Organizations at the University of Southern California; members of the Factory of the Future group at HP, and personnel of HP engaged in leading and carrying out the development of new products, who were dealing with intense competitive pressures and were attempting to establish teams to improve this process. The authors describe the streams of theoretical and practical knowledge that converged in this collaboration, and the multiple trajectories of collaborative research that resulted. The chapter includes the individual voices of the authors, who interviewed one another for the purpose of this chapter.

The last chapter in this section, by Mohrman and Shani (Chapter 25), is an attempt to draw on the learning from the four chapters in the section. The authors argue that collaborative management research aimed at changing the dynamics and performance of a system must pay careful attention to the voices of the participants. The voices of the varied collaborators are rarely heard in reported research. Reflecting across the varied cases in which the voices of the collaborative management research actors were shared and explored, Mohrman and Shani identify and briefly explore four issues: alignment and purpose as the basis for true collaboration, the institutional context of collaboration, the voices around learning mechanisms, and the convergence of the language of practice and theory.

Enablers, Challenges, and Skills

The final section of the *Handbook* offers some thoughts about the state of the art of collaborative management research, including a critical appraisal of its strengths, weaknesses, and future potential. Adler and Beer (Chapter 26) describe and analyze experiences from building a tradition, a capacity, and a competence for R&D in management in organizations and explore the value of these experiences for management research and management practice. The authors use 15 years of collaborations and experimentation, primarily by Truepoint and FENIX, as the basis for the chapter. Truepoint has primarily been using a systematic collaborative methodology known as strategic fitness profiling (SFP). FENIX has primarily been training executive Ph.D.'s (active managers in organizations working in research projects, writing

scientific articles, and defending a Ph.D. thesis) and setting up collaborative workshops (management laboratories) and collaborative research projects exploring specific managerial challenges. Adler and Beer argue that R&D in management could become a functional process in complex organizations enabling the discovery, validation, and legitimization of new management approaches—and simultaneously contributing to academic research meeting international standards.

Pasmore, Woodman, and Simmons (Chapter 27) argue that to make collaborative management research more valuable to the parties involved, it must become more rigorous, reflective, and relevant. After briefly reviewing the evolution of collaborative management research and the definition of scientific methods, the authors define rigor as "upholding the standards of scientific proof in assessing the impact of leadership practices or organizational arrangements on organizational performance." By reflective, the authors mean "reflection in collaborative management research as the process of jointly creating new insights and theories by referring to the related work of others and the investigation of intervention effects over time." Finally, the authors define relevant research as providing "significant value to the organizations in which it is conducted, as well as provid[ing] opportunities for reapplication of the insights gained to other settings." Pasmore, Woodman, and Simmons review the elements of rigorous, reflective, and relevant research and then offer helpful suggestions to collaborative researchers about how to achieve these ends.

In the next piece, Bradbury (Chapter 28) discusses quality and actionability in action research, which refers to people's ability to use knowledge to produce the actions they want. Bradbury reviews the history of science and points out that the goal of many scientists is to produce knowledge, but not necessarily knowledge that has practical value. Pragmatists started a tradition of placing concern with outcomes over concern with method. In action research, the dimensions of quality that affect actionability include practical value, insider/outsider social interaction in defining the research effort, cycles of reflection and action, active experimentation, and representation (how the work is published). Bradbury cites learning histories, which are rich descriptions of the shared inquiry process, as especially helpful in capturing insights and sharing them with others to make a difference.

Coghlan and Shani (Chapter 29) next examine the challenges of collaborative management research communities that confront insiders and outsiders as they endeavor to collaborate. The authors note that there are three distinct activities that deserve special attention by the parties involved in collaborative management research: defining the task, defining the process, and attending to the relationship. Coghlan and Shani argue that the researcher must bring the expertise that can facilitate the design of the collaborative management research community. The designer is challenged to reflect on the many choices that are available and search for the fit among the cultural context, the research content, and the scientific discovery process. Finally, this chapter provides a window into the issues of quality within the collaborative management research community.

The section ends (Chapter 30) with a reflection by the editors of the book on the current state of the art of collaborative management research and some of the challenges it must face as it continues to develop. We also reflect on the insights we have gained from undertaking this effort in the hope that by doing so we create a larger and more tightly knit community of interest in this topic.

CONCLUSION

Our decision to edit a handbook on collaborative management research was driven by our assessment that this approach is maturing rapidly but possesses no uniform and accepted description, methodologies, or standards that clearly define it. Thus, it is in some scholars' minds currently not differentiated from participative inquiry, collaborative inquiry, action research, or other related communities of interest, which carry out work that may or may not yield knowledge for both the practice and theory of managing complex systems. Our sense at the time was that collaborative management inquiry was beginning to take on a character of its own, and that it was beginning to emerge as a viable strategy to bridge the academic relevancy gap. We felt that establishing a clearer identity for this approach would be important, especially in strengthening opportunities for collaboration with managers who might not be familiar with the approach or its contributions to date. We also thought that it would be important to provide a single compendium of current methods and issues for interested scholars, so that they could more easily build upon what exists in moving ideas forward. We certainly hope that this *Handbook* adds visibility to the many excellent efforts that have taken place and are under way, and raises issues in the field to a level of discourse in the community that will stimulate its further advance. We don't believe we have succeeded in precisely nailing down the boundaries of the approach, although we have put a stake in the ground asserting that for collaborations, inquiries, and/or research to constitute collaborative management research, there are some minimum standards that should be achieved. We will say more about that in our closing chapter. For now, we hope that we have launched this volume in a way that encourages the reader to take in the full richness of what our contributors have to say, and perhaps inspires a few to join the community of those interested in this important topic.

REFERENCES

Adler, N., Shani, A. B. (Rami), & Styhre, A. (2004). *Collaborative research in organizations: Foundations for learning, change, and theoretical development.* London: Sage.

Argyris, C. (1980). *Inner contradictions of rigorous research.* New York: Academic Press.

Argyris, C., Putnam, R., & Smith, D. (1985). *Action science.* San Francisco: Jossey-Bass.

Argyris, C., & Schön, D. (1982). *Theory in practice.* San Francisco: Jossey-Bass.

Argyris, C., & Schön, D. (1989) Participatory action research and action science compared. *American Behavioral Scientists, 32,* 612–623.

Berger, P., & Luckmann, P. (1966). *The social construction of reality.* Garden City, NY: Doubleday.

Bourdieu, P. (1990). *The logic of practice.* Palo Alto, CA: Stanford University Press.

Brown, L. D. (1990). Participative action research for social change. *Human Relations, 46*(2), 249–273.

Coghlan, D., & Brannick, T. (2005). *Doing action research in your own organization.* Thousand Oaks, CA: Sage.

Evered, R. D., & Louis, M. R. (1981). Alternative perspectives in the organizational sciences: Inquiry from the inside and inquiry from the outside. *Academy of Management Review, 6,* 385–395.

Gergen, K. (1982). *Toward transformation in social knowledge.* New York: Springer-Verlag.

Ghoshal, S. (2005). Bad management theories are destroying good management practices. *Academy of Management Learning & Education, 4,* 75–91.

Giddens, A. (1993). *New rules of sociological method.* Palo Alto, CA: Stanford University Press.

Hoffman, A. (2004). Reconsidering the role of the practical theorist: On (re)connecting theory to practice in organization theory. *Strategic Organization, 2,* 213–222.

Huff, A. S. (2000). Changes in organizational knowledge production: 1999 presidential address. *Academy of Management Review, 25,* 288–293.

Kaplan, A. (1964). *The conduct of inquiry: Methodology for behavioral science.* San Francisco: Chandler.

Kuhn, T. (1962). *The structure of scientific revolutions.* Chicago: University of Chicago Press.

Lincoln, Y., & Guba, E. (1985). *Naturalistic inquiry.* Newbury Park, CA: Sage.

Mitroff, I. (1974). *The subjective side of science: A philosophical inquiry into the psychology of the Apollo moon scientists.* Amsterdam: Elsevier.

Pfeffer, J., & Sutton, R. (2006). *Hard facts, dangerous half-truths and total nonsense: Profiting from evidence-based management.* Cambridge, MA: Harvard University Press.

Reason, P. (1988). *Human inquiry in action.* London: Sage.

Reason, P., & Torbert, W. R. (2001). The action turn: Towards a transformational social science. *Concepts and Transformation, 6*(1), 1–37.

Roethlisberger, F. J., & Dickson, W. J. (1939). *Management and the worker.* Cambridge, MA: Harvard University Press.

Shani, A. B. (Rami), David, A., & Wilson, C. (2004). Collaborative research: Alternative roadmaps. In N. Adler, A. B. (Rami) Shani, & A. Styhre (Eds.), *Collaborative research in organizations* (pp. 83–100). Thousand Oaks, CA: Sage.

Simon, H. (2001). *The sciences of the artificial* (3rd ed.). Cambridge: MIT Press.

Stymne, B. (2006). The innovative research enterprise. In J. Löwstedt & T. Stjernberg (Eds.), *Producing management knowledge: Research as practice*. London: Routledge.

Susman, G. I., & Evered, R. D. (1978). An assessment of the scientific merit of action research. *Administrative Science Quarterly, 23*, 583–603.

Tandon, R. (1989). Participatory action research and social transformation. *Convergence, 21*(2/3), 5–15.

Taylor, F. W. (1911). *The principles of scientific management*. New York: Harper & Brothers.

Torbert, W. R. (1976). *Creating a community of inquiry: Conflict, collaboration and transformation*. London: Wiley.

Torbert, W. R. (1999). The distinctive questions developmental action inquiry asks. *Management Learning, 30*(2), 189–206.

Trist, E., & Bamforth, K. (1951). Some social and psychological consequences of the longwall method of coal getting. *Human Relations, 1*, 3–38.

Weick, K., & Quinn, R. (1999). Organizational change and development. *Annual Review of Psychology, 50*, 361–386.

Whyte, W. (1991). *Participatory action research*. Newbury Park, CA: Sage.

CHAPTER 2

From Actionable Knowledge to Universal Theory in Management Research

ALBERT DAVID

ARMAND HATCHUEL

ABSTRACT

In classic social research, scientists often attempt to generalize from a representative sample to a larger population. This classic process is less helpful in understanding how innovation in managerial practice occurs. Instead, we need an alternative approach to research that can provide actionable knowledge at the very moments when management practices and theories are invented. This chapter aims at proposing a framework for better understanding the contribution of management research to the production of actionable knowledge and to the process of moving from actionable knowledge to universal theory. After characterizing management as a practice and defining the concepts of "management model," "actionable knowledge," and "universal theory," we distinguish (1) between the discovery and validation stages in the design of management models and (2) between the respective contributions of the academy and the organizations[1] to these stages. Examining the two dimensions in a 2×2 matrix, we generate four ideal-typical configurations for academy/organizational collaboration. Our main conclusions are twofold: (1) At the discovery stage, the researcher must be able to simultaneously capture the new management model in its actionable form and create a theory that gives the model its general, universal value, and (2) only collaborative management research with pioneering organizations permits the joint production of actionable and universal forms of new management models.

There are two complementary questions about the links between actionable knowledge and universal theory in management research. The most frequently addressed is how to make scientific results more actionable. Creating actionable knowledge (Academy of Management Conference, 2004), making theories more actionable, and bridging the gap between theory and practice (Hatchuel, 2005; "Relevance," 2001) are a few formulations of this problem, among many others. A classical answer to this first question is to draw managerial implications from theoretical conclusions. Managerial implications do constitute a step toward actionability; the researcher makes recommendations about possible applications of the research results in real management situations. By doing so, the researcher targets certain types of management situations and organizational contexts. He or she formulates more or less precise and relevant hypotheses concerning future situations and contexts. Such managerial implications are an interesting but subjective effort to conceive of contextual problems for which the application of the research results would be appropriate.

The second question—how to create universal theories from actionable knowledge—is often understood as "how to generalize from empirical data toward more universal theories." Inductive inference has long been identified as a means by which general-level propositions can be made from empirical data. Abductive and inductive reasoning (Peirce, 1931) are well known stages of this process of scientific generalization, but constitute only a part of the answer because "empirical data" and "actionable knowledge" are separate notions. That is, data are not necessarily "knowledge," and empirical knowledge is not necessarily "actionable." Hence, there is no reason why "actionable knowledge" should necessarily be "empirical." In management research, as in management practice,

moving from actionable knowledge to general, universal theories is not just a matter of generalizing from a representative sample to a larger population. Such a generalization protocol only works at validation stages, not at the discovery or invention stages of the process of management innovation. Instead, we need an alternative process that affords actionable knowledge a more central position and reconsiders the role of management research at the discovery stage, that is, at the very moments when management practices and theories are invented. This chapter aims at proposing such a framework to better understand the contribution of research to the production of actionable knowledge and to the process of moving from actionable knowledge to universal theory. After characterizing management as a practice and defining the concepts of "management model," "actionable knowledge," and "universal theory," we distinguish between the stages of discovery/invention and validation in the design of management models. Examining these two dimensions, discovery/invention and validation in the academy and/or in organizations, in a 2×2 table, we distinguish four types of academic contributions: (1) researchers and actors in the field discover/invent a new management model and create the theory that gives the model its universal value; (2) researchers discover/invent a new management model, within the academy, that could be made actionable in some management contexts; (3) researchers create a theory that gives universal value to a model already discovered/invented by pioneering organizations; and (4) researchers work at commenting on, comparing, testing, or improving a management model that has already been discovered/invented and validated and for which the relevant universal theory has already been formulated. We then go on to analyze why only collaborative research with pioneering organizations permits the joint production of both actionable and universal forms of management models.

MANAGEMENT, MANAGEMENT MODELS, AND MANAGEMENT RESEARCH

According to Drucker (2001), the founding contributions to management were made by Taylor, Fayol, Rathenau, Shibusawa, Gantt, Follett, and Sloan. In contrast, Hamel (2006) identifies the role of pioneering companies in the invention of the main management innovations of the 20th century: General Electric perfected Edison's industrial research laboratory, DuPont made a major contribution to the development of capital-budgeting techniques, Procter & Gamble formalized their approach to brand management, Visa International created one of the most ubiquitous brands by putting together a web of more than 20,000 financial institutions, and Linux developers pioneered open source development. Examining earlier history, Hatchuel and Glise (2003) uncovered three key revolutions that shaped management: (1) the Italian *compania* with profit centers, accounts, and collective ventures; (2) the management of manufacturers with corporate bodies and technical departments; and (3) the foundation of the modern enterprise, resulting from the efforts of Fayol and Taylor. Each of these breakthroughs in the evolution of management doctrines constitutes a wave of rationalization (Hatchuel & Weil, 1995) that addresses the essence of management, giving birth to a new management model.[2]

A *management model* is a set of management principles that govern managerial action. Hence, implementing a new management model means changing the governing variables, that is, addressing the "theories in use" level of double-loop learning (Argyris & Schön, 1978). This occurred in 1954, for instance, when Ohno's "lean production"

management principles replaced the classical supply management model. A management model is composed of a set of tools and techniques—a technical substratum—that makes it actionable (Hatchuel & Weil, 1995). Each of the new management models both expands on previous models and ultimately makes them obsolete as they redefine the principles underlying efficiency.

While *management* is a practice, *managing* is using management techniques, be they explicitly or implicitly related to a management model. Hence, managing also results in testing, improving, expanding, criticizing, or discarding management models and techniques.

Linking actionable knowledge to universal theory would be easy in a world where models and techniques are discovered/invented by the academy and then applied within practical organizational contexts. But in a world where management models are invented by pioneering organizations, and where a part of the activity of validating, expanding, and diffusing management models is taken on by those in the "practical" world, what is left for academic management research? Drucker (2001) contends that researchers cannot do much in the early stages of discovery:

> Management is a practice like medicine or law. And in a practice the basic work and foundations are always done and laid by practitioners and not by academicians. Not until a practice is very mature can academicians—who are not themselves practitioners—make major contributions. (p. 1)

Should management research be limited to describing and commenting on what managers do? Should management researchers be devoted exclusively to analyzing regularities and correlations, discovering factors of performance, or establishing typologies once mature practices are commonly adopted by a large enough sample of organizations? We argue against Drucker's restriction and defend a wider vision: "The essence of management research is understanding, inventing and criticizing models of collective action" (Hatchuel, 2001, p. S36).

ACTIONABLE KNOWLEDGE AND UNIVERSAL THEORIES

The concept of actionable knowledge is widely used, but rarely precisely defined. Basically, actionable knowledge is knowledge that allows the implementation of a singular solution to a contextual problem. According to Argyris, actionable knowledge is that which allows actors to effectively implement their intentions. This definition seems very broad, but within the conceptual framework of double-loop learning and action science experiments (Argyris, Putnam, & McLain Smith, 1985), actionable knowledge is knowledge produced within a group once barriers to free, confident, and informed communication have been overcome. It is knowledge within a context freed from the rhetoric of management, from the excesses of "muddling through" (Lindblom, 1959), and from various kinds of power games.[3]

The restriction imposed by Argyris's definition of actionability on the nature, scope, and purpose of knowledge production through double-loop learning has an equivalent in the context of the discovery/invention of new management practices. When managers behave as designers, their commitment to designing singular solutions to a critical management problem leads them to produce actionable knowledge. In so doing, they may invent a new management model. At the same time, we must recognize that actionable knowledge is necessarily contextualized: This is why there are no universal criteria that can be used *ex ante* to decide whether a given proposition is actionable knowledge or not.

A universal theory is a theory that is not conditioned to one context. Each of the great management models, and each of the management

tools and techniques they are composed of, carries a universal vision of collective action. A universal model aims at challenging existing theories of action and mobilizing organizations for radical change. Great management models have a universal reframing power: The new theory of action they embody seems able to embrace *all* the aspects of the firm's processes and to propose changes to them. Scientific management, lean production management, project management, and quality management, for example, have had, and in many cases still have, the power to question any process within any organization and to redesign organizational processes because they address basic principles of management.

Hence, the actionable knowledge with the highest value in management is not everyday knowledge produced to solve routine problems in an adaptive way. It is the knowledge produced when a pioneering company invents—consciously or not—a new management model. This is the moment when the potential of actionable knowledge produced for theoretical innovation is the highest, the moment when the disjunction between the actionable knowledge produced and the existing universally accepted principles is at its maximum.[4] At this moment, the same set of new knowledge is used by managers for practical purposes, to radically transform their organizational world, and by researchers to promote scientific discovery. Hence, on both sides, a validation process begins: practical validation in the world of organizations and scientific validation within the academy.

PRACTICAL DISCOVERY/INVENTION

The process of practical discovery/invention comes to an end when the set of practices put together by managers as a solution to a contextual problem can be bracketed and labeled as a "model." Sometimes invention and labeling are simultaneous, as in the case of Taylor's scientific management principles or Ohno's lean production models. In other cases, labeling comes later because the way actors handled their problem appears *ex post* as a pioneering experience of what will later be called model X or Y. In other words, *ex post* labeling occurs when someone else later makes more general sense of the actionable knowledge produced by managers who successfully handled a particular challenge. Labeling occurs at the moment when a model is "officially" discovered or invented—even though it is still a hypothesis at that stage. It also constitutes the early stage of the validation process: Labeling a set of practices a "model" means that some kind of a generalization process has begun. The new object has been named, "abstracted," and can hence circulate in various design and implementation spaces. The labeling process is a process of decontextualization that by necessity generates additional knowledge of the type of context within which the model would be relevant and efficient. This additional knowledge can be implicit or explicit. However, labeling a set of practices "a model" provides actionable knowledge produced at the discovery stage some of its universal value.

PRACTICAL VALIDATION

Practical validation begins when actors think that an existing model or set of existing tools could be successfully implemented within their organization. More precisely, practical validation supposes that a local way of doing would be considered *ex ante* or evaluated *ex post* as relevant and efficient; the knowledge that has been produced is actually actionable. Implementing the new model may, for example, lead to prototyping, testing, and experimenting in a few units before generalizing to the whole company. Diffusion and implementation of the model within a population of organizations generates discourses on the model's relevance,

reports on its efficiency, and lessons learned from experience, all of which contribute to its practical validation and to some kind of analytical generalization. Wide diffusion of the model is a sign of its practical validation on the market of management models, although the "fads and fashion" side of the process (Abrahamson, 1991) and its "political" side (Waring, 1991) come to limit its depth and reliability.

SCIENTIFIC DISCOVERY/INVENTION AND SCIENTIFIC VALIDATION

Scientific discovery occurs when a researcher discovers or invents a new management model or builds a theory that gives the model its universal value. This discovery follows the rules of scientific research. While the process of practical invention is guided only by conditions of existence and feasibility, scientific discovery is driven by the researcher's obligation to "clarify" his or her inferences. Some kind of "proof" must be provided so that the academy will recognize the validity of the propositions made.

Scientific validation begins when researchers investigate an existing management model using scientific methods. Research is a controlled process of knowledge production. In the discovery/invention stage, for example, the difference between a researcher and an actor validating a model is in the purpose pursued and in the techniques used. The overall purpose of the researcher is to build a theory that gives the model its universal value. The techniques used aim to produce reliable analyses of the genealogy, structure, dynamics, diffusion mechanisms, and implementation processes of the model.

Scientific validation begins with the labeling of a set of practices discovered or invented by actors in a practical situation. At later stages of the model's life, it consists of analyzing the model's dynamics, testing its relevance in various situations, extending its scope, specifying its domain of validity, specifying how to steer changes to make them more successful, measuring the model's efficiency and its diffusion, and analyzing its life cycle.

MANAGEMENT RESEARCH BETWEEN DISCOVERY/INVENTION AND VALIDATION: FOUR DIFFERENT CONTRIBUTIONS

The academy can discover/invent management models, as can pioneering organizations. The academy can also validate management models, while organizations adopt, diffuse, and implement them, hence validating the models in practice. Crossing the developing/validating and academic/organizational dimensions produces four ideal-type cases (see Table 2.1). In the first case, researchers and a pioneering company together discover/invent a new management model. In the third, researchers create the theory behind a model after it has been invented by one or several pioneering organizations. In the second, researchers discover

or invent a new model, within the academy, that could be actionable in organizational contexts. And in the fourth, researchers work on a model that has already been discovered/invented and diffused in both worlds.

Joint Discovery/Invention by the Academy and by One or Several Organizations

When pioneering managers invent a management model, the model is generally not yet recognized as such, it is not implemented in another organization, and it is not referenced in the academic or in the professional literature. There are very few moments in the history of management when a radically new management model is invented. Even less often do the same people invent the management model and create the theory that gives the model its universal value (see Table 2.2).

When Taylor invented scientific management, he did it as an engineer, as a researcher, and as a manager. As an innovative engineer, he redesigned the very heart of technical tasks—for example, pig-iron handling,

Table 2.1   The Four Contributions of Management Research

		Organizations	
		Discovery/Invention	*Validation*
Academy	*Discovery/Invention*	**1. The researcher and the actors in the field together discover/invent a new management model.** The academic contribution is to co-invent the model and to build the theory that gives the model its universal value.	**2. The researcher discovers/invents a management model within the academy.** The academic contribution is to design the model.
	Validation	**3. The researcher creates the theory of a model after it has been invented by one or several pioneer organizations.** The academic contribution is to build the theory that gives the model its universal value.	**4. The researcher adds value to an existing model.** The academic contribution is to clarify, refine, test, and extend the model, and/or to clarify, refine, test, and extend the theory that gives the model its universal value.

bricklaying—thanks to time-and-motion studies. As a theoretician, he was able to design a total system of management and to build the theory—principles of scientific management— that gave the model its universal value. As a manager, he designed and steered the experimentation and implementation of the method at the Bethlehem Steel Company and succeeded in overcoming the numerous barriers to radical change. So did Ohno as an assembly line manager at Toyota in the 1950s. Ohno and Taylor share the privilege of having given their names to the management revolution they initiated; after "Taylorism," "Ohnism" (or "the Toyota system") is recognized as the second most important revolution in production management of the 20th century.

A second family of discoveries corresponds to a hybrid situation in comparison to Taylor or Ohno. Neither Mayo nor Roethlisberger, both academics, were members of Western Electric before the "Hawthorne experiments" began,[5] but a close cooperation between Western Electric and the research team led to major advances in the understanding of behaviors at work (though controversies appeared in the validity of the research apparatus), thus creating the "human relations" school of management thought. Even if Mayo's intervention is different (close to classical experimentation), his contribution can also be understood as the discovery, by a research team, of a universalizing theory with large-scale managerial implications. We could say that the "human relations" model was discovered at Western Electric just as Taylorism was invented at Bethlehem Steel Company or lean production at Toyota. But we cannot really say that the human relations model was invented "by" Western Electric, while we could say that scientific management was, to some extent, invented "by" Bethlehem Steel Company and lean production "by" Toyota. In other words, Taylor and Ohno can be considered innovative intrapreneurs, their

respective companies having let them design and test a new management model. Mayo, Roethlisberger, and Dickson, though leading a long cooperation with Western Electric, were not intrapreneurs but rather "experimenters" who happened to discover a new factor within an experimental plan that had not been designed for that purpose. This is also why Taylor's and Ohno's contributions are closer to invention while Mayo's contribution is closer to discovery.

Kurt Lewin's action research experiments with Harwood Manufacturing Corporation are another example of a research team inventing new universal theories through close cooperation with an organization. An important difference between the Hawthorne and Harwood experiments is that while Lewin's research apparatus was made for producing actionable knowledge, Mayo's protocol was a classical experimental research design. In other words, even if their perceptions and opinions could be taken into account, the workers from the relay assembly line at Hawthorne did not produce knowledge in a participative way; the knowledge was gained by observing the workers' reactions to various changes in the context and organization of their work. Workers at Harwood, on the other hand, were invited to take part in the design and experimentation of possible paths to overcome barriers such as the difficulty for the youngest of them to reach higher productivity rates or the belief that no worker older than 30 should work on the assembly line.

Argyris's action science studies (Argyris et al., 1985) clearly refer to the Lewinian tradition of action research. Since Argyris, like Mayo and Lewin, is also an academic, his model can be considered to be invented by the academy. Argyris invented a new management model—the double-loop learning organization—through numerous collaborations with organizations, but his early works on motivation and his later work with Schön on organizational learning led him to design

Table 2.2   Main Examples of Academic Contributions in the Four Cases

<table>
<tr><td colspan="3" align="center">Organizations</td></tr>
<tr><td rowspan="2">Academy</td><td>Discovery/Invention</td><td>Validation</td></tr>
<tr>
<td>

1. The researcher and the actors in the field invent/discover a new management model.

Taylor with Bethlehem Steel Company: **scientific management**

Ohno with Toyota: **lean management**

Kurt Lewin: **the unfreeze-change-refreeze model of change; the participative model of the management of change**

Argyris: **double-loop learning model and action science experiments**

Hawthorne experiments: **the "human relations"** model

Peter Drucker: **management by objectives and self-control**

</td>
<td>

2. The researcher discovers/invents a management model within the academy.

Classical OR: **optimization methods**

Soft OR: **Checkland's problem structuring methods**

Roy: **multicriteria decision aid**

Katz and Kahn: **systems theory applied to organizations**

</td>
</tr>
<tr>
<td rowspan="2">Validation</td>
<td>

3. The researcher creates the theory of a model after it has been invented by one or several pioneer organizations.

Chandler: **the M-form**

Burns and Stalker: **the mechanistic and organic structures**

Cohen, March, and Olsen: **the garbage-can model**

Chapel (1997), Hatchuel, Lemasson, and Weil (2002): **design-oriented organizations**

</td>
<td>

4. The researcher adds value to an existing model.

The majority of scientific publications

</td>
</tr>
</table>

a part of the model and also the related intervention protocol within the academy before it was tested in real organizations.

Another practitioner of this approach is Peter Drucker, who is considered the inventor of "management by objectives." Part of Drucker's model came from the experience of General Motors. "Alfred P. Sloan had used at GM something very similar to management by objectives since the 1920s. Donaldson Brown had given the method theoretical expression in a 1927 paper entitled 'Decentralized Operations and Responsibilities With Coordinated Control'" (Waring, 1991, p. 87). Drucker later adapted the idea through a collaboration with General Electric. The leading principle was that employees would efficiently work under self-control if and only if "goals and methods were jointly defined" (Waring, 1991, p. 88). The method was labeled "management by objectives and self-control," implemented at General Electric in 1952, and described by Drucker in *The Practice of Management* (1954).

Discovery/Invention by the Academy, Validation in Organizations

Few management models were the result of purely academic discovery or invention. "Operations research" first appeared as a set of tools and techniques invented in the academy and then applied to the practical world. Operations research was born in the late 1930s in Britain, in the Royal Air Force. An interdisciplinary team was formed, not to design new equipment but to optimize the deployment of existing equipment. Hence, operations research was not born strictly in a scientific ivory tower. Scientists and mathematicians worked at designing optimization models from practical problems, in a Gibbons's Mode II type of research (Gibbons et al., 1994). From then on, however, due to the sophistication of the mathematical models involved, most of the advances in operations research techniques came from the academy. Managers were not skilled in mathematical modeling, and the growth in academic interest (scientific societies, teaching programs) was very quick. Following the Second World War, and especially after the publication of Morse and Kimball's *Methods of Operations Research* in 1951, operations research broadened its ambition and its scope:

> The British and American scientists and mathematicians who invented the new tools during and after the Second World War claimed that they had created the first positive management science that could overcome some of the failings of Taylorism; their methods could, they said, direct complex organizations by integrating specialized operations and formulating strategies without resort to politics. (Waring, 2001, p. 20)

From a practical standpoint, management scientists "assumed that managers faced only a few types of quantitative problems, so they developed a set of standardized tools [in order to solve] inventory, allocation, queuing, sequencing, routing, replacement, competition and search problems" (Waring, 1991, p. 27). Operations research is a complex case; its invention is rooted in collaboration between scientists and the military on practical problems. The main families of techniques were discovered/invented through collaboration in real situations, but then the majority of the academy worked separated from the practical world. The symptom of the so-called "operations research crisis" in the 1970s (Ackoff, 1979) can be summarized by one recurrent question: "Why are so many models designed and so few used?"

In another development, Katz and Kahn (1966) promoted the application of open systems theory to the world of organizations. Conducting and supervising surveys at the Survey Research Center of the Institute for Social Research, they did not directly collaborate with organizations, though some surveys did take place within a given corporation (Katz & Kahn, 1951; Katz, Maccoby, & Morse, 1950). The open systems approach did renew the way organizations were conceptualized. There is no doubt that open systems theory and the project to apply it to organizations came from the academy and received scientific validation. But practical validation in the world of management supposes that a technical substratum—a set of tools and techniques—is designed, so that local solutions to a contextual problem can be found; that is, according to our definition, so that actionable knowledge is produced. Katz and Kahn do propose a "systemic check on irrationality" (1966, pp. 294–298), but the question remains: Is the application of open systems theory actionable? And is it able to give birth to management models? Certainly, the work by Peter Senge and his colleagues (*The Fifth Discipline* [Senge, 1990] and *The Fifth Discipline Fieldbook* [Senge, Kleiner, Roberts, Ross, & Smith, 1994]) is one such attempt. While Senge and others have applied these tools to organizations, the extent to which managers have applied them independently to solving organizational issues and adapted them further remains unclear.

Discovery by an Organization, Validation by the Academy

Chandler (1962) did not invent the M-form. He did, however, build the theory that gave the model, invented by General Motors and a few other pioneering companies, its universal value. As a historian, Chandler put into perspective several decades of "naturally" occurring incremental design processes that led to the divisionalization of large corporations. As an organization theorist, by labeling the structure he had been studying the "M-Form," he made a major contribution to theory on the link between strategy and structure in the contemporary firm.

From a practical standpoint, Burns and Stalker (1961) did not invent mechanistic and organic structures. But, by labeling as "mechanistic" the structures in which hierarchical communication, formalized routines, and strategic stability are dominant, and as "organic" the structures in which horizontal communication, mutual adjustment, and strategic adaptation are dominant, and further pointing out the relationship between "organic" and "made for innovation," they contributed to a general theory of how companies willing to innovate should be organized, thus constructing a part of the theory that gives the actionable form of the model its universal value. From a scientific standpoint, they "created" mechanistic and organic structures insofar as they made them abstract objects that could be identified and diffused both within the academy and in organizations.

Likewise, Cohen, March, and Olsen (1972) did not invent the random meeting, in a semi-organized space, of problems, solutions, decision makers, and occasions to take decisions. But the garbage-can model of decision making was a major contribution to both the academy and the practical world. From a theoretical standpoint, Cohen et al. added a new way of thinking about the nature and efficiency of decision processes. They built the theory that gives the model much of its universal value. From a practical standpoint, the model is applicable because its representation of the world is closer to reality and therefore more accurate for use in designing solutions and managing projects. It is also actionable in the Argyris sense of enabling a more effective implementation of actors' intentions, and in our own sense of enabling the design of a singular solution to a contextual problem. Managers can have a better understanding of how to build a network so that problems, solutions, decision makers, and occasions to decide come together in an effective manner to improve the performance of decision processes within their organizations.

Paul Rivier, CEO of Tefal from 1979 to 1999, was aware that his company was probably a very singular case with respect to how innovation was organized. Hatchuel, Lemasson, and Weil did not create the Tefal structure and organization, but they engaged in close collaboration with Tefal in the middle of the 1990s. Chapel, a Ph.D. student working under Hatchuel's supervision, went to work at Tefal as a product manager, thus analyzing the "Tefal model" from the inside. The several years of research partnership between the Centre de Gestion Scientifique and Tefal led the research team to confirm the uniqueness of Tefal's organization for innovation. They asserted the hypothesis that Tefal was among the pioneers of a new organizational form, which they labeled "design oriented organizations" (DO2; Hatchuel, Lemasson, & Weil, 2002).

Design oriented organizations are not matrix structures. We enter the world of DO2 precisely when two types of situations occur repeatedly and with a high frequency in a competitive context: a new body of knowledge is identified and could be explored, yet nobody knows which concepts could be linked to this exploration and could convey new products (for example the case of "technical" textiles or the "WAP" standard in mobile telephony). New concepts are easily identified but nobody knows which body of knowledge will be necessary to transform the concept into acceptable products (for example designing a way to stop a car on a very short distance even at a relatively high speed).

What are the organization principles that guide effective work and adequate work division in such conditions? Classical bureaucracy will not help: Its basic entries miss the mark (standards, output, and skills are not yet defined, since they are the target of the design work). Mutual adjustment, the principle of adhocracy, has no operational meaning (who is going to adjust to the other if no network yet exists?). What therefore, is the logic of collective action in such contexts? It is to increase the work on Design strategies, principles and rules and to manage the non-routinized metabolism associated with these strategies, *i.e.*, without simply adding to the existing routines in an additive or complementary way. . . . Tefal is very close to this DO2 model. (p. 18)

Validation by the Academy, Validation by Organizations

Most of the time, the researchers' contribution consists of validating a management model that has already been discovered/invented and has already been reported by previous scientific research. Once a new model has been discovered/invented, the validation process that follows includes tests, experimentation, and extensions of various kinds. The validation process can be a joint process if both the academy and managers work, together or separately, on the model. The first step of the validation phase might consist of extending the model to a larger scope of management situations. The successors of Taylor, for example, extended the scientific management model to any kind of activity; Drucker extended management by objectives and self-control from managing managers to managing knowledge workers (Waring, 1991). In Drucker's view, further diffusion is possible only when the model and the related tools and techniques are mature enough, that is, validated from a practical standpoint thanks to a large diffusion within relevant contexts.

DISCOVERY STAGES: A CHALLENGE FOR MANAGEMENT RESEARCH

The act of moving from discovery to theory poses significant challenges to management researchers. Three out of the four cases in Table 2.1 include discovery/invention.

In Case 3, the researchers create the theory that gives universal value to a management model after it has been invented in organizations, thereby challenging management researchers to capture models in their actionable forms. Researchers have to be able to locate singular problems and to analyze the contextual solutions that have been designed to cope with these problems. Neither the idea of a "problem" nor that of a "solution" are simple concepts. Fortunately, practitioners are generally reflexive (Schön, 1983) and the knowledge base of management theories and practices is generally wide, thus allowing comparisons that are essential to a grounded scientific abstraction process.

In Case 2, the academy discovers/invents a management model that later is or could be validated by organizations, thereby presenting a challenge to management research insofar as the researchers must be able to discover/invent models that effectively are or could become widely adopted management models. The theory that gives the model its universal value is created in advance of its application in organizations. Operations researchers did not invent the principle of optimizing an economic function under constraints. Katz and Kahn, as mentioned above, did not invent open systems theory. But additional value was added to these theories through their tentative application to management situations. In this sense, operations researchers or the researchers who applied open systems theory to management transformed universal theories into potentially useful management models.

In Case 1, the academy and one or several pioneering organizations together discover/ invent a new management model and create the theory that gives the model its universal value. This is the most challenging situation for management research. Case 1 combines the challenges of Case 2 and Case 3: The researchers must simultaneously invent (not just capture) the model in its actionable form *and* create the theory that gives the model its universal value. The difficulty is twofold: First, at the very beginning of the process, the model is not yet observable (it is being invented), and second, the theories that give the model its universal value are not clearly identified. In the ideal-typical Case 1, an iterative and interactive process takes place. Actionable knowledge and hypotheses regarding theoretical concepts that could give the model under construction its universal value are coproduced in a design space in which there is no clear difference between collaborative researchers and reflexive practitioners. Case 1 discovery/ invention requires a transformation in R&D logic: Collaborative researchers and reflexive practitioners must together design innovative singular solutions to unprecedented contextual problems. When problems and solutions are already referenced in the academy and already diffused in the population of organizations addressed by the model, the actionable knowledge produced has no added value. On the contrary, when contextual problems are

unprecedented, solutions have to fit with new formulations and constraints. Actionable knowledge corresponds to local solutions but may be innovative and give rise to a general, universal discovery: a new management model. When singular solutions are innovative answers to new contextual problems, the actionable knowledge they produce has universal added value.

CONCLUSION: DISCOVERY STAGES AND COLLABORATIVE MANAGEMENT RESEARCH[6]

Separating the discovery and validation stages of management models and distinguishing whether these stages take place in the academy or in organizations leads to formalizing four different and complementary possible contributions of the academy to management research.

Of course the four cases are ideal types: Real contributions, though we have clearly positioned them in one case, could, in fact, belong to more than one case or be positioned at an intermediary place. For instance, Chapel (1997) and Hatchuel et al. (2002) were able to capture the Tefal "organizing for innovation" model in its actionable form and then create the DO2 (*Design Oriented Organizations*) theory that gives the model its universal value. Chandler wrote "chapters of the history of the American industrial enterprise" thanks to numerous historical sources.[6] Chandler did not have to discover the model in its actionable form to the extent that Hatchuel et al. did in the case of Tefal: The concept of multidivisional structure was already partially validated as a model both in the academy and in the world of organizations, at least in the industrial sectors to which the pioneers—for example, GM and DuPont—belonged.

Thanks to the proposed framework, the nature of each academic contribution, in terms of discovery or validation, is made clear, and the question of how actionable knowledge is produced and related to universal theories is better formulated. "Bridging the relevance gap" ("Relevance," 2001) involves neither making academic knowledge more practical nor being able to generalize formalized empirical facts to higher-level theories. Such formulations are epistemological traps. In fact, any knowledge can be discovered as actionable *ex post*. And going back to a model in its actionable form after it has been discovered and formulated in its academic, general form is adding to the genealogy of an already identified object. *Ex ante,* no universal criteria can help us to recognize actionable knowledge. At the discovery stage, the actionability of knowledge can be assessed only if research, in the tradition of the experimental method, is also a form of action. Collaborative forms of research that follow a rigorous academic protocol offer the opportunity to introduce some actionability criteria in their methodology, thus scientifically grounding the process of linking actionable knowledge to universal theories.

NOTES

1. The "academy/organizations" distinction is preferred to the "research/practice" distinction: In this chapter, we need to suppose that management research, as well as practice, can be on both sides.

2. See also Hatchuel and David's Chapter 7 in the present volume.

3. This restriction on the knowledge produced is a common characteristic of intervention methods affiliated with action research or, in the operational research community, problem structuring, "soft OR" methods (Rosenhead & Mingers, 2001), or multicriteria decision aiding (Roy, 1996). For a deeper analysis of the differences between action research and intervention management research, see also in the present volume Hatchuel and David, Chapter 7, and Bartunek, Chapter 4.

4. In routine contexts, on the contrary, there is a conjunction between the actionable knowledge produced and the universal principles it refers to.

5. The Hawthorne experiments began in 1923 when the president of the engineering division of the National Research Council, Frank Jewett, who was also in charge of Western Electric labs, decided to add to the activities of the division some research on the human relations model in industry. Jewett first worked with two engineers from MIT. Elton Mayo had arrived from Australia in 1923 and was already well known for several studies on "the man at work" and especially on fatigue. From 1926, Mayo was a member of the industrial research section of the Harvard Graduate School of Business. Having been told about what was taking place at Hawthorne by an engineer from Western Electric, Mayo took control of the experiments in 1928, one year after the Relay Assembly Test Room experiment began (Roethlisberger & Dickson, 1939; Desmarez, 1986; O'Connor, 1999). Fritz Roethlisberger was a Harvard University professor, and William Dickson was a Western Electric executive.

6. Including Sloan's memoirs and a number of works on GM history written by GM's managers themselves (for instance, Brown, 1927).

REFERENCES

Abrahamson, E. (1991). Managerial fads and fashions: The diffusion and rejection of innovations. *Academy of Management Review, 16*(3), 586–612.

Academy of Management Conference. (2004). *Creating actionable knowledge.* New Orleans: Author.

Ackoff, R. L. (1979). The future of operational research is past. *Journal of the Operational Research Society, 30,* 93–104.

Argyris, C., Putnam, R., & McLain Smith, D. (1985). *Action science.* San Francisco: Jossey-Bass.

Argyris, C., & Schön, D. (1978). *Organizational learning: A theory of action perspective.* Reading, MA: Addison-Wesley.

Brown, D. (1927). Decentralized operations and responsibilities with coordinated control. *Annual Convention Series* (Vol. 57). New York: American Management Association.

Burns, T., & Stalker, G. (1961). *The management of innovation.* London: Tavistock Institute.

Chandler, A. (1962). *Strategy and structure: Chapters in the history of the American industrial enterprise.* Boston: MIT Press.

Chapel, V. (1997). *La croissance par l'innovation intensive: De la dynamique d'apprentissage à la révélation d'un modèle industriel—le cas Téfal.* Unpublished doctoral dissertation, École des Mines de Paris.

Cohen, M. D., March, J. G., & Olsen, J. P. (1972). A garbage can model of organizational choice. *Administrative Science Quarterly, 17*(1), 1–25.

David, A. (2000). Intervention-research as a general framework for management research published in French. In A. David, A. Hatchuel, & R. Laufer (Eds.), *Les nouvelles fondations des sciences de gestion.* Paris: Vuibert.

Desmarez, P. (1986). *La sociologie industrielle aux Etats-Unis.* Paris: Armand Colin.

Drucker, P. (1946). *The concept of the corporation.* New York: John Day.

Drucker, P. (1954). *The practice of management.* New York: Harper and Row.

Drucker, P. (2001). Management is practice. Retrieved from http://gurusonline.tv/uk/conteudos/drucker4.asp

Gibbons, M., Limoges, L., Nowotny, H., Schwartman, S., Scott, P., & Trow, M. (1994). *The new production of knowledge: The dynamics of science and research in contemporary societies.* London: Sage.

Hamel, G. (2006, February). The why, what, and how of management innovation. *Harvard Business Review,* 72–84.

Hatchuel, A. (2001). The two pillars of new management research. *British Journal of Management, 12*(S1) [Special Issue], S33–S39.

Hatchuel, A. (2005). Towards an epistemology of collective action. *European Management Review, 2,* 36–47.

Hatchuel, A., & Glise, H. (2003). Rebuilding management. In N. Adler, A. B. (Rami) Shani, & A. Styhre (Eds.), *Collaborative research in organizations.* Thousand Oaks, CA: Sage.

Hatchuel, A., Lemasson, P., & Weil, B. (2002). From knowledge management to design-oriented organizations. *International Social Science Journal, 171,* 25–37.

Hatchuel, A., & Weil, B. (1995). *Experts in organizations.* Berlin, Germany: Walter de Gruyter.

Katz, D., & Kahn, R. L. (1951). *The Caterpillar Tractor Co. study: Vol. VI. Factors related to job satisfaction.* University of Michigan (mimeographed).

Katz, D., & Kahn, R. L. (1966). *The social psychology of organizations.* New York: Wiley.

Katz, D., Maccoby, N., Gurin, G., & Floor, L. (1951). *Productivity, supervision and morale among railroad workers.* Ann Arbor, MI: Institute for Social Research.

Katz, D., Maccoby, N., & Morse, N. (1950). *Productivity, supervision and morale in an office situation.* Ann Arbor, MI: Institute for Social Research.

Lindblom, C. E. (1959). The science of muddling through. *Public Administration Review, 19,* 79–88.

Morse, P., & Kimball, G. (1951). *Methods of operations research.* Cambridge: MIT Press.

O'Connor, H. (1999). The politics of management thought: A case study of the Harvard Business School and the human relations school. *Academy of Management Review, 24*(1), 117–131.

Peirce, C. S. (1931). Kinds of reasoning. In *Collected papers: Vol. 1. Principles of philosophy* (Chapter 2, §10). Cambridge, MA: Belknap Press.

The Relevance of Management Research. (2001). *British Journal of Management, 12*(S1) [Special Issue].

Roethlisberger, F., & Dickson, W. (1939). *Management and the worker.* Cambridge, MA: Harvard University Press.

Rosenhead, J., & Mingers, J. (Eds.). (2001). *Rational analysis for a problematic world: Problem structuring methods for complexity, uncertainty and conflict* (2nd ed.). Chichester, UK: Wiley.

Roy, B. (1996). *Multicriteria methodology for decision aiding.* Dordrecht, The Netherlands: Kluwer.

Schön, D. (1983). *The reflective practitioner.* New York: Basic Books.

Senge, P. M. (1990). *The fifth discipline.* New York: Doubleday.

Senge, P. M., Kleiner, A., Roberts, C., Ross, R., & Smith, B. (1994). *The fifth discipline fieldbook.* New York: Doubleday.

Waring, S. P. (1991). *Taylorism transformed: Scientific management theory since 1945.* Chapel Hill: University of North Carolina Press.

CHAPTER 3

Following the Second Legacy of Aristotle

The Scholar-Practitioner as an Epistemic Technician

RAMKRISHNAN (RAM) V. TENKASI

GEORGE W. HAY[1]

ABSTRACT

In our Western scientific tradition, Aristotle's first legacy has conventionally been invoked to justify the separation of theory and practice. In contrast, we draw attention to a second, less recognized legacy of Aristotle, one where he argues for the integration of universals (theory), with the particulars (experience and practice) of a situation as the basis of true knowledge and understanding. Scholar-practitioners, we suggest, are the contemporary carriers of the Aristotelian second vision, who skillfully integrate theory, experience, and practice to create actionable scientific knowledge, or knowledge that advances the causes of both the organization and the larger scientific discourse. Our study of 11 scholar-practitioners and their efforts in organizational projects to generate actionable scientific knowledge suggests that they employ six strategies for interrelating theory and practice: framing, influencing and legitimizing, sensemaking, demonstrating, turns, and scaffolding. We discuss implications from our findings for the design of collaborative management systems that strive to produce knowledge outcomes with such dual relevance.

The true "technê" [practice] implies not merely the possession of this or that ability, but also the "epistêmê" [theory] of why this particular "technê" works and yields the desired results.

Aristotle (*Metaphysics*, 1961, p. 981b)

Much akin to the Greek god Janus and his two opposing heads, theory and practice have frequently been at loggerheads, evoking the image of incommensurable opposites (Astley & Zammuto, 1993). These oppositional images have been and continue to be part of mainstream management discourse in the oft-repeated separations between theory and practice, scholar and practitioner, or knowledge and action—a legacy that can be traced back to the Aristotelian separation between *epistêmê* and *technê*, where we "find the basis for the modern opposition between epistêmê as pure theory, and technê as practice" (Parry, 2003). Less acknowledged is that there is another legacy of Aristotle, one where Aristotle advocates the importance of integrating theory and practice by blending the universals with the particulars as the basis for true knowledge and understanding. In following this second legacy of Aristotle, we can not only understand the importance of integrating theory and practice but also derive some insights on the kinds of practice and theoretical elements that have to come together to produce fruitful, relevant knowledge of events and situations, a principal aim of collaborative management research systems.

A primary focus of this chapter is to highlight this less-traveled second image of Aristotle that stands in contrast to his widely held first image of knowledge creation, and speak to his legacy and contributions as an early enthusiast of theory-practice integration. In furthering the Aristotelian second legacy and relating it to current times, we focus on scholar-practitioners as contemporary carriers of Aristotle's second vision. Scholar-practitioners are defined as actors who have one foot each in the worlds of academia and practice and are pointedly interested in advancing the causes of both theory and practice (Huff & Huff, 2001; Tenkasi & Hay, 2004). Much akin to the

implications of studying insider/outsider research teams (Bartunek, Chapter 4 in this volume) for collaborative management research, following the efforts of scholar-practitioners in organizational projects to create actionable scientific knowledge, or knowledge that strives both to meet the practical demands of the organization and advance the causes of the scientific community (Adler, Shani, & Styhre, 2003), can provide us a deeper understanding of the hows of theory-practice integration. In sketching out implications from our study of individual scholar-practitioners to collaborative management systems, we will highlight the processes and strategies of scholar-practitioners in creating actionable scientific knowledge as they strive to move back and forth between the local and the general, or in Aristotelian terms, the universals and the particulars, in interrelating theory and practice. An insight into these dynamics can help inform the design of collaborative management systems that strive to produce outcomes relevant for practice while concomitantly advancing the causes of theory.

THE FIRST LEGACY OF ARISTOTLE AND THE THEORY-PRACTICE DIVIDE

Aristotle initially distinguished the spheres of scientific knowledge and craft as two separate and different domains in his writings in Book VI of the *Nicomachean Ethics* (Parry, 2003). His reasoning was that scientific knowledge, or *epistêmê,* concerns itself with the world of universal truths or judgments, which stands apart from the world of everyday contingencies, which is the province of experience, or *empeiria,* and craft, or *technê.* And thus the initial basis of separation between theory and practice, scholar and practitioner was created. Aristotle's logic in creating this separation was informed by his quest for how best to establish enduring truths or universal judgments that can form the basis of true knowledge of events. Aristotle contrasted experiences and the practice of craft with inquiry, or the acquisition of knowledge, as representing fundamentally different domains. Experience, or *empeiria*, and the practice of craft, or *technê*, are ends in themselves, such as playing the flute, or making something such as a physical object, be it a flute or a ship. These he distinguished from *epistêmê*, which is an understanding of the underlying rules and principles governing why something happens and how it happens beyond a single event or instance. For example, how does the playing of a flute make beautiful music happen (i.e., what are the underlying laws of creating beautiful music)? Or how does a ship come to be (i.e., what are the principles of construction of a strong, floatable ship)? Answers to these questions, he felt, fell within the province of *epistêmê theoretike*, or scientific knowledge, which he defined as the ability to know the real as it is.

Epistêmê is translated as "true and scientific knowledge as opposed to opinion, an organized body of knowledge, and as theoretical knowledge" (Peters, 1967, p. 59). In Aristotle's view, *epistêmê* is concerned with first causes, which are *"knowledge of the factors that are primary"* (Aristotle, 1961, p. 983a). First causes are the ultimate explanation for phenomena. All other causes flow from first causes; no other causes explain first causes. Because of this, *epistêmê* is different from other forms of knowledge like *empeiria* and *technê* that are focused on (immediate) useful outcomes. *Technê* is knowledge of that which can be changed, which is what makes *technê* useful. What makes *epistêmê* unique is that it concerns knowledge of that "which cannot be other than it is" and is, consequently, "eternal" and

therefore "real (Aristotle, 1962, p. 1139b). This was a process that required scholars who, through their careful and systematic inquiry, produce universal truths about underlying laws of nature by considering data beyond a single instance or experience, to unearth the causal laws that are universally applicable to events and situations. As Aristotle (1961) eloquently clarifies in the following passage,

> That this science [*epistêmê*], moreover, is not one of production is clearly illustrated in those who first began to philosophize. For it was their curiosity that first led men to philosophize and that still leads them. In the beginning, they were curious about the difficulties close at hand. Then they progressed little by little in this respect and raised difficulties about matters of greater consequence; for example, about the behavior of the moon and the sun and the stars and of all becoming. . . . Therefore, inasmuch as men philosophized in order to escape ignorance, it is evident that they learned in the pursuit of knowledge, and not for some useful [immediate] end. (p. 982b)

This classical division between the purely theoretical and the purely practical was such a powerful image that a thought that originated in roughly 347 B.C.E. has been carried through as the dominant and unquestioned view of knowledge till the latter half of the 20th century. This early distinction between theory and practice not only influenced subsequent Greek philosophers such as Plotinus, who found little use for technê or craft "because it is so far from reality" (Parry, 2003, p. 1), but also had an impact on important later figures of our Western scientific legacy: John Locke, David Hume, Auguste Comte, and more recently Karl Popper,[2] who, in questioning the value of experience as a reliable source of knowledge, upheld the preeminence of theory and, by inference, the scientist-scholar as the objective producer of knowledge of the physical and the social worlds. This point of view further perpetuated the separations between *epistêmê* on the one hand, and *empeiria* and *technê* on the other hand, in turn deepening the chasm between the scholar and the practitioner.

It has taken 2000-odd years for this influential image of Aristotle to be forcefully challenged. Such was the dominance of Aristotle's first image that the early management literature questioning the separation between theory and practice (such as Astley & Zammuto, 1993; Lawler et al., 1985; and Rynes, Bartunek, & Daft, 2001) focused on pointing out the "great divide" between theory and practice in academic knowledge production and on actively building the case for theory-practice integration. It is only recently that the field of organizational studies has moved to systematic investigations of what it means to link theory and practice, particularly inspired by the seminal work of Gibbons et al. (1994) and their distinction between Type 1 and Type 2 knowledge production models. Of special import are the writings of Adler and Shani (2001) and Adler et al. (2003) to the current call for collaborative management research that seeks to integrate theory and practice in the production of actionable scientific knowledge and to further understand the underlying knowledge-creation processes involved.

THE SECOND LEGACY OF ARISTOTLE AND THEORY-PRACTICE INTEGRATION

Ironically, in recovering a place for the integration of theory and practice in knowledge production, we need look no further than Aristotle himself. One of the first thinkers to question the separation of practice and theory and challenge the scholar, and by implication

the practitioner, as the unilateral producer of knowledge was none other than Aristotle in his later reflections on the nature of knowledge in the classic work *Metaphysics*. Here inspired by ideas of his mentors Socrates and Plato, Aristotle presents a radically different image of what it means to create true knowledge of events and situations. And in this second, less renowned "image" presented by Aristotle, we find compelling claims that the bedrock of true understanding emanates from the creative integration of knowledge based on theory, practice, and experience. Aristotle's latter position about ascertaining the true nature of knowledge involved merging the worldviews of the scholar and the practitioner. His striving was in understanding how the experience of the practitioner in doing things, or the *empeiria* or experience of playing a flute, and the practical knowledge and craft or *technê* of how a flute is played or made, are merged with the theoretical knowledge of the scholar who inquires into how things come to be, which is *epistêmê*. In other words, either one or the other form of knowledge is not sufficient. True knowledge and understanding, according to Aristotle, have a basis in experience (*empeiria*), craft (*technê*), and theory (*epistêmê*). As Aristotle explains in *Metaphysics* (1961),

> The master craftsman (*technitês*) is wiser than the person only of experience, or only of technique, because he knows the cause, the reasons (*epistêmê*) why things are to be done or why things happen the way they happen. The mere artisan (*cheirotechnês*) or practitioner acts without this knowledge. (pp. 981b–982a)

He also contrasts the *technitês* (the ones with *empeiria*, *technê*, and *epistêmê*) with the inexperienced scholar who has only *epistêmê*, and relies on the rational accounting of why things happen the way they happen without a basis in experience (*empeiria*) or craft (*technê*). According to Aristotle, this is equally ineffective in producing true knowledge (Parry, 2003). Aristotle (1961) goes on to explain why this is so:

> On the contrary, we see [sometimes] experienced men succeeding even better than those who know the reasons, but who lack experience. The reason is that experience, like action or production, deals with things severally as concrete individuals, whereas art deals with them generally. Thus, a physician does not cure "man" but he cures Callias, Socrates or some other individual. . . . If then someone lacking experience, but knowing the general principles of the art, sizes up a situation as a whole, he will often, because he is ignorant of the individuals within that whole, miss the mark and fail to cure; for it is the individuals who must be cured. (p. 981b)

In these two statements of the second Aristotelian legacy, we clearly see the necessity and importance of inquiry designs such as collaborative management research that seek to blend theory and practice and, by implication, the scholar and the practitioner.

According to Aristotle, both these sets of competencies are necessary to realize true knowledge that can inform a situation. If either one is separately applied without support from the other, true knowledge will not be realized. The scholar's forte is in appealing to scientific knowledge. Her strength is in uncovering the generalizable principles and explanatory reasons that may underlie a situation derived from the larger scientific discourse that incorporates multiple contexts and experiences. In contrast, the practitioner derives knowledge from her experience with the particulars of the situation. Her strength is drawn from *empeiria*, which is grounded in the experience of humans who populate a particular system and the craft, or *technê*, derived from those experiences. *Empeiria*

and *technê* deal with the specifics, the individuals, and particular contexts of those experiences. It is as significant a form of knowledge that informs understanding and action as the theoretical knowledge of *epistêmê* that deals with underlying causes. This kind of integrated knowledge is the practical wisdom of *phronesis*.

For Aristotle, *phronesis* represents the ideal integration of experience, craft, and theory. The ancient Greek word *phronesis* is defined as wisdom, practical wisdom, and prudence (Peters, 1967, p. 157). A major theme throughout *phronesis* is its concern with morals and ethics (Adler, 1978). But, for Aristotle, *phronesis* also involved knowledge of the particulars, or *empeiria*, the *technê* or craft derived from those experiences, and the invocation of universals, or *epistêmê theoretike* (Dunne, 1993), the generalizable knowledge that may apply to those particulars. And it is here we find his most compelling claim for the creative integration of theory and practice as the basis for true understanding and action. Aristotle (1962) writes: "Practical wisdom does not deal only with universals. It must also be familiar with particulars, since it is concerned with action, and action has to do with particulars [while not missing the general]"(p. 1141b).

Aristotle (1962) explains his logic with the following contrast between a man of scientific, universal knowledge about health and a man with practical knowledge about foods:

> This explains why some men who have no scientific knowledge are [sometimes] more adept in practical matters, especially if they have experience, than those who do have scientific knowledge. For if a person were to know that light meat is easily digested, and hence wholesome, but did not know what sort of meat is light, he will not produce health, whereas someone who knows that poultry is light and wholesome is more likely to produce health. (p. 1141b)

Clearly the optimal solution for health, opines Aristotle, is to have knowledge of both the universal, or the scientific knowledge that light meat is easily digested, and the particulars, arising from the experience that poultry is light. According to Dunne (1993), the ability to blend the universal with the particulars (or theory with experience) is the stunning achievement of *phronesis*: "*Phronesis* does not ascend to a level of abstraction or generality that leaves experience behind. It arises from experience and returns into experience" (p. 293).

Another important consideration that *phronesis* speaks to is action that is based not merely on an integrative understanding but also on ethical and moral dimensions. While *phronesis* or "practical wisdom issues commands, its end is to tell us what we ought to do and what we ought not to do," which is the hallmark of virtue, or *arete* (Aristotle, 1962, p. 1143a). Those who are deemed the most knowledgeable in *phronesis,* Aristotle states, are also "good at deliberating. . . . They can, by reasoning, aim and hit the best thing attainable to man by action, [and] have the capacity for seeing what is good for themselves and for mankind" (p. 1141b).

And in this statement we see the ethical responsibilities Aristotle places on scholar-practitioners and collaborative management research communities. In invoking the particular and the general in their knowledge-creation activities, they should be equally concerned about contributing to the local good and about advancing the causes of theory, which is the larger good.

In many ways, Aristotle and his mentors Socrates and Plato are often believed to have loved knowledge for the sake of knowledge, not caring about its practical applications (Dunne, 1993; Parry, 2003). However, in exploring the second image of Aristotle, it is clear that he considered the highest result in every concern to be the achievement of true practice, a practice that draws on wisdom (*phronesis*) that arises from an integral complex of experience (*empeiria*), craft (*technê*), and theory (*epistêmê*), because in his opinion it is only "this kind of knowledge that enables a conscious choice possible between true and false, good and bad, benefit and hurt, and, generally, between 'good' and 'evil'" (Parry, 2003, p. 12).

THE SCHOLAR-PRACTITIONER AS AN EPISTEMIC TECHNICIAN

Beyond highlighting this second image of Aristotle and speaking to his legacy and contributions as an early advocate of theory-practice integration, another goal of this chapter is to relate the Aristotelian second legacy to current times and its application to organizational research. We regard scholar-practitioners to be ideal contemporary carriers of Aristotle's second vision. As individuals who have a foot each in the worlds of academia and practice and who are familiar with the universal and particulars, these actors view as equally important the advancement of organizational causes and the scientific profession. They strive to create actionable scientific knowledge through useful research (Lawler et al., 1985) that enhances the theoretical understanding of the phenomena as well as provides for a better resolution of business problems (Tenkasi & Hay, 2004). Astley and Zammuto (1993) describe them as an intermediate cadre of professionals, who by virtue of membership in both the academic and practice worlds can act as effective bridges between the otherwise incommensurate communities of scholars and practitioners. Graduates of executive doctoral programs who continue working in organizations during and after education are one example of this intermediate cadre of "boundary spanners," those "who have the potential to close the relevance gap from both ends of science and business" (Huff & Huff, 2001, p. S50).

In following the efforts of scholar-practitioners in organizational projects to create actionable scientific knowledge, we can further the Aristotelian vision by extending our understanding from the need to integrate theory and practice to comprehending the processes involved in blending the universals with the particulars in which *phronesis* or theory-practice integration is realized. For this, we turn to an inductive study reported in some detail in earlier publications (Hay, 2003; Tenkasi & Hay, 2004) that sought not only to understand the elements of theory and practice that the scholar-practitioner brings to the table but also to grasp how the scholar-practitioner goes about linking them in organizational projects to create actionable scientific knowledge that meets scientific criteria and influences business results.

STUDY METHODOLOGY

Interviews were completed with 11 scholar-practitioners, who were asked to recount successful organizational projects that had effective theory and business outcomes and that applied their knowledge of theory and practice. These project experiences related to 11 organizations located in the East Coast and Midwest regions of the United States. All interviews were taped and transcribed. All the scholar-practitioners were Ph.D.'s; two were members of consulting organizations, two were academics with extensive consulting interaction with industry, and seven were graduates of an executive doctoral program in organizational development who continued their employment as internal organizational change agents. All of the 11 projects selected had tangible business outcomes such as a customized business model, a new technique or process that was implemented and used as a result of the project, or, in some cases, evidence of material impacts of these interventions on financial indices such as return on investment

(ROI), profitability, and other metrics of effectiveness such as reduction in product development cycle time. Theoretical outcomes from these projects were academic presentations, journal publications, books, and, in some cases, dissertations that advanced the state of knowledge in arenas such as self-managing teams, leadership assessment and development, mergers and acquisitions, and sociotechnical systems design for knowledge work. Six contrast interviews were also completed, four with business researchers who had no scholarly affiliations and two with academics who had minimal experience with organizations (see Table 3.1).

Our analytical strategy employed an iterative approach of traveling back and forth between the data and emerging theory to develop our model. The cornerstones of our analyses were (1) to develop a narrative sequence of events for each case (Elsbach & Sutton, 1992; Silverman, 2001); (2) to employ a within-and-across case analysis of all cases to identify similarities and differences across events (Eisenhardt, 1989); and (3) to systematically develop and employ an emergent coding system to methodically discern and elaborate on the common dynamics of theory-practice integration observed across the cases based on the logic of replication (Yin, 1994). The logic of replication treats a series of cases as a series of experiments with each case serving to confirm or disconfirm an emergent relationship, where the emphasis is on retaining the common relationships found across all the cases (Eisenhardt, 1989; Yin, 1994).

In following the sequence of these 11 successful projects, we found that scholar-practitioners, in order to successfully realize project outcomes, employed a set of actions motivated by their knowledge of theory and a set of actions motivated by their experiences and knowledge of practice conventions endemic to the system. Instead of the traditional views of practice as involving action and theory as involving abstract thinking, much in line with activity theory[3] (Vygotsky,

Table 3.1   A Description of Scholar-Practitioner Projects and Outcomes of Dual Relevance

Purpose of Project	Practical Outcomes	Theoretical Outcomes
1. Increasing the innovation effectiveness of the R&D center of a high technology firm	A practical model of the critical deliberations that new product development projects should undertake based on the project life stage and the essential knowledge domains required at each stage Key impact: reduction in product development cycle time	Several presentations at forums such the Academy of Management, and journal publications
2. Leadership alignment across a multidivisional global consumer products firm	A training program and a model that could be used to assess and develop transformational leadership behaviors among the many managers/supervisors of each division/unit Key impacts: observed uniformity in transformational leadership behaviors across the different business units	Presentations at academic and practitioner conferences, journal publications, and working papers that assess the relationship between transformational leadership and emotional intelligence
3. Establishing a Center for Manufacturing Excellence in a heavy engineering firm	An internal organizational model of the stages involved in realizing self-managing team effectiveness and training interventions that will accelerate movement to each stage Key impacts: improvements in cost and quality indices	Paper presentations at practitioner and academic conferences on self-managing teams, a book chapter, and a dissertation
4. Creating effective practices and processes for mergers and acquisitions (M&A) in an electrical products firm	An internal workbook highlighting procedures, processes, and training interventions for post-M&A integration drawing on social constructionist principles. A major aspect of the model was achieving strategy or vision consensus about the merged organization. Key impacts: quicker and more effective cultural integration as indicated in postsurvey measures	Presentations at Academy of Management, a journal article, and a dissertation
5. Transitioning four brownfield manufacturing units into high performance work systems of a global equipment manufacturing firm	An internal process model based on Appreciative Inquiry and incorporating best practices and training interventions drawn from a study of four pilot sites, to help evolve other brownfield manufacturing sites into high performance work systems Key impacts: improvements in cost, quality, and productivity indices	Presentations, conference proceedings, and a dissertation

Purpose of Project	Practical Outcomes	Theoretical Outcomes
6. Piloting a whole-systems design model for radical organizational change in one region of a multiregional wireless company	A process model for whole systems design developed from learnings of the pilot region for use in other regions Key impact: increased market share based on restructuring of business operations, particularly the customer service function	Presentations, journal articles, and a book on large group interventions
7. Assessing differential implementation success rates among four business units/regions of a corporate-driven global organizational change program in a worldwide food services firm	An internal model of change communication that takes into account interpretive differences among the multiple constituents who are parties to the change Key impact: a revised change communication protocol from the corporate office for tailoring change messages by taking into account the cultural/interpretive background of regions/units	Presentations, publication in several conference proceedings, and a dissertation
8. Designing optimal organizational structures for new product development effectiveness and efficiency in a global communications firm	An internal organization design model for structuring new product development units largely derived from a meta-analysis of existing new product development research literature	Presentations, journal publications, working papers, and a dissertation
9. Improving restaurant effectiveness and efficiency in the midwestern region of a worldwide food services firm	An internal process model based on Appreciative Inquiry and a template that can be implemented in other regions for improving restaurant effectiveness and efficiency Key impacts: improvement in restaurant service effectiveness	Presentations, publication in conference proceedings, and a dissertation
10. Transitioning a centralized global IT company into decentralized customer-focused business teams	Successful reorganization of a company, with buy-in of key stakeholders	Working papers, presentations at practitioner conferences, and a dissertation
11. An assessment of the impact of peer mentoring on effective sharing of organizational knowledge in a global communications firm	Evaluation of a peer mentoring program and identification of best practices in knowledge sharing	Conference presentations, journal article, and a dissertation

1962, 1978), we found scholar-practitioners using knowledge drawn from theory, experience, and technique as different kinds of tools and resources to inform different kinds of action as the projects progressed. There were actions that were informed by theoretical precepts represented in the form of formal domains of knowledge available in books, articles, expert opinion, and principles of research. Scholar-practitioners regularly invoked their broad knowledge of the scholarly and practical literature on how people and organizations work, and also accessed specific publications within academic or practitioner outlets that pertained to the topic of interest, such as designing team-based organizations or creating a leadership assessment process. And there were other actions arising out of the scholar-practitioners' awareness of and experience with organizational conventions, history, norms, and power relationships and their mastery of the techniques of getting things done in the organization. These practice-mediated streams of actions frequently invoked organizational, political, and rational conventions to influence key decision makers controlling resources for the project, to secure cooperation of employees responsible for implementation of the project, and to ensure that projects were framed to conform to local project management conventions (see Tenkasi & Hay, 2004, for a comprehensive description).

STRATEGIES FOR INTERRELATING THEORY AND PRACTICE

Of more interest is how these practitioner-scholars linked their understanding of theory and practice to produce actionable scientific knowledge or, in Aristotelian terms, the achievement of *phronesis* (Dunne, 1993). Our analysis of the 11 cases revealed that scholar-practitioners tended to interrelate theory and practice as strategies for (1) framing, (2) influencing and legitimizing, (3) sensemaking, and (4) demonstrating. We elaborate on each of these dynamics.

Framing

Framing effects were most commonly observed in defining the nature and scope of the project. Framing was typically employed to bound and structure an otherwise equivocal phenomenon in more concrete and precise

terms (Weick, 1979). In several cases, we noticed the use of theory and research findings to frame and give direction to a broadly expressed change mandate from the leadership as a possible solution to an organizational crisis or toward achieving a desired future state. The scholar-practitioners relied on several knowledge elements, such as social science knowledge and current literature on theories of organizational effectiveness, as informing forces to frame a general organizational mandate in more bounded and specific terms. In one case the scholar-practitioner took the vision of the CEO to move a manufacturing plant into a center of excellence and helped define the project as one of reorganizing the workforce into self-managing teams. Another scholar-practitioner took the broad mandate of leadership alignment and helped "frame" and "define" the project as one of implementing a leadership assessment and development process for the organization. Infrequently, we also found instances where the scholar-practitioner used a practically mediated opening to frame a theoretical niche. In these cases, the practical opportunity provided the right conditions to test a theoretical model and/or develop new theory to answer a practical question. In one of the cases, the CEO's desire to make the R&D organization more effective at knowledge management opened up the opportunity for the scholar-practitioner to pilot test a new process that took the principles of sociotechnical theory and applied them to knowledge work. In addition to practical ramifications, the project had theoretical ramifications in terms of charting new ground for sociotechnical theory by extending its application from routine work to nonroutine work.

Influencing and Legitimizing

Influencing and legitimizing were used to justify a concept, idea, model, or course of action as the most appropriate for a situation.

Legitimizing was typically exercised by the scholar-practitioner in convincing and informing key stakeholders of the need for change, the model and attributes of change, and the process involved in the change. We found that legitimization actions involved cases both where theory informed practice and, conversely, where practice informed theory. Theory was used as a tool to legitimize the need for a certain kind of practical action. In addition to the practical justification for change driven by the leadership mandate, or organizational crisis, this frequently took the shape of using as a tool the theoretical knowledge that the scholar-practitioner garnered from a review of current literature around the topic of interest. In one case, the scholar-practitioner, in his quest to understand leadership alignment, read the current literature and determined that the most appropriate way to achieve alignment was through a "leadership assessment and development" process and convinced the stakeholders of the rationality of this approach based on his knowledge of the current literature. In contrast to using theory as a tool to legitimize practice, we also found the practical demands of a situation/context as an opportunity to legitimize a certain kind of theoretically informed action. This was evident in a case where the scholar-practitioner, after a review of several models of knowledge management, indicated that the sociotechnical systems (STS) approach applied to knowledge work might be most suitable, because it not only considered the interface of knowledge elements pertaining to the social, technical, and environmental systems but also engaged the workforce in designing such a system, a most appropriate strategy given the CEO's interest in involving a large population of the R&D workforce in the change process. The scholar-practitioner was able to skillfully match the practical requirements of the CEO that called for broad employee engagement with a theoretical model that allowed the same. The

justification behind asking managers from the several research functions to be part of the central design team was attributed to the CEO's mandate, although it was also clearly a requirement of the STS design model.

In both framing and legitimizing, scholar-practitioners are engaging in the search for appropriate causal mechanisms or pathways that will enable realization of the outcomes desired by the CEO in light of the contextual constraints and opportunities afforded by the organization. Top management, at least in the cases we studied, expressed the desire or mandate for a future state based on a vision or organizational crisis, but not a clear sense of how to get there. We frequently noticed that this is where the scholar-practitioner steps in and uses her expansive knowledge of theory, experience, and craft in analyzing the situation and conjecturing the pathways that may help realize the desired outcomes. Scholar-practitioners are aware that the fit between mechanisms or pathways and their functional outcomes is not necessarily concrete, and that their relationship as expressed in theory is inherently ambivalent (Bunge, 2004). It is through a review of several potential pathways that they choose what they believe might be the most appropriate mechanism, after giving due consideration to the situational context. This is where theory, experience, and understanding of organizational conventions (rational and political) are useful. While theory and research findings are often used to frame and assess the potential pathways through which the desired outcomes can be realized, it is frequently the particulars of the local environment that dictate the choice of the pathway. For example, the CEO's quest for the firm to become a center for manufacturing excellence could have been addressed through various mechanisms such as improved manufacturing processes or better materials management, all scientifically validated pathways to realize manufacturing excellence (*Best Manufacturing Practices*

Report, 1998). However, the scholar-practitioner chose self-managing teams as the most viable mechanism based on several local considerations. These included the high levels of camaraderie and collective identity as a distinct group among an older workforce that contrasted itself with the supervisors, and a recognition that potentially the best way to infuse a sense for quality, cost, and schedule would be by making the employee group take ownership for these issues through self-governing work teams rather than relying on supervisory mandates, which had proven ineffectual in the past. Other factors were the multiskilling and job rotation that come with a team-based design, which would allow team members variety and challenge in their jobs in an otherwise routine manufacturing environment. Alternative pathways such as technological enhancements to the old assembly line format or improved material management techniques would not have decreased the boredom or reduced the quality problems, because these designs would have failed to take into account the social dynamics of the situation.

Conjecturing the pathways and thinking through why one mechanism might be more appropriate than others also helps in subsequently legitimizing the pathway since it is based on both theoretical and practical considerations. This stance of reflection and pondering about appropriate causal mechanisms that considers the general and the local was a defining quality of scholar-practitioners that enabled them both to produce outcomes of consequence for the organization and to advance the larger state of knowledge. This quality essentially distinguished the scholar-practitioner from practitioners who would mimic the latest technique or fad and apply it indiscriminately to the local environment with which they were familiar without really understanding the underlying theory or conducting research to direct their efforts. This

approach was also in contrast with the scholar who, familiar with theories of organization, applies her theoretical understanding of how organizations work and conducts research on an abstract problem without due consideration of the local dynamics or a reflection of how useful the findings may be to improving the causes of the organization (Tenkasi & Hay, 2004).

Sensemaking

Once the causal pathway is established, the third strong function of interrelating theory and practice was its role in mutual sensemaking. The scholar-practitioner relies on theory as a tool to make sense of practice, and practice elements as instruments in making sense of theory. This mutual dynamic often took the form of co-informing, reciprocal cycles of invoking theory to inform practice and invoking practice to inform theory, which were evident in all project stages. While framing was a unique type of sensemaking activity often related to the project definition stage, sensemaking patterns pertaining to project execution and project realization were also frequently observed. A clear instance of theory informing practice was the application of systematic research principles in the assessment/diagnosis and sensemaking preceding the implementation of the intervention. This was a common pattern across all the cases, where scholar-practitioners used a combination of survey instrumentation, interviews, systematic observations, and, in one case, personal diary recordings of the participants for data collection. The leadership assessment and development project used a pretest-posttest design, while the self-managing team project involved a constant-comparison qualitative design where the scholar-practitioner compared and contrasted the evolutionary journey of six natural workgroups as they transitioned into effective self-managing teams at different speeds. The use of systematic approaches enabled more accurate diagnosis and sensemaking prior to implementation. In many respects, scholar-practitioners were engaging in fact-based decision making (Pfeffer & Sutton, 2006) using evidence-based approaches (Leslie, Loch, & Schaninger, 2006). Realizing that their observations might be contaminated by what they expected to see, they relied on data collected through systematic and scientific approaches. They were aware that it is easy to be trapped by ideologies, beliefs, and conventional wisdom instead of paying attention to the data (Pfeffer & Sutton, 2006).

Practice informing theory followed a similar rigor and was most evident in the process of implementing the change. Respondents mentioned that they learned from the process of doing, or implementing the change. Making sense of the implementation experience frequently drew on a background of theoretical knowledge, including literature reviews and the use of research data acquired through scientific research methods. Coexistent with this approach was the inductive dynamics of practice reinforcing theoretical knowledge, particularly when there were anomalous experiences provided by the data from implementing the model that could not be explained by current theoretical precepts. These variations in practice were mediational tools that frequently reinforced the current dominant theoretical conceptualization. A salient case is the scholar-practitioner who initially applied a traditional sociotechnical system framework to analyze knowledge work. In applying the model to a pilot sample, he found that the linear transformation processes of routine work and their variances were not applicable to nonroutine knowledge work and that the best way to understand transformation processes in knowledge work required a focus on the deliberations or sensemaking conversations of the scientists. He realized that these conversations were the

principal transformational activities in knowledge work and that variances arose from factors such as not having the right members who had relevant knowledge involved in the conversations, or the lack of an appropriate process to hear everyone's opinion in the deliberations. These revised understandings helped him design an effective knowledge management model for nonroutine work.

Demonstrating

The final commingling of theory and practice was in demonstrating impact. Theory informing practice was most evident in providing empirical evidence and demonstrating proof that the organizational project was successful in terms of achieving practical results— that there was a change in mindsets, in behavior, and in profitability or other metrics. Providing proof of business impacts relied on data collected and analyzed through systematic research designs. Scholar-practitioners frequently used quantitative evidence to indicate behavior and/or attitude change in survey scales pre- to postintervention, or indicated shifts in financial measures pre- to post-change. Qualitative data, particularly context-sensitive quotes or verbatim comments, were employed to demonstrate changes in perspective or new behaviors. For example, the scholar-practitioner involved with the implementation of self-managing teams made use of extensive quotes from team members to demonstrate that the teams were engaging in self-managing behaviors and highlight the kinds of new behaviors that were involved in team self-management. Practice informing theory was typically in the form of using the practical business impacts to provide proof of the theoretical model. A reduction in new product development cycle time was conclusive evidence for the scholar-practitioner to demonstrate in subsequent academic publications that the knowledge management model based on sociotechnical systems was clearly valid.

TURNS AND SCAFFOLDING
AS UNIQUE DEVICES
IN INTERRELATING THEORY
AND PRACTICE

Of the 11 projects we studied, in only a few cases did the scholar-practitioner explicitly inform the organization that he was seeking to advance his theoretical interests alongside business outcomes. One case involved a project that was seeking to determine why the research efforts of an R&D organization were not producing consequential results. In this context, research on why research was not producing intended outcomes was seen as a legitimate enterprise. However, in the majority of cases, it was clearly the business problem that was most salient in the minds of management and that had to be ddressed. In this situation, the scholar-practitioners, whether external consultants or internal change agents employed by the firm, were aware that addressing business issues was most important for personal legitimacy in the corporate world and approached these projects as consulting assignments rather than research endeavors. Our interviews with these scholar-practitioners suggest that, at least in the corporate environments they worked in, consulting is seen as adding value to the organization, while research is viewed as an abstract act that is not of practical relevance. Approaching the assignments from a consulting angle helped them gain access since they were viewed as practical problem solvers. Furthermore, the word *research* for many of these scholar-practitioners was a term they would prefer not to use but would rather build in as part of the background. In their view, research and principles of research entail considerable background education that corporate executives do not have the time or patience for, although they are tolerant of research and publications as long as they do not come in the way of achieving practical results. In some cases, the publications have to be cleared by the appropriate legal departments.

As aptly summarized by one scholar-practitioner, "My CEO wants us to become a center of manufacturing excellence. . . . I have convinced him that the best way to achieve it is to create self-managing teams. He wants them to happen, and if I tell him I want to conduct a research project on testing a theory of self-managing team effectiveness, I will probably be out of the door tomorrow. . . . We don't have the luxury of presenting a research proposal but have to build research principles into the way we consult. But if I do write a few articles or get my dissertation from this project he is OK with it as long as I show practical results— that is what is most important to him. If I gain research knowledge that is fine as long as it does not come in the way of organizational needs" (author interview).

Despite the lack of explicit emphasis on research, intriguingly all 11 projects managed to produce outcomes that were of relevance to the organization and the scientific community. Our interest was in understanding how these scholar-practitioners were able to create theory-practice linkages to realize dual outcomes of relevance to both practice and research. In Aristotelian terms this is another aspect of *phronesis,* being able to deliberate about the situation and aim for creating knowledge that not only is good for the particulars but also considers the universals, or the larger good of humankind. We found that it was in this spirit that many scholar-practitioners approached their organizational projects. They wanted to create knowledge through these projects that could be communicated to the larger professional community in addition to helping the organization practically.

Across all 11 cases we found evidence for two dominant types of strategies through which theory-practice linkages were created, enabling the embedding of systematic research. These dual strategies were the use of *turns* and *scaffolding*. These two moves enabled the scholar-practitioners to set the conditions favorable for theory-practice linkages and enact these linkages to produce both practical and research outcomes.

Turns

Turns are reframing moves and tools that help make an element more familiar, more legitimate, and potentially more palatable to the concerned audience by locating it within a respective community's "systems of meaning" (Fleck, 1935/1979). In our observations, successful scholar-practitioners skillfully employed "theory to practice" turns to make the unfamiliar familiar to the practitioner community. We found several instances of theory-to-practice turns that facilitated the acceptance of theoretically informed activities, including principles of research, and enabled their linkage with practically informed activities. Some self-evident examples of theory to practice turns were (1) turning the knowledge of current literature into information from best practices in the industry and other organizations; (2) turning representative sampling that called for sampling across levels, functions, and gender into a strategy for broader involvement of employees; (3) turning action research processes of implementation into learning from experience; and (4) turning principles of valid and reliable research (including systematic data collection, comparative research designs, and rigorous analytical strategy) into a foolproof strategy to assess bottom-line impact. The goals of these turns were to influence an audience—a business rather than an academic audience. Reframing for the business rather than the academic audience has more of a pragmatic goal to it. The goal is not to change the academic import of the theoretical action but rather to present it in such a way that the

business audience does not misunderstand it and is motivated to construe and continue with the research as having practical relevance.

The dynamic of turns may be best understood by invoking the concept of "thought worlds" (Fleck, 1935/1979). Thought worlds appeal to the social basis of cognition and meaning making in any community. The organizational participant community can be construed as a unique thought world and the academic/research community as another. A community's thought world is characterized by two aspects: their "fund of knowledge," or what they know, and their "systems of meaning," or how they know. Complex ideas cannot be shared easily across thought worlds, and different thought worlds will attempt to interpret each other's ideas based on their unique funds of knowledge. If such interpretation fails, then they may view the other's central issues as esoteric, if not meaningless (Dougherty, 1992). For a community of knowing to adopt an idea, information, or knowledge from a different community of knowing, the information or knowledge has to be reconfigured or adapted to fit in with the recipient community's meaning systems (Boland & Tenkasi, 1995; Tenkasi & Mohrman, 1999). Acceptance of new knowledge or an innovation by a local community would vary depending upon the innovation's location in a knowledge space consisting of "local cultural objects of knowledge" of varying degrees of similarity to the proposed innovation. Actors in a community would behave toward new objects or received knowledge in ways similar to how they behave toward existing cultural objects that have been judged to be similar to the new objects (Stefflere, 1972). And this process of locating research activities in terms similar to familiar corporate activities informs the underlying logic of turns that the scholar-practitioner uses to legitimate activities informed by theory and/or principles of research. These forms of translation facilitate acceptance among the organizational community.

Scaffolding

Scaffolding, a term most commonly associated with construction, typically denotes "a platform made for workers to stand on when they want to reach higher parts of a building to add on to or modify the structure of the building" (Cambridge Dictionaries Online, 2003). This notion of a platform that helps in subsequent building activities probably best conveys the image of scaffolding as a mediational tool employed by scholar-practitioners to enable theory-practice linkages. Scaffolding, which typically involved the creation and use of a theory-based or a practice-based platform at an earlier stage to influence its complement at a subsequent stage, formed a critical linking mechanism between theory and practice.

A role particularly served by practice-to-theory scaffolding was in ensuring knowledge outcomes of the organizational project. The scholar-practitioner may enact the current event to meet practice needs but does so in anticipation of a future use on the theoretical side. Sometimes, these activities may exceed what is required to meet practice needs, but in building them in, the scholar-practitioner increases the odds of subsequent theoretical outcomes. For example, a scholar-practitioner involved in a leadership assessment and development process used several validated leadership instruments, such as the Multifactor Leadership Questionnaire MLQ; Bass & Avolio, 1995), to evaluate transformational leadership behaviors in order to assess existing leadership behavior and styles within the organization. The practical agenda was to create an aligned leadership model across the organization and train managers in transformational leadership behaviors. The program and process employed a well-established leadership development program and would not have realized any research outcomes beyond stating that the leadership training intervention worked and there was an increase in self-reports of transformational leadership behaviors by the managers and in their assessments by subordinates. However, the scholar-practitioner also had a long-standing research interest in understanding the links between emotional intelligence and leadership behaviors, particularly in whether there was an overlap between the two constructs, and if levels of emotional intelligence moderated the practice of transformational leadership. Although this was not part of the leadership alignment program or process, he used the opportunity to collect data on emotional intelligence, and while incorporating it as part of the feedback to managers, he subsequently used the data to write papers suggesting that transformational leadership and emotional intelligence are independent constructs, and that transformational leadership behaviors of managers are moderated by their levels of emotional intelligence.

The common pattern with scaffolding from theory to practice was the inclusion of a theory-based platform at an earlier stage of a project that, while helping guide practice, also ensured subsequent theoretical outcomes in seeking to answer new research questions. This was typically the case when theory was used to frame the nature and scope of the project. An illustrative case is the scholar-practitioner who was able to frame the CEO's vision to move the manufacturing plant into a center of excellence as one of reorganizing the workforce into self-managing teams. The theory-based platform of self-managing teams enabled the practitioner not only to direct action but also to do systematic research on what she identified as a gap in the self-managing teams research and literature, i.e., that is, to discover the evolutionary pathway to becoming a self-managing team; why some teams are able to more successfully transition into self-management than are others; and further, why some are faster at it.

Scaffolding is an important mechanism that scholar-practitioners use to realize theory-practice linkages. Theory-based platforms not only engender practice patterns that help generate practical outcomes but also ensure the embedding of theoretical elements to generate scientific outcomes. Likewise, practice-based platforms are skillfully appropriated or enacted by the scholar-practitioner such that they not only meet the practice requirements of the current situation but also enable future use on the theoretical side (see Table 3.2).

IMPLICATIONS FOR COLLABORATIVE MANAGEMENT RESEARCH

In both Aristotle's notion of *phronesis* and the scholar-practitioner's role as the contemporary carrier of the Aristotelian second vision, we see single individuals holding the knowledge and responsibilities for integrating theory and practice to produce actionable scientific knowledge. On the other hand, collaborative management research seeks to produce actionable scientific knowledge through partnerships between researchers and members of a living system (Shani, Wilson, & David, 2003). Nevertheless, we believe there are some lessons to be gleaned from the actions of these single actors that could apply to collaborative management research projects involving multiple actors.

First, producing actionable scientific knowledge requires the commingling of experience, practice, and theory-mediated streams of actions. Although these are embodied in a single individual in the case of the scholar-practitioner, what clearly came out in our analysis was that these are different

sets of competencies based on different kinds of "know-that" and know-how. Gilbert Ryle (1949) distinguished between "know-that" (knowing about something) and know-how (knowing how to do something), both essential components of knowledge. In the case of the scholar-practitioner, theory-informed actions involve certain kinds of "know-that" (current literature, social science theory, principles of research design) and certain kinds of know-how (framing, designing, and analyzing a survey). Practice-mediated actions similarly invoke other kinds of "know-that" (contextual conventions, norms, rules, power relationships, routines, established procedures) and know-how (influencing, legitimizing, project management) that allow the scholar-practitioner to use these contextual conventions as enabling forces or, when required, to work around them. It is in this creative intersection of the two different types of competencies that the scholar-practitioner realizes theory-practice linkages and further uses them to make possible the dual outcomes associated with actionable scientific knowledge.

In designing collaborative research systems it is crucial that these different sets of know-how and "know-that" are well represented in the community of collaborative researchers. We see at least four different roles in collaborative research communities that invoke these different sets of competencies. First, there is a need for actors familiar with the particulars of the organization, specifically local theories of action including knowledge of organizational history, social dynamics, interpretive conventions, norms, and power relationships. Second, there is a need for a set of actors familiar with the universals or the larger scientific discourse pertaining to both theory and research who can bring forth an awareness of what is known and what needs to be known to advance knowledge from a research/knowledge point

Table 3.2   Strategies for Interrelating Theory and Practice

Strategy	Relating Theory to Practice	Relating Practice to Theory
Framing: A strategy employed to bound and structure an otherwise equivocal phenomenon in more concrete and precise terms	Using theory and research findings to frame and give direction to a broadly expressed change mandate from leadership as a potential solution to an organization crisis or a desired future state	Using a practically mediated opening to frame a theoretical niche, where a practical opportunity provides ideal conditions to test a theoretical model and/or develop new theory to answer a practical question
Influencing and Legitimizing: A strategy used to justify and convince relevant stakeholders that a concept, idea, model, or course of action was most appropriate for a situation	Using theory as a tool to influence and legitimize the need for a certain kind of practical action often garnered from a review of current literature around the topic of interest	Using the practical demands of a situation/context as a mediating tool to legitimize a certain kind of theoretically based action
Sensemaking: A reciprocal dynamic where theory is used as a tool to make sense of practice, and practice to make sense of theory	Using theory as a tool to make sense of practice, applying systematic principles in the assessment, diagnosis, and sensemaking preceding the implementation of interventions, and making sense of implementation experiences by drawing on a background of theoretical and research knowledge	Using practice experiences to re-inform theory, particularly recognizing anomalous experiences provided by the data that could not be explained by the current dominant theoretical framework and using them as opportunities to revise theory
Demonstrating: A strategy that commingles theory and practice elements to demonstrate impact and results	Using research-based quantitative and qualitative evidence to demonstrate that the organization project was successful in terms of achieving practical results—that there was a change in mindsets, behavior, or metrics of effectiveness such as ROI or profitability	Using practical business impacts to provide supporting evidence and legitimate the veracity of the theoretical model
Turns: A strategy of reframing that helps make a theoretical element more familiar, legitimate, and palatable to a practitioner audience by locating it within the community's systems of meaning	Turning the knowledge of current literature into information from best practices in the industry and other organizations, or turning representative sampling into a broader strategy for involvement of employees	
Scaffolding: A strategy that can be likened to a platform that helps in subsequent building activities	Including a theory-based platform at an earlier stage of a project that, while helping in guiding practice, also ensures subsequent theoretical outcomes in seeking to answer new research questions	Adding practical elements to a project that may exceed current practice needs but that will increase the subsequent odds of theoretical outcomes

of view. In the union of these two sets of actors, collaborative research communities can arrive at appropriate causal mechanisms that can move the system to its desired state enabling practical outcomes, while also elaborating scientific theory. Third, to put these causal pathways into motion, we need actors who enjoy credibility, legitimacy, and influence in the organizational system, particularly with top management and other relevant stakeholders. We see these actors as having deep practical knowledge of how to move these projects within the organization. A fourth and critical role involves actors who are adept at translating theory with respect to its practice implications and can frame practice contingencies in terms of their theoretical potentials, a role that we elaborate in the next section.

Our second implication is motivated by the observation that the majority of the cases began without a clear mandate to integrate theory and practice and yet each of them resulted in the delivery of actionable scientific knowledge. Thus, what transpired between the beginning and end is of significance given that it points to the active involvement of the scholar-practitioner in the creation and use of theory-practice linkages, a form of "expert practice" in and of itself. The scholar-practitioners were able to seamlessly integrate theory and practice, revealing a fair amount of dexterity in being able to sense opportunities for interrelating and act on them right away. The scholar-practitioners were able to turn potential theory mediators such as current literature into practice mediators by reframing them as best practices in order to legitimate them. The scholar-practitioners also engaged in scaffolding by creating a theoretical platform and using this tool to make sure that there would be a realization of future theory elements out of practice mediators, while also ensuring that the reframed theory mediators would lead to practice elements. The goal is

to create an agenda for pursuing theory and practice aims and to secure the organizational resources required to realize those aims, which in turn comes from an intimate familiarity with both the practical and theoretical contexts of the project. We believe collaborative research communities can benefit by including at least a few such members, who in addition to their valuable skills of integration can play the role of "semiotic brokers" and thus act as effective bridges between the research and practice contingents of the community. The particular skills of this role lie in translating between communities and locating concepts within the respective communities' systems of meaning. In essence the role involves the ability to take theoretical elements and express them in terms that would be more familiar and legitimate to a practice-based community, while also taking practical contingencies and framing them for their theoretical and research possibilities to a research community.

Third, we found that one of the strongest functions of interrelating theory and practice was their role in mutual sensemaking. Theory was frequently used as a tool to make sense of practice, and practice elements mediated in making sense of theory. It was through this important reciprocal dynamic that outcomes of relevance to practice and theory were realized, and it is in facilitating these dynamics that we see the critical contribution of collaborative research systems. Further, we believe that collaborative research communities should deliberately structure such sensemaking forums to optimally draw on the strengths of the different sets of know-how and "know-that" represented in the community.

An excellent example of one such structure is provided by Mohrman, Gibson, and Mohrman (2001) in their depiction of joint interpretive forums that bring together scholars and practitioners in mutual pursuit of useful research and practical outcomes. Set as forums to facilitate mutual perspective taking (Boland & Tenkasi, 1995), they are intended to bring together members of different communities to jointly reflect and interpret information. By enabling the surfacing of different knowledge structures, the parties can self-reflect on their own views of a situation, collectively reexamine it, and come away with altered and enhanced interpretations and perspectives. This mutual perspective-taking process that takes each other's viewpoints into account should facilitate each community to translate between, and at least partially

integrate, their own and the other's frameworks. In the context of a research project, sessions to craft the research effort to ensure that both a focal organization's and the researchers' issues are taken into account, sessions to jointly examine and interpret data patterns, and sessions in which the possible action implications of research findings are collectively drawn and discussed could be topics for deliberations (see Table 3.3).

A final and related implication is that in almost all of the cases we studied, the practice/business contingencies were the primary mediators of the project. The project would

Table 3.3 Potential Roles for Collaborative Management Research Communities Seeking to Produce Actionable Scientific Knowledge by Interrelating Theory and Practice

Roles	Knowledge and Skills
Actors familiar with the *particulars* of the organization	Knowledge of local theories of action, including awareness of organizational history, insights into social dynamics, interpretive conventions, norms, and power relationships within the organization
Actors familiar with the *universals* or the larger scientific discourse pertaining to both theory and research	Knowledge of generalizable theories of action derived from mastery of theory and research in domains such as organizational behavior, organization theory, strategy, organizational development and change, and research methods, including qualitative, quantitative, and mixed
Actors who have *influence* in the organizational system to move projects within the organization	Understanding of how to build credibility and legitimacy with top management and relevant stakeholders and the skills to influence them; practical knowledge and skills to move projects toward completion within organizations
Actors who can play the role of *semiotic brokers* and act as effective bridges between the research and practice contingents of the collaborative management research community.	Skills in translating between communities and locating concepts and ideas from one community within the meaning systems of another; includes the ability to take elements of theory and express them in terms that would be more familiar and legitimate to a practice-based community, while also taking practical contingencies and framing them for their theoretical and research possibilities to a research community

have gone on without the inclusion of theory-based mediators had it not been for the agential involvement of the scholar-practitioner. Linkages were actively created, often inconspicuously, and nurtured and leveraged by the scholar-practitioner as the sole instigator. Aside from the fact that inclusion of theory-based elements advanced the practical aims of the organization, it also rose from their desire to create knowledge that could advance the causes of the larger scientific community. However, worthy of note is that the scholar-practitioners' primary access to the project and organization was as internal or external consultants. At least in the organizational contexts we pursued, consulting was seen as adding value to the organizations, because consulting was associated with solving practical problems faced by the organization, while research was construed as an abstract act far removed from practical realities. This observation holds a few implications for collaborative research communities that bring together practitioners from the inside and researchers/academics from the outside to create actionable scientific knowledge. Depending on the receptiveness of the organization to research, such collaborative research communities can propose an overt process of negotiation between scholars and practitioners to develop a shared agenda of investigating organizationally hot theoretical and practical issues such as exemplified in the table-tennis model of collaborative research of Adler and Shani (2001). In some contexts this may require targeted education of key managers in advance on the benefits of systematic research in creating desired organizational outcomes (while also advancing scientific outcomes) as well as on the unique strengths provided by a collaborative community of practitioners and academics in enabling these outcomes. In organizations with low receptivity to research, an alternative is to frame the collaborative enterprise between practitioners and researchers as predominantly a consulting

project and skillfully build in elements of theory and research in that background in a manner that does not compromise the practical needs of the organization (see Werr & Greiner, Chapter 5 in this volume). A caveat is that the organization should see these research by-products as legitimate, and the collaborative team should seek appropriate permissions for publications from the data. Of course the viability of this strategy will also depend on the organization's willingness to include academics as part of the project.

CONCLUSION

Although our 2000-year-old legacy of separating theory from experience and knowledge from action has been traditionally associated with Aristotle (Parry, 2003), we have drawn attention to a second, albeit underrecognized, legacy of Aristotle, one that argues for the integration of the universals and particulars as the basis of true understanding and knowledge. We regard scholar-practitioners, another important focus of this chapter, as contemporary carriers of the Aristotelian second vision. Being familiar with the universals and the particulars, they are able to integrate this knowledge to produce consequential results for the organization and the larger scientific discourse by relying on six predominant strategies of integration. Had this second Aristotelian legacy received even some attention compared to the popularity of his first pronouncements, we would have potentially inherited an additional model of doing science, one that celebrates the union of theory, experience, and practice as the bedrock of useful knowledge. Nonetheless, we are increasingly evolving as a field in ways consistent with Aristotle's second legacy through research designs such as collaborative management research systems and roles such as scholar-practitioners and insider/outsider researchers. We look forward to a future that delivers on the promise of theory-practice integration as we now knowingly embrace and continue to refine the Aristotelian second legacy.

NOTES

1. Our gratitude to Kala Visvanathan for insightful and valuable comments on earlier versions of this chapter.

2. Sir Karl Popper, a world-renowned 20th-century philosopher of science, wrote an influential book, *The Logic of Scientific Discovery* (1972), which had considerable impact on the practice of both the natural and the social sciences. In this seminal work, Popper decries the value of learning from experiences because, in his view, experiences are inherently fallible as a source of true knowledge. He illustrates with a now-classic, much-quoted example why this is the case: Even a simple statement drawn from experience, such as "all swans are white, or all ravens are black, can be logically refuted by the observation of one swan that is black, or one raven that is white" (Chalmers, 1999, p. 60). Popper's notion that experience is immaterial in deriving immanent knowledge about events and situations is aptly summarized in the following statement: "Because of the logical situation that renders the derivation of universal laws and theories from observations impossible, but the deduction of their falsity possible, falsifications [of theory] become the important landmarks, the striking achievements, the major growing points in science" (Chalmers, 1999, p. 61). Popper, instead of using experience as a basis of knowledge, suggests in its place the construction of theories and testing whether the theories hold or are falsified by experience. True to the Aristotelian first legacy, he believes that it is only carefully constructed theories derived from prior theories that can generate true scientific knowledge and, by implication, holds the scholar-scientist as the objective producer of knowledge.

3. Lev Vygotsky, an influential Soviet developmental psychologist, formulated *activity theory* as an antidualist solution to the crisis of psychology during the first decades of the 20th century. The cognitivists studied cognition as the activity of an autonomous agent independent of observed behavior. On the other hand, the behaviorist program was not as much concerned about mental processes; instead, behavior as manifested in action was the object of interest. Vygotsky formulated a new solution to transcend these two opposing but equally unsatisfactory explanations through his concept of mediated action (Vygotsky, 1978, p. 40). The concept of mediated action was based on the principle of unity and inseparability of consciousness and activity (Vygotsky, 1962, 1978). In its simplest terms, an *activity* is defined as the engagement of a subject toward a certain goal or objective, which is in turn determined by some kind of knowledge that serves as a tool to enable the activity. Tools can be *psychological,* such as language and symbol systems that include models, theories, frameworks, cognitive norms, standards, and object-hypotheses; *physical,* such as technical artifacts; and *social,* such as norms, contingencies, conventions, rules, routines, and established procedures. In a previous paper (Tenkasi & Hay, 2004), we point out that theory has often been equated with abstract ideas, laws, and principles that are removed from the realm of action, and in contrast, practice has been seen as the execution of actions with the goal of achieving something concrete. Drawing from activity theory, we suggest that instead of the traditional views in which practice is equated with action and theory with abstract thinking, we view them as different kinds of tools and resources that mediate different kinds of action. There are actions that are mediated by theoretical precepts and other actions that are mediated by contextual contingencies and conventions.

REFERENCES

Adler, M. J. (1978). *Aristotle for everybody: Difficult thought made easy.* New York: Macmillan.

Adler, N., & Shani, R. (2001). In search of an alternative framework for the creation of actionable knowledge: Table-tennis research at Ericsson. In R. W. Woodman & W. A. Pasmore (Eds.), *Research in organizational change and development* (Vol. 13, pp. 43–79). Oxford, UK: Elsevier Science.

Adler, N., Shani, A. B. (Rami), & Styhre, A. (2004). *Collaborative research in organizations.* Thousand Oaks, CA: Sage.

Aristotle. (1893). *Nicomachean ethics* (F. H. Peters, Trans.). Oxford, UK: Oxford University Press.

Aristotle. (1961). *Metaphysics* (Books I–IX, Books X–XIV, H. Tredennick, Trans.). Cambridge, MA: Harvard University Press.

Aristotle. (1962). *Nicomachean ethics* (M. Ostwald, Trans.). Englewood Cliffs, NJ: Prentice-Hall.

Aristotle. (1975). *Posterior analytics* (J. Barnes, Ed.). Oxford, UK: Clarendon Press.

Aristotle. (1999). *Nicomachean ethics* (2nd ed., T. Irwin, Trans.). Indianapolis, IN: Hackett.

Astley, W., & Zammuto, R. (1993). Organization science, managers, and language games. *Organization Science, 3*, 443–460.

Bass, B. M., & Avolio, B. (1995). *MLQ: Multifactor Leadership Questionnaire* (Technical Report). Redwood City, CA: Mind Garden.

Best Manufacturing Practices Report. (1998). Retrieved October 1, 2006, from http:// www.bmpcoe.org/bestpractices/surveys.html

Boland, R. J., & Tenkasi, R. V. (1995). Perspective making and perspective taking in communities of knowing. *Organization Science, 6*(4), 350–372.

Bunge, M. (2004). How does it work? The search for explanatory mechanisms. *Philosophy of the Social Sciences, 34*(2), 182–210.

Cambridge Dictionaries Online. (2003). Available from http://dictionary.cambridge.org/

Chalmers, A. F. (1999). *What is this thing called science?* Indianapolis, IN: Hackett.

Dougherty, D. (1992). Interpretive barriers to successful product innovation in large firms. *Organization Science, 3*(2), 179–202.

Dunne, J. (1993). *Back to the rough ground: 'Phronesis' and 'techne' in modern philosophy and in Aristotle.* Notre Dame, IN: University of Notre Dame Press.

Eisenhardt, K. (1989). Building theories from case study research. *Academy of Management Review, 14*(4), 532–550.

Eslbach, K., & Sutton, R. (1992). Acquiring organizational legitimacy through illegitimate actions: A marriage of institutional and impression management theories. *Academy of Management Journal, 35*(4), 699–738.

Fleck, L. (1979). *Genesis and development of a scientific fact.* Chicago: University of Chicago Press. (Originally published in German in 1935)

Gibbons, M., Limoges, C., Nowotny, H., Schwartzman, S., Scott, P., & Trow, M. (1994). *The new production of knowledge.* London: Sage.

Hay, G. W. (2003). The nature and significance of the executive doctoral scholar-practitioner of organizational development and change: A morphogenetic account of theory-practice linkages for the achievement of scholarly knowledge and business results. *Dissertation Abstracts International, 64*, 1747A.

Huff, A., & Huff, J. (2001). Refocusing the business school agenda. *British Journal of Management, 12*(S1) [Special Issue], S49–S54.

Lawler, E., III, Mohrman, A. M., Jr., Mohrman, S. A., Ledford, G., Cummings, T., & Associates (Eds.). (1985). *Doing research that is useful for theory and practice.* San Francisco: Jossey-Bass.

Leslie, K., Loch, M. A., & Schaninger, W. (2006). Managing your organization by the evidence. *McKinsey Quarterly, 2006*(3), 32–41.

Mohrman, S. A., Gibson, C. B., & Mohrman, A. M., Jr. (2001). Doing research that is useful to practice: A model and empirical exploration. *Academy of Management Journal, 44*(2), 357–375.

Parry, R. (2003). Epistêmê and technê. In E. N. Zalta (Ed.), *Stanford Encyclopedia of Philosophy* (Summer 2003 ed.). Retrieved from http://plato.stanford.edu/archives/sum2003/entries/episteme-techne/

Peters, F. E. (1967). *Greek philosophical terms: A historical lexicon.* New York: New York University Press.

Pfeffer, J., & Sutton, R. I. (2006). *Hard facts, dangerous half-truths, and total nonsense.* Boston: Harvard Business School Press.

Popper, K. R. (1972). *The logic of scientific discovery.* London: Hutchinson.

Ryle, G. (1949). *The concept of mind.* London: Hutchinson.

Rynes, S., Bartunek, J., & Daft, R. (2001). Across the great divide: Knowledge creation and transfer between practitioners and academics. *Academy of Management Journal, 44*(2), 340–355.

Shani, A. B., Wilson, C., & David, A. (2003). Collaborative research: Alternative roadmaps. In N. Adler, A. B. Shani, & A. Styhre (Eds.), *Collaborative research in organizations.* Thousand Oaks, CA: Sage.

Silverman, D. (2001). *Interpreting qualitative research* (2nd ed.). Thousand Oaks, CA: Sage.

Stefflere, V. J. (1972). Some applications of multidimensional scaling to social science problems. In A. K. Romney & S. C. Weller (Eds.), *Multidimensional scaling theory and applications in the behavioral sciences* (pp. 211–243). New York: Seminar Press.

Tenkasi, R. V., & Hay, G. W. (2004). Actionable knowledge and scholar-practitioners: A process model of theory-practice linkages. *Systemic Practice and Action Research, 17*(3), 177–206.

Tenkasi, R. V., & Mohrman, S. A. (1999). Global change as contextual-collaborative knowledge creation. In D. L. Cooperrider & J. E. Dutton (Eds.), *Organizational dimensions of global change: No limits to cooperation* (pp. 114–136). Newbury Park, CA: Sage.

Vygotsky, L. S. (1962). *Thought and language.* Cambridge: MIT Press.

Vygotsky, L. S. (1978). *Mind in society: The development of higher psychological processes.* Cambridge, MA: Harvard University Press.

Weick, K. (1979). *The social psychology of organizing.* New York: McGraw-Hill.

Yin, R. (1994). *Case study research: Design and methods* (2nd ed.). Beverly Hills, CA: Sage.

CHAPTER 4

Insider/Outsider Team Research

The Development of the Approach and Its Meanings

JEAN M. BARTUNEK[1]

ABSTRACT

In this chapter, I clarify the central criteria of insider/outsider (I/O) team research and summarize recent uses of this approach. I explore what is new in I/O research, focusing on creative composition of I/O teams, the social construction of insider/outsider roles, and new research methods that incorporate I/O components. I then describe several process issues encountered in conducting I/O collaborations, as well as means of addressing them. Finally, I consider advantages and disadvantages of an I/O approach and what is next for development of the approach.

In this chapter I discuss collaboration between academics and practitioners who are jointly conducting research in the practitioners' setting. Meryl Louis and I (Bartunek & Louis, 1996; Louis & Bartunek, 1992) have referred to this as *insider/outsider team research*.

Insider/outsider (I/O) team research is an unambiguous manifestation of collaborative research. Most of the chapters in this *Handbook* use it in some way. It involves external researchers and internal members of a setting collaborating in various ways throughout a research project, including determining what should be studied, developing methods of carrying out the study, collecting data and analyzing them, and then telling the story to various publics, ideally both academic and practitioner. The stages of I/O research as Louis and I defined them are presented in Table 4.1.

Table 4.1   The Stages of Insider/Outsider (I/O) Research

Stages	Key Issues
I. Composing the I/O research team	Those who initiate the research choose insider or outsider partners. Criteria for choosing insiders include wide access in the setting, interest in the research, and ability to appreciate others' perspectives. Criteria for choosing outsiders include trust, ability to work jointly, and research skill.
II. Developing a working relationship	Mutual respect and influence are essential in the development of the working relationship. The research addresses the goals of both parties.
III. Formulating research questions to orient the study	Insider and outsider researchers develop questions to orient the study. Together, they may decide on a common set of questions. One group may have more say than the other, or they may have equal say in this decision.
IV. Designing data collection procedures	Insider and outsider researchers design the data collection process. Insiders may give an external researcher guidance in methods and specific questions to be addressed, or the groups may jointly design these.
V. Collecting data	Insiders and outsiders may collect the same types of data or complementary data. Insiders, with guidance from outsiders, may collect the data. Outsiders may collect the data.
VI. Analyzing and interpreting data	Insiders and outsiders may analyze the data together. One party may provide a tentative interpretation, and the other may critique and advance the interpretation.
VII. Writing reports and presenting results	One party may write the report and obtain comments on drafts from the other party. Insiders and outsiders may author the report jointly, or parties may write separate reports.
VIII. Taking action	Action is undertaken based on the research and aimed at benefiting participants in the setting.
IX. Making scholarly contributions	The research makes a contribution to scholarly literature in some area.
X. Tracking outcomes	Researchers assess the extent to which project goals were achieved.

SOURCE: Bartunek and Louis (1966, p. 26).

Since publication of the Bartunek and Louis book in 1996, several authors have used insider/outsider research approaches and, in doing so, have contributed to an expanded understanding of the method. Some have applied the ideas in ways that were consistent with our original meanings, and some have made partial use of the approach. Some have used different terms to describe equivalent approaches. Others have developed new research methods that incorporate I/O collaboration. Yet others have developed new ideas about possible meanings underlying components of I/O research.

Here I will first summarize Bartunek and Louis's (1996) primary arguments regarding

I/O team research, clarifying the central criteria of this approach and summarizing recent illustrative uses of it. Second, I will explore what is new in I/O research, focusing on creative composition of I/O teams, the social construction of insider/outsider roles, and new types of research methods that incorporate I/O components. Third, I will describe several process issues encountered in conducting contemporary I/O collaborations, as well as some means of addressing them. Fourth, I will consider both advantages and disadvantages of an I/O approach. Finally, I will consider what is next for development of the approach. As is the case with the 1996 book, this chapter will incorporate work from multiple scholarly disciplines, since the use of and insights into I/O research come from so many social science fields.

WHAT IS I/O RESEARCH?

Summary of the Argument From Bartunek and Louis

Bartunek and Louis (1996, p. 3) defined I/O research as an approach to research in which members of a setting under study work together as co-researchers with outsider researchers. In this approach, insiders and outsiders jointly examine the setting and jointly author public accounts of life in the setting. Together they produce the sense made of the setting and knowledge to be gleaned from it. In working jointly with outsiders, insiders contribute directly to public understanding of events in the setting.

As Evered and Louis (1981) made evident, insiders are the individuals for whom the personally relevant social world is under study. They often are members of the setting being studied who hope to understand and act more effectively in the setting. (Other characteristics of insider researchers are discussed by Coghlan & Coughlan, Chapter 21 in this

volume; Coghlan & Shani, 2007; and Roth, Shani, & Leary, in press). In contrast, outsiders are typically external researchers who seek to create knowledge that generalizes across settings. Consistent with Weick's (1989) argument that greater heterogeneity among conjectures or thought would lead to more robust theorizing, we believed that by combining insider and outsider perspectives, a more robust picture of a setting could be produced.

We argued that insiders did not necessarily have to be totally within a setting, but had to be closer to it than the outsider. For example, a consultant to a setting might be a (comparative) insider. An I/O research team is, thus, composed of people who differ in their connectedness to the setting.

We also described the phases of I/O research that are summarized in Table 4.1. This description of phases makes evident that insiders are involved throughout the research process; they are not the equivalent of research assistants to external researchers for part of the study.

We briefly summarized several practical and ethical challenges of conducting such research. Practical challenges include managing interpersonal differences that arise in conjunction with the heterogeneity of theorizing as well as maintaining adequate separation between insider and outsider team members in order to retain their differing perspectives. Ethical dilemmas include the possibility that study participants and internal researchers might not feel comfortable or "safe" talking honestly with each other about the research, as well as difficulties associated with gaining informed consent of those participating in the research, since I/O studies are typically longitudinal and it is not always possible to determine all events that will occur. In the years since we published the book, the expansion of the role of institutional review boards in universities in which many outside researchers work has made the complexities of gaining informed consent more salient.

We also described an I/O study I was then conducting with a Network Faculty Development Committee (NFDC), a committee of teachers in a network of independent schools whose aim was to empower teachers in the network. Several scholarly articles have been published from that study, including Bartunek and Lacey (1998); Bartunek, Walsh, and Lacey (2000) (discussed below); and Meyer, Bartunek, and Lacey (2002). For example, Bartunek and Lacey (1998) described how the NFDC's confrontation of the alcoholism of one of its members resulted in what Turner (1974) called a "social drama" that surfaced tensions in the NFDC, and Meyer et al. (2002) demonstrated the difficulties of maintaining-memory of the initial values and norms of a group once turnover of members takes place.

In addition, I wrote a book about the NFDC (Bartunek, 2003), and I invited everyone who had been a member of the NFDC at any time to contribute to the book. About half accepted this invitation, and their reflections are included in the book. Sometimes these reflections included group members' analyses that differed from mine. For example, in its early years when the NFDC had co-leaders, the co-leaders and I saw the co-leadership model as collaborative. Other NFDC members, however, were more aware than I was of how much time the co-leaders spent talking solely with each other or me, and experienced co-leadership as excluding the rest of the NFDC members.

Recent Illustrative I/O Studies

I will summarize some recent studies that embody an I/O approach. I will track these studies through an abbreviated version of some of the stages in Table 4.1, composing the research team, collecting the data, and analyzing the data. I will also suggest some of their contributions to scholarly knowledge.

Engwall, Kling, and Werr (2005)

In order to determine the extent to which formal models that are used during product development actually affect product development practice, Engwall et al. (2005) studied how such models are interpreted by their users during new product development. The authors had different backgrounds and different preconceptions of product development. One had a long career in the practical management of product development and was the most internal of the researchers, one was a researcher of project management, and one was a researcher of management consulting, the most external researcher.

The data collection involved an I/O approach: "Two researchers, part-time employees in different units of [a] telecom manufacturer, conducted interviews in units other than those where they normally worked. An external researcher was used to gain an outsider perspective" (Engwall et al., 2005, p. 430).

The data were analyzed by the three authors, who identified how their different backgrounds helped to contribute to the trustworthiness of the analysis. They commented that "these different backgrounds, combined with an awareness of the risk for bias and testing the validity of the identified conceptions with practitioners and scholars not engaged in the study, represent an attempt to limit bias as much as possible" (Engwall et al., 2005, p. 431).

The researchers found that the employees they studied had five different conceptions of the roles of formal models in product development. These different conceptions challenge typical assumptions of direct links between formal models and product development practice.

Börjesson, Dahlsten, and Williander (2006)

Börjesson et al. (2006) explored challenges associated with idea generation and product expansion proposals at Volvo, especially in terms of environmental scanning.

> The research team consisted of three researchers—two insiders simultaneously employed at Volvo Cars and one outsider. The insider perspective offered detailed know-how about typical practices in the automotive industry, as well as enabled access to participation in the project. The outsider perspective allowed a critical distance to the empirical material and forced "reflection in action" (Schön, 1983). (Börjesson et al., 2006 p. 778)

The authors' data collection process (Börjesson et al., 2006) involved considerable observation:

> Two researchers participated as team members in the scanning project for its full duration of half a year, acting as observing participants. Notes were taken in all meetings, then exchanged between the insider researchers, reflected and commented upon, and shared with the outsider researcher. (p. 779)

Finally, for data analysis, the empirical material was coded according to categories that made sense to the practitioners and were used in the practitioners' typical speech patterns. Research findings were reported back to the participants in the project and then interpreted and tested with them, as well as with the department responsible for the annual environment-scanning activity. The results of the study made evident that environmental scanning was useful not only for strategy purposes but also for idea generation that could foster long-term planning.

Thomas et al.

Thomas, Beaven, et al. (1999) and Thomas, Hagerott, et al. (1999) studied the meaning of work for nurses employed in two state psychiatric hospitals and how nurses coped with the challenges they faced at their hospitals. Thomas, Blacksmith, and Reno (2000) reflected on what it meant to conduct an I/O study.

The coauthors of the Thomas, Beaven, et al. (1999) and Thomas, Hagerott, et al. (1999) papers were from the University of Washington and the two state hospitals in which the study was conducted. Nurses at both hospitals participated with university faculty in designing and carrying out the research. Somewhat similar to the approach used by Engwall et al. (2005), nurses at one hospital collected data at the other hospital; thus, they had some, but not total, insider knowledge of the setting. Thomas et al. (2000) commented that the nurse participants "were all outsiders in the sense that the focus was on data from the other hospital. However, in contrast to the university team member, the state hospital nurses brought insider insights to these discussions from their perspective as state hospital insiders" (p. 821).

The findings of the studies were reported back and discussed with nurses in feedback sessions at both hospitals, and the results of the discussions were taken into account in writing the report. Reviews of the reports by the insider research team members were used to make refinements prior to publication.

Results of the Thomas, Beaven, et al. (1999) study indicated that the dilemmas nurses experienced in state psychiatric hospitals were in clinical decision making, personal control, and maintaining professional standards. The Thomas, Hagerott, et al. (1999) study indicated that the means nurses used to cope with the challenges encountered included maintaining watchfulness about potential dilemmas, narrowing their focus, taking pride in their ability to cope with the challenges, and constructing personal meanings about the challenges.

Bartunek, Walsh, and Lacey (2000)

Bartunek et al. (2000) conducted a study of leadership succession as it unfolded over five years of the NFDC in order to explore the kinds of dynamics and dilemmas associated with leading a group based on feminist principles. Bartunek and Walsh were outsiders. Lacey was an insider, one of the founders of the NFDC and a member during its first six years. Both the insider and outsider authors were involved in data collection:

> [The third author] kept extensive journal notes of events occurring there. The first author was an external observer at NFDC meetings. . . . She interviewed the founders prior to the beginning of the NFDC, took as close to verbatim notes as possible of what was said during each meeting, collected working documents, and tape-recorded a session near the end of each meeting in which members of the group reflected on its high and low points. . . . The second author provided a totally external perspective on the group's events. (p. 594)

The data for the study consisted primarily of transcripts of meetings in which the NFDC discussed leadership succession. The authors divided the tasks for the content analysis of these transcripts. The third author carried out initial coding for one research question, and the first and second authors checked the text for agreement with this coding. The first author carried out initial coding for the other research questions, and the second and third authors then checked these for accuracy. In other words, both insider and outsider coauthors took primary responsibility for different parts of the analysis.

The results of the study indicated that, over time, as the group used consistently participative methods designed to empower its members, the members experienced less and less power. This was obviously very different from what had been expected and suggested possible contradictions associated with empowerment efforts.

As these illustrations suggest, I/O team research as Louis and I described it focuses on contributing to academic knowledge about the phenomena studied. The findings of the studies benefit the settings as well, often as results are fed back to setting members. However, the primary emphasis is on the importance of the findings for scholarly knowledge. Thus, this approach is similar to that of Hatchuel and David (Chapter 7 in this volume) in that it focuses primarily on contributions to scholarly research. The expected contributions of the studies differ from those of other chapters in this *Handbook* that emphasize action research almost exclusively and whose findings primarily benefit the organization in which the research takes place.

Partial Use of the I/O Research Method

Some studies have also made use of part of the I/O approach. For example, in studying community agencies from a community psychology perspective, Foster-Fishman, Salem, Allen, and Fahrbach (2001) described how "a committee of eight ICC and interagency team members worked collaboratively with the research team on survey development, data collection, and data interpretation" (p. 881) in order to increase the local relevance of the questions asked and methods employed.

I/O Research by Other Names

There are other names for what Louis and I considered I/O research. For example, Ospina and Dodge (2005) use the term *interactive social science* to refer to "a style of activity where researchers, funding agencies and 'user groups' interact throughout the entire research process, including the definition of the research agenda, project selection, project execution and the application of research insights" (p. 419). Hartley and Benington (2000, 2006) describe their "co-research methodology" as encompassing a research program that includes case studies of organizational processes. For each case study, there are three researchers. First is the academic, who is responsible for the overall research. Second is the host manager in the organization being researched, who arranges interviews and amasses the relevant organizational documentation and contextual data required by the researchers. Third, there is a co-interviewer from a different organization who is in a senior and corporate job similar to that of the host manager, but is an outsider in terms of the specific organization being studied.

Other chapters in this *Handbook* include additional illustrations of what Louis and I would see as I/O partnerships. For example, members of the ARC Research Team (Chapter 22) discuss the development of an action research partnership between representatives of a college and its neighboring community, and Knights, Alferoff, Starkey, and Tiratsoo (Chapter 19) describe industry-academic networks.

WHAT'S NEW IN I/O RESEARCH?

Quite a bit is new in I/O research. One new aspect is signaled by Hartley and Benington's (2006) approach, in which someone is a "partial" insider who has familiarity with a type of organization setting, but is an outsider to the particular setting under study. This represents a creative composition of an I/O team. A second new aspect is increased understanding of what it might "mean" to be an insider or outsider, including how much the roles of insider and outsider are fixed and/or socially constructed. Third, some new I/O research methods have been developed since the 1990s.

Creative Composition of the I/O Team

As Louis and I initially discussed the concept, there were relatively clear distinctions between insiders and outsiders. However, work by Engwall et al. (2005), Hartley and Benington (2006), Thomas, Beaven, et al. (1999), and Thomas, Hagerott, et al. (1999) has shifted these boundaries, indicating ways that researchers may be both insiders and outsiders. For instance, Easterby-Smith and Malina (1999) discussed an interesting pairing of researchers in studies taking place in both China and the United Kingdom. The research was designed and conducted by a team comprising seven Chinese academics and eight UK academics. Thus, in both national settings studied, the research team contained both insiders and outsiders, and the academics who were insiders in China were outsiders in the UK and vice versa.

Taken together, these studies suggest how insider and outsider roles may be paired and combined in ways that give multiple researchers both insider and outsider experiences, thus increasing the likelihood of heterogeneity in their theorizing (Weick, 1989). This loosening of the boundaries of insiders and outsiders is accompanied by enhanced understandings of how insider/outsider roles are socially constructed.

The Social Construction of Insider/Outsider Roles

Recently, some authors (Ganiel & Mitchell, 2006; Garland, Spalek, & Chakraborti, 2006) have argued that the categories of insider and outsider are socially constructed and include many more components than is typically realized. For example, Ganiel and Mitchell found that the categories of insider and outsider were socially constructed by the participants in their research. The two authors were conducting fieldwork regarding religious experience in

Northern Ireland. One of the authors identified herself as evangelical, the other as agnostic (and, thus, more of an outsider than the people they were interviewing). While the authors had somewhat fixed understandings of what their religious identifications meant, they found that the terms *evangelical* and *agnostic* took on varying meanings for their interviewees, who interpreted the labels according to their own religious beliefs and then responded to the researchers based on the meanings they attributed to the terms.

In addition, the researchers found that they had "multiple identities": their insider/outsider status based on their religious beliefs was not the only dimension that mattered to those they were interviewing. The interviewees also attended to the researchers' gender, educational status, institutional affiliation, and national identity. These combinations of characteristics meant that the researchers' insider/outsider status was on a continuum. Researchers were more or less similar to their interviewees in several different ways, each of which might be salient (or not) at any time, and each of which evoked responses based in part on the interviewees' social constructions of the researchers' multiple characteristics.

Garland et al. (2006) described similar dilemmas and issues facing criminology researchers who investigate the experiences of "hard to reach" minority ethnic households. They suggested that one way of doing this would be to involve the minority ethnic groups in all stages of the research process as a way of breaking down cultural, religious, or ethnic barriers that may exist between the researcher and the researched. However, they note that even for researchers from minority group backgrounds, self-identity (and thus insider status) is complex: "Issues of ethnicity, class, gender, sexuality, age and religion are just some of the factors that can influence identity constructions, and indeed these perceptions can, in any case, fluctuate temporally" (p. 434).

These scholars make evident that I/O identity issues for researchers are much more mutable and complex than previously discussed. Moreover, the formal I/O status of a researcher may sometimes be less important to research participants than other researcher characteristics.

New Types of Research Methodologies That Make Use of I/O Teams

Several new collaborative research approaches that use some type of I/O methodology have been developed. Two that have received considerable recent attention are *Mode 2* approaches to research and *design research*.

Mode 2 Research

In 1994, Gibbons et al. distinguished between Mode 1 and Mode 2 knowledge in the natural sciences. Their distinction was brought into management by Tranfield and Starkey (1998) and Starkey and Madan (2001). Briefly, Mode 1 knowledge is what is typically created using a scientific research approach, most often in universities. It is typically disciplinary and cognitive, focused more on theory than on practice. In contrast, Mode 2 knowledge is less concerned with a discipline base or with theory; it might be called transdisciplinary. It is particularly focused on knowledge in practice. Kelemen and Bansal (2002) noted that if the aim of Mode 1 research is to construct or test theory that can be replicated elsewhere, Mode 2 research aims at gaining insights into a particular context with the view to providing a practical solution to identified problems. Thus, Mode 2 research is a form of action research that engages practitioners at all stages of the research process. Although Mode 1 researchers (Kilduff & Kelemen, 2001) sometimes challenge the value of the knowledge Mode 2 research produces, this research has received considerable attention, especially by those concerned about research creating value for managers (e.g., Van de Ven, 2007).

MacLean, MacIntosh, and Grant (2002) presented an example of Mode 2 research. It was initiated shortly after the authors presented a research seminar for the Scottish Health Advisory Service (SHAS) on complexity theory and corporate transformation. During the seminar, questions concerning "the roles of reflexivity, intuition and emotion in influencing emergent outcomes of corporate transformation projects were raised, giving rise to related research questions and the desire to investigate them empirically" (p. 193).

Subsequently, at the request of the chief executive of SHAS, university-based researchers became involved in a complexity-based transformation project that allowed the researchers to pursue their research interests while aiming to help SHAS develop a more distinct identity and more effective ways of working. In particular, the chief executive felt that there was a need to transform working practices so that key decisions and initiatives depended less on her direct involvement. SHAS personnel also wanted to develop a more coherent external identity in tandem with SHAS's new internal processes.

The project was thus concerned with the strategic transformation of SHAS both internally in terms of its management processes and externally in terms of sharpening its identity and image. The desire of the chief executive and the rest of the core team to apply concepts from complexity theory to organization and management enabled a convergence of interests between the academic researchers and the SHAS staff.

Several events took place during the project that, with the researchers' help, made SHAS participants more conscious of dysfunctional patterns into which they often fell. This greater awareness led them to articulate "ground rules" concerning how SHAS members should interact with each other more functionally than in the past. In turn, these ground rules allowed those present to respond more effectively when dysfunctional patterns started to emerge. The researchers used complexity theory and management and psychoanalytic perspectives to help interpret events and patterns, foster new responses, and ultimately develop agreement among SHAS personnel on practical steps forward.

After some time, SHAS personnel noted that patterns of behavior and relating had changed significantly since the start of the project. In particular, SHAS now had a clearer external identity, and several of its internal processes were now working more effectively. There was growing coherence apparent in its activities, especially in the initiation of new areas of action, though this was intermittently overwhelmed by a "return to the old ways."

Consistent with Mode 2 emphases, this study was context-based and employed applicable theoretical perspectives in the service of an action-research project. SHAS members were fully involved as participants throughout the study. In addition, the authors noted that from an academic perspective, their understanding of transformational processes within organizations developed considerably. They came to understand (MacLean et al., 2002) how new organizational patterns or strategies may emerge when "individuals reflexively interact to transform their own emotionally stimulating unplanned experiences into collective interpretations and coordinated interactions" (p. 197).

Design Research

Herbert Simon (1996) was the first to suggest the idea of design science, in his book *The Sciences of the Artificial*. There Simon distinguished between natural sciences and artificial, or design, sciences, stating that natural sciences (e.g., chemistry, physics) are concerned with how things are, while design sciences are concerned with how things ought to be. A key feature of the design sciences is that, in collaboration with members of a client system, one or more investigators try both to expand their knowledge of a system and to improve its functioning. Disciplines such as architecture, medicine, engineering, and education (cf. Trullen, Bartunek, & Harmon, in press) often use a design approach; they focus not only on what is (e.g., what causes particular diseases), but also on creating something new (e.g., how to cure the diseases).

Those who have done the most to define design approaches for management are Boland (e.g., Boland & Collopy, 2004), van Aken (2004), and Romme (Romme, 2003; Romme & Endenburg, 2006). As van Aken notes, "the ultimate objective of research in these sciences is to develop valid and reliable knowledge to be used in designing solutions to problems" (2004, p. 225). Thus, the design sciences aim at intervening in particular situations, not just understanding the situations.

The knowledge created in design approaches is often slightly different than the knowledge created in more standard research approaches, and the validity of such knowledge is pragmatic. Knowledge from design science research results in what van Aken (2004, 2005) and Romme (2003) refer to as field-tested and grounded technological rules, action guides for how to accomplish intended outcomes. Technological rules for design approaches typically are stated in this form: "In situation s, to achieve consequence c, do action a" (Argyris, Putnam, & Smith, 1985, p. 81). An illustration will be provided below.

A practitioner may play a lead role in design approaches to knowledge generation. For example, Romme and Endenburg (2006) have described and analyzed a particular type of intervention called *circular organizing* that was pioneered by Gerard Endenburg, the CEO of an electrotechnical company in the Netherlands. Endenburg has been developing this approach for over 30 years, and Romme has been studying it with him for over nine years.

Their paper describes the conceptual basis for circular organizing, some history of its development in Endenburg's company, the kinds of technological rules initially developed in conjunction with it, and how these were revised based on particular critical experiences. Based on Endenburg's experience, Romme and Endenburg (2006) suggested that for circular organizing to succeed in an organization, particular situational conditions must be present ("in situation s"). For example, "All members of the organization (must) have access to information systems and flows" (p. 296). Given this condition, to build organization capacity for self-regulation (to achieve consequence c), "decisions about policy issues are taken by informed consent" (p. 296): do action a. The paper also describes several learnings that occurred in conjunction with implementing circular organizing first in Endenburg's company and then in other organizations.

Process Issues Associated With Creating Knowledge Through I/O Collaboration

Multiple process issues need to be addressed for I/O collaborations to succeed. I will briefly introduce three important dimensions: conflict, power, and intergroup dynamics. I will also suggest ways problems associated with these dynamics may be addressed.

Conflict and Its Potential Sources in I/O Teams

Difficult process issues that are likely to be present early in I/O collaborations may create conflict that seriously interferes with these collaborations if they are not resolved. Speaking from the perspective of community psychology, Israel, Schulz, Parker, and Becker (1998, cited in Trickett & Espino 2004) indicate several of these, including lack of trust and respect between researchers and community members, inequitable distribution of power and control, questions about who represents the community, and differing priorities, values, and expectations of the role of a researcher. Trickett and Espino suggest that other potential conflicts include questions of who owns and controls the project and the data, tensions between the research agenda of scholars and the practice agenda of insiders, and differing time perspectives of academic researchers and community agencies.

Thomas et al. (2000) described a source of conflict arising from the fact that the nurses participating on the I/O team came from different hospitals. They noted:

Having two institutions with parallel missions in a public sector environment with limited funds could lead to occasional strains between nurses from the two hospitals. For example, nurses from one hospital felt that . . . nurses at the other hospital . . . had more autonomy. On the other hand, nurses who were farther away and served a more rural clientele felt that those who were in an urban area and closer to the capital had better access to resources." (pp. 823–824)

While, as noted above, combining multiple perspectives on an issue is the primary mechanism for I/O research, Thomas et al. (2000) make evident that there might be conflict among the holders of the different perspectives, and the ability to manage the conflict productively is necessary for a successful I/O effort.

Studying the workings of their own I/O team, Amabile et al. (2001) found that, consistent with Jehn's (1997) conflict theory, their I/O team performed more effectively when they experienced *task-related* conflict stemming from different perspectives on a problem. But their performance suffered when differences between I/O team members caused negative *process* conflict or *relationship* conflict. Amabile et al. found that incompatibility of problem-solving styles appeared to lead to unproductive process conflict in their team, that leader skill in managing team communications appeared to strongly influence the I/O team's functioning, and that cultural differences between the academics and the practitioners in the group were frequently mentioned as the culprits behind process conflict.

The Relative Power of Insider and Outsider Members of the Research Team

I have already referred to some power issues with regard to possible sources of conflict. Outsider members often have more power than insider members on a research team, especially if they are academics and the insiders are not. This is simply because academics are likely to be more cognizant of the domain in which much publishing (especially academic publishing) takes place. Thus, insider researchers sometimes defer to academics even when they have knowledge that is crucial for the research.

Easterby-Smith and Malina (1999) described another dimension of power dynamics in their discussion of the joint UK-China investigations in which they were involved. They became aware that "perceptions of status were based on different considerations in the two countries" (p. 79). They reflected on how, "when researchers conduct fieldwork, external perceptions of status may conflict with the internal pecking order of a research team" (p. 81), and how this can complicate relationships on the team.

Intergroup Dynamics

Conflict and power differences are likely to be related to different explicit or implicit "groups" represented in an I/O team. For example, Easterby-Smith and Malina (1999) observed,

> [When] the Chinese team members adapted the focus of the research to their context, the U.K. group realized how much the draft proposal already reflected the U.K. context; we in the United Kingdom also started to appreciate how each group was attributing purely academic motives to itself but attributing slightly less positive, practical and commercial motives to the other national group. (p. 79)

In other words, the collaboration had characteristics of the kinds of intergroup dynamics described by Tajfel (1982), whose work indicated that when an event—such as an I/O project—happens that makes group membership salient, people identify with their own groups and view members of other groups less favorably. This may happen even if a sole individual (an insider or outsider) is aware of the group that he or she is "representing."

The group differences surfaced by Easterby-Smith and Malina (1999), differences equivalent to those between academics and practitioners, suggest the likelihood that insiders and outsiders may belong to different communities of practice, and that awareness of these communities may be surfaced when representatives from one group collaborate with representatives of another group. Brown and Duguid (2001) describe communities of practice as "groups of interdependent participants [that] provide the work context within which members construct both shared identities and the social context that helps those identities. . . . Members of such groups collectively develop an outlook on work and the world" (p. 202). Considerable learning and sharing of tacit knowledge occurs within them, but it is often difficult for this learning to go beyond them. Rather, different communities of practice often develop different terms and different types of cultural manifestations.

It may be helpful to think of apparently "individual" academics and practitioners as identifying with different communities, not operating solely as individuals. They may not only differ individually, but also embody differences that have been learned communally, and how the differences unfold may depend in part on how strong the identification is with a particular group at any given time. For example, if Ganiel and Mitchell (2006) were primarily identified with their religious affiliations and related communities of practice, their different identities would be likely to evoke difficulties that flow from their different communities of practice. Differences would be particularly likely to surface during tense times in the collaboration.

Characteristics and Actions of Team Members That Affect How Well Concerns Might Be Addressed

Amabile et al. (2001) found that effective use of member capabilities and frequent meetings that are well planned in advance appear to facilitate the functioning of the I/O teams and the success of their projects. Hartley and Benington (2006) found that several characteristics of people and groups participating in their collaborative research teams affected how well the teams could work together. These included "a culture of curiosity and respect for diversity of views, a conscious interest in gaining the different perspectives from each of the groups . . . and a commitment to explore the tensions which arise from these differences" (p. 105).

An example of a successful effort to foster I/O collaboration is presented by Easterby-Smith and Malina (1999). I noted above some of the differences that occurred between the researchers from China and the

UK in their study. That the various difficulties came to be resolved over time gives hope that, when they are made explicit, problematic issues that emerge in I/O collaborations might be successfully addressed. For example, issues of differences surfaced during writing research reports:

> With regard to outputs, research team members began to realize through the experience of working alongside foreign colleagues that in each country different assumptions were being made about the requirements of the audiences for this research. U.K. team members were under pressure to publish theoretical work in refereed journals, and any practical implications were seen as secondary. In contrast, the Chinese team members were expected to demonstrate how theoretical observations could be implemented in Chinese enterprises. (p. 81)

As the groups continued to work together they were able to make these differences more explicit and to empathize with the demands on each other.

Ospina and Dodge (2005) suggested that as preconditions of successful collaboration, academic researchers need to appreciate the knowledge base that practitioners bring as insiders, trust practitioners' ability to be reflexive and sophisticated about their practice and to locate practice within a broader context, believe that practitioners' perspectives can enhance their research design and contribute to building theory, and create incentives for practitioners to participate in research, whether through compensation or by committing to create concrete products or processes to improve their work. Practitioners need to appreciate the reasons and logic behind research standards, accept a different pace and rhythm in the collaboration process, and respect researchers' expertise and availability to carry on the research process.

Both parties need to recognize that they must negotiate their collaborative relationship, including how they will accommodate, adapt, and integrate their different perspectives on a problem or question being examined (cf. Van de Ven, in press, Chapter 9).

Taken together, this literature makes evident that there will be conflicts, power differences, and intergroup dynamics within I/O teams; there are too many potential sources of difficulties for this not to happen. Characteristics of the members of the I/O team and processes used in the group to address process issues affect how successfully these are dealt with and how successful the group's work will be. The ARC Research Team (Chapter 22 in this volume) and Coghlan and Coughlan (Chapter 21 in this volume) suggest additional processes instrumental to the development of I/O groups.

Advantages and Disadvantages of Applying an I/O Approach to Research

There are both advantages and disadvantages to I/O research. Werr and Greiner (Chapter 5 in this volume) suggest some common advantages. Another frequently cited advantage is the marginal perspective generated by the combination of insider and outsider roles that "penetrates the culture as no insider could" (Handy, 1989, p. ix). Common disadvantages include the possibility that scholars will not trust the objectivity and validity of the results because they cannot be sure of the researchers' objectivity. I will suggest some advantages and disadvantages that have received considerable attention in recent years.

Advantages

There are important advantages to I/O research, many of them predicated on Bartunek and Louis's (1996) assertion that a diversity of theorizing improves theory. For example, Hartley and Benington (2006, p. 105) noted that differences in perspective in their study (when recognized and addressed) helped to generate new insights and fresh knowledge. Thomas et al. (2000, p. 827) argued that new knowledge was generated in their hospital study because the insider/outsider approach they used provided multiple lenses with which the researchers could view the data.

However, diversity in an I/O team will only contribute to more effective theorizing when trust is present and the ability and willingness exist to resolve process problems (Amabile et al., 2001; Hartley & Benington, 2006). Otherwise, as Jehn (1997) has found, process difficulties will interfere with the ability to use differences productively.

Academic researchers involved in an I/O collaboration can often collect more and richer data and gain important insights into the meaning of the data collected because of their interactions with practitioners (Rynes, Bartunek, & Daft, 2001) than would be the case without such collaboration. I/O collaboration has also been valuable to practitioners. Macduff and Netting (2000), for example, argue that practitioners often need expertise in research methods that can only be obtained through collaboration with academics or equivalent others. Heyl (1997) argued that academic-practitioner research increases the value and relevance of research findings for the practitioners involved.

More generally, as Bartunek, Trullen, Bonet, and Sauquet (2003) noted, the expectation is that I/O research facilitates learning and enhances the likelihood of achieving both research quality and relevance for scholars and practitioners (Hatchuel, 2001; Pettigrew, 2001). I/O teams may not only improve research by fostering better theorizing; they also may improve practice because practitioners are an integral part of the research effort and contribute to the relevance and actionability (Argyris, 1996) of the findings.

Disadvantages

There are also disadvantages to the approach. Dutton, Worline, Frost, and Lilius (2006), in a recent study of compassionate organizing that partially used an I/O approach, note that one possible disadvantage "arose from the research team's intimate familiarity with the context. . . . Some members might have been too steeped in the organization's culture to adequately or objectively describe it or might disregard important information because it was overly familiar" (p. 63). Having multiple research team members from different universities helped to minimize the impact of this bias. A second disadvantage involved possible conflicts of interest if a negative picture of the organization arose. This reflected a more general concern sometimes voiced by academics, that working with practitioners might violate objectivity and jeopardize their ability to generate truth (Mohrman, Gibson, & Mohrman, 2001; Rynes et al., 2001). However, Dutton et al. (2006) attempted to be aware of such potential conflicts and report results vigilantly and accurately.

Thus, while there are advantages to be gained from I/O research, there are disadvantages as well. Achieving the advantages and limiting the disadvantages is one of the challenges for I/O researchers.

NEXT STEPS IN THE DEVELOPMENT OF I/O RESEARCH

Several steps might be taken to further the development of I/O methods. I will suggest three areas surfaced by the exploration in this chapter. These are the understanding of I/O collaboration as including intergroup dynamics, ethical issues particularly associated with this type of approach, and insider/outsider status as a social construction.

Understanding I/O Collaboration as a Form of Collaboration Across Groups

The work presented here makes evident that I/O research is a viable and important approach, one with the capacity to contribute to both academic and practitioner knowledge creation and one that represents a larger world of collaboration. As Amabile et al. (2001) argue,

> Cross-profession collaboration, of which academic-practitioner collaboration is one form, is a fruitful arena for future research. Broadly defined, such research would encompass collaborations between individuals from different professions and different organizations who come together primarily as individuals . . . to accomplish a particular work project. (p. 429)

Thus, greater understanding of the dynamics that occur in academic-practitioner collaborations has the potential to inform a wider range of cross-profession scholarship, as well as to contribute to more enhanced I/O collaborative practice. Some topics that might be explored include how much researchers truly participate as individuals or, really, as part of larger communities of practice; the range of relationships among academics and practitioners that might be present in a more or less effective manner; and how the process issues associated with I/O collaboration might be better understood if individual inside and outside researchers are viewed in terms of the communities of practice that they represent.

In addition to study of the I/O relationship and its effectiveness, it is important to develop ways of making I/O teams more effective. One possible way to address this issue is to take a design science approach and to develop technological rules that could be applied in I/O relationships. These might take forms such as

this: "In situations where there are likely to be differences of perspective present, to successfully accomplish I/O team relationships, insiders and outsiders must learn mechanisms that enable them to deal productively with process conflicts." As Amabile et al. (2001) showed, process differences are very likely to interfere with the successful accomplishment of I/O work; addressing them successfully is crucial for I/O collaboration to be productive.

Ethical Issues Associated With I/O Research

Some complex issues regarding how researchers deal with research participants emerge when insider members of a setting study it with an outsider. Thomas et al. (2000), for example, described how, in the Thomas, Beaven, et al. (1999) and Thomas, Hagerott, et al. (1999) studies,

> Some of the insider nurses on the research team were in leadership positions and, because of human participation considerations, could not seek participants from among those they supervised because it could imply coercion. Yet, we wanted nurses to understand that they were free to leave their wards to participate in the research and that their responses would be anonymous. (Thomas et al., 2000, p. 825)

They solved the predicament in a creative way by providing communication channels to nurses other than through their supervisors. For example, university faculty sent letters to all nurses that invited their participation and assured them of anonymity.

A second potential issue they encountered was anonymity and confidentiality. Although participants were instructed not to use personal names as they described situations, it was possible that individuals might be identifiable from the situations described or by their handwriting. The researchers solved this issue by insuring that insiders at each hospital did not see data collection tools from their own hospital.

A third issue arose during data collection. Occasionally respondents used data collection to communicate a specific problem in the hope that action would be taken. No follow-up of any situation identified on the data collection tools was done because of confidentiality. In one focus group the nurses asked a researcher who led the group to communicate to their supervisor that it was affirming of their identity as nurses to come together as they did in the focus group and that they would like other opportunities to do so. In the latter situation, the leader did agree to inform the supervisor.

These are all ethical concerns that are particularly likely to occur in settings in which participants are also researchers. More exploration of the range of ethical issues involved and of ways of addressing them is very important for the development of this methodology.

Insider/Outsider Status as a Social Construction

Two of the studies discussed here, Ganiel and Mitchell (2006) and Garland et al. (2006), made evident that insider/outsider status is in part a social construction. While Louis and I did not originally claim that insider/outsider status was entirely fixed, we implicitly treated it as role-based and thus relatively fixed. These studies have made evident, however, that attributes that most stand out for participants in a study may not be the more or less "fixed" characteristics of the I/O role, but other personal characteristics. In addition, even if a characteristic is relatively fixed, its meaning may be very different for different participants in a study.

This raises important questions about the characteristics of researchers to which research participants respond, not only, but particularly, in I/O studies, where the expectation of some similarities between respondents and insider researchers is taken for granted. What characteristics of a researcher are most salient under these circumstances? How do the characteristics most salient to research participants affect data gathering?

CONCLUSION

In this chapter, I have described characteristics of I/O team research, illustrated its contemporary uses, and explored processes usually evoked by it and advantages and disadvantages of its use. On the basis of this exploration, I have recommended areas that should be addressed for further development of the method. This chapter has shown the vitality of the approach as well as ways to open up the broader kinds of academic-practitioner collaboration that it is designed to enable. I/O team research has the potential for a very positive future.

NOTE

1. I am very grateful to Ian Walsh for his very helpful comments on earlier drafts of this chapter, and to Meryl Louis for her foundational work in the areas addressed here.

REFERENCES

Amabile, T. M., Patterson, C., Mueller, J., Wojcik, T., Odomirok, P. W., Marsh, M., & Kramer, S. J. (2001). Academic-practitioner collaboration in management research: A case of cross-profession collaboration. *Academy of Management Journal, 44*(2), 418–431.

Argyris, C. (1996). Actionable knowledge: Design causality in the service of consequential theory. *Journal of Applied Behavioral Science, 32*(4), 390–406.

Argyris, C., Putnam, R., & Smith, C. M. (1985). *Action science: Concepts, methods, and skills for research and intervention.* San Francisco: Jossey-Bass.

Bartunek, J. M. (2003). *Organizational and educational change: The life and role of a change agent group.* Mahwah, NJ: Lawrence Erlbaum.

Bartunek, J. M., & Lacey, C. (1998). The roles of narrative in understanding work group dynamics associated with a dramatic event: Confronting alcoholism. In J. Wagner (Ed.), *Advances in qualitative organizational research* (Vol. 1, pp. 33–66). Greenwich, CT: JAI Press.

Bartunek, J. M., & Louis, M. R. (1996). *Insider/outsider team research.* Thousand Oaks, CA: Sage.

Bartunek, J. M., Trullen, J., Bonet, E., & Sauquet, A. (2003). Sharing and expanding academic and practitioner knowledge in health care. *Journal of Health Services Research and Policy, 8*(Suppl.2), 62–68.

Bartunek, J. M., Walsh, K., & Lacey, C. A. (2000). Dynamics and dilemmas of women leading women. *Organization Science, 11*(6), 589–610.

Boland, R. J., & Collopy, F. (Eds.). (2004). *Managing as designing.* Stanford, CA: Stanford University Press.

Börjesson, S., Dahlsten, F., & Williander, M. (2006). Innovative scanning experiences from an idea generation project at Volvo Cars. *Technovation, 26*(7), 775–783.

Brown, J. S., & Duguid, P. (2001). Knowledge and organization: A social-practice perspective. *Organization Science, 12*(2), 198–213.

Coghlan, D., & Shani, A. B. (Rami). (2007). Insider action research: The dynamics of developing new capabilities. In P. Reason & H. Bradbury (Eds.), *The Sage handbook of action research* (2nd ed.). London: Sage.

Dutton, J. E., Worline, M. C., Frost, P. J., & Lilius, J. (2006). Explaining compassion organizing. *Administrative Science Quarterly, 51*(1), 59–96.

Easterby-Smith, M., & Malina, D. (1999). Cross-cultural collaborative research: Toward reflexivity. *Academy of Management Journal, 42*(1), 76–86.

Engwall, M., Kling, R., & Werr, A. (2005). Models in action: How management models are interpreted in new product development. *R&D Management, 35*(4), 427–439.

Evered, R., & Louis, M. R. (1981). Alternative perspectives in the organizational sciences: "Inquiry from the inside" and "inquiry from the outside." *Academy of Management Review, 6*(3), 385–395.

Foster-Fishman, P. G., Salem, D. A., Allen, N. A., & Fahrbach, K. (2001). Facilitating interorganizational collaboration: The contributions of interorganizational alliances. *American Journal of Community Psychology, 29*(6), 875–905.

Ganiel, G., & Mitchell, C. (2006). Turning the categories inside-out: Complex identifications and multiple interactions in religious ethnography. *Sociology of Religion, 67*(1), 3–21.

Garland, J., Spalek, B., & Chakraborti, N. (2006). Hearing lost voices: Issues in researching "hidden" minority ethnic communities. *British Journal of Criminology, 46*(3), 423–437.

Gibbons, M., Limoges, L., Nowotny, H., Schwartman, S., Scott, P., & Trow, M. (1994). *The new production of knowledge: The dynamics of science and research in contemporary societies.* London: Sage.

Handy, C. (1989). *The age of unreason.* Boston: Harvard Business School Press.

Hartley, J., & Benington, J. (2000). Co-research: A new methodology for new times. *European Journal of Work & Organizational Psychology, 9*(4), 463–476.

Hartley, J., & Benington, J. (2006). Copy and paste, or graft and transplant? Knowledge sharing through inter-organizational networks. *Public Money & Management, 26*(2), 101–108.

Hatchuel, A. (2001). The two pillars of new management research. *British Journal of Management, 12*(Suppl.1), S33–S40.

Heyl, B. S. (1997). Across the differences in collaborative fieldwork: Unanticipated consequences. *Sociological Quarterly, 38*(1), 1–18.

Israel, B. A., Schulz, A. J., Parker, E. A., & Becker, A. B. (1998). Review of community-based research: Assessing partnership approaches to improve public health. *Annual Review of Public Health, 19*, 173–202.

Jehn, K. A. (1997). A qualitative analysis of conflict types and dimensions in organizational groups. *Administrative Science Quarterly, 42*(3), 530–557.

Kelemen, M., & Bansal, P. (2002). The conventions of management research and their relevance to management practice. *British Journal of Management, 13*(2), 97–108.

Kilduff, M., & Kelemen, M. (2001). The consolations of organization theory. *British Journal of Management, 12*(Suppl.1), S55–S59.

Louis, M. R., & Bartunek, J. M. (1992). Insider/outsider research teams: Collaboration across diverse perspectives. *Journal of Management Inquiry, 1*(2), 101–110.

Macduff, N., & Netting, F. E. (2000). Lessons learned from a practitioner-academician collaboration. *Nonprofit and Voluntary Sector Quarterly, 29*(1), 46–60.

MacLean, D., MacIntosh, R., & Grant, S. (2002). Mode 2 management research. *British Journal of Management, 13*(3), 189–207.

Meyer, J., Bartunek, J. M., & Lacey, C. (2002). Identity change and stability in organizational groups: A longitudinal investigation. *International Journal of Organizational Analysis, 10*(1), 4–29.

Mohrman, S. A., Gibson, G., & Mohrman, A. M., Jr. (2001). Doing research that is useful to practice: A model and empirical exploration. *Academy of Management Journal, 44*(2), 357–375.

Ospina, S. M., & Dodge, J. (2005). Narrative inquiry and the search for connectedness: Practitioners and academics developing public administration scholarship. *Public Administration Review, 6*(4), 409–423.

Pettigrew, A. (2001). Management research after modernity. *British Journal of Management, 12*(Suppl.1), S61–S70.

Romme, A. G. L. (2003). Making a difference: Organization as design. *Organization Science, 14*(5), 559–573.

Romme, A. G. L., & Endenburg, G. (2006). Construction principles and design rules in the case of circular design. *Organization Science, 17*(2), 287–297.

Roth, J., Shani, A. B. (Rami), & Leary, M. (in press). Insider action research: Facing the challenge of new capability development within a biopharma company. *Action Research.*

Rynes, S. L., Bartunek, J. M., & Daft, R. L. (2001). Across the great divide: Knowledge creation and transfer between practitioners and academics. *Academy of Management Journal, 44*(2), 340–355.

Schön, D. A. (1983). *The reflective practitioner: How professionals think in action.* San Francisco: Jossey-Bass.

Simon, H. A. (1996). *The sciences of the artificial* (3rd ed.). Cambridge: MIT Press.

Starkey, K., & Madan, P. (2001). Bridging the relevance gap: Aligning stakeholders in the future of management research. *British Journal of Management, 12*(Suppl.1), S3–S26.

Tajfel, H. (1982). Social psychology of intergroup relations. *Annual Review of Psychology, 33*, 1–39.

Thomas, M. D., Beaven, J., Blacksmith, J., Ekland, E., Hein, J., Osborne, O. H., et al. (1999). Meanings of state hospital nursing I: Facing challenges. *Archives of Psychiatric Nursing, 13*(1), 48–54.

Thomas, M. D., Blacksmith, J., & Reno, J. (2000). Utilizing insider-outsider research teams in qualitative research. *Qualitative Health Research, 10*(6), 819–828.

Thomas, M. D., Hagerott, R. M., Hilliard, I. A., Kelly, J., Leichman, S., Osborne, O., et al. (1999). Meanings of state hospital nursing II: Coping and making meaning. *Archives of Psychiatric Nursing, 13*(1), 55–60.

Tranfield, D., & Starkey, K. (1998). The nature, social organization, and promotion of management research: Towards policy. *British Journal of Management, 9*(4), 341–353.

Trickett, E. M., & Espino, S. L. R. (2004). Collaboration and social inquiry: Multiple meanings of a construct and its role in creating useful and valid knowledge. *American Journal of Community Psychology, 34*(1–2), 1–69.

Trullen, J., Bartunek, J. M., & Harmon, M. (in press). The usefulness of design research in elementary and high schools for management education. In S. K. Piderit, R. E. Fry, & D. L. Cooperrider (Eds.), *A handbook of transformative cooperation: New designs and dynamics*. Stanford, CA: Stanford University Press.

Turner, V. (1974). *Dramas, fields, and metaphors: Symbolic action in human society*. Ithaca, NY: Cornell University Press.

van Aken, J. E. (2004). Management research based on the paradigm of the design sciences: The quest for field-tested and grounded technological rules. *Journal of Management Studies, 41*(2), 219–246.

van Aken, J. E. (2005). Management research as a design science: Articulating the research products of Mode 2 knowledge production in management. *British Journal of Management, 16*(1), 19–36.

Van de Ven, A. H. (in press). *Engaged scholarship: Creating knowledge for science and practice*. New York: Oxford University Press.

Weick, K. E. (1989). Theory construction as disciplined imagination. *Academy of Management Review, 11*(4), 516–531.

CHAPTER 5

Collaboration and the Production of Management Knowledge in Research, Consulting, and Management Practice

ANDREAS WERR

LARRY GREINER

ABSTRACT

For managers looking for management knowledge beyond their own experience, academics and consultants are two main resources. In this chapter, we focus on academic researchers and management consultants as producers of management knowledge and ask what the two can learn from each other. We suggest that there is a strong potential for collaboration in the triad manager–researcher–consultant, but we also acknowledge the institutional forces that make it difficult and discuss how they may be overcome. The chapter begins with an investigation into the knowledge-creating systems of academia and consulting, goes on to successful examples of knowledge creation in collaboration, and ends with a discussion of the tensions to be overcome, especially in the collaboration between academics on the one hand and practitioner-managers and consultants on the other.

The world of managers is increasingly knowledge intensive. Competition is growing and large organizations are becoming more global and complex, resulting in a proliferation of new management models and tools. This makes it difficult for managers to keep up with the latest developments (Huczynski, 1993). Although the main source of managers' learning is their own experience, this is becoming increasingly insufficient. Today's managers must search widely beyond their own experience for management knowledge that is relevant to their unique situations. They hire consultants, study for MBAs, attend executive education programs, and buy management books. As the demand for and debate about management knowledge has grown, so too have the supply and the number of actors involved in producing knowledge about management.

Management consultants and academic researchers from business schools are the main sources of management knowledge available to managers who want to obtain external knowledge input. Traditionally, management consulting and academic research have been depicted as distinct but complementary knowledge systems, with business schools and other disciplines acting as producers of knowledge that is turned over to consultancies, who then serve as disseminators to managers as the final customers. However, the past decade has seen this role division alter dramatically with academics and consultants now going separate ways to generate their own knowledge. Mainstream academics are now pursuing empirical research and publishing in their own journals for their own reading. The larger consultancies are also engaged in the creation of management knowledge (Davenport & Prusak, 2005) to enhance their marketing and provide solutions for clients. Managers, too, have occasionally become engaged in publishing knowledge from their experience in the form of books (Bossidy, Charan, & Burck, 2002; Welch, 2001). The popularity of these books indicates that many managers prefer the often simplified and unambiguous "practical" advice and knowledge presented in such books from consultancies and their managerial peers to the more ambiguous and complex knowledge disseminated from universities and business schools (Pfeffer & Fong, 2002). Many channels for disseminating

management knowledge are currently dominated by management consultants and practitioners. In a study of the German management magazine *Manager Magazin,* for example, practicing managers and management consultants were more often referred to as experts than were academics (Kieser, 2002b). Also, many consultancies publish journals containing informative articles written by their consultants based on research and consulting experience, which are widely subscribed to by executives and even academics. Examples include *McKinsey Quarterly* and *Strategy and Business*, published by Booz Allen Hamilton.

This chapter focuses on academics and consultants as producers of management knowledge. We acknowledge that in an increasingly complex world, professions and organizations need to specialize. But specialization also creates a need for integration. We consider the relative strengths and limitations of academics and consultants as current knowledge creators, and the potential value of collaboration between them and with managers in the conduct of future research. While the focus of our argument above has been on the drifting apart of consulting, research, and practice, there are examples of successful integrations of these systems, which have inspired our current argument. Influential researchers, such as Michael Porter, Michael Beer, and Susan Mohrman, have set up their own research institutes in which they integrate research and practice, and which increasingly (and successfully) compete with large consulting organizations. Also, some of the most influential developments in management research have been generated through consulting work, and breakthroughs in consulting organizations' knowledge have been created in collaboration with researchers. These collaborative activities will be exemplified by testimonials from Edward E. Lawler, Chris Argyris, and Edgar Schein later in this chapter.

It is useful to compare academics with consultants because each party has different concepts of the nature of knowledge and the best ways to produce it. We also recognize the third party to collaboration, the manager-practitioner, who holds the keys to access and data and is the ultimate judge of the usefulness and validity of the knowledge produced by consultants and researchers. Managers are the prime experimenters who put researchers' and consultants' knowledge to the test.

Our argument is structured as follows: After a brief discussion of how we view relevant knowledge in management research, we turn to the academic and consulting systems, respectively, in trying to understand their differing approaches to knowledge creation and collaboration. We then turn to a discussion about how collaboration between consultants, academics, and practitioners may be enhanced and provide testimonials of three successful cases, carried out by well-reputed academics. We conclude with a discussion of some of the tensions inherent in collaboration and how they may be overcome.

Our view throughout is that research collaboration involving all parties, given proper safeguards, is a highly useful way to produce new knowledge. Business school academics have much to give from their scientific theories and research methods, and consultants can provide their advantage of extensive experience with real-world issues, while practitioner-managers can offer access to their complex reality. Collaboration is the only way to expose researchers to (1) richer data about the total situation, (2) observation of the underlying dynamics at hand, (3) the uniqueness and specificity of each situation, and (4) the ability to test one's findings and conclusions through feedback from the subjects of study.

Unfortunately, as we shall see, many academics have withdrawn from collaboration with consultants and practitioners in their research efforts; furthermore, as a result, the latter two parties have avoided contact with academics for their perceived lack of relevance. Perceived relevance is key to making one's knowledge heard among practitioners, and both researchers and consultants have to compete with the hard school of business life from which managers derive most of their management knowledge.

Multiple Meanings of Relevant Knowledge

The question of what is and is not knowledge often provokes debate among the different producers; they each have different criteria for what passes as "real" knowledge. In academia, knowledge is usually defined by the theories and methods used to produce it. In consulting, the focus is on the practical results that knowledge produces. For the purposes of this chapter, we view knowledge in terms of its perceived relevance (not always immediately apparent) to various consumers, who include not only managers but consultants and academics as well. This does not mean that knowledge must be stated in "how to do it" terms, but its consequences should enlighten and cause other reactions. This knowledge can appear in a variety of forms:

- *Research findings* from using scientific methods, usually conducted by academics
- *New theories and concepts* about the managerial world, generated by academics and consultants from their research and experience (e.g., Drucker, 1955; Porter, 1980)
- *Applied techniques, tools, and methods* created through experience, usually by consultants and managers (e.g., BPR from Hammer & Champy, 1993)
- *Best practices* developed from looking across several organizations to see what actions are associated with effective results, often by consultants and packaged as popular management books (e.g., Peters & Waterman, 1982)
- *Personal accounts* from experience, usually by CEOs (e.g., Bossidy et al., 2002; Welch, 2001)
- *Case histories* derived from a firm's experience, usually incorporated within the

knowledge management system of consulting firms or in teaching cases

- *Project reports* prepared by consulting companies based on client-specific data and general knowledge to solve a specific organization's problems
- *Critical reviews and commentaries* based on critiques of the literature and its research, largely done by academics such as in this book

No doubt some skeptics will claim that many of the above examples do not qualify as knowledge. Business schools have been frequently questioned about the usefulness of their research (Pfeffer & Fong, 2002; Starkey & Tempest, 2004), and consultants are often criticized for the standardization and faddishness of their knowledge. Negative assessments range from failure to adhere to the scientific method to publishing meaningless statistics to succumbing to personal bias and placing fashion over objectivity. Despite these criticisms, our preference is to regard all of the above examples as forms of relevant knowledge because each depicts and informs a slice of reality. Different forms of knowledge are often created by different producers, each having unique strengths and limits, and even different methods for creating knowledge. In the following we will look more closely at the different knowledge standards of academics, consultants, and researchers, as inherent tensions between these standards limit the opportunities for collaboration. Backing off the standards in one system to adapt to the standards in another involves considerable risk for the actors involved.

ACADEMIC PRODUCERS

Management research began as an applied science in which the worlds of academics and practitioners were closely interwoven, with each informing the other. The academic community developed through generating new concepts from field research in organizations, the first classic exemplar being *Management and the Worker* (Roethlisberger & Dickson, 1934). Later came Peter Drucker (e.g., 1955) in his long career and series of popular books on management. These scholars were interested in helping both managers and themselves to understand better such topics as leadership, organizations, and markets by creating new frames of reference with many practical implications. Their research methods consisted largely of observations, interviews, and discussions with practitioners as they went out into organizations, spent considerable time, conducted field experiments, and even consulted with them. A few managers also made notable intellectual contributions through reflecting on their experience (e.g., Barnard, 1938; Fayol, 1917). Much of this early work was published in books, not journals, to be read by scholars, consultants, and managers. Authors were inclined to view knowledge as part of a systemic whole, which required the full length of a book to describe and document the realities of organizational life (Argyris & Schön, 1978; Bennis, Benne, & Chin, 1970; Lawrence & Lorsch, 1967; Miles & Snow, 1978). Many disciplines, from psychology to economics, adopted this approach to knowledge generation and distribution (Blau, 1963; Galbraith, 1958; Gouldner, 1954; Homans, 1951; Selznick, 1949), and it was highly influential on practice. The Hawthorne studies reported in *Management and the Worker* (Roethlisberger & Dickson, 1934), for example, led to a whole new era in management—the human relations movement—that transformed the way management was perceived (Perrow, 1986).

However, beginning in the late 1960s, the academic community in business schools became increasingly concerned with gaining more respect as "scientists." In the United States, Gordon and Howell (1959) criticized business schools for their lack of rigor and academic legitimacy. This made management researchers look for more "scientific" approaches. Some turned to a field of research that had long been operating in the background with roots traceable to Frederick Taylor's management engineering (Taylor, 1911). In this field, researchers were occupied with finding the optimal way to organize work, based on the scientific principles of the natural sciences.

This quest for the "scientification" of management was driven by a desire to legitimate the managerial occupation by providing it with a "rigorous" knowledge base. In mimicking the "big (natural and physical) sciences," the professional status of management was to be established. The manager was to be made an "expert" who would use his or her own scientific knowledge base for taking action. A hierarchy of knowledge production was therefore established (or assumed), with the academic acting as provider and the manager as the consumer-technician (Kenworthy-U'Ren, 2005). At the same time, those in other scholarly disciplines, notably economists and behaviorists, similarly began to organize themselves into professional associations with their own in-house journals.

Academic research, in its drive to become a "real science," has increasingly pursued the values of the natural and physical sciences, including universality (the "truth" of a certain knowledge should be established through universal criteria—irrespective of particular interests), commonality (results of research are a common good/property), unselfishness (the altruistic search for knowledge), and organized skepticism (refraining from premature judgments; reliance on scientific method and data) (Kieser, 2002b). For many scholars, the truth is to be found through adhering to the orthodoxy (theories and vocabulary) of a chosen discipline, which serves as one's professional identity.

Our informal survey of the leading academic journals suggests that well over 90% of the articles are concerned with establishing basic causality behind certain phenomena, such as what factors lead to greater commitment or motivation. Very few studies investigate whether a certain method or intervention used by management is effective or not, such as the introduction of a new goal-setting or reward system. This is in contrast to the medical field, where there is extensive investigation of the efficacy of experimental drugs.

While contemporary mainstream management research thus may have little to say to management practitioners, it is unfair to claim that the past 30 years of management research have passed unnoticed by management practitioners. Some instances of management research have been instrumental in shaping the managerial world by introducing new ways of understanding practice. Examples include modern finance theory, which has enabled the creation of a whole new financial industry, and the view of business as socially constructed, which has enabled new approaches to the challenge of innovation.

Collaboration and Academics

In striving for scientific ideals imported from the basic sciences, a set of criteria for "good management research" was created that has gradually moved academia away from practice, making it difficult for researchers to engage in such practice-oriented activities as consulting (Engwall, Furusten, & Wallerstedt, 2002; Stymne, 2004). This search for "objective" knowledge has created distance between academics and those being studied. Scholars are today pursuing large samples generated from archival or survey data, which are analyzed using sophisticated statistical methods. The advantage of this type of research is its ability to identify and describe certain patterns across large populations of people and/or organizations, which can be portrayed and compared at single or longitudinal points in time. Disadvantages, however, include the inability to pinpoint causality behind surface numbers, and statistical levels of significance that become too easy to obtain in large samples, without representing practically meaningful relations. Studies of this kind also make it difficult to find applications to a particular organization.

Another "distancing" approach is the use of laboratory experiments under artificial conditions, especially when involving students with no prior relationship established. While these studies may reveal important aspects of interaction within a limited range of researcher-defined variables, they often overlook the more complex and systemic aspects of business reality (e.g., real managers and organizations) that may in fact explain more of the variance in real-world settings than do the experimental variables.

Engagement with practice through consulting is today viewed negatively by many academics. Collaboration with the subject of research is to be avoided because it produces bias and wastes time in data gathering. Academics are rewarded for staying away from managers. Prior to the 1960s, academic evaluations for tenure in Sweden, took into account engagement with practice, but thereafter only the scientific merits were considered (Engwall et al., 2002). As one might expect, managers have added to the distance gap because they attribute lack of relevance to academic research.

Kieser (2002b) identifies several characteristics that have shaped knowledge creation in the academic world, resulting in barriers between theory and practice. First, the academic system is to a large extent a self-referential system, where relevance and quality criteria are internally created and controlled by one's scholarly peers. Only knowledge certified from within the system is regarded as "real" knowledge. The main vehicle for knowledge diffusion in academia is the scientific article, which is published for members of the academic system rather than for practitioners, who rarely read these articles. Second, success in the world of management research is closely linked to publication and citations in a limited number of highly reputed "A" journals, as ranked by other academics. The success of a researcher in addressing the practical needs of managers is generally not regarded as a source of scholarly reputation. Instead, extensive engagement and popularity among practitioners might be a threat to one's academic reputation. Consulting is typically treated negatively as an "income-earning activity" and a diversion from serious research. Third, a growing degree of specialization in management research, based on (most often) refined statistical methods, has resulted in a level of complexity that makes management knowledge increasingly hard to access and understand for outsiders to the academic system. The journal system rewards rhetoric that is abstract and full of technical terms. Academics, acting out of a need to demonstrate technical competence, impersonality, and systematic skepticism, make communication with practicing managers especially difficult. Finally, the dynamics of the scientific system and the protocol of many of its "A"-rated journals prohibit researchers from discussing applied implications and recommendations. Expressing disdain for the practical world, while not explicitly encouraged, is tolerated by editors of the academy's publications.

These characteristics further isolate the academic world from practice, preventing collaboration with consultants and managers. As a result, the latter assume a reverse relationship between practical relevance and academic value (Kieser, 2002a). This in turn makes it hard for researchers to gain access to organizations where they might otherwise obtain rich data, much of it qualitative, for explaining the dynamics lying behind their statistical findings (Schein, 2001, 2004).

Another negative consequence of this ingrown academic system occurs subtly in the quality of research revealed in statistically based articles. On close inspection of statistical tables in most articles, one finds that the hypothesized predictions of the researcher frequently explain less than 10% of the relationship between causal variables and predicted outcomes such as productivity and motivation. All of this unexplained variance raises further questions about the relevance of research engaged in by academics. Distance from management phenomena is clearly inhibiting the development of more complete and enlightening academic knowledge.

CONSULTANT PRODUCERS

The second major group of producers of knowledge, management consultants, are often depicted by academics as downstream actors in the supply chain of management knowledge. Presumably, consultants take the knowledge produced by academic research and apply it to the practice of management (Kenworthy-U'Ren, 2005; Suddaby & Greenwood, 2001). Like the management sciences, consulting has its roots in Taylorism, with the central idea of designing more efficient work. In the early 20th century, the first consulting companies grew out of industrial engineering to make recommendations based on time-and-motion studies (Kipping, 2002). Ironically, for many decades that followed, consulting research closely resembled today's academic research, which is engaged in stand-off studies that rely on extensive data gathering and analyses presented in written reports.

However, in the 1990s the large consultancies became increasingly involved in the production of their own knowledge for wider distribution and public consumption. Continuing today, consultants publish books and their own journals under a rubric they call "thought leadership" (Davenport & Prusak,

2005; Pasternack & Viscio, 1998). These consultancies have exploited their vast bases of experience gained from client projects to offer "brandable" models, such as McKinsey's "7S," Porter's "Five Forces," and the BCG "Growth Matrix." Many popular books advocating models and methods for solving managerial problems have resulted from these efforts (Maister, 1997; Nadler & Nadler, 1998; Slywotzky, 2002). These publications not only serve as useful marketing and branding tools for the consulting firms, but also function as a learning mechanism for consultants and clients (Werr, 1999). In one notable and highly popular book, *In Search of Excellence,* the collaborating authors were a consultant and an academic (Peters & Waterman, 1982). Interestingly, academic research has been stimulated by these models, which, ironically, are frequently taught by academic researchers in MBA classrooms.

Knowledge production within management consulting takes place within a different context than the academic world. In consulting firms, two types of knowledge are emphasized (Greiner & Poulfelt, 2005): (1) functional knowledge about topics and issues (e.g., strategic planning and compensation systems), and (2) specific industry knowledge (e.g., financial services and biotechnology). While functional knowledge overlaps with traditional academic disciplines, specific industry knowledge is to a large extent lacking in academic research. In addition to the production of management theories and concepts, consultants are involved in developing detailed methods, tools, and approaches to solving contemporary problems, representing a different kind of knowledge, such as BPR and Six Sigma (e.g., Werr & Stjernberg, 2003). These practical accomplishments have often gone unrecognized or criticized by the academic world (Salaman, 2002).

Consulting projects and the resulting knowledge are generally aimed at implementing systems and "inducing action" by clients

(Kieser, 2002b). "Inducing action" means that knowledge may be used for a number of different ends, even including less legitimate ends such as focusing only on data that justifies a priori decisions made by management (Kieser, 1998). The focus of consultants on action can easily lead to oversimplification by portraying an organizational world that is formally structured with clear roles and controls (Huczynski, 1993). Although this knowledge may attract popular attention, its methodological underpinnings in scientific terms are frequently regarded as weak, and its conclusions dubious (e.g., Alvesson, 1993; Furusten, 1995). Consulting knowledge is seldom subjected to formal evaluation and scientific critique. Critics explain that managers, under pressure to succeed, embrace popular and simplified solutions from consultants that are anxiety reducing (Abrahamson, 1991; Huczynski, 1993). In uncertain situations, managers seek "quick fixes" (e.g., Micklethwait & Wooldridge, 1996; O'Shea & Madigan, 1997). Beyond simplification, the rhetoric of consulting knowledge is characterized by a certain level of mystification and personalization that underpins the consultant's reputation of having superior expert knowledge and enhances his ability to extract fees (Clark, 1995; Clark & Salaman, 1996, 1998). This codification of consultant knowledge has even been criticized by clients for being too standardized and ill adapted to their needs (Greiner & Malernee, 2005).

Collaboration and Consultants

As the consulting industry has matured, it has developed a unique set of values that have pulled it closer to management practice, clearly distinguishing it from academic values. In the 1990s, with a strong focus on "client service," the work of consultants has shifted from writing reports toward implementing solutions (Nanda & Morrell, 2002). Creating measurable value for clients is now an overarching goal of management consulting (Maister, 1993). Academics, on

the other hand, are governed more by the twin goals of creating what they regard as "true" knowledge and enhancing their reputations among academic colleagues.

Knowledge creation and learning in consulting are to a large extent based on collaboration between consultants and organizations where they consult. It is a customer-driven business, with client questions serving as a trigger for knowledge development. In dealing with short-term deliverables, consultants frequently use cross-functional teams composed of consultants and client employees to share and leverage their knowledge and expertise (Fosstenlökken, Löwendahl, & Revang, 2003). Besides being a source of consultant learning, collaboration is used to bring about learning for the client, an added example of value creation (Kubr, 2002; Schein, 1988, 1999).

Much of the consulting literature is devoted to understanding the characteristics of the consultant-client relationship, which facilitates results and applied learning. Kubr (2002) identifies three dimensions to this relationship: First, he emphasizes that "without client-consultant collaboration there is de facto no effective consulting" (p. 66). The second is knowledge transfer from consultant to client and vice versa. This leads to trust, the third ingredient, which is needed for achieving an open relationship that allows for knowledge exchange and mutual learning.

Table 5.1 summarizes and makes clear that academics and consultants indeed live and work in very different worlds, with unique task demands and goals that produce different kinds of knowledge (Kubr, 2002, p. 58). The comparison indicates that academics are scientific yet removed from the phenomena being studied, and that consultants are overly close to the action but lacking in scientific rigor. We next address this question: Can collaboration between these producers and with practicing managers help to build on their different strengths and correct for their deficiencies in the production of relevant knowledge?

Table 5.1   The Different Logics of Research and Consulting

	Research	*Consulting*
Main values	Universality, communality, unselfishness, organized skepticism	Client service, profitability
Structuring of knowledge	Disciplines	Functions and industries
Problem	Mainly fashioned by researcher, formulated and based in the scientific community	Mainly fashioned by client, sometimes on joint basis
Time scale	Usually flexible	Tighter and more rigid
End product	New theories and models, new knowledge, publications, and citations (and better management practice?)	Organizational action, happy clients, and repeat business (and better management practice?)
Ownership of information	Usually publicly available	Often confidential
Academic rigor	Methodology tight	Minimum level appropriate to problem
Evaluation	External, by peers in scientific community, policy makers	Internal, by company

SOURCE: Adapted from Kubr (2002, p. 58).

MANAGEMENT CONTEXT FOR RESEARCH

To better assess the conditions that are likely to facilitate or obstruct collaborative research between consultants, academics, and practitioners, we need to understand the nature and context of the management environment, its required skills, and its working processes. Whitley (1989) identifies five common characteristics of managerial tasks, which he defines as (1) highly interdependent, contextual, and systemic; (2) relatively unstandardized; (3) changeable and developing; (4) combining maintenance of administrative structures with their development; and (5) rarely generating visible and separate outputs that can be directly connected to individual inputs.

The above view of management as a local and idiosyncratic practice is further elaborated upon by Kotter (1982) in his study of general managers, where he found that most successful leaders had substantial experience in a specific organization or industry sector. This implies that general management knowledge needs to be adapted to the specific situation for it to prove valuable (Clegg & Palmer, 1996; Whitley, 1989). In addition, the reviewers of management practice point out that managerial skills are about dealing with a series of interconnected problems in a single system, where solutions to one problem may create new and unanticipated problems and solutions. Under these conditions, the situational validity of general management theories and models becomes problematic, resulting in a lack of applicability in solving management problems. Generalized findings and theories, if they are to be useful, require inductive adjustment to account for local and systemic data.

Against this background of work characteristics, Schön (1983) severely criticizes the scientific/rationalistic model underlying most current academic research. Two central assumptions of this model are identified, which fit awkwardly with managerial practice: First, the model separates knowledge from action, implying that knowledge needed for competent action can be unambiguously stipulated by academic experts and then directly transferred to practitioners for implementation. The local and systemic character of management expertise makes this assumption highly questionable. A second criticism is the model's purported division between means and ends, which implies that a specific situation can be unambiguously identified as a specific problem to be solved (end) by the application of general knowledge (means). This assumption appears to be unrealistic, given the complexity and ambiguous character of today's management challenges. Instead, Schön emphasizes the constructive and interactive nature of the problem-solving process adapted to the situation. Scientific models and theories can play a role in this process through acting as a source of inspiration and insight for a manager's sensemaking. In this vein, Stymne (2004) argues for the conditional utility of academic research:

> The management researcher, who has the ambition to contribute to the competence of managers, has to produce theories that are not necessarily fully based on empirical facts. Instead they should be suggestions to practitioners about suitable ways of reasoning on which to base their actions. (p. 51)

Both academics and consultants will find some comfort in the above observation.

Consultants can resonate with the importance of local knowledge, since they are required to operate in close proximity to managers and organizations. Academics, too, will find support in the notion that formal management knowledge and management research are needed to help consultants and practitioners to make better sense of the reality facing them (Czarniawska, 2001; Stymne, 2004).

TOWARD COLLABORATIVE KNOWLEDGE

These various descriptions of the managerial world suggest that complete and valid management knowledge cannot by itself be developed at a distance, but rather must be integrated with insights from more intensive exposure to organizational life (Schein, 1987; Schön, 1987; Van de Ven & Johnson, 2006). In our opinion, this means that collaboration in research must be moved to the forefront of the producers' mindset and approaches to knowledge creation. Schein (1987, 2001, 2004), in this vein, talks about "clinical research/process consultation," and Van de Ven and Johnson (2006), about "engaged scholarship." But this won't be easy, given the institutional barriers and personal limits mentioned earlier. We now turn to a discussion of what the various parties might do to learn and benefit from each other as they move toward collaborative research. In particular, we consider alternative ways in which the strengths of each can be combined to produce new knowledge.

Collaboration is composed of both an individual's attitude and his or her behavior intended to produce a "win-win" outcome for all parties. But this ideal condition is not easily achieved. For collaborative research to advance, the various collaborators must recognize their own personal limits and know their strengths; they also need to respect each other and value the others' strengths; and they must be skillful in acting to bring synergy to the relationship (Amabile et al., 2001). This makes it important to carefully negotiate objectives and identities, roles of participants, rules of engagement and disengagement, and the dissemination and use of the findings of the collaborative research endeavor (Hatchuel, 2001). Figure 5.1 depicts the key parties involved in collaboration for knowledge creation, along with their potential contributions and gains.

While each of these collaborators clearly experiences a different reality, they all have something important to give to the others and share a common interest, around which they may unite, in better understanding the world of business. If one can satisfy both his or her own and the others' needs, it should advance the cause of collaborative research. We explore now what each party wants and has to give back through interaction. Table 5.2 gives a summary of the various needs and strategies to satisfy the different needs of each party.

Alternative Forms of Collaborative Research

Personal and institutional limits often prevent full and complete collaboration. We previously have noted that academics are limited by university reward systems and journal requirements. Consultants are constrained by the client situation and pressure for immediate results, and practitioners by their involvement in a complex and demanding reality. So it helps to keep in mind a set of alternative approaches and sometimes more modest arrangements for achieving collaboration.

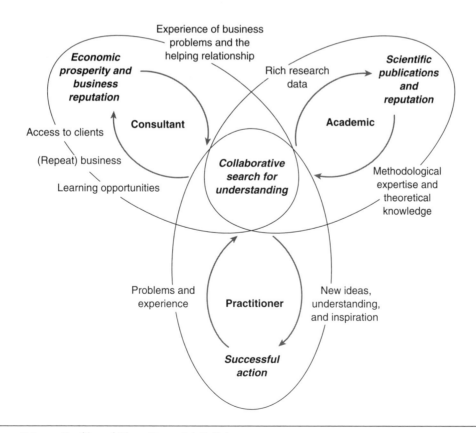

Figure 5.1   Profiles of Three Potential Collaborators

Table 5.2   Needs and Strategies for Collaboration

The Academic and the Practitioner

What the academic needs from the practitioner:

- Access to rich (real-world, dynamic) data
- Time with practitioners to review and validate the data (inductive + deductive)

What the academic can do to further collaboration:

- Involve the practitioner in designing research questions to ensure a relevant result
- Respect the confidentiality and time constraints of the practitioner

What the practitioner needs from the academic:

- Collaboration must be relevant to the issues facing the practitioner
- Approach and methods must be made clear to the practitioner

What the practitioner can do to further collaboration:

- Willingness to consider a long-term relationship with the academic, especially where problems are systemic or could benefit from the broader perspective that the academic has

The Academic and the Consultant

What the academic needs from the consultant:

- Invitation to participate in a research project
- Access to consultant and client data

What the academic can do to further collaboration:

- Help with research on the client's problem
- Engage in joint publications that are intended for a practitioner audience (and not solely an academic one)
- Follow the consultant's lead and respect his or her sensitivities

What the consultant needs from the academic:

- Provide rigor to the data collection/methods
- Write up or extend findings/insights from a portfolio of consulting projects

What the consultant can do to further collaboration:

- Invite the academic to work on a project
- Provide data from consultant files and the client
- Be open to academic topics and research methods

The Consultant and the Practitioner

What the consultant needs from the practitioner:

- Project with revenue
- Interesting problem
- Willingness to cooperate

What the consultant can do to further collaboration:

- Include the practitioner on consultant team
- Seek mutual agreement on problem definition and recommendations

What the practitioner needs from the consultant:

- Insights into the problem at hand
- Inclusion in the project
- Specific recommendations leading to positive results

What the practitioner can do to further collaboration:

- Participate on consultant team and provide guidance
- Provide sensitive data to the consultant
- Arrange for frequent feedback from the consultant

Central to making collaboration of any kind happen is the practitioner-manager, who controls access and is concerned about solving a problem. Nothing will happen unless he or she is willing to invite academics and consultants into the setting. Many practitioners are skeptical about consultants who have a partly deserved reputation for high fees and questionable value. Managers are also likely to be skeptical of academics, whom they are inclined to perceive as wasting their time by asking theoretical questions and requesting certain kinds of data not easily available. This skepticism has to be overcome by helping practitioners to see the potential benefits of collaboration in terms of new ideas, new ways of understanding the situation, and inspiration to act.

For a research project to be perceived as relevant by managers, collaboration must possess a number of characteristics, several of which are often overlooked by academics, though rarely by consultants. First, any collaborative attempt needs to be perceived as addressing the reality of the issues facing the manager-practitioner. Van de Ven and Johnson (2006) advise us to focus on the "big questions" that "have no easy answers and seldom provide immediate payoffs to practitioners or academics" (p. 810). Second, the approach and methods of the collaboration must be understandable and workable from the manager's point of view. Third, the collaboration must add to the manager's knowledge base, that is, question or confirm some of the manager's "taken for granted" assumptions (Weick, 1979). This may be achieved by formulating different versions of the problem and examining them from different perspectives (Van de Ven & Johnson, 2006). Mohrman, Gibson, and Mohrman (2001) note that practitioners are more inclined to view the results of research as useful when they are involved in discussing and interpreting the findings. Taken together, researchers and consultants alike must demonstrate to the practitioner that their efforts can yield greater insight and more successful action.

For the needs of the consultant, who ultimately struggles for economic prosperity and business reputation, the practitioner can offer the revenue from a sale, a problem to be solved, and a willingness to cooperate in a study. From this collaborative process, the consulting firm can add to its revenue and its knowledge base—and, if the client is satisfied, to its reputation. The consultant may bring to both practitioner-managers and academic research a rich experience of business problems and knowledge and skills of how to realize the helping relationship. Consultants are generally highly skilled in how to interact with their clients in order to create perceptions of value (Clark & Salaman, 1996).

As for the academics, who are driven by a quest for scientific publication and consequential reputation, the practitioner can open the door to the "real world," which includes rich data from observations and interviews about the dynamics of events that are taking place. This may provide material with good publishing potential. The academic might be easily satisfied by simply gaining access to an organization with its data. However, to get even closer to the phenomena in ways that earn trust from the manager, the academic must become more involved; he or she has to be willing to listen and to give and receive feedback in a spirit of reflective learning. Research projects should be designed as collaborative learning communities in which the diverse knowledge of practitioners and academics, possibly from different disciplines, may interact to form an understanding of the problem (Van de Ven & Johnson, 2006). This exchange requires academics to use terminology that resembles the practitioner's lexicon in helping to solve a client's problem. The academic will not gain much cooperation if he or she is perceived as lacking respect for the practitioner. Instead, academics can add value to knowledge creation with their methodological skills as well as their knowledge from research findings in areas of concern to the practitioner.

Academics can further collaborate in research with the consultant without even having to become involved with managers. They can incorporate their research questions into a data-gathering process that is being conducted by a consultant for a client. Further, although the fact is often unrecognized by academics, consultants possess a reservoir of untapped knowledge about management, which because of their project demands they don't find much time to write up and publish. Academics can therefore work with consultants to draw out their knowledge and jointly publish it, potentially adding to the reputation of both the consultant and the academic. They can also ask consultants to suggest researchable problems and solicit their feedback and alternative explanations to those they have proposed in journal drafts they are preparing for scientific publication.

A more complete form of collaboration involving all knowledge producers is advocated by Schein (1987, 2001, 2004) with a model he calls "clinical research/process consultation." According to Schein, management knowledge cannot be produced *for* managers; rather, it needs to be produced *with* them. In this truly collaborative model, the elements of knowledge production, research, consulting, and practice are integrated into a joint effort to better understand and deal with issues of concern to all parties. The nexus of this relationship is a practitioner's problem and the consultant's and researcher's genuine willingness to help the practitioner understand and solve the problem (see also Van de Ven & Johnson, 2006).

Paramount to Schein's mode of full collaboration is a genuine search by all parties for mutual understanding about what is "really" going on in the situation; this objective is in line with the basic academic value of searching for truth, with the consultants' striving to earn reputation by demonstrating true commitment to solving the client's problem, and with

the practitioners' search for more successful action. However, unlike in positivistic academic research, practitioners (consultants and managers) become involved in the process as both providers and interpreters of data. Data in this process comes voluntarily as all participants gain by revealing more about themselves as they seek to understand their reality. Even though academic involvement in the research site violates the values of "objective" research, we all remember Lewin's famous axiom that by trying to change a system one learns more about it. This knowledge is produced from richer and deeper data than is typically available in surface statistical data (see also Schein, 1987, for a more thorough discussion of the "quality" of knowledge produced through a clinical approach). Another scholar, Donald Schön (1983), calls this process "reflection in action," which emphasizes openness, spirit of inquiry, and authenticity of communication. Client anxieties related to revealing more about themselves are overcome by establishing an open and trustful relationship. Van de Ven and Johnson (2006), in their discussion of collaboration between researchers and practitioners, further emphasize the potential of having actors with different perspectives look into the same problem in the collaborative research process. This may require collaboration not only between academics, practitioners, and consultants but also between academics from different disciplines. Such a process may create conflict, but this is likely a prerequisite for more productive inquiry.

To conclude, there are multiple advantages for academics to engage in high levels of collaboration, including the identification of research questions, access to organizations, and availability of a test site to interpret findings (Amabile et al., 2001). Prior research suggests that academics who spend more time in organizations report greater personal learning and a higher frequency of citations for their publications (Rynes, McNatt, & Bretz, 1999). They also find that academics' involvement in organizations increases the likelihood that their findings will be implemented by manager- practitioners. The academics' theoretical and methodological skills become valuable by ensuring the quality of management knowledge produced, although the quantitatively oriented management researcher may need to add some qualitative tools (see also Schein, 2001, 2004). Clinical researchers can still engage in surveys, perform interviews, or act as participant-observers. The difference from mainstream research is that "total collaboration" is accomplished with a focus on a problem defined by the practitioner and with a mindset to help the client deal with that problem.

EXAMPLES OF COLLABORATION: ACTING AS BOTH CONSULTANT AND ACADEMIC

The overarching implication of this chapter is for academics and consultants to reevaluate their roles and identities as participants in the research process. So far we have discussed each party as if they are separate people, which is usually the case. But there is evidence that the two roles can be integrated within a single person and that such a combination may be a powerful enabler of a collaborative knowledge creation process. Many well-known management scholars have produced some of their most influential findings through acting at the same time as both consultant and researcher; examples include Chris Argyris, Michael Beer, Warner Burke, Thomas Cummings, Edward Lawler, Paul Lawrence, Jay Lorsch, Henry Mintzberg, Susan Mohrman, David Nadler, Jeffrey Pfeffer, Michael Porter, Robert Quinn, Edgar Schein, Noel Tichy, and Dave Ulrich in the United States and Andrew Pettigrew, Richard Normann, and Eric Rhenman in Europe. We have asked three of these— Edgar Schein, Chris Argyris, and Edward Lawler—all highly regarded in academic and consulting circles, to provide personal

examples of how they have used the combined role to create collaborative processes toward creating new knowledge. While their experiences are different, they all take advantage of gaining access to field situations, and they use collaboration to create not only local solutions but also broader knowledge.

LIVING WITH LIMITS AND BRIDGING TENSIONS

The above comments by three successful researcher-consultants illustrate the potential for collaboration in producing new knowledge. They illustrate that collaboration may simultaneously contribute to the creation of more valid *and* more useful management knowledge. The cases illustrate how collaboration with practice may alert academics to new and important research areas (such as HR business process outsourcing), and how it creates a more complex (but probably also more valid) understanding of organizational phenomena. Both in the case of Exult and HR BPO and in the case of the bank and its resistance to technological innovation, a complex set of systemic and cultural factors, such as skills, role perceptions, occupational identity, and assumptions of authority and career development, were found to interact in creating barriers to change. These factors, and their interaction, were identified based on a thorough and longitudinal engagement with the research sites and would have been difficult to identify through a more distanced research approach. As illustrated in the story told by Edgar Schein, other kinds of explanations, covering up the underlying cause, would have been readily available to a more distanced researcher. Furthermore, the collaborative process gave researchers such as Chris Argyris the opportunity to test and refine research-based tools and techniques to help consultants in Monitor become more efficient, both internally, as a learning organization, and externally, in providing value to their clients.

Example 1
Edward E. Lawler III—
Understanding Business
Process Outsourcing in HR

When the Exult Corporation was founded in 1998, there were no companies focused on human resources business process outsourcing (HR BPO). HR then, as it is now, was frequently criticized for its failure to become a strategic partner with line management, and for being mired in administrivia. Exult saw an opportunity to change this situation and built a business model based on their taking over the administrative parts of the HR function for major corporations.

I heard about Exult in 2000 from a number of HR executives who were intrigued by their business model. I made contact with them and was invited to join their advisory board. It was a distinguished group, including Dave Ulrich and Jac Fitz-enz.

At the time I joined the board, I had already done a number of studies on the role of the HR function in U.S. corporations. These studies consistently showed that HR was not transforming itself from an administrative function to a strategic function.[1] The Exult approach appeared to me to offer an opportunity to reposition the HR function in major corporations as a high value-added strategic partner. My initial role with Exult was to meet with clients, consult with Exult on the design of their HR systems, and give talks about HR outsourcing.

As I learned more about HR BPO, it became apparent to me that there was an opportunity to do a research study that evaluated the effect of utilizing HR BPO in major corporations. After some discussions with me, Jim Madden, the president of Exult, was eager to support a research project. Discussions with Dave Ulrich and Jac Fitz-enz led to an agreement that the four of us would do research and write a book on the impact of Exult's HR BPO system in four of their major corporations: BP, Prudential, International Paper, and Bank of America. We got a financial grant from Exult to fund our work and hired a case writer to do in-depth reports on each of the four cases. In addition, I used the Center for Effective Organizations at the University of Southern California to collect survey data from HR executives in each of the four companies.

We were able to collect enough change data to justify publishing a research-based book on business process outsourcing.[2] It was the first book to focus on the impact of HR BPO and to make a significant contribution to our understanding of its impact on the HR function.

There is no doubt in my mind that if I hadn't had a consulting relationship with Exult, the opportunity to do this piece of research would never have appeared. The consulting relationship helped build trust with the management of Exult and made them more receptive to our needs for financial support in order to do the research.

On the personal side, I learned a great deal about HR BPO from my consulting work with Exult that greatly enriched the book. There were a number of unexpected findings that I most likely would not have identified if I had not had a good working relationship with Exult. Just to mention one, we found a type of co-dependency between HR managers and line management in the companies we studied. Both decried the traditional relationship between HR and the line as mired in administrative trivia and, at times, even conflict, but when freed of this, both parties were unable to abandon the old. In many cases, they simply did not have the skills or the concepts needed to redefine their relationship to one where HR was more of a strategic support function for the line.

Example 2:
Chris Argyris—Understanding
the Learning Organization[3]

About two decades ago, the top board members of the Monitor Group, a consulting firm, invited me to assist them in becoming a first-class learning organization. I asked, and they agreed that we should begin with the board.

The major research procedures that were used were observing and tape-recording their meetings. We were able to map the board members' interactions to show how they inhibited the kind of double-loop learning they sought.

We also used this knowledge to create an intervention, at the top, to strengthen their productive interactions as well as to create new ones. As the success of this intervention was documented (through the tape recordings and observations), it was used throughout the company, beginning with the immediate reports to the board members. The intervention, changed through our learning, continues to be used in the hiring and training procedures.

A second result was the development of diagnostic and change instruments and procedures that would be offered to clients. I believe that it is fair to say that these procedures created a quality of services that benefited the effective implementation of the recommendations in the client organization.

I believe that the foundation of my two decades with the firm as well as the continued deepening and expansion of our relationship after I became less active was due to the fact that the research was based upon a model of consulting. This made it necessarily acceptable for Monitor to continually confront us on the advice that they were receiving. It also made it possible for us to make demands to collect data (e.g., through tape recordings) and to design interventions that, in addition to helping them, could be used to test out theories of effective action and learning.

Example 3:
Edgar Schein[4]–Deciphering a Failure to Implement a New Technology

For several years, I was a process consultant to a senior manager in a bank operations department, helping him with a variety of projects. One of his main goals was to introduce an effective new information technology system for handling various financial transactions. Several years had already been spent on developing the technology, and contract research had been done to determine the feasibility of introducing the technology to the clerical workforce. The essence of the new technology was to have fewer clerks handling many more tasks rather than having specialists for each task.

As the new technology was being installed, it became evident that many fewer clerks would be needed, and it was then discovered that the bank had an unbreakable norm that nobody would be laid off. Everyone was to be retrained and given other jobs in the bank. At the same time, it was discovered that my client would not be able to relocate or retrain the many persons who would be displaced by the new technology because either the retraining would not suit given clerks or there were no alternate jobs available. The existence of the "no-layoffs" norm was well known, but no one had any idea of how powerfully held it was until the technological change was attempted. No one realized how overstaffed all the other departments of the bank were. The new technology was at this point abandoned as impractical.

In the traditional research model the existence of this norm would be a sufficient "explanation" of the observed phenomenon that a potentially useful technology failed to be adopted. But what I learned as a consultant to the head of this unit "deepens" our understanding considerably. Once we discovered that the no-layoffs norm was operating, I began inquiries about the source of the norm and learned that it was strongly associated with my client's boss. He had been in his job for a long time, and for him "no layoffs" was a central management principle that he had made into a sacred cow. I had assumed from prior knowledge of social psychology that norms are upheld primarily by group members themselves. I found, instead, that in this situation it was the boss's fanaticism that was really the driving force, an insight that was confirmed three years later when he retired. All the attitudes about layoffs changed rapidly, the department was now ready to lay off people, but, surprisingly, the new technology was still not introduced. My previous two explanations had both been wrong.

It should also be noted that, as a traditional researcher, I would not have been allowed to hang around for so long, so I would not even have discovered that the constraint on the new technology was something other than the no-layoffs norm and the presence of its powerful originator. To explain further what was happening, I had to draw on some other knowledge I had gained as a member of the design team for the initial change. I remembered that the group had had great difficulty in visualizing what the role of the new operator of such a computer program would be and especially what the role of that person's boss would be. The group could not visualize the career path of such an operator and could not imagine a kind of professional organization where such operators would be essentially on their own. I asked a number of people about the new technology and confirmed that people did not see how it could work, given the kinds of people who were hired into the bank and given the whole career and authority structure of the bank. Low-level clerk specialists were easy to manage and their careers were well understood. Superclerks of the kind that would be created by this technology would have to be better educated, would want more pay, and would be autonomous operators operating essentially from a principle of "self-control" instead of managerial control.

So what was really in the way of introducing the new technology was not only the norm of no layoffs, but some deeper conceptual problems with the entire sociotechnical system, specifically an inability to visualize a less hierarchical system in which bosses might play more of a consultant role to highly paid professional operators who, like airline pilots, might spend their whole career in some version of this new role. In fact, the no-layoffs norm might have been a convenient rationalization to avoid having to change deeper cultural assumptions about the nature of work and hierarchy in this bank.

What the clinical process revealed was that the phenomenon was "overdetermined," multiply caused, and deeply embedded in a set of cultural assumptions about work, authority, and career development. We were dealing with a complex system of forces, and once this system was understood as a system, it became obvious why the bank did not introduce the new technology. Attributing it to the boss with his norm of no layoffs would have been a misdiagnosis even though all the surface data indicated that this was a sufficient explanation.

The clinical process also revealed the interaction of forces across hierarchical boundaries, the operation of power and authority, the role of perceptual defenses, the linkages of forces across various other organizational boundaries, and the changing nature of those forces as the situation changed. Human systems are complex force fields, and many of the active forces are psychological defenses and cultural assumptions that will not reveal themselves easily to uninvolved observers, surveyors, testers, or experimenters. It is too much to ask of the traditional research process to reveal this level of dynamics, yet without understanding organizations at this level, how can we possibly make any sense of what we observe around us?[5]

The cases also illustrate what practitioners and consultants may have to gain from a deeper collaboration with academics. In all cases, the actions by the researchers were informed by academic thinking and methodology, pushing practitioners to search for solutions to their problems beyond the obvious. In the cases of both Exult and the bank, the collaborative process created an understanding of the causes of observed problems, which went beyond what the organizations themselves would have been able to achieve on their own. In the case of Monitor, the research-based interventions by Chris Argyris directly helped the organization become more efficient, internally as well as externally.

Finally, the cases illustrate some of the enabling factors of successful collaboration. In all three cases, the academic researcher's primary goal is to be helpful to the manager-practitioner and the organization. In the case of Exult, it was about helping to design and sell the product; in the case of Monitor, to create a learning organization and more effective procedures for creating client value; and in the case of the bank, to help senior management with the implementation of a new IT system. This initial focus on being helpful created trust between academics and the organization, which opened up an opportunity for the academics to address more of their research agenda—and gain both access and financing for pursuing it.

While the above cases illustrate successful examples of knowledge development in collaboration, achieving this is not always easy. Both the amount of time needed to realize such collaboration and the focus on a single or a few organizations may be important barriers. Research universities and "A" journals today are unlikely to accept articles based on exclusive use of such a research model, unless the sample of firms is larger and the patterns in findings across them appears profound. Nor are skeptical consulting firms and practitioners likely to open their doors wide to academics for conducting extensive collaboration. Interestingly, the authors above are all senior professors who have attained tenure and successful reputations, which allows them to take risks by engaging in collaboration.

Still, some modest movement toward promoting collaboration can be made, though it takes political will and a sense of personal security. On the institutional front, editors of top-rated journals can insist on accepting only studies that support and interpret the dynamics behind the reported statistics, which would likely cause more field research involving collaboration. These editors could also ask for more articles that evaluate interventions by management or consultants, using methodologies like field experiments. They should require a section at the end of each article that discusses and speculates about the practical implications of an article's findings—presently, only passing and rather superficial references are made to what managers might do with the findings. In addition, the reward and promotion systems of universities could be adjusted slightly to elevate the status of books with theoretical significance, as well as according articles in highly regarded publications such as *Harvard Business Review* (*HBR*) the same status as articles in "A" journals. The acceptance ratio for *HBR* is likely more rigorous than for most "A"-level journals. Business schools can also act to remove "faculty consulting" from their "dirty word" list, making these schools more congruent with the warm welcome they typically extend to consulting firms during recruiting season.

As for consulting firms and their consultants, they can reach out to receptive academics to encourage books and articles to be written jointly with them. They might also invite academics to serve in residence during sabbaticals while performing research on the firm's knowledge system. They could ask academics to join them as part-time research advisers to their projects on relevant methods and theory, as was illustrated by the role of Chris Argyris in relation to Monitor above. They could further evaluate a project's results, since consultants rarely ask for an assessment of their work. In reaching out to clients, as in action research (Reason & Bradbury, 2001), consultants can include client members on the consulting team to conduct interviews and provide and interpret data. They can also give lectures of practical significance and organize retreats with intensive discussion and problem solving.

Even these minor changes are likely to threaten the status quo now producing resistance, so consultants and academics will need to make up their own minds about how far they are willing to proceed. No doubt some small steps are possible for many of us, which can lead to major results. For example, one of the authors of this chapter, Larry Greiner, had an MBA student, who became a consultant and then a CEO, who invited him in to help in a collaborative way to solve some strategic problems. Greiner and his colleague Arvind Bhambri kept detailed notes on what happened, leading eventually to an academic paper that won the McKinsey prize at an SMS (Strategic Management Society) conference, and to a publication in *Strategic Management Journal* (Greiner & Bhambri, 1989). Another example is provided by the other author of this chapter, Andreas Werr, who was involved through an executive Ph.D. student in an insider/outsider action research project (Bartunek & Louis, 1996) in the student's organization. While helping the organization deal with the issue at hand, the project also resulted in several academic papers, one of which was eventually published in *MIT Sloan Management Review* (Sandberg & Werr, 2003). Other small steps for academics to take include occasional uses of collaboration with consultant friends to explore what's behind statistical findings. Also, going out to write a

teaching case can lead indirectly to interesting research ideas for follow-up. Academics might also initiate a larger study of "consultant knowledge" about management, industries, and implementation, since consultant experiences are much closer to these phenomena.

In all these efforts at collaboration, the involved parties will likely encounter and confront tensions that are not easily resolved. Everyone will have to find his or her own resolutions. Academics and consultants who fall at the extreme ends of these tensions might occasionally consider moving more toward the middle, which would be beneficial for both research quality and knowledge creation. Some of the major tensions facing these various producers of management knowledge are presented in Figure 5.2.

Involvement Versus Distance. At one extreme is the academic value of assuring objectivity through distance from the subject being studied. In order to gain "true" knowledge, the system must be studied "unobtrusively" (as if the act of studying has no effect) so as not to influence its "real" workings. For resolution, academics need to recognize that involvement may be not only unavoidable but also a source of important questions (Van de Ven & Johnson, 2006) and rich data (Schein, 2001, 2004). At the other extreme, consultants are not always conscious of how their involvement and desire to please the client can bias their objectivity. To overcome this problem, consultants can invite academics to advise them on research methods, such as triangulating interviews with numerical data. Weick (1979) argues for diversity in research approaches and perspectives to match the diversity and complexity in the phenomena being studied (see also Van de Ven & Johnson, 2006).

Academic Versus Practical Relevance. Academic reputation is currently derived from contributions to intellectual discourse

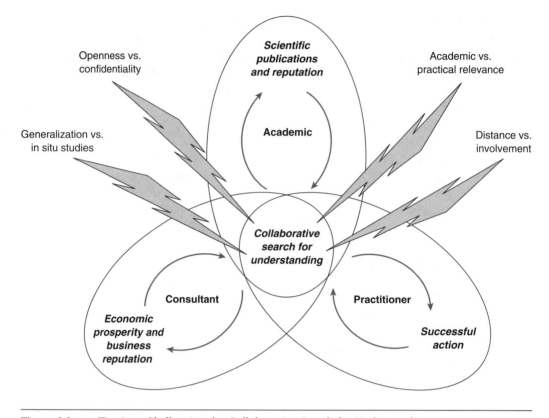

Figure 5.2   Tensions Challenging the Collaborative Search for Understanding

rather than to practice. Academics purposely avoid normative conclusions in their research, which makes it hard for them to be perceived as relevant to practitioners. Ironically, academics teaching cases in the classroom typically ask students for their "action plans" and are not reluctant to give their own remedies to problems. This suggests that academics are not immune to an interest in practical consequences. So, if interested, academics might approach consultants to indicate their willingness to work with them in framing research projects to deal with both practical and theoretical problems simultaneously. On the other hand, consultants can improve their analyses of client problems by gaining additional insight from academics drawing on the latest research.

Openness Versus Confidentiality. Practitioners understandably want to protect information, either positive or negative, from leaking out within the firm or to the public. This causes problems for both academics and consultants who may be interested in publishing research based on client data. Academics must respect the confidentiality concerns of both consultants and practitioners. This responsibility can be dealt with by aggregating data over several cases while making the sources anonymous.

Generalization Versus In Situ Studies. Universality is a strong value in the academic community that causes academics to shy away from generating deep knowledge from a single case. However, several cases can be compared in order to identify patterns that yield more generalizable insights (Eisenhardt,

1989). Single cases can be used to refine theories and conceptual models. Turning to consultants, they too have a mutual interest in discovering generalizable knowledge, such as "best practices," which they can brand, publish, and use in other engagements. Both parties should be open to the opportunity for joint publication.

MOVING AHEAD

As we have seen, collaborative research may involve three distinct professions—academia, consultation, and management—all operating from different thought worlds (see also Amabile et al., 2001). We have argued for the potential benefits of knowledge creation through collaboration across these worlds while working singly or in pairs or triads. However, as we have observed, there are serious institutional obstacles to making collaborative research happen. Recognizing these limits, individuals must decide how far they personally wish to go. As one ventures forward, it is important to realize that collaboration involves additional responsibilities such as understanding the other party's frame of reference in searching for a "win-win" outcome.

It is an advantage that all the knowledge producers are united by their common focus on knowing better the managerial world, which still remains a combination of science and art. For practitioner-managers, individual success is linked to their organization's growth and success (Whitley, 1989). They are judged by the results they produce, which, it is hoped, will stimulate a search for better understanding of the messy reality being faced. The problems encountered by practitioners become the motor and enabler for collaborative research. In addition, academics and consultants must carefully select among practitioners for those who have a keen appreciation for the importance of

research, and who enjoy working with and learning from people different from themselves (Amabile et al., 2001). The kinds of processes we have discussed above bring together different perspectives and thus make conflict an unavoidable but potentially rewarding part of the inquiry process (Van de Ven & Johnson, 2006).

The consultant's world is dominated by an overall need to secure an inflow of new assignments, which means keeping clients satisfied while building the firm's reputation and brand image in the business world. In their relationships with clients, consultants derive knowledge from their experience with numerous cases, which is sometimes formalized into books, tools, and methodologies. They hope for satisfied clients who will purchase their services again and refer them to new clients. However, not all attempts at collaboration by consultants live up to being "helpful" because the pressure to sell becomes a barrier to achieving a truly helpful relationship (Schaffer, 2000; Schein, 1988, 1999). Consultants who engage in a collaborative relationship will have to give up some of their need for control and make themselves more open and vulnerable to influence from academics and manager-practitioners. Engaging in collaborative processes with academics can also help consultants to validate their models and experience, allowing them to improve their concepts and methods (Suddaby & Greenwood, 2001). Both academics and consultants are likely to gain through joint publications, a commonly shared goal that enhances both their reputations (Davenport & Prusak, 2005).

This nexus and spirit of helpfulness and risk taking in bringing together academics, practitioners, and consultants in collaborative research relationships promises, we believe, to open up new opportunities for further learning and the production of valuable and useful knowledge that will benefit all involved.

NOTES

1. Lawler, Boudreau, and Mohrman (2006).
2. Lawler, Ulrich, Fitz-enz, and Madden (2004).
3. Argyris (1993, 2004) and Edmonson and Moigeon (1996).
4. Schein (1999, 2001).
5. See also Schein (2003) for another illustration of how one extensive longitudinal case study may produce genuine new theory.

REFERENCES

Abrahamson, E. (1991). Managerial fads and fashions: The diffusion and rejection of innovations. *Academy of Management Review, 18*(3), 586–612.

Alvesson, M. (1993). Organizations as rhetoric: Knowledge-intensive firms and the struggle with ambiguity. *Journal of Management Studies, 30*(6), 997–1015.

Amabile, T. M., Patterson, C., Mueller, J., Wojcik, T., Odomirok, P. W., & Kramer, S. J. (2001). Academic-practitioner collaboration in management research: A case of cross-profession collaboration. *Academy of Management Journal, 44*(2), 418–431.

Argyris, C. (1993). *Knowledge for action.* San Francisco: Jossey-Bass.

Argyris, C. (2004). *Reasons and rationalizations.* Oxford, UK: Oxford University Press.

Argyris, C., & Schön, D. (1978). *Organizational learning: A theory of action perspective.* Reading, MA: Addison-Wesley.

Barnard, C. I. (1938). *The functions of the executive.* Cambridge, MA: Harvard University Press.

Bartunek, J. M., & Louis, M. R. (1996). *Insider/outsider team research.* Thousand Oaks, CA: Sage.

Bennis, W. G., Benne, K. D., & Chin, R. (Eds.). (1970). *The planning of change.* London: Holt, Rinehart & Winston.

Blau, P. (1963). *Dynamics of bureaucracy* (2nd ed.). Chicago: University of Chicago Press.

Bossidy, L., Charan, R., & Burck, C. (2002). *Execution: The discipline of getting things done.* London: Random House Business Books.

Clark, T. (1995). *Managing consultants.* Buckingham, UK: Open University Press.

Clark, T., & Salaman, G. (1996). Telling tales: Management consultancy as the art of story telling. In D. Grant & C. Oswick (Eds.), *Metaphor and organizations* (pp. 167–184). London: Sage.

Clark, T., & Salaman, G. (1998). Creating the "right" impression: Towards a dramaturgy of management consultancy. *Services Industries Journal, 18*(1), 18–38.

Clegg, S. R., & Palmer, G. (1996). Introduction: Producing management knowledge. In S. R. Clegg & G. Palmer (Eds.), *The politics of management knowledge* (pp. 1–18). London: Sage.

Czarniawska, B. (2001). Is it possible to be a constructionist consultant? *Management Learning, 32*(2), 253–266.

Davenport, T. H., & Prusak, L. (2005). Knowledge management in consulting. In L. Greiner & F. Poulfelt (Eds.), *The contemporary consultant* (pp. 305–326). Mason, OH: Thomson South-Western.

Drucker, P. (1955). *The practice of management.* London: Heinemann.

Edmonson, A., & Moigeon, B. (1996). When to learn how and when to learn why. In B. Moigeon & A. Edmonson (Eds.), *Organizational learning and competitive advantage* (pp. 17–37). London: Sage.

Eisenhardt, K. M. (1989). Building theories from case study research. *Academy of Management Review, 14*(4), 532–550.

Engwall, L., Furusten, S., & Wallerstedt, E. (2002). The changing relationship between management consulting and academia: Evidence from Sweden. In M. Kipping & L. Engwall (Eds.), *Management consulting: Emergence and dynamics of a knowledge industry* (pp. 167–183). Oxford, UK: Oxford University Press.

Fayol, H. (1917). *Administration industrielle et générale*. Paris: Dunot et Pinat.

Fosstenlökken, S. M., Löwendahl, B. R., & Revang, Ö. (2003). Knowledge development through client interaction: A comparative study. *Organization Studies, 24*(6), 859–879.

Furusten, S. (1995). *The managerial discourse: A study of the creation and diffusion of popular management knowledge*. Uppsala, Sweden: Department of Business Studies, Uppsala University.

Galbraith, J. K. (1958). *The affluent society*. London: Hamish Hamilton.

Gordon, R. A., & Howell, J. E. (1959). *Higher education for business*. New York: Columbia University Press.

Gouldner, A. (1954). *Patterns of industrial bureaucracy*. Glencoe, IL: Free Press.

Greiner, L., & Bhambri, A. (1989). New CEO intervention and dynamics of deliberate strategic change. *Strategic Management Journal, 10*(Summer), 67–86.

Greiner, L., & Malernee, J. K. (2005). Managing growth stages in consulting firms. In L. Greiner & F. Poulfelt (Eds.), *The contemporary consultant* (pp. 271–291). Mason, OH: Thomson South-Western.

Greiner, L., & Poulfelt, F. (Eds.). (2005). *The contemporary consultant*. Mason, OH: Thomson South-Western.

Hammer, M., & Champy, J. (1993). *Reengineering the corporation: A manifesto for business revolution*. New York: HarperCollins.

Hatchuel, A. (2001). The two pillars of new management research. *British Journal of Management, 12*(Suppl.1), S33–S40.

Homans, G. C. (1951). *The human group*. London: Routledge & Kegan Paul.

Huczynski, A. (1993). *Management gurus*. London: Routledge.

Kenworthy-U'Ren, A. (2005). Toward a scholarship of engagement: A dialogue between Andy Van de Ven and Edward Zlotkowski. *Academy of Management Learning & Education, 4*(3), 355–362.

Kieser, A. (1998). Unternehmensberater: Händler in problemen, praktiken und sinn. In H. Glaser, E. F. Schröder, & A. v. Werder (Eds.), *Organisation im wandel der märkte* (pp. 191–226). Wiesbaden, Germany: Dr. Th. Gabler Verlag.

Kieser, A. (2002a). On communication barriers between management science, consultancies and business organizations. In T. Clark & R. Fincham (Eds.), *Critical consulting* (pp. 206–227). Oxford, UK: Blackwell.

Kieser, A. (2002b). *Wissenschaft und beratung*. Heidelberg, Germany: Universitätsverlag C. Winter.

Kipping, M. (2002). Trapped in their wave: The evolution of management consultancies. In T. Clark & R. Fincham (Eds.), *Critical consulting* (pp. 21–27). Oxford, UK: Blackwell Business.

Kotter, J. P. (1982). *The general managers*. New York: Free Press.

Kubr, M. (2002). *Management consulting: A guide to the profession* (4th ed.). Geneva: International Labour Office.

Lawler, E. E., Boudreau, J. W., & Mohrman, S. A. (2006). *Achieving strategic excellence: An assessment of human resource organizations*. Stanford: Stanford University Press.

Lawler, E. E., Ulrich, D., Fitz-enz, J., & Madden, J. C. (2004) *Human resources business process outsourcing: Transforming how HR gets its work done*. San Francisco: Jossey-Bass.

Lawrence, P. L., & Lorsch, J. (1967). *Organization and environment: Managing differentiation and integration*. Boston: Harvard University.

Maister, D. (1993). *Managing the professional service firm*. New York: Free Press.

Maister, D. (1997). *True professionalism*. New York: Free Press.

Micklethwait, J., & Wooldridge, A. (1996). *The witch doctors: What the management gurus are saying, why it matters and how to make sense of it*. London: Heinemann.

Miles, R. E., & Snow, C. C. (1978). *Organizational strategy, structure, and process*. New York: McGraw-Hill.

Mohrman, S. A., Gibson, C. B., & Mohrman, A. M., Jr. (2001). Doing research that is useful to practice: A model and empirical exploration. *Academy of Management Journal, 44*(2), 357–376.

Nadler, D., & Nadler, M. B. (1998). *Champions of change: How CEOs and their companies are mastering the skills of radical change*. San Francisco: Jossey-Bass.

Nanda, A., & Morrell, K. (2002). *McKinsey & Company: An institution at a crossroads*. Boston: Harvard Business School Publishing.

O'Shea, J., & Madigan, C. (1997). *Dangerous company*. London: Nicholas Brealey.

Pasternack, B. A., & Viscio, A. J. (1998). *The centerless corporation: A new model for transforming your organization for growth and prosperity*. New York: Simon & Schuster.

Perrow, C. (1986). *Complex organizations: A critical essay* (3rd ed.). New York: McGraw-Hill.

Peters, T. J., & Waterman, R. H. (1982). *In search of excellence: Lessons from America's best-run companies*. New York: Warner Books.

Pfeffer, J., & Fong, C. T. (2002). The end of business schools? Less success than meets the eye. *Academy of Management Learning & Education, 1*(1), 78–95.

Porter, M. (1980). *Competitive strategy: Techniques for analyzing industries and competitors*. New York: Free Press.

Reason, P., & Bradbury, H. (Eds.). (2001). *Handbook of action research: Participative inquiry and practice*. London: Sage.

Roethlisberger, F. J., & Dickson, W. J. (1934). *Management and the worker: Technical vs. social organization in an industrial plant*. Boston: Graduate School of Business Administration, Harvard University.

Rynes, S. L., McNatt, B. D., & Bretz, R. D. (1999). Academic research inside organizations: Inputs, processes, and outcomes. *Personnel Psychology, 52*(4), 869–899.

Salaman, G. (2002). Understanding advice: Towards a sociology of management consultancy. In T. Clark & R. Fincham (Eds.), *Critical consulting: New perspectives on the management advice industry* (pp. 347–360). Oxford, UK: Blackwell.

Sandberg, R., & Werr, A. (2003). The three challenges of corporate consulting. *MIT Sloan Management Review, 44*(3), 59–66.

Schaffer, R. H. (2000). Rapid-cycle successes versus the Titanics: Ensuring that consulting produces benefits. In M. Beer & N. Nohria (Eds.), *Breaking the code of change* (pp. 361–380). Boston: Harvard Business School Press.

Schein, E. H. (1987). *The clinical perspective in fieldwork.* Newbury Park, CA: Sage.

Schein, E. H. (1988). *Process consultation: Its role in organization development.* Reading, MA: Addison-Wesley.

Schein, E. H. (1999). *Process consultation revisited.* Reading, MA: Addison-Wesley.

Schein, E. H. (2001). Clinical inquiry/research. In P. Reason & H. Bradbury (Eds.), *Handbook of action research: Participative inquiry and practice* (pp. 228–237). London: Sage.

Schein, E. H. (2003). *DEC is dead, long live DEC: The lasting legacy of Digital Equipment Corporation.* San Francisco: Berrett-Koehler.

Schein, E. H. (2004). *Organizational culture and leadership.* San Francisco: Jossey-Bass.

Schön, D. (1983). *The reflective practitioner: How professionals think in action.* Aldershot, UK: Avebury.

Schön, D. (1987). *Educating the reflective practitioner.* San Francisco: Jossey-Bass.

Selznick, P. (1949). *TVA and the grass roots.* Berkeley: University of California Press.

Slywotzky, A. J. (2002). *The art of profitability.* New York: Warner.

Starkey, K., & Tempest, S. (2004). Researching our way to economic decline. In N. Adler, A. B. (Rami) Shani, & A. Styhre (Eds.), *Collaborative research in organizations: Foundations for learning, change and theoretical development* (pp. 23–36). Thousand Oaks, CA: Sage.

Stymne, B. (2004). Travelling in the borderland of academy and industry. In N. Adler, A. B. (Rami) Shani, & A. Styhre (Eds.), *Collaborative research in organizations: Foundations for learning, change and theoretical development* (pp. 37–53). Thousand Oaks, CA: Sage.

Suddaby, R., & Greenwood, R. (2001). Colonizing knowledge: Commodification as a dynamic of jurisdictional expansion in professional service firms. *Human Relations, 54*(7), 933–953.

Taylor, F. W. (1911). *The principles of scientific management.* New York: Harper & Brothers.

Van de Ven, A. H., & Johnson, P. E. (2006). Knowledge for theory and practice. *Academy of Management Review, 31*(4), 802–821.

Weick, K. E. (1979). *The social psychology of organizing* (2nd ed.). New York: McGraw-Hill.

Welch, J. (2001). *Jack: Straight from the gut.* New York: Warner Books.

Werr, A. (1999). *The language of change: The roles of methods in the work of management consultants.* Doctoral dissertation, Stockholm School of Economics, Stockholm.

Werr, A., & Stjernberg, T. (2003). Exploring management consulting firms as knowledge systems. *Organization Studies, 24*(6), 881–908.

Whitley, R. (1989). On the nature of managerial tasks and skills: Their distinguishing characteristics and organization. *Journal of Management Studies, 26*(3), 209–224.

Part II

COLLABORATIVE RESEARCH MECHANISMS AND PROCESSES

Publications about collaborative research attest to the difficulties associated with creating and maintaining collaborative relationships that support significant, sustained research leading to transformation in organizational performance and meaningful additions to the body of scientific knowledge (Adler, Shani, & Styhre, 2004). Research also suggests that the challenges of collaborative management research intensify as we increase the scope of concern from understanding single organizations to complex networks of organizations, regions, and even societies. Part II of this *Handbook* is devoted to the exploration of a variety of approaches to the conduct of collaborative management research that can establish the foundation to support significant and sustainable research. McGuire, Palus, and Torbert offer us the guiding theory of developmental action inquiry, along with the notions of engaging in 1st-, 2nd-, and 3rd-person research/practice, single-, double-, and triple-loop learning, and an interweaving of collaborative research and collaborative practice. To enhance the potential for academia to contribute to future theoretical breakthroughs, Hatchuel and David propose the intervention-research in management (IRM) approach and outline some critical principles that must be followed by IRM researchers and the organizations they collaborate with. Docherty and Shani argue that there are various ways to design and manage collaborative management research via organizational learning mechanisms that could be cognitive, structural, or procedural in nature, or some combination of the three. Holmstrand, Härnsten, and Löwstedt describe the research circle approach with a set of guiding principles and a road map for action. Mirvis examines and contrasts three different forums and the design parameters in which collaborative management research takes place. Table II.1 provides a high-level guide to the theoretical foundations and focus of the chapters in this section.

At the center of collaborative management research is the active involvement of managers and researchers, agents and populations of agents, and communities of practice that together form a community of inquiry in the framing of the research agenda, the selection of methods, and the development of implications for action. The complex nature of the inquiry system requires an understanding of the mechanisms and processes of collaborative management research. This need stems from the challenge of designing and managing the collaborative relationships among different actors, agents, networks, and communities of practice, such that they will support significant and long-term research. In the chapters of this *Handbook*, we can find a variety of approaches to designing both the community of inquiry and the inquiry process. The authors in this section describe a variety of different approaches, which are only samples of the many permutations and combinations of the elements of inquiry, reflexivity, research, and action/practice focus that are inherent in collaborative management research. This section gives a small peek into the many different approaches that will be evident in the later exemplar chapters—each of which fits with and/or constrains the purposes and outcomes intended by the participants. That different approaches achieve different outcomes suggests that different kinds of communities of inquiry may be appropriate for different situations and when the participants are striving to achieve different purposes. For example, the learning circles of Holmstrand et al. are appropriate when the desired outcome is to engage and empower people to participate in improving their work system. The contractual and formal study process advocated by Hatchuel and David fits when the intent is to discover or invent new management models.

Because the collaboration is formed by multiple parties, each of which has aspirations and purposes for the collaboration, they must together determine which collaboration approach is appropriate. Underlying this choice are a set of design dimensions (and decisions), each of which fulfills a necessary design requirement for achieving a desired outcome. Several design requirements that seem to constitute the minimal critical specifications for collaborative management research include (1) constituting a community of inquiry that has representatives from the communities of practice that are relevant to the achievement of the practice and theory outcomes; (2) specification of inquiry and learning processes that facilitate ongoing participation, dialogue, and conversations; and (3) research processes and methodologies to facilitate the scientific discovery process. We can see from the examples in this section that just as the purposes and approaches to collaborative management research differ, so too do the decisions along these three dimensions. For example, bringing together people from multiple companies in a network to explore and learn about a topic involves a group with members who are not tied to each other in a particular workplace, but who are trying to learn from each other's practice and from individuals who are experts on the topic. The collaborations in this type of group will follow quite a different process from collaborative research in a setting where the members of a work system are trying to examine and change their norms and process of interaction in order to become an effective learning system that is able to change its performance outcomes. The research processes followed in these two kinds of settings will differ substantially from the learning processes that might be carried out if academic researcher/consultants are asked to work with an internal design team to conduct a deep, academically rigorous analysis of a work system and to discover and test ways to make it more effective at attaining new levels of performance.

Table II.1   Part II: Overview of Chapters

	Chapter 6	Chapter 7	Chapter 8	Chapter 9	Chapter 10
	Developmental Action Inquiry, 1st-, 2nd-, and 3rd-person research/practice (McGuire, Palus, & Torbert)	Intervention-Research in Management (IRM) (Hatchuel & David)	Design and Management of Learning Mechanisms (Docherty & Shani)	Research Circles (Holmstrand, Härnsten, & Löwstedt)	Academic-Practitioner Learning Forums (Mirvis)
Theoretical roots	* Human development theory * Action science theory * Experiential learning theory	* Theory of collective action * Engineering science * Organization theory	* Organization design theory * Organization development theory * Organization learning theory	* Theory of communicative action * Democratic dialogue * Organization development theory	* Organization development theory * Network learning theory
Essence of the approach	* An approach that integrates developmental action inquiry with 1st-, 2nd-, and 3rd-person research/practice, and with single-, double-, and triple-loop learning	* A protocol for collaborative revelation or invention of a practice in the local context that can be generalized and diffused as a radically new theoretical management model for collective action	* Purposeful design of the community of inquiry, using specific structural and procedural configurations and processes in order to facilitate sustainable scientific discovery and action	* Purposeful design of research circles in which researchers facilitate democratic study and joint exploration of contentious issues that empower participants to take individual action in their ordinary roles	* Purposeful design of network-based learning forums—seminars, roundtables, self-study—where different kinds of knowledge creation of variant nature takes place

Another important design consideration of collaborative management research is whether the collaborative research is intended to be an integral part of the work system or a parallel or even temporary approach. Does collaborative management research take place in the formal structures of the organization as part of its permanent working routines, or does it occur in specially formed study teams, research circles, or parallel teams? The approaches in this section differ along this dimension as well.

Sustaining collaborative management research and collaborative management research capabilities is a complex task. It entails building into the routines of the organization the processes and mechanisms through which both continuous scientific discovery and improved performance of the firm and all the actors, agents, networks, and communities of practice involved are achieved. The ongoing commitment of the parties depends on the outcomes of the collaboration, and on ongoing commitment of resources—time, attention, funding, and access to data and participants—that get consumed and have to be regenerated. This raises the question of whether the collaborative research is seen as a temporary partnership or an ongoing relationship. From the point of view of the hosting organization or system, it raises the question of whether the capability to engage in collaborative management research is viewed as a competence that is situation-specific or that should be built into the fabric of the organization. The illustrations that follow present different views about the duration of the collaboration and intentions with regard to embedding the collaborative research capabilities.

In sum, the nature of collaborative management research suggests that while each participant brings different knowledge about practice, about the scientific discovery process, and about what might work, careful exploration and choices must be made about the most appropriate collaborative approach. The chapters in this volume and in this section illustrate diverse approaches, mechanisms, and processes and will, we hope catalyze consideration of the issues of design, sustainability, and mechanisms for those interested in pursuing collaborative management research.

REFERENCE

Adler, N., Shani, A. B. (Rami), & Styhre, A. (2004). *Collaborative research in organizations: Foundations for learning, change, and theoretical development*. Thousand Oaks, CA: Sage.

Toward Interdependent Organizing and Researching

JOHN MCGUIRE

CHARLES J. PALUS

BILL TORBERT

ABSTRACT

This chapter introduces both the theory and practice of developmental action inquiry, along with the notions of engaging in (1) 1st-, 2nd-, and 3rd-person research/practice; (2) single-, double-, and triple-loop learning; and (3) an interweaving of collaborative research and collaborative practice that attempts to help move individuals, leadership cultures, and whole organizations from a dependent, through an independent, to an interdependent orientation. These notions are illustrated through a longitudinal case study of individual, interpersonal, team, and organizational transformations.

This chapter illustrates how developmental action inquiry (DAI) theory, method, and practice (Torbert, 1991; Torbert & Associates, 2004) can be used both to assess and to transform leaders, teams, and organizations simultaneously, through a participatory action research process (Reason, 1994; Reason & Bradbury, 2001) that attempts to become increasingly self-transforming and collaborative as it evolves. The chapter first introduces the DAI theory and method. Next, we introduce the case example of a leadership development organization we have worked with, which we will call LDR (an actual case with some confidential details changed). We show the application at LDR of DAI as a theoretical lens as well as a source of modes of intervention, leadership practices, and research methods that interweave efforts at individual, interpersonal, and organizational transformation. In conclusion, we suggest that we have illustrated how interweaving 1st-, 2nd-, and 3rd-person research in the midst of practice can generate both valid knowledge and transforming action.

A central aim of collaborative management research is to overcome the barriers that tend to divorce research from context, action, results, and learning in organizational settings. In this chapter we explore a further aim supported by DAI, in which the interdependence of the various organizational actors, including researchers, is developed as a new long-term capability of the organizational system. In the case of LDR—and in many other organizations also grappling with complex knowledge work in contexts of organizational and social transformations—mere cooperation or local alignment of interests is not enough. We define *interdependence* in stage-developmental terms, as action-logics that allow groups of people with shared work to deliberately integrate and mutually transform toward desired ends their otherwise fatally diverse roles, functions, identities, visions, and worldviews (McCauley, Drath, Palus, O'Connor, & Baker, in press).

DAI requires and cultivates a high voluntary commitment by all its actors, as well as increasing mutuality and collaboration among them. According to developmental theory and our previous findings (Torbert & Associates, 2004), only under such conditions will the trust develop that is necessary for sustainable individual, team, and organizational transformations. In this chapter and especially in the case illustration we explore practical issues of leadership associated with DAI, such as building and sustaining commitment and trust among diverse actors; collaborating with (and telling truth to) those in power; and building coalitions in support of deep change.

DEVELOPMENTAL ACTION INQUIRY AS A COLLABORATIVE RESEARCH METHODOLOGY

The theory, practice, and research methods associated with DAI originate in the work of Bill Torbert and his colleagues (Torbert, 1976, 1987, 1991; Torbert & Associates, 2004). DAI integrates developmental theory (Kegan, 1994; Loevinger, 1976; Piaget, 1954) with action science (Argyris, Putnam, & Smith, 1985). DAI is a model of research that integrates the ongoing development of its subjects, including the researchers themselves. While having much in common with other models that stress collaborative forms of inquiry coupled with action (Reason, 1994) and reflective practice (Schön, 1983), DAI is distinctive in its rigorous developmental emphasis and its integral awareness (Wilber, 2000) of the interplay of subjective, intersubjective, and objective qualities in experience. Especially, DAI supports the awareness, development, and enactment of mature "postformal" stages (Commons & Richards, 2003) or modes (Basseches, 1984) of human development as necessary for mindful and sustainable individual, organizational, and social transformations.

DAI has four distinct features as a research model. In this chapter we will focus on two of these (the first and last as presented below) as windows into the model illustrated by the case. The reader will find further elaboration of all features of the model in Torbert and Associates (2004).

The first distinctive feature of DAI is that its theory, practice, and research methods all point toward the capacity of individuals, teams or communities of practice, and larger organizations and institutions to interweave 1st-person, 2nd-person, and 3rd-person research *in the midst of their daily practice* (Chandler & Torbert 2003; Foster & Torbert, 2005; Torbert, 2000).

First-person research here refers to studying "myself" in the context of the overall inquiry, in the midst of practice. First-person research serves the related purposes of self-understanding, self-development, presence of mind, and being able to effectively apply one's own subjectivity to the larger research effort. Thus 1st-person research connects the researcher's inner self with the outer research project and its larger aims, and in general requires reflecting on and adapting one's own thoughts, emotions, intuitions, behaviors, and effects. Without a 1st-person research aspect, the process of action inquiry can become stuck in the limits, lack of integrity, or blind spots of its individual actors.

Research groups with various collaborating actors are inevitably diverse in perspectives and worldviews. *Second-person research* refers to studying and developing "ourselves"—as a social body with integrity—in the midst of practice and in the context of the overall inquiry. Developing the collective abilities of inquiry partners as reflective practitioners allows more sufficiently complex, accurate, nuanced, and mutually shared understanding and coherent action to be constructed. Without a 2nd-person research aspect, the process of action inquiry can too easily become trapped in unexplored assumptions and norms, be limited in perspective, and lack the mutual trust that underlies commitment to larger aims.

Third-person research refers to studying and developing "it" and "them"—the world as relatively objective systems, structures, and processes. Third-person research ranges from empirical measurement and analysis of defined objects (as in "traditional" research) to the creation of sustainable systems and institutions beyond the local subjective worlds of the researchers and actors. Without a strong 3rd-person research aspect, inquiry becomes divorced from its extended effects in space and time.

The interweaving of 1st-, 2nd-, and 3rd-person research in action (hence "action inquiry") creates useful triangulations in perspectives and methods. For example, DAI encourages all participants in a given action inquiry project to self-diagnose their individual "action-logics" (1st-person), compare their self-diagnosis to a reliable and valid leadership development profile (LDP) (3rd-person), and explore the action implications with a coach or community of practice (2nd-person). Likewise, in the case of LDR we will see how the development of the shared and individual (1st-person) perspectives in a strategic team (2nd-person) accompanies the reform of organizational systems (3rd-person). Overall, such interweaving of stances aims at evolving more adequate and transformative marriages of objectivity, subjectivity, and intersubjectivity, and thus more adequate ways of deeply paying attention to what we are doing and the effects we produce.

A second distinctive feature of DAI's epistemology and ontology is that instead of seeing "outside reality" as the "territory" where research is done and science as the "map" of that territory, DAI holds that there are four distinct "territories of experience." These may be found either to be aligned with, or incongruent with, one another at any given moment or period of time, and thus are the basis for learning, knowledge creation, and effective action. For the individual, these four territories or qualities can be thought of and experienced as (1) the outside world, (2) one's own sensed behavior, (3) one's thinking and feeling, and (4) one's attention and intention. To listen in to all four territories at once now means that you, our reader, become aware, not just of your thinking of these words, but also of this page as a physical presence, while sensing your breathing, and playing with your newly widened attention. For an organization, these same four territories are likewise the basis for learning, knowledge creation, and effective action and can be thought of and experienced as (1) the organization's tangible inputs, outputs, and environment; (2) its operations or performance; (3) its espoused strategy and structure, as well as its norms-in-use; and (4) its vision and mission.

A third distinctive feature of DAI is that progress occurs not just by incremental single-loop hypothesis testing but also by double-loop (Argyris & Schön, 1974) and triple-loop learning and change. When, during our personal, relational, and collective actions and inquiries, incongruities are found across the four territories of experience (e.g., an unintended result, an ineffective performance, a strategy that feels inconsistent with one's integrity, a lie), action inquiry gradually generates the capacity for these three distinct orders of change. First, we may master (relatively speaking) a capacity for reliable *single-loop change,* whereby unintended outcomes lead us to experiment with changes in our performance to achieve our goal. Next, we may develop a capacity for occasional double-loop change. *Double-loop change* occurs when the human system's enacted strategy or action-logic transforms (with associated changes in goals, performance choices, and outcomes). Finally, *triple-loop change* occurs when the human system's very way of attending (the fourth territory) itself changes, acquiring greater capacities for intentionally moving among the other three territories and across more than one at a time. For example, instead of blinding or defending itself against the incongruities in its practices, an organization and its members might actively seek them out, based on an ongoing commitment to greater integrity of mission, strategy, performance, and outcome.

The fourth distinctive feature of DAI (the D in DAI) is the developmental theory shown in Table 6.1. This version of constructive-developmental theory (McCauley et al., in press; Piaget, 1954) hypothesizes a specific sequence of action-logics through which any human system can (but perhaps may not) transform as it gradually gains the capacity to monitor all four territories of its activity

and to develop greater congruity and integrity among them. According to this theory, human systems develop a reliable capacity for intentional single-loop learning at the *Achiever/Systematic Productivity* action-logic. (Any level of learning may occur sporadically at earlier action-logics but without the ability to sustain or intentionally direct it.) At the *Strategist/Collaborative Inquiry* action-logic the person or organization develops the capacity for intentional double-loop learning, and finally, at the *Alchemist/Foundational Community* action-logic, the capacity for triple-loop awareness and learning. A 3rd-person psychometric measure of developmental action-logics—the LDP—has shown high validity and reliability in predicting which individual CEOs and consultants have developed to the point of double-loop, transformational learning and of successfully leading organizational transformation (Rooke & Torbert, 2005; Torbert & Associates, 2004). A growing body of empirical research confirms that only those few leaders and organizations that reach the *Strategist/Collaborative Inquiry* action-logic can reliably create conditions for their own and others' transformation (Bushe & Gibbs, 1990; Fisher & Torbert, 1991; Manners, Durkin, & Nesdale, 2004; Merron, Fisher, & Torbert, 1987; Rooke & Torbert, 1998; Torbert & Fisher, 1992).

The overall path of development, as illustrated in Table 6.2, is from relatively "dependent" orientations that tend to resist change (up through the *Diplomat* action-logic), through relatively "independent" orientations that support incremental, single-loop change (*Expert* through *Individualist* action-logics), to relatively "interdependent" orientations that welcome not just incremental change but also transformational, double- and triple-loop change when appropriate (*Strategist* action-logic and above).

To summarize, DAI represents a scientific and political paradigm for integrating inquiry and action, profoundly different from

Table 6.1   Parallels Between Personal and Organizational Developmental Action-Logics

Personal Development	Organizational Development
1. Impulsive Impulses rule behavior	1. Conception Dreams about creating a new organization
2. Opportunist Needs rule impulses	2. Investments Spiritual, social network, and financial investments
3. Diplomat Norms rule needs	3. Incorporation Products or services actually rendered
4. Expert Craft logic rules norms	4. Experiments Alternative strategies and structures tested
5. Achiever System effectiveness rules craft logic	5. Systematic Productivity Single structure/strategy institutionalized
6. Individualist/Pluralist Reflexive awareness rules effectiveness	6. Social Network Portfolio of distinctive organizational structures
7. Strategist Self-amending principle rules reflexive awareness	7. Collaborative Inquiry Self-amending structure matches dream/mission
8. Alchemist Mutual process (interplay of principle/action) rules principle	8. Foundational Community of Inquiry Structure fails, spirit sustains wider community
9. Ironist Intergenerational development rules mutual process	9. Liberating Disciplines Structures encourage productivity and transformational learning through manageable conflict and vulnerable power

SOURCE: Adapted from Torbert and Associates (2004).

modernist empiricism, postmodern constructivism, and "realpolitik." DAI leads to increasingly timely and transformational action across multiple time horizons of particular situations, not just to valid generalizations or to instrumentally efficient actions.

THE LDR CHALLENGE

LDR is a medium-sized company providing leadership development services and research-based knowledge to organizations and individuals. For several years, LDR had faced a changing marketplace. Client demand for the development of individual leaders had become a slower-growth and more saturated market. Demand was accelerating for forms of development that integrate the development of leaders with the strategic development of organizational culture and human systems. Individual leader development was increasingly viewed as quite necessary but insufficient in itself for meeting complex organizational challenges (Day, 2000; Van Velsor & McCauley, 2004). This market shift had been recognized

Table 6.2 The Relationship Between LDR's Three Leadership Cultures and Torbert's Developmental Action-Logics

Leadership Cultures	Individual Action-Logic	Organizational Action-Logic
Dependent	Opportunist	Investments
Foundational Learning as Survival	Diplomat	Incorporation
Independent	Expert	Experiments
Functional Learning as Utility	Achiever	Systematic Productivity
	Individualist	Social Network
Interdependent	Strategist	Collaborative Inquiry
Future Learning as Desire	Alchemist	Community of Inquiry

by LDR executives for several years through strategic investment in research and development toward a new business with the capability to deliver organizational leadership development products and services.

However, this shift in focus from the core business of individual leader development to include the new business of organizational leadership development would prove to be a complex organizational challenge itself, with both technical and organizationally adaptive aspects (Heifetz, 1994). The challenge was threefold. First were the technical business challenges of implementing a new line of services. Second, the new business capability needed to include and integrate the existing core capability in order to provide comprehensive solutions. Finally, a shift toward interdependence was needed in the culture of LDR. That is, a shift was needed beyond the existing action-logics of *Experimentation* (supporting initial development of the new business prototypes) and *Systemic Productivity* (supporting productivity of the core business), and toward *Collaborative Inquiry*

(supporting long-term, mutually transformational engagements inclusive of diverse client constituencies and of LDR core and new capabilities; see Table 6.1).

LDR's new business in organizational leadership seemed to require advancement to an interdependent stage of culture and to late-stage action-logics for two reasons. First, the nature of long-term, transformative client engagements is dialogical, aimed at cultural root causes and deep assumptions, rather than solely transactional. Therefore, LDR's staff and its systems needed the capability to sustain this dialogue across complex organizational boundaries over time. Second, the complexity of the work in organizational leadership requires a horizontal business-process orientation that is inherently interdependent. Developing new products and services requires a client-centered flexibility that crosses most boundaries within the organization (Womack & Jones, 2003) and explores cultural root causes and deep assumptions within one's own organization.

In response to this new strategic direction, the R&D division formed a workgroup tasked with creating new knowledge, practices, and prototypes for this emergent market where leadership and organizational development had merged. This group adopted grounded theory and action-research methods (Eisenhardt, 1989; Strauss, 1987) coupled with rapid prototyping methods (Schrage, 2000) for the development of research-based tools and services. The group conducted its initial research within highly customized client contracts that promised collaborative learning for both clients and LDR.

Based on the first year of collective work, this R&D group decided to explore three different, but related, promising avenues. They divided into three workgroups and assigned a project manager to maintain the core of an integrated project. But after about a year they were struggling with how to more deeply integrate the work of the three R&D teams. One key area of common ground was that most core team members had been using constructive-developmental theories as part of the foundation for building this new capability for several years (Drath & Palus, 1994; McCauley et al., in press; Palus & Drath, 1995), including Robert Kegan's constructive-developmental theory and practices (Kegan, 1994; Kegan & Lahey, 2001; Drath, 2001); Bill Torbert's DAI theory and practices (Torbert & Associates, 2004); Clare Graves's meme theory (Beck & Cowan, 1996); and Ken Wilber's integral theory (Wilber, 2000). Therefore, constructive-developmental theory in the form of DAI was an attractive organizing principle for the growing community of practice. The group decided to adopt the DAI model and to incorporate Bill Torbert's parallels between personal and organizational stages of development (Table 6.1), with LDR's stages of culture theory and practice (Table 6.2). The shared intent among the three R&D teams was to understand and develop leadership in organizations as it functions interdependently. It was also the stated aspiration of the three R&D teams themselves to work together interdependently, moving their subcultures from Independent to Interdependent, for reasons including authentically participating in the change envisioned for the LDR culture at large, as well as to effectively address the complexity inherent in the new business.

But the teams fell frustratingly short of this aspiration. They also had doubts as to whether the LDR executive team and the organization as a whole would continue to endorse the degree of change required to integrate the new business into the core business.

LDR MEETS DEVELOPMENTAL ACTION INQUIRY

At this point, the research and development group at LDR invited Bill Torbert to visit for a two-day retreat, seeking input and feedback to their projects and the challenges of integrating the three workgroups.

As his way of introducing DAI to the retreat as a "live process" rather than as a "canned product," Torbert played back his initial interpretations of both the culture of the three teams and the culture of the executive leadership of LDR. Having reviewed a 30-year history of LDR and its presidents, Torbert suggested that LDR had mastered the industry niche of its core business and was functioning at the *Systematic Productivity* organizational action-logic (see Table 6.1). If this was so, then LDR's leadership culture as a whole was likely of an Independent orientation and therefore, theoretically, not likely to support the Interdependent culture and the *Collaborative Inquiry* orientation that the three teams were seeking.

The inability of the three teams to ally strongly with one another, as well as the fact that they felt more stymied than challenged by a lack of systemic support for their strategic initiative, suggested that they were themselves operating at the *Individualist/Social Network* action-logic. This orientation placed the larger R&D group and its three teams on the cusp between the Independent and Interdependent cultures (again, see Table 6.2), but falling short of the *Strategist/Collaborative Inquiry* action-logics necessary to sustain the new and more complex business model. Torbert predicted that the three teams would not succeed in influencing the larger organization's operating structure unless they found a stronger common cause, common theoretical foci and methodological tools, and a common strategy. These ideas were emerging in dialogue at different meetings during the day, with Torbert asking all present to offer evidence that they saw as confirming or disconfirming his interpretations. Partly because of this 2nd-person-in-the-present form of research, a convergence of shared commitment around this diagnosis, and a commitment to using DAI emerged among the three teams.

LDR WORKSHOP

Soon, a three-day workshop was organized for 18 members of the organization (most of them members of the three R&D teams). During the workshop each member filled out and received feedback and coaching on the LDP (Cook-Greuter, 1999; Rooke & Torbert, 2005). Each member also began to learn how to diagnose the action-logic informing his or her choices during actual "difficult conversations" with colleagues at the workshop and clients (Argyris & Schön, 1974; Rudolph, Taylor, & Foldy, 2001). Moreover, the group as a whole used the organizational action-logics to help them

design and implement further strategic steps toward LDR's new business.

Not too surprisingly, given their interests and vocations, the 18 LDR leaders scored, on average, at much later action-logics than larger professional and managerial samples. Whereas the larger samples (Rooke & Torbert, 2005) found 85% of respondents at the early action-logics up to *Achiever,* with the *Expert* action-logic as the mode, 66% of this LDR group scored at the post-*Achiever* action-logics. The average score for the group was *Individualist,* eight scored as *Strategists* (median and modal group score), and two scored as *Alchemists.*

All participants were asked to make an estimate (*1st-person*) of their own action-logic before they received the feedback (*3rd-person*) from the LDP. Then, part of the coached debriefing session (*2nd-person*) was devoted to exploring the difference, if any, between the 1st- and 3rd-person estimates. Each participant maintained control of whether others learned his or her score on the LDP (supporting a proactive rather than a merely compliant 1st-person stance).

To get an impression of how 1st-, 2nd-, and 3rd-person research can interweave to generate personal and organizational transformations, we can follow one thread of the action. During the first day of the workshop, one participant whom we will call Ray became distressed when the LDP measured him at the *Achiever* action-logic, whereas he had diagnosed himself at the *Alchemist* action-logic, three transformations later. The visibly distressed but nonetheless professional participant (1st-person) asked for a public discussion of the validity and ethics of the LDP measure (3rd-person). All agreed to such a discussion, scheduled after small group work on each participant's "difficult conversation" case (2nd-person). During the subsequent public discussion, the group was thus able to actively triangulate among

1st-, 2nd-, and 3rd-person forms of research (Reason & Bradbury, 2001; Reason & Torbert, 2001; Chandler & Torbert, 2003).

Ray's "difficult conversation" case showed that he felt like a "lone ranger" committed to creativity within a larger organization that expected him to conform in a number of ways. Strikingly, Ray felt isolated and powerless in spite of having so many late action-logic colleagues who were participating in this strategic initiative, one of whom he was in fact addressing in his difficult conversation. Here is the difficult conversation case Ray wrote up, followed by a summary of the small group discussion of the case by another member of the small group, and concluding with Ray's afterthoughts.

"Difficult Conversations" Case From the Workshop

Ray himself wrote both columns in the grid below describing the brief episode, or "case," as he remembered it.

Ray's Challenge: To find a way to influence LDR's ability to be customer-focused.

Context: LDR is intent on routinizing its business practices, policies, and systems. This can conflict with the creative, entrepreneurial instincts of employees, so that some of them at times become disengaged, angry, and less productive.

Ray's thoughts and feelings (unspoken "left column" from a remembered discussion)	The remembered discussion between the participant Ray and his LDR colleague "George." Speaker in italics.
From the first weeks that I came to LDR I was encouraged to bring my creativity and business experience to my work. Yet time after time I feel isolated, angry, unappreciated, and wondering how to influence this organization. Do they even want my ideas?	*Ray*: George, I'm going crazy again. I just don't understand why LDR does not get the customer focus proposition.
Framing my frustration in the context of the "church of enlightened leadership" helps me to put a frame around my frustration, but it does not help me to work more effectively within the organization. Am I so underdeveloped with a sense of the body politic that I continue to just make the same mistakes over and over? It is just not good enough to feel that you are right!	*George*: Ray, when are you going to get it? You work for the "church of enlightened leadership." It has its high priests, its rules, and its inner circle. And you are not in it yet.
Whether I fit is a lifelong struggle no matter what organization I have been in. I see things differently, I have good intentions to bring this sense to the organization, and I have been ineffective.	*Ray*: I don't know if I fit here any more. LDR doesn't value what I bring to our work. I wonder if I will ever be accepted for what I bring?
This is good advice . . . do what you can do well. If you can't do that, then consider a change in work.	*George*: Why not just keep turning (as you've always done at LDR) your focus to the clients you serve. When that doesn't work any more, then it may be time to consider other options.

Our work at LDR has the potential of bringing real change into the world. We touch thousands of leaders each year. Yet we do not engage them on the issues of the day. We are happy to bring them to new levels of self-awareness and not fully draw out their potential to act as awakened and conscious leaders regarding the environment or in the pursuit of their own sense of purpose in this earthly walk.

It helps to realize that many of us who work for LDR may feel the same way. However, it's hard to realize that those in control don't really care about whether we feel connected to them and their purpose.

When I was in my own consulting practice I operated as a "lone ranger." It was lonely work and I realize I had never worked for such a hard boss: myself. I came to LDR to be part of a posse. I came to LDR to not feel isolated. How is it that I find myself isolated again? Is there something about me that brings isolation and rejection about?

I feel for the first time in a while that a person of substance (yourself) recognizes that I have something to bring to the party. I feel gratitude for this comment. I also wonder what is behind the reference of being years ahead of the organization.

My hunger for intellectual intercourse with my colleagues is high. I see George as a big thinker. I see him as deeply engrossed in the interdependent leadership work. Yet I wonder if he too has short patience for my push to have influence in LDR? Is my need to be recognized within LDR really impacting my one relationship of depth within LDR? There are so few at LDR that I can have a focused, rich discussion with. Everyone is just too busy.

Ray: I have worked to bring new approaches to leadership around newer methodologies for systemic change. But there doesn't seem to be much interest in these ideas. Am I off base?

George: It's hard to have much influence in LDR's culture. We were often hired because we are strong independent practitioners. And at the same time we have developed a centralized control structure that often disenfranchises people. I don't think you are alone in your feelings.

Ray: Sometimes it feels like the only way to survive here is to be a lone ranger, riding off to do good without much alignment with others. (Without a posse!) But I would still like to have influence within our organization. More and more, I am feeling isolated from others.

George: Ray, you may not perceive it, but your ideas on newer methodologies for systemic change may have their day yet. You are years ahead of the organization.

Ray: Even with you, George, I wonder whether you prefer that I shut up about these newer models and methods. You are so focused on your own work you don't seem to have patience for other ideas.

Ray's framing assumptions in the case did not seem *Achiever*-like, either to him or to his colleagues; rather, they seemed *Individualist*-like. The dialogue shows that Ray was enthusiastically willing to critique his own assumptions and outcomes ("whether I fit is a lifelong struggle . . . I have good intentions . . . and I have been ineffective"). At the same time, Ray was effective in engaging the group to go more deeply into learning. Moreover, he and those with whom he was debriefing the case felt an analogy between his attitude of isolation within the larger organization and the situation of the team as a whole in the larger organization. This reignited the question of how the R&D work-group could move beyond its three-team confederation with its *Individualist* (and therefore personally isolated) way of operating within an *Independent* culture, and move toward a more unified strategy for influencing the larger organization.

During the public conversation that occurred after the small group meetings, Ray's initial distress had transformed into a display of humor, tears, and positive passion in leading a discussion about

1. the change of perspective he had personally experienced, from viewing himself as enacting an *Alchemist* action-logic to viewing himself more realistically as enacting an *Individualist* action-logic (still post-conventional as he had believed, but now with a clear developmental agenda of actually learning to exercise the political skills of mutually enhancing, transforming power);

2. the importance to the community of practice gathered at the workshop of interweaving 1st-, 2nd-, and 3rd-person action and research in an artistic, compassionate, timely manner; and

3. the need for the community to take a more proactive, influential stance with LDR's senior management.

Consistent with his open approach to life, Ray subsequently requested peer coaching from his colleagues.

Buoyed by a strongly positive participant assessment of the workshop, the DAI methodology became central to the R&D group's research and its simultaneous efforts to shift LDR's culture.

LDR'S R&D-DRIVEN STRATEGY FOR CHANGE

LDR's research and development effort then was redesigned to integrate the three R&D subteams as a single team. The goal was to establish a practice emphasizing development toward more interdependent leadership cultures and leadership practices in client organizations and in global society. Yet it was now even more clearly understood within this community that for LDR as a whole, the organizational action-logic of *Systematic Productivity* and its Independent culture would have to advance toward an Interdependent culture with a *Collaborative Inquiry* action-logic in order to rise up to the challenges inherent in the new business.

The newly integrated R&D group faced three related challenges:

1. to conduct valid research and develop related services and tools for the benefit of clients and constituents;

2. to foster change in basic systems, business processes, and associated organizational capabilities such that the core business integrated effectively with the new business; and

3. to support the development of LDR's culture.

Because these challenges were understood to be constructive-developmental in nature, combining LDR's new methods and tools for organizational leadership with DAI methods and tools (Table 6.3) provided a promising pathway for sustained progress.

The following five initiatives were explicitly defined within LDR's R&D-driven change effort:

1. Establishing a new community of practice

2. Cocreating the organization's new business strategy and plan

3. Developing requisite organization capabilities

4. Pursuing an integrated research agenda

5. Transforming the organizational culture

With emphasis on the first two initiatives, we will discuss how they have been informed and enhanced by DAI.

Initiative 1: Establishing a New Community of Practice

The R&D project's overall mission had been to establish a new professional practice

Table 6.3 Methods and Tools Supporting Developmental Action Inquiry and Interdependent Organizing in the LDR Case

Method or Tool	Description	Source or Reference
Difficult Conversations (two-column exercise)	Examining the assumptions, frames, and feelings left unspoken in a conflictual conversation	Argyris, Putnam, & Smith, 1985; Senge et al., 1994
Learning Pathways Grid	Systematic analysis of a difficult conversation in terms of actual vs. desired frames, actions, and outcomes	Taylor, Rudolph, & Foldy, 2006
LDP instrument with coaching groups	Assessment of individual action logics, supported by trained coaches and peer dialogues	Rooke & Torbert, 2005; Cook-Greuter, 1999, 2004
Mapping organizational action-logic history	Understanding LDR by tracing its history of development in action-logics	Torbert & Associates, 2004
Culture Mapping Tool	Group exercise in which the "Culture Crew" at LDR mapped, and reflected upon, their appraisal of the organization's actual and desired culture, according to two dimensions and four types	Cameron & Quinn, 1999; Slobodnik & Slobodnik, 1998
Business Process Analysis & Mapping	Analysis of value-creating activities for specific products and services and aligning them into a "value stream" while eliminating activities that don't add value	Womack & Jones, 2003
Culture Evaluation Tool	Survey instrument developed at LDR for assessing the relative strength of current organizational action logics; used as an internal assessment at LDR, with coaching	Ongoing research at LDR
Team Workstyle Continuum	Tool that helps a team self-assess current and future required functioning on a continuum from earlier to later action-logics; used in the LDR culture-change discovery process	Tool created by LDR
Four Parts of Speech	Encourages *framing, illustrating, advocating,* and *inquiring* for effective communication in support of collaborative inquiry	Torbert & Associates, 2004
Group Dialogue	Conversation models that support the construction of shared meaning through exploring diversity in assumptions and perspectives	Isaacs, 1999; Palus & Drath, 2001; McGuire & Palus, 2003
Visual Explorer	A tool that uses visual imagery and the resultant metaphors to mediate group dialogue	Palus & Horth, 2007
First- and second-person journaling	Research staff keep personal as well as group journals of observations and experiences related to projects	LeCompte & Schensul, 1999

Method or Tool	Description	Source or Reference
Body Sculpting of Roles and Relationships	Group workshop exercise in which people from diverse roles in LDR collectively, physically modeled their actual and desired interdependencies with each other, using physical postures in relation to one another as a metaphoric device to support group reflection	Moreno, 1977
Culture Walk-About Tool	LDR-designed ethnographic tool to capture subjective and objective observations in 1st-, 2nd-, and 3rd-person modes	LeCompte & Schensul, 1999
Open Space Technology	A tool for establishing effective affinity groups amid diverse interests; used in a variety of ways at LDR, including forming discussion groups at workshops and seeding idea communities	Owen, 1997
Idea Communities	Interest- and passion-driven greenhouses of future R&D efforts, leading in some cases to fully established communities of practice such as the one described in this chapter	Lave & Wenger, 1991

area in the development of leadership cultures and leadership practices (Drath, 2003). Essential to this had been the growth of a community of practice to collectively own the work (Lave & Wenger, 1991; Wenger & Snyder, 2000). LDR has for some time been intentional about fostering internal, voluntary "idea communities" around shared professional interests and passions and across functional roles, with the goal of innovation. This latest community-building initiative used three additional techniques:

1. *Formal project assignments.* These included a significant number of faculty from across diverse functions and geographies. In addition, there were a number of volunteers who became involved simply based on their interests. This was becoming less of a "project team" and more of a confluence of interests, opportunities, and abilities.

2. *Differentiating and integrating community membership.* The original R&D group of 15 faculty started making progress when subgroups were formed around promising avenues of specific ideas, grounded

theory, and rapid prototypes within the larger (and more vague) whole. At this earlier point the R&D project group was understood as a "federation" of three independent teams with related interests, rather than a true community of practice. Total membership expanded as people both internal and external to LDR were drawn to work with specific prototypes in these increasingly successful subteams. Subsequent steps for including DAI within capability development efforts have substantially reintegrated this body of people under shared frames and purposes.

3. *Shared client work.* The most powerful impact on group cohesion and extended community building has been the result of tangible shared work, typically driven by client engagements. The abstract and conceptual part of the R&D-generated frameworks has not been sufficient to unite a diverse community. Tangible client work around rapid prototyping, on the other hand, has the potential to draw people into common experience and shared language (Schrage, 2000). The danger was that the specific prototypes would produce cliques

of enthusiasts, generating independent groups, rather than an interdependent community and a unified practice. Steps were taken to avoid this danger and are woven throughout the five initiatives.

Initiative 2: Cocreating the Organization's New Business Strategy and Plan

A detailed strategy and plan for the new business was still missing. The new business would require not only a whole new depth and range in human resources but also significant business investments in systems, structure, and business process creation. Core members of the R&D group thus engaged key directors and vice presidents in a strategy and planning process by creating a new cross-functional Strategy Team. The work of the team was first to inform and engage each other (2nd-person) and then target the Executive Team and provide the objective business case (3rd-person), leading to ways that would shift the understanding of each individual (1st-person).

One difficulty was that the *Systemic Productivity* action-logic of LDR primarily supported the core business. Innovations outside the core required heroic advocacy and fostering of an Independent culture. This naturally generated a "them versus us" competitive mindset. The Strategy Team, mindful of these cultural patterns at LDR, explicitly aspired to a *Collaborative Inquiry* action-logic, in part by using DAI methods as leadership practices. In its first meeting, a profound reframing occurred within both several individuals and the group as a whole. While previously the mental model of the shift in services was understood as "from individual to organizational leadership," the co-inquiry process and consequent reframing resulted in the recognition that we are in "the transformation business" at both the individual and collective organizational levels simultaneously. This "transcend and include"

recognition was a significant breakthrough from either/or thinking toward both/and, more complex thinking among a group of independent, largely siloed players.

Initiative 3: Developing Requisite Organizational Capabilities

The new business at LDR needed new organizational capabilities to support new knowledge, services, and tools, as well as enhancement of the existing core capability (Beer & Nohria, 2000). These capability development efforts at LDR had three primary aspects. First, a client-services architecture was built in support of a client strategy focused on broad and deep, long-term, research-grounded client relationships. The growing R&D-generated body of experience, knowledge, tools, and services was organized around a small number of specific client problems and LDR's solutions to those problems. Next, the core systems, structures, and business processes of LDR needed to interact with this new services architecture in a way that would transform old and new into one whole. Third, and to these ends, a series of workshops were held in order to provide organization-wide awareness of the emerging practice and its frameworks, along with the new business opportunities. Competencies, people needed to staff the new work, and pathways for further development were identified. These workshops combined 1st-, 2nd-, and 3rd-person inquiry using methods and tools from LDR's and DAI's repertoire (Table 6.3). Each capability-development workshop became a learning forum that furthered the development of individuals, the community of practice, and LDR's approaches to the new business.

Initiative 4: Pursuing an Integrated Research Agenda

Most of the people in the broader community of practice do not identify themselves as researchers. Rather, they identify themselves as educators, designers, or client-relationship specialists. For many the notion of "research" includes some negative connotations as an esoteric notion that excludes their own expertise and gets in the way of pragmatic client relations. The question for them becomes "How do I participate meaningfully in research?" Thus DAI has begun to serve as a research framework that honors their (considerable) 1st- and 2nd-person inquiry skills in support of the creation, testing, and refinement of objective knowledge. The participative and developmental nature of DAI has helped to unify the broader community.

As the R&D subgroups were integrated, DAI was explicitly adopted as an overarching methodology for primary research projects. For example, a new series of case studies included not only 3rd-person methods of surveys, assessment instruments, and subject matter interviews but also the intra- and intersubjective 1st- and 2nd-person methods of journaling, cultural ethnography, and dialogue (Table 6.3). Measurement tools (3rd-person) conceived within the practice were focused on the existence and nature of interdependent leadership cultures and practices. One of these measures is a 10-question Cultural Evaluation Tool (CET) that asks respondents to allocate 10 points among three answers to each question. In each case, one of the answers reflects a more Dependent orientation in the organization, one reflects a more Independent orientation, and one a more Interdependent orientation.

Initiative 5: Transforming the Organizational Culture

Following some disturbing results from an internal climate survey, the LDR president decided to apply R&D's organizational leadership development services approach to developing the culture of LDR. An internal team including one of the authors entered into a consultative relationship with the senior management team and a representative

stakeholder group ("the Culture Crew") made up of directors, vice presidents, and board members. A discovery and diagnosis process for LDR's culture, incorporating 1st-, 2nd-, and 3rd-person action inquiry methods combined with LDR's new business services and tools, revealed largely Dependent cultural systems within headquarters and administrative staff, and a primarily Independent culture within the faculty, business managers, and campuses. These Dependent and Independent action-logics often clashed, and yet the learning opportunities in this were muted by strong norms of conflict avoidance. To begin to address these gaps between the actual cultures and the desired culture of interdependence, and in an effort to "practice what we preach," a discovery process and a workshop were held with the Culture Crew for identifying and understanding the organization's future core capability and strategic direction (3rd-person), while also engaging team development (2nd-person) and the evolution of individual points of view (1st-person). As a result, the president sponsored a series of activities to better define leadership strategy, customer identity, vision, core capabilities, and cultural norms. Within a few months, these project groups made significant progress with the issuance of a vision statement and the identification of seven cultural pillars, or normative behaviors, which were then tied to the organization's performance and development process.

Whether LDR can fully realize an interdependent culture and integrate its core and new businesses remains to be seen. It has done so in pockets, and for periods of time, directly leading to positive results in each of the five change initiatives described above. But there are both encouraging and disappointing results from these efforts. LDR continues to maintain a hierarchical, Dependent-type structure that harbors silos and disables cross-boundary work. Senior management is in flux with the imminent retirement of a senior executive. Action-logics variance in management appears to forestall a robust and aggressive advancement toward the new business. Readiness is appropriately questioned as a new flagship service launch is postponed. The threat of evolving from LDR's core identity gives pause to management's considerations of change; and the commensurate investments required are considerable.

And yet there have been substantial advances. As of this writing, LDR's executive team has significantly engaged in the process, deepening their knowledge of the business challenge, and has accepted the initial business strategy and plan. A dedicated team has been assigned to advancing the work in interdependent process creation and services development. LDR's culture work has advanced a set of values tied to performance management, and the research work has a coherent center of gravity. In fact, the postponement of the key new service has reverberated throughout the organization, which is actively questioning "why wait?" There seems to be a reinvigorated collective expectation that we will move in this new business direction toward organizational leadership development.

CONCLUSION

As both the extended personal case of Ray at the initial DAI workshop and this latest example of the Strategy Team suggest, the Interdependent action-logics, beginning with *Strategist/Collaborative Inquiry*, generate transformation not by elaborating and selling a plan and then implementing it via the use of unilateral forms of organizational power, but rather by beginning to enact collaborative inquiry from the outset. Individuals, teams, and larger systems increasingly experiment with and may begin to adopt a *Strategist/Collaborative Inquiry* action-logic as they experience incidents such as Ray's and the Strategy Team's creation of new insight and shared vision.

The special challenge of the Interdependent action-logics is that they cannot be routinized. They invite and require all participants to seek repeated, ongoing contact with the four territories of experience (vision, strategy, performance, outcome) in order to express in a timely manner the mutual dilemmas and incongruities that can motivate incremental and transformational change. This does not mean that the Interdependent collaborative inquiry approach is powerless to influence the earlier, more unilateral action-logics. Collaborative inquiry uses all available forms of unilateral power to invite organizational members into collaborative modalities, while simultaneously using multiple 1st-, 2nd-, and 3rd-person inquiry methods to confront gaps in organizational efficacy, to explore incongruities among mission, strategy, performance, and outcomes, and to test the efficacy of the new modalities themselves. According to developmental theory and to our prior statistical findings (Torbert & Associates, 2004), unilateral power alone is powerless to transform individuals, teams, or organizations. While collaborative inquiry cannot guarantee transformation, it is the only process that makes it possible.

Since this 18-month organizational transformation process is still very much under way at LDR, perhaps the most powerful conclusions we can offer at this point are the 1st-person reflections of two of its most engaged internal participants and of the external researcher/consultant.

First-person reflection #1 (internal LDR participant): Prior to the first DAI workshop, we had long been cultivating a 2nd-person practice of working collaboratively with clients, with goals of mutual learning and development, using forms of action research including rapid prototyping. But we had found that 2nd-person practice seemed to pull us away from 3rd-person research or what we sometimes refer to as "traditional research." Also hampering 3rd-person research was a diversity of expert models within our community so that realms of expertise would compete, or be insensible to one another. The dilemma was, How could we create shared frames of expertise for our traditional research while sustaining the mutual inquiry we value in our action research process with clients? The DAI framework allowed us to prioritize 3rd-person methods in our Case Studies Project (e.g., building survey instruments; coding and analyzing interviews), while also using 1st-person methods (e.g., journaling by investigators; using personal perceptions and hunches as a source of raw data) and 2nd-person methods (e.g., dialogue sessions between investigators and subjects, and between pairs of investigators). DAI is useful in observing and interpreting, in a systematic way, my own and others' actions, and highlights the ongoing dilemmas that Dependent and Independent action-logics can create. I notice that I am asking myself more often: What would an Interdependent action-logic intervention look like, right now? I notice others doing the same, and sometimes enacting those action-logics. At the time of writing this it is still not clear whether we will attain and sustain the needed level of interdependence and integration of our work (or even what that level should be at any time).

First-person reflection #2 (internal LDR participant): The three R&D teams were formed as semi-independent subteams from a core group that decided differentiation and experimentation were in order. Splitting up seemed paradoxical and even troubling to us at the time because our task implied collaborative work. Were we simply feeding our inclination toward independent work? Torbert's notion of collaborative inquiry helped us think about these issues without stopping our momentum.

In the capability-development work we encountered the fact that our colleagues varied in the roles they wished facilitators to play. What I have had to begin to learn more about recently is how to combine the "expert" leadership role that colleagues and clients often expect in a workshop or meeting with the *Collaborative Inquiry* action-logic. I have to remember that each new meeting or organizing process will proceed through the developmental action-logics all over again. While we often attempted to lead with a co-inquiry style, many audiences insisted that we play at least two other roles. Often we were led to take on a subject matter expert role for more Dependent audiences. Other more Independent audiences requested that we just supply them with the data, and they would independently use the information as required. Even though I can exercise Interdependent action-logics within myself at any time, the question of how to act in a group and organizational setting is also influenced by the developmental trajectory of the other persons, groups, or organizations involved.

REFERENCES

Argyris, C., Putnam, R., & Smith, D. (1985). *Action science: Concepts, methods, and skills for research and intervention.* San Francisco: Jossey-Bass.

Argyris, C., & Schön, D. (1974). *Theory in practice: Increasing professional effectiveness.* San Francisco: Jossey-Bass.

Basseches, M. (1984). *Dialectical thinking and adult development.* Norwood, NJ: Ablex.

Beck, D., & Cowan, C. (1996). *Spiral dynamics: Mastering values, leadership and change.* Malden, MA: Blackwell Business.

Beer, M., & Nohria, N. (2000). Cracking the code of change. *Harvard Business Review, 78*(3), 133–141.

Bolman, L. G., & Deal, T. E. (2003). *Reframing organizations* (3rd ed.). San Francisco: Jossey-Bass.

Bushe, G., & Gibbs, B. (1990). Predicting organization development consulting competence from the Myers-Briggs Indicator and stage of ego development. *Journal of Applied Behavioral Science, 26*(3), 337–357.

Cameron, K. S., & Quinn, R. E. (1999). *Diagnosing and changing organizational culture.* Reading, MA: Addison Wesley Longman.

Chandler, D., & Torbert, W. R. (2003). Transforming inquiry and action: Interweaving 27 flavors of action research. *Journal of Action Research, 1*(2), 133–152.

Commons, M. L., & Richards, F. A. (2003). Four postformal stages. In J. Demick & C. Andreoletti (Eds.), *Handbook of adult development* (pp. 199–220). New York: Kluwer Academic.

Cook-Greuter, S. R. (1999). Postautonomous ego development: A study of its nature and measurement. *Dissertation Abstracts International, 60,* 06B. (UMI No. 993312)

Cook-Greuter, S. R. (2004). Making the case for a developmental perspective. *Industrial and Commercial Training, 36,* 275–281.

Day, D. V. (2000). Leadership development: A review in context. *Leadership Quarterly, 11*(4), 581–613.

Drath, W. (2001). *The deep blue sea: Rethinking the source of leadership.* San Francisco: Jossey-Bass.

Drath, W. (2003). Leading together: Complex challenges require a new approach. *Leadership in Action, 23*(1), 3–7.

Drath, W., & Palus, C. J. (1994). *Making common sense: Leadership as meaning-making in a community of practice.* Greensboro, NC: Center for Creative Leadership.

Eisenhardt, K. M. (1989). Building theories from case study research. *Academy of Management Review, 14,* 532–550.

Fisher, D., & Torbert, W. R. (1991). Transforming managerial practice: Beyond the achiever stage. In R. Woodman & W. Pasmore (Eds.), *Research in organizational change and development* (Vol. 5). Greenwich, CT: JAI Press.

Foster, P., & Torbert, W. R. (2005). Leading through positive deviance: A developmental action learning perspective on institutional change. In R. Giacalone, C. Dunn, & C. Jurkiewicz (Eds.), *Positive psychology in business ethics and corporate responsibility* (pp. 123–142). Greenwich, CT: Information Age Publishing.

Heifetz, R. A. (1994). *Leadership without easy answers.* Cambridge, MA: Harvard University Press.

Isaacs, W. (1999). *Dialogue and the art of thinking together.* New York: Random House.

Kegan, R. (1994). *In over our heads: The demands of modern life.* Cambridge, MA: Harvard University Press.

Kegan, R., & Lahey, L. L. (2001). *How the way we talk can change the way we work: Seven languages for transformation.* San Francisco: Jossey-Bass.

Lave, J., & Wenger, E. (1991). *Situated learning: Legitimate peripheral participation.* Cambridge, UK: Cambridge University Press.

LeCompte, M. D., & Schensul, J. J. (1999). *Analyzing and interpreting ethnographic data.* Walnut Creek, CA: AltaMira Press.

Loevinger, J. (1976). *Ego development.* San Francisco: Jossey-Bass.

Manners, J., Durkin, K., & Nesdale, A. (2004). Promoting advanced ego development among adults. *Journal of Adult Development, 1*(1), 19–27.

McCauley, C. D., Drath, W. H., Palus, C. J., O'Connor, P. M. G., & Baker, B. A. (in press). The use of constructive-developmental theory to advance the understanding of leadership. *Leadership Quarterly.*

McGuire, J. B., & Palus, C. J. (2003). Using dialogue as a tool for better leadership. *Leadership in Action, 23*(1), 8–11.

Merron, K., Fisher, D., & Torbert, W. R. (1987). Meaning making and management action. *Group and Organizational Studies, 12*(3), 274–286.

Moreno, J. L. (1977). *Psychodrama* (4th ed.). New York: Beacon House.

Owen, H. (1997). *Open space technology* (2nd ed.). San Francisco: Berrett-Koehler.

Palus, C. J., & Drath, W. H. (1995). *Evolving leaders: A model for promoting leadership development in programs.* Greensboro, NC: Center for Creative Leadership.

Palus, C. J., & Drath, W. H. (2001). Putting something in the middle: An approach to dialogue. *Reflections: The SoL Journal, 3*(2), 28–39.

Palus, C. J., & Horth, D. M. (2007). Visual explorer. In P. Holman, T. Devane, & S. Cady (Eds.), *The change handbook: The definitive resource on today's best methods for engaging whole systems* (2nd ed.). San Francisco: Berrett-Koehler.

Piaget, J. (1954). *The construction of reality in a child.* New York: Basic Books.

Reason, P. (1994). *Participation in human inquiry.* London: Sage.

Reason, P., & Bradbury, H. (2001). *Handbook of action research: Participative inquiry and practice.* London: Sage.

Reason, P., & Torbert, W. R. (2001). The action turn: Toward a transformational social science: A further look at the scientific merits of action research. *Concepts and Transformation, 6*(1), 1–37.

Rooke, D., & Torbert, W. R. (1998). Organizational transformation as a function of CEOs' developmental stage. *Organization Development Journal, 16*(1), 11–28.

Rooke, D., & Torbert, W. R. (2005, April). Seven transformations of leadership. *Harvard Business Review,* 66–77.

Rudolph, J. W., Taylor, S. S., & Foldy, E. G. (2001). Collaborative off-line reflection: A way to develop skill in action science and action inquiry. In P. Reason & H. Bradbury (Eds.), *Handbook of action research: Participative inquiry and practice.* London: Sage.

Schön, D. (1983). *The reflective practitioner: How professionals think in action.* New York: Basic Books.

Schrage, M. (2000). *Serious play: How the world's best companies simulate to innovate.* Boston: Harvard Business School Press.

Senge, P. M., Roberts, C., Ross, R. B., Smith, B. J., & Kleiner, A. (1994). *The fifth discipline fieldbook: Strategies and tools for building a learning organization.* New York: Doubleday.

Sherman, F., & Torbert, W. R. (2000). *Transforming social inquiry, transforming social action.* Boston: Kluwer Academic.

Strauss, A. L. (1987). *Qualitative analysis for social scientists.* New York: Cambridge University Press.

Taylor, S. S., Rudolph, J. W., & Foldy, E. G. (2006). Teaching reflective practice: Key concepts, stages, and practices. In P. Reason & H. Bradbury (Eds.), *The Sage handbook of action research* (2nd ed.). London: Sage.

Torbert, W. R. (1976). *Creating a community of inquiry*. London: Wiley.

Torbert, W. R. (1987). *Managing the corporate dream: Restructuring for long-term success*. Homewood, IL: Dow Jones-Irwin.

Torbert, W. R. (1991). *The power of balance: Transforming self, society, and scientific inquiry*. Newbury Park, CA: Sage.

Torbert, W. R. (2000). A developmental approach to social science: Integrating first-, second-, and third-person research/practice through single-, double-, and triple-loop feedback. *Journal of Adult Development, 7*(4), 255–268.

Torbert, W. R., & Associates. (2004). *Action inquiry: The secret of timely and transforming leadership*. San Francisco: Berrett-Koehler.

Torbert, W. R., & Fisher, D. (1992). Autobiography as a catalyst for managerial and organizational development. *Management Education and Development Journal, 23*, 184–198.

Van Velsor, E., & McCauley, C. D. (2004). Our view of leadership development. In C. D. McCauley & E. Van Velsor (Eds.), *The center for creative leadership handbook of leadership development* (2nd ed., pp. 1–22). San Francisco: Jossey-Bass.

Wenger, E., & Snyder, W. M. (2000). Communities of practice: The organizational frontier. *Harvard Business Review, 78*(1), 139–145.

Wilber, K. (2000). *Integral psychology*. Boston: Shambhala.

Womack, J. P., & Jones, D. T. (2003). *Lean thinking: Banish waste and create wealth in your corporation*. New York: Simon & Schuster.

CHAPTER 7

Collaborating for Management Research

From Action Research to Intervention Research in Management

ARMAND HATCHUEL

ALBERT DAVID

ABSTRACT

In this chapter, we present the institutional and academic contexts that gave birth to intervention research in management (IRM) and its major differences with standard action research. IRM tightly combines a *theoretical perspective* and a *collaborative protocol*. Both are necessary to characterize the relevance and universality of the knowledge produced through IRM. The theoretical perspective defines the basic issues and object of management research. Introducing the notions of *contextual theory-in-use* (CTU) and *established theory-in-use* (ETU), we show how local configurations of CTUs and ETUs indicate a research potential for an IRM project. The *collaborative protocol* warrants research-oriented partnerships with pioneering organizations. We describe the preconditions and monitoring principles of IRM partnerships. To conclude, we discuss a recent IRM project concerning innovation management at Renault.

INTRODUCTION: A COLLABORATIVE PROGRAM FOR MANAGEMENT RESEARCH

In this chapter, we present the principles and outputs of a specific collaborative approach between academics and practitioners called *intervention research in management* (IRM). These principles emerged progressively from more than three decades of fieldwork at the *Centre de Gestion Scientifique*[1] (CGS), one of the oldest French research teams with extensive experience with IRM in companies and state agencies.[2] The principles of IRM were also an outcome of a wider academic work aimed at revisiting the foundations of management science (David, Hatchuel, & Laufer, 2001) and at specifying the academic contribution of collaborative approaches in management research (see David & Hatchuel, Chapter 2 in this *Handbook*). In 1999, the Swedish *FENIX Centre for Innovations in Management* (Adler, Shani, & Styhre, 2004) was created, which included IRM perspectives in its academic background and program.[3] Since then, intense cooperation between CGS and FENIX has allowed cross-fertilization of our approaches in different institutional contexts. In this chapter, we focus on IRM's main theoretical and methodological aspects.

IRM tightly combines a *theoretical perspective* and a *collaborative protocol*. The theoretical perspective defines the basic issues and object of management research; the collaborative protocol warrants research logic stimulated by management issues in pioneering organizations. These two "pillars" (Hatchuel, 2002) are needed to establish precisely *why* and *how* management scholars can be fruitfully involved in research-oriented partnerships with organizations.

IRM does not aim at having a planned impact on organizations or at creating some emancipatory social change (Burnes, 2004). It is a research program that seeks to improve the theoretical and instrumental management capabilities of contemporary societies. A basic assumption of IRM is that, in contemporary organizations, including not-for-profit ones, management theories and techniques are not only instruments that serve preexisting pragmatic or political goals; they also shape the content and processes of social change. Modern history shows that management doctrines have now achieved the same influential role that political theories played during earlier periods in the transformation of nations and states. This has a major social consequence: Established management theories are most often theories-in-use (i.e., theories that shape "action" or at least discourse) in organizations (Argyris, 1995). Therefore, local management problems may signal the shortcuts, pitfalls, and limitations of established theories. These assumptions strongly determine the issues, partners, and expected outputs of IRM that are discussed in this chapter.

IRM Issues: Problems That Suggest Potential Management Breakthroughs

The collaborative logic of IRM is not oriented toward the solution of the management problems of a client organization. Countless management problems could be investigated scientifically without offering any valuable research potential. Thus, an IRM program selectively targets those local problems that potentially require theoretical revision or a breakthrough in management theory. We will indicate analytical criteria for such selection.

IRM Partners: Management Pioneers

IRM is possible only when a research issue in management becomes the core motivation for a collaborative protocol between academics and a host organization. Research in management is an unusual commitment for an organization. In fact, IRM is possible only in organizations where an interactive relationship between problem solving and research is possible. This built-in bias of IRM is not a methodological weakness but rather a central condition for its fruitfulness and discovery power. Therefore, IRM is an appropriate research methodology for the study of organizations that can be viewed as "management pioneers" and is suited to research designed according to a discovery logic and not an *ex post* validation or confirmatory logic (this point is discussed further in David & Hatchuel, Chapter 2 in this *Handbook*).

IRM Outputs: Improving "Models of Action," not "Action"

IRM does not directly attempt to improve "action" (Coghlan, 2004). It is an academic investigation of *models of action*, that is, artifacts (symbolic or material) that partly constitute and shape (collective) action.[4] Ideally, the result of a fruitful IRM project is not purely an empirical description; it is a theoretical revision of existing models of action.

In the sections of this chapter, we begin by presenting the institutional and academic contexts that gave birth to IRM, and then we distinguish IRM from action research (AR). We argue that AR is more a model of enlightened and democratic action than a research program. Extending Argyris and Schön's concept of theory-in-use, we introduce the notions of *contextual theory-in-use* (CTU) and *established theory-in-use* (ETU). We show that local configurations and tensions between existing CTUs and ETUs are good indicators of research potential in management. We define management science as a basic research program aimed at the study and discovery of "models of collective action" (David et al., 2001; Hatchuel, 2002, 2005). We then present the collaborative principles of IRM, distinguishing between the preconditions for IRM partnerships and the monitoring principles of IRM processes. To conclude, we discuss a recent IRM project concerning innovation management at Renault.

The Sources of IRM: An R&D Logic in Management

IRM emerged progressively at CGS (Moisdon, 1984; Hatchuel & Molet, 1986; David, 2002).[5] CGS was created at the end of the 1960s to teach management to engineering students at l'École des Mines de Paris.[6] Be it in the natural or the social sciences,[7] l'École des Mines de Paris already had a two-century-old tradition of intellectual cooperation with state administrations and private industries. This legacy offered resources and opportunities to build a new management research program and to test it with a large number of organizational partners.

In the early years of CGS, "management science" was mainly equated with operations research (OR), decision studies, and cost analysis. During the 1970s, the crisis of operations research stimulated intense and varied efforts to redefine the Center's area of research. As in many other OR teams of that time, a more comprehensive and actionable approach to management science was under development (Checkland, 1985; Hatchuel & Molet, 1986; Meredith, Raturi, Amoako-Gyampah, & Kaplan, 1989; Mintzberg, 1979). After a period of maturation, a new academic program emerged, including a critical perspective on major international trends in management research. The main assumption of this program was that management research was not an applied field for economics or sociology. Rather, it should grow as a basic research area focusing on theoretical issues or new empirical problems that were neglected or implicit in older social sciences (Hatchuel, 2002, 2005). This "foundationist" perspective has been discussed elsewhere (David et al., 2001; Hatchuel, 2005) and will be briefly developed below.

Partners in companies and public services supported this view of management and welcomed "interventions" of academics that could be seen as R&D projects in management. The notion of "intervention" was borrowed from the French tradition of social psychology. It described the fact that the researcher participates in an organizational inquiry while keeping his or her academic identity, ethics, and purpose. Collaborative research protocols supporting these interventions appeared feasible and were progressively structured. Actually, dramatic changes in management issues also paved the way for IRM.

Business historians may consider the end of the 1980s as a turning point in the history of management doctrines. Major facts signal such a turning point: the diffusion of Japanese management doctrines; the organizational revolution brought on by computerized information; the rising criticism of management consultants and MBAs; and the new battlefields for competitive advantage (innovation, global supply chains, alliances, environmental issues, and so on). Management science no longer comprised a set of universal Fayolian and Taylorian principles to be tempered by human and political relations. A new "unexplored continent" appeared where invention and theory played a major role. In the early 1980s, French companies as well as major state-owned organizations began to criticize standard consultant recipes and welcomed a research spirit in management.[8,9] Thus, IRM is not only the result of an academic vision and would have seemed unrealistic without the stimulus of innovative organizations. The fact that a foundationist program in management theory[10] received continuous grants from practitioners is certainly a surprising and crucial aspect of the history of IRM. It directly explains why IRM grew with a different logic and purpose than AR. Yet, in order to highlight the specificities of IRM, we need to take a detour through AR.

BEYOND ACTION RESEARCH: THE RESEARCH POTENTIAL OF COLLABORATIVE PROGRAMS

IRM's collaborative protocol was designed to support research in real management contexts. Therefore, collaborative projects are appropriate for IRM only when local management issues have a research potential for management theory. This strong precondition limits the scope of IRM but bypasses the "controversy and confusion" (Robinson, 1993) that characterized the academic development of action research approaches. Even in a recent survey of AR literature, Cassell and Johnson (2006) still emphasized that "the diverse action research families must only be evaluated from within their particular webs of knowledge constituting assumptions" (p. 808). Acknowledging different "knowledge-constituting assumptions" is simply saying that there are different research programs under the same AR label. We will go a step further and argue that IRM does not have the same type of collaborative methodology as AR.

Action Research: A Model of Enlightened and Democratic Action[11]

In spite of a variety of "alternative roadmaps" for collaborative research in organizations (Coughlan, Harbison, Dromgoole, & Duff, 2001; Schein, 1995; Shani, David, & Wilson, 2004), AR is still the most widely discussed framework. Several handbooks, special issues, and academic surveys about AR are available. Muddling through this large body of literature, AR appears defined as a small set of versatile propositions constantly repeated over several decades. Even if substantial varieties of AR have actually emerged, they all maintain this initial set of assumptions (Baker, 2000; Baskerville & Wood-Harper, 1996; Coghlan, 2004; Davison, Martinsons, & Kock, 2004; Dickens & Watkins, 1999; Elden & Chisholm, 1993; Huxham & Vangen, 2003; Kates & Robertson, 2004; McCutcheon & Jung, 1990; Robinson, 1993). We will argue that the core principles of AR do not define a research program but an idealistic model of action.

A Participatory and Humanistic Intervention

AR's primary aim is to implement an impact-seeking intervention in organizations that face complex problems (Halbesleben, Osburn, & Mumford, 2006; Reason & Heron, 1986). During such interventions,

AR seeks constructive dialogue and a reflexive spirit from members in the host organization. A central assumption of AR is that increased participation and empowerment will enhance practitioners' reflexivity and favor their personal development (Bartunek, 1993; Fals-Borda & Rahman, 1991; Kidd & Kral, 2005). It is also a repeated belief that pursuing humanistic values in organizations in the long run constitutes a major factor of organizational motivation and performance. Most papers about AR describe cycles of participative investigation, action, and learning (Torbert, 1976). Expected signs of effective AR are commonly organizational improvements, better awareness of members' potentials and competencies, and, it is hoped, increased performance.

A Knowledge-Seeking and Research-Oriented Intervention

Concurrent with its impact-seeking logic, AR advocates a *knowledge-generating intervention,* and learning is seen as a constitutive component of reflexive action (Gustavsen, 1993; Marsick & Gephart, 2003; Raelin, 1997). This interplay between knowledge and action is one of the most important ideas of AR. Yet research logic should also be introduced as a controlling and guiding protocol for effective learning (Eden & Huxham, 1996). This dimension of AR has led several authors to interpret AR as a methodology that could be applied to research in specialized areas such as information systems, accounting, or marketing (Baskerville & Myers, 2004; Halbesleben et al., 2006; Lindgren, Henfridsson, & Schultze, 2004).

If we combine the impact-oriented and learning-oriented logics put forward in AR, do we obtain a research program? With other authors (Robinson, 1993), we argue that these principles do not define a research program. We maintain instead that AR principles describe an *enlightened and democratic*

"model of action." AR calls for resistance to local beliefs or pressures and for accurate descriptions and critical thinking (Wilson, 2004). AR's participatory and humanistic values set the stage for democratic, pluralist, and dialogic decision processes. Authoritarian expertise, even coming from academics, should be avoided, and knowledge of organization members should be a central resource for reflexivity and action. Therefore, AR can rightly claim that it offers a challenging stimulus for change. However, as we elaborate below, we do not find that it aims at contributing to management models valid outside the investigated context, which would be required to build a research program.

Action and Theories-in-Use: Restoring a Research Issue

More generally, when do contextual improvements produce knowledge advancement or breakthroughs? At this point, a short discussion of the word *action* will underline the theoretical difficulties of action as an object of study.

Action as an Object of Study

Action seems a simple and straightforward notion, yet it is not easy to explore it with consistency. Hatchuel (2005) has developed an "epistemology of action" that underlines that action is neither an observable entity nor an easy test for theories. Let us take the example of coordination: How can we observe coordination? We need models of coordination and some procedure that confronts observations with these models. The problem is that this procedure will itself use the model of coordination we want to observe. If we ignore some types of coordination, our procedure will miss them or even hide them. This is the main reason why there is no universal protocol to study action. What we can study is how *models of action* are generated, tested, discussed, and revised. These models are both inter-preters of the action made observable and shaping tools that create action. For example, accounting, which is a model of action, makes business observable and simultaneously shapes and orients it.

The issue left for research becomes the fol-lowing: When does the revision of a model of action become interesting for research? Implementing a scientific and democratic pro-cedure should have led AR to offer an enriched theory of this procedure. Yet the AR literature often raises such issues without offering convincing treatment (Eden & Huxham, 1996; Robinson, 1993; Thompson & Perry, 2004). Our point of view is that the traditional framework of AR is not tailored to answer such questions. Revising a model of action leads to valuable research only if some well-established assumptions are rigorously revised. To further elaborate this idea, we define a model of action as a specific form of theory-in-use (Argyris & Schön, 1978) and introduce a crucial distinction between two types of theories-in-use.

Contextual and Established Management Theories-in-Use

The notion of theory-in-use (Argyris & Schön, 1978) describes the knowledge, beliefs, and conceptual frameworks that shape or enforce practice (through power relations). Models of action as we define them are theories-in-use from the field of management. Moreover, if we distinguish two types of management theories-in-use—CTUs and ETUs—we can clarify and evaluate the research potential of a local management issue.

Contextual Management Theory-in-Use (CTU)

We label a set of management assump-tions, rules, and schemes that are common to members of an organization (or part of it) a "contextual management theory-in-use." This CTU is not necessarily the official dis-course of the organization (the *espoused* theory, according to Argyris & Schön). This means that members of the organization are familiar with it, use it in some way, and expect others to do so.

Established Management Theory-in-Use (ETU)

ETUs describe the same type of material as CTUs, when this material is actually legit-imized and validated *outside the organization* by a widely referenced set of academic and professional supports. ETUs also include man-agement theories that are actively mobilized by consultants or by leading organizations even if they have not yet been fully discussed in the literature. Each classical field of management (accounting, marketing, strategy, control, and so on) attempts to shape and support ETUs. AR has given no central attention to ETUs, and the improvement of a CTU is its primary goal. IRM, on the contrary, defines its purpose as *the potential revision of ETUs,* and improv-ing CTUs is therefore interesting *only if* it leads to such a revision. Therefore, local tensions or configurations of ETUs and CTUs offer major signals of a research potential for IRM.

Assessing the Research Potential of Local Management Issues: The ETU/CTU Grid

The various configurations of CTUs and ETUs that can be observed in organizations can be described through a simple grid that is also an easy-to-use tool for appraising the research potential of a local management problem. It can be synthesized into a 2×2 matrix (see Table 7.1), indicating the existence (or absence) of a CTU (the columns) and the existence (or absence) of an ETU (the rows). Let us briefly indicate how each cell of the matrix corresponds to a different research potential.

Table 7.1 A Typology of Research Potential Defined by the Joint Analysis of Existing CTUs and ETUs

		Contextual Theory-in-Use (CTU)		
		Yes		*No*
Established Theory-in-Use (ETU)	*Yes*	ETU and CTU are different: explain the discrepancy	ETU and CTU are identical: a natural experiment	Avoid the case of lack of expertise and the lack of organizational maturation
	No	Existing or revised CTU as a new model?		Open exploration for a new management model

The "Yes-No" Case[12]

There is an ETU for the management problem but no CTU. In this case, we must ensure that this is not due to a lack of expertise or a lack of problem maturation. Many organizations are kept informed about management methods (ETUs) through the media, students, or consultants. This often leads to the question "Could it be good for us?" regardless of the organization's needs or without any clarification of the assumptions of the method. This is a very common situation, but not an appropriate situation for IRM.

Example 1: A company being told about activity-based costing (ABC), an ETU (Kaplan, 1998), would like to know from independent academics whether this could be a profitable method. The academic team informs the company that a possible research issue would be to better define the type of activities that should be targeted by ABC, an issue not very clear in the existing literature. But the company sees ABC only as a quick cost reduction method. No room is left for research issues.

The "Yes-Yes" Case

Both an ETU and a CTU exist. They can be identical or different. If they are different, we may again face a local lack of expertise, and a clarification of the reasons for this discrepancy is needed. If ETUs and CTUs are identical, and they appear ineffective, we may benefit from a possible "natural field experiment." In this case, an IRM partnership is promising, as we can expect at least some revision of the existing ETU. A wide literature on management uses case study research to describe the pitfalls of well-known management methods. The advantages of an IRM approach in these situations are mainly due to the special access to data and exploratory power ensured by the collaborative protocol discussed below.

Example 2: A company that favored the development of expert systems and knowledge-based tools, an ETU, faced disappointing or surprising results, instilling skepticism of knowledge management. CGS is asked to investigate. After a first study, it appears that the investigation should not be limited to a classical analysis of the successes and failures of a project. It seems that there was an increasing gap between newly required knowledge-creation processes and existing management of expertise. The company accepted the issue, and the ensuing case study was a contribution to a research program on the dynamics and crisis of expertise in contemporary high-tech competition. The outputs of this program are discussed in detail in Hatchuel and Weil (1995).

The "No-Yes" Case

If there is no ETU and if the existing CTU is not clear or controversial, the case becomes complex and the research potential substantial. Why is there no ETU? In some cases, research may prove that some hidden CTU is locally efficient and innovative. If the theoretical assumptions behind such a CTU can be clearly identified, this is a good case for a potential breakthrough.

Example 3: Scholars have asked to interview managers of a company that has shown successful innovative capabilities. The company rejects the first proposal, arguing that in order to understand its methods, academics should participate directly in its innovation processes. This research challenge was taken on by a Ph.D. student from CGS who showed that the company had invented a successful and rarely described management model for product innovation. This finding led to a broad program about repeated innovation strategies (Hatchuel, Le Masson, & Weil, 2001).

The "No-No" Case

The problems faced by the organization appear to be new and disturbing. The research area seems open and has high stakes, but the exploration process is also very risky. This is a challenging area for IRM. An example of such situations will be described in more detail in the last section of the chapter.

This grid is far from being complete. We have left aside ambiguous cases and situations where several competing ETUs and CTUs exist. Simple as it is, however, this grid underlines a central difference between AR and IRM. The content and academic value of knowledge produced through AR has remained controversial and with limited research aims: "It would be unusual for action research to deliver fundamental new theories. Rather, the research insights are likely to link with, and so elaborate, the work of others" (Eden & Huxham, 1996).

Such limitations do not hold or, at least, should be tempered for IRM. The research logic of IRM is directed not toward the improvement of CTUs but toward the revision or regeneration of ETUs. Moreover, the ETU/CTU grid offers the possibility to restrict IRM to local situations where a clear set of ETUs are challenged.

Ensuring a Common Field of Knowledge

Still, what proves that CTUs and ETUs can influence each other and can be related to the same field of knowledge? In other words, collaborative research is only possible when and where practice or action is prescribed, shaped, and legitimized, at least partially, by accepted theories or doctrines; or conversely, if these theories or doctrines are justified by the type of practice they shape.[13] In the following section, we analyze why the history of management ensures this mutual influence between CTUs and ETUs.

THE SCIENTIFIC PERSPECTIVE OF IRM: A FOUNDATIONIST PERSPECTIVE IN MANAGEMENT

Management Science as a Theory of Collective Action

The principles of IRM are largely dependent on how "management" is theoretically elaborated. Most often management is defined by a number of social roles and powers (managers) or by functional issues (accounting, marketing, strategy). These definitions have their value, but it has been argued (Hatchuel, Le Masson, & Weil, 2001; Hatchuel, 2005) that they do not clarify the identity and foundations of management science. From a foundationist perspective, management science is not a conventional set of social issues or organizational functions. It is a basic field of research devoted to the study and design of theories, models and tools of collective action (Hatchuel, 2002, 2005). From this standpoint, classic organizational typologies (e.g., companies, networks) and classic repertoires of rationalities (e.g., truth, interest, solidarity) as well as functions (production, marketing, accounting) are not invariant categories. They cannot be grounded in some basic social or economic science. They are historically designed models of action. For instance, for an economist, a "firm" may designate any business-oriented group. For management science, as we defined it, "firms" as we know them emerged first as *companias* in the early Renaissance. The latter innovatively combined older management models: the Roman legacy of associations, the family structure of merchant activities, and traditional trade rules. The Italian *compania* is a major managerial discovery that later became the ETU that was revised by the manufacturing model of the industrial revolution (Hatchuel & Glise, 2004). These innovations had a major impact on Western civilization, as many other civilizations experienced trade without inventing innovative models for collective business as we know them. Therefore, the history of management models is a permanent dialectic between practice and doctrine, innovation and theory.

Such a perspective establishes the scientific logic of IRM. Management science can solidly claim to be the study of models of action that are shaped by a dynamic and critical evolution. Likewise, physics is not the study of "reality," but the study and revision of physical models. Consequently, the dialectics between established management theory-in-use and contextual management theory-in-use can be assessed as an important main driver of management theory and history. Finally, IRM is not a research program designed to study whether a management method once widely used is a significant statistical factor of performance[14] (Hatchuel, 2005). The aims of IRM are precisely to study the theoretical assumptions of existing management models (ETUs), to detect and validate innovative ones in pioneering organizations, or to design new ones whenever possible.

Therefore, the collaborative protocol of IRM defines a set of prerequisites and shared commitments that may warrant and protect a specific investigation process. This research protocol may affect the history of the host organization, but it cannot enforce it. And, in some cases, the research results may be of little value for the host organization, yet provide important theoretical insights. This protocol is presented in the next section.

The Collaborative Protocol for IRM: Protecting Research and People

The collaborative protocol of IRM is a set of principles designed to *select* appropriate partners and to *contractually commit* these partners to the application of a specific *scientific investigation*. It is therefore necessary to distinguish two sets of principles: those that define the preconditions of an appropriate partnership and those that define the monitoring of the cooperation process (see Table 7.2).

THE PRECONDITIONS FOR IRM

A Partner With a Pioneering Logic

Who makes a good partner for IRM? Not all organizations are appropriate or suitable for IRM. A *pioneering logic* is required from the partner. Such logic can be plausibly assessed, though always with some uncertainty, when the following conditions hold and are agreed on by both partners before the launching of a project:

An "Open Management Issue"

We define as an "open management issue" a question that (1) can be formulated by managers (and in special cases, also by workers and employees) as a management problem, (2) is shared or could be shared with their staff and personnel, and (3) is perceived as a research issue for which there is no immediate solution. These are restrictive conditions. Managers are usually under pressure and, when they formulate problems, feel the need to immediately announce solutions that could be implemented. What enables them to resist such pressures and to declare that a management issue should be investigated with a research spirit and methodology? There is no universal answer to this question. However, two contextual elements have played a crucial role in the history of collaborative research in French and Swedish contexts. The first one is the progressive institutionalization and legitimation of management as an autonomous field of research. The second element can be described as a good window of opportunity or political agenda for management research due to increased competition and less belief in consultant recipes (Björkman & Sundgren, 2005). Indeed, the management issue that fosters IRM cannot be a hot, short-term issue, but must nevertheless be a mobilizing issue (e.g., future threats or opportunities). These restrictions are not unbearable biases imposed on research. Management research, as we define it, is only possible when there are sufficient resources and autonomy in the organization to reject existing ETUs or to discuss existing CTUs.

Assessing Research Potential: A Phase of Exploratory Collaboration

We have shown that an investigation of existing CTUs and ETUs is necessary to permit the assessment of a research potential. The study of actual ETUs can be done through literature review and examination of current professional norms and doctrines. Yet before any contractual commitment, the identification of CTUs needs a collaborative exploratory phase. This exploratory phase is also required to build a collaborative agreement that meets the expectations of both parties.

Contractual Commitment to a Research Issue: A Minimum Duration

If such an agreement can be reached, a contractual partnership becomes possible. It should be underlined that this is not a consulting contract. An IRM contract clearly states the research purpose of the partners during the program. The academic team should not commit to solving a problem or conducting some planned change. It should be accountable only for designing a process of investigation, not for any performance or impact resulting from this process. The term of the contract is a significant indicator of this orientation. It is very unlikely that a real research project can be conducted in less than one year, while management consulting or expertise is usually delivered in a few weeks. In the French context, CGS has usually signed partnerships for a minimum duration of one year, but many have actually lasted several years.

An Academic Team With a Legitimate Research Potential in Management

Which academic team is appropriate for IRM partnership? We want to emphasize those specific skills that are required for an IRM project. Obviously, they are different from those required for handling classical questionnaires and data treatment. One can think of the social and political competencies needed to negotiate contractual commitments with managers and employees, but these skills are more or less required by any social or qualitative field research. What is really specific for IRM may be surprising: It is the capacity of an academic team to build, share, and maintain updated management knowledge in order to capture the research potential of an "open management issue" and to transform it into an innovative investigation process.

Example 4: In 1979, CGS was contacted by car manufacturers to discuss the validity of new manufacturing models coming from Japan. While Toyotism, TQM, and Quality Circles were already a reference-in-use for professionals, the academic literature on the subject was in its infancy. A research team with no knowledge of these new management models, and thus unable to relate them to Taylorism and Fordism, may have missed the research potential of these models and would have appeared a noncredible partner for organizations perceiving this potential.

For an individual researcher, these competencies are difficult to build. Doing so requires a collective and enduring research project that goes beyond standard research teams, which gather multidisciplinary experts for one project. There is also a need for apprenticeship in the field to introduce young researchers to IRM. In France and Sweden, it appears that introducing such apprenticeship into the doctoral program was both necessary and fruitful.

All these preconditions help to establish a partnership suitable for an IRM project. Once the project is launched, monitoring principles are also necessary.

MONITORING PRINCIPLES FOR IRM[15]

While IRM preconditions seek to warrant a pioneering logic and a credible research potential, monitoring principles aim to support an investigating process for the academic team as well as to protect members of the organization participating in the problem.

Principle of Free Academic Investigation

The most challenging issue is to afford all members of the organization an equal opportunity to express their views about the reasons and logic behind an existing CTU. This leads to a participatory investigation scheme, not necessarily to a democratic process. Its rules should be as follows:

Free interviewing of concerned members of the organization: This could be a jointly agreed-upon list of persons to be interviewed, but it should be possible for the academic team to revise the list if the research work proves it necessary.

Confidentiality of all individual interviews: This is a classic ethical condition (Owen, 2004) to ensure freedom of expression. Academics should know, however, that this confidentiality may not be foolproof in organizations where certain ideas or proposals may be easily attributed to individuals.

Principle of isonomy between members of the organization: This principle does not aim to implement a democratic process or complete empowerment of the members. This would mean that the academic team preconditions its intervention to such a normative management model. We have already signaled that this was one of the pitfalls of standard AR. However, IRM should warrant that all members of the host organization have an equal right to freely describe and discuss existing CTUs or ETUs with the academic team. In return, the academic team should protect the interests of each member by maintaining the confidentiality of the interviews when research results are presented to management. This is not democracy, nor even full participation in the knowledge produced. It is only the equal right to discuss the order of a collective process even if there is no equal right to rule it. We call this the principle of *isonomy*, from the Greek *isonomia*, in the sense of the *iso* (equal) right to express *nomos* (the order of the world). Isonomy allows us to build a rigorous and ethical investigation process while not enforcing a democratic model of action.

Capacity to create research-oriented empirical material: Interviews are often an insufficient source of information for establishing unknown facts or collective phenomena that may be the unintended result of several individual behaviors. Research often demands measures or investigations that are not part of the standard information systems and procedures of the organization. This is a research opportunity that is not easy to obtain in standard field research limited to interviews and the consultation of existing documents. The collaborative structure makes it more feasible and also gives IRM its exploratory power.

Principle of controlled design processes: New models of action do not emerge easily from purely analytical work of CTUs or ETUs. They need the design of a management experiment (Shani & Docherty, 2003; Ayas, 1996; Heron, 1981). But research needs to clearly distinguish between a *controlled design process* and the search for a *satisfactory solution.* A short comment on "design" will clarify this distinction: According to Herbert Simon (1981), design is problem finding and problem solving. Hatchuel (2002) argues that design also requires that some concepts be revised or discovered in the process, and thereby implies some form of invention. On the one hand, the academic team will be primarily interested in all the theoretical implications and potential of these new concepts; on the other hand, the organization will investigate a satisfactory and politically acceptable solving procedure. The task of the academic team is not to justify those solutions selected by the organizations but to control this design process. This means evaluating the innovativeness of the new concepts and the full potential of solutions unveiled, including those actually implemented.

Management innovations evaluated as "rational myths": Most people who promote a new management model are naturally tempted to declare it a success. An overly critical attitude from organizational members could be interpreted as defeatism or unjustified skepticism.

Thus, new management models act as *rational myths* (Hatchuel & Molet, 1986; Hatchuel & Weil, 1995). They combine two aspects: (1) a rational response to a management issue and (2) a mobilizing myth that should create trust, energy, and commitment. The role of academics is to carefully monitor a review process that distinguishes these two aspects.

Principle of Joint and Continuous Monitoring[16]

All that we have said about IRM portrays a fragile and complex cooperation process between two partners with different logics, tasks, and goals. Yet the value of the entire project lies in these differences and in the capacity to create fruitful, continuous cooperation while fully respecting the different identities of the partners. Cooperating in difficult and uncertain contexts requires continuous and intensive monitoring. Suggesting and implementing such monitoring is a central requisite of IRM. In most cases, this is done in the form of a steering committee whose members come from the academic team and from the organization. The task of the steering committee is to protect and warrant the successful fulfillment of IRM principles and commitments; it is also to discuss all conflictual issues that emerge during the project (see Table 7.2).

Before concluding this chapter and discussing the limitations of IRM, let us illustrate the logic of an IRM project through a recent program with Renault.[17]

AN EXAMPLE: REVISITING THE MANAGEMENT OF INNOVATION

Renault is a French car manufacturer. It gained a global reputation through its successful alliance with Nissan. Renault has been a major partner for collaborative management research.[18] CGS, as well as other research teams, have been working almost permanently with

Table 7.2   IRM Collaborative Protocol: A Synthesis

Preconditions for IRM	A partner with a pioneering logic An open management issue An assessed research potential A contractual commitment to a research issue An academic team with a legitimate research potential in management
Monitoring principles for IRM	Principle of free academic investigation • Free interviewing • Warranted isonomy • Confidentiality of all individual interviews • Capacity to create new empirical material • Controlled design • Management innovations evaluated as rational myths Principle of joint and continuous monitoring
Outputs of IRM	Local contribution to potential management breakthroughs Publishable case studies Revision or discovery of management models and theories

Renault for the two last decades. Renault also has a long tradition of innovation. Several Renault cars created a new concept that was rapidly followed by all the industry. The famous R4 and R5 gave new life to the concept of the small "city car"; the Espace, Twingo, and Scenic invented the monospace architecture. Maintaining this innovative capability is a major strategic intent at Renault.

An Issue About the Management of Innovation

In 2003, however, managers from the R&D departments began to think that important challenges lay ahead. Renault-Nissan was a global player and faced new markets. The identities and values of cars were changing. New invading technologies were on the shelf: X-by-wire, fuel cells, hybrids. New design offers had to be made. Yet, why do management research in this battlefield? The R&D executives shared the feeling that some innovative projects didn't work well. The projects were risky and uncertain and thus some percentage of failure was normal. But these executives were convinced that their problems also originated

from management methods. What exactly had to be improved?

Research Potential Assessed

This situation was a good candidate for an IRM project. Clearly, there was no problem that called for immediate action, and the horizon for investigation was consistent with research requirements. Regarding management theory, the situation was ambiguous. From the point of view of management handbooks, Renault was in line with existing ETUs, that is, good project management and new product development (NPD). However, after a phase of exploration, we came up with the idea that the situation could be seen from a reverse perspective. Renault was facing a challenging situation where there was no clear CTU and no ETU available.

A research partnership was signed that was going to continue for at least four years. It included an empirical analysis of innovative projects and an investigation of the relations between the literature on creativity and the literature on innovation and engineering design. It is worth noting that these bodies of literature are usually separate and that there are very few theoretical works that tend to reach unified results across these fields. A clear suggestion by Renault's head of advanced engineering and research led to an attempt to attain this unified view.

First Discovery: A New Typology of Design Ventures

To summarize, after a first series of investigations, we had to make a distinction between two types of design situations. Type 1 could be an innovative car or an innovative component but with rather classical functions and skills. Yet this was not necessarily an incremental innovation: Twinge and Scenic were highly innovative cars, but such architectural and conceptual innovations were not disturbing for Renault's design rules and project management. We defined Type 1 design as *rule-based design*. For these projects, ETUs (project management and NPD) and CTUs were identical and relevant. In contrast, Type 2 situations required *innovative design* and presented features that did not fit with rule-based design. These design situations were based on a powerful initial idea that needed much more exploration and for which new skills and new partners as well as market research were required. For these situations there was no clear CTU and no ETU.

Second Discovery: Managing Innovative Design Is Not Managing a Project

The collaborative program was oriented toward Type 2 design situations. We studied in detail a panel of about 10 Type 2 innovative situations with detailed information about the engineering, industrial design, or market issues; in a few cases, we participated in the early phases of the "project" itself. But a difficult issue presented itself. We were supposed to learn from observing these innovation ventures, but what did "observing" innovative projects mean? Which framework should be used in order to make valuable phenomena visible? Research on innovation had evolved progressively from the quest for good structures to the identification of "collective learning" models. On the one hand, greater attention was given to networks and communities of practice; on the other hand, knowledge brokers, sensemaking events, and experimentalism were also highlighted. The literature is still distributed between these perspectives.

Our empirical work confirmed that design teams had difficulties in managing all these perspectives in the same course of action. Our main discovery was that managing innovative design was not managing a project. What had to be managed was not the attainment of a set of requirements through preestablished gates and phases. Instead, innovative design teams had to simultaneously expand and structure several conceptual orientations and various new skill developments. Yet there was no available model in the literature about innovation, engineering design, or NPD that could guide such ventures. These observations triggered a wider research program that led to a new model of innovative design that could inspire and guide managers and designers. This new model for the management of innovative design (inspired by a new design theory called C-K theory) has been explored with Renault and is now discussed with other pioneering companies (Le Masson, Weil, & Hatchuel, 2006).

CONCLUDING REMARKS

The Renault program illustrates some of the main features of IRM that we synthesize as a conclusion to this chapter.

In IRM, the collaborative work is not built around a "hot" problem. Renault shared with us a basic research issue in management theory. The impact on the organization was not predictable at the beginning of the program. However, these results stimulated several cascading developments: new management tools for Type 2 design situations, creation of a support unit for innovative projects, and creation of specialized units in charge of "innovation fields" (Hatchuel, Le Masson, & Weil, 2006). Such impacts are not the direct consequence of the research program. They reflect a complex and ongoing political appropriation of the innovation issue in the company. The IRM project is only one part of this change process. This supports our assumption that research is not about action but about models of action. *Action* is the name that we should give to the complex set of changes that was only partly influenced by these new models of action.

The principles of free interviewing, confidentiality, and isonomy have been of crucial importance. Innovations are often major political projects. Careers, rewards, influence, and power are dependent on the signs of success or failure from such projects. Therefore, designers, engineers, researchers, product planners, and purchasers all expect that any IRM program on innovation would carefully account for their experience and ideas about innovative projects. Also, Renault and CGS agreed on a publication policy that permits publishing research material excepting information that could endanger the competitive advantage of the company.

Partners May Trigger Theoretical Ambitions

Now, could classic qualitative research reach the same results? We claim that the unifying view of innovative design processes that we have looked for in this program is precisely an effect of the collaborative scheme. Research on innovation usually analyzed isolated cases from different companies. Moreover, each researcher tended to stick to his or her own problematic. A researcher interested in social issues would highlight the political problems created by innovations; if interested in learning, he or she would insist on prototyping and knowledge creating processes; if studying collective processes, he or she would look for communities, cooperation and networking, and so on. From the point of view of management, however, each of these aspects only highlighted classic models of action that could be found in any change process. What was needed was a model of action specific to highly innovative situations. Therefore, the theoretical impetus for a unified logic of innovative design was driven by the collaborative context itself.

Some Limitations of IRM

IRM is a research method that cannot be easily repeated by all management students. It requires heavy resources both from academia and from companies. Much more than standard research based on questionnaires or qualitative research (Glaser & Strauss, 1967), IRM requires management research teams that are credible and reliable partners for pioneering organizations. Also, it is unlikely that an IRM project could be conducted by a young and inexperienced student on his or her own. For many academic settings in the field of management, all this will appear as a very demanding type of research organization. Yet the stakes are also quite different. After 100 years of management research, it has often been noted that the main revolutions in management (major ETUs) came from innovative firms and not from academic research. This indicates that academic research is not yet a major player in management history and plays more of a filtering and disseminating role than an exploratory one (see David & Hatchuel, Chapter 2 in this *Handbook*). IRM offers a complementary and consistent approach to fill this gap. However, is it a reasonable endeavor? On the one hand, IRM needs pioneering partners with uncommon management thinking. It seeks theoretical breakthroughs for management, and these are necessarily rare. On the other hand, it offers access to empirical situations presenting a high exploratory power and ambitious theoretical challenges. Are there many other alternatives that give to management research a small chance to influence management history?

NOTES

1. In English, "Center for Management Science."

2. Most of the literature produced about this program has been published in French.

3. Armand Hatchuel has been a permanent guest professor at FENIX since its creation. Niclas Adler, director of FENIX, has been a senior researcher at CGS during the same period.

4. For the sake of simplicity, "action" designates "collective action" throughout the chapter.

5. IRM has been described in several papers, most of these in the French academic literature.

6. A "grande école" for public servants and people in executive engineering.

7. To date, the sole French Nobel Prize recipient in economics was Maurice Allais, who spent his entire academic career at l'École des Mines.

8. For example, during the 1980s, Renault published a series of documents on the major authors in management theory. The Paris transport authority later launched a major research program entitled "Réseau 2000," which spanned several academic fields, including management research.

9. AP-HP, the Paris Hospitals authority, has been a partner of CGS for three decades. The authority's management institute for doctors acting as department heads was cofounded and is cochaired by CGS.

10. CGS reached its present scope of scholar and collaborative activities at the end of the 1980s when it launched joint doctoral and graduate programs with major academic institutions in the Paris area (e.g., Université Dauphine, Université de Marne la Vallée, Université de Nanterre). The principles of IRM have been taught and applied by doctoral students in management since 1990.

11. Concerning action research, see also Bradbury, Chapter 28 in this *Handbook*.

12. The local rejection of an existing ETU in an organization is a CTU. This case is treated in the Yes-Yes cell of the matrix.

13. Following Michel Foucault's work in *Les Mots et les Choses* (English title: *The Order of Things*), the notion of a "common field of knowledge" can be interpreted as a common "episteme": a set of concepts that are active both as knowledge and as models of action.

14. See also David and Hatchuel, Chapter 2 in this *Handbook*.

15. See also Pasmore, Woodman, and Simmons, Chapter 27 in this *Handbook*.

16. See also Bartunek, Chapter 4 in this *Handbook*.

17. The results of this research were presented in a keynote presentation by Armand Hatchuel and Dominique Levent at EURAM 2005, Munich. Dominique Levent is in charge of innovation management issues at Renault.

18. This tradition has even interested historians. See Perriaux's book on Renault and the social sciences (Perriaux, 1999).

REFERENCES

Adler, N., Shani, A. B. (Rami), & Styhre, A. (2004). *Collaborative research in organizations*. Thousand Oaks, CA: Sage.

Argyris, C. (1995). Action science and organizational learning. *Journal of Managerial Psychology, 10*(6), 20–27.

Argyris, C., & Schön, D. (1978). *Organizational learning: A theory of action perspective*. Reading, MA: Addison-Wesley.

Ayas, K. (1996). Design for learning and innovation. *Long Range Planning, 29*(6), 898–901.

Baker, C. R. (2000). Towards the increased use of action research in accounting information systems. *Accounting Forum, 24*(4), 366–379.

Bartunek, J. (1993). Scholarly dialogues and participatory action research. *Human Relations, 46*(10), 1221–1233.

Baskerville, R. L., & Myers, M. (2004). Making IS research relevant to practice: Foreword. *MIS Quarterly, 28*(3), 329–335.

Baskerville, R. L., & Wood-Harper, A. T. (1996). A critical perspective on action research as a method for information systems research. *Journal of Information Technology, 11*(3), 235–246.

Björkman, H., & Sundgren, M. (2005). Political entrepreneurship in action research: Learning from two cases. *Journal of Organizational Change Management, 18*(5), 399–415.

Burnes, B. (2004). Kurt Lewin and the planned approach to change: A re-appraisal. *Journal of Management Studies, 41*(6), 977–1002.

Cassell, C., & Johnson, P. (2006). Action research: Explaining the diversity. *Human Relations, 59*(6), 783–814.

Checkland, P. (1985). From optimizing to learning: A development for systems thinking for the 1990s. *Journal of the Operational Research Society, 36*, 757–767.

Coghlan, D. (2004). Action research in the academy: Why and whither? Reflections on the changing nature of research. *Irish Journal of Management, 25*(2), 1–10.

Coughlan, P., Harbison, A., Dromgoole, T., & Duff, D. (2001). Continuous improvement through collaborative learning. *International Journal of Technology Management, 22*(4), 285–303.

David, A. (2002). *Intervention methodologies in management research*. Paper presented at EURAM Conference, Stockholm, Sweden.

David, A., Hatchuel, A., & Laufer, R. (Eds.). (2001). *Les nouvelles fondations des sciences de gestion* [The new foundations of management science]. Paris: Vuibert Fnege.

Davison, R. M., Martinsons, M. G., & Kock, N. (2004). Principles of canonical action research. *Information Systems Journal, 14*(1), 65–86.

Dickens, L., & Watkins, K. (1999). Action research: Rethinking Lewin. *Management Learning, 30*(2), 127–141.

Eden, C., & Huxham, C. (1996). Action research for management research. *British Journal of Management, 7*(1), 75–86.

Elden, M., & Chisholm, R. F. (1993). Emerging varieties of action research: Introduction to the special issue. *Human Relations, 46*(2), 121–142.

Fals-Borda, O., & Rahman, M. A. (Eds.). (1991). *Action and knowledge: Breaking the monopoly with participatory action research*. New York: Intermediate Technology/Apex.

Glaser, B. G., & Strauss, A. L. (1967). *The discovery of grounded theory: Strategies for qualitative research.* Chicago: Aldine.

Gustavsen, B. (1993). Action research and the generation of knowledge. *Human Relations, 46*(11), 1361–1365.

Halbesleben, J. R. B., Osburn, H. K., & Mumford, M. D. (2006). Action research as a burnout intervention: Reducing burnout in the federal fire service. *Journal of Applied Behavioral Science, 42*(2), 244–266.

Hatchuel, A. (2002). Towards design theory and expandable rationality: The unfinished program of Herbert Simon. *Journal of Management and Governance, 5*(3/4), 260–273.

Hatchuel, A. (2005). Towards an epistemology of action. *European Management Review, 2,* 36–47.

Hatchuel, A., & Glise, H. (2004). Rebuilding management. In N. Adler, A. B. (Rami) Shani, & A. Styhre (Eds.), *Collaborative research in organizations: Foundations for learning, change, and theoretical development* (pp. 5–21). Thousand Oaks, CA: Sage.

Hatchuel, A., Le Masson, P., & Weil, B. (2001). *From R&D to R-I-D: Design strategies and the management of innovation fields.* Paper presented at the 8th International Product Development Management Conference, Enschede, The Netherlands.

Hatchuel, A., Le Masson, P., & Weil, B. (2006). From NPD to NDS: The management of innovation fields. *Proceedings of the IPDM conference* (Vol. 2, pp. 759–775). Milan: EIASM.

Hatchuel, A., & Molet, H. (1986). Rational modelling in understanding human decision making: About two case studies. *European Journal of Operational Research, 24*(1), 178–186.

Hatchuel, A., & Weil, B. (1995). *Experts in organizations.* Berlin, Germany: Walter de Gruyter.

Heron, J. (1981). Experiential research methodology. In P. Reason & J. Rowan (Eds.), *Human inquiry: A sourcebook of new paradigm research.* Chichester, UK: John Wiley & Sons.

Huxham, C., & Vangen, S. (2003). Researching organizational practice through action research: Case studies and design choices. *Organizational Research Methods, 6*(3), 383–404.

Jae, E. Y. (2004). Reconsidering participatory action research for organizational transformation and social change. *Journal of Organisational Transformation & Social Change, 1*(2/3), 111–141.

Kaplan, R. S. (1998). Innovation action research: Creating new management theory and practice. *Journal of Management Accounting Research, 10,* 89–118.

Kates, S. M., & Robertson, J. (2004). Adapting action research to marketing: A dialogic argument between theory and practice. *European Journal of Marketing, 38*(3/4), 418–433.

Kidd, S. A., & Kral, M. J. (2005). Practicing participatory action research. *Journal of Counseling Psychology, 52*(2), 187–195.

Koch, N. (2004). The three threats of action research: A discussion of methodological antidotes in the context of an information systems study. *Decision Support Systems, 37*(2), 265–286.

Ledford, G. E., Jr., & Mohrman, S. A. (1993). Looking backward and forward at action research. *Human Relations, 46*(11), 1349–1360.

Le Masson, P., Weil, B., & Hatchuel, A. (2006). *Les processus d'innovation.* Paris: Hermés Science Publishers.

Lewin, K. (1948). Action research and minority problems. In G. W. Lewin (Ed.), *Resolving social conflicts.* New York: Harper & Row.

Lewin, K. (1951). *Field theory in social science.* New York: Harper & Row.

Lindgren, R., Henfridsson, O., & Schultze, U. (2004). Design principles for competence management systems: A synthesis of an action research. *MIS Quarterly, 28*(3), 435–472.

MacLean, D., MacIntosh, R., & Grant, S. (2002). Mode 2 management research. *British Journal of Management, 13*(4), 189–207.

Marsick, V. J., & Gephart, M. A. (2003). Action research: Building the capacity for learning and change. *Human Resource Planning, 26*(2), 14–18.

McClintock, D., Ison, R., & Armson, R. (2003). Metaphors for reflecting on research practice: Researching with people. *Journal of Environmental Planning & Management, 46*(5), 715–731.

McCutcheon, G., & Jung, B. (1990). Alternative perspectives on action research. *Theory Into Practice, 29*(3), 144–152.

McKernan, J. (2006). Choice and quality in action research: A response to Peter Reason. *Journal of Management Inquiry, 15*(2), 204–206.

McSweeney, B. (2000). Comment: "Action research": Mission impossible? *Accounting Forum, 24*(4), 379–391.

Meredith, J. R., Raturi, A., Amoako-Gyampah, K., & Kaplan, B. (1989). Alternative research paradigms in operations. *Journal of Operations Management, 8*(4), 297–326.

Mintzberg, H. (1979). An emerging strategy of "direct" research. *Administrative Science Quarterly, 24*(December).

Moisdon, J. C. (1984). Recherche en gestion et intervention [Management research and intervention]. *Revue Française de Gestion,* September–October.

Owen, M. (2004). Conflict and convergence: The ethics review of action research. *Journal of Research Administration, 35*(2), 21–30.

Perriaux, A. S. (1999). *Renault et les sciences sociales.* Paris: Seli-Arslan.

Raelin, J. A. (1997). Action learning and action science: Are they different? *Organizational Dynamics, 26*(1), 21–34.

Reason, P., & Heron, J. (1986). Research with people: The paradigm of co-operative experimental inquiry. *Person Centred Review, 1,* 456–475.

Robinson, V. M. J. (1993). Current controversies in action research. *Public Administration Quarterly, 17*(3), 263–290.

Schein, E. H. (1995). Process consultation, action research and clinical inquiry: Are they the same? *Journal of Managerial Psychology, 10*(6), 14–20.

Shani, A. B. (Rami), David, A., & Wilson, C. (2004). Collaborative research: Alternative roadmaps. In N. Adler, A. B. (Rami) Shani, & A. Styhre (Eds.), *Collaborative research in organizations: Foundations for learning, change, and theoretical development* (pp. 83–100). Thousand Oaks, CA: Sage.

Shani, A. B. (Rami), & Docherty, P. (2003). *Learning by design: Building sustainable organizations.* Malden, MA: Blackwell.

Simon, H. A. (1981). *The sciences of the artificial.* Cambridge: MIT Press.

Thompson, F., & Perry, C. (2004). Generalising results of an action research project in one work place to other situations: Principles and practice. *European Journal of Marketing, 38*(3/4), 401–417.

Torbert, W. R. (1976). *Creating a community of inquiry: Conflict, collaboration, transformation.* New York: John Wiley.

Wilson, Hugh N. (2004). Towards rigour in action research: A case study in marketing planning. *European Journal of Marketing, 38*(3/4), 378–400.

CHAPTER 8

Learning Mechanisms as Means and Ends in Collaborative Management Research

PETER DOCHERTY

A. B. (RAMI) SHANI

ABSTRACT

Learning mechanisms are viewed as a critical component of collaborative management research. In this chapter, the authors review the evolution of a variety of learning mechanisms within four streams of research. Three types of learning mechanisms—cognitive, structural, and procedural—are explored as both ends and means in collaborative management research. Utilizing a five-year research project with Skandia, the nature of the learning mechanisms tapestry, or combination of different types of mechanisms being used at any time, is described, and the role that it played in the collaborative management research is discussed. The last part of the chapter focus on the exploration of three challenges: the multiple roles of learning mechanisms in collaborative management research, the design choices in the formation of learning mechanisms and their potential consequences, and learning mechanisms and the voices of inquiry and practice.

LEARNING MECHANISMS: AN IMPORTANT COMPONENT IN COLLABORATIVE RESEARCH

The raison d'être of collaborative management research is conducting research *together with* practitioners in industry, commerce, and the public sector, as distinct from

conducting research *on* them. The focus of the research is on issues that are important to the practitioners, and the aim is, on the one hand, to generate knowledge that is directly relevant to their needs and ambitions, and on the other, to generate new general scientific knowledge for academia and society at large. Engaging in collaborative research entails or implies change or development: solving a problem, realizing an opportunity, or taking action on or with the results of the research. These changes or developments may concern the participating organization's products or services, its structures or processes, its relations to its environment or business context, or any combination of these.

By definition, collaborative research entails involvement, action, and decision making on the part of the researchers and the practitioners. It entails a continuous dialogue between researchers and practitioners, involving "cycles of reflection on experience that lead to desired experiments and action" (Bradbury, Chapter 28 in this volume). The conduct of the research itself becomes a learning process for those involved. For both parties, the research process may require that they take on new roles or reassess and possibly modify certain values or attitudes; for example, new participatory practices may require participants to reassess their views of each other (see Bartunek, Chapter 4 in this volume; Coghlan & Shani, Chapter 29 in this volume). The models, methods, and tools used in the collaborative research may be new experiences for the parties, requiring new knowledge and skills.

The dialogue between researchers and practitioners, the collective reflection on their experience, the discussion and interpretation of members' insights regarding events and processes in the research work, and the emergence of a common understanding of the project constitute collective reflection and learning in the collaborative research (Boud, Cressey, & Docherty, 2006). An important conclusion from such learning at work is that the learning process is much more effective if the conditions and process for the learning are designed in a planned and systematic way rather than being allowed to evolve without any conscious attention (Elkjaer, 2005; Ellström, 2001; Fenwick, 2003; Shani & Docherty, 2003). The specific features of the context and processes in the collaborative

research situation that are designed to promote, support, and facilitate scientific processes and learning we refer to here as *learning mechanisms*. An integral part of the collaborative activity centers on scientific inquiry. As such, learning is taking place in many different groups within and between organizational levels, and even between organizations (see Mohrman, Mohrman, Cohen, & Winby, Chapter 24 in this volume; Stebbins & Valenzuela, Chapter 23 in this volume).

Figure 8.1 illustrates schematically the typical structure of European collaborative research programs. The central group or community in a collaborative research project is the project group studying the main issue. While there are usually two parties collaborating in the group, the researchers and the practitioners, there may be three or more, with different values, cultures, and agendas (see Werr & Greiner, Chapter 5 in this volume). The researchers may come from different disciplines or institutions, and the practitioners may come from different organizations or stakeholder groups such as management, unions, or customers (see, for example, Huzzard & Gregory, Chapter 16 in this volume). The parties in the collaborative project have their own forums for discussion: the representatives from the unit being studied will be conducting a dialogue with their organizational unit as a whole and even with other groups in the organization. There will also be forums for the exchange of experiences between projects in a program, usually for researchers and for all stakeholders.

The thesis of this chapter is that mechanisms to promote and support learning at different levels and across levels of an organization are the internal way of organizing collaborative scientific inquiry and the way of organizing, acting on, and developing the firm's differentiated capabilities. In the context of collaborative management research, learning mechanisms concern both the learning in the actual scientific inquiry process, in which they are "means," and also the

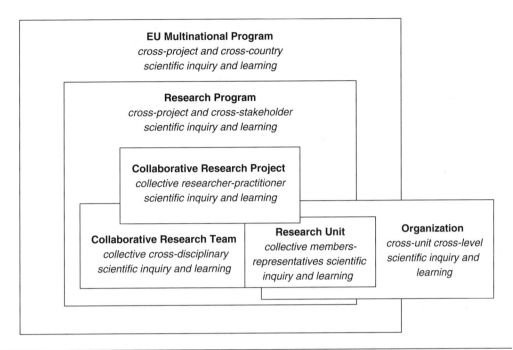

EU Multinational Program
cross-project and cross-country
scientific inquiry and learning

Research Program
cross-project and cross-stakeholder
scientific inquiry and learning

Collaborative Research Project
collective researcher-practitioner
scientific inquiry and learning

Collaborative Research Team
collective cross-disciplinary
scientific inquiry and learning

Research Unit
collective members-
representatives scientific
inquiry and learning

Organization
cross-unit cross-level
scientific inquiry and
learning

Figure 8.1   Schematic Organization of Past and Ongoing European Collaborative Research
Programs

efficiency of the learning processes in the organization that constitute part of the research outcome(s); in this latter context, the learning mechanisms are an "end."

In the next section of this chapter, we outline how different research streams that address change and learning in organizations have contributed to the design of learning mechanisms for use in collaborative management research. Next, we explore the nature and role that different learning mechanisms—cognitive, structural, and procedural—play in the facilitation and support of such research, and present an illustration of how the mechanisms contribute to the generation of "local" knowledge for the practitioners and general knowledge for academia. Finally, we discuss the contributions that the study of learning mechanisms as means and ends has made to science and to practice, and the types of issues that remain for further research and development.

THE USE OF LEARNING MECHANISMS IN COLLABORATIVE MANAGEMENT RESEARCH, BUILDING ON DIFFERENT RESEARCH STREAMS

Research, change, and *learning* are ubiquitous terms in the behavioral, social, and management sciences; no single discipline can claim priority of their use. They are allotted major importance in all disciplines. Many phenomena in which they feature are common to different disciplines. We identify four broad streams of applied research in which collaborative research has played an important role.[1]

The "Work Organization" Stream

This stream started during the 1940s and 1950s among social psychologists and organizational behaviorists in the fields of group dynamics (e.g., Lewin, 1997) in the United States and sociotechnical systems (STS) at the Tavistock Institute in London (e.g., Trist & Murray, 1990, 1993). Their approach from the beginning was to work together with members of an organization, especially at the operative level, on issues of health, well-being, and personal development as well as the productivity and effectiveness of the organization. Their research was focused on the organization of teams that would enable self-management.

This required systematic and collective reflection and discussion within these teams. Together with multiskilling, this entailed much training for the workers. Researchers also developed frameworks, tools, and methods that may be utilized as learning mechanisms in the introduction and development of sociotechnical systems (see Kolodny & Halpern, Chapter 13 in this volume).

However, Tavistock's participative, collaborative approach attracted more attention outside the UK than within it. Different STS schools emerged around the world. Fred Emery and Philip Herbst moved from Tavistock to the Work Research Institute in Norway. There they joined Einar Thorsrud to gradually extend the approach from a focus on the operational level to the organization as a whole and the interplay between levels and functions (Thorsrud & Emery, 1969; Emery & Emery, 1974). This process was continued by Björn Gustavsen. An important feature of this development was the focus on the participation of the unions, management, and employer federations in the development process and in the resulting organizations. This entailed the development of "search conferences" and "democratic dialogue," which are learning mechanisms organizing the structures and the processes of collaborative research (Emery, 1982; Gustavsen, 1992). These methods played a central role in the Swedish collaborative research

program on "Leadership, Organization, and Codetermination," which produced several doctoral dissertations.

The next step in the development of this school was to enlarge the system from individual organizations to clusters of organizations within a region. In a cluster, the companies work together with agencies, authorities, and offices of the unions or employer federations at the regional or national levels. This has required the development of network-based learning mechanisms in order to establish and maintain a more sustainable collaborative research activity system (Fricke & Totterdill, 2004; Gustavsen, Colbjørnsen, & Pålhaugen, 1998; Huzzard & Gregory, Chapter 16 in this volume; Nielsen & Lundvall, 2003; Nilsson, 2005).

The "Organizational Learning" Stream

Organizational learning has addressed both the character of learning and the coupling between levels in the organization. Research in this field is usually conducted in business school or institutes of behavioral or social science. Many researchers have formulated classifications of learning with respect to the depth and character of the learning process (see Pavlovsky, Forslin, & Reinhart, 2001, for a current overview). The pioneering work of Argyris and Schön (1996) regarding single- and double-loop learning is a well-known example. The conceptualization of different types of learning is an important cognitive learning and design mechanism for the conduct of collaborative management research projects.

The research program led by Peter Senge, William Isaacs, and George Roth at the Massachusetts Institute of Technology has focused on longitudinal case studies. Representatives from the different organizations met at regular intervals to exchange and discuss experiences. This research group focused considerable resources on the development of methods, models, and tools to promote and support the learning processes facilitated by the researchers within and between the organizations (DiBella, 2001; Isaacs, 1993; Senge, 1991). The MIT group's collaborative management research approach underlines the need for dialogue, openness, and system dynamics (see Roth, Chapter 17 in this volume). Senge suggests that learning in organizations may be thought of as a flow process that often needs to be unlocked or released within individuals and organizations. Others, such as Crossan, Lane, and White (1999), have provided models for the development and diffusion of learning from individuals to groups and, eventually, to the organization as a whole.

The "Learning at Work" Stream

The third stream, "Learning at work," is formed by the educationalists, educational psychologists, and human resource experts studying issues of adult and vocational learning. Their interest has evolved from the study of the formal training of individuals in the classroom milieu to the experiential learning of individuals and groups (teams) in the workplace. Two important factors have contributed to this shift in focus. First was a growing conviction by some researchers, such as Reg Revans (1982), that classroom teaching was ill suited to the development of important behavioral skills such as leadership. This led to his development of the Action Learning Ph.D. program. Second, the implementation of management models such as lean production has made the necessary integration of learning in the workplace more difficult. Collaborative research has focused on the development of learning mechanisms to provide opportunities for reflection at work and to improve the efficiency of problem-solving

and decision-making processes in collaborative research forums (Bjerlöv, 1999; Wilhelmson, 1998).

Fenwick and Rubenson (2005) review collaborative research on learning in work. Learning is shown to be prompted by particular individuals (guides, mentors), events (conflicts or disturbances), leaders (encouraging inquiry, supporting improvisation), or conditions (learning mechanisms) (see, for example, Boyatzis, Howard, Rapisarda, & Taylor, Chapter 11 in this volume). Learning in the communities-of-practice model is affected by relational stability (trust), variety (new ideas, risk), and group structure (networks, competence). Power and politics are given relatively little attention in the literature. However, the sensemaking and reflective dialogue approaches address this issue by differentiating sensemaking between managers and their staff from sense-giving by managers and sense-taking by their staff (Pettigrew et al., 2003).

The "Organizational Design" Stream

Many of the people in this stream have been and are active in the streams previously mentioned here. They have, however, focused on the research conclusion mentioned in our introduction: Conditions for learning need to be designed, not left to emergence. The design process may concern culture, structures, and processes that initiate, promote, facilitate, and maintain learning. Collaborative research on this topic started in the late 1980s and early 1990s and was led by Dale Zand, Gervase Bushe, and Rami Shani, who focused on parallel learning structures as an organization development intervention strategy that optimizes both learning and inquiry within systems (Zand, 1981; Bushe & Shani, 1991). Parallel learning structures were viewed (Bushe & Shani, 1991) as "a generic intervention where: (a) a structure is created that (b) operates 'parallel' with the formal hierarchy and structure and (c) has the purpose of increasing an organization's learning through scientific inquiry" (p. 9). This stream of research integrated sociotechnical system and action research perspectives for the purpose of a system's continuous change and improvement.

This orientation was further advanced in the mid-1990s by Raanan Lipshitz, Micha Popper, Victor Friedman, and their colleagues in Israel, who advanced the concept of organizational learning mechanisms (Lipshitz, Popper, & Oz, 1996; Popper & Lipshitz, 1998; Friedman, Lipshitz, & Overmeer, 2001). Their research led them to argue that organizational learning mechanisms (OLMs) are institutionalized structures and procedural arrangements that allow organizations to learn nonvicariously, that is, to collect, analyze, store, disseminate, and use systematically information that is relevant to their members and their performance. OLMs link learning to learning by organizations in a concrete, directly observable, and malleable fashion (Lipshitz, Friedman, & Popper, 2006).

The need for "space for research" was advanced by Nonaka & Konno (1998), based on the Japanese concept of *ba,* which is defined as the context in which knowledge is created, shared, and utilized. *Ba* does not necessarily mean a physical space. The notion advanced by Nonaka, Konno, and Toyama (2001) is that *ba* can be a physical space, a virtual space, a mental space, or any combination of these. The most critical aspect of *ba* is creating the space for interaction between people. The essence of collaborative management research is embedded in the nature of interaction between people within and outside the firm. Learning mechanisms are viewed as such a space within and through which people co-inquire into an organizational phenomenon of mutual interest. Learning mechanisms serve as the engine that nurtures the community of inquiry (Coghlan & Shani, 2007, and Chapter 29 in this volume).

TYPES OF LEARNING MECHANISMS IN COLLABORATIVE MANAGEMENT RESEARCH

The literature suggests that learning mechanisms are organizational features that can foster scientific inquiry (Bushe & Shani, 1991; Popper & Lipshitz, 1998) and learning processes. Literature on learning mechanisms identifies three focuses: cognitive, structural, and procedural (Shani & Docherty, 2003). Although we argue that a tapestry of the three different kinds of learning mechanisms can trigger ongoing collaborative scientific inquiry and organizational action, we will first briefly discuss learning mechanisms with each of these focuses.

Cognitive Learning Mechanisms

Cultural or cognitive mechanisms are the bearers of language, concepts, symbols, theories, frameworks, and values for establishing thinking, reasoning, and understanding that are consistent with the organization's strategy. Cognitive mechanisms are management's main means for creating an understanding among all employees on the character, need, and priority of the strategy and the learning and changes required to realize it. They include company value and mission statements, strategy documents, policies and plans, and management-union or company-partner joint agreements. These are among the systemic frameworks that underpin generically subjective sensemaking (Weick, 1995) and enable various elements of the organization and its activity system to operate with shared meaning. Cognitive learning mechanisms are a foundational part of the emergent multilevel and cross-community social fabric of the firm and underpin the dispersed practice-based learning processes. As an illustration, value and mission statements have been shown to be important stable reference points and new capability enablers for organizations in complex, ever-changing, high-speed growth industries, such as the information and communication technologies (ICT) industry and certain investment services (Lapidoth, 1996).

Specific cognitive learning mechanisms play a special role in collaborative research, especially in Europe. They are usually formalized in written agreements between research institutions and the participating organizations, and specify the issues and goals of the research, the stakeholders concerned and those participating in the research, the decision discretion and resources available to the different parties, and the theoretical frame of reference of the project. These agreements may state management's influence on the formulation of research issues and protect their information of a sensitive social or commercial nature. Researchers' influence on the conduct and analysis of the studies is defined, and their right to publish their results is confirmed. Such agreements are usually a condition for receiving public research funding.

Structural Learning Mechanisms

Structural mechanisms are organizational, physical, technical, and work-system infrastructures that facilitate collaborative management research and encourage practice-based learning. Organizational mechanisms house and enable the collaboration and discourse required for collective learning of new practice: the intersubjective or person-to-person sensemaking that is entailed as individuals and groups learn from experience (Weick, 1995). These mechanisms may include communication channels; the establishment of lateral structures to enable learning of new practices across various core organizational units; changes to the work organization, including the delineation of roles and the establishment of teams with

shared accountability and thus a mutual need to learn; formal and informal forums for joint exploration and debate; networks for mutual learning; and learning-specific structures such as parallel learning structures, bench-learning structures, and process improvement teams (see Stebbins & Valenzuela, Chapter 23 in this volume). The physical structure may be laid out to facilitate contact between members of various units or multiple organizations for sharing and combining knowledge (Bushe & Shani, 1991; Dilschmann & Berg, 1996).

Technology mechanisms may include learning centers, e-learning programs, databases and data warehouses, e-mail, and document and data sharing systems that enhance the collaborative management research process. Technology mechanisms facilitate virtual contact between members that stimulates collective sensemaking, or provide access to key process and content documents that provide generic frameworks that are generated to guide the enactment of the strategy.

The work organization can be designed to facilitate collaborative management research, collective reflection, and learning (Roth, Chapter 17 in this volume). For example, new knowledgeable experts may be temporarily or permanently added to a unit, or new units or teams may be composed that combine different knowledge bases to work together on specific topics. If these are cross-community groupings, they will facilitate learning both in their home unit and in the collaborative grouping. For example, joint expert problem solving brings together temporary groups of discipline experts with varying kinds and degrees of experience of the new capability to learn from one another in the process of addressing real problems of practice (Dixon, 2001). Cross-level groups can be established to facilitate the institutionalization of new knowledge and practice at the larger organizational level.

Procedural Mechanisms

Procedural mechanisms concern the rules, routines, methods, and tools that can be institutionalized in the organization to promote and support collaborative management research and learning (Pavlovsky et al., 2001). These may include tests and assessment tools and methods, standard operating procedures, and methods for specific types of collective learning, such as action learning or debriefing routines. Learning processes may be built directly into practice routines if steps are defined in the work processes where people share knowledge or combine it. The focus of the routine or work process will influence the degree to which the procedural learning mechanism is multilevel and crosses community boundaries.

Organizations may also adopt collaborative management research methodologies to facilitate the conduct of dialogues for collective reflection in groups, and build these as pervasive core routines to carry out the learning required to implement the organization's strategy (see Mohrman et al., Chapter 24 in this volume). These may be within an organization or may be cross-organizational. "Start conferences" (Emery, 1982), democratic dialogues (Gustavsen, 2001), work-based dialogue (Bjerlöv & Docherty, 2006), and debriefing procedures (Lipshitz, Popper, & Friedman, 2002) are different methods that have been successfully applied to allow participants to systematically learn from each other's experience through reflection and the encoding of new scientific knowledge in new practices and repositories.

Building a Tapestry of Learning Mechanisms

Most collaborative management research requires a tapestry or combination of different types of learning mechanisms. The cognitive mechanisms often form the value base for the structural and procedural mechanisms. Many mechanisms are combinations of structural and procedural ones, for example, democratic dialogue conferences. The work with the design of learning mechanisms in a collaborative research project may concern both the conduct of the project, that is, a means of the research, and part of its outcome, in the form of learning mechanisms implemented in the activity system under study, that is, an end. It may entail the formation of stable relationships with researchers to engage in collaborative R&D projects over time. Such relationships can well extend over several decades (see Mohrman et al., Chapter 24 in this volume, and Stebbins & Valenzuela, Chapter 23 in this volume).

Particular learning mechanisms often entail cognitive, structural, and procedural dimensions. For example, Emery's "start conferences" and Gustavsen's democratic dialogues, which were developed for use in collaborative research and are used to facilitate learning in cross-community, cross-level, and interorganizational groups, have both structural and procedural components. The structure includes the main stakeholders in the organization(s), levels, and communities. The process includes analysis and specification of the new capability, identification of the facilitating and obstructing conditions in the organization(s), and agreement on the key tasks to be addressed. These are discussed in different constellations during a two-day workshop. Cognitive frameworks are shared and emerge, and behavioral action plans are created. Such dialogues are carried out at regular intervals during the transformation or development process.

Common to the three types of learning mechanisms is that they stimulate the development of new shared meaning and enable learning and the generation of scientific knowledge across multiple networks and communities, across the different hierarchical levels of the organization, and across organizational boundaries. What follows is one illustration of a collaborative research project that used one configuration or tapestry of learning mechanisms.

AN ILLUSTRATION OF COLLABORATIVE MANAGEMENT RESEARCH: SKANDIA INSURANCE COMPANY

This project was conducted in the early 1970s, when the zeitgeist of the Scandinavian labor markets was strongly influenced by the work of Fred Emery and Einar Thorsrud, in Norway, who launched a collaborative research program on increased employee participation in working life. The program research was based on sociotechnical theory. The political impact of the program was such that the Joint Development Council between the central (national) union and employer bodies in Sweden (URAF) decided to conduct a similar program, comprising 10 projects that would cover participation and codetermination issues in different functions and different sectors. A program board was formed that included senior representatives from academia, the unions, and the employers' confederations. They selected which companies and researchers would be approached to participate. Skandia Insurance Company was chosen to represent the service sector, and the Stockholm School of Economics was chosen as the relevant research institution. The research was financed by Riksbanksfonden, a government research financing body.

P. G. Gyllenhammar, the CEO of Skandia (and later of Volvo), was supportive of the company's participation, and management/union steering committees were appointed at the head office and a regional office to follow and discuss the study. The main field experiment was carried out in Gothenburg in a department with about 100 employees engaged in corporate insurance work.

The leader of the research project was Professor Bengt Stymne, whose full-time team of five researchers had backgrounds in finance, organizational theory, organizational behavior, and clinical psychology. Their research model was composed of 17 propositions based primarily on sociotechnical theory. The research issues included

the design of work organization for increased participation;

the roles of researchers in such change processes;

the relations between change processes and people's quality of life;

the impact of involvement in "conditions of work" on unions' organization; and

factors affecting the design and usability of information systems.

The project entailed collaboration among researchers from different disciplines, and among researchers, managers at different levels, union representatives, and staff. A number of the intangible factors were formalized in various documents. This management research relied on testing a model in practice, though comparisons were made with corresponding units in other regions.

The strategic goal of the project was to realize the first research objective. This and the issues of resources and control over the development of the project were spelled out in a formal agreement among the parties involved. Thus, management or staff could veto any action proposed by the other. The conduct of the research experiment in the unit chosen had to be ratified by a secret staff ballot.

Two of the researchers were primarily responsible for the collaborative research study on the transformation of the operational department. They wrote two reports that were research reports, very similar to the "learning histories" developed and used as a learning mechanism by the Society for

Organizational Learning (see Bradbury, Chapter 28 in this volume). One report was an analysis of the obstructing and facilitating factors in the organizational development experiment (Stjernberg, 1975). The other was a detailed description of the collaborative researchers' roles and activities in the project, which included roughly 50 major interventions recommended by the researchers to the project group responsible for planning and implementing the transformation. These mostly took the form of suggestions regarding organizational design and activities in the project. Interventions also took place in staff units and management at higher levels, such as by arranging meetings between the management of the department unit and representatives of staff responsible for, for example, rationalization processes that were thought to interfere with the development processes. Other examples of interventions were to initiate meetings with the department's employees to discuss the development and the suggested new work organization, to initiate a discussion of conflicts between existing salary norms and the new organization, and to argue for including also the low-status tasks, such as typing, in the integrated workgroups. The impact of the suggestions and interventions varied from not being acted upon to being of importance. The roles of the collaborative researchers and their associated activities are shown in Figure 8.2.

The company had no previous experience of researcher-supported participative development projects. Thus, "selling the project" entailed the researchers making as clear as possible the norms for participation and what the project would mean for individuals in the department—not least, in terms of additional tasks. The "selling" ended in a secret ballot in the department where the employees voted to accept the researchers' involvement, and where they appointed six employee representatives who would share

the power of the change process with the management team of the department. The project group, at first, felt that it had plenty of time for their task of developing a new work organization, and therefore the researchers tried to transfer their notion of this task as more than redrawing the boundaries of the responsibilities of the different teams and their members.

The researchers "pushed" the project group to intensify their work, often in hard competition with the day-to-day workload. The researchers came to be active participants in the project group and argued their ideas as intensely as others argued theirs. This active participation eliminated, probably, the hopes of finding shortcuts through adapting "scientifically" proven solutions. The researchers managed to show, by contributing their knowledge, that most of the relevant knowledge for the design process was available within the department and within Skandia. By honestly contributing as much of their knowledge as possible at project meetings, the researchers managed to demystify the relevant knowledge sufficiently and eliminate the need for additional workshops. This is a very important lesson—it is *not* by contributing, but by holding back one's potential contributions that the academic researchers tend to create an unbalanced power in the development. Thus, their "consulting" did not take on the form of merely giving advice, or carrying out studies on behalf of the project group, but rather by contributing on equal terms.

Any local development process tends to run into conflicts with higher-level developments. In insurance, the production technology is computer-based information technology (IT). The URAF project was defined as being an organizational development project. In the 1970s, IT was the prime mover of change even more than today: IT systems were developed; then organizations were adapted to be able to use them. The project group was

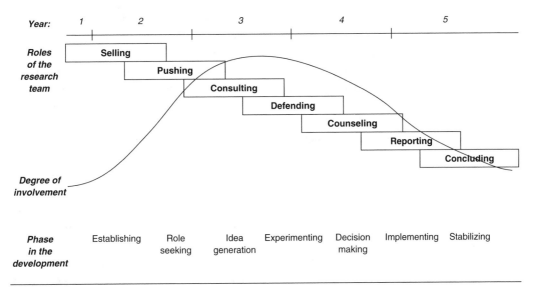

Figure 8.2   The Main Phases and Activities of the Collaborative Research Team in the Skandia Project

SOURCE: Based on Docherty (1976, p. 20).

informed that new systems were being developed that would be used in the department's business. Some of the proposed features of the new systems were seen to clearly interfere with important features of the organizational development of the project group planned for the department. The researchers became strongly involved as spokespersons defending the interests of the department, utilizing their academic legitimacy, their sociotechnical framework, and their understanding of the commitment expressed by the CEO at the start of the democratization project to give room for the local development activities. Their stance at this stage of the project gave rise to immediate and considerable irritation in some parts of management, but agreement was reached relatively quickly.

The radical ideas about new work roles and about sharing power in the department between the management team and the employee representatives meant that many issues surfaced, some of which were rather

personal. The trustful relationship between the project team, especially the department manager, and the researchers meant that they became partners, "counseling" in the discussions and deliberations during the implementation of these ideas. The development work led to semiautonomous groups, where most tasks were integrated rather than separately handled by functional specialists as before. It also led to the transfer of the department manager's formal rights to take decisions to a joint body, where that power became equally shared between management and employee representatives.

The researchers formed their own "reflection forum," meeting every Friday morning throughout the project to discuss, evaluate, and plan the research work. They also met in regular seminars with the researchers involved in the other nine projects to exchange experiences. Similarly, they met with the steering committees at Skandia regional and head offices and with the program steering committee.

The researchers were involved in reporting within Skandia, and in writing academic texts on each of the research issues. Separate drafts were discussed in the project group, in which the unit manager was most active, formulating conclusions from the project to the academic world—a process that had been going on all through the research project, but that intensified toward the end.

Researcher legitimacy was built up over time as the researchers and practitioners worked through their roles in the project group. As noted above, the researchers took a very active role, establishing dialogues between the representatives in the project group and their constituencies and promoting the carrying out of experiments with partial solutions to the new organization to generate experience and stimulate innovativeness. The researchers conducted "force field analyses" (Lewin, 1997), questionnaires, and interviews, the results of which were fed back for discussion in the project group. Some of the methods and tools constituted structural and procedural learning mechanisms in the project group. The most important factor, however, was the development of an open, trustful, risk-taking, and tolerant climate that came to characterize the work among all the members in the project group. The group allocated much of its meeting time to reflection on experiences gained and implications for the direction in which the project should develop.

The outcomes of the project reflected the researchers' sociotechnical framework. Single-task groups were replaced by multi-task groups that were responsible for specific groups of customers. Even the simpler tasks were included in the groups—a result of experimentation and much discussion. The value base of the change program, its cognitive mechanism, was confirmed in the new organization. The groups were given broad discretion in the planning and conduct of their work and the development of their

members. This entailed guidelines for individual members' and the team's competency development, giving priority to the team's needs, a key learning mechanism. An innovation from the project was the creation of a management group for the department made up of three managers (the department manager and two assistant managers, each responsible for half the teams) and three representatives elected by the personnel in the same way the project group was originally elected. This was a forum for collective reflection and for joint formulation of lessons and decisions on further development, that is, a further learning mechanism. Considering scientific inquiry, the researchers conducted performance comparisons between this department and departments in other regions in the company as part of the evaluation of the development process. This involved the development of a special organizational climate questionnaire.

The researchers experienced a number of the classical balancing dilemmas in collaborative research that have to do with the researchers' expert role, namely, the risk of manipulation or coercion and problems of value and goal conflicts (White & Wooten, 1986). These dilemmas concern balancing the researchers' ambitions for the practitioners with the latter's own ambitions for themselves. Are the researchers pushing them too far? How do researchers continue collaborative research in the face of opposition? How should the "advocate" role play out? How does the cost-benefit relationship for proposed changes appear for different parties? Who are the winners and losers in the short, medium, and long term? The line between researchers being politically astute and unethical is very fine. For example, their advice and argumentation to suit the needs of one stakeholder may lead to decisions of which the more or less foreseeable consequences may have very negative consequences for other stakeholders.

DISCUSSION

The relationships among collaborative management research, learning, learning mechanisms, and change are at the heart of this chapter. Collaborative management research is a matter of design, not just natural evolution of a research paradigm (Kolodny & Shani, 2006). Design in this context means conscious, active decisions on the space and measures to promote, facilitate, and support collaborative scientific processes, reflection, and learning (Nonaka et al., 2001). However, the issues of research, reflection, and learning are often not formally allotted clear priority on the management agenda in many organizations, and the prerequisites for these activities will in fact be steered by values, norms, and practices that have simply evolved and are not given a thought (Boud et al., 2006).

The Skandia project illustrated the proactive measures for the scientific process, reflection, and learning via tapestry of learning mechanisms that created the space for research and learning. It also illustrated some of the dilemmas in the utilization of learning mechanisms in collaborative management research. Within the context of framing some key issues for the rest of this *Handbook*, in this section we will discuss three challenges, namely, the multiple roles of learning mechanisms in collaborative management research; the design choices in the formation of learning mechanisms and their potential consequences; and learning mechanisms and the voices of inquiry and practice.

The Multiple Roles of Learning Mechanisms

Learning mechanisms, in one variation or another, are an integral part of most collaborative management research efforts. Learning mechanisms seem to play a variety of roles in collaborative management research. As the Skandia project illustrated, the tapestry of learning mechanisms that was created served as the engine that nurtured the community of inquiry (see Coghlan & Shani, Chapter 29 in this volume); as the space where the scientific process was designed and managed; as the place where experimentation with different organizational solutions was tested; as the space where sensemaking of the data that was collected was done and interpreted; and as the place where organizational changes were developed based on the results from the scientific studies.

As we will see in the chapters in this *Handbook*, while many collaborative research efforts use variations of learning mechanisms, many unresolved issues around learning mechanisms as means for collaborative inquiry require further scientific investigation. Examples include the role of the collaborative researcher(s) in the design of learning mechanisms (see, for example, Hatchuel & David, Chapter 7 in this volume); the dynamics of insider and outsider collaborative researchers and their effect on the creation and management of learning mechanisms (see, for example, Stebbins & Valenzuela, Chapter 23 in this volume); and the compatibility of the values and frames of reference of the collaborative researchers and practitioners in the design and facilitation of learning mechanisms in the pursuit of actionable knowledge creation (see, for example, Tandon & Farrell, Chapter 14 in this volume).

The Design of Learning Mechanisms

Just as there are many types of organizational designs, there are also various ways to design and manage organizational learning mechanisms. Collaborative researchers shoulder the responsibility of the design and facilitation of such a process. The design of a specific configuration is viewed as a rational choice among alternatives. Thus, the researcher brings expert knowledge about design criteria and about possible design configuration alternatives. As the Skandia example illustrated, the initial dialogue among the few individuals who initiate a project centers on the research focus and the most appropriate learning mechanisms through which the collaborative management research will be conducted (see, for example, Olascoaga & Kur, Chapter 12 in this volume).

The design of the learning mechanisms must meet the demands for learning that are deemed to exist in the collaborative research context. These may well include such factors as trust and respect, equitable distribution of power and control, basic skills and knowledge to participate in the research project, and adequate representation of different functional, hierarchical, and organizational interests in the activity system concerned in the research. Thus, in the Skandia illustration, the formal agreement specified equitable power distribution via the right of veto for all participants, and all the members of the project group participated in a four-day course on basic project management, group processes, and research methodologies. The work in the initial stages of the project focused on honing skills and building trust, respect, and self-confidence in the project group.

Other learning mechanisms focus on the elements of individual and collective learning in the collaborative research process: the character of the social climate, the communication process, the sensemaking, the time allotted for discussion of experiences and researchers' formal inputs, and the planning and decision making regarding further action. In the Skandia case, the researchers conducted climate surveys in the unit and parallel units regarding openness, risk taking, social and managerial support, readiness for change, perceived influence, and perceived satisfaction. These factors increased throughout the project. Researchers in collaborative research have differed in the extent to which they have become engaged in the basic tasks of the project or functioned as facilitators in the project group, regarding the reflection, sensemaking, and decision-making processes.

Regarding the different types of learning mechanisms, the cognitive mechanisms give the value base for the collaborative research. They define the degrees of freedom and participative character of the research and the extent to which the knowledge generated is of a general scientific character or a local, actionable character primarily of benefit to the participating organization(s). They also define whether the design of learning mechanisms is confined to the research process itself or even to the design of learning mechanisms in the organizations participating in the research. The structural and procedural mechanisms facilitate learning within the determined resource and power frameworks.

The Utilization of Existing Learning Mechanisms

Most organizations over time develop distinct routines, structures, and specialized resources to conduct development dialogues in the normal course of events. These can be fruitfully utilized in the collaborative management research context (see, for example, Kolodny & Halpern, Chapter 13 in this volume, and Olascoaga & Kur, Chapter 12 in this volume). This approach tends to utilize existing resources and thereby increase the efficiency of launching and maintaining the collaborative research process and diffusing its results throughout the organization. One of the risks associated with this approach is that the competencies and skill levels of specialist resources will be increased instead of those of line personnel in the units or departments involved.

Learning Mechanisms and the Voices of Inquiry and Practice

Collaborative management researchers face a wide array of challenges. Recently, the skills and challenges of collaborative action researchers in terms of the three voices and practices of inquiry were explored (Coghlan & Shani, 2007; Torbert & Taylor, 2007). There are several modes by which we can participate and inquire into our experience. Through *first-person voice/practice,* we can reflect on our own values and assumptions and how we behave, and so develop self-reflective skills.

Through *second-person voice/practice,* we engage in inquiry with others and work to create a community of inquiry. This involves not only the actual processes of collaboration but also the design and management of shared responsibility for the design and execution of the project, which enhances co-inquiry. The collaborative nature of the inquiry is central to the quality of the collaborative research process and its outcomes (Shani & Pasmore, 1985).

Through *third-person voice,* we move beyond immediate first- and second-person audiences to the impersonal wider community and make a contribution to the body of knowledge of what it is really like in these systems and how we can learn to manage change while being in the middle of it. Within the context of a collaborative management research project, individual contributions might include shared knowledge and continuous learning via the systematic facilitation of shared sensemaking. Individual contributions also might include interpretation and continuous experimentation and the ability to suspend preconceived and well-indoctrinated categories and analytic rules such that new knowledge can be created and acted upon. Through *third-person practice,* we work to extend the scale of the first- and second-person practice to a wider system such as other organizations or to influence policy making and implementation (see McGuire, Palus, & Torbert, Chapter 6 in this volume).

CONCLUSION

This chapter makes the case that learning mechanisms are critical features that foster collaborative management research and

learning processes and at the same time can be viewed as important outcomes of a collaborative research project. Four broad streams of applied research literature, namely the work organization, organization learning, learning at work, and organization design streams are reviewed, and the learning mechanisms that are utilized are identified. Based on the literature, the chapter identifies three types of learning mechanisms: cognitive, structural, and procedural (Shani & Docherty, 2003). The authors further argue that a tapestry of the three different kinds of learning mechanisms seems to have emerged in most collaborative management research projects.

The Skandia collaborative management research program was formally anchored in a research program initiated by the central employers' federation and unions in Sweden that resulted in a five-year partnership of ongoing scientific processes and learning. The researchers in the project had multidisciplinary backgrounds and created a community of inquiry together with managers, union representatives, and organizational members. A unique tapestry of learning mechanisms emerged during the project: for example, the formal agreement on the participative character of the project with the right to veto by all parties involved (an illustration of a cognitive learning mechanism). The project group functioned as a forum for the development of cycles of reflection on experience that led to scientific experiments and action (an illustration of structural and procedural mechanisms). And the discussions were based on data that was collected using scientific data collection methods (an illustration of procedural mechanisms).

The interplay between learning mechanisms and collaborative management research is complex. While we argued (and illustrated) the importance of the learning mechanism role, we also identified some of the challenges and the unresolved issues. The approach presented in this chapter complements some of the other approaches advanced in this section of the

Handbook. It also presents an additional lens through which one can examine the exemplar chapters that illustrate distinct collaborative management research projects.

NOTE

1. In the framework of this chapter, only a few references may be given in any area. The areas themselves are multidisciplinary and overlapping, so that many researchers have been active in several streams.

REFERENCES

Argyris, C., & Schön, D. A. (1996). *Organizational learning II: Theory, method and practice.* Reading, MA: Addison-Wesley.

Bjerlöv, M. (1999). Om lärande i verksamhetsanknytna samtal: En studie av prat och lärande i möten på en arbetsplats [Learning in work-related conversation in meetings at a workplace] (Work and Health series, No. 1999:1). Stockholm: National Institute for Working Life.

Bjerlöv, M., & Docherty, P. (2006). Collective reflection under ambiguity. In D. Boud, P. Cressey, & P. Docherty (Eds.), *Productive reflection at work: Learning for changing organizations* (pp. 93–105). London: Routledge.

Boud, D., Cressey, P., & Docherty, P. (Eds.). (2006). *Productive reflection at work: Learning for changing organizations.* London: Routledge.

Bushe, G., & Shani, A. B. (Rami). (1991). *Parallel learning structures.* Reading, MA: Addison-Wesley.

Coghlan, D., & Brannick, T. (2005). *Doing action research in your own organization* (2nd ed.). London: Sage.

Coghlan, D., & Shani, A. B. (Rami). (2007). Insider action research: The dynamics of developing new capabilities. In P. Reason & H. Bradbury (Eds.), *The Sage handbook of action research* (2nd ed.). London: Sage.

Crossan, M. M., Lane, H. W., & White, R. E. (1999). An organizational learning framework: From intuition to institution. *Academy of Management Review, 24*(3), 522–537.

DiBella, A. J. (2001). *Learning practices: Assessment and action for organizational improvement.* Upper Saddle River, NJ: Prentice Hall.

Dilschmann, A., & Berg, H. (1996). *Learning: Have we time to learn? Can we afford not to? Regional Employment Council in Gothenberg and Bohus County.* Stockholm: National Institute for Working Life.

Dixon, N. (2001). *Common knowledge.* Boston: Harvard Business School Press.

Docherty, P. (1976). *Forskarroller in en aktionsforskningsprojekt* [Researcher roles in an action research project]. *Delrapport 6 i serien Organisationsutveckling för ökat medinflytane i tjänstemannaföretag.* Stockholm: EFI and PA-Rådet.

Docherty, P. (1996). *Läroriket: Vägar och vägväl i den lärande organisationen* [Learning roadmaps: Roads and crossroads for the learning organization]. Stockholm: Arbetslivsinstitutet and Utbildningsradion.

Docherty, P., Ljung, A., & Stjernberg, T. (2006). The changing practice of action research. In J. Löwstedt & T. Stjernberg (Eds.), *Producing management knowledge: Research as practice* (pp. 221–236). London: Routledge.

Elkjaer, B. (2005). *När laering går på arbejde: Et pragmatisk blik på laering i arbejdslivet* [When learning goes to work: A pragmatic look at learning in work life]. Fredriksberg, Denmark: Forlaget Samfundslitteratur.

Ellström, P.-E. (2001). Integrating learning and work: Conceptual issues and critical conditions. *Human Resource Development Quarterly, 12*(4), 421–435.

Emery, F., & Emery, M. (1974). *Participative design: Work and community life.* Canberra: National University of Australia.

Emery, M. (1982). *Searching in new directions in new ways for new times.* Canberra, Australia: Office of the Ministry of Labour and the Office of the Quality of Working Life Centre.

Fenwick, T. (2003). Professional growth plans: Possibilities and limitations of an organization-wide employee development strategy. *Human Resource Development Quarterly, 14*(1), 59–77.

Fenwick, T., & Rubenson, K. (2005, December). *Taking stock: A review of research on learning in work, 1999–2004.* Paper presented at the Fourth International Conference on Research on Work and Learning, University of Technology, Sydney, Australia.

Fricke, W., & Totterdill, P. (Eds.). (2004). *Action research in workplace innovation and regional development.* Amsterdam: John Benjamins.

Friedman, V. J., Lipshitz, R., & Overmeer, W. (2001). Creating conditions for organizational learning. In M. Dierkes, A. Berthoin Antal, J. Child, and I. Nonaka (Eds.), *Handbook of organizational learning and knowledge* (pp. 757–774). Oxford, UK: Oxford University Press.

Gustavsen, B. (1992). *Dialogue and development.* Assen/Maastricht, The Netherlands: van Gorum.

Gustavsen, B. (2001). Theory and practice: The mediating discourse. In P. Reason & H. Bradbury (Eds.), *Handbook of action research: Participative inquiry and practice* (pp. 17–27). London: Sage.

Gustavsen, B., Colbjørnsen, T., & Pålhaugen, Ø. (Eds.). (1998). *Development coalitions in working life: The "Enterprise Development 2000" program in Norway.* Amsterdam and Philadelphia: John Benjamins.

Isaacs, W. N. (1993). Taking flight: Dialogue, collective thinking, and organizational learning. *Organizational Dynamics, 22*(2), 24–39.

Kolb, D. (1984). *Experiential learning: Experience as a source of learning and development.* Englewood Cliffs, NJ: Prentice Hall.

Kolodny, H., & Shani, A. B. (Rami). (2006). Researching organization design: Comparative versus collaborative approaches. In J. Löwstedt & T. Stjernberg (Eds.), *Producing management knowledge: Research as practice* (pp. 199–220). London: Routledge.

Lapidoth, J., Jr. (1996). *Organisatoriskt lärande i ett tillväxtföretag* [Organizational learning in a high-growth company]. Stockholm: National Institute for Working Life.

Lewin, K. (1997). Field theory and learning. In K. Lewin, *Field theory in social science* (D. Cartwright, Ed., pp. 212–230). Washington, DC: American Psychological Association.

Lipshitz, R., Friedman, V., & Popper, M. (2006). *Demystifying organizational learning.* Thousand Oaks, CA: Sage.

Lipshitz, R., Popper, M., & Friedman, V. J. (2002). A multifacet model of organizational learning. *Journal of Applied Behavioral Science, 32*, 292–305.

Lipshitz, R., Popper, M., & Oz, S. (1996). Building learning organizations: The design and implementation of organizational learning mechanisms. *Journal of Applied Behavioral Science, 32*(2), 292–305.

Nielsen, P., & Lundvall, B.-Å. (2003). *Innovation, learning organisations and industrial relations.* Aalborg: Danish Research Unit for Industrial Dynamics, Working Paper No. 03-07. Aalborg University.

Nilsson, T. (2005). Arrangerade nätverk för kompetensutveckling: Fackets roll i lokal utvecklingsarbetet [Arranged networks for competence development: The union's role in local development work] (Work Life in Transition series, No. 2004:6). Stockholm: National Institute for Working Life.

Nonaka, I., & Konno, N. (1998). The concept of "ba": Building a foundation for knowledge creation. *California Management Review, 40*(3), 1–15.

Nonaka, I., Konno, N., & Toyama, R. (2001). The emergence of "ba": A conceptual framework for the continuous and self-transcending process of knowledge creation. In I. Nonaka & T. Nishiguchi (Eds.), *Knowledge emergence: Social, technical, and evolutionary dimensions of knowledge creation* (pp. 13–29). New York: Oxford University Press.

Pavlovsky, P. (2001). The treatment of organizational learning in management science. In M. Dierkes, A. Berthoin Antal, J. Child, & I. Nonaka (Eds.), *Handbook of organizational learning and knowledge* (pp. 61–89). Oxford, UK: Oxford University Press.

Pavlovsky, P., Forslin, J., and Reinhart, R. (2001). Practices and tools of organizational learning. In M. Dierkes, A. Berthoin Antal, J. Child, & I. Nonaka (Eds.), *Handbook of organizational learning and knowledge* (pp. 775–793). Oxford, UK: Oxford University Press.

Pearson, M., & Smith, D. (1985). Debriefing in experience-based learning. In D. Boud, R. Keogh, & D. Walker (Eds.), *Reflection: Turning experience into learning* (pp. 69–84). London: Routledge.

Pettigrew, A., Whittington, R., Melin, L., Sanchez-Runde, C., van den Bosch, F. A. J., Ruigrok, W., et al. (Eds.). (2003). *Innovative forms of organising: International perspectives.* London: Sage.

Popper, M., & Lipshitz, R. (1998). Organizational learning mechanisms: A structural and cultural approach to organizational learning. *Journal of Applied Behavioral Science, 34,* 161–179.

Revans, R. W. (1982). *Origins and growth of action learning.* Bromley, UK: Chartwell-Bratt.

Richtner, A. (2004). *Balancing knowledge creation: Organizational slack and knowledge creation in product development.* Stockholm: Economic Research Institute at Stockholm School of Economics.

Senge, P. M. (1991). *The fifth discipline: The art and practice of the learning organization.* New York: Doubleday/Currency.

Shani, A. B. (Rami), & Docherty, P. (2003). *Learning by design: Building sustainable organizations.* Oxford, UK: Blackwell.

Shani, A. B. (Rami), & Pasmore, W. A. (1985). Organizational inquiry: Towards a new paradigm of the action research process. In D. Warrick (Ed.), *Contemporary organization development* (pp. 438–448). Glenview, IL: Scott, Foresman.

Stebbins, M., Shani, A. B. (Rami), & Docherty, P. (2006). Reflection during a crisis turnaround: Management use of learning mechanisms. In D. Boud, P. Cressey, & P. Docherty (Eds.), *Productive reflection at work: Learning for changing organizations* (pp. 106–119). London: Routledge.

Stjernberg, T. (1975). Hindrande och stödjande factorer i ett förändringsförlopp inom Skandia. [Obstructing and supportive factors in a change process in Skandia] (Organizational Development for Increased Co-determination in Service Companies series, No. 2). Stockholm: EFI and PA-Rådet.

Thorsrud, E., & Emery, F. (1969). *Medinflytande och engagemang i arbetet: Norska försök med självstyrande grupper* [Influence and commitment at work: Norwegian experiments with autonomous workgroups]. Stockholm: Utvecklingsrådet för samarbetsfrågor.

Torbert, W. R., & Taylor, S. (2007). Action research methods: Unilaterally creating mutuality. In P. Reason & H. Bradbury (Eds.), *The Sage handbook of action research* (2nd ed.). London: Sage.

Trist, E., & Murray, H. (Eds.). (1990). *The social engagement of social science: Vol. I. The socio-psychological perspective.* Philadelphia: University of Pennsylvania Press.

Trist, E., & Murray, H. (Eds.) (1993). *The social engagement of social science: Vol. II. The socio-technical perspective.* Philadelphia: University of Pennsylvania Press.

Weick, K. (1995). *Sense-making in organizations.* Thousand Oaks, CA: Sage.

White, L. P., & Wooten, K. C. (1986). *Professional ethics and practice in organization development.* New York: Praeger.

Wilhelmson, L. (1998). *Lärande dialog: Samtalsmönster, perspektivförändring och lärande i gruppsamtal* [Learning dialogue: Conversation patterns, perspective changes, and learning] (Work and Health series, No. 1998:16). Stockholm: National Institute for Working Life.

Zand, D. (1981). *Information, organization and power.* New York: McGraw-Hill.

CHAPTER 9

The Research Circle Approach

A Democratic Form for Collaborative Research in Organizations

Lars Holmstrand

Gunilla Härnsten

Jan Löwstedt

ABSTRACT

The research circle approach (RCA) is an example of collaborative research based on two explicit values: the belief in the power of knowledge and the need for democracy in the workplace. The RCA builds on a tradition of vocational education and has its roots in the modernization of Sweden. Four examples of quite different change efforts are used to present how research circle work is conducted and the kind of practical as well as scientific knowledge that is developed from working with this approach.

The Research Circle Approach (RCA) is an approach to collaborative research that aims to increase the ability of the participants to make a difference in organizational change projects as well as, more generally, to increase their preparedness to act when the need or opportunity arises, to influence the system of action in an organization. The RCA builds on "study circles," a well-established education tradition with roots in the modernization of Swedish society. The circles are founded on two basic values. One is a belief in the power of knowledge. In the study circle, you gain knowledge and experience. The other is a belief in democracy, in the sense that a better society can be built if everyone has a voice and is allowed to participate. A research circle is a study circle where a researcher plays an important role as a source of knowledge, as a liaison to academic knowledge, and as an organizer.

The RCA has many points in common with action research and related schools of participatory research such as participatory action research (PAR). However, in addition to involving relatively disadvantaged groups in research, the PAR school of thought generally takes a distinctly normative and ethical position in asserting that research is needed in order to make social inequality and injustice visible. These conditions, moreover, require that the researchers take action to bring about change (Reason & Bradbury, 2001). The RCA also finds that there is good reason to make research more collaborative and participatory. In contrast to action research, the RCA's justification for participation is that it improves the democratic process by creating and sharing knowledge. In this chapter, we interpret the RCA from the perspective that practitioners participate in research circles in order to gain knowledge in order to be better equipped to influence the system of action they are part of, be this a firm, a hospital, or a local community. The RCA does not make a distinction between managers and workers or between the resourceful and the disadvantaged; all can take part in the circle. What is essential, though, is that the work in the circle reflects democratic values that allow everyone to have a say and that the more powerful participants are not there to command but to listen, understand, and explain.

A main argument for participatory research is that the knowledge construction, the inquiry, is conducted in cooperation with the people concerned. As a consequence, the latter are regarded as important knowledge sources and not as passive spectators or objects that may, possibly, eventually be given the opportunity to take part in the usually largely arranged and filtered research findings. By including the groups affected by the research in the research process, not only are the research resources considerably enlarged; the research itself is also democratized. The hierarchy between the researcher and the researched-upon people is radically changed. It is all about the raison d'être of collaborative research, which is doing research *with* each other and not *for* or *on* others (see Docherty & Shani, Chapter 8 in this volume). In this context, we thus find the concept of "actionable knowledge" useful, since a key argument for this kind of approach is to take the practitioners' knowledge interest seriously. For us, actionable knowledge implies a deeper understanding of the relevant contexts that can supply the grounds for action where and when conditions make that possible.

The benefits to social science of engaging in collaborative research methods such as the RCA are above all radically enlarged empirical knowledge and a contextually based understanding against which theoretical perspectives can be tested. Thus, scientific knowledge will often be challenged, modified, and developed.

The RCA has been used in this type of research for a variety of research and development projects in Swedish organizations. Research circles can take different shapes (Holmstrand & Härnsten, 2003), but characteristic for all of them is the collaboration between practitioners and researchers and the dialogue between the different knowledge bases these two types of participants represent (cf. Holmstrand, Lindström, Löwstedt, & Englund, 1994).

In this chapter, we begin with a brief presentation of a theoretical background for collaborative research circle work in organizations. We then describe some vital aspects of the Swedish experience with research circles from the 30 years they have existed, to provide a background for the presentation that follows: four research circle project cases chosen from different contexts. These stories are followed by a discussion of what characterizes the role of the researcher, the types and sources of knowledge, and the process of the RCA. Finally, we draw some preliminary conclusions about the actionable knowledge and the scientific knowledge gained from our examples.

A THEORETICAL BACKGROUND

From a micro-oriented view on knowledge in organizations (Knorr-Cetina, 1981), knowledge is enacted in an organization's organizing processes. According to this view, all members of an organization are carriers of organizational knowledge in their day-to-day activities and act accordingly, both in the production of institutionalized behavior and in what are considered to be new and unique situations (Löwstedt, 1993). Such knowledge is neither explicit nor independent of time and space. The use of knowledge in a specific situation is dependent on the interpretations and negotiations made by coacting organizational members. The knowledge used in a situation is also shaped by the institutionalized perception these actors have of questions such as these: What business are we in? What is the purpose of this activity? And how do we achieve our (my) goals? (Löwstedt & Stymne, 2002). Knowledge is also dependent on relations between the actors in the organization because knowledgeable action presupposes that it is perceived to be mutual and legitimate.

Taking this route to the analysis of knowledge in organizations where knowledge is considered emergent, distributed, situated, and activity- and relation-dependent (Löwstedt & Stymne, 2002), one must ask how organizational processes can be supported and researched by the researcher in collaboration with the practitioner. In educational research, there is a tradition that focuses on the democratic aspects of this type of day-to-day knowledge in organizations.

Building on many years of work in study circles, research circles, and other situations where a group of people has the opportunity to engage in a constructive dialogue for social change, educational research has been important for the development of the concept of democratic knowledge processes (cf. Holmstrand & Härnsten, 2003). Our understanding of democratic knowledge processes is embedded in how we view democracy. Arenas where different types of knowledge and experience are blended, managed, developed, challenged, and questioned can be arenas for innovative thinking. We are referring here to processes that stem from and respect knowledge, experiences, and conditions that have been silenced in many contexts. The point, then, is to challenge structures that hinder development and oppress and diminish the inherent strengths and capabilities of people and groups.

Such democratic knowledge research processes can lead to several possible outcomes. In the process of improving insights on the specific situation at hand, approaches are used to infuse the experience gained from these processes with knowledge from research. The research circle thereby provides an opportunity for the practitioners to improve their capacity to act with an improved knowledge base and from an empowered position in the organization.

For the researcher, the RCA is not only a way to get rich and thick descriptions about knowledge development and change processes in organizations. First, with its focus on problems defined by the practitioners, it is a means by which to overcome the relevance gap discussed in management research. Second, there are epistemological arguments that can be found in the constructionist view of knowledge in organizations. From this point of view, developing knowledge about organizational and managerial issues using the RCA recognizes the emergent, context-dependent, and situated nature of organizational knowledge. Third, using the RCA is also one way to address the fact that researching social processes in organizations is also a social and often messy practice (Löwstedt & Stjernberg, 2006) and must therefore be conducted in a collaborative mood.

Research Circles: The Work Process

The research circle is a meeting place, a forum, where organized knowledge construction takes place and knowledge development is established in cooperation with all participants. It is a place to create an exchange of ideas and experiences to develop new insights needed for problem areas chosen for the research circle project. Participants have the opportunity to give expression to their own experiences and knowledge and to discuss and modify them in the light of other perspectives. Different types of knowledge can be contrasted, thereby challenging simplistic or narrow perspectives. This mutual influence entails a kind of democratization because more people participate in the knowledge construction. The open and critical but simultaneously constructive attitude toward knowledge constitutes an important basis for the democratic knowledge process. The objective of the research circle is to study a problem in order to understand it better and be able to "attack" it from the new knowledge base developed in the circle. Core values in collaborative research conducted according to the RCA are summarized as follows:

- Collaboration between researchers and practitioners needs to be based on equal standing.
- Developing knowledge in organizations is embedded in how we view democracy.
- Structures that hinder development and diminish the inherent capabilities of people and groups are to be challenged.

- Actionable knowledge implies a deeper understanding of relevant contexts, which can supply grounds for action.
- There is no one best way—there are a wide range of ways to approach organizational problems using the RCA.

How to approach a project with the RCA can naturally vary considerably depending on the problem under study, the participants, and the resources available for the work. There are, however, some conditions and routines that are usually present. As with any study circle, the recommendation is to not include more than seven or eight participants and to meet regularly a number of times. Larger change programs can be organized into several coordinated research circles.

First of all, it is important to consider the different knowledge resources that can be used. Here, the knowledge and experience of the participants relevant to the issue under scrutiny are given special priority. The researcher's knowledge about the issue is also valuable, as is his or her general professional competence to structure and systematically study a problem in a critical and distanced manner. Further, it is possible that the knowledge of other researchers (or experts of some kind) may be needed, and here the researcher has the added task of finding the right person to invite to one of the circle meetings.

There are no rules for how the work of a research circle should be organized. It is the responsibility of each new circle to come up with its own way of working. The participants themselves should decide on the organization and content of the circle, but there are a few routines that have proved to be useful.

When the work begins, there usually exist considerable cultural gaps to bridge between two different worlds. The first meeting of a research circle is therefore often devoted to developing trust, a common understanding of the problem, and getting to know one another. It is important for the researcher to be open and receptive to the viewpoints of the other participants. Often the problem that has been identified by the participants to be worked with needs further clarification, and it can be a good idea to systematically chart the experiences and viewpoints the participants already have. Here, the researcher has a kind of moderator role.

In principle, anyone in the circle can take the role of circle leader, in the sense of chairing meetings and being responsible for the progress of the work. However, this is a task that is frequently handed over to the researcher. Another important task is to document the proceedings of the circle sessions in some way to capture at least the essence of the knowledge exchange and discussion that takes place. This can be done by the researcher or another participant, and the task is often rotated so that all participants contribute to writing circle minutes or notes that are distributed to all circle participants. These notes can then be reviewed at the beginning of the following session.

The specific competence of the coordinating researcher in a research circle is not only his or her area of expertise but the researcher's skills in formulating questions that are possible to investigate and find answers to in the specific situation, and also his or her knowledge about where to find knowledge or expertise that can be brought into the circle to support the work on the problem it is trying to solve. These skills are important to facilitate the development in a research circle and for the researcher to get a close and detailed understanding of the development process in the organization under study.

In addition to the knowledge resources mentioned, research circles often undertake systematic inquiries of their own. For example, if the issue in focus concerns a work environment, the participants might interview workmates or distribute a questionnaire. In order to widen the perspective or to get a deeper understanding of some aspect of

the problem under study, the researcher often contributes by reading relevant research literature and presenting an overview. The following are some guiding principles of RCA work:

- There are a variety of ways to conduct collaborative research in accordance with the RCA—no formal procedures.
- The problems formulated by the participants are in focus to the knowledge development process.
- The expertise of the researcher is to translate conceptions of problems and ideas of solution into research questions for a scientific investigation.
- The role of the researcher is to be a liaison to academic knowledge and an organizer of the discovery process.
- Research circles are small and in larger projects are organized into several coordinated research circles.
- Research circle work recognizes that there are considerable cultural gaps between the world of researchers and the day-to-day life of practitioners.
- Research circles preferably undertake inquires of their own.

BACKGROUND: 30 YEARS OF EXPERIENCE WITH THE RESEARCH CIRCLE

The research circle stems from the tradition of study circles, a popular education movement that was an important form for adult education in Sweden in the early 20th century. The current labor-market context in which the research circle was introduced during the late 1970s is also important. This was a period of radical labor rights reform in Sweden (e.g., the Co-determination Act and the Work Environment Act). The Swedish labor market is further characterized by a model that includes collective bargaining and a high degree of trade union organization (on average, 80% of the workforce, according to

Kjellberg, 2001), as well as a strong preference for rational arguments, facts, and consensus (Berglund & Löwstedt, 1996).

Most people in Sweden have participated in some kind of study circle. It is hardly a coincidence that the study circle tradition is still important. The popular movements with their roots in the second half of the 19th century depended to a great extent on this form of education to develop their own knowledge and perspectives.

The research circle was introduced some 30 years ago in the context of cooperation between universities and the trade union part of the labor movement (see, e.g., Holmstrand & Härnsten, 2003). An important element was to give participants access to all the research that could contribute to their understanding of the issue under study. Research circles have been used all over Sweden in various contexts. However, although several hundred research circles have been documented, knowledge about this collaborative form has not spread outside a rather limited network of researchers. It has shown such great promise as an interesting and challenging meeting place for researchers and practitioners that it deserves to be known to a larger audience.

Different Research Circles

The idea of using research circles as a link between unions and universities originally developed in southern Sweden, with Lund University as its base, and then spread to other parts of Sweden. After some time, research circles began to be initiated by actors other than trade unions, and it is probably fair to say that, today, they are an established way of working with knowledge development in organizations.

There seem to be no restrictions as to what kinds of topics or issues research circles might be arranged around. Circles have been formed to study issues as varied as work environments, the professional knowledge of women

in low-paid jobs, general problems of the public sector, and opportunities for a municipality to find ways forward in a particular situation of crisis. Although it is extremely difficult to estimate the total number of research circles that have been started, a rough estimate would be approximately 400. Since the issues under study in the circles can vary considerably, researchers from many disciplines (e.g., sociology, education, economics, business studies, social and economic geography, history, and economic history) have been involved. But even if the disciplinary ties of these researchers differ, they tend to have in common a similar curiosity and willingness to listen to other people.

Research About Research Circles

Research about research circles is relatively scarce. More systematic and detailed research about the knowledge process and the results that can be achieved under different conditions has only just begun. In an early evaluation of their use, Gunnarsson and Perby (1981) found research circles to constitute a fruitful method in the cooperation between unions and researchers. In 1990, the Swedish Centre for Working Life organized a conference on research circles with contributions from several researchers (Arbetslivscentrum, 1990); Holzhausen states in the preface to the proceedings that practitioners and researchers are participating "in a mutual work to develop new knowledge." He notes that they bring to the circle their respective knowledge, skills, and insights and together define the conditions for research circle work. The contribution made by the researchers was considered to be composed of reflections based on their own experience of research circle work. Härnsten (1994) discusses the educational roots and characteristics of the research circle against the background of research information, adult education, and study circles. She concludes that a vitalization is needed in all three of these areas in order to reach the basic intentions, and that the research circle may be able to offer this. A few limited but systematic studies about the process in research circles (Bracken & Lindström, 1993), the experiences of participants (Lundh, 1995), and the experiences of researchers (Schüldt, 1996) all point to the fruitfulness of this kind of work. But judging from these studies, it also seems obvious that the research circle format places considerable demands on the researcher, who has a delicate and difficult task, and who should be a multiskilled person. Lundberg (1997), who describes the research circle from an empowerment perspective, writes in a similar vein about the importance of the researcher's "personality, social talent, willingness to listen and other similar characteristics" (p. 56) for the possible outcomes of the circle work. He also emphasizes that the research circle needs to be nurtured and used in a sensible way, based on participatory and democratic ideas. He also writes that "with favourable conditions" the results can be astonishing. Recently, the RCA has been used also in research reported in doctoral theses (Wingård, 1998; Enö, 2005), and several works are in progress.

FOUR CASES OF THE RESEARCH CIRCLE APPROACH

Next, we present four examples of projects where the RCA has been central. The examples are chosen to illustrate how this approach can be used in a wide range of organizational contexts. The first two cases are R&D projects of relatively short duration conducted in different kinds of companies. The third example is a project that concerned a more far-reaching organizational change and lasted more than two years. The fourth project included in principle most inhabitants of a (small) municipality. We have named the cases the Engineering Plant, the Insurance Company, the Hospital, and the Municipality.

The case of the Engineering Plant concerns a family-owned small or medium-sized enterprise (SME) where two research circles met regularly for one year, focusing on issues concerning production planning and product development. The practitioners involved were manufacturing managers and employees. In the case of the Insurance Company, the entire private insurance department, consisting of 50 employees, met in seven study circles over the course of a year to start a process of on-the-job learning from each other and to create a more flexible and integrated organization. Both of these cases were part of the Work Environment Fund Program for Learning at Work and had the additional aim of studying the application of the RCA in this context.

The Hospital case concerned a special hospital for mentally retarded criminals, a unit that was under threat of being closed. In this project, the tacit knowledge of the employees was the focus of the six research circles that met over a period of two years. In the Municipality project, gender issues and education in a thinly populated rural community were in focus. Here, seven research circles and a number of other collaborative research activities were organized.

The Engineering Plant

The first case presented concerns a development effort in a family-owned SME and its engineering plant in Eskilstuna, Sweden. The initiative for these projects came from a group within the Work Environment Fund Program for Learning at Work in cooperation with regional unions looking for a suitable industrial company to work with. Two parallel research circles were formed in this company: one focusing on production planning and the other on achieving shorter lead times in product development.

Representatives for different functions in the manufacturing organization, including management, participated in the circles. The aim of these circles was to improve company practices through collaborative learning in these specific areas of interest. The role of the coordinator was to design, together with the participants, a learning process able to match the local formulation of problems and possible solutions to these problems with research-based knowledge and other types of expertise. More specifically, the researcher's task was to act as a facilitator to the process of problem formulation and to act as a knowledge broker with expertise to visit the research circle meetings to present and discuss the possibilities of transforming their ideas of best practice to the actual setting in the company.

The two circles met on a monthly basis and lasted for approximately one year. The first meetings were dedicated to discussion of development issues surrounding the areas of knowledge the participants identified as areas they wanted the circle to look into. These meetings resulted in a proposed structure for the following meetings and ideas on the content. The role of the researcher in this planning process was to help the participants formulate their needs for new knowledge into questions and themes that could be covered during the following meetings—for example, by inviting other researchers or consultants to provide input to the work in the circle. The work in the circles finished off with a one-and-a-half-day workshop, where ideas for improvements from the two circles were presented to the management group.

The results from the project show that the participants were very pleased. They report that they have gained important knowledge from the circles about problems and questions that they themselves formulated in the beginning of the research circle process.[1] When it comes to the outcomes to improve

the production planning process and the product development process, the results were not as noticeable, though the participants gained an increased capacity to analyze potential prospects for change and more salient knowledge about alternative ways to organize, respectively. The lack of implementation was due to several factors. The most obvious was that it was not the aim of the research circles in this company to implement changes in the organization, only to infuse ongoing discussion in the company with up-to-date knowledge on important issues for the company.

The Insurance Company

In this case, the research circles approach was used to start an R&D project and a developmental process of learning at work in an insurance company in Uppsala (Holmstrand, Englund, & Lindström, 1995). The company has a special profile—it is a locally oriented nonprofit organization owned by its customers. The background of this project was the growing competition in that particular part of the industry, which was considered a long-term threat to this kind of enterprise with a traditional and somewhat old-fashioned structure. The activities concerned the entire private insurance department consisting of approximately 50 employees.

The aim of the project was to contribute to a change in the organizational culture toward a more flexible and learning-oriented climate and to achieve closer integration between the various professional groups within the department. The idea was also to use the project to initiate a process of learning from each other on the job. For this purpose, seven study circles with researcher support were started, each with six to eight participants.

Prior to commencement, 14 volunteers from the employees were given a two-day circle leader education by three of the researchers in the project. A steering group consisting of representatives from the company management, the local union, and the project then decided how to compose the seven circles. Each circle group had one circle leader and one backup. The seven circles held their first session in late winter, and then a total of five meetings before the summer vacation and four more during the autumn. After every session, the circle leaders met with the project group (the company project leader and the project secretary, the scientific leader of the project, and the two evaluators of the project). The evaluators had then been following the work of all the circles as observers. A continuous exchange of experience between the circle leaders and between the project group and the circles was thus possible. At these meetings, the possible need for additional researchers or other experts to participate in the following session of each circle was also discussed.

Most of the circles had visiting researchers or other experts on at least one occasion. Another type of support for the work of the circles was provided in the form of four special seminars/lectures given by researchers for all the participants (and open to the rest of the company as well).

The project was carefully evaluated and documented. Each circle was responsible for writing brief minutes from every session. At the more than 60 sessions, an observer/evaluator was present and noted things such as the kind of interaction taking place and what topics were discussed. At the end of each session, a short questionnaire was distributed to all participants. Before the circles began and after their last sessions, more elaborate questionnaires were completed. In-depth interviews were also carried out with 12 participants before and after the circle work.

The results clearly show that a process of change had started and that the majority of the employees supported and actively participated in it. There was a marked change in attitudes toward a greater openness and understanding of other professional groups and the company as a whole. Most of the participants expressed satisfaction with the circle method. Some of them felt that it provided a way of developing creativity and solidarity. The participants also emphasized the great knowledge potential that had become visible at the individual level as well as at the group level. Higher confidence in the future of the company was also noted as a result of the circles.

There appear to be several circumstances of importance for the relatively successful outcome of this project. There can be no doubt about the fundamental contribution made by the collaborative approach of the project. The links to research and the participation of researchers provided a critical and fruitful perspective. The active support by the management and their demonstrated confidence in the employees grew as the project went on. The nonprofit nature of the company and broad participation in the circles were additional conditions of utmost importance. These factors provided many advantages—above all, the firm belief among the employees that they themselves had achieved something together. Or as they put it, *we have done it ourselves; we own the process.* Thus, what was initiated in this project would appear to be nothing less than democratic knowledge processes.

The Hospital

In the third case, the so-called "Salberga project," six research circles were organized with 6 to 10 participants and one researcher each. The participants were all employees working with mentally retarded criminals at a special hospital. The aim of the project was to systematically chart the tacit knowledge of these employees and thereby also strengthen their professional identity in order to improve care. The research circles had meetings regularly during two years.

The Salberga project used research circles as a central ingredient. It took place at the Salberga Special Hospital for mentally handicapped criminals in Sala over a period of 18 months (see Lönnheden, 1997). Research circles had been used there before (Härnsten, 1994), initiated in part through the trade union (the Swedish Municipal Workers' Union). The background was that the existence of the special hospital was threatened. The Security Foundation for Municipalities therefore financed the project in order to address and develop the knowledge and experience of the personnel and simultaneously strengthen their opportunities in the labor market.

In preparation for the research circles, two days of search conferences were arranged in order to formulate the themes for the different circles to work with. The background and the idea of the project were presented to the participants, and it was made clear that the knowledge and experience of the employees was the intended basis for the activities. The democratic spirit of the project was also emphasized. In spite of the suspicions and discouragement resulting from the closure threat, the participants left the conference in a slightly more hopeful frame of mind. The group work and discussions of the search conference made it possible to identify the themes for the research circles to continue to work with.

At another introductory meeting with the circles, two participants from each circle were chosen to serve as circle leaders. These people were given one day of training. After these preparations, the six research circles worked with their chosen themes over the two-year period. The participating researchers had multifaceted backgrounds and represented a diversity of disciplines including education, psychology, psychiatry, medical jurisprudence, and criminology. In between the circle meetings, the two project leaders met with the circle leaders to exchange experiences and to coordinate the work. The researchers also had similar meetings.

The results of each research circle are documented in separate leaflets. It is evident that much of the previous tacit knowledge of the employees was made visible through the project. It can further be noted that the participating researchers developed scientific knowledge within their respective disciplines. It is also a fact that the special hospital for mentally handicapped criminals was not closed but integrated into a larger department for forensic psychiatry. For all involved, the project represented a bewildering experience of trying to achieve something constructive under the threat of closure. It was a great challenge for us as researchers to find ways of development for the participants, who were used to being treated as unimportant and objects of reorganization. The project report (Lönnheden, 1997), entitled "When the Silent 'Knowledge Shapers' Start Speaking," captures some of the essence of this kind of work. Lönnheden concludes the report by emphasizing the strength of research circles in providing time for reflection and discussion of important issues. It was clear that considerable tacit knowledge had now become visible and been made explicit. Knowledge from patients as well as employees was developed in the project. The extent of this new knowledge was impressive, and there is reason to believe that this case is not unique and that there are similar hidden resources of tacit knowledge in many other contexts.

The Municipality

In the fourth case, the Municipality or "Jokkmokk project," the focus was on gender issues and education in a rural municipality. A starting point was the gender pattern indicating that boys were noted to achieve considerably less well at school than girls, and that girls to a great extent and to a much higher degree left the municipality for further studies at the university level. This pattern meant that, in the long run, the whole existence of the municipality was threatened. The aim of the project was thus to start a broad knowledge process around these issues. Could involving the wider issues of quality of education, quality of life, and survival of a rural community in general help to develop an emancipating collective knowledge?

The Municipality of Jokkmokk is situated at the Arctic Circle. With an area of 19,474 square kilometers, it is the second largest municipality in Sweden and two-thirds the size of the Netherlands. Half of Jokkmokk's area is made up of an extensive mountain region with national parks and a number of nature reserves. When the area was settled and the exploitation of hydroelectric power began, there was a great expansion. In the early 1960s, the population was about 12,000; today it is 5,800.

The Jokkmokk project was initiated by some teachers, but was authorized and put forward through the Swedish Agency for Education (SAE), which had observed that in most rural areas boys on average attain lower school grades than girls. In 2003, the Municipality of Jokkmokk stood out in this respect, and this became an evident problem for the local school authority.

The project began with a two-day search conference in which more than 200 persons participated. In the process that was initiated, gender, school achievement, and societal issues were the focus of a large number of study circles, seven research circles, and other groups involving more than 100 participants. In the circles, the participants widened the question to be a societal problem. Questions concerning historical patterns, gender, power, and social structures were addressed to the inhabitants when this local resource mobilization project started in Jokkmokk. Teachers, principals, parents, and students took part, as well as pensioners,

people from sports and recreational activities, and other community members. Four researchers and two master's students were also involved in the project. Because of changes in the SAE, the project was only able to continue for one year. In spite of this very short time, some interesting results can be noted.

A number of interesting preliminary conclusions that can be drawn from this collaborative research project. Most important, it can be noted that in spite of the short duration of the project, the general approach and design proved to be powerful. Through the work in the research circles, gender patterns and hierarchies were challenged on different levels. The complexities of the problems under scrutiny became obvious for the many participants. A growing collective body of knowledge around these matters was developed. Many people were reflecting, discussing, and searching for more knowledge individually or with others. This must be considered a result as good as any.

Many participants obviously felt very strongly and experienced very deeply the importance of history and power structures. They gained insights into their own roles and also into their capacity to change patterns. Some of these insights were transformed into action: To give just one example, the content in the preschool and in the school was changed by some of the participants in the circles, to be more gender neutral. For the researchers, the project principally produced relevant insights about the relationship between agency and structure and the influence of educational activities characterized by genuine democratic knowledge processes.

DISCUSSION

The initiatives taken to start the four cases of research circles presented above were led by different types of actors: organizational members (the Municipality), unions (the

Hospital), and government-funded research programs (the Engineering Plant and the Insurance Company). Furthermore, these cases could also be said to differ in areas such as scale and scope, type of organization, issues targeted by the research circles, and to some extent also in how the circles were conducted. Still, there are some important commonalities in the approaches taken to the change and development process at hand in the participating organizations and in the views of knowledge and knowledge creation in these organizations. In the following, we will discuss the role of the researcher, experiences from the process types, and the outcomes from the process in terms of actionable versus scientific knowledge.

Learning From the Process and the Role of the Researcher

Knowledge in organizations is considered here to be emergent and situated in the social and technical reality that organizational members perceive. Change and development in organizations must therefore depart from knowledge that can be identified by the people involved in a certain organizational situation, even when the need for knowledge resources is identified to be external to the organization. The research circle process makes it possible to organize an iterative knowledge development process, facilitated by the researcher, between what is known in the organization and what could be learned from external sources. Depending on the situation, the problem, and the people involved, the role of the researcher takes somewhat different routes.

In the first case, the Engineering Plant, the researcher was given an active role in the initial phases of the circle when the participants made inquiries into their ways of working and in the process whereby this analysis fostered ideas of areas where the group needed new knowledge. Later, the researcher's role

became more one of a knowledge broker, in which he could bring external experts to the group.

In the Insurance Company, researchers participated in some of the circle sessions and in the coordinating meetings when the circle leaders reported from their previous sessions. Other researchers coordinated the whole project and provided, among other things, a link to management. Researchers did not have a very prominent or outspoken role here, but were key in integrating the different activities of the project.

The Hospital project had a stronger representation of researchers than did the Insurance Company. Researchers participated and contributed in all circles. Circle leaders met with the researchers and the project management. The researchers in the circles also had their own meetings. On the whole, the project had a more distinct and developed organization. Furthermore, the Municipality project, which is a more recent example, was characterized by extension to several groups and circles and broad participation from all sectors of the municipality. Many researchers were also involved.

In a critical review of the experience from processing research circles, Holmstrand and Härnsten (2003) analyzed both the possibilities and the difficulties in using this approach. Their review indicates the seemingly inherent potential of the research circle concept in providing interesting opportunities for a knowledge meeting of a somewhat new kind—a democratic knowledge process. To realize this potential, however, an awareness of some crucial conditions is considered to be required.

First, all evidence indicates the great importance of creating conditions that are as equal as possible for the knowledge meeting, and of striving for a climate that supports participation and engagement by every participant. Here, the researcher has a special responsibility to demonstrate a humble attitude and not to exploit his or her normally attributed status. On the other hand, the researcher has a delicate task in trying to obtain a balance between a restrictive use of research perspectives and making the appropriate contributions to the discussions. It is only by considering and utilizing the experiences and viewpoints of every participant in the circle work that we can talk about "democratic" knowledge processes.

Second, the researcher can contribute to the knowledge process of the circle by using his or her professional skill as a researcher to systematically handle the issue in focus. All trained researchers should also be competent in searching for already existing knowledge and in finding methods for obtaining new knowledge. This constitutes a considerable extra resource for the circle. Lönnheden (1997) draws attention to the important skill and partly tacit knowledge of researchers in having "a competence in summarising and developing categories, lifting secret or undreamt-of stones, presenting questions and hypotheses that might scare, tickle, provoke or appeal" (p. 33).

Third, the researcher can relatively easily contact other researchers who might contribute to the understanding of the theme in focus. Thus all possible existing research knowledge can in principle be made accessible for the research circle.

Finally, it is important for the researcher to use the best features of academic research traditions to demonstrate a critical attitude toward all contributions in the knowledge work of the circle. This includes maintaining a self-critical attitude.

Actionable Knowledge Versus Scientific Knowledge

In all the cases presented, the participants of all the circles and their knowledge and experience about the themes under study were the primary knowledge sources. The researchers also contributed in the circle work. In the Engineering Plant, the Hospital, and the Insurance Company, seminars or lectures were held as a kind of knowledge supplement. In the Municipality, all the people who participated in the project met several times to exchange questions and interim results. In connection with this, there were also short lectures. In the Engineering Plant, the Hospital, and the Municipality projects, some of the circles conducted systematic studies of their own in order to find out more about the problems in focus.

To varying degrees, critical knowledge characterized the work in all the circles. The essence of this is above all the interaction between the different kinds of knowledge brought forward and discussed in the groups. Here, the researcher plays a vital role in keeping an attitude of critical distance to all kinds of knowledge, including his or her individual contribution. In the Insurance Company, this aspect was not as intense as in the other cases. In the Hospital and Municipality cases, there are examples of this critical knowledge work that illustrate its importance.

Several things could be learned from our cases. In the case of the Engineering Plant, the capacity of the participants to analyze and suggest solutions to new challenges was enhanced by the research circle project. In the Insurance Company, the project resulted in an abundance of knowledge to be used in the process of making the organization more flexible and customer oriented. Some of these changes, learning from each other and broadening of the repertoire of work tasks, began during the project. The Hospital project prepared for and resulted in organizational change as well as an enhanced quality of work due to the employees' increased awareness and broadened perspectives. In the Municipality, there was substantial growth in knowledge concerning gender issues and gender patterns, with action beginning to be taken in some areas as a result.

Where scientific knowledge is concerned, the observations from the use of the RCA in the Engineering Plant support what is reported in the research literature, that is, that knowledge development in an SME like this is highly dependent on a small number of key actors and open to many types of interferences. Research shows that change efforts in organizations are often hindered by resistance to change and new ideas or new ways of approaching old problems. The "not invented here" syndrome is well known. More specifically, this case adds to this area of knowledge by describing how participants in the research circle projects both appreciate and are willing to learn and develop new ways of looking at existing issues and that it is mainly the organizational inertia (Child, Loveridge, & MESS Research Team, 1990) that is difficult to overcome.

From the Insurance Company project, we note that a broad participation and a kind of bottom-up process took place. This created a lot of learning in the organization and revealed a great knowledge potential. These results indicate that the characteristics of the context are important. In this case, the spirit and the culture of the nonprofit, customer-owned company seem to have been a crucial condition for the basically democratic knowledge in the project. The potential of this kind of approach in emancipating knowledge strengthens the theoretical assumptions about democratic knowledge processes.

The Hospital project demonstrates the large amounts of tacit knowledge that can be found among employees in this kind of organization and the vital importance of making this knowledge visible. This result is in line with much working life research. It is also interesting that researchers from different fields added to their scientific knowledge. The project is a clear illustration of the advantages of fusing different kinds of

knowledge and thus supports the choice of approach used. It became evident that in this case the research-based knowledge is not meaningful without the human and contextual aspects.

In the Municipality project, scientific knowledge was gained regarding the complexity of gender patterns and their dependence on historical and structural conditions. Deeper insight into the individual construction of gender identities and patterns was also added. Again, the collaborative research approach with broad participation proved to be fruitful. The project also led to new knowledge about conditions and obstacles for democratic knowledge processes.

More important, though, is the integrated view of the situated knowledge of the participants and the generalized and process knowledge of the researchers involved. The researcher is considered to channel scientific knowledge into the circles, which blends with practical knowledge, enabling the practitioners to act better and obtain better results than without this input. The practitioners contribute to the knowledge development process by adding their detailed knowledge of the situation and experience of the social and technical systems at hand. This knowledge can form the basis for the researchers' need for more general theorizing about the specific issue dealt with in the circle or about the process of conducting change or knowledge development in organizations.

Using the RCA to develop knowledge may perhaps be criticized for the risk of not being innovative, or for making only minor contributions to social science. From a traditional researcher standpoint, it may be argued that collaborative research such as the RCA merely contributes to developing common sense among participants in the organization by sharing the researcher's know-how or "know-what." However, it is the conviction of the authors of this chapter that this approach to collaborative research is an effective means of developing knowledge that is actionable as well as scientific.

CONCLUSIONS

Our four examples of the RCA illustrate that the methodology is flexible and can be adapted to circumstances that vary over a circle's lifetime, as well as varying by the type of project involved, the composition of the circle, and the focus of the work.

The readiness of organizations to get involved in collaborative research may be limited by doubts about the ability of social science research to contribute anything useful and by the costs and trouble of committing an organization's scarce resources to collaborative research. In this respect, a project using the RCA is less risky than a major action research project. This way of viewing the circles may be one of the reasons why they have been able to go on for as long as one to two years. The circle may be seen as a non-threatening activity with positive historical and cultural connotations. There is little danger that the circle will become an instrument of forceful but unwelcome interventions by the researcher. The action that comes about is up to the participating practitioners. The main output of the circles that we have described is not a set of reports that higher management must accept or reject. Instead, the output of the circles is embodied in the knowledge and attitudes that the participants carry with them and apply in their day-to-day jobs. In this way, the product of the circles works like a yeast, giving rise to the fermentation of future activities in the organization.

The willingness of the social science research community to accept that researchers can collaborate with organizations, especially their management, varies according to the social and political climate. The RCA also has a comparative advantage in this respect, as it can be associated with the positively value-loaded concept of popular education.

Perhaps it is the modest format and inconspicuous appearance of the RCA that have kept it less known than it deserves to be, judging from the figures that show the extent to which it is in fact being applied. We see great potential for this specific branch of collaborative work, however, owing to its many attractive characteristics.

The important contributions that we have observed from the RCA are all related to the situated aspects of organizational knowledge. The participants have acquired widened perspectives on the issues under study and development. Results that could not be attained in other ways now occur as a consequence of the continuity and the closeness to the specific situation in the organization that the participants bring to the circle. Since the results are also shaped gradually in the process of collaboration in the circle, the participants can gradually transfer what they have learned to others in the organization. Thus, there is no need to inform practitioners after the completion of the research project and to sell them its results. Implementation of new ideas and practices is therefore much easier.

The RCA is a way of doing research that reduces the risk of getting results of limited relevance. For the researcher, it is an excellent opportunity to discover and develop new and interesting research questions. There are also rich opportunities to gain more traditional scientific knowledge from the experience generated by using the RCA.

The experience from the circles referred to above clearly suggests that, in general, the participants of a research circle gained very substantive insights into the issues that were studied. It also appears that the circle participants managed to spread their new knowledge and insight to others. As a consequence, the circles also resulted in new and changed collective knowledge. We think we have found ample evidence for the validity of the two basic premises of the RCA: that knowledge is power, and that knowledge created in a democratic process is relevant in shaping the context in which the participants work. Knowledge development that takes place in research circles—a collaboration on equal terms in which the researcher sees to it that all participants have access to relevant knowledge—enhances development of a new kind of emancipating knowledge.

NOTE

1. These research circles were evaluated by external examiners (see Holmstrand, Englund, & Lindström, 1995).

REFERENCES

Arbetslivscentrum. (1990). *Lokal facklig kunskapsuppbyggnad i samverkan med forskare: Bidrag till en konferens om forskningscirklar* [Local union knowledge building in collaboration with researchers: Contributions to a conference on research circles]. Stockholm: Author.

Berglund, J., & Löwstedt, J. (1996). The fate of human resource management in a folkish society. In T. Clark (Ed.), *International perspectives on human resource management*. Oxford, UK: Blackwell.

Bracken, R., & Lindström, K. (1993). *Arena för problemhantering? Studie av två forskningscirklar 1992–3* [An arena for problem solving? A study of two research circles]. Arbetsrapporter från Pedagogiska institutionen (No. 179). Uppsala, Sweden: Uppsala Universitet.

Child, J., Loveridge, R., & MESS Research Team. (1990). *Information technology in European services*. Oxford, UK: Blackwell.

Enö, M. (2005). *Att våga flyga: Ett deltagarorienterat projekt om samtalets potential och förskolepersonals konstruktion av det professionella projektet* [Daring to fly: A participant-oriented project about preschool personnel construction of the professional project]. Malmö, Sweden: Malmö Studies in Educational Sciences.

Forsberg, E., & Starrin, B. (Eds.). (1997). *Frigörande kraft: Empowerment som modell i skola, omsorg och arbetsliv* [Emancipating power: Empowerment as a model in school, care, and working life]. Stockholm: Gothia.

Giddens, A. (1984). *The constitution of society: Outline of the theory of structuration*. Cambridge, UK: Polity Press.

Gunnarsson, L., & Perby, M.-L. (1981). *Forskningscirklar: En metod i facklig kunskapsuppbyggnad* [Research circles: A method of trade union knowledge building]. Stockholm: Arbetslivscentrum.

Härnsten, G. (1994). *The research circle: Building knowledge on equal terms*. Stockholm: Landsorganisationen.

Härnsten, G., Holmstrand, L., Lundmark, E., Hellsten, J.-O., Rosén, M., & Lundström, E. (2005). *Vi sätter genus på agendan: Ett deltagarorienterat projekt i en glesbygdskommun* [Putting gender on the agenda: A participatory-oriented project in a rural municipality]. Pedagogisk kommunikation (No. 6., IPED). Växjö, Sweden: Växjö University.

Holmstrand, L. (1993). The research circle: A way of co-operating. In K. Forrester & C. Thorne (Eds.), *Trade unions and social research* (pp. 106–114). Aldershot, UK: Avebury.

Holmstrand, L., Englund, A., & Lindström, K. (1995). *Forskningscirklar som en modell för kunskapsarbete och lärande i två verkstadsföretag* [Research circles as a model for knowledge work and learning in two workshop companies]. Stockholm: Swedish Work Environment Fund.

Holmstrand, L., & Härnsten, G. (1996, July). *Democratic knowledge processes in working life*. Paper presented at the Fourth Conference on Learning and Research in Working Life, Steyr, Austria.

Holmstrand, L., & Härnsten, G. (2003). *Förutsättningar för forskningscirklar i skolan: En kritisk granskning* [The conditions for research circles at school: A critical review]. Stockholm: National Agency for School Improvement.

Holmstrand, L., Lindström, K., Löwstedt, J., & Englund, A. (1994, June). *The research circle: A model for collaborative learning at work*. Paper presented at the International Conference on Learning at Work, Lund, Sweden.

Holmstrand, L., Olsson, A.-C., & Ekstav, C. (1995). *Lärande på Länsförsäkringar: Forskningscirklar som stöd i en lärandeprocess* [Learning at Länsförsäkringar: Research circles as support for a learning process]. Stockholm: Swedish Work Environment Fund.

Kjellberg, A. (2001). *Fackliga organisationer och medlemmar i dagens Sverige* [Trade unions and members in today's Sweden]. Lund, Sweden: Arkiv.

Knorr-Cetina, K. (1981). Introduction: The micro-sociological challenge of macro sociology: Towards a reconstruction of social theory and methodology. In K. Knorr-Cetina & A. Cicourel (Eds.), *Advances in social theory and methodology*. Boston: Routledge & Kegan Paul.

Lönnheden, C. (1997). *När de tysta "kunskaparna" börjar tala! Forskningscirklar: Ett möte mellan praktiker och teoretiker* [When the silent "knowledge shapers" start talking! Research circles: A meeting between practitioners and theoreticians]. Stockholm: Swedish Employment Security Fund.

Löwstedt, J. (1993). Organizing frameworks in emerging organizations: A cognitive approach to the analysis of change. *Human Relations, 46*(4), 501–526.

Löwstedt, J., & Stjernberg, T. (Eds.). (2006). *Producing management knowledge: Research as practice*. London: Routledge.

Löwstedt, J., & Stymne, B. (Eds.). (2002). *Scener ur ett företag: Organisationsteori för kunskapssamhället* [Scenes from a company: Organization theory for the knowledge society]. Lund, Sweden: Studentlitteratur.

Lundberg, B. (1997). *Forskningscirklar: Makt över kunskapandet* [Research circles: Power over the knowledge work]. In E. Forsberg & B. Starrin (Eds.), *Frigörande kraft: Empowerment som modell i skola, omsorg och arbetsliv* [Emancipating power: Empowerment as a model in school, care, and working life]. Stockholm: Gothia.

Lundh, H. (1995). *Perspektivknuten: Kvalitativ studie av en forskningscirkel* [The perspective knot: A qualitative study of a research circle]. Arbetsrapporter från Pedagogiska institutionen (No. 191). Uppsala, Sweden: Uppsala Universitet.

Reason, P., & Bradbury, H. (Eds.). (2001). *Handbook of action research: Participative inquiry and practice*. London: Sage.

Schüldt, U. (1996). *Forskningscirkeln: Ur forskarens perspektiv* [The research circle: From the researcher's perspective]. Undergraduate research paper, Department of Education, Uppsala University.

Wingård, B. (1998). *Att vara rektor och kvinna* [To be a principal and a woman]. Uppsala: Uppsala Studies in Education.

CHAPTER 10

Academic-Practitioner Learning Forums

A New Model for Interorganizational Research

PHILIP H. MIRVIS

ABSTRACT

This chapter examines the purposes and operations of three different forums joining academics and practitioners together to create actionable knowledge. Each case involves multiple companies with their distinct as well as common interests, and multiple researchers with different agendas. The work concerns how research and practice interests are defined, combined, and realized in a collaborative interorganizational relationship. Of particular interest is how learning occurs between academics and practitioners through processes of knowledge transfer, translation, and transformation. The chapter concludes with a look at the relevance of each of these three different kinds of forums for serving particular academic and practical interests.

Case 1: Forum on Corporate Citizenship

At Petro-Canada, the northern nation's largest oil company, managers seeking to develop a more holistic approach to corporate citizenship noted that many of the issues were being addressed within the company, but in functional silos. Hazel Gillespie, community investment manager, and David Stuart, of Environment, Health, Safety, and Security, recalled that their own activities were "contributing to the company's internal and external reputation," but observed, "We weren't doing it in a coordinated, concentrated, focused, strategic way." Even when efforts were aligned, Stuart noted, "it was largely because of personal relationships, rather than any kind of systematic management system."[1]

These concerns were echoed by other business leaders who had joined the Executive Forum on Corporate Citizenship (EFCC), hosted by Boston College, to explore ways to advance and institutionalize citizenship in companies. Reeta Roy, a divisional vice president for Abbott, stated, "I was hired for a job in 'issues management,' in the public affairs department, and different elements of citizenship were handled by different parts of the group. When I took on the position, I did some internal research with senior executives, interviewing them about the issues confronting our business and our industry, and did some external benchmarking." Roy recognized that what Abbott really needed was not a stronger issues management unit but a unified policy function. She and the team from Petro-Canada were soon swapping experiences and strategizing together, with the aid of a member of the BC team, on how to integrate citizenship into the business.

Case 2: Initiative on Corporate Branding

Novo Nordisk, a Danish-based pharmaceutical company, is the worldwide leader in the treatment of diabetes, an illness of pandemic proportions that now kills more people than AIDS. Like any pharma company, Novo Nordisk faced heightened public scrutiny about issues such as access to medicine and product affordability. In presentations to the other members of the Corporate Branding Initiative (CBI), hosted jointly by the Copenhagen Business School and McIntire School of the University of Virginia, its representatives felt reasonably assured on these matters, pointing to the company's founding tradition of getting insulin to patients without profit and its long-standing commitment to the triple bottom line. The problem was that, outside of diabetes professionals, few outside of Denmark knew of Novo-Nordisk and often confused its good works with those of Novartis, a main competitor with a similar sounding name.

An effort at corporate branding by Novo Nordisk was bollixed up by the conflicting viewpoints and priorities of the media relations, internal communications, and public affairs functions of the company. One executive summed up the situation thusly: "We are our own worst enemies. We cannot agree what is corporate branding and why we need it." Two other companies, Johnson & Johnson and ING, chimed in with some lessons on how to link branding to identity, a favored subject among the academics present. This led to collective model building on the "cycles" of branding within companies.

Case 3: A Sustainability Consortium

The Sustainability Consortium was founded in 1999 as a part of the Society for Organizational Learning (SoL). It is a voluntary association of about a dozen member organizations that have an interest in embracing a broader business mandate. The idea behind it traces to 1996 when meetings led by consultants and MIT researchers, and even a conference among committed CEOs, failed to catalyze energy. There were many presentations at these gatherings, but no group of people stepped forward who were committed to building a learning community for sustainability. Finally, in a meeting hosted by BP and Interface, a critical mass was reached and the consortium was launched.

According to the organizers of the 1999 founding meeting (Senge, Bradbury, Carroll, & Kaeufer, 2004), the participants were invited not because of their work on sustainability but because of their experience in using organizational learning tools and methods to lead change efforts. What then would be the mission of the consortium and the agenda for future meetings? What would it take to create interorganizational learning? Would the group have any impact on sustainability in member companies, let alone on a larger scale? All of this would be left to the "self-organizing" consortium.

These cases come from three different academic-practitioner learning forums. The idea that professors and practitioners might cooperate in research-and-practice endeavors is well established. There is, for example, a long tradition of researchers studying workers, managers, and even companies with mutual

benefit in the form of advances in theory for academia and some practical learning for the companies and personnel involved (see Mohrman, Gibson, & Mohrman, 2001). Academics and practitioners also combine in participatory research efforts, where both sides have some say-so over what is studied, and how, and to some extent codetermine what is learned and how it is applied in the situation at hand (see Chisholm & Elden, 1993; Reason & Bradbury, 2001).

These three cases, however, involve multiple companies, with their distinct as well as common interests, and, in some cases, multiple researchers with different agendas. This chapter shows how knowledge can be developed in a joint academic-practitioner forum. It concerns how research-and-practice interests are defined, combined, and realized in this complex, collaborative interorganizational relationship (cf. Ring & Van de Ven, 1994). Of particular interest is how learning occurs between academics and practitioners through processes of knowledge transfer, translation, and transformation (see Powell, Koput, & Smith-Doerr, 1996; Van de Ven, 2006). The chapter concludes with a look at the actionable knowledge that was developed in these cases and some considerations on the relevance of each of these three different kinds of forums for serving particular academic and practical interests.

BACKGROUND: THREE LEARNING FORUMS

There are distinct features in the creation of each of these three learning forums. In the case of the Executive Forum, for instance, the project was initiated by the Center for Corporate Citizenship of Boston College with the research purpose of understanding how the aims and processes of citizenship were developing in a sample of companies that had already developed some aspects of citizenship but had neither integrated it into the business nor institutionalized it in the company structure or culture (Manga, Mirvis, Rochlin, & Zecchi, 2005). Participants in the Forum, all drawn from North America, included Abbott, Advanced Micro Devices (AMD), Agilent Technologies, JPMorgan Chase, Levi

Strauss & Co., Petro-Canada, Unocal Corporation, and Verizon. The sample companies were chosen to reflect different industries, sizes, and customer bases and to encompass a variety of economic, social, and environmental challenges.

On the practice end, the companies were already part of the Center's general membership body of some 400 companies. The research team of Steve Rochlin, Julie Manga, and Kristen Zecchi, based on the general sampling criteria, identified company representatives who had expressed motivations to advance citizenship in their companies and a desire to learn from other companies. At the first meeting, in September of 2003, each of the eight companies sent a two- to-three-person "team" of managers representing, for example, community affairs, public affairs, environment, safety and health, issues management, communication, and myriad other functions—wherever the various responsibilities for citizenship were located in the firm. The author joined the team at this first meeting. Thereafter, the Center's research team engaged regularly with the representatives from each company, individuals who, despite their diversity of titles and functions, had taken a high degree of ownership of their companies' corporate citizenship activities, strategy, and/or implementation.

The Corporate Branding Initiative was launched by Professors Mary Jo Hatch, of the McIntire School of Commerce, University of Virginia, and Majken Schultz, of the Copenhagen Business School. The member companies, a sample of convenience from around the world, included Novo Nordisk, LEGO, Johnson & Johnson, ING, Telefonica, and Nissan. Boeing and SONY, initial members, dropped out in the first year. The author joined the CBI to facilitate meetings, and James Rubin joined in the role of case writer.

An initial communiqué to members highlighted the practice, research, and educational agendas of the CBI:

- Form a network of executives involved in corporate brand development and execution who lead the corporate branding efforts for their companies and who are committed to developing the best corporate branding practices in the world through the exchange of ideas and experiences (practice agenda)
- Capture the real-time processes the company uses to implement brand vision as it moves from strategy into practice, and gather personal brand experience stories from key stakeholders (research agenda)
- Disseminate the knowledge this initiative produces by, for example, publishing a book of corporate brand management cases, coteaching students in the classroom, or being involved in an interactive Web site (educational agenda)

Both the Executive Forum and the CBI held biennial meetings over the course of three years that featured a combination of theory and idea presentations by the academics and select thought leaders, case presentations by the companies, and interactive dialogue. At the outset of the citizenship project, the research team conducted baseline interviews in each company among a range of individuals knowledgeable about or relevant to their company's efforts. The team also completed a similar set of interviews as the project was ending. The Center also hosted 10 conference calls in which the participants were able to interact with each other while the project team gathered data on their perceptions and progress. The CBI project, by comparison, had less engagement among member companies, but the research team made site visits to select companies to prepare case studies.

Most of the members of the SoL Sustainability Consortium are large corporations, including Ford, GM, Nike, Shell, BP, and Unilever. Exceptions include Plug Power, a small fuel cell company, and the World Bank. The Consortium's purpose statement states that its goal is "to nurture the desire and capacity . . . to build knowledge for achieving . . . sustainability [through] engaging

people committed to leadership and learning to collectively [redirect] commerce, education, and technology" (Laur & Schley, 2004). Its members have, in turn, "applied principles of organizational learning and dialogue to develop and institute new business practices that incorporate concern for broader social and environmental issues."

According to meeting reflections (Senge et al., 2004),

> Approximately 50 representatives meet for two or three days, about one-third of whom are new to the Consortium. Roughly 200 individuals from the member companies have participated in meetings since 1999, including executives, line managers, internal consultants, and engineers and other individual contributors. Meetings include opportunities to create new projects, that have grown over time in numbers and size. Not all organizations participate in all projects, but the organizers encourage such participation.

A research team, including Peter Senge, Hilary Bradbury, John Carroll, John Ehrenfeld, and other SoL affiliates, assumed responsibility for studying the consortium and its operations, as well as helping to facilitate meetings and collate learnings. The author was not a member of the Sustainability Consortium but was connected to at least a part of its work through his association with environmental affairs at a member company, Unilever. This consortium was selected for consideration in this chapter as it offers yet another variation on an academic-practitioner learning forum.

WHY COMPANIES CHOOSE TO LEARN TOGETHER

There are many reasons for and types of voluntary collaboration between organizations (Oliver, 1990). Apart from common motives of sharing costs or risks, and formally combining through a merger, joint venture, or alliance, there is increasing evidence of firms coming together in multicompany associations to share knowledge and develop new insights in an uncertain environment. When academics enter the mix, these associations often take the form of research or practice consortia where there is joint interest in, for example, professional or industry developments, new social or market trends, or advances in science and technology.

The stakes are raised, however, when there is interest in mutual learning in these arenas and the potential application of new knowledge to practice. This means that organizational members may have to disclose more in-depth information about their circumstances, operations, and problems, some of which might be deemed private or even proprietary. What leads companies to join an interorganizational forum where they might divulge such details and share information and learning with others that could otherwise be a source of competitive advantage? And what motivates academics to "get their hands dirty" in a "messy" research milieu where their theorizing might be inapt and prior understandings of the subject might prove naive or even irrelevant in practice?

A New Situation

On the practice end, key factors that stimulate companies to consider joining with academics and peers to explore a common problem are the relative novelty of the approach combined with its importance to the firm. It is well established that new situations, particularly when they pose potential risks or opportunities to an organization, spur a search for a better understanding of what is happening and ways to respond to it. This search takes the form of exploration where it is believed that past experiences and prior knowledge within an organization provide insufficient tools for members to fully grasp or

creatively address the situation at hand (Levitt & March, 1988; March, 1991).

Big questions about corporate brands and reputation, the role of business in society, and the very survival of the planet have exploded in the media, education, politics, and certainly the corporate world in the past decade. In the three forums studied here, every company was facing new expectations from stakeholders, including broad-based and industry-specific consumer movements, watchdog NGOs and media coverage, regulatory pressures, and reporting requirements, and all this was occurring in a context of heightened mistrust of business overall and increasing calls for transparency and responsiveness. At the same time, there has been growing recognition of the economic and commercial value of corporate branding, of the social-and-business case for corporate citizenship, and of the cost savings, market potential, and sheer necessity of sustainable business practices.

This amalgam of heightened risk and opportunity, given a paucity of past experience and best practice to draw upon, made the practitioners especially responsive to the call to join with other companies in an academic research forum. Naturally, the prospect of learning something clarifying about all these developments "in action" was behind the academic researcher's calls to them.

Intangible Knowledge

The university, with its knowledgeable faculty, data bases, and traditions of open inquiry, is of course one source for learning about the new (Rynes, Bartunek, & Daft, 2001). So why not just a seminar or conference? Although connection to a university provides practitioners with, potentially, a broader look at a subject of interest, models of its characteristics and contours, and an open space to explore it more deeply, much of the knowledge needed in practice is more tacit and situated within an organizational space (cf. Lave & Wenger,

1991). To access this kind of knowledge means connecting regularly and deeply with fellow practitioners in a knowledge-sharing environment. That was another feature motivating the companies to join these forums.

Knowledge about branding, citizenship, and sustainability has both explicit and implicit dimensions (Nonaka, 1994; Krogh, Ichijo, & Nonaka, 2000). Models, case studies, and practical guidelines for each of these subjects could be found on both the academic and practice sides of these consortia. To get at some of the implicit "know-what" information would, however, require more intensive and sustained dialogue among the practitioners and academics. Just as important was the know-how to act on this knowledge (cf. Cohen, 1991). Responsibilities for these matters in companies span hierarchical and functional boundaries. To be successful in their endeavors, practitioners need not only subject matter expertise but also a sense of organizational politics and culture. To get at this kind of implicit knowledge requires thick description, as in storytelling, reciprocal interaction, even visits to one another's organizations. Further, considerable time would be spent in each forum developing open work processes and increasing levels of trust and engagement among the participants.

It should be noted, moreover, that academics also need firsthand and trustful connections to practitioners to gain access to such implicit knowledge. The chance to interact with so many practitioners, with their unique understandings and varied responses to their job demands, yields a cornucopia of anecdotes and insights to inform theory building. My own sense is that practice is in some respects ahead of academia in these three arenas. Indeed, some of the analytic models used by the practitioners were more conceptually sophisticated than those that the academics proffered and certainly showed greater sensitivity to practical concerns. Thus, academics needed practitioners in these areas

not only for data but also as interpreters and even cotheorists.

Shared Professional Identity

It is important to note, however, that companies did not attend these three forums: individuals were the attendees. Although members brought their own ideas, interests, needs, and, of course, styles to these associations, one of the ties binding them was a common professional identity. Certainly they faced common problems on their jobs, but more than this, they had a shared interest in and professional identity around the subject matter.

In many respects, these forums joined members in a self-styled "community of practice" (Brown & Duguid, 1991; Wenger & Snyder, 2000). This growing sense of commonality was evident in the forums in two ways. First, in their conversations and interactions, many practitioners began to attach less to their corporate identities and more to the concerns and interests they faced in common with their peers. The forum became an "us." As a result, members began to spend less time and energy on the formal face work required when speaking as representatives of their company, and they would spend more on the informal, unrehearsed give-and-take that is characteristic of peer exchange. In addition, the members would, over time, talk less about their individual on-the-job issues and more about the common concerns reported by the group.

Needless to say, this community-of-practice model would require role flexibility from the academics, who, after all, had self-assigned and member-valued roles as outside experts. The author's initial role, in the two university-business forums, was to serve as a facilitator of the meeting and also offer inputs as a "thought leader." Over time, however, the other researchers assumed this facilitation role and in so doing became "insiders" in the conversation. The capacities to think and act as both scholar and practitioner is a new kind of identity for academics and essential to this work.

Mutual Support

Needless to say, a final factor motivating companies to join an interorganizational relationship is the payoff. Obviously, the most important payoff is the chance to learn and then apply new ideas. But these forums also served two other important functions for members. First, fellow members were a source of social support to one another. Corporate work, particularly in these arenas, takes an emotional and physical toll on people. The chance to share the joys and frustrations and simply the fellowship of others in similar circumstances was, for many members, a welcome inducement. Second, that fellow members were from respected companies also lent legitimacy to membership in what might otherwise been seen as an inessential activity and unwelcome corporate expense.

Interestingly, the idea of their own faculty interacting with and learning from practitioners was also attractive to the schools involved in these joint forums. Again, the expectation of providing social, not simply intellectual, support to practitioners meant a redefinition of traditional research roles. A joint learning forum won't work if the academics see members as "subjects" of their study. It helps, too, when academics have an affinity for practice and a sincere desire to see practitioners do better.

VARIETIES OF LEARNING FORUMS

There are many variations of academic-practitioner learning forums that differ in terms of conception, roles of academics and practitioners, and purposes. The forums studied here approximate three distinct types (see Figure 10.1).

Seminar

One type of forum is the *seminar,* where, in the classic *American Heritage Dictionary* (2000) definition, "a small group of advanced students in a college or graduate school engage in original research or intensive study under the guidance of a professor who meets regularly with them to discuss their reports and findings." This model, common in professional education, also has relevance to research, where, for instance, a community of scientists might gather to explore new ideas in their discipline or practitioners might participate in a "clinic" to investigate a new technology, therapy, or practice that has potential for application in their field. In generic form, academics drive the content in a seminar and, insofar as practice is concerned, theory is applied to the "real world."

Of the three forums here, the CBI had the greatest amount of this flavor. The academic conveners had conducted a series of case studies in corporate branding in the 1990s and developed an integrative branding model (Hatch & Schultz, 2001). In their framework, brands are shaped by the images held by multiple stakeholders, the internal identity of the company, and the firm's longer term strategic vision. The research agenda was to test and amplify this model through the guidance of practitioners, the top brand managers in their companies (Schultz & Hatch, 2005).

As the CBI agenda unfolded, practitioners expressed an interest in knowing more about brand measurement and valuation. The academics shared the state of knowledge from their vantage point, and then representatives from Nissan and Johnson & Johnson showed the approach used in their companies and a sampling of developments in the practice community. This kind of mutual exchange, common to the CBI, shows the group shifting from a seminar to the more egalitarian mode of a roundtable.

Academic/Practitioner Forums

Structure	Agenda	Purpose
Seminar	Roundtable	Self-study
Academics drive content	Shared agenda Dual purpose	Practitioners drive content
Apply theory to "real world"	Theory from practice, practice from theory	Solve problems

Figure 10.1   Academic-Practitioner Forums: Structure, Agenda, and Purpose

Roundtable

The *roundtable* model "pertains to a conference, discussion, or deliberation in which each participant has equal status, equal time to present views, etc." (*American Heritage,* 2000). The Executive Forum certainly had this flavor, in that academics and practitioners developed a shared agenda and established a mutually beneficial purpose of bridging the theory-practice gap. In this case, however, there was no established model of integrating citizenship to proffer; indeed the hoped-for result for the academics was to develop the theory from practice. At the same time, practitioners were hungry for theory and welcomed Center ideas on, for example, developing an internal value proposition for citizenship and early thinking on stages of citizenship in companies (Mirvis & Googins, 2006; Rochlin & Googins, 2005).

The academic's dual role in this roundtable format is evident in the timeline of events in the Executive Forum (see Figure 10.2). It shows that through regular phone check-ins, members of the research team would serve as forum facilitators by culling "progress, successes, issues, challenges, and requests" from members and using these inputs to shape the

agenda of subsequent conference calls and plenary sessions. After each session, in turn, the team would write up notes, including a summary of learnings for its own use and for review by the participants.

Self-Study Group

The dictionary defines *self-study* as "a form of study in which one is to a large extent responsible for one's own instruction" (*American Heritage,* 2000). In the academic-practitioner learning model, this would mean that practitioners drive more of the content and that it is aimed more at meeting their needs. The SoL Sustainability Consortium had more of this flavor and in a sense aimed to help practitioners to solve problems in their worlds.

Consistent with the SoL tradition that favors self-organizing communities, the Sustainability Consortium took a different shape than its original intention. Although the original vision was for an inclusive group of the "whole ecology of organizational life," including nongovernmental organizations, most of the members are corporations. Again, as part of the SoL ethos, consortium members have established a steering committee, goals, membership fees, and an evolving set of practices around meetings and projects.

The self-study flavor of the consortium is very much evident in its agenda. One key difference between this and the other two forums was the early emphasis on knowledge application. As one interviewee expressed the aspiration, "We've got to get value, and one way to do that is developing projects that address business concerns while evolving some of the social and environmental issues— on-the-ground-type projects, real things that you can touch, feel, show results." Another reflected on the emergence of this emphasis in the consortium in this way: "The first meeting was very open-ended. It was sitting in the question and seeing what emerged. By the [third meeting] there were working groups starting to emerge, focusing on issues relevant to a number of companies in the room." Eventually, working groups were formed that addressed toxicity in raw material use, pollution in manufacturing, and waste in packaging, while another focused on why an environmentally preferred product (polypropylene) is not captured and reused more extensively.

A number of factors might help explain the differences in structure, agenda, and purposes of these three groups. As for conception and structure of these learning forums, the CBI was founded and organized by well-known professors who were recognized experts in corporate branding. By comparison, the citizenship researchers were not professors, nor did they purport to offer the kind of theorizing associated with academic research.

Indeed, to this point the Center was better known for its "member services" than its contributions to knowledge. In the case of the Sustainability Consortium, its leaders were recognized experts, but chiefly in organizational learning rather than the content of sustainability. As noted, it took a long time for this body to take shape and even, when

formed, to find its direction through action projects.

As for agenda, the CBI participants were comparatively high-level executives located in different parts of the world. Arguably, this would make it more difficult for them to assume dual responsibility for the operations of the branding initiative. The executive forum participants were busy, too, but nonetheless were invited and chose to contribute more of their time and talents to the operations and learning agenda of their body. The Sustainability Consortium had, by comparison, a core group of organizers that would steer its operations and a variable roster of participants who would attend one or another meeting or conference.

Finally, it is worth noting that corporate members in the CBI were not charged any fees to join, whereas Forum members were charged $20,000 to support facilitation and the research agenda. Members of the Sustainability Consortium paid roughly $40,000 to join. To what extent factors such as the relative status of organizers and participants, the time demands, and the financial support of such a body shape its organization and operation is open for speculation. Here, at least, it is evident that both the research team and participants in the citizenship forum had more time to devote to ongoing engagement and showed greater willingness to codefine and cofacilitate the agenda. In the case of the Sustainability Consortium, a paid SoL staffer provides ongoing support, and it is the corporate members who more or less run the show.

DEVELOPING WORKING PROCESSES

Considerable time and attention, in each forum, was given to developing the task agenda and operating effectiveness of the community. On the task side, the agenda of the citizenship forum was developed by the

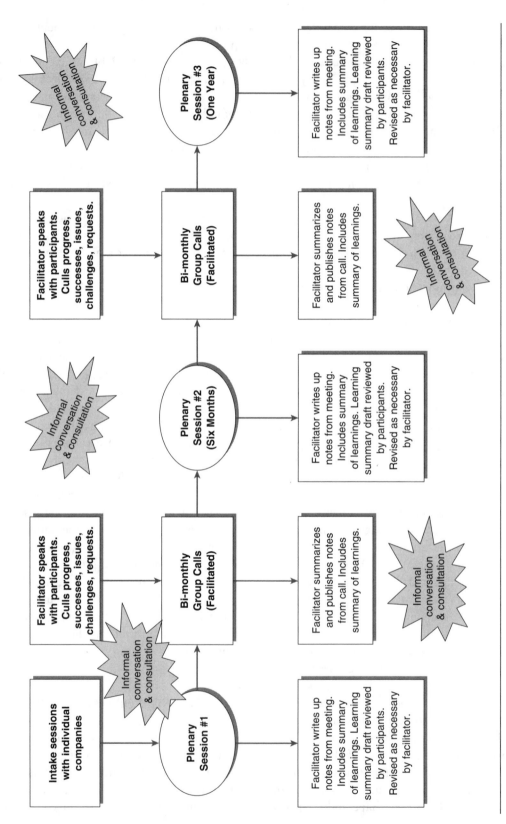

Figure 10.2

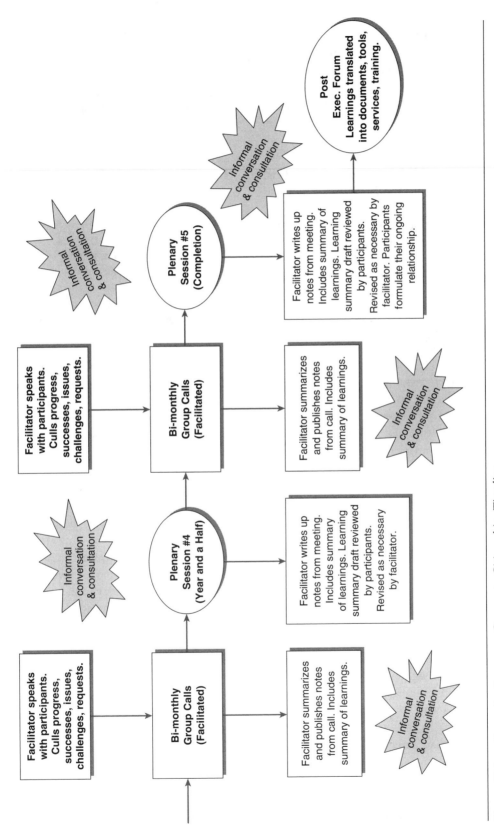

Figure 10.2 Executive Forum on Corporate Citizenship: Timeline

211

researchers and participants jointly, as noted, through regular conversation and give-and-take. This was similar in the other groups, with the academics taking the lead in CBI and practitioners doing so in the sustainability body. In all cases, content experts or thought leaders were brought in to develop thinking and respond to specific needs. In the CBI, for instance, external thought leaders shared the latest research on corporate branding in multi-brand companies such as GE, Procter & Gamble, and Unilever and on valuation of the brand in market capital. In the Sustainability Consortium, an expert from Xerox told how he and his team had developed a copier that was over 90% remanufacturable and recyclable. It had only about 200 parts, was put together with screws or clips for easy disassembly, and replaced a machine with about 2,000 parts. He also showed a short video based on interviews with members of the team that showed just how meaningful and emotionally powerful the project had been to many involved (see Bradbury, 2003). Such attention to content ensured that the meetings themselves proved to be meaningful experiences.

In each forum, moreover, members were invited to attend meetings hosted by member companies. The CBI traveled to SONY headquarters in Berlin, a LEGO Group design studio in New York, and Telefonica HQ in Madrid, along with meetings near the two host business schools. The Executive Forum went to Calgary, hosted by Petro-Canada, and San Francisco, hosted by Levi Strauss & Co. There, the forum members conducted a "live" case study interviewing people about citizenship throughout the corporation. The sustainability meetings, in turn, are routinely hosted by member companies. All of this lends variety to the task agenda and gives members a chance to "be there" and see first-hand what is happening in peer companies.

On the process side, the author, who is reasonably well-versed in group dynamics and principles of experiential learning, helped the

CBI and Executive Forum get off to a good start. This meant establishing "ground rules" for members that would cover matters of open and honest sharing, management of air time, norms for constructive engagement and disagreement with one another, and so on. In the case of the CBI, some additional "rules of engagement" were developed. These addressed matters of meeting participation and the use of information about other companies:

- Participation is personal—do not nominate "proxies."
- If you want to bring in colleagues (as an exception), all members should be informed beforehand.
- ALWAYS check whether you can use information from the CBI meetings in other contexts BEFORE you use it or refer to it.

As for research, it was agreed in the Executive Forum that all material and information generated would be available for publication. In cases where individuals or host companies indicated that material was confidential, an effort would be made to disguise it or ensure that it was reported in such a way as to guarantee anonymity. Failing joint agreement on those counts, the material would not be published. In the case of the CBI, the research rule was that companies would have the right of prior review of published materials and, in the case writing, final approval over descriptions of the firm.

There was, not surprisingly, given SoL's traditions, more concerted and sustained attention to the social process in the Sustainability Consortium. SoL promulgates a set of conversation principles and tools that emphasize the role of dialogue, as contrasted with debate or ordinary discussion, for encouraging organizational learning (Isaacs, 1999; Mirvis, 1996). In turn, Senge, Kleiner, Roberts, Ross, and Smith (1994) suggest that relationships characterized by trust, intimacy, and honesty are crucial for learning. Thus, consortium members spent considerable time looking at social and work processes and modes of communication.

An assessment of the consortium's process, reported by Bradbury, Powley, and Carroll (2003), addressed four dimensions of what they termed *peering* among the participants: (1) an emotional sense of trust that often developed into a sense of friendship, (2) a cognitive ease with each other because of shared capacity for complexity, (3) physical proximity through face-to-face meetings at least twice a year, and (4) permission, without expectation, to speak of personally held aspirations. One participant summarized the difference between the Sustainability Consortium and other cooperative business ventures thusly: "What you really have are people who are interested in relationships rather than transactions and contracts. Those [transactions and contracts] are the traditional modes of relating between organizations and their vendors, which makes the Sustainability Consortium different."

Reflecting on these findings, Bradbury et al. (2003) report, "Research on organizational collaborative learning has been developed with little reference to the emotional tenor of the context in which cognition is occurring." They go on to say, "Because learning is primarily social . . . a deeper appreciation of the role of human relationships in learning is required." That was certainly stressed in the process of the Sustainability Consortium and to some extent in the CBI and the Executive Forum.

KNOWLEDGE EXCHANGE

In all three forums, the raison d'etre for membership was the exchange of experiences and knowledge. As one member of the Sustainability Consortium remarked,

> I have to argue for the budget to cover our time and meetings with the Consortium. This is not that easy to do, even in a rich company. The availability of information

and a network, along with the capacity building, make the case.

On the academic side, of course, a central aim was the development of theory.

Development of the working processes within each group enabled members to talk to and with one another more openly and fully. Additional effort would be needed, however, for them to understand one another and learn together. This would mean exchanging knowledge across communication boundaries—among the varied practitioners, and certainly between them and the academics.

In several studies of communication in innovation, Carlile (2004) highlights three progressively more complex boundaries that affect the exchange of knowledge—syntactic, semantic, and pragmatic. He proposes, in turn, three communication processes—transfer, translation, and transformation—to cross them. Each of these boundaries would be evident in these academic-practitioner forums and would require appropriate communication processes to cross.

TRANSFER OF KNOWLEDGE

One barrier to knowledge exchange is the syntactic boundary—the parties simply speak a different "language" and need common vocabulary to exchange information. This barrier first cropped up in the Executive Forum during a discussion on how to effect change in member organizations. The researchers, and many of the practitioners, spoke of change in terms of organization development—where an inside consultant would typically work through a hierarchy and change would be effected through a rational, linear, step-by-step process of, for example, diagnosis, analysis, intervention, evaluation, and feedback (cf. Beckhard, 1969). But this didn't match the role or experience of several of the practitioners who, after all, didn't see themselves as consultants, couldn't rely on a top-down approach, and used more organic methods to exercise influence and advance change in their companies. Using a rock-climbing metaphor, Laurie Regelbrugge, manager of corporate responsibility at Unocal, described the use of "handholds" to effect change in her company:

> In scaling a wall of rock, a rock climber must find and make effective use of the meager or substantial handholds along that wall. Some handholds that seem promising may ultimately lead the climber to a dead end, while others allow the person to reach the desired destination. Different climbers, presented with the same rock face, may choose a different set of handholds and, therefore, follow a slightly different path. The key is that there are often many options, and climbers choose certain holds for reasons having to do with their skills, experience, what results they can anticipate, and the plan they have for scaling the rock face.

In conversation, it was discovered that most of the Executive Forum participants operated with this highly pragmatic approach of identifying and seizing opportunities for demonstrating success, rather than establishing and adhering to an overarching strategy with prescribed steps and activities. Based on this exchange, the academics thereupon pictured this ad hoc process versus the top-down model extant in the field as shown in Figure 10.3.

This model was a stimulus to theory building on "leading change from the middle." The research team made a connection between the practitioners' stories of building coalitions and creating coordination structures to support integration of citizenship in their companies with the emerging literature on complex adaptive systems (CAS). Mirvis and Manga (2006), in turn, put theory into practice by devising a framework on leading change from the middle. It likened the practitioners to "tempered radicals" (cf. Meyerson, 2003) to identify three different CAS-based change strategies they adopted:

Small Wins. Most accounts of organizational transformation emphasize how interventions necessarily have to be bigger, deeper, and

Traditional Top-Down

- Fixed plan
- Top-down, change from one source
- Managers as implementers
- Directive
- Predictable outcomes assumed

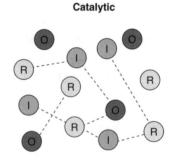

Catalytic

- Adaptive and responsive
- Multidirectional, multisource change
- Mangers as strategists and catalysts
- Emergent
- Lack of predictability recognized as part of process

Figure 10.3   Two Models of Organization Change: Executive Forum on Corporate Citizenship

wider. CAS advises thinking again about small changes—the movement of a butterfly's wing—and thus the importance of small wins. At almost every Executive Forum company, the practitioners started small, advanced operational initiatives to demonstrate the value of citizenship, and then built on successes with more comprehensive efforts. As Petro-Canada put it, "slow and steady wins the race."

Reusing Structures. Abrahamson's (2004) analysis of the value of more incremental, as opposed to transformational, change in organizations shows that by "reusing" structures or "recombining" processes, managers can employ already culturally approved mechanisms, build on past precedents, and thus allay at least some resistance to change. The practitioners here "piggy-backed" on existing measurement schemes, assessment and control systems, reputation projects, and the like by adding citizenship content and thereby moving their agendas forward. Adding this new input into existing activities set the system, in CAS language, on a new course. Practitioners prospected new areas of opportunity in their companies, such as, in one case, injecting citizenship materials into an executive development program and, in another, experimenting with cause-related marketing.

Balancing Acts. Brown and Eisenhardt's (1998) studies of complexity in strategy highlight several catalytic interventions that affect strategic change. They frame these in the form of complex balancing acts, wherein managers have to, for example, balance past precedents versus future needs or movement toward intended directions versus available opportunities. In the citizenship case, to illustrate, managers had to balance corporate interests against those of line managers, trade off the benefits of conforming to external codes versus developing ones unique to their own businesses, help their companies

navigate through risks versus opportunities of taking a bolder stance on social issues, and formulate a business case for larger initiatives versus moving quickly to gain quick wins. This involved improvisation, time pacing, and what Brown and Eisenhardt term *co-adapting* among the many interests in their companies.

TRANSLATION OF KNOWLEDGE

A second barrier to knowledge exchange is the semantic boundary—where words and ideas mean different things to different people. This barrier was significant in the CBI effort in a discussion of how companies adapt their brand to signals from stakeholders. For example, Francesco Ciccolella, former global brand manager of the LEGO Group, observed during one meeting that a brand manager can be either an "arrogant bastard" (focused inwardly on the company) or a "headless chicken" (enslaved by consumer trends and preferences). This seemed to make sense to the other practitioners but didn't resonate with the academics, who had an organization-level frame of reference on corporate branding. The academics needed to translate these practice observations into organizational analogues to understand the implications for the corporate brand. Hatch and Schultz's meeting notes on analogues contain the following:

> *Hyper-Adaptation.* Overreaction to undesired stakeholder images creates confusion in the internal activities of the firm because change with little regard for what must be retained to maintain identity (e.g., the organization's unique heritage of past practices and prized traditions) can destroy the organization's soul. Some companies have fallen into the trap of changing their identity claims every time they gather new data about one or another of their key stakeholder groups. Desiring to be profitable, and

knowing the importance of customer opinion, these companies become obsessed with responding to each and every criticism or suggestion they hear. Like adolescents who try to change themselves into whatever they think others want them to be, the hyper-adaptive organization has no strong sense of itself or its purpose to guide its choices.

Narcissism. Narcissism exists wherever organizational members infer their identity solely on the basis of how they express themselves to others rather than also on the basis of how others respond to them. What initially might appear to be attempts at impressing outsiders via identity claims turn out to be expressions of self-understanding formed without the benefit of external validation or refutation. Hence the members mistakenly believe that others see them as they see themselves. Even though organizational members may espouse concern for external stakeholders as part of their cultural self-expression processes ("Our company is dedicated to customer service!"), if they do not listen to external stakeholders who are willing to tell them otherwise, their identity dynamic will be internally focused and self-contained.

A variation of this "translation" problem racked the Sustainability Consortium. The technical interests of many from the environmental side of the consortium, and the initial emphasis on environmental issues, case studies, and projects, was somewhat off-putting to members with a more psychological or humanistic background and greater interest in social sustainability. Then John Ehrenfeld, an engineer at MIT, recast the three dimensions of sustainable development developed by the Bruntland Commission—equity, environment, and economics (the basis for the triple-bottom-line management practices)—in a new light. The consortium then began to speak of the three fundamental dimensions of "true sustainability"—the ethical, the natural, and the human (Ehrenfeld, 2005). This translation seemed to "level-set" the interests, as one described it, and gave the consortium new energy and purpose.

TRANSFORMATION OF KNOWLEDGE

A third barrier to knowledge exchange is what Carlile (2004) called the pragmatic boundary—where one group's knowledge impedes the development of knowledge among another. This barrier was a factor leading up to and throughout the CBI effort.

In several of their writings, the hosts of the CBI have spoken to the difficulties of reconciling knowledge about branding across disciplines and interests. In an account of bringing together academics who study brands and identity, Schultz and Hatch (2005) describe the experience as follows:

> We invited scholars with different disciplinary backgrounds and interests to write about organizational identity, image, culture, reputation and corporate branding. While we experienced high agreement among the members of this group that all these constructs were important and interrelated, it turned out to be an immense struggle to define even basic terms such as identity and image, because the different disciplines on which we drew clung to their own definitions. . . . In our struggle to make sense of interrelated conceptual differences we ended up using the Tower of Babel myth to describe the belief the group held that they were looking for a lost—or not yet found—common language. More specifically, we used a spatial metaphor to argue that the meaning of each term depends on where in the conceptual landscape an observer stands, each discipline preferring a different position. This experience gave us firsthand knowledge of the cross-functional

difficulties managers face when implementing corporate initiatives. (p. 340)

The experience from the CBI brought these difficulties to life and stimulated reflection on "building theory from practice." The hosts offered this kind of advice to practitioners based on their CBI experience:

- Managers need simple integrated frameworks that enable them to link internal and external stakeholders and related business functions. This means linkages between key stakeholders as well as between business functions. If we continue to equate higher levels of conceptual disaggregation with more profound knowledge, we face the risk of remaining irrelevant to practitioners.
- To develop theoretical constructs that reflect everyday managerial concerns, we need to develop frameworks that bring together insights from different theoretical disciplines and accept the necessary loss of conceptual refinement this requires when seen from any single disciplinary perspective.

In addition, they also saw dilemmas in "simplifying" messages for practice. Again, Schultz and Hatch (2005) write:

Paradoxically, even as management researchers drift toward increasing complexity in their theorizing, we also find reason to accuse them of naïve simplicity. This happens when management researchers oversimplify the implications of their findings for managerial action. We find that many management researchers from areas such as institutional theory, resource based theories, networks and identity, often translate profound theoretical ideas and empirical findings into a few straightforward, conflict-free implications for practice in the mistaken belief that this is what practitioners want. This elimination of conflicts in management implication may originate from researchers' assumptions about the limited time, scope and attention span of managers. The preference for straightforward implications may find further support in the request from many editors of management journals to limit the implications for practice to a few paragraphs at the end of a paper. By reducing implications for management to a few guidelines, researchers risk underestimating the tensions and paradoxes that are basic conditions for managers, particularly when they work across functional boundaries as is the case with managers involved in corporate branding. (p. 341)

Throughout the CBI, the research team kept notes on the many paradoxes that divided members of the group along disciplinary as well as academic-practitioner lines. The key ones noted included (1) language barriers (languages don't always translate clearly or beautifully into each other); (2) art versus natural science (aesthetic versus rational perceptions of things); (3) hard versus soft disciplines; (4) tangible versus intangible representations (economics versus values in branding); (5) linear versus multivariate ways of understanding; and (6) inductive versus deductive approaches. For each of these dichotomies, the members of the CBI spent considerable time talking through their differences and the assumptions behind them.

Certainly one important role of the academics was to transform differences into common understanding, where possible, through higher-order theorizing. On this count, Schultz and Hatch (2003) proposed a set of ideas on "balancing" the paradoxes of brand management (see Figure 10.4). Their balancing model highlights the risks associated with maintaining one's position on corporate branding and the benefits of adopting a both/and perspective.

In their analysis of what makes for successful knowledge exchange, Bradbury et al. (2003) developed a thoughtful and relevant model of the relationship between the "relational space"

Balancing the Paradoxes of Brand Management

Strategic Direction	Inside-Out	Outside-In
	Risk: Arrogant Bastard	*Risk: Headless Chicken*
Brand Foundation	Timeless cultural heritage and brand identity	Current relevance and emotional appeal
	Risk: Brand blindness	*Risk: Brand Hype*
Brand Coherence	Coherence	Local adaptation
	Risk: Brand Isolation	*Risk: Brand Fragmentation*
Organizing Process	Centralization	Decentralization
	Risk: Brand Policing	*Risk: Brand Turfs*

Figure 10.4 Balancing the Paradoxes of Brand Management

SOURCE: Schultz and Hatch (2003).

and "action space," showing how, for instance, frustration with the status quo among the participants, coupled with an aspiration to do better, led to more self-disclosure and, though a series of conversational loops, into proposals to take action through the consortium. Certainly, efforts to create a high-quality relational space made a difference here. One participant commented on the results as follows: "This is a special group of people with high capacity for telling the truth, thinking about complexities without oversimplifying. They can see the big picture." Another reported, "I didn't understand before the Sustainability Consortium the real power of getting in the room with other folks and actually speaking the truth rather than trying to bullshit each other like we do at conventional business meetings."

Generalizing beyond the relational space, Bradbury et al. (2003) also analyzed the characteristics of the consortium as a *proto-institution*. Here they speak to fellow theorists about this new institutional form:

Lawrence, Hardy, and Phillips define proto-institutions as new practices, rules, and technologies that transcend a particular collaborative relationship and may become a new institution if they diffuse sufficiently (2002: 281). . . . Agency and (proto) institutionalization involves both action and meaning. . . . [A] social constructionist lens on institutional agency suggests that meanings attract actors to action; hence, actors are carriers and creators of institutional meanings that are embodied in their action. . . . We believe proto-institutions are built on the paradigmatic human event of reciprocal and reciprocated speaking, through which meanings can evolve and participants can learn to produce new actions and lived realities.

REFLECTIONS ON THE FORUMS

Each of these three types of academic-practitioner learning forums followed a different path after their first years. As of this writing, the Sustainability Consortium continues to evolve, with myriad conferences and a European working group formed to convene more regularly. A new volume titled

Learning for Sustainability, by Senge, Kleiner, Laur, Schley, and Smith (2006), summarizes key lessons to date.

The branding initiative concluded as a working group; but the research team is now engaged in the preparation of teaching cases from several of the companies. Interestingly, many of the ideas brewed in the CBI are evident in Novo Nordisk's "changing diabetes" branding effort and Nissan's new approach to the American market.

The Executive Forum has evolved into a "network" with many more members but less emphasis on research per se. In reflecting on the value of the experience, one member spoke of the intangible benefits as follows: "You always come back energized from meetings like the Executive Forum." Several of the members continue in this network, serving as mentors to new entrants. Summing up the whole experience, Theresa Fay-Bustillos of Levi Strauss & Co. said of the personal, group, and institutional benefits:

> This is a very collegial environment to work in. We don't always appreciate what we can accomplish just by networking and being part of different external organizations that are interested in moving the agenda. You learn. You get ideas. You get encouragement. You have a group of people you can call up, and they will help you. There are people at other companies who are more than willing to collaborate. Being a part of these external groups is a way to move the internal agenda at your company.

To conclude, it may be useful to review some of the similarities and differences among these three forums and consider their relative strengths and weaknesses for advancing theory and practice (see Table 10.1).

As noted, in the CBI, the academics defined more of the content and took a larger hand in setting the agenda, convening meetings, and pursuing their interests; in some respects, this was for them like a seminar or, more aptly, a clinic for testing theory in practice. The corporate members were senior executives at the cutting edge of practice who, by position and temperament, had a broad view of their enterprise and took a holistic perspective on their work: corporate branding. They seemed comparatively comfortable with periodic bouts of collective theorizing and individually defined their own desired "takeaways." It may be that senior-level executives in integrative functions have more tolerance and even an appetite for a more exploratory, theory-driven approach to developing practical knowledge—particularly, as in this case, when it is leavened by practitioner-oriented content and peer interaction. As for deliverables, three members launched major branding efforts over the course of the CBI, informed by theory and the counsel of their peers.

By comparison, the Executive Forum was designed as more of a roundtable where practice-minded researchers and reflective practitioners worked together on a shared agenda. Absent a strong going-in theory about how to embed citizenship in companies, the research team acted variously as observers, subject matter experts, and peer problem solvers to support the practitioners and develop grounded theory. This suited the members, middle managers who were drawn to practice-oriented theory but also steered the agenda from the get-go to address their everyday concerns. The members seemed most animated during sessions when their cases were subject to peer commentary and most engaged in small group coaching sessions. It is understandable why mid-level managers, with a wide scope but a pressing agenda, might gravitate more toward practical knowledge and particularly to knowledge that helps them move their own agendas forward. Many made substantial progress moving citizenship deeper into their companies. They also made good use of one another for benchmarking, counsel, and social support.

Table 10.1   Comparing Three Learning Forums

	CBI	ExecForum	SoL Sustainability
Participant's objective	Develop holistic approach to corporate branding	Integrate corporate citizenship into the company	Apply organizational learning tools to sustainability
Researcher's objective	Apply and refine vision-image-culture model in "live" setting	Develop theory on integrating corporate citizenship; how multiple parties move agenda	Develop an understanding of sustainability in companies
Members	Senior level corporate executives, academic researchers	Mid-level staff executives, Research Center team (most nonacademic)	Mix of midlevel businesspeople and consultants; academic and professional researchers
Structure and degree of collaboration	Seminar/clinic: Academics set agenda and define more of the content than practitioners	Roundtable: Joint agenda and influence over content	Self-study: Practitioners set agenda and define more of the content than the academics
Practical results achieved	Three corporate-wide brand launches informed by theory and peer input	Progress in all cases on integrating corporate citizenship; benchmarking; varied innovations	Lessons on implementing sustainability; some collaborative projects
Research results achieved	Insights into rigidity vs. adaptability of branding; roster of paradoxes	Model of leading change from the middle; input into stages of corporate citizenship;	Best-practice examples; insights into research and practice space
Risks to be managed in this type of effort	Misapply theory to practice; issues of time/engagement of participants	Mis-theorize from experience; overgeneralize; issue of power of participants	Develop "lay" theory that depends on tacit knowledge; issue of continuity of people
Strengths of this approach: when to use	Best for testing and refining theory; for thinkers and doers	Best for generating theory-in-action; for doers and reflective practitioners	Best for modifying general theory in specific circumstance; action learning
Weaknesses of this approach: when to avoid	Depends on robust theory; not suited for exploratory research	Knowledge from inductive experience; not suited for theory testing	Knowledge depends on generalization; not suited for deep theory building or rigorous research
Skills/resources needed	Ability to apply theory	Ability to induce theory	Ability to learn with others

The SoL Sustainability Consortium was almost wholly practitioner directed. Its members included businesspeople, change consultants, subject matter specialists, and assorted others, as well as a mix of academic and independent researchers. Given

SoL's long-standing emphasis on action learning, "lessons" that were distilled on implementing sustainable practices in companies were as likely to emerge from the practitioners or consultants as from the research members of the consortium. It is difficult to catalog the results for participants, because membership in this forum varied from meeting to meeting. In any case, sustainability efforts in member companies or consultations were shaped by myriad factors, of which the consortium was a modest one.

How about knowledge exchange and development? On the academic side of the CBI, beyond testing their culture-vision-image model in practice, the researchers gained insights into problems of narcissism versus hyper-adaptation in corporate branding. Case studies of select member companies added to both the scholarly literature and classroom teaching. It should be noted, however, that there can be problems with knowledge exchange in this kind of theory-driven forum. There is a risk, for example, that academics will misapply their comparatively abstract theories to practice. This is a generic problem in any joint academic-practitioner knowledge exchange, but is complicated in this case because the branding scholars were applying theory drawn from the fields of identity and culture to an arena heretofore defined by theorizing from marketing and communications. It is worth wondering whether a more pragmatic or professional discipline-based audience would have been as open to the theorizing Hatch and Schultz offered. Interestingly, the researchers used knowledge translation problems to theorize more broadly about other paradoxes in corporate brand management.

The research team in the executive forum originally set out to catalogue how practitioners *align* their citizenship efforts with business strategies, *integrate* citizenship into their organization structure and processes, and *institutionalize* it into the mindsets, values, and culture of their organization. But there can be a gap between theoretical assumptions about the situation at hand and the practically difficult and politically charged realities of organization life. Thus, in this instance, the research agenda turned to theorizing about leading change from the middle.

If there are risks of misapplying theory in theory-driven exercises, the risks in practice-driven research are in "mis-theorizing" from observation. The research team was understanding of, but disappointed by, the lack of progress in the first months of the forum on corporate citizenship—and comfortably attributed this lack of progress to the lack of senior management support and competing corporate priorities that blocked the practitioners' agendas. It was only when, over time, the researchers were able to get close to practice and witness the incremental, pragmatic, handhold strategy of forum members that a new theory of practice emerged.

That said, there can also be problems in overgeneralizing from observed experience. An in-depth look at 10 companies provides plenty of grist for interpretation and theorizing. But it cannot match the varieties of experience found in a larger sample. In addition, a small sample may not feature dominant behavior patterns that might be observed in a larger one. The Executive Forum study demonstrated how leadership from the middle is important. But, in a multiwave survey of over five hundred companies, the Center for Corporate Citizenship found top managers' attitudes about citizenship to be a far more consistent and crucial predictor of the degree to which citizenship was integrated into companies (Rochlin, Jordan, Mirvis, Witter, & Thome Beevas, 2004–2006).

The self-study emphasis in the SoL Sustainability Consortium yielded a roster of broadly generalizable lessons for practice. A risk in these kinds of practical, problem-oriented forums is that the lessons that emerge are, at best, based in "lay theories" that bespeak truths but are packed with tacit knowledge. The ideas seem simple when expressed in a model or formula but are complicated and fraught with significance when expressed in practice. My own sense is that research generated from practitioner-driven forums is best suited for modifying general theories to specific circumstances. This kind of forum is, even more than the others, well suited to participatory action research—as evidenced by the action projects stimulated by the Sustainability Consortium.

Interestingly, there was a formal research arm to this consortium that was organized separately and funded externally by the National Science Foundation. It developed an interesting model of linkages between reflective spaces and action spaces that is conceptually interesting and generalizable to many kinds of collaborative research and action learning endeavors.

What are the implications for academics in these kinds of forums? A taste and feel for practice and a genuine interest in practitioners are required in all three types. But a CBI-type forum depends on robust theory. Thus, academics with a gift for theorizing would fit best here. In their catalogue of scholarly types, Mitroff and Kilmann (1978) identify the *conceptual theorist*, who relishes abstract ideas and how they fit together. This may work on the theorizing side of interorganizational research, but my sense is that to be successful in a collaborative forum, conceptual theorists also need a practical bent that expresses itself in a genuine interest in applying theory and making a difference in practice.

A practitioner-based group, like the SoL Sustainability Consortium, depends on developing knowledge in action. A researcher who has been around many organizations and seen diverse changes therein is right at home here. Many of the scholar-practitioners in SoL fit the type Mitroff and Kilmann (1978) term *particular humanists*, who can theorize but are most concerned with developing practical knowledge and with applying it with humanistic values.

In groups like the Executive Forum, which give equal attention to theory and practice, the ideal scholarly type is the *conceptual humanist*. As a member of the research team in two of these three bodies, I found myself going from theory to practice and from practice to theory. Real insight, however, seemed to emerge from immersion in and then deep reflection on the experience (cf. Schön, 1983). That, plus peer exchange with academics, with practitioners, or with both together provided a rich source of insight and social support for this researcher as well.

NOTE

1. Quotations not otherwise referenced are from unpublished field notes of the author. Some may be found in Manga, Mirvis, Rochlin, and Zecchi (2005).

REFERENCES

Abrahamson, E. (2004). *Change without pain*. Boston: Harvard Business School Press.

American Heritage dictionary of the English language (4th ed.). (2000). Available online at http://www.bartleby.com/61

Beckhard, R. (1969). *Organization development: Strategies and models*. Reading, MA: Addison-Wesley.

Bradbury, H. (2003). Integrating sustainability into business strategy and operations: Personal and group (re)vitalization as catalysts for action. In S. Waage (Ed.), *Ants, Galileo and Gandhi: Re-shaping business through nature, genius, and compassion* (pp. 223–241). Sheffield, UK: Greenleaf.

Bradbury, H., Powley, N., & Carroll, J. (2003). *The importance of relational space for interorganizational learning: Taking on a broader business mandate.* Paper presented at the Academy of Management Annual Conference, Seattle, WA.

Brown, J. S., & Duguid, P. (1991). Organizational learning and communities-of-practice: Toward a unified view of working, learning, and innovation. *Organization Science, 2*(1), 40–57.

Brown, S., & Eisenhardt, K. (1998). *Competing on the edge: Strategy as structured chaos.* Boston: Harvard Business School Press.

Carlile, P. R. (2004). Transferring, translating, and transforming: An integrative framework for managing knowledge across boundaries. *Organization Science, 15*(5), 555–568.

Chisholm, R. F., & Elden, M. (1993). Features of emerging action research. *Human Relations, 46*(2), 275–298.

Cohen, M. D. (1991). Individual learning and organizational routine: Emerging connections. *Organization Science, 2*(1), 135–139.

Ehrenfeld, J. (2005). The roots of sustainability. *Sloan Management Review, 46*(2), 23–25.

Hatch, M. J., & Schultz, M. (2001, February). Are the strategic stars aligned for your corporate brand? *Harvard Business Review,* 128–134.

Isaacs, W. (1999). *Dialogue: The art of thinking together.* New York: Doubleday/Currency.

Krogh, G. von, Ichijo, K., & Nonaka, I. (2000). *Enabling knowledge creation.* New York: Oxford University Press.

Laur, J., & Schley, S. (2004). *The SoL Sustainability Consortium: Society for Organizational Learning.* Report on consortium activities available at http://www.solonline.org

Lave, J., & Wenger, E. (1991). *Situated learning: Legitimate peripheral participation.* Cambridge, UK: Cambridge University Press.

Lawrence, T. B., Hardy, C., & Phillips, N. (2002). Institutional effects of interorganizational collaborations: The emergence of proto-institutions. *Academy of Management Journal, 45*(1), 281–290.

Levitt, B., & March, J. (1988). Organizational learning. *Annual Review of Sociology, 14,* 319–340.

Manga, J., Mirvis, P., Rochlin, S., & Zecchi, K. (2005). *Integration: Critical link for corporate citizenship.* Boston: Center for Corporate Citizenship.

March, J. G. (1991). Exploration and exploitation in organization learning. *Organization Science, 2,* 71–87.

Meyerson, D. (2003). *Tempered radicals: How everyday leaders inspire change at work.* Boston: Harvard Business School Press.

Mirvis, P. H. (1996). Historical foundations of organizational learning. *Journal of Organization Change Management, 9*(1), 13–31.

Mirvis, P. H., & Googins, B. (2006). Stages of corporate citizenship: A developmental framework. *California Management Review, 48*(2), 104–126.

Mirvis, P. H., & Manga, J. (2006, May). *Integrating corporate citizenship: Leading from the middle.* Paper presented at the Conference on Corporate Responsibility and Global Business: Implications for Corporate and Marketing Strategy, London Business School.

Mitroff, I., & Kilmann, R. (1978). *Methodological approaches to social science.* San Francisco: Jossey-Bass.

Mohrman, S. A., Gibson, C. B., & Mohrman, A. M., Jr. (2001). Doing research that is useful to practice. *Academy of Management Journal, 44*(2), 347–375.

Nonaka, I. (1994). A dynamic theory of organizational knowledge creation. *Organization Science, 5*(1), 14–37.

Oliver, C. (1990). Determinants of interorganizational relationships: Integration and future directions. *Academy of Management Review, 15,* 241–265.

Powell, W. W., Koput, K. W., & Smith-Doerr, L. (1996). Interorganizational collaboration and the locus of innovation: Networks of learning in biotechnology. *Administrative Science Quarterly, 41*(1), 116–145.

Reason, P., & Bradbury, H. (Eds.). (2001). *Handbook of action research: Participatory inquiry and practice.* London: Sage.

Ring, P. S., & Van de Ven, A. H. (1994). Developmental processes of cooperative interorganizational relationships. *Academy of Management Review, 19*(1), 90–118.

Rochlin, S. A., & Googins, B. K. (2005). *The value proposition for corporate citizenship.* Boston: Center for Corporate Citizenship.

Rochlin, S. A., Jordan, S., Mirvis, P., Witter, K., & Thome Beevas, D. (2004–2006). *The state of corporate citizenship in the U.S.* Boston: Center for Corporate Citizenship.

Rynes, S. L., Bartunek, J. M., & Daft, R. L. (2001). Across the great divide: Knowledge creation and transfer between practitioners and academics. *Academy of Management Journal, 44*(2), 340–355.

Schön, D. A. (1983). *The reflective practitioner: How professionals think in action.* New York: Basic Books.

Schultz, M. S., & Hatch, M. J. (2003). The cycles of corporate branding: The case of the LEGO Company. *California Management Review, 46*(1), 6–26.

Schultz, M. S., & Hatch, M. J. (2005). Building theory from practice. *Strategic Organization, 3*(3), 337–347.

Senge, P., Bradbury, H., Carroll, J., & Kaeufer, K. (2004). *Requisite complexity: Organizing for problems of unprecedented complexity* [Unpublished working paper]. Cambridge, MA: Society for Organizational Learning.

Senge, P., Kleiner, A., Laur, J., Schley, S., & Smith, B. (2006). *Learning for sustainability.* Cambridge, MA: Society for Organizational Learning.

Senge, P., Kleiner, A., Roberts, C., Ross, R., & Smith, B. (1994). *The fifth discipline fieldbook: Strategies and tools for building a learning organization.* New York: Doubleday/Currency.

Van de Ven, A. H. (2006). *Practicing engaged scholarship.* Paper presented at the Academy of Management Annual Conference, Atlanta, GA.

Wenger, E., & Snyder, W. (2000). Communities of practice: The organizational frontier. *Harvard Business Review, 78,* 139–145.

Part III
EXEMPLARS
Cases and Projects
IIIA. Collaborative Research in a Single System

The first two sections in this volume have been focused on providing arguments for the use of collaborative management research and on illustrating different types of mechanisms and processes for pursuing this type of research. So far, our contributors have described the character, features, and functioning of an alternative and complementary research approach—a new camera. Now we move into Part III, where the prime focus will be on showing the pictures that can be taken with this new camera, the exemplars: the cases and projects pursued by researchers and managers exploring collaborative management research approaches in different settings.

In planning this volume, we asked for recent or contemporary case studies on "collaboration and the creation of knowledge through research in order to improve the capacity to effectively manage complex systems so they can attain their goals." From the different stories we received from our colleagues, we have chosen to include a portfolio of exemplars that together are intended to illustrate the multiplicity of setups, groups of actors, applied processes, and possible outcomes fitting within our statement above. The authors of each exemplar have all been asked to answer a series of questions such as the following:

- Who were the practitioners, what were they trying to accomplish, and why were they engaging in the collaborative research process?
- Who were the scientists/scholarly researchers, and what is the scholarly knowledge that they were trying to create?
- What was the collaborative research process, and what were the roles played by various stakeholders?
- What scientific knowledge was created?

- What actionable knowledge was created, from the practitioners' perspective?
- How was the knowledge implemented or acted upon?
- How did the collaboration lead to betterment or accomplishments of both sets of goals, for example, what learning processes took place? What enabled learning or inhibited it?
- How did the knowledge of practitioners and the knowledge of researchers combine to yield an effective knowledge-producing collaboration?

The exemplars are grouped under three subheadings: collaborative research in a single system, collaborative research in complex networks, and collaborative research in government and society. Table III.1 gives an overview of the 10 chapters that make up this section of the *Handbook*. A striking characteristic of almost all of these cases is that they involve the application of a model, more or less in the way David and Hatchuel defined management models in Chapter 2. Such models contain some kind of philosophical justification, a conceptual/theoretical description of the model, and a set of techniques, tools, and instruments that makes the model actionable. This observation leads to two further reflections.

One is that collaboration is far from the image of practitioners and scientists sitting down at a tabula rasa, scratching their heads, and asking each other how to collaborate. Instead, the model in practice is more similar to that used by consultants. Practitioners have needs to improve their system and are seeking ways to do so; scientists bring models and methodologies that could be applied to help and also generate new knowledge. When the interests of the two parties align, collaboration begins, but doesn't always succeed. The relationship between the parties and the ability of each party to provide what the other is looking for ultimately determine the fate of the collaboration. The second reflection is that consultants are often successful in what they do because they base their work on models that have been tested and shown to be useful to managers. Sometimes these models have been honed to make them simple, understandable, and applicable. In contrast, scientists often seek to build new models rather than simply apply existing ones. In this respect, they have no "goods" to sell and cannot promise in advance how useful their discoveries may be. Managers, to avoid risk and achieve rapid results, could understandably prefer working with consultants to engaging in collaborative management research.

Nevertheless, as these exemplars attest, some managers are willing to take the risks that accompany collaborative management research. Some of these managers may have been disappointed with the results of other approaches they have tried for addressing their issues or opportunities. Others may enjoy participating in collaborative inquiry. A few may be seeking the recognition that comes with being a successful innovator. Each of the stories that is told by the contributors in this section reveals different motivations on the part of the parties involved. What is important for readers to understand, we believe, is that there is not one best way to approach collaborative management research, and that the intangible elements in relationships often influence the strength of collaborative efforts as much as the logic behind the research.

FORMS OF COLLABORATION

Apel, Heikensten, and Jansson (Chapter 18 in this volume) suggest that the collaboration between academic economists and the practitioners who govern the monetary system takes three forms: interaction, formal collaboration, and integration. When it comes to central banking, the trend is clearly the latter; there is a strong trend toward integrating economists who have academic credentials and who publish in the best academic journals into the banks' own

Table III.1 Overview of the Chapters in Part III

Chapter	System Studied	Model Used	Form of Collaboration	Associated Pactical Outcome
Boyatzis, Howard, Rapisarda, & Taylor	Authoritarian CEO	Intentional change theory (Reinforcing positive social behavior)	Manager + coach + researcher	CEO became more considerate
Olascoaga & Kur	Manufacturing pilot plant	Dynamic strategic alignment (Collaboration a component)	Management + consultant/ researcher	More understanding of the need to be responsive to customers
Kolodny & Halpern	Manufacturing plant	Socio-technical system theory	Management/staff + consultant/ researcher	Doubling of productivity
Tandon & Farrell	Gender discrimination in NGOs	Organization development for mainstreaming	Specialized organization advising other NGOs	Improved practical awareness of gender issues and preparedness to act
Walshok & Stymne	Region	Collaborative game	Arenas for the meeting of scientists, entrepreneurs, and service providers	Commercially highly successful innovations
Huzzard & Gregory	Unions in social partnership with employers	Boxing and dancing	International group of unionists + researchers form policy based on local cases	Actionable ways for unions to handle a key sensitive issue
Roth	University-industry collaboration in technology development	Different models for industry collaboration have been tried and are described and evaluated in the chapter		Recommendation that university creates policy; researchers have to understand different cultures in industry
Apel, Heikensten, & Jansson	The monetary policy component of the nation's economic system	A model for how to relate today's interest level to the desired inflation level	Central bank managers + university and in-house economists	Radical lowering of inflation
Knights, Alferoff, Starkey, & Tiratsoo	Business school collaboration with industry	Actor network theory	Research forums	Ways to make forums more attractive for practitioners
Bammer & the Goolabri Group	Uncertainty and ignorance in an area of practice, e.g., illicit drug prevention	Systems theory	Symposium bringing specialists from different areas together	Book, at least one company representative incorporated ideas in practice

staff. Our impression is that there is a similar trend among consultancy firms. However, even if there is some mention of internal consultants among the exemplars, there is no general trend visible of integrating management researchers in industrial firms, as called for by Adler and Beer (Chapter 26). Having management scientists working on R&D in management in industry would of course lead to closer contacts between university-based management research and in-house management researchers. This was certainly the case in the banks studied by Apel and his colleagues. Why does this form of collaboration not happen more often in other settings? This is worth thinking about, and perhaps with additional thought we might find convincing arguments to begin to change the status quo.

The remainder of the exemplars described by the contributors to this section take the form of informal or formal collaboration between individuals or institutions. In the example offered by Tandon and Farrell (Chapter 14) concerning gender issues in India, the collaboration was between a specialized nongovernmental organization (NGO), set up with the explicit goal of assisting other NGOs, and the NGOs the organization served. In the Huzzard and Gregory chapter dealing with unions (Chapter 16), a two-level approach to collaboration was used to create social partnerships. First, at the local level, experience was gathered in real instances of attempts to form social partnerships between the union and employers, often with the participation of a researcher. Second, at the international level, unionists from Europe and the United States collaborated with researchers to formulate both union practice and theories for the unions' handling of "social partnerships" in the national or local arena. Roth's analysis (Chapter 17) of the collaboration of MIT scientists with industry since the Second World War shows that collaboration took many forms within the scope of formal contracts between the companies and the university. Roth's research into the history of collaborative efforts found that designing the contracts and the specific forms of collaboration was highly problematic. Collaboration became even more difficult as funds from companies became scarce, so the university began to shift its research to government-sponsored contracts. Nevertheless, industry-university partnerships continue, and at least some that Roth describes have had quite positive results. The same is true of the industry-university collaborations that Walshok and Stymne (Chapter 15) describe in the San Diego region, where such collaborations helped to found several highly successful startup companies. Roth concludes that the relationship between the company and individual scientists or university representatives is often the deciding factor in determining whether companies renew their collaborative research contracts.

In the Walshok and Stymne case regarding the University of California, San Diego, it is obvious that a different approach was used than was used by Roth and his colleagues at MIT. The San Diego form of collaboration involves the establishment of a multitude of arenas where scientists, entrepreneurs, venture capitalists, and representatives of other business services meet in different constellations that create opportunities for the participants to form collaborative relationships, for example, in order to commercialize a scientific discovery. The collaboration is not designed in detail, but there are "rules" to be followed in the collaborative game that takes place on the regional playing field. These rules are partly formalized and partly emergent, and consist of such things as different types of forums that are created to familiarize companies with the work of scientists. Moreover, the history of success of such approaches in the region has created expectations for success in collaborative efforts that help the efforts get off the ground and overcome issues that would otherwise derail them. The creation of a "collaborative region" therefore creates a more fertile ground for collaborative efforts to take root than is available in other settings.

The three chapters dealing with government and society reveal that forms of collaboration have been sought that could overcome the natural boundaries between researchers, managers, and society. The business school studied by Knights, Alferoff, Starkey, and Tiratsoo (Chapter 19) opened up interactions among these parties by creating "research forums" for encounters between the financial world and academics. Knights and his colleagues show that the forums took more than just inviting people to a gathering to be successful. In fact, they required professional leadership and the creation of an ongoing network. The network in this case consisted of different actors in the financial sector who used the forums to meet people and enter into discussions of issues that they could not have held elsewhere.

Bammer (Chapter 20), in her discussion of the implementation of scientific discoveries, starts from the observation that there is a lack of knowledge related to important societal issues because existing knowledge is hidden in "silos" and is not communicated across these boundaries. Examples of such issues are found in the areas of achieving environmental sustainability and stopping the flow of illegal drugs. Bammer therefore arranged symposia for scientists from different disciplines and practitioners who were concerned about these issues. In advance, each participant had to write a paper on uncertainty and knowledge in his or her field and to read the corresponding papers from two other fields. Then two days of discussion ensued on how to decrease ignorance and uncertainty in the different fields and by doing so, make society more competent in handling its present and future challenges. The general outcomes from the symposia were that people from the different silos were quite interested in trading information about their situation and felt enriched by getting information from the others. When it came to discussing how a framework could be created to establish a new science of integration and implementation, the reactions of participants were less positive and even hostile. Experiments in collaboration such as this one indicate that we are making progress but still have much to learn about supporting the deeper and longer-lasting efforts that will be required to affect global events.

OUTCOMES OF COLLABORATION

Most of the exemplars of collaborative research report impressive results. As an example, let us train the camera on what happened to the CEO described in the chapter by Boyatzis, Howard, Rapisarda, and Taylor (Chapter 11): As the film opens, the CEO knows that he is an authoritarian person who dominates his subordinates, but he wishes to be better liked by them, as well as by his first grandchild. The coaching process is carried out collaboratively and is based on research in similar situations. To better understand the client's strengths for establishing positive relationships with others, the researchers developed a technique for evoking happy incidents rather than focusing on the weaknesses that the client wanted to change. The next sequence of the "film" shows how the client is advised to start using his hitherto hidden social intelligence in a less-demanding and less-engrained context than work. We then observe him doing so in his church. And just before the film's end, the researcher is listening to a subordinate of the CEO express positive astonishment that the CEO has started to listen to the opinions of others in the firm and to treat them with consideration. As the audience viewing these productive transformations, we conclude that collaborative research with individual managers can produce powerful developmental experiences.

In addition to the case just cited, four of the remaining cases report clear measures of their associated outcomes: Doubling productivity was the outcome of work using sociotechnical systems design in a Canadian manufacturing organization in the chapter by Kolodny and Halpern (Chapter 13). Product innovations that created some of the most spectacular cases of profitable growth in the history of U.S. companies during the last 15 years were reviewed by Walshok and Stymne (Chapter 15). Finally, lowering inflation from double digits to 2% was associated with the collaborative research described in the chapter by Apel, Heikensten, and Jansson (Chapter 18). The other chapters report better understanding and more awareness of, for example, the need be responsive to customers (Olascoaga & Kur, Chapter 12); gender issues (Tandon & Farrell, Chapter 14); actions unions should take to improve social partnerships (Huzzard & Gregory, Chapter 16); recommendations for helping scientists get a better appreciation of the culture of industry to be practically useful (Roth, Chapter 17); advice on how to go about exactly that when it comes to business schools (Knights et al., Chapter 19); and a practical demonstration of how to get people from different knowledge silos to collaborate on key societal issues (Bammer and the Goolabri Group, Chapter 20).

Since most of the chapters in this section are based on the application of existing models, the scientific payoffs from these chapters are twofold. First, they verify the models in use. One interesting verification is the finding of Knights et al. (Chapter 19) that the actor network theory developed by Callon and Latour was useful when they designed a well-functioning research forum. All the cases mentioned above that report quantitative figures as measures of their success can also be regarded as having achieved a strong verification of the models underlying the approach in use. The second type of scientific payoff from the collaborative research efforts in this section is that either the model used was improved or information was generated that will be helpful in future revisions of the model. There is also one example of the discovery of a new model of "boxing and dancing" for application in the context of unions (Huzzard & Gregory, Chapter 16).

Together, these chapters represent some of the cutting-edge practice that is occurring in collaborative management research. What is clear to us, and quite honestly a bit unexpected, is the range of application represented here. From assisting with individual development to addressing societal issues, collaborative management research has been applied with promise. In each case, the approach and methods used were different, but still within the spirit and definition of what now can be more clearly defined as the boundaries of this discipline. We are excited by the potential these exemplars represent for the future development of the field, as well as for our ability to use collaborative management research to make headway on some complex and long-standing issues.

CHAPTER 11

Coaching for Sustainable Change

RICHARD E. BOYATZIS

ANITA HOWARD

BRIGETTE RAPISARDA

SCOTT TAYLOR

ABSTRACT

Coaching is one of the most-used methods for helping people develop. But research on coaching, what works and what does not, is often missed. Such research can and should be collaborative for many reasons. First, coaching requires a trusting, collaborative relationship. Second, coaching with compassion engages the human body, neurologically and hormonally, in a healthy process of renewal. It is contagious, and most easily spread in collaborative relationships. Third, research on coaching, and probably any form of management and leadership development, is better when it occurs in the midst of a collaborative relationship.

Longitudinal research has shown that coaching can lead to significant improvement in the emotional and social intelligence competencies that enable managers and leaders to be effective. This occurs through a process described by intentional change theory. The theory explains that people develop through cyclical iterations of five discontinuous discoveries: (1) the Ideal Self; (2) the Real Self; (3) a Learning Agenda; (4) experimentation and practice; and (5) forming close, trusting, resonant relationships.

While sitting on the long flight to Samoa, Roger Selden was nervous.[1] It was not the flying, nor was it the challenge of building a schoolhouse with friends from his church. He was about to try being sensitive to others and a compassionate leader. For 30 years, Roger had refined and used his gruff style. He built and sold two companies and was now cofounder and CEO of United Health Services, a 1-billion-dollar-a-year healthcare company. His fast-paced, hard-nosed style and relentless drive had served him well over the years. But lately he had been worried. The company had recently lost its CFO and its VP of sales. Turnover was becoming costly. The culture reflected Roger's style—it had become cutthroat and survival oriented. It had always worked, but Roger had begun to wonder if there was a better way. This process of the leader slipping into dissonance with others, as well as with himself or herself, is described in detail in Boyatzis and McKee (2005). What Roger did not realize or even appreciate is how sensitivity to others is required for collaboration, and collaboration is required for sustainable behavior change, as the reader will learn later in this chapter. Let's look at how Roger got into this situation.

Fortunately for Roger and United, the COO decided to begin a leadership development program. A key feature of the program was to work with an executive coach. A few months later, Roger found himself on the flight to Samoa and considering experimenting with a dramatically different leadership style. And it happened through building of resonant relationships with others, including a coach.

Roger's experience is typical of a new wave of an old practice—the use of coaching for development. In the past, people in these roles have been called mentors, guides, trainers, therapists, and sometimes friends. The articles appearing in *The Wall Street Journal* and *The Economist* about coaching signal the arrival of a practice that used to be relegated to the athletic field. When effective coaching relationships evolve, they are collaborative relationships in which the coach and the person being coached develop trust and caring for each other. They typically move further into a resonant relationship in which they are in sync with each other. A resonant relationship is one in which the two people, or leader and group, are in synchrony

with each other (Boyatzis & McKee, 2005). It is a relationship filled with a positive emotional tone, best characterized by the concept of "hope." It is also a relationship in which people feel compassion toward each other. More than mere empathy, compassion invokes caring, and action based on that caring. Collaborative relationships also require a degree of mindfulness on the part of all people in the relationship. Effective leaders have such relationships with the people around them, as do effective coaches and helpers.

It is likely that if Roger had not begun working with a coach, his style would have remained the same. Or more accurately, he might have tried to change, but it either would not have worked or would only have lasted a few days. This challenge of helping someone change his or her behavior, style, or perspective requires a collaborative relationship. It requires a relationship in which both parties have the same overarching goals, the same degree of mutual care and compassion, and the same vision and hope and are spreading a contagion of positive emotion (Boyatzis & McKee, 2005; Goleman, 2006). As most readers will acknowledge, it is difficult to sustain such a collaborative and resonant relationship in an organizational atmosphere consumed by fear, threat, or the animosity often associated with competition against other people. But it all starts at the level of individuals and their relationships.

ENTER THE COACH

People change. Recent research has established that people can change in desired ways—and the changes can be sustained over years (Ballou, Bowers, Boyatzis, & Kolb, 1999; Boyatzis, 2006; Boyatzis, Stubbs, & Taylor, 2002; Cherniss & Adler, 2000; Goleman, Boyatzis, & McKee, 2002). But the research has revealed an old axiom—we need others to help us develop. Enter the coaches. Professionals in these roles range from consultants who add a trusted-adviser aspect to their practice, to social workers and therapists who decide to use their skills with people facing work challenges instead of anxiety attacks or eating disorders. The ranks of coaches are growing at a prodigious rate all over the world. The personal attention is both attractive and private. It does not require disclosing one's foibles or vulnerabilities in front of others. In many countries and cultures in which the "boss" is to be respected, feared, and not addressed with informality, executive coaches provide a convenient and safe way to explore development and change. This can also work for those whose style is not accessible to others, like Roger. Is there a form of coaching that is most appropriate in a collaborative management research setting? An issue with the growing popularity of coaching is that the field seems full of competing approaches, and it's difficult at times to separate the gurus from the quacks. The best antidote seems to be a careful review of a coach's past clients—who were they, did they change, were the time and effort well spent? Of course, the ultimate test would be an empirical longitudinal study, but few people have the skills or the patience for such research, so recommendations and referrals may be the most expedient approach to quality assurance.

Scott Taylor was Roger's coach as part of a company-sponsored program. His first challenge was to earn Roger's trust and build a collaborative relationship. Based on his training, he used an approach designed to engage a client's motivation. It was to ask Roger what he wanted out of life and what he wanted for his future and the company's future. Roger, like many crusty executives, does not often talk openly about his own future and might not even have considered what life and work might be like in 10 years or more. Roger had announced his intention to hand over the CEO role to the current

COO in a year or two. So Scott asked what he looked forward to doing after that, what kind of life he wanted to lead, and what he hoped his legacy in the company would be. Roger did not hesitate in his answer. He wanted to be seen as a great leader of the company, but without the additional complaints about his intimidating style and Machiavellian tactics. He hoped his family would enjoy spending more time with him, but even that would involve his family seeing him as a different person than they did.

The tipping point in his willingness to change came when they talked about him learning that his only son and daughter-in-law were going to have a child. Roger wanted to become the kind of grandfather who would be fun, approachable, and respected. He knew this meant change. If Scott had not asked about Roger's life and his aspirations outside of work, the key opening to his new desire to change would not have been found. The path to opening a trusting relationship is to engage each other in a common desire or emotion. In this case, it was developing an image of a desired future. As Roger talked about this desired future, Scott shared some of his own thoughts and feelings. After all, a collaborative relationship requires mutuality and sharing, in addition to trust. It seems that Roger was pretty open after all.

FINDING YOUR PERSONAL VISION: YOUR IDEAL SELF

In workshops, courses, and lectures on coaching over the past three years, a group of us from Case Western Reserve University have made several discoveries about when coaching is and is not effective. It required us to develop collaborative relationships and to engage in research to help develop and refine concepts of what works and what does not. This study group did not occur from thin air;

the context was a series of similar relationships among people in the past. This follows 18 years of longitudinal studies showing adults can change their habits and develop both cognitive and emotional intelligence competencies (Boyatzis et al., 2002; Ballou et al., 1999). A comparison of results from these studies and averages of other graduate management programs and training in government and industry is shown in Figure 11.1. This comparison shows that a program with coaching using intentional change theory shows substantial improvements in emotional and social intelligence competency behavior (Boyatzis et al., 2002; Goleman et al., 2002). These changes last for at least five to seven years. Meanwhile, training programs in government and industry show poor results of about a 10% improvement from three to 18

months after the programs (Cherniss & Adler, 2000). This effect atrophies even more over time.

When adults change their behavior, they follow a series of epiphanies, or discoveries, that Richard Boyatzis described with his intentional change theory (Boyatzis, 2001, 2006; Boyatzis & McKee, 2005), which was called self-directed learning theory in earlier works (Goleman et al., 2002). Intentional change theory is presented in Figure 11.2. The research and theory development were a part of the process of helping people change and grow. So there were two levels of collaboration involved, one among the researchers and teaching and coaching staff and one between the teaching and coaching staff and the participants and students. Let's look at the theory to see how it works.

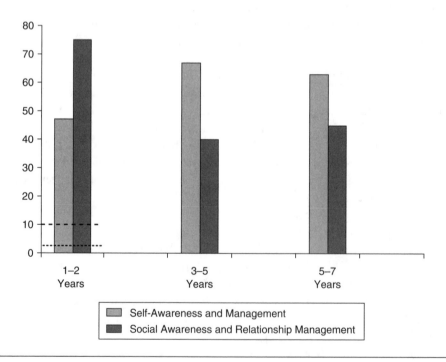

Figure 11.1 Percentage Improvement of Emotional and Social Intelligence Competencies of Different Groups of MBA Graduates Taking the Intentional Change Course

NOTE: - - - - - - - - Indicates impact of company and government training programs 3–18 months after training on multiple emotional and social intelligence competencies.

--------------- Indicates impact of a variety of above-average MBA programs.

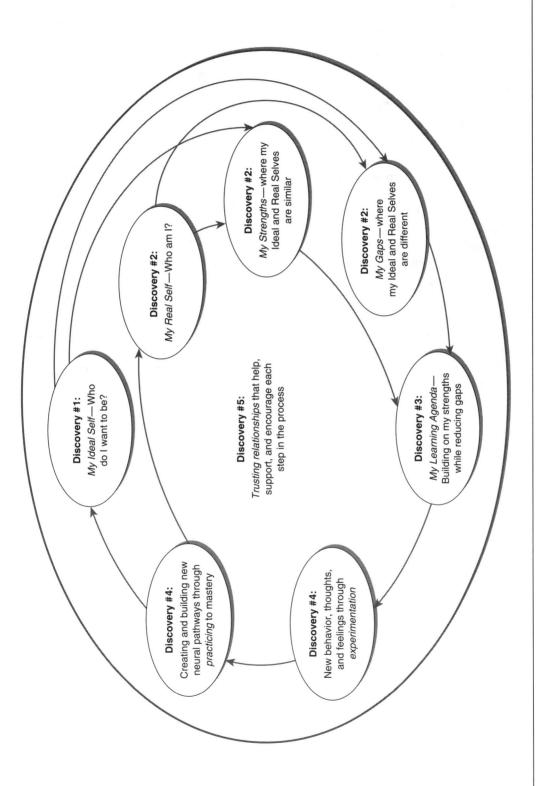

Figure 11.2   Boyatzis's Intentional Change Theory

235

Based on complexity theory concepts, intentional change theory shows that sustainable, desired change is most often a series of discoveries or experienced discontinuities, called emergence in complexity theory (Boyatzis, 2006). When the process of change is studied over time, five specific discoveries, or epiphanies, seem always to be present: (1) the Ideal Self, or personal vision, a discovery of who you want to be and what you want out of life (Boyatzis & Akrivou, 2006); (2) the Real Self, a personal balance sheet with a sense of your strengths and weaknesses (your present behavior as compared with your Ideal Self) (Taylor, 2006); (3) the Learning Agenda, your approach to getting closer to your personal vision using strengths and possibly working on a few weaknesses close to the tipping point; (4) experimentation and practice with the new behavior or perspective; and (5) development of resonant relationships: close, trusting relationships that enable you to experience and move into each of the discoveries (Boyatzis, 2006).

If the first discovery does not occur, people don't change. That is the reason most people think leaders are born, not made. On the whole, those of us who try to help are lousy at developing people. Despite well-intentioned, sensitive, thoughtful people as consultants, teachers, or coaches, most education and training does not produce sustainable changes in behavior. To explore why this occurs, let us suggest an exercise. Take a moment and do the following reflective exercise.

When managers, executives, and advanced professionals do this exercise, they have warm, emotional reactions to the memories of the people who helped them. The feelings come back strongly as they remember moments that may have been tender or challenging but had a lasting impact. When we recorded these reflections and coded them for which aspect of the change process was primarily involved, we discovered that 80% of the moments people recalled involved someone helping them extend their dreams, reach for new aspirations, or consider what it means to be successful or a good person. In other words, these people help us re-create a new Ideal Self (i.e., personal vision) or endorse our strengths and capability in a way we doubted or never considered.

When we examined the moments people recalled of others trying to help them in the last year or two, most instances (typically 50% to 67%) involved someone giving us feedback and focusing on what we needed to do to improve; that is, focusing on our weaknesses. The application of the business practice of "gap analysis" was rampant as the tactic most used to help someone else work on his or her "development or performance improvement plan."

Reflection

Think about the people in your life who helped you the most. Think of the people who helped you achieve what you have in life and work and who helped you become the person you are. Write their names on a sheet of paper. Next to each name, describe moments you remember with them that had a lasting impact on you. What did they say or do? Thinking back to these moments, what did you learn or take away from them?

Now think of the people who tried to help, manage, or coach you over the last two years. Think of the moments with them. What did they say or do?

Go back to each of the moments remembered from the first list and ask yourself which stage of the intentional change model was involved.

No wonder many people do not change. We are often doing the wrong things to encourage and support the exploration of a change. In fact, we are often doing the opposite of what has worked so well for most of us. We often try to help "fix the problem" or prove to the person that he or she has to change. Such relationships seldom involve collaboration and its components, such as a deep trust, mutuality, and interest in discovering the truth (often the role of research or other forms of inquiry).

This is what happened to Roger Selden. Scott asked him about his desired future and what kind of person he wanted to be. Using several exercises and tests, Roger began to develop an image of his future. He smiled as he thought about it. "Wouldn't it be great if I could do that?" he asked Scott, but then quickly followed, "But it's too hard and I'm too old for this. Besides, no one would believe me if I started acting that differently." Scott pointed out that developing the desired image was the first step. Then he had to consider his strengths before attacking a weakness. Roger kept getting caught in what was likely and began to conclude it was impractical.

THE POSITIVE AND NEGATIVE EMOTIONAL ATTRACTORS

Roger got excited and then almost as quickly began to dampen his enthusiasm. He was setting in motion an orientation that would inhibit any change or limit its sustainability. As he worried about the feasibility of the change, he emotionally focused on his weaknesses. His smile dropped as he began to frown. You could see him becoming tense and worried. He had entered the realm of the negative emotional attractor.

Research on neuroendocrine processes and their relationship to psychological and behavioral patterns shows that people can find themselves involved in moving toward a positive or negative emotional attractor (PEA or NEA) (for more on the PEA, see Boyatzis, 2006; Dyck, Caron, & Aron, 2006; Howard, 2006). The PEA involves arousing the parasympathetic nervous system, a set of neural circuits predominantly emanating through the left prefrontal cortex. When you consider your dreams, hopes, and desired vision for the future, your breathing slows, your blood pressure drops, your immune system increases its activity, and you feel calm, elated, happy, amused, optimistic, and hopeful (Boyatzis, Smith, & Blaize, 2006; for more on the Ideal Self, see Boyatzis & Akrivou, 2006). This appears to also occur when we consider our strengths.

In contrast, when you invoke the NEA, you focus on weaknesses, fear, and being "realistic," or you dwell on what happened in the past and what went wrong. You feel nervous, anxious, depressed, pessimistic, or filled with despair. The NEA arouses and is aroused by your sympathetic nervous system and neural circuits emanating predominantly through your right prefrontal cortex. Your blood pressure increases, as does your breathing. Your facial muscles tighten. Your body prepares for stress or injury, and in doing so elicits the stress response. You get set to defend yourself. In eliciting the stress response, you prepare for "fight or flight" and send blood to large muscle groups as well as closing off neural circuits not necessary to survival (for more on the NEA, see Boyatzis, 2006; Dyck et al., 2006; Howard, 2006).

The PEA not only allows you to open yourself to new possibilities and relationships but, because emotions are contagious (Goleman, 2006; Hatfield, Cacioppo, & Rapson, 1994), draws others into positive, supportive relationships with those in the situation. The NEA pushes you to fix things that are wrong. It creates distance between people. Did you ever wonder why it is so hard to lose weight? We believe it is because it is a negatively conceived goal. It would be different if you wanted to feel vibrant and look good—and losing weight were part of the way to get there. So the PEA allows you to move toward your aspirations. The NEA inhibits forward movement—it, quite literally, turns you off.

To make a sustainable change in one's habits or behavior, a person needs to start with the PEA and move through the NEA. And it is difficult, if not impossible, to do this alone. Roger did this with the help of his coach. After soliciting a refined image of Roger's desired future from him—his personal vision—Scott then felt that Roger was ready to look at some feedback. The research they had collected as part of the assessment contained data on Roger's behavior and the ways many others around him viewed his behavior. Roger's feedback from the Emotional Competence Inventory (ECI; Boyatzis & Sala, 2004) was not surprising to him. He had heard it before. His direct reports stated in the verbatim comments that Roger was a stubborn man, bullied people with his strong opinions, dominated discussions, constantly made decisions that lower-level employees were charged to make, and rarely appeared to listen to others' opinions. He had tried to change before but was always afraid that if he got "soft," results would fall, and he with them.

Scott had to redirect Roger during the discussion. Roger wanted to focus on and explain his weaknesses. This is a common mistake. Once people become embedded in analyzing their weaknesses, they are solidly arousing the NEA and have a hard time keeping the context hopeful and part of the PEA. Scott reminded Roger that he yearned to leave a legacy of doing something important *and doing it the right way*. He asked Roger to describe the person who acted the way Roger had said he always wanted to act. His ideal was someone people felt close to; someone by whom others felt valued in their ideas; a leader who was able to help people achieve their potential and get incredible results because of his confidence in them and impact he had on them. Once they summarized his strengths of determination, initiative, influencing others, and adaptability, they turned to the "bad news." An image of using his strengths to build a new style began to appear to Roger. But he was cynical about pulling it off. This ideal became more salient because he was going to step down as CEO in a year and wanted to be remembered differently, if possible.

EXPERIMENTING WITH A NEW ROGER SELDEN

Scott suggested that maybe the workplace was not the best setting in which to experiment with the change. Relationships at work invoked people's memory of his past habits. Roger was the boss at work, and people deferred to his authority because they had suffered from the consequences of not doing so in the past. Scott thought it best to build new relationships in a new setting as a way for Roger to practice his sensitivity to others.

Scott suggested that the church congregation Roger often talked about might be a better place. Roger leaned back in his chair and his face lit up. He had not thought of starting outside the organization, but the perfect opportunity to try a new leadership style was being planned. A small group of people in his congregation were going to go to Samoa to build a schoolhouse for a village. Roger could see himself getting into his natural command and control mode and taking over the leadership for the project. He decided instead to set up a plan to be like his ideal leader. "These church members don't know what I am like, they don't know I am a CEO of a company; they have not experienced my command style. This is a clean slate," he said. Roger and Scott crafted a specific Learning Agenda. Although it might sound like a semantic quibble, a learning plan documents experimenting and trying things. This feels different than a performance improvement plan—the former arouses the PEA and the latter arouses the NEA.

After the trip to Samoa, Roger could not wait to tell Scott that the project was a tremendous success. He viewed the experience as an experiment, a form of research. He discovered that they had worked as a team and he was not carrying the load alone. When he was called on to lead a piece of the work, he asked questions and listened to others before solving the problem and laying out the solution. He was amazed at the capability of the others. He said he did catch himself once or twice when he was on the verge of interrupting someone or arguing about a choice someone else had made.

Roger felt transformed. For the first time, he had experienced himself influencing others in a way that strengthened others but still brought out tremendous results. Even at home, Roger focused on "being patient and listening completely to family members." His son told Scott a few weeks later that he saw a difference in his father: "He seems quieter; you can tell he is really trying to listen."

Now it was time to take it back to the workplace. Roger had enough "small wins" outside of work. He was excited about the challenge, he realized it would not be easy and that he would have setbacks, but he was eager to try. A month later, in a coaching session with the head of sales, Scott asked the sales vice president (SVP) how Roger seemed to be doing. The SVP asked, "What have you done to him? He is not interrupting me as much. He has a few times, but catches himself and apologizes. He is really trying and, amazingly, making a little progress. People can't believe it. It's nice." Roger was becoming the kind of person he wanted to be, in a transformation that had eluded him for years. Roger was becoming his ideal leader.

Collaborative relationships breed collaborative relationships. Cooperation, like emotions, is contagious. In fact, as humans, we are hardwired for collaboration (Goleman, 2006). It is the most natural form of social relationship. In this example, the building of the collaborative relationship between Scott and Roger mirrored other relationships Scott had with members of the coaching study group at the university—other people involved in teaching and coaching and studying the process. Once Roger started being sensitive to others at the schoolhouse building site, he formed collaborative relationships—and this pattern spread. He was then able to change the nature of his relationships at home and at work.

Because people compete and block out collaboration only when they have learned to do so, we suggest that a natural model for doing research with humans, and by extension with our social institutions— whether they be teams, organizations, or communities—would be to use a collaborative model. This often means building a trusting and mutually beneficial relationship between the researcher and the "subjects." Some scholars extend this into an actual partnership with the people in the organization or in management. In our case, almost all of our research on coaching and helping to provoke sustainable, desired change involves collecting data and helping people develop at the same time.

To maintain intellectual integrity, those of us helping others change should engage in systematic research on the effects or impact of the change efforts. In contrast to what people may think, longitudinal research is a great candidate for collaborative research. It requires careful development of comparison conditions. But even cumbersome comparison conditions can be avoided by using time-series models. For example, suppose you were assessing the impact of a coaching intervention to help managers develop. You could assess a cadre of managers or leaders once a year over six years with a 360, to capture what others around them think about the frequency of their use of desired managerial or leadership competencies. Meanwhile, you could enroll them in a development program using coaching in the second or third year. The time series design allows you examine the impact of the coaching program. Even more important, it allows you to engage the managers and leaders in a collaborative relationship with the researchers. This helps them to feel a part of the effort, not "guinea pigs" of the consultants. It allows the consultants to explore the nature and degree of change without more intrusive and labor-intensive qualitative methods.

COLLABORATION ENABLES SUSTAINABLE CHANGE

To complete the picture, the process adults go through when they sustain improvements in their habits is described in Figure 11.2. As Roger Selden did, people go through five discoveries, or epiphanies (Boyatzis, 2006). The first, as described, is the development of your Ideal Self—your image of your desired future and the person you want to be (Boyatzis & Akrivou, 2006). The second discovery is the assessment of your strengths and weaknesses, which emerge when comparing how you appear to others (i.e., the Real Self) with your Ideal Self (Taylor, 2006). The third discovery is the development of a Learning Agenda and plan. How will you get closer to your Ideal Self, building on strengths and working on a few weaknesses? The fourth discovery is the experimentation and practice with the new behavior. The fifth discovery, which in many ways is the first, is the establishment of a trusting, collaborative relationship with someone who can help you through each of the steps in the process. This is where the coach of today becomes an essential element in the growth process, by helping people like Roger capture and become their dreams. The coaching relationship must be collaborative to be effective, and to induce compassion in both the coach and the person being coached (Boyatzis et al., 2006). This sets the stage for another level of collaboration, between the researcher and those being studied. People feel a part of helping others. The neuroendocrine, emotional, perceptual, and behavioral benefits of coaching are contagious. The collaboration allows both the researcher and the people being studied, both the coach and the people being coached, to develop while working together.

NOTE

1. Roger Selden's name and the name of the company have been changed to protect his privacy.

REFERENCES

Ballou, R., Bowers, D., Boyatzis, R. E., & Kolb, D. A. (1999). Fellowship in lifelong learning: An executive development program for advanced professionals. *Journal of Management Education, 23*(4), 338–354.

Boyatzis, R. E. (2001). Developing emotional intelligence. In C. Cherniss & D. Goleman (Eds.), *The emotionally intelligent workplace* (pp. 234–253). San Francisco: Jossey-Bass.

Boyatzis, R. E. (2006). Intentional change theory from a complexity perspective. *Journal of Management Development, 25*(7), 607–623.

Boyatzis, R. E., & Akrivou, K. (2006). The ideal self as a driver of change. *Journal of Management Development, 25*(7), 624–642.

Boyatzis, R. E., & McKee, A. (2005). *Resonant leadership: Renewing yourself and connecting with others through mindfulness, hope, and compassion.* Boston: Harvard Business School Press.

Boyatzis, R. E., & Sala, F. (2004). Assessing emotional intelligence competencies. In G. Geher (Ed.), *The measurement of emotional intelligence* (pp. 147–180). Hauppauge, NY: Novas Science Publishers.

Boyatzis, R. E., Smith, M., & Blaize, N. (2006). Sustaining leadership effectiveness through coaching and compassion: It's not what you think. *Academy of Management Journal on Learning and Education, 5*(1), 8–24.

Boyatzis, R. E., Stubbs, E. C., & Taylor, S. N. (2002). Learning cognitive and emotional intelligence competencies through graduate management education. *Academy of Management Journal on Learning and Education, 1*(2), 150–162.

Cherniss, C., & Adler, M. (2000). *Promoting emotional intelligence in organizations: Make training in emotional intelligence effective.* Washington, DC: American Society of Training and Development.

Dyck, L., Caron, A., & Aron, D. (2006). Working on the positive emotional attractor through training in health care. *Journal of Management Development, 25*(7), 671–688.

Goleman, D. (2006). *Social intelligence.* New York: Bantam Books.

Goleman, D., Boyatzis, R., & McKee, A. (2002). *Primal leadership: Realizing the power of emotional intelligence.* Boston: Harvard Business School Press.

Hatfield, E., Cacioppo, J. T., & Rapson, R. L. (1994). *Emotional contagion.* New York: Cambridge University Press.

Howard, A. (2006). The role of positive and negative emotional attractors in intentional change. *Journal of Management Development, 25*(7), 657–670.

Taylor, S. (2006). Why the real self is fundamental to intentional change. *Journal of Management Development, 25*(7), 643–656.

CHAPTER 12

Dynamic Strategic Alignment

An Integrated Method

ERNESTO OLASCOAGA

ED KUR

ABSTRACT

This study improved the alignment of members of a Mexican manufacturing corporation (MMC) with the strategy of that organization and simultaneously advanced what is known about ways to increase strategic alignment. This was accomplished using a new process called Dynamic Strategic Alignment (DSA). DSA is a collaborative action research process built on sociotechnical systems and information technology. MMC is a multisite corporation that had been severely affected by a national economic downturn. Multiple stakeholders collaborated in the process: a change coordinator, directors, plant managers, supervisors, information systems experts, and internal and external change agents. The study employed a collaborative approach to scientific data collection and analysis to generate actionable knowledge and increase organizational capability through continuous learning. The process substantially improved strategic alignment and performance, increased members' collaboration capabilities, strengthened the DSA process itself, and demonstrated the utility of a specific software package, Platform EJE®, for increasing strategic alignment. Conducted during a period of unusually high threats to organizational survival, the study demonstrates the ability of collaborative research to simultaneously advance the body of knowledge and facilitate organizational productivity and effectiveness.

PURPOSE OF THE PROJECT

MMC (a pseudonym) is a Mexican multi-plant manufacturing company that was in the midst of a major crisis brought on by global competition, reduced sales, and increased raw material prices. The CEO was interested in working with us to discover ways to enhance company performance. He was clear that the company would not survive unless it reduced its costs, redesigned its core manufacturing processes, and enhanced alignment among its leaders. He believed that we, as collaborators and researchers, would bring ideas, tools, and frameworks that would spark discussion and action. With his support, we entered the system and began the process of collaborative research.

MMC was a key supplier in the automotive industry. When it confronted a severe economic crisis in 2002, management began making major changes, including improving marketing, increasing process orientation in the company, restructuring certain components, improving strategic alignment, developing better performance indicators, involving people more, focusing on organizational learning, and reducing headcount. By March 2004, the company began using proprietary software called Platform EJE to support these changes. The first author is a partner of the consulting firm that developed and implemented this software.

Several needs converged in a manner that supported collaboration. MMC needed to support its change process; the consulting firm wanted to expand the use of its software and other services; and the authors wanted to further develop a process called Dynamic Strategic Alignment (DSA), which one of them had started to develop for the purpose of improving strategic alignment and execution.

MMC had used Platform EJE for two years in two plants and now wanted to use it in all of its business units as part of an alignment, deployment, and execution process (ADEP) for strategic planning that had already been initiated. Management hoped the software and the communication processes associated with it would help to reverse a breakdown in organizational climate that was under way. The ADEP team, formed by the HR director in charge of the alignment, an internal consultant, and an internal facilitator, was under enormous pressure because it was absolutely necessary for MMC to significantly increase quality, productivity, and sales.

During March 2004, with these forces in place, the parties agreed to conduct a collaborative research project. They believed that in order to execute strategy in the current environment, it would be necessary for people to improve their understanding of that strategy, to see how actual results compared with intended results, and to develop high levels of flexibility. The collaborative research process was conducted in one plant of the company as a pilot project that was to form the basis for further changes in other plants and divisions.

RESEARCHERS' FOUNDATIONAL FRAMEWORKS

The change process both utilized and contributed to the development of Dynamic Strategic Alignment, a process that rests on four foundations that we briefly discuss below. Figure 12.1 presents these foundations graphically and links them to the research methods used in this study. The foundations of DSA are the following:

1. STS, or sociotechnical systems

2. SDM, or the self-design model

3. CR, or collaborative research

4. IT, or information technology

The first foundation, sociotechnical systems theory (STS) and the sociotechnical systems change model (Pasmore, 1988), provides a basis for analyzing and understanding organizations (p. 120) as well as a specific protocol for identifying variables that affect alignment. For a rich historical perspective on how sociotechnical thinking has been applied in many other organizational studies and in practical change work, see Kolodny

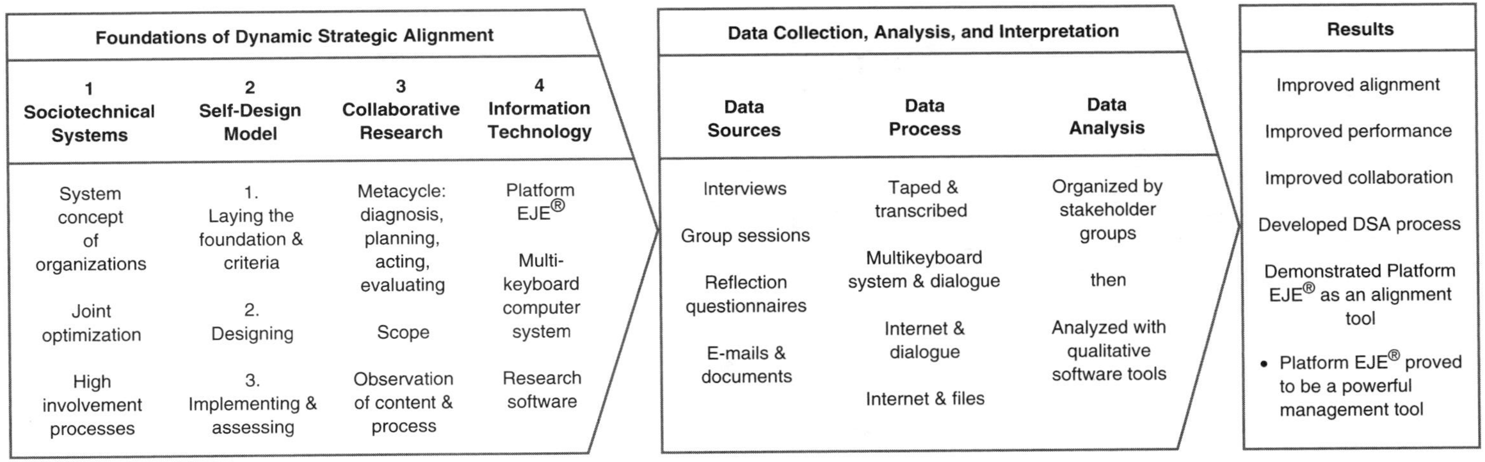

Foundations of Dynamic Strategic Alignment

1 Sociotechnical Systems	2 Self-Design Model	3 Collaborative Research	4 Information Technology
System concept of organizations	1. Laying the foundation & criteria	Metacycle: diagnosis, planning, acting, evaluating	Platform EJE®
Joint optimization	2. Designing	Scope	Multi-keyboard computer system
High involvement processes	3. Implementing & assessing	Observation of content & process	Research software

Data Collection, Analysis, and Interpretation

Data Sources	Data Process	Data Analysis
Interviews	Taped & transcribed	Organized by stakeholder groups
Group sessions		
Reflection questionnaires	Multikeyboard system & dialogue	then
E-mails & documents	Internet & dialogue	Analyzed with qualitative software tools
	Internet & files	

Results

Improved alignment

Improved performance

Improved collaboration

Developed DSA process

Demonstrated Platform EJE® as an alignment tool

• Platform EJE® proved to be a powerful management tool

Figure 12.1   Elements and Flow of the Dynamic Strategic Alignment Process

and Halpern (Chapter 13 in this *Handbook*). In our study, a tool developed for STS work, the Sociotechnical Systems Assessment Survey (STSAS; Pasmore, 1988), was used to identify variables in need of special attention, to identify social and technical training needs, and to help determine priorities for change and for implementing and using the alignment software. The STS framework helped participants to conceptualize the organization and provided the bases for many questions and ideas. For example, it was helpful to conceptualize the organization as a series of agreements among people (Pasmore, 1988, p. 4) and to recognize that organizational improvement often requires changing some past agreements. Furthermore, during the project the collaborators rediscovered that joint optimization of social and technical variables (i.e., the sociotechnical criterion) was more likely to lead to improved performance than optimizing these subsystems separately. STS also helped us understand that the ultimate objective of the design process should be to add learning capacity within the organization so that continuous self-redesign can take place.

The self-design model (SDM) developed by Mohrman and Mohrman (2004, p. 317) and Mohrman and Cummings (1989) was our second foundational framework. It provided a three-step approach to process design and organization design. SDM describes the roles and tasks carried out by the various parties involved in collaborative research. It also explains the key activities and products during each of three stages: (1) laying the foundation and criteria, (2) designing, and (3) implementation and assessment. As a change method, it supports the incorporation of existing knowledge, generation of new knowledge, translating knowledge into practical approaches, and testing these in practice. Mohrman, Docherty, and Shani (2006) explain that it provides a road map of the elements of action that were found to be predecessors of successful redesign in a series of change and research projects. Basically, it stresses the need to lay a foundation for strategy-driven redesign by (1) identifying the values that are to guide both the design process and the new organization, (2) learning about what is known in organization science and from practice that is relevant to the task at hand, and (3) diagnosing the functioning of the current system and identifying the gap between the current and desired states. Design criteria are generated from the learning that results as the foundation is constructed.

Literally hundreds of elements, processes, tools, arrangements, models, roles, tasks, and positions were designed in the course of this project. The self-design model reminded us that for each of these a foundation must be set, criteria established, care taken during implementation, and assessment conducted, if we were to learn. Indeed, our work suffered most during those moments when we disregarded that reminder.

Our third foundational framework, collaborative research (CR), proved critically valuable. It facilitated disengagement from various "silos" and reengagement in a collective process of creating actionable knowledge regarding strategy, alignment, and execution. Here we were especially influenced by Shani, David, and Willson (2004) and by Coghlan and Brannick (2001). Shani and his colleagues view "collaborative management research . . . as an emergent and systematic inquiry process, embedded in a true partnership between researchers and members of a living system for the purpose of generating actionable scientific knowledge" (p. 83). As they see CR, it is not a single unified perspective on management research; rather, it is characterized by both shared elements and divergent views used to leverage partnerships between the organizations that are being studied and the researchers who lead the studies.

Coghlan and Brannick (2001) provided a framework for collaborative research (see Figure 12.1) consisting of three interdependent parts. The first is called the *metacycle of inquiry*, which considers the context and purpose of the research and which includes four basic steps: diagnosis, planning action, taking action, and evaluating action. The second part is the scope of the project. It is typically not confined to one individual or team, but involves interdepartmental or interteam dynamics. The third part includes observations on content, process, and premise issues.

Turning to our fourth foundation, information technology (IT), management believed that user-friendly, online, paperless software could enhance performance by enabling people to become more involved in the design, deployment, implementation, and follow-up of strategy and plans. Their previous experience with Platform EJE and related tools taught them that IT could provide a monitoring system that would encourage self-control, alignment, and empowerment by tracking performance and capturing and classifying opinions and preferences of various participants in the process. Furthermore, it could give leaders information they need to provide coaching, direction, and support. It already provided information that supported decision making and facilitated alignment with strategy and could do even more of this. EJE in Spanish means axle or shaft, suggesting coordination, balance, centering, and alignment. The three letters form an acronym of three words associated with alignment: Equipos (Teams), Juntas (Meetings), and Estrategia (Strategy), all of which are also key aspects of collaborative research.

Strategic Alignment

The four foundational frameworks discussed above are the core of Dynamic Strategic Alignment (DSA), the name we've given to the overall process. Together they serve to increase strategic alignment, a term with at least three meanings: (1) an organization's strategic fit with the requirements of its environment, (2) the match between organization design and strategy, and (3) people's understanding of and/or agreement with the goals of the organization. Both this study and DSA focused on the third meaning, specifically on Fonvielle and Carr's (2002) use of the term: "alignment is not only a matter of individuals agreeing on goals and means; it also refers to the need for business processes and functions to rally their actions around the flagpole of the organization's strategy" (p. 12).

Mintzberg, Ahlstrand, and Lampel (1998) lent indirect support to the importance of this aspect of alignment when they challenged the largely rational basis of strategic planning:

> The formal systems could certainly process more information, at least hard information, consolidate it, aggregate it, move it about. But they could never internalize it, comprehend it, synthesize it. . . . It is not worthwhile to realize that everything went according to plan but no strategic thinking came about. (pp. 73–74)

Early in the process, MMC decided to expand its use of one tool, Platform EJE, to adopt another tool, collaborative research and design, and to do this using a partly formed process called DSA that existed in the mind of one of the authors. Under these circumstances, unplanned emergent changes were expected, and du Plooy's (2003) argument "that transformation occurs through the ongoing, gradual and reciprocal adjustments, accommodations and improvisations enacted by the members of the organization, and to which the information systems must respond" (p. 45) readily applied.

Going in, we knew that team members with collaborative research competencies would be needed for this project and that simultaneously the project itself would be the vehicle that developed these competencies.

HOW THE WORK UNFOLDED

In this section we describe key steps of the project, identify who was involved in these steps, indicate when the steps were taken, and explain the key insights generated. We considered presenting this information as a linear or sequential process such as this: "We did X; from X we learned XX; then we did Y; from Y we learned YY." Originally, we thought this would simplify communication. Furthermore, describing it this way is partially accurate: For example, we gathered data before we analyzed it. However, most learning in this project developed in a nonlinear, free-flowing, organic fashion. It was typical for us to finish X with little clarity about what we learned from doing it (i.e., XX) until after we also finished doing and learning from other steps. According to Fisher and Phelps (2006), finding ways to communicate this nonlinear learning is an ongoing problem in action research. The nonsequential nature of this particular project may become more apparent after considering the sheer number of collaborating groups and the complexity of the relationships among them (see Figure 12.2). This research is an example of the type of complex academic-practitioner collaboration described by Bartunek (Chapter 4 in this *Handbook*).

We gathered data from several sources at various points during the project. During the first stage of the self-design model (laying the foundation and criteria), the first researcher interviewed the members of the ADEP

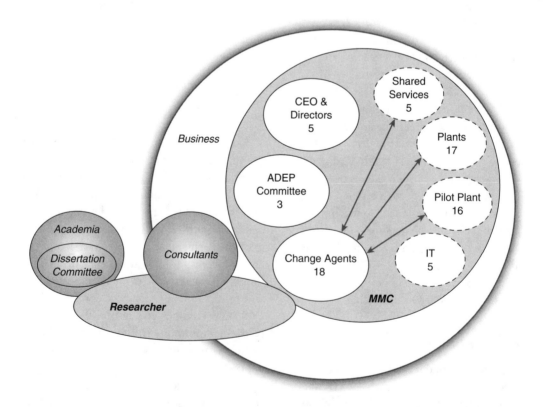

Figure 12.2　Principal Collaborators

committee in order to define the scope of the change process and the method to follow. The entire company—four regions, 17 plants, 7,000 employees, four shared services departments—was undergoing very significant change. However, the CR process would focus on learning and increasing alignment and performance in one pilot plant. Work there would focus on directors, plant managers, and internal change agents. What was learned there would be shared across the rest of the company at a later time, after the conclusion of the formal collaborative research project. Table 12.1 identifies the significant data gathering steps and group sessions that occurred in the pilot plant study and with other stakeholders in each of the three stages of SDM. Aside from these sources, the first author wrote extensive field notes of his observations.

Three main issues were analyzed during the laying foundation and criteria stage with the CEO, directors, and ADEP committee members: Why is an alignment process needed? What are the sociotechnical requirements for the process to be successful? What doubts exist regarding the change process? ADEP committee members and the researcher reviewed and adapted the DSA method to fit their needs. During this stage, two questionnaires on sociotechnical systems and alignment to strategy were administered through the Internet to ADEP committee members, pilot plant supervisors, and internal change agents. Results were used to raise awareness and stimulate reflection during collaborative sessions.

Plant managers, pilot plant supervisors, and internal change agents were accountable for implementing the change. They participated in meetings in which they provided input on key issues that should be considered in the designing stage. Their input was used to design and support the alignment process and the training and use of the alignment software.

Table 12.1   Research Stages and Stakeholders

Stages and Stakeholders Involved	n	Group Sessions	Interviews
1. Laying foundation and criteria			
CEO and four directors	5	May 04	
ADEP committee	3	August 04	
2. Designing			
Internal change agents	18	August 04	
Plant managers	20	September 04	
Pilot plant supervisors	16	May 05	
ADEP committee	3	Ongoing	
3. Implementing and assessing			
CEO and four directors	5		May 05
Pilot plant supervisors	16	May 05	
IT consultants	5	May 05	
Alignment consultant	1		May 05
Internal change agents	23	June 05	
ADEP committee	3	Ongoing	

In the implementing and assessing stage, we interviewed the CEO, directors, and external consultant, who was simultaneously leading a balanced scorecard implementation. We also held group sessions with the pilot plant supervisors, internal change agents, IT consultants, and ADEP committee members. Work in this stage focused on many topics that affected multiple stakeholder groups, such as successes during the process, obstacles and headaches, group dynamics during the CR sessions, and both productive and unproductive experiences with the software.

During the three stages of the self-design model, as part of the work outlined in Table 12.1, we examined two general types of documents: those written by various participants (e.g., e-mails, reports, comments generated at group sessions using a multikeyboard computer system, results of questionnaires) and transcripts of interviews. We analyzed all of these documents as follows:

1. We grouped documents into 10 families or groups of sources.

2. We coded the contents (such as words, phrases, or paragraphs) of each document using ATLAS.ti qualitative research software, which also elaborates various groupings, queries, counts, and searches. We coded in three stages: (1) according to a previously developed list; (2) according to super codes (combinations of codes) related to the three stages of the SDM; and (3) according to each purpose of the study.

3. The third step in analyzing documents was to make a comparative quantitative analysis of opinions in the different families. To do this, we developed an Excel table based on the main issues or questions addressed in each of the three stages of the SDM.

4. Using the software tools mentioned, we calculated the extent to which similar opinions were expressed by various participants at various points during the process.

A Comment on Research Method

Two issues associated with our research method were especially important to us: (1) the accuracy of the information we collected, that is, its match with reality; and (2) the evolutionary or emergent nature of the research design.

Accuracy of the Information Collected

Even though qualitative researchers do not share a stance on most research methods, Creswell (1994, p. 158) suggests that it is especially important to address internal validity, the accuracy of information, and whether it matches reality. Throughout this research, we employed several procedures to address this issue.

For example, to neutralize bias, we involved other researchers in designing research methods and we utilized multiple methods of data collection and analysis. We selected data sources and participants from groups likely to hold a variety of perspectives. These varied stakeholders were active participants in all phases of the research. We included their perspectives along with those in the academic literature (Stringer, 1999). As a check on accuracy, we either taped and transcribed interviews or took notes directly from participants' comments and then validated these notes with the participants at the end of each session. To assure consistency of coding, we coded all text files using a qualitative software package that identified text segments and allowed researchers to attach category labels to each segment and sort data by category, participant group, or step of the process. We developed matrices to count and compare opinions from different stakeholders. Participants themselves helped analyze questionnaire data, drew their own conclusions, and helped to define next steps.

These procedures followed the rigor suggested by Stringer (1999, p. 176) and reinforced the trustworthiness of the study. We established credibility through prolonged engagement with participants, triangulation of information from multiple data sources, member checking, and peer debriefing procedures. We established transferability by recording the step-by-step method and ideas about how it could be applied in the rest of MMC and other settings. Finally, we addressed the issues of dependability and confirmability by thoroughly describing the data collection and analysis processes and by keeping the raw data for future use.

Emergent Nature of the Research Design

Consistent with our comments above concerning how the work unfolded, we continuously adapted our methods to the changing needs and flow of events. At the outset, the ADEP committee agreed that when adjustments were needed, research methods would be adjusted to help MMC achieve its goals, and not the other way around. Initial expectations were very broad. For example, the CEO emphatically described MMC as heavily injured. He called for cleaning what was dirty, developing awareness, enforcing alignment, deploying information for shared decision making, and assuring a culture change. He also insisted that EJE software be used to help people focus on strategic issues (interviewee No. P0, personal communication, May 23, 2004).

ADEP committee members believed that in order for MMC to survive it would have to build a culture of effectiveness, measurement, focused results, and creativity and that "everyone involved in the goal achieving process has to understand his or her role, consolidate information, make action plans and assure the results we all need" (interviewee No. P5, personal communication, May 24, 2005). It was clear that in this situation there would be overlapping, multilevel, and interdependent CR cycles and that the exact number of cycles and the exact scope of the project could not and should not be fully predefined.

One of the earliest shifts in method and focus occurred when the ADEP committee decided the research should center on installing Platform EJE. This shift resulted in choosing a plant in which Platform EJE had been used effectively for two years as the pilot plant for the entire study. We had not considered this to be so central in our original thinking; however, it became critical because pressures were so intense that the ADEP committee believed that focusing the CR process on this installation would bring about the greatest change in the least time.

The ADEP coordinator recognized the need to use several data gathering tools. However, because the organization was under enormous uncertainty and pressure, the ADEP committee wanted control over decisions regarding applying surveys and running collaborative sessions. ADEP members wanted to make these decisions based more on the evolution of the change process than on a formal research design. They also wanted to avoid extra work, minimize risks of increasing resistance to change, and avoid inappropriately raising expectations.

ADEP committee members agreed that the main participants would be pilot plant members, change agents, and key IT people from MMC, its outsourcing IT office, its server outsourcing, and the IT department from its consulting firm. These IT stakeholders developed, after several attempts, a master plan to implement Platform EJE. The immediate objective at this stage was to install Platform EJE in all business units using the methods of the IT outsourcing company. Although at first this seemed just to be a technology implementation supported by CR, it resulted in other complex changes in both the action and research sides of the CR process. As in other research reported by Werr and Greiner (Chapter 5 in this *Handbook*), at several points the researchers and consultants involved in our project needed to reevaluate their roles and identities as participants in the research process.

ADEP committee members, with the support of the consultant, reviewed all strategy maps and recommended changes before capturing them in the IT database. In order to align the shared services maps with those of the plants, "catch-up" sessions were designed to negotiate the needs of the plants and shared services areas. These sessions, though not a part of the original plan, led to development of a new software module to keep track of the generated agreements. This is an example of a technical design made to respond to a social need of the system as well as an example of the emergent nature of the action research method.

Another change in method that evolved during the project involved designing new user training sessions. The first two training sessions and posttraining evaluations allowed us to identify a number of needed changes. For example, we designed a case study enabling users to learn through experience. An outsourcing help desk service was also suggested to support users in resolving their doubts about how to do what.

The DSA method that we originally proposed suggested several kinds of interventions, tools, and questionnaires to generate data for awareness and learning about the integration of STS, SDM, CR, IT, and alignment to strategy. However, we needed to continuously change our research expectations and methods in order to respond to MMC needs and to generate the actionable knowledge that was required. A number of similar sociotechnical journeys are described by Kolodny and Halpern (Chapter 13 in this *Handbook*).

Results and Learnings

Below we list and briefly discuss selected results in three categories: (1) results in line with our original intentions and objectives; (2) unexpected results; and (3) results for collaborative management research in general.

Results That Were in Line With Our Original Intentions and Objectives

The most important results in this category were the following:

- Strategic alignment improved through the use of DSA.
- Teamwork and collaboration improved at all levels in the pilot plant.
- Platform EJE proved to be a powerful management tool.

At least seven findings indicated that alignment improved. Perhaps the most telling was that area strategy maps developed during and immediately after this collaborative research process were consistent with the overall corporate strategy map. Furthermore, near the end of the project, 96% of the change agents, 100% of pilot plant members, and 40% of directors said they understood the strategy and were aligned with it. Furthermore, several change agents mentioned their skepticism early in the process (August 2004), yet less than a year later all of them recognized strategic alignment as a main achievement of the project.

Other indicators of increased alignment include (1) shared understanding of the need to change, to become productive and customer focused; (2) shared and explicit recognition of the need for a common vision, strategy, and direction; (3) shared desire to deal with the environment and suppliers as one company, not as isolated plants anymore; (4) shared awareness that providing business information to employees will improve interaction and teamwork; (5) reduced skepticism and increased recognition by change agents that the alignment of goals and indicators of all plants had been achieved; and (6) awareness by most directors of the need for them to change and improve their teamwork in order to lead the alignment process.

During a session with participants from the pilot plant, one ADEP committee member noted,

In the pilot plant they have gotten to a point in which the organizational culture allows them to align very quickly. . . . They are very united and have faith in the results they can achieve. (P5, personal communication, May 24, 2005)

Another comment is representative of data gathered from many participants in this process:

We used to be below our targets. Now, with the same people and the same machinery we are above what we planned. . . . It is incredible what people are doing for the plant. . . . In our meetings the managers remain silent and let their employees present by themselves their results and plans using EJE. (P4, personal communication, May 12, 2005)

As for confirming the power of Platform EJE, at the end of the project the change agents were nearly unanimous in their decision to use only this software for their periodic balanced scorecard reviews. In the pilot plant 89% of participants used the software at least weekly and 83% considered it to be a good or excellent tool. Furthermore, people in the pilot plant were able to execute one specific deployment process in record time of less than eight hours using Platform EJE (P5, personal communication, May 24, 2005).

Finally, we note that the 16 pilot plant participants identified 51 achievements emanating from this project. Out of those, 41% were centered on the alignment gained through strategy definition, goals, and the metrics-identification process.

Unexpected Results and Learnings

The most important results and learnings in this category were the following:

- Plant managers learned that more commitment, energy, patience, and understanding than they originally expected are required to lead change of this magnitude.
- Managers learned the importance of the role of directors and other key managers in implementing changes of this magnitude.
- Role ambiguity among change agents greatly limited their effectiveness.
- Managers were more comfortable with and more effective in making technical changes than social changes.
- The need for learning requires that people who simultaneously conduct research and manage the business in which they conduct that research must communicate much more frequently and in much greater depth than would be needed if they only managed the business or only conducted research.

We've listed the items above under the heading "unexpected" because most members of MMC who participated in this project did not expect them and were somewhat surprised by them. On the other hand, as experienced consultants who have participated in change projects in perhaps 90 organizations, we (the authors) tend to think of most of them as basic principles or truths. Nonetheless, they typically require learning by managers in organization after organization, and MMC was no exception.

In retrospect, we might have addressed the need for learning these truths more thoroughly than we did. For example, the importance of managing role ambiguity among participants is among the most critical of the learnings listed above. Our own past experience, the self-design model, and the sociotechnical perspective all led us to clarify the roles and responsibilities of each of the collaborators and stakeholders early in the project. However, after the project ended it became clear that addressing these issues in greater depth would have been beneficial.

As another example, consider the last point in the list above, the need for more extensive communication conducted for the purpose of maximizing in-process learning.

At least five distinct groups of internal and external stakeholders were involved in the process of installing and configuring software. Yet, there was no team building or formal coordination of the IT effort. Many issues associated with coordinating IT efforts were identified and considered in the first master plan; however, far more issues emerged during this complex process. At one point, the ADEP coordinator finally organized a meeting to focus on the need to respond as one IT team to the demands of the change process. That meeting proved to be critical as IT stakeholders agreed to a number of changes in their interactions. More meetings of this type should have been included as learning mechanisms in the original research design instead of being left so much to emergence. Docherty and Shani (Chapter 8 in this *Handbook*) point out that oversights such as this are, unfortunately, frequently the case, as managers and researchers get caught up in responding to more immediate and tangible demands.

Results for Collaborative Management Research in General

The most important results and learnings in this category were the following:

- A critical contribution of principal investigators and consultants in CR is to provide frameworks, tools, and methods.
- The four foundational frameworks, STS, SDM, CR, and IT, contributed substantially to the changes and to the learning.
- There is value in staying primarily focused on the issues that most concern the members of the organization and secondarily focused on research objectives when it is necessary to choose one focus over the other.
- Regardless of focus, it is appropriate, even critical, to maintain rigor in research processes by attending to internal validity, triangulating data sources, and using appropriate tools for coding and quantifying data.

- Principal investigators in CR projects must be granted (by their research institutions, grant providers, dissertation committees, and institutional review boards) the authority to deviate from initial research proposals and plans as CR unfolds.
- One of the ultimate goals of collaborative research in management or organizations is to increase organizational capability through learning.
- Strategic alignment increases as one conducts collaborative research on strategic alignment.
- The DSA itself, now more fully refined than when we began the project, is a valuable tool.

Space does not permit a discussion of all of the learnings and results above. However, the last two items merit comment. After this research we now see alignment as a *result*, a *process*, and a *design*. It is a *result* when the customer, due to the impact he or she experiences, perceives it. It is a *process* (of ongoing learning cycles) when members of the organization perceive that it is under way. It is a *design* when the organization has been configured to maintain focus and execution. Perhaps it is easier to see lack of alignment than alignment itself.

We discovered that improving strategic alignment in an organization can begin with organization members actively and collaboratively trying to learn how to improve it and how to engage in double-loop learning. Improvement in strategic alignment need not wait until they have completed the learning. This is consistent with Docherty and Shani's observation (Chapter 8 in this *Handbook*). They indicate that explicit development of learning mechanisms that increase capability to change, as opposed to those that maintain a sense of stability, are too often left to chance in collaborative research work. Meanwhile, the work of "trying to learn how to improve it" is itself enhanced by the presence of preliminary ideas about how to accomplish this. In this research project, these preliminary ideas existed initially in the mind of one of the researchers who gave them the label "Dynamic Strategic Alignment." In the course of the research these "rough ideas" became more refined because of collaboration between the researcher and others, including members of MMC, external consultants, and other researchers. In this truly collaborative model, "the elements of knowledge production, research, consulting and practice are integrated into a joint effort to better understand and deal with issues of concern to all parties" (Werr & Greiner, Chapter 5 in this *Handbook*).

Implications for Collaborative Management Research

In this section we reflect on how the project reported in this chapter might influence future collaborative management research. We begin this reflection by identifying some of the mechanisms that promoted collaboration and helped ensure rigor in data gathering and analysis. We also identify some of the mechanisms that might have been employed but that we did not employ, or did not employ as extensively as hindsight suggests we should have. We have listed some of these mechanisms in Table 12.2. They provide a basis for consideration in planning future collaborative management research.

Based on our experience—of both what worked well and what we and our collaborators may have overlooked—we offer the following suggestions for future collaborative management research.

Suggestion 1: Clarify What Each Group of Collaborators Hopes to Bring to the Process

First, clarify and document among the collaborators themselves the general nature of the contributions each group of collaborators is likely to make as well as the types of limitations each is likely to bring to the process. Usually the principal groups are the members of the host organization and the researchers. The challenges of emergent dynamics between the insider/outsider roles need to be addressed (for example, see in this *Handbook* Bartunek, Chapter 4; Hatchuel & David, Chapter 7; and Coghlan & Shani, Chapter 29). From our perspective, insiders or members usually bring focus, urgency, financial and human resources, and most of all, a bias for action. Experience has taught them to perform, to produce, and to act decisively and quickly even in the face of uncertainty. Their skills and biases benefit CR to the extent that some decisions cannot be postponed, some risks must be taken, and members of the organizations are most primed to take them. On the other hand, the researchers, usually from the outside, bring a bias for rigor, a commitment to note taking and recording, and a preference for taking the time to reflect deeply and critically when interpreting data and anticipating consequences of plans. They are also usually much more inclined than insiders to draw on theory, models, frameworks, and formalized bodies of knowledge to provide alternative courses of action and to anticipate consequences. The depth of their thinking often provides a sound starting point—a first draft of a statement of where to begin, what to consider, and what first steps to take, while the insiders' penchant for action provides the urgency to move beyond that starting point.

Suggestion 2: Identify Conceptual Foundations

Second, select a handful of appropriate foundational frameworks, concepts, models, theories, and research tools to influence the process. Then provide early education and training to the collaborators in the use of these. In this project, we were constantly sensitive to the value of basing our work on

Table 12.2   Mechanisms in Collaborative Research

Mechanisms That Facilitated Collaboration	Mechanisms That Ensured Rigor
• Purposeful design with significant, clearly defined goals	• Outside researchers participated in method design
• Insider/outsider research team	• Multiple methods of data collection and analysis
• Sensitivity sessions	• Relevant literature consulted in all phases
• ADEP committee coordinator functioning as a liaison	• Evidence gathered and analyzed systematically
• Joint decision making between ADEP committee and researcher	• Many interviews taped and transcribed
• Multikeyboard system for gathering and validating opinions	• Other interview notes written directly and validated with participants
• Stakeholders engaged as active participants in all phases	• Text files coded and recoded as necessary to ensure consistency
• Joint data analysis through entire process	• Qualitative research software used to analyze data
• Attention to sense of ownership	• Matrices used to count and compare opinions from various stakeholders
• Technology that facilitated contact, sensemaking, and action	• AR cycle used at end of every stage of SDM to identify changes or next steps
	• Academic experts provided theoretical input to improve DSA model
	• Local knowledge tested against local problems

Mechanisms That Might Have Facilitated Collaboration, but Were Underutilized	Mechanisms That Might Have Ensured Rigor, but Were Underutilized
• More consistent follow-up of sensitivity sessions	• More triangulation to deepen analysis
• More frequent formal meetings between more insiders/outsiders	• More complete, thorough use of qualitative software
• Identify learning design dimensions and requirements at the outset (Shani & Docherty, 2003)	• More complete analysis of data supplied by Platform EJE®
• A more clear and complete description of DSA	

relevant literature and theory. The overarching framework we used, Dynamic Strategic Alignment, was our own and was largely untested. However, we used it to integrate other frameworks that were established and respected within the body of knowledge, specifically STS, SDM, CR, and IT. Critics may rightfully point out that we did not use any of these frameworks or tools in a "perfectly correct" manner; however, constantly referring to them in our work with other collaborators and in our private reflections helped us to stay on track during a complex and demanding process. So, this knowledge was "produced from richer and deeper data than what is typically available in surface statistical data" (Werr & Greiner, Chapter 5 in this *Handbook*).

A special note regarding one of our foundational frameworks, STS, is appropriate here. Over the years we have become aware of a special advantage of using and teaching sociotechnical principles in environments dominated by technologists, engineers, accountants, and others trained in fields that emphasize analytical processes. The advantage is that sensitivity to human social and behavioral dynamics rises among these people once human issues are described in systems language. The work at MMC reconfirmed this learning. Throughout the project, participants who were predominantly oriented toward manufacturing, engineering, technology, and finance became sensitive to and responded to a wide variety of human issues, needs, and opportunities and were supported in this effort by their newly acquired orientation to STS thinking.

Suggestion 3: Provide Training to Build Both Skill and Confidence

Third, early in collaborative research, provide extensive training on new skills, procedures, software tools, or job content likely to be used during and following the change process. For example, in this project we knew in advance that Platform EJE and a multikeyboard system for tracking preferences would be used during meetings. Though software and other IT implementation was not an end in itself, it was always expected to be part of this project. None of the collaborators knew at the outset all the ways these IT tools would be used or how central EJE in particular would become, but we knew they would be part of this work. As the project drew to a close, 50% of plant managers mentioned that in future work of this kind, a communication

and training strategy regarding the software should be implemented earlier. They saw IT not only as an alignment tool, but also as a means of dealing with resistance to change and adopting new working methods.

Suggestion 4: Attend to Human Dynamics Among the Collaborators

Fourth, attend to the social or human dynamics within and among the groups and individuals who collaborate on the research. We have already discussed the importance of clarifying roles and providing training to increase skill and confidence in fulfilling those roles. In addition, consider the need for emotional support among participants, especially in the midst of enormous pressure—pressure on executives to improve their business, pressure on operating managers to improve performance, pressure on researchers to complete dissertations or publish, pressure from funding agencies to demonstrate relevance, and pressure on internal change agents to enable change. Each of these groups can increase the pressure on every other group—alternatively, each can provide valuable and needed support and encouragement to the others. In our project, after several months of performing as change agents, 96% said they still needed more support from their managers and 70% believed the project would succeed only if directors, managers, and supervisors were truly involved and committed. Change agents (67%) also said they must start changing themselves. We believe that in the face of complexity and uncertainty, maintaining high levels of emotional support within the research team itself fosters the very involvement, commitment, and personal change to which the change agents referred. It may very well also enable the researchers to more effectively handle the social side of the sociotechnical changes within the larger client system. This discussion is supported by findings from Mohrman et al. (2006). They concluded that effective interaction among leaders, project team members, and change agents is fundamental for success in this kind of work.

Suggestion 5: Consider Using a New Model for Strategic Alignment

Future researchers on strategic alignment should consider using the model shown in Figure 12.3 that emerged in the course of this project. This model presents alignment as a continuous balancing act. The figure can be seen as an eye, representing the vision, perspective and focus necessary for the full alignment of the system. The circles and oval rotate around an interconnecting axle. Customers and other stakeholders set their rhythm and speed. In order to ensure a dynamic balance, the circles need to be realigned constantly. The five S's of this

model emphasize that customer and stakeholder *satisfaction* requires an alignment of the whole system. The specific environment and *situation* define key *strategic* elements to be established so that *staff* (people) and all required *structural* aspects may be constantly realigned. The rotating circles are consistent with the interacting cycles of collaborative research.

Suggestion 6: Put Organizational Capability on the Front Burner

Finally, keep the notion of increasing organizational capability alive throughout collaborative research projects. CR typically requires continuously changing research methods because of changing needs within the systems in which research is conducted. This was precisely our experience, and we believe that continuously redesigning the methods used in this

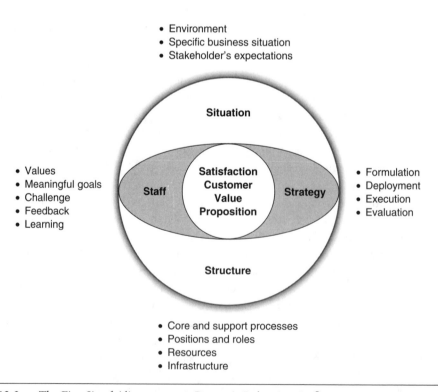

Figure 12.3 The Five S's of Alignment as a Dynamic Balancing Act®

project moved MMC toward mastering a continuous learning process that is on its way to becoming a new organizational capability. Dosi, Nelson, and Winter (2000) (cited in Mohrman et al., 2005) say that "organizational capabilities are the know-how that enables an organization to achieve its intended outcomes" and affirm that "relatively little is known about how firms actually develop new capabilities" (p. 3). Mohrman et al. conclude that "developing new capabilities entails approaches that lead to the necessary modifications of the company's cognitive traits and activity patterns" (p. 7). Bradbury (Chapter 28 in this *Handbook*) affirms that "actionability will likely seem familiar at first, yet it is not easily practiced because it requires multiple competencies."

In our view, the kind of collaborative research reported in this chapter approached the ideal of implementing an explicitly designed learning mechanism. We say "approached" this ideal because throughout this project we focused much more on increasing alignment and on processes for doing so than on processes for increasing organizational capability. In retrospect, it seems to us that we might have couched all of our work at MMC in terms of "increasing organizational capability" and "explicitly designed learning mechanisms" as well as in terms of "strategic alignment." DSA might be as much a tool for learning how to learn as it is a tool for increasing alignment.

CLOSING COMMENTS

The MMC participants in this project believed that their interpretations of data and their conclusions were valid. They trusted their own research findings and tended to see these findings as facts. We believe this is because they—the internal stakeholders identified in Table 12.1—gathered and analyzed all data along with the outside researcher. They were not constrained or minimized by that researcher; rather, he was their partner in the process, providing leadership for some aspects of the work and giving support in others. He was influenced by the other participants as readily as he influenced them. Similar experience is reported by Werr and Greiner (Chapter 5 in this *Handbook*). They refer to Mohrman, Gibson, and Mohrman (2001), who said that practitioners are more inclined to see the results of research as useful when they are involved in discussing and interpreting the findings.

Those of us who engage in collaborative action research must be realistic about the degree or quality of collaboration that is feasible. For example, in MMC's case, habit, culture, and competence limited the time available for collaboration on some issues and assumed that time would be made available for collaboration on others. However, even though it was difficult for people to attend work sessions, once there, they focused on the task at hand. Collaboration had far less to do with interaction time than with the quality and depth of the interaction.

At MMC, people took great strides forward at a time when they were under enormous pressure. They did so through collaboration and inquiry. Throughout this collaborative research process, they and we increased capability, strengthened the scientific understanding of strategic alignment, and improved organizational and individual performance.

REFERENCES

Antonacopoulou, E. (2004). The dynamics of reflexive practice: The relationship between learning and changing. In M. Reynolds & R. Vince (Eds.), *Organizing reflection* (pp. 47–64). Aldershot, UK: Ashgate.

Bartunek, J. M., & Louis, M. R. (1996). *Insider/outsider team research.* Thousand Oaks, CA: Sage.

Coghlan, D., & Brannick, T. (2001). *Doing action research in your own organization.* Thousand Oaks, CA: Sage.

Creswell, J. W. (1994). *Research design: Qualitative and quantitative approaches.* Thousand Oaks, CA: Sage.

Dosi, G., Nelson, R. R., & Winter, S. G. (2000). *The nature and dynamics of organizational capabilities.* New York: Oxford University Press.

du Plooy, N. F. (2003). The social responsibility of information systems developers. In S. Clarke, E. Coakes, M. G. Hunter, & A. Wenn (Eds.), *Socio-technical and human cognition elements of information systems* (pp. 41–59). London: Information Science Publishing.

Fisher, K., & Phelps, R. (2006). Recipe or performing art? Challenging conventions for writing action research theses. *Action Research, 4*(2), 143–164.

Fonvielle, W., & Carr, L. P. (2002). *Gaining strategic alignment: Making scorecards work, Part 1.* Downloaded from http://www.bettermanagement.com/Library/Library.aspx?LibraryID=4241

Mintzberg, H., Ahlstrand, B., & Lampel, J. (1998). *Strategy safari: A guided tour through the wilds of strategic management.* New York: Free Press.

Mohrman, J. A., & Mohrman, S. A. (2004). Self-designing a performance management system. In N. Adler, A. B. (Rami) Shani, & A. Styhre (Eds.), *Collaborative research in organizations: Foundations for learning, change, and theoretical development* (pp. 313–332). Thousand Oaks, CA: Sage.

Mohrman, S. A., & Cummings, T. (1989). *Self-designing organizations: Learning how to create high performance.* Reading, MA: Addison-Wesley.

Mohrman, S. A., Docherty, P., & Shani, A. B. (Rami). (2006). *The development of new organizational capabilities.* Paper presented at the Annual Conference of the Academy of Management, Atlanta.

Mohrman, S. A., Gibson, C. B., & Mohrman, J. A. (2001). Doing research that is useful to practice: A model and empirical exploration. *Academy of Management Journal, 44*(2), 357.

Pasmore, W. A. (1988). *Designing effective organizations: The sociotechnical systems perspective.* New York: Wiley.

Shani, A. B. (Rami), David, A., & Willson, C. (2004). Collaborative research: Alternative roadmaps. In N. Adler, A. B. (Rami) Shani, & A. Styhre (Eds.), *Collaborative research in organizations: Foundations for learning, change, and theoretical development* (pp. 83–100). Thousand Oaks, CA: Sage.

Shani, A. B. (Rami), & Docherty, P. (2003). *Learning by design: Building sustainable organizations.* Oxford, UK: Blackwell.

Stringer, E. T. (1999). *Action research* (2nd ed.). Thousand Oaks, CA: Sage.

CHAPTER 13

From Collaborative Design to Collaborative Research

A Sociotechnical Journey

HARVEY KOLODNY

NORMAN HALPERN

ABSTRACT

Sociotechnical systems and collaborative research share common beginnings in the participation of people in the design of their own work and their organizational arrangements. This chapter traces through the history of sociotechnical systems with a special emphasis on the organization design aspects of the field. The chapter calls on several Canadian case studies to illustrate the degree of collaboration that is inherent in the design of organizations when the design approach is a sociotechnical one. Through the case illustrations and the historical journey, a compelling argument is made for sociotechnical systems as one of the important building blocks on which the new field of collaborative research is being developed.

As a methodology, collaborative management research has developed and evolved on the foundations of other disciplines. This chapter will focus on sociotechnical systems (STS) theory as one of the disciplines and particularly on the collaborative design aspects of STS that have contributed to the development of collaborative research.

Both STS and collaborative research had early origins in the psychiatric groups that Wilfred Bion and Eric Trist and others established to treat shell-shocked United Kingdom victims of the Second World War. There were insufficient counselors to treat the many in need, and participation in self-managed groups arose as a way to handle the shortage of personnel (Bion, 1961). That experience strongly influenced a set of researchers associated with the Tavistock Institute in London, England, and self-managed groups and their accompanying approaches to participation and collaboration became the modus operandi of the many research activities that followed (Trist & Murray, 1990b, 1993, 1997).

Collaborative research appeared soon after, when a researcher from the Tavistock Institute and a worker from the coal mining industry collaborated to develop the seminal study, described below, that gave STS its name (Trist & Bamforth, 1951). STS and collaboration share a long history and build heavily on each other.

The Trist and Bamforth study explicitly identified the interdependence of the social and technical systems in the coal mines in the United Kingdom. Researchers from the Tavistock Institute in London followed with an extensive set of research studies in the United Kingdom, Norway, the Netherlands, and India that fleshed out the field of STS. Some of the classic studies of the STS field were produced during this period (Emery, 1959; Emery & Trist, 1965; Miller, 1959; Rice, 1958; Trist, Higgin, Murray, & Pollock, 1963). The research studies and related conceptual articles provided a comprehensive foundation for the STS field.

The publications excited researchers around the world, and Tavistock and British coal mines became regular visiting locations for international research scientists. In the 1970s, a further flurry of STS-based research and conceptual articles and books were published, which this time included works by many North American authors (Cherns, 1976; Cummings, 1976; Davis & Taylor, 1979; Emery & Trist, 1978; Englestad, 1970; Miller, 1975; Pasmore & Sherwood, 1978; Susman, 1976; Taylor, 1978; Trist, Brown, & Susman, 1977). The published articles and working papers were later assembled into three volumes, edited by Eric Trist and Hugh Murray, and titled *The Social Engagement of Social Science*. The first volume was published in 1990, subtitled *The Socio-psychological Perspective*, the second in 1993, subtitled *The Socio-technical Perspective*, and the third in 1997, subtitled *The Socio-ecological Perspective*. The three volumes have provided a thorough and comprehensive history and background of the field of STS theory. More recently, Van Eijnatten (1993) published an insightful overview of the different schools of STS thought that have arisen around the world, as STS has diffused from the first set of countries cited above to Canada and the United States, France, Belgium, Italy, Mexico, and a host of other countries.

STS has also diffused widely through conferences, workshops, roundtables, and study groups where applications and management knowledge have been extensively shared. There was a strong attraction between the researchers who were excited about the opportunity to link a social systems perspective with the technical systems perspective that had begun to dominate the workplace (e.g., from Frederick Taylor's "scientific management" perspective in the early 1900s through to the "learning curve" that management consulting firms propagated widely after the Second World War). STS was an equally strong attraction for practitioners who believed there had to be a better solution than the narrow technical system[s] perspective that prevailed. Collaboration between researchers, consultants, and practitioners began to show up often in this public context of conferences and workshops.

A SOCIOTECHNICAL SYSTEMS PRIMER

The published literature of STS research, STS case studies, and STS concepts is probably more comprehensive than that of almost every other managerial organizational innovation of the last 50 years, with the possible exception of Total Quality Management (TQM) systems. For readers unfamiliar with the sociotechnical field, we provide a brief primer on STS design, the perspective of this chapter. STS design consists of several components:

1. STS design acknowledges that organizations are composed of two subsystems: a social system (individuals' skills/roles/ responsibilities, personnel policies, reward systems, norms, values, and so on) and a technical system (equipment, technology, operating procedures, layout, and so on). Both are simultaneously considered in organization design through a process of joint optimization.

2. STS design embraces an explicit set of human values related to meeting workers' preferences in the following areas (Emery, 1959):
   - Workers want their work to be reasonably demanding (not in physical terms)— that is, to require some mental effort and to provide variety.
   - They would like the job to provide opportunity to learn new skills on a continuing basis.
   - They would like it to provide opportunities to make decisions and exercise discretion.
   - They would like to be part of a group upon which they can depend for assistance when needed.
   - They would like a system whereby their performance and contributions can be assessed, so that they have some idea of what they have accomplished as a result of their efforts and can get appropriate recognition.
   - They would like to know that they are not dead-ended in their careers.

3. STS design includes a set of design principles (Cherns, 1976). Two of the principles most relevant to this discussion are discussed later in this chapter.

4. STS design provides a design methodology— a set of tools for both social and technical systems analysis.

The endurance of STS design to this day is largely attributable to its focus on the human element and the fact that many have undertaken leadership roles in keeping it current and relevant through conferences, roundtables, and public workshops. This is one of the interesting and delightful enigmas of STS— namely, that it has endured so well and been adopted so widely despite the fact that, unlike other similar managerial innovations such as TQM and Business Process Reengineering (BPR), STS was not adopted and advocated by major professional consulting groups. International consulting groups were largely responsible for the worldwide diffusion of TQM and BPR and, in turn, both TQM and BPR were critically important underpinnings of the growth and development of these groups. STS never acquired that international consulting support, possibly because it preceded TQM by a generation, and at that time these groups were early in their formation. A more likely reason is that the human element that informed STS was not a part of the values of the many consultants who composed these international consulting groups. It may also be that industry leaders were more inclined to pay for the quick-fix productivity efficiencies that TQM and BPR espoused, but less inclined to pay for the social and human benefits that STS espoused, even though the technical side of STS offered most of the same process improvements as did BPR.

STS endured at a lower level of adoption probably because so many of its adherents were so strongly committed to the sociopsychological side of the activities of the workplace, that is, the human element. In each other, they found common beliefs and values that were not widely accepted in the workplace. STS provided them with one of the few forums where they could find others who were interested in innovating the design of the social systems of the workplace as well as the technical systems. However, STS never caught the imagination of industry leaders in the way that other managerial innovations did, and it has slowly faded from the attention of the organizational management field.

THE DESIGN FOCUS

STS theory has built a foundation on principles of job and organization design, on action research to collect data on which to apply those design principles, and on the participation of members of the organization in the action research or the process of design or both. This participation has sometimes been at the level of the top managers, sometimes at the level of a work-group or a job, sometimes involving these and other levels of work, and often cutting diagonally across all these levels.

On most occasions, this participation has also made the design process a collaborative one between those doing the work itself and those designing or redesigning the work. The collaboration in STS design and redesign processes has at times been conducted entirely within the boundaries of the organization, at other times with consultants outside the organization, and in some instances with academics from outside the organization who served in both research and consulting roles with respect to STS principles or STS methodology or both. STS, then, has focused on design and specifically on participative and collaborative design, which still leaves the question about the relationship of collaborative STS design to collaborative STS research to be addressed.

In gathering data to design or redesign an organization or an organizational unit, the organizational research that is carried out is a collaborative process between the designers and the members of the organization. If the designers are external to the organization, their involvement with the organization could be in the form of collaborative consulting or collaborative research or both. If the designers and the organization disseminate and share the knowledge of the research process, we refer to this as "collaborative research," and if this takes place at the management level of the organization, we refer to it as "collaborative management research." In situations where adversarial parties, for example, management and union, jointly explore opportunities for STS application (as described in the Shell case below), and publicly share their knowledge of this process, this is also collaborative research.

This chapter will explore the path to collaborative research that has been well worn by those who chose a sociotechnical approach on their journey to designing better organizations. In the Canadian cases described here, there are some clear illustrations of organization design carried out primarily, and sometimes exclusively, by members of the organization in question. There are other cases where consultants and academics were involved in a collaborative design process as well as in collaborative research processes. Collaborative research is an evolving field and there are, and probably always will be, some definitional dilemmas associated with what is called a collaborative research process. In addition to the roles played by academic scholars, this chapter includes collaborative research with consultants and others, as long as the results of the collaborative research process have become publicly shared so as to advance our knowledge about organizational research.

Three specific phases of STS will be discussed in this chapter and related to collaborative research:

1. The early developments in STS, when it evolved as a conceptual scheme out of the coal-mining studies conducted by Eric Trist and others at the Tavistock Institute

2. The strong organization design phase of STS that began with Fred Emery's and Einar Thorsrud's experiments in concert with four manufacturing facilities in Norway, which continued with the North American greenfield and redesign initiatives that have been described by Louis Davis, Jim Taylor, William A. Pasmore, and others, as well as the European and North American initiatives

that were documented and disseminated by professional organizations such as the Swedish Employers' Confederation and the Work in America Institute, among others

3. A collaborative design phase that emphasizes the participative nature of organization design and, in so doing, distinguishes it from other initiatives that focus only on the organization design issues

Phase 1: The Early Development of STS

One of the earliest articles to put forward the basic ideas of the STS school is the classic study of the British mining industry by Eric Trist and Ken Bamforth (1951). In 1948, the British government formed an Industrial Productivity Committee, which had a Human Factors Panel (Trist & Murray, 1990a). One set of grants made to the Tavistock Institute under this program was for the study of improved productivity in coal mines. Many of the mines in Britain had adopted "longwall" methods of mining to improve efficiency, an "underground" version of the assembly processes that had evolved in the automobile industry. However, the projected efficiencies were largely unrealized, primarily because of a number of social and organizational dysfunctions resulting from the long-wall technology, which the 1951 article captured extremely well. Trist teamed up with an ex-miner in Bamforth and they proceeded to collect data about the different approaches used in the various coal mines that they observed, particularly mines that had realized significant production improvements, but had done so by designing joint social and technical organizational arrangements rather than through the long-wall design. Their project led to the discovery of self-regulating groups in coal mines.

This seminal study established the idea that there were better ways to organize than just those that followed a technical rationality.

There was a demonstrable interdependence between the social systems in the mines and the systems of technology that, if appropriately integrated through self-regulating workgroups, could result in superior economic performance in addition to creating a better working environment. This conceptual idea remained at the heart of all subsequent STS studies and applications. It continues today as STS's primary appeal, especially to technically oriented engineers who have found themselves dissatisfied with purely technical solutions to organizational issues.

While Ken Bamforth was not a coal miner in any of the particular mines they examined, his long experience in the mines allowed him to act as a surrogate for the miners they studied. This classic research study could be considered a tentative step toward collaborative management research because, while Trist and Bamforth did not go on to initiate changes in the mines studied, as a consequence of their research they did offer specific organizational design recommendations to the Coal Board to pass on to the mine owners and managers.

Phase 2: The Organization Design Phase

Building on Einar Thorsrud's strong influence with the Norwegian government after World War II, Fred Emery of the Tavistock Institute and Thorsrud initiated a set of redesign experiments in four Norwegian factories and mills (Emery & Thorsrud, 1969). The studies led to a design methodology and design procedures that stimulated many subsequent STS adherents and continue today as exceptionally strong organization design approaches (Emery, 1959).

One of those who followed was Albert Cherns, a United Kingdom researcher who built on the Norwegian studies but went further to capture some of the North American experience while working with Louis Davis, an American researcher and consultant, in California. Cherns's (1976) STS design principles espoused value-based and participative approaches. For example, his Principle of Compatibility states,

> The process of design must be compatible with its objectives. If the objective of design is a system of self-modification, of adapting to change, and of making the most of the creative capacities of the individual, then a constructively participative organization is needed. A necessary condition for this to occur is that people are given the opportunity to participate in the design of the jobs that they are to perform. (p. 785)

Consistent with Cherns's Principle of Incompletion, the process of design does not end abruptly. In effective STS designs, it evolves indefinitely. In many instances, provision for this is built into the process through formation of boards of employees for the explicit purposes of continuous evaluation and redesign (see examples cited below).

The Norwegian sites were redesigns or "brownfield" sites. The early North American STS designs were also brownfield sites; however, the great STS success stories were mostly with "greenfield" sites—new organizations with new employees. Two kinds of greenfield designs evolved. In one kind, the sites were largely designed by third parties and the odd internal manager without any involvement from those who would do the work, in part because employees did not exist at the time of the plant's design. Collaboration in design was relatively limited.

Perhaps because of the heavy involvement of external consultants and relatively little involvement from those who would eventually operate the plant, an "expert knowledge" mentality prevailed in many STS designs. Nevertheless, the widespread diffusion of STS design was a product of this

expert knowledge, as consultants, conferences, and publications became avenues to share this expertise.

At the same time, there were some extremely successful examples of greenfield design that were done in concert with early employees together with third parties or, in some cases, with relatively little involvement of third parties, as expert knowledge was evolving rapidly behind the scenes as managers and practitioners met to share their experiences and expertise. This chapter will describe two such greenfield sites: Shell Canada's polypropylene/isopropyl alcohol plant in Sarnia, Ontario, and Continental Can's "Vista" plant in Mississauga, Ontario. A third Canadian example described here is a brownfield or redesign example: Celestica Inc.'s electronics assembly plant in Toronto, Ontario.

Beginning with some of Volvo's creative design work in the late 1970s and early 1980s (Aguren, Bredbacka, Hansson, Ihregren, & Karlsson, 1984; Aguren, Hansson, & Karlsson, 1976), there was considerable sociotechnical design in a variety of Swedish manufacturing facilities, mostly in automotive and mechanical assembly plants (Aguren & Edgren, 1980). A variety of third-party persons, mostly academics and consultants, worked with many of the employers to adopt these STS designs. When the innovations were described, they were often published through Swedish professional associations (e.g., Swedish Employers Confederation and The Swedish Work Environment Fund), mostly in Swedish, but many were also translated into English.

Though many of the Swedish examples would be classified as collaborative designs, there were also many early examples of collaborative research here (e.g., Edgren, 1974). A quote describing one research project illustrates this (Göranzon et al., 1982):

> This project was based primarily on a research design from a larger international project, and the Swedish report primarily emphasizes

automation and work organization since these aspects were relevant to the Swedish situation. The main theoretical issue is to assess to what extent work organization designed according to sociotechnical theory and supported in practice by more automated technology affects workers and their attitudes (in terms of job design criteria such as learning and decision-making, job satisfaction), social relations, stress, wages, training opportunities, participation, relation to the company and the union, and other quality of work life variables. (p. 31)

While there was a hiatus in collaborative design and research activity in the 1990s in Sweden, the current collaborative research activity centered in Sweden builds heavily on the foundation that was established in that country in the 1970s and 1980s.

Collaborative Design in Canada

Shell Canada. One of the earliest examples of a participative STS design in Canada was the Shell polypropylene/isopropyl alcohol plant in Sarnia, Ontario. This was a facility built adjacent to an older oil refinery. Technical design commenced in 1974 with plant startup in 1978. While the plant was new, it wasn't quite "greenfield," since it was part of a larger complex with existing policies, practices, and a Union Collective Agreement. A comprehensive description of the design process was published by Norm Halpern in 1985. It describes Shell management's early initiatives to examine best practices in social systems design in manufacturing processes around the world.

The process followed in the Shell Sarnia plant was to establish a steering committee of four general managers and a design team. The latter was composed of individuals who were initially assigned to do the engineering design and construction, along with management and supervisory staff associated with

this facility and union representatives. As new members were added to the project, they were incorporated in the STS design process, through membership in either the design team or various subteams.

Because of the stage at which the design was started, this group had an opportunity to influence not only the social system design but also the technical side. This was a true STS "joint optimization." By the time of plant startup, every employee was involved in some aspect of the final design.

The process was facilitated by an external consultant who taught design team members the process of organizational analysis and design in accordance with STS principles, but all ultimate decisions were those of employees of the site.

To maintain continuous design post startup, a Team Norm Review Board (TNRB) was formed, consisting of six operators, a team coordinator, an operations manager, and a union representative. The role of the group was to continuously assess, through various forms of surveys, where further changes were appropriate, and to arrange for their implementation. Ongoing design by the TNRB, without external consultation, was substantial.

Lou Davis had worked with the design team to teach them the principles of STS analysis and design, and Stu Sullivan, as the international representative for the union (then called the Oil, Chemical, and Atomic Workers union), joined the design team along with the president of the union local. An article by Davis and Sullivan (1980) describes what was learned about the intense collaboration of management and the union in the design process.

It was initially presumed by management that the union would be highly resistant to the sociotechnical design effort, and much consideration was given to unilateral approaches that would exclude the union from the process. Ultimately, however, it was concluded that success would be realized only if the union was involved and supportive.

As expected, initial overtures to the union were met with resistance and total lack of interest to participate. There were expressions of mistrust—that management merely had an objective of workforce downsizing. It was only after the union was given assurances that there would be no job loss as a consequence of the design and was persuaded that management had no specific outcomes in mind—that they were seeking to explore jointly with the union approaches that would jointly improve quality of working life and organizational effectiveness—that the latter agreed to collaborate.

The process began with education related to methodology and principles of sociotechnical design. There was comfort within the union since it was agreed that all decisions within the design team would require members' consensus. No decision would be made without everyone's agreement to support it. This was followed by collaborative exploration of alternatives to existing organization design structures, which were consistent with sociotechnical principles.

The process of collaborative research without preconceived notions led to unexpected results, which undoubtedly would not have occurred if management had proceeded on their own. These included elimination of job jurisdictional boundaries, advancement based on acquisition of skills rather than seniority, multiskilled employees, a work schedule providing shift workers the opportunity to spend considerable time on "days," and high levels of self-regulation. Perhaps the most unanticipated outcome was a unique collective agreement. Consistent with the Principle of Minimum Critical Specification (Cherns, 1976), both parties agreed that the Agreement should specify only what was considered to be absolutely necessary to provide a framework and set of guidelines for employees to work within. Responsibility for filling in details would be left with the workforce outside of formal collective bargaining. As a consequence, an eight-page collective agreement was developed that did not even include a grievance procedure. This was a major innovation in collective agreements in North America and came about because of the high trust levels established within the self-managed teams.

As described below, Shell management undertook many initiatives to disseminate the learning from their experience in this endeavor. Reception was generally very favorable. The union made several presentations at conventions of the Canadian Federation of Labour, which were met with mixed reviews. Several unions, however, were impressed and subsequently participated in sociotechnical designs.

Celestica. Celestica was a stand-alone subsidiary of IBM that was spun off in 1992. Located in Toronto, Ontario, Celestica designs and manufactures equipment for customers in the computer and communication sectors. In 1994, Celestica embarked on an STS redesign process, with a workforce of approximately 2,500 employees.

It is common in large organizations to sequentially roll out an STS redesign, starting in one or two areas and working through the remainder as the earlier ones get under way. This approach is generally followed because of insufficient experienced resources to facilitate a larger process and to allow some learning to take place in a smaller portion before expanding the scope.

At Celestica, however, because of a sense of urgency, it was decided to tackle the entire organization at once. The following structure was established for this purpose:

- A Resource Team, composed of nine members who would act as facilitators and internal consultants. This group received extensive training in STS methodology and process consultation. It was aided by an experienced external consultant.

- Twenty-one Design Teams, made up of representatives of the departments being redesigned, to conduct the STS analysis and formulate change recommendations.
- A Central Design Team, comprised of a member from each design team, to ensure consistency and dissemination of learning across the site.
- A Steering Committee, made up of senior management, to provide resources and approve recommendations.
- Swarm Teams for each redesigned work area, to accelerate implementation of change initiatives. These were short-term multidisciplinary groups, with representatives from manufacturing and engineering, whose task it was to get the newly formed work cells up and running to a point where predetermined stretch performance targets were achieved.

Once the initial design recommendations were implemented, a number of Continuous Design Teams were formed, as in the Shell case described above, to continue the redesign process.

The Celestica design process advanced knowledge about the use of parallel processes in organization design, particularly simultaneous, comprehensive parallel processes. Celestica's design interventions elaborated on the use of design teams to include new practices such as Swarm Teams and Continuous Design Teams, as described in an article by Dyck and Halpern (1999), with Norm Halpern serving the dual role of consultant and academic in leading the initiative to capture the learning from Celestica's efforts.

The redesign led to such changes as these:

- Establishment of customer-focused teams, which included most of the functions required to fully support each customer
- Skills transfer, primarily from engineering, supply chain management, and maintenance to manufacturing, to improve response capabilities

- Substantial modifications to operational training, to enhance skills
- Introduction of an open job-posting process
- Increased emphasis on housekeeping and "showcasing"
- Improved data transfer from the customer to permit more rapid response to meeting customers' needs
- Modified work schedules to better accommodate manufacturing requirements

As a result, significant benefits were realized:

- Productivity doubled, with the consequent increase in manufacturing without additional labor requirements or capital expenditures.
- Cycle times, from customer ordering to product delivery, were reduced eightfold.
- Product quality, as measured by defects per unit, improved by a factor of two.
- Operating costs decreased substantially.

Crown Cork & Seal. In 1986, Continental Can (subsequently purchased by Crown Cork & Seal) built a greenfield facility in Mississauga, Ontario, to manufacture end units for beverage cans. In an effort to gain an advantage in a very competitive field, it was decided to proceed with an STS design at this site. This facility ultimately produced units with higher quality at a lower cost than any of the sister plants.

To provide a high level of participation and develop a sense of ownership, employees were brought in while there was still nothing more than an empty building. These people were given training in STS design and, concurrent with serving on the design team along with two management personnel, actually participated in the installation of the equipment. This group, along with two management personnel, formed the initial design team. As others were hired, they joined the design process. An external consultant provided training in STS methodology.

Because this facility was truly "greenfield," in addition to establishing multi-skilled, self-regulating work teams similar to those described in the two preceding cases, this design team had the opportunity to influence considerably more than in the two examples cited above. This group formulated some very unique policies in such areas as compensation, benefits, discipline, overtime regulation, and promotion. As in the Shell and Celestica cases described above, an organization review board was established here for the purpose of continuous redesign. In addition, once per year, the plant shut down for two to three "STS days," at which time all employees gathered off-site to work in small groups on various redesign projects identified by shop-floor workers.

Phase 3: Collaborative Design

In a direct challenge to the many expert-oriented approaches that had begun to diffuse widely, Fred and Merrilyn Emery argued strongly for what they referred to as "design principle two"—an approach to organization design that was built on employees of a unit under study being involved in the data gathering and analysis aspects as well as being directly involved in the redesign of the unit itself (Emery, 1976; Emery & Emery, 1969). It was called "participative design," and the case can be made that it too is a strong forerunner of current collaborative research approaches. However, participative design, or PD, tended to be limited to design at the shop-floor level or in clerical situations at the lower levels of the organization. Few, if any, examples of its successful application beyond these levels have been published.

Collaborative research, in contrast, found its early applications in the knowledge areas of the organization with professional scientists and engineers. It remains to be seen if applications of collaborative research at lower levels of the organization will differ from the initiatives and methodologies developed under the participative design phase of STS.

Some of the early collaborative designs in North America were considered so superior to conventional designs that the organizations that fostered them considered them as competitive advantages and held their design processes as well as their implementation proprietary. Only selected visitors were allowed, and publication of any part of the design process was forbidden. The occasional time when a violation of the ban occurred became a cause célèbre within the organization design field (Krone, 1975). However, others did make their way to publication, but mostly as case studies that described the design process and its implementation. While the Trist and Bamforth (1951) description of how coal mines in the United Kingdom were designed was published as an academic research article, as were subsequent organization design interventions that emanated from the Tavistock Institute in the United Kingdom, a large number of the case descriptions in North America were published in more pragmatic journals or as compendiums of case studies (Davis & Cherns, 1975; Cunningham & White, 1984) or by professional associations (e.g., the Work in America Institute).

COLLABORATIVE RESEARCH

The collaborative designs described above were built on a foundation of considerable shared management knowledge about organization design. In each of these cases, there was much effort invested by those within the organizations being redesigned to learn of similar efforts elsewhere, their methodologies, how impediments were dealt with, steps for success, and lessons learned "if we had to do it all over again." Furthermore, in each instance there was extensive sharing and dissemination of experiences through various media, even if these experiences did not always fit the traditional definition of collaborative research. Some examples follow:

- In the Shell case, prior to undertaking the STS design process, over a period of more than a year, several members from the organization visited numerous sites in Europe and North America where innovative designs had been reported. A detailed report was issued outlining what was done and ultimately achieved. It was this internal research report that was the stimulus for Shell Canada to proceed. Much of the learning from that report was subsequently published (Halpern, 1985).

- In all cases, management, union members (Shell), and design team members undertook to research accomplishments of others through visits, articles, videos, and attendance at conferences, to learn of organizational design alternatives.
- Every one of these organizations allowed outsiders (managers, union members, academics, practitioners) who expressed an interest in STS to visit their facilities—often at great inconvenience and cost—to share their experiences and learning. (Of interest, Celestica's decision to follow an STS approach in redesigning its organization was stimulated by a visit to Crown Cork & Seal. The suggestion for the visit was made by a recently hired new graduate who had taken an STS design course at the University of Toronto.)
- Articles were published in various journals and books by Celestica and Shell authors (e.g., Davis & Sullivan, 1980; Halpern, 1984, 1985; Dyck & Halpern 1999; Halpern & Ward, 2000).
- Members from each of these organizations made frequent presentations at public conferences such as Ecology of Work, Work in America, Productivity Inc., and the Personnel Association of Ontario.
- All of these organizations volunteered their time to present case studies at various university organization design classes and workshops.
- The Shell case was the subject of two doctoral dissertations—at the University of Toronto (Halpern, 1983) and the Wharton School of Management (Rankin, 1990).
- The Celestica design exemplified a particularly interesting collaboration. Two independent groups of consultants—one with STS design expertise and the other expert in

lean manufacturing—were engaged to jointly work on the project. Results were excellent, with each side admitting to have learned much from the other.

While the up-front research for other STS design projects might not be as extensive as that conducted by Shell, primarily because there is much more information on STS readily available these days, it nevertheless invariably takes place. For example, public workshops and seminars describing STS methodology were conducted at the University of California and the University of Toronto. Case studies were presented to the public in large, well-attended conferences produced by a variety of organizations such as Ecology of Work and Work in America. Sharing of information continues through a variety of additional channels. A series of STS videos, describing experiences of several organizations, is now available, thanks to Modern Times Production and Blue Sky Productions. The STS roundtable, consisting of consultants, academics, and industry representatives, meets annually to share such experiences. Several consultants and academics, such as Lyman Ketchum and Barry Macy, conducted roundtables, open to the public, that described the learning from these various design innovations.

CONCLUSION

The Canadian cases we have described here, both greenfield and redesign, have illustrated the solid foundation of collaborative design in sociotechnical system undertakings. They have also illustrated how this ethic of collaboration, coupled with a sociotechnical tradition of knowledge sharing, has resulted in publications that have made important contributions to collaborative research.

Organizational research through data collection is a basic step in STS organizational design methodology (Emery, 1959). With the value orientation of STS practitioners and academics, that data collection is usually carried out by organizational members in a participative process. It is that culture of participation that has usually resulted in collaborative design between those undertaking a redesign or a new design, usually managers in concert with external consultants or academics.

It is interesting that so many of the early founders of STS thinking (Emery, Trist, Thorsrud, Rice, Miller) were associated with research institutes (e.g., Tavistock Institute of Work Relations, Oslo Work Research Institute) rather than traditional universities. As such, they were a little closer to practice than academics usually are. It is also interesting to note how prolific some of these early STS researchers, such as Eric Trist and Fred Emery, were. This has probably set a high standard for publishing that links the collaborative design of STS so closely to collaborative research. It might also explain the amount of sharing of management knowledge among practitioners who frequented the conferences, forums, and workshops that were so prevalent in the STS arena. The ethic of sharing knowledge was widely accepted, and perhaps because so many of these practitioners did not have the research and writing backgrounds of academics, the opportunities to meet and share knowledge in a more verbal way at conferences and workshops or through site visits were their ways of enacting collaborative research.

REFERENCES

Aguren, S., Bredbacka, C., Hansson, R., Ihregren, K., & Karlsson, K. G. (1984). *Volvo Kalmar revisited: Ten years of experience.* Stockholm: Efficiency and Participation Development Council.

Aguren, S., & Edgren, J. (1980). *New factories: Job design through factory planning in Sweden.* Stockholm: Swedish Employers' Confederation, Technical Department.

Aguren, S., Hansson, R., & Karlsson, K. G. (1976). *The Volvo Kalmar plant.* Stockholm: The Rationalization Council SAF-LO.

Bion, W. (1961). *Experiences in small groups and other papers.* London: Tavistock Institute.

Cherns, A. B. (1976). The principles of sociotechnical design. *Human Relations, 29*(8), 783–792.

Cummings, T. (1976). Sociotechnical systems: An intervention strategy. In W. Burke (Ed.), *Current issues and strategies in organization development.* New York: Human Sciences Press.

Cunningham, J. B., & White, T. H. (Eds.). (1984). *Quality of working life: Contemporary cases.* Ottawa: Labour Canada.

Davis, L. E., & Cherns, A. B. (Eds.). (1975). *The quality of working life.* New York: Free Press.

Davis, L. E., & Sullivan, C. S. (1980). A labour-management contract and quality of working life. *Journal of Occupational Behaviour, 1,* 29–41.

Davis, L. E., & Taylor, J. (1979). *Design of jobs.* Santa Monica, CA: Goodyear.

Dyck, R., & Halpern, N. (1999). Team-based organization redesign at Celestica. *Journal for Quality and Participation, 22*(5), 36–40.

Edgren, J. (1974). *With varying success: A Swedish experiment in wage systems and shop floor organization.* Stockholm: Swedish Employers' Confederation, Technical Department.

Emery, F. E. (1959). *Some characteristics of socio-technical systems.* London: Tavistock Institute.

Emery, F. E. (1976). Active adaptation: The emergence of ideal seeking systems. In F. E. Emery (Ed.), *Futures we are in* (pp. 67–131). Leiden: Martinus Nijhoff.

Emery, F. E., & Emery, M. (1969). *Participative design: Work and community life.* Canberra: Centre for Continuing Education, Australia National University.

Emery, F. E., & Thorsrud, E. (1969). *Form and content in industrial democracy.* London: Tavistock Institute.

Emery, F. E., & Trist, E. L. (1965). The causal texture of organizational environments. *Human Relations, 18*(1), 21–32.

Emery, F. E., & Trist, E. L. (1978). Analytical model for sociotechnical systems. In W. Pasmore & J. Sherwood (Eds.), *Sociotechnical systems: A sourcebook* (pp. 120–131). San Diego: University Associates.

Englestad, P. (1970). Sociotechnical approach to problems of process control. In F. Bolam (Ed.), *Papermaking systems and their control.* London: British Paper and Boardmakers Association.

Göranzon, B., Elden, M., Hammarström, O., Forslin, J., Viklund, B., Hedberg, B., et al. (1982). *Job design and automation in Sweden.* Stockholm: Center for Working Life.

Halpern, N. (1983). *Strategies for dealing with forces acting on the process of organization change in a unionized setting.* Unpublished doctoral dissertation, University of Toronto, Canada.

Halpern, N. (1984). Sociotechnical systems design: The Shell Sarnia experience. In J. B. Cunningham & T. H. White (Eds.), *Quality of working life: Contemporary cases.* Ottawa: Labour Canada.

Halpern, N. (1985). *Organization design in Canada.* In A. Brakel (Ed.), *People and organizations interacting.* New York: John Wiley and Sons.

Halpern, N., & Ward, J. (2000). Values-based organization design. *Target, 16*(3), 6–21.

Krone, C. G. (1975). *Open systems redesign.* In J. D. Adams (Ed.), *New technologies in organization development* (pp. 335–356). La Jolla, CA: University Associates.

Miller, E. (1959). Technology, territory and time: The internal differentiation of complex production systems. *Human Relations, 12*(3), 245–272.

Miller, E. (1975). Sociotechnical systems in weaving, 1953–1970: A follow-up study. *Human Relations, 28*(4), 349–386.

Pasmore, W., & Sherwood, J. (Eds.). (1978). *Sociotechnical systems: A sourcebook.* San Diego: University Associates.

Rankin, T. (1990). *New forms of work organization: The challenge for North American unions.* Toronto: University of Toronto Press.

Rice, A. (1958). *Productivity and social organization: The Ahmedabad experiment.* London: Tavistock Institute.

Susman, G. (1976). *Autonomy at work.* New York: Praeger.

Taylor, J. C. (1978). *Studies in participative sociotechnical work systems analysis and design: Service technology work groups* [Paper CQWL-WP-78-1-B]. Los Angeles: UCLA Center for the Quality of Working Life, Institute of Industrial Relations.

Trist, E. L., & Bamforth, K. W. (1951). Some social and psychological consequences of the longwall method of coal-getting. *Human Relations, 4*(1), 3–38.

Trist, E. L., Brown, G., & Susman, G. (1977). An experiment in autonomous working in an American underground coal mine. *Human Relations, 30*(3), 201–236.

Trist, E. L., Higgin, G. W., Murray, H., & Pollock, A. B. (1963). *Organizational choice: Capabilities of groups at the coal face under changing technologies: The loss, rediscovery and transformation of a work tradition.* London: Tavistock Institute.

Trist, E. L., & Murray, H. (1990a). Historical overview: The foundation and development of the Tavistock Institute. In E. L. Trist & H. Murray (Eds.), *The social engagement of social science: Vol. 1. The socio-psychological perspective* (pp. 1–34). Philadelphia: University of Pennsylvania Press.

Trist, E. L., & Murray, H. (Eds.). (1990b). *The social engagement of social science: Vol. 1. The socio-psychological perspective.* Philadelphia: University of Pennsylvania Press.

Trist, E. L., & Murray, H. (Eds.). (1993). *The social engagement of social science: Vol. 2. The socio-technical perspective.* Philadelphia: University of Pennsylvania Press.

Trist, E. L., & Murray, H. (Eds.). (1997). *The social engagement of social science: Vol. 3. The socio-ecological perspective.* Philadelphia: University of Pennsylvania Press.

Van Eijnatten, F. M. (1993). *The paradigm that changed the world.* Assen, The Netherlands: Van Gorcum.

IIIB. COLLABORATIVE RESEARCH IN COMPLEX NETWORKS

Collaborative Participatory Research in Gender Mainstreaming in Social Change Organizations

RAJESH TANDON

MARTHA FARRELL

ABSTRACT

Unequal gender relations in societies, especially in developing countries, have been a focus of development programs for decades. Much of this focus has been on changing gender relations in communities. However, organizations—governmental and private—also reflect similar patterns of gender relations. Advocacy for gender mainstreaming in organizations has had limited success due to its prescriptive approach. The Society for Participatory Research in Asia (PRIA) has adopted a learning-process approach to gender mainstreaming in development NGOs in India. Collaborative research methodology has been utilized toward this end. This chapter describes one such case and draws implications for future research and practice.

GENDER CONTEXT

Women's marginalization, exclusion, and deprivation are pervasive in many societies around the world. Women's participation in social spheres is constrained and restricted through a wide variety of cultural and religious practices and taboos; women's economic participation generally keeps them in low-paid, low-skilled occupations and jobs; women's political participation is generally

invisible and inconsequential. Women continue to perform several roles simultaneously (e.g., as homemakers, biological mothers, and care providers much of this work is invisible, unaccounted for, unpaid, and undervalued. In addition to work at home, women work in fields, mines, factories, and offices as earning members of the family (Farrell, 2004).

Those involved in the women's movement worldwide began to question and protest against the unequal status of women and resist the discrimination they faced in all spheres of life—at home, in the community, and at workplaces. As a consequence, legislation, programs, and schemes began to be formulated by governments in many countries to address such issues of inequality and discrimination (Kabeer, 1994).

Over the past two decades, many development agencies and programs have also been attempting to provide resources for transforming the conditions and status of women around the world, especially in the developing countries of the South. In the early days, these programs had a Women-in-Development (WID) focus (Kardam, 1991); later it became Women-and-Development (WAD)-focused; now, it is focused on gender—Gender-and-Development (GAD) (Moser, 1993). The WID perspective attempted to develop programs aimed at improving services for women (such as education and healthcare); the WAD approach took a holistic view of women's development (including such aspects as livelihood, water, and sanitation); the GAD perspective attempts to change unequal relations of power between women and men—gender relations—in a given social context.

Perceptions of gender characteristics and capabilities are the result of social construction of roles and responsibilities (Glaser & Strauss, 1967). Gender discrimination, therefore, is open to change and is the focus of many current interventions in development programs. Rooted in the ideology of patriarchy, gender discrimination is still widespread in many societies—in the North and the South. According to Farrell (2004),

> The word *patriarch* means the rule of the father. *Patriarchy* therefore refers to a social system where the father controls all members of the family, all property, all economic and other major decisions. The traditional form of patriarchy is based on the assumption that "men" are superior to "women," that women should be controlled

by men and are part of a man's property. So we can define patriarchy as "the system that subordinates and oppresses women in both private and public spheres." (p. 57)

Over the past two decades, analysis of programs established to overcome gender discrimination has largely been carried out by those involved in the women's movement, civil society, and development NGOs (nongovernmental organizations). Documentation and analysis of such programs clearly established that women's low status in the family and society is closely related to many other development deficits such as malnutrition among children, lack of education for girls, poor immunization and healthcare, inadequate water conservation, absence of sustainable livelihoods, and so on (Moser, 1993). Thus, many international agencies and governments have formulated and implemented several programs that attempt to enhance the status and improve the condition of women in different societies.

Many civil society and nongovernmental organizations have been implementing development projects aimed at addressing such gender discrimination in rural and urban areas. These projects cover a wide spectrum of issues—education, health, savings and credit, microfinance, livelihood, and so forth. Various frameworks and methodologies have been formulated for undertaking systematic gender analysis in particular locations; likewise, many methods and tools have been designed to formulate projects that address the conditions and interests of women from a gendered lens (Kabeer & Subramaniam, 1996). Thus, mainstreaming gender in development planning, programming, and monitoring has now become commonplace, especially among NGOs.

However, very little attention has been paid to the issue of mainstreaming gender within the very same organizations that address gender discrimination in society through their own interventions.

This chapter describes a collaborative research and change effort in a network of NGOs where institutional gender mainstreaming was attempted over a period of two years (2002–2004). A collaborative approach to this research was chosen because it seemed appropriate to the learning-process orientation needed to bring about organizational change.

GENDER AND ORGANIZATIONAL CHANGE

Organizational change efforts began in a planned and systematic manner nearly 40 years ago. Organizational development (or OD as it came to be known) is a field of theory and practice that evolved from change efforts in for-profit, private sector corporations in the United States and elsewhere (Beckhard, 1992). Over the years, participatory diagnosis and change methodologies, utilizing collaborative research and inquiry, also gained considerable currency (see Pasmore, Stymne, Shani, Mohrman, & Adler, Chapter 1 in this volume). The values and processes in OD attempted to change organizations in ways that would enhance employee motivation and empowerment, as well as organizational productivity, efficiency, and results. OD methods, therefore, seem well suited to address gender issues that are rooted in the design and process of organizations, including NGOs.

The impact that institutional design and functioning have in mainstreaming gender in development programs has begun to be reported only recently (Goetz, 1997). The mainstay of many of these arguments is the separation of life from work, and nonrecognition of women's reproductive responsibilities in society. It has been clarified that institutions not only affect the manner in which programs are delivered in the field, but the functioning of their internal processes as well. Thus, many theorists have argued for

an engendered view of organizations in general, and development organizations in particular. Such analysis helps to clarify the institutionalization of patriarchy in organizations. Acker (cited in Kelleher & Gender at Work Collaborative, 2002) sums it up succinctly:

> The gendered substructure lies in the spatial and temporal arrangements of work, in the rules prescribing workplace behavior and in the relations linking workplace to living place. These practices and relations, encoded in arrangements and rules, are supported by assumptions that work is separate from the rest of life and that it has first claim on the worker. Many people, particularly women, have difficulty making their daily lives fit these expectations and assumptions. (p. 255)

In recent years, some interesting and positive experiences of organizational change efforts through a gender lens have been reported in the literature. These indicate how challenging and uncommon such efforts are within development organizations themselves (Macdonald, Sprenger, & Dubel, 1997). Rao, Stuart, and Kelleher (1999) describe a number of case studies where organizational change was introduced by uncovering roots of gender inequality in organizations: "Our explorations focus on the institutional arrangements of organizations, on what Joan Acker calls the 'gendered substructure' of organizations. This she characterizes as being built on a fundamental separation, and consequent devaluation, of 'life' from 'work'" (p. 2).

In promoting awareness of and sensitivity to gender discrimination, many activists and protagonists have successfully utilized aggressive advocacy and sustained pressure from below. Most international agencies and governments were made to listen to these voices due to such campaigns. The "women's rights are human rights" campaign had to take on religious institutions as well in achieving results during the Convention on the Elimination of All Forms of Discrimination Against Women (CEDAW) after the UN Conference in Cairo (1994). In local situations, women's groups had to mobilize themselves in the face of extreme resistance from both their families and society to impress upon men and authorities that their experiences of gender discrimination were real and that their analysis of such experiences had convinced them that such discrimination was systemic and institutionalized.

When issues related to gender mainstreaming in organizations were raised, these feminist activists attempted a similar assertive advocacy approach. In raising the question of gender mainstreaming within development organizations themselves, such an aggressive approach has typically resulted in denial, rejection, and justifications of such practices in their organizations from the leadership (and many times from the rank-and-file men). In the context of NGOs from the South, many donors have recommended the use of "gender experts" to prepare gender policies for mainstreaming gender in their organizations. In our experience, such an externally "imposed" gender agenda has caused harm to the cause of gender mainstreaming in development organizations in the long run, as resistance to internal change and transformation has been built into the leadership of such NGOs.

However, newly "engendering" organizations have generally adopted a different strategy. Rao et al. (1999) describe their perspective on organizational change succinctly:

> Our approach is different in two important ways. First, our understanding of organizational change marries insights from feminist and organizational change theory. Although power and accountability are important, we believe that change requires more than getting power and then telling people what to

do or training them to do it. It requires both power and participation. We describe a change process to do this, elements of which underlie the five cases. Second, our goal is not simply to improve existing structures. We don't want to play by the rules; we want to change them fundamentally and contribute to the evolution of a new way of thinking about organisations. (p. 3)

In a similar vein, Howard (2002) critiques the expert-driven methodology of gender mainstreaming:

> However, there is much that is unproductive in the characterization of (most) planners as resisters, which implies that people (both men and women) and organisations are resistant, static, tradition- and interest-bound, and inherently and unconsciously (structurally) biased. These characterizations, no matter how well founded, tend to lead to prescriptions that are top down, based upon ("correct") expert input, and managerial and administrative coercion. On the other hand, the characterization of planners as passive recipients leads to somewhat different strategies, where at least it is recognized that, in an enabling environment, they have the capacity to learn, understand the need for change, and implement procedures that will improve the outcomes for women. (p. 167)

Thus, our own commitment to institutional gender mainstreaming was translated in practice through a collaborative learning and inquiry process.

NGOS AND COLLABORATIVE RESEARCH

The Society for Participatory Research in Asia (PRIA) is a nonprofit, nongovernmental support organization, which has been supporting learning and strengthening of civil society organizations for the past 25 years (http://www.pria.org). Its focus on organizational renewal has been a holistic one. Its approach to capacity building in individuals and organizations is based on the theories of participatory research, adult education, and experiential learning. It has evolved its unique approach to organizational renewal of mission-oriented social change organizations, specially suited to the realities of NGOs in the South (Tandon, 1997). An organizational learning approach (Argyris & Schön, 1978) to mainstreaming gender, in our view, offers durable possibilities for creating organizational capabilities for ongoing renewal and transformations in such situations.

PRIA's founding philosophy is based on the principles of participatory research. In its core meaning, research is described as a systematic process of understanding a given reality. Knowledge, in this perspective, is not merely that which is recorded in books and documents; knowledge is the understanding of realities in order to act upon them. Thus, participatory research has evolved methods, tools, and techniques that enable actors to articulate their existing knowledge about a reality (or a set of issues within that reality). Popular knowledge, indigenous knowledge, knowledge in use, and tacit knowledge are valued and recognized as valid in this perspective. Thus is propagated a belief that all human beings are knowledgeable and capable of knowing more. Knowledge production and utilization do not reside in experts alone, and ordinary folks are knowledge producers and users as well (Tandon, 2002).

In this approach, PRIA has worked with local communities and their organizations to facilitate articulation of knowledge by systematizing their own experiences. It has also supported them in accessing expert knowledge in a manner that builds on what they already know. In doing so, PRIA has learned that knowledge production is not merely a cognitive exercise; feelings and emotions are equally legitimate modes of knowing, just as action (as espoused by action research theories) is a legitimate mode of knowing. Thus, PRIA's methodology of knowledge production utilizes cognition, emotion, and action as equally relevant modes of knowing about a given reality.

In its program of work with NGOs, PRIA has found ready resonance for this methodology. As social change mission-oriented organizations, NGOs identify and act on societal problems based on their own values, inspirations, and commitments. Such actions generate huge insights, which remain largely hidden within the experiences of their staff and volunteers. Systematization of this knowledge requires some facilitation, which PRIA has undertaken during these 25 years in numerous settings and on various issues. NGO staff thus find participatory research methodology, practiced in a collaborative manner, very helpful in articulating and synthesizing their experiences in the form of "usable" knowledge. PRIA facilitators establish a relationship of mutuality with NGO staff in undertaking such an exercise: they emphasize the collaborative nature of this effort at building knowledge. NGO staff are encouraged to take ownership of the processes of collective reflection and analysis, while PRIA facilitators act as stimulators, questioners, and supportive synthesizers. PRIA facilitators also bring to the notice of NGO staff other relevant knowledge that may already exist, which may have a bearing on the synthesis being attempted. Thus, the process of systematization can benefit from knowledge produced by others, too.

This process of working together with NGOs resonates with their own style of functioning, which is more cooperative and collective, more informal than formal, and more subjective and intuitive. Thus participatory research perspectives and principles, when applied in a collaborative mode, make it exciting for NGOs to make the effort toward knowledge building. Their commitment to knowledge production increases as they see a clear link with use of knowledge thus produced in this collaborative approach. Their historical antipathy to the ivory-tower ways of intellectual, academic, and research enterprises melts away in the face of such a methodology. It enhances their willingness to undertake systematic and rigorous reflections of their practices.

Thus, collaborative research, carried out within the above perspective of participatory research, is found valuable and meaningful in PRIA's work with NGOs.

We now describe such a collaborative inquiry and learning approach to bring about institutional gender mainstreaming in a group of Indian NGOs.

COLLABORATIVE INQUIRY PROCESS

As a support organization for other civil society groups and NGOs, PRIA regularly facilitates their empowerment efforts. PRIA's mission clearly recognizes the agenda of gender equity in society; its programs and interventions have been focusing on addressing such gender inequity and discrimination over the past 25 years. In recent times, PRIA began to address gender mainstreaming in its own organizational context.

PRIA's vision (PRIA, 2003, pp. 16–19) articulates a world where equity and justice characterize relations that include "gender justice as a cornerstone of such relations in the family, community and society." Its mission, among many others, recognizes that "gender discrimination necessitates focusing upon changing women's roles and status as agents and leaders of change." Core values, on the other hand, include "mainstreaming gender justice and equity through analysis of social reality, organizational policies, systems and structures, program priorities and plans . . . integral to our vision."

CASH: COMMITTEE AGAINST SEXUAL HARASSMENT

On August 13, 1998, the supreme court of India passed a judgment making it binding for all institutions, whether private or government, to institute certain rules of conduct and preventive measures to stop sexual harassment at the workplace. The judgment also made it mandatory for all organizations to constitute a committee against sexual harassment. The purpose of this committee would be to protect women and prevent sexual harassment in the workplace and to take action against the perpetrators of such abuse.

In December 1998, the PRIA Governing Board mandated the formation of its Committee Against Sexual Harassment (CASH). Its main concern was to play a role in developing a positive work environment that would act as a preventive measure to counteract sexual harassment. However, the committee did not limit its mandate to the issue of sexual harassment alone, but took a deliberate decision to facilitate gender mainstreaming in all aspects of the institution.

Though the law made it mandatory for all organizations to set up such committees, the structures to enforce implementation were initially weak. As a result, many organizations chose to ignore the directive, and where they were compelled to do so (this happened primarily when the organizations were government offices), the committees remained nonfunctional and existed only on paper. Committee members were often unaware that they represented such a committee until a circular was issued. A total of six persons representing various levels of the organizational hierarchy constituted PRIA's committee, which had a two-year term. Gender balance was also ensured in the selection of its members; in accordance with the supreme court's ruling, the committee's chairperson was a woman. The members were selected on the basis of their having worked in PRIA for at least two years, having a clear understanding of gender issues, being mature and responsible in their behavior, and having an ability to work in an inclusive and collective manner. This core group of six persons was the working committee, but there was an option of inviting other members of the organization to form referral groups when this was required.

However, the larger objective went beyond just the institution of CASH within PRIA. It was felt that if PRIA as an organization were to attempt to persuade others to set up their own committees, then PRIA itself should set up CASH, which was an active and functioning body. New legal provisions are not readily implemented by all, unless persuasion happens. In addition, it was also seen to be important that the experience of institutionalizing CASH would help in providing some lessons to initiate the process in other organizations.

Challenges Facing CASH

The first task that confronted CASH was to create an awareness of the supreme court's ruling regarding the formation and scope of such a committee. This implied that each and every member of the staff irrespective of his or her sex would have a clear understanding of the definitions and constitutions of sexual harassment.

The second and more difficult task was to help the entire staff understand that even though the environment of PRIA was positive and there were so far no reported or known cases of sexual harassment, this fact did not obviate the need for such a committee.

For most of the male staff in PRIA, the committee was seen as an unnecessary body and not needed in an NGO. Several of them felt vulnerable and threatened by having such a body. Claims were made that there were no instances of sexual harassment in the workplace within an NGO, since most organizations with their liberal and advanced thinking worked on development issues, which

included the empowerment of women in society. Women, on the other hand, welcomed such a move and were eager to talk about the roles, functions, and mandate of the committee.

The initial six months were a stormy period for CASH and the organization. Orientation programs about CASH, workshops on sexual harassment, discussions on norms of acceptable behavior—verbal and nonverbal—created a very subdued atmosphere. There was a visible physical distancing between male and female staff at informal events, including lunch breaks. Dirty jokes were shared in small private groups, and public announcements were made to the effect that no one was risking his or her job or reputation by sharing these openly (in case some women took offense).

However, consistent efforts were made to discuss these issues in an open manner. There was a focus on discomfort levels of men occasioned by the dress and certain behaviors of women in the office, as well as in the field.

"Who decides limits" was discussed, which helped establish norms of behavior for both the sexes. Slowly, the environment came back to normal in terms of interactions among the staff. However, there was a difference—very clearly there was an awareness of norms of behavior, respect for each other as colleagues, and an understanding of what kinds of behavior constituted sexual harassment.

Conscious efforts were also made to include sessions on gender discrimination and sexual harassment in some of the ongoing training programs of PRIA.

Review

At the end of 2000, the staff of PRIA were invited to review and critique the functioning of CASH since its inception. The feedback was positive and encouraging, with constructive suggestions for the future.

Everybody across the organization unanimously reiterated that CASH had positively been able to create a broader awareness and sensitivity to issues regarding gender in the organization.

One of the key contributions of CASH was that it was regarded as a forum through which the organization had provided space to discuss various issues related to gender inequality and discrimination. Structured events had offered everyone in the organization a common platform to come together and hear and share each other's views and perspectives.

The general opinion was that CASH had been very effective in strengthening and maintaining a conducive environment for women in the organization. However, both men and women also said that they felt a degree of comfort in knowing that there was an existing forum to be approached if anything untoward happened to them.

Challenges

A number of colleagues raised the issue that CASH should play a much greater role in extending this model beyond the organization. The CASH members themselves felt that even the internal role entailed a large amount of time commitment, and if CASH were to play a more proactive external role as well, then this would have some implications on time planning as well as appointment of additional staff recruited specifically for the purpose of gender mainstreaming within the organization.

The issue of size and diversity within the organization was another factor that needed to be considered while planning for and conducting programs.

It was further suggested that, given the turnover within the organization, issues and themes related to gender should be reiterated as an orientation to newcomers regarding the importance of gender within the organization. There were suggestions to deepen efforts to integrate gender concerns into programmatic planning and interventions. Everyone

lauded the role of the existing CASH in fulfilling a statutory commitment as well as in playing a larger role in institutionalizing gender mainstreaming within the organization.

However, several persons expressed their reservations regarding the use of the name Committee Against Sexual Harassment, as they felt that it had very negative implications and prevented people from openly approaching the committee not only with their complaints but also for a more open discussion. There was also the general impression of those outside PRIA who thought that CASH had been established because sexual harassment was rampant within the organization and that this was the official way of dealing with the problem. It was suggested that the committee be given a name reflecting a more positive message and a wider scope of functioning.

In 2001, CASH evolved into the Committee for Gender Awareness and Mainstreaming in PRIA (CGAMP), and it continues to operate as such.

Gender Audit Study

The next milestone in the evolution of gender history in PRIA was the decision to have a gender audit study conducted both within PRIA and also within its regional support organization (RSO) partners. The audit, to be conducted jointly with an external facilitator, would assess the role, scope, and future of the committee and the process of gender mainstreaming within PRIA and its RSO partners.

Following through on the strong organizational mandate in pursuit of gender justice, this study was commissioned by PRIA in late 2002 in order to (1) document current practices and efforts in mainstreaming gender in PRIA and RSOs in order to address the question of how a gender perspective is understood, negotiated, and articulated in both formal and informal structures and processes within the organizations; and (2) generate recommendations that further promote the gender mainstreaming process within PRIA and help initiate and further facilitate these processes in the RSOs.

The study also hoped to identify factors that facilitate as well as those that constrain gender mainstreaming and that can serve as the basis for formulating recommendations on methods and strategies that will serve to further promote the gender mainstreaming agenda.

Process

An external facilitator was identified to join some members of PRIA's CGAMP team in undertaking the study. The reasons for inviting an external facilitator were manifold:

- To enhance professional understanding of gender in organizations
- To bring additional perspectives in looking at internal realities to which organizational members may be "blind"
- To increase the effect of recommendations for organizational changes on top management, should such recommendations arise

The study team designed a process of data collection and analysis spread over several weeks. It utilized a modified version of the organizational analysis framework developed by PRIA (Tandon, cited in Chadha, Jagadananda, & Lal, 2003, pp. 6–7). The analytical categories included the following:

- Vision-mission
- Decision-making structures
- Personnel system
- Internal mechanisms
- Culture
- Capacity

The data gathering began with documentary review and was followed by semistructured interviews of key organization members and two sets of focus group discussions (FGDs) with staff located in different levels of the organization, one exclusively with women and another with men. A set of questions served as the starting point and helped guide the assessment.

In some cases, the external facilitator alone conducted interviews with key individuals, namely, the president, the coordinator of CGAMP, and the person in charge of personnel and administration. Group discussions were also held with other key individuals, such as members of the CGAMP and the top management committee. Individual interviews were also held with two staff members each at the level of program coordinators, technical specialists, and unit heads (one woman, one man), and two members from support staff (one woman and one man), who were selected randomly. Two FGDs, one with female staff and another with male staff, were conducted after participants were drawn from the ranks of program secretaries, assistants, helpers, drivers, and field staff through stratified random sampling. The objective of the FGDs was to undertake a rapid organizational appraisal of staff understanding of the term *gender,* draw out their ideas on gender mainstreaming within the organization, and generate suggestions for improvement of this process. Semistructured interviews were used to ensure that participants' responses were not fragmented into preconceived categories.

Analysis and Feedback

After completion of data gathering, the study team did a preliminary analysis of findings. It then discussed the same with the president of PRIA and the entire CGAMP team. These discussions further enriched the analysis of the secondary data and external facilitator, and the researchers began to formulate recommendations for further mainstreaming gender institutionally in PRIA. Another round of feedback and sharing of analysis was held with staff, and further suggestions were invited.

Box 14.1

Institutional Aspects of Gender Mainstreaming in PRIA

1. Organizational philosophy: vision-mission "to address gender-based inequality."

2. Decision-making structures: governing board's composition (40% women); bylaws of the governing board that suggest "gender balance" criteria in its composition.

3. Top management team: composition (40% women).

4. Personnel systems: recruitment of women, paternity leave, women with young children enabled to take them to the field, focused attention to Human Resource Development (HRD) of women staff to take up leadership positions.

5. Internal mechanisms: Committee on Gender Awareness and Mainstreaming in PRIA (CGAMP), headed by senior female staff, with representation from all levels in the organization; mandated by the governing board of PRIA, and presenting a biannual report to it.

6. Culture: The most significant aspect of gender mainstreaming is cultural change in the organization's norms, values, symbols, and meanings. In PRIA, this has focused upon such aspects of sexual harassment as language, dress, and gestures, in the field and in offices. An effective mechanism of handling any such incident of harassment is put in place in all offices.

7. Capacity: One of the important ways to sustain such processes of inquiry and change is to invest in the capacity of individuals and groups. Gender focal points in each partner and field location are mandated with this role and provide proper orientation on matters such as gender, grievance handling, and facilitating reflections and change.

A revised report containing analysis and findings was submitted to the president of PRIA. After deliberating upon the recommendations in the top management team, the president asked the chair of CGAMP to share the findings of the study and recommendations in the next meeting of the governing board of PRIA.

Key Findings and Recommendations

The key findings about institutional aspects of gender mainstreaming in PRIA are shown in Box 14.1.

Further findings and recommendations from the study included the following:

- A gender disparity was recognized in the composition of PRIA staff. The ratio of

men to women needed to be reviewed in the context of the representation of women in the decision-making process of the organization. The statistics revealed a very interesting picture. It is generally assumed that in most organizations women are more dominant at a support level; in PRIA, it was the opposite.

- The institutional policies of PRIA are gender sensitive. The credit for the change in policies goes largely to CGAMP, as it was their persistent efforts in taking recommendations from the staff and following up the same with management. The management and governance structures were also supportive of the process, which finally culminated in these positive changes.

- CGAMP/CASH workshops were successful, and these led to the creation of a gender-sensitive climate within the institution, where women can work in an atmosphere of comfort and security.

- A working environment was created where women feel they can generally compete with their male colleagues in terms of work opportunities based on merit and competence.
- A thorough and systematic review of personnel, systems, and other processes was instituted with a view to making these gender sensitive.

The following are some recommendations for institutional changes suggested by the study:

- Flextime/part-time arrangements should be made available for mothers-to-be and those with young children.
- Formalize facilities that are already in practice such as compensatory leave and flexible working hours for all staff.
- Build capacity of all levels of staff on gender issues; CGAMP members should be given additional inputs to enhance their capacity as well.
- Review existing gender training modules and customize PRIA's own module.
- Include other gender development concepts in trainings.
- Develop child care facilities in the head office.
- Retain women in the organization, especially married and pregnant women.
- Provide reassurance of job security to young and married women.

There were also specific recommendations for the improvement of CGAMP:

- Reconstitute CGAMP as a committee to address grievances related to sexual harassment and awareness on gender issues. In addition, the committee should be responsible for taking gender-related programs with other NGOs and projects at a community level including conducting research and other studies.
- Identify a full-time person responsible for gender issues at the head office.
- Identify gender focal points at the program level. Use the expertise and learning of female PRIA board members.

FOLLOW-UP

Several of these recommendations have since been implemented in PRIA. CGAMP continues to function and monitor ongoing issues in gender mainstreaming institutionally in PRIA.

Based on its own learning, PRIA initiated a process of collaborative inquiry with its partner NGOs during the past three years to assess the reality of gender issues in their own organizations. This gender study methodology (as practiced in PRIA first) entails a process of joint inquiry where internal members join with external PRIA facilitators to undertake a process of diagnosis.

PRIA approaches the leadership of NGOs to consider undertaking a process of "gender study" in their own organizations. Once a commitment to do so is secured, a team of two PRIA facilitators undertakes a collaborative inquiry of the various organizational dimensions viewed through a gender lens. The inquiry process generates data on existing gender-related practices in the organization. Many of these evolve as pressures for change mount from inside and outside. However, many such practices remain informal practices. The inquiry then identifies areas where new practices need to be evolved. The collaborative inquiry process then shifts the onus of renewal and decision making onto the organization itself—its leadership, its internal decision-making structures, and its people.

PRIA facilitators share experiences from PRIA and similar organizations that have initiated and implemented gender mainstreaming. Options and ideas are generated together, but decisions to change and improve are made by the specific organization.

The PRIA team then assists the organization in implementing those decisions. It helps to enhance the internal capabilities for implementing those changes. It provides some follow-up support to assist the institutionalization of those changes. It also attempts to strengthen internal commitment and capabilities to undertake collaborative research with other field-based partners of that organization.

By so doing, PRIA is able to promote the use of collaborative inquiry as a methodology of gender mainstreaming in development organizations.

CONCLUSIONS

One may ask why collaborative inquiry was instrumental in organizational change in the above cases?

Several lessons from the above interventions can be drawn for future inquiry and practice:

1. Gender mainstreaming "out there"— in government, community, and other organizations—is a lot easier to define and promote than "in here"—in one's own life, family, and organization. This is particularly so in development organizations that have been actively promoting gender equality in society. They often pay little attention to the means—the instruments within their own organizations—of achieving those normative ends. Hence, development organizations, especially NGOs, typically remain "outward-focused" and rarely make the link between their inner workings and outer impacts (Tandon, 1997).

2. By its very nature, gender construction is socially learned over decades in families, society, schools, and other cultural institutions. Such deep-rooted socialization affects men and women alike; values, norms, and traditions are the essence of gender, and changing these is generally very difficult. Attempting to change such core dimensions through dictates or aggressive confrontation ends up increasing resistance. Harigopal (2001) describes many aspects of such cultural resistance in the imposed organizational change process. Thus, a learning-process approach to cultural change in organizations may facilitate addressing such sensitive issues as gender.

3. Leadership of many development NGOs in the South continues to be male-dominated.

In general, these are men of vision, integrity, and commitment, including commitment toward gender equality. However, when using the gender lens uncovers patterns of power hitherto hidden under their leadership, there is a tendency on the part of male leaders to deny or simplify the data. The analysis of power relations viewed through the gender lens in a development NGO tends to make its findings discomforting to the male leadership. Plowman (2000) explains:

> Identifying where women and men are situated in the broader political, social and economic spheres immediately raises consciousness about the institutionalized and structured nature of unequal gender relations. It also makes very clear what it is that we are up against. The analysis can then shift from the bigger picture to the level of the organisation which is, of course, shaped in so many ways by the external environment, unequal gender relations included. (p. 193)

Describing a similar change effort in another Indian NGO, Sarah Ahmed (2002) focuses her attention on gender-sensitive leadership:

> Translating the organizational commitment to gender equity into practice requires gender-sensitive leadership, which is not necessarily vested in one individual, but more broadly includes the head of the organisation as well as those involved in senior management positions who are able to influence the direction, style, and values of an organisation. (p. 303)

Building a collaborative and learning-process-oriented inquiry on the theme of gender mainstreaming makes it possible for the organizational teams to discover their own reality of structures and practices that are gender-fair or gender-unfair. Interpretation of data by the teams themselves makes it possible for the analysis to be owned by the organization, thereby enhancing the possibilities for fundamental change to happen. For example, when confronted with the need for male responsibility in child rearing, male staff in an RSO initially went into denial mode. But examination of data generated through focus group discussions brought them to realize the importance of institutional support (in the form of paternity leave) for shared responsibility in child rearing. Such difference in perceptions and meanings is not uncommon in organizations. However, interpretation of an act by a man toward a woman as "sexual harassment" is charged with emotions and meanings. Thus, learning-process orientation in an organization can facilitate innovation and change. When such a learning orientation is carried out with the gender lens, the internal motivations, attitudes, values, and culture of an organization can be transformed.

4. Finally, collaborative modes of inquiry can help uncover dynamics that may well be invisible to outsiders. In the case described above, aspects and nuances of sexual harassment in a field setting were uncovered through such a collaboration. Women field workers in the role of researchers began to articulate dynamics of harassment that their male, urban counterparts could not perceive. Thus, systematic knowledge about sexual harassment in the workplace could not be gathered without collaborative research. Farrell (2004) described sexual harassment in organizations with the following example:

> What may appear friendly and social behaviour for some may be perceived as sexual misbehaviour for others. For example, complementing a person on their figure/looks may appear friendly, but to the receiver it may be inappropriate behaviour in that particular context. (p. 79)

Thus, preventing such harassment in the workplace is only possible when both women and men are engaged in analyzing the existing realities and developing norms of behavior and organizational standards that are acceptable and enforceable.

It thus becomes apparent that gender mainstreaming in social change organizations (and southern NGOs in particular) requires an approach to change that begins with collaborative research on the nature of gender dynamics and analysis of gender-fair organizational practices. Such collaborative modes of documentation and inquiry then generate organization-specific diagnoses for actions (as opposed to universal prescriptions of gender equality). The leadership (even when embodying male stereotypes) is then able to take some responsibility for bringing about relevant and meaningful changes that address the underlying dynamics of power relations based on gender.

IMPLICATIONS

This chapter has argued for gender mainstreaming in social change organizations, especially those that focus their programs of intervention toward addressing gender discrimination in society. The chapter describes a theory of collaborative participatory research that has been widely utilized in social change efforts as an appropriate methodology for learning about and changing certain aspects of organizational realities. The case study of PRIA presents a detailed account of the practice of this methodology.

Several implications for future research and organization practice can be drawn from the conclusions made in the previous section. One key implication for knowledge production is the acknowledgment of hidden and sensitive dimensions in organizational life. Sexual harassment is clearly one such issue; discriminatory norms and values, which ignore multidimensional responsibilities of women, is another. Exploring such issues is only possible through a collaborative participatory research methodology that values emotions and feelings as legitimate modes of knowing, which encourages a learning-process orientation of all actors in inquiry.

Another implication for practice concerns the capacity of gender experts and activists in facilitating such a collaborative inquiry process. There is a real shortage of trained professionals who bring in a gender lens to inquiry and change. Those knowledgeable about gender issues often lack competencies in collaborative inquiry.

Thus, addressing problems of social change such as gender discrimination entails more concerted efforts at promoting the use of collaborative participatory research in mainstreaming gender in organizations.

REFERENCES

Acker, J. (2002). Hierarchies, jobs and bodies: A theory of gendered organizations. *Gender and Society, 4*(2).

Ahmed, S. (2002). Engendering organisational practice in NGOs: The case of Utthan. *Development in Practice, 12*(3/4), 298–311.

Argyris, C., & Schön, D. (1978). *Organizational learning*. Reading, MA: Addison-Wesley.

Beckhard, R. (1992). *Organization development: Strategies and models*. Reading, MA: Addison-Wesley.

Chadha, P., Jagadananda, & Lal, G. (Eds.). (2003). *Organisational behaviour: A framework for non-government development organisations*. Bhubaneswar, India: Centre for Youth and Social Development.

Farrell, M. (2004). *Gender on agenda*. New Delhi: PRIA.

Glaser, G., & Strauss, A. L. (1967). *The discovery of grounded theory: Strategies for qualitative research*. Chicago: Aldine.

Goetz, A. M. (1997). *Getting institutions right for women in development*. London: Zed Press.

Harigopal, K. (2001). *Management of organisational change*. New Delhi: Response.

Howard, P. L. (2002). Beyond the "grim resisters." *Development in Practice, 12*(2), 164–176.

Kabeer, N. (1994). *Reversed realities: Gender hierarchies in development thought*. London: Verso.

Kabeer, N., & Subramaniam, R. (1996). *Institutions, relations, and outcomes: Frameworks, tools, and gender-aware planning* [IDS discussion paper]. Brighton, UK: IDS.

Kardam, N. (1991). *Bringing women in: Women's issues in international development*. Boulder, CO: Lynne Reinner.

Kelleher, D., & Gender at Work Collaborative. (2002). Organisational learning: A borrowed toolbox? *Development in Practice, 12*(3/4), 312–320.

Macdonald, M., Sprenger, E., & Dubel, E. (1997). *Gender and organizational change*. Amsterdam: Royal Tropical Institute.

Moser, C. O. N. (1993). *Gender planning and development theory, practice and training*. London: Routledge.

Plowman, P. (2000). Organisational change from two perspectives: Gender and organisational development. *Development in Practice, 10*(2), 189–203.

PRIA. (2003). *Strategic plan of PRIA: Governance where people matter.* New Delhi: Author.

Rao, A., Stuart, R., & Kelleher, D. (1999). *Gender at work.* West Hartford, CT: Kumarian Press.

Tandon, R. (1997). Organisational development in NGOs: An overview. *Institutional Development: Innovations in Civil Society, 4*(1), 3–19.

Tandon, R. (2002). *Participatory research: Revisiting the root.* New Delhi: Mosaic Books.

CHAPTER 15

Collaboration in the Innovative Region

MARY LINDENSTEIN WALSHOK

BENGT STYMNE

ABSTRACT

Science-based, commercially successful product innovations represent a highly desirable but extremely hard-won fusion of scientific and business knowledge. The capability of nations and regions to bring about that fusion varies considerably and, as a consequence, so does their economic growth and prosperity. This chapter suggests that collaboration among the scientific, business, and professional communities and access to mechanisms for commercialization and innovation set the scene for innovation that contributes to regional economic growth. Innovative regions offer a playing field for a collaborative game in which scientists, practitioners, and capital providers take part. A model is presented that posits the region's innovative capabilities as an outcome of interactions between a set of essential resources and a set of collaborative mechanisms. The chapter provides a number of micro examples of innovations, though the focus is less on collaboration in specific projects than on the regional conditions that are conducive to continuous and sustainable collaboration between science and business across many scientific domains. The actions of four different participants in this collaborative game are described: the enabler, the entrepreneur, the scientist, and the research institute. We conclude by suggesting ways in which individuals in a region can collaborate in order to contribute to product innovation by facilitating or engaging in interaction between science and practice.

THE MOMENT OF INNOVATIVE COLLABORATION

Peter Farrell is in many ways the epitome of a San Diego manager. In 1998 he was honored as the Ernst and Young "San Diego Entrepreneur of the Year." In 2005 he was named the Nation's Entrepreneur of the Year in the health sciences category.

In 1964, at age 22, Peter Farrell received a bachelor's degree in chemical engineering from the University of Sydney. After a stint with Union Carbide he joined the research group of Professor Ed Merrill at MIT and wrote a master's thesis on dialysis techniques which could potentially be applied to hemodialysis. He then worked for a period in MIT's industrial liaison office (see Roth, Chapter 17 in this *Handbook*) before moving to the University of Washington in Seattle, where he finished his Ph.D. thesis on membrane transport characteristics in hemodialysis in record time. In 1972, Farrell was recruited back to Sydney to take up a teaching position at the University of New South Wales. In parallel, he assisted the Baxter company as a consultant. Headquartered in Chicago, Baxter specializes in pharmaceuticals and medical devices for the treatment of complex medical conditions including hemophilia, immune disorders, kidney disease, cancer, and trauma. Its worldwide sales for 2006 were over US$10 billion. During a 10-year period, Farrell assisted Baxter in opening up new markets by traveling to Japan and Europe to talk to doctors and scientists about different forms of hemodialysis and peritoneal dialysis. In 1984, he was appointed by Baxter as vice president of R&D to set up and run their R&D facility in Japan. Eighteen months later, Farrell moved back to Australia to set up an R&D center for Baxter in Sydney, while he continued to oversee Japanese R&D for Baxter. His mission was to "find out where the low-hanging fruit was, pick what you think makes sense and take it on to the world market using Baxter's global marketing and financial muscle!" (Quotations in this section are from an interview of Peter Farrell by Bengt Stymne, March 17, 2005.)

A meeting with Professor Colin Sullivan at the University of Sidney spawned Farrell's opportunity to collaboratively link basic science and technology to the practice of product development. The professor showed him a video of a snoring man on a hospital bed. On the top of the picture were indicators of heart rate and blood pressure. Suddenly the snoring stopped and it was clear that the upper airway was blocked and that the man had experienced acute respiratory failure. His blood pressure and heart rate dropped like stones with the onset of the asphyxiation. After 35 to 40 seconds, he inhaled with a stentorian snore and the heart rate and blood pressure doubled. A pattern of many similar episodes followed.

"Do you think that is good for him?" Sullivan asked.

"Next question!" answered Farrell.

The professor explained that he was quite sure that this blocking of the airways, and the ensuing hypoxia, were a cause of hypertension. "And if that were the case, that would mean that untreated obstructive sleep apnea could be associated with a high incidence of stroke and heart failure," he further ventured. Then he fast-forwarded the video a ways. The sleeper was now fitted with a gargantuan mask attached by a hose to a sort of reverse vacuum cleaner which blew rather than sucked room temperature air. The machine was noisy, but the snoring and the obstructions were eliminated. Sullivan explained that positive air pressure from the device formed a pneumatic splint for the upper airway and let the patient breathe normally. He had several patients who were attached to such machines every night with the same positive results.

After having shown the video, Sullivan left the room and returned with a patient who was using Sullivan's device. He explained that the man had been using the machine for some time. As the treatment had progressed, the patient had lost weight and appeared to be healthy; and he had a normal body mass index. He told Farrell,

> "Before, I used to wake up in the morning feeling as though I had not slept. I fell asleep at breakfast and on the way to work, I was depressed. I had morning headaches. The treatment saved my life, my marriage and my job."

Professor Sullivan explained that these severe symptoms of sleep apnea were not yet taught in medical schools. He complained that in spite of his spectacular success, he had failed to arouse the interest of others outside the research community in his findings and their potential market. Farrell saw the possibilities of designing a marketable product on the basis of Professor Sullivan's invention. He proposed developing the professor's technology further and compensated him and the University for the right to do so.

Farrell founded the company ResMed in 1989, which focused its activities on respiratory medicine based on Sullivan's discovery. In 1992 its headquarters were set up in San Diego, when ResMed bought the equity interests of Medtronic, a cardiac pacemaker company with whose Nortech division, in San Diego, Farrell and ResMed had been working. ResMed's adaptation of Sullivan's machine and its introduction into the market went well, and by 2007 the company had 3,000 employees. It reported a net income of US$133 million before taxes in 2006 (ResMed, 2006, p. F3). The current sales run rate (over $700 million) grew over 30% and has led to an impressive run of 11 consecutive years of uninterrupted growth. Farrell saw a formidable market potential for his product. At least 20% of the world's adult population is estimated to suffer from sleep-disordered breathing. Clinical data show that a majority of people with drug-resistant hypertension, atrial fibrillation, stroke, type 2 diabetes, or congestive heart failure also are afflicted by

such sleeping disorders (ResMed, 2004, p. 4). The largest barrier to the firm's expansion is lack of knowledge about sleep apnea and its health consequences in the medical profession and among patients. For example, over 40 million Americans suffer from sleep-disordered breathing, but 9 out of 10 have never been diagnosed. "It's time to wake up to sleep," Farrell says.

What we want to illustrate with this case of the innovation of a treatment for obstructive sleep apnea is that the moment of decisive collaboration between a scientist and a manager can take place in a single afternoon. However, that moment was not a freak accident. Farrell's education had prepared him for it, as had his close to 20 years of consulting and employment with Baxter, where he had maintained connections on their behalf with scientists and M.D's all over the world in order to exchange business and scientific information and find and pick "low-hanging fruit."

THE REGION AS A CONTEXT FOR COLLABORATIVE RESEARCH

Farrell's success resulted from identifying an exciting opportunity after his time with scientists around the globe, enabled by his role in a multinational corporation. Increasingly, these sorts of productive interactions can occur in regional contexts characterized by a lot of good scientists and a lot of technology entrepreneurs. Science and practice both have the task to innovate. The core of science is discovery, theory, and new methods for solving problems. The core of practice is new products, improved processes, and better ways to organize production and distribution. In today's globally competitive economy, both basic scientific domains and industrial applications face innovation imperatives. The innovative knowledge developed through science creates opportunities for the development of innovations in practice. The problems and opportunities emerging from practice often stimulate new scientific questions and discoveries.

The interaction between science and practice is not just a bilateral, linear process but involves a multitude of actors and intermediaries. They include the creative intellectual capital involved in the process of research and discovery; the public- and private-sector investors in the R&D process; the innovators and entrepreneurs who can translate promising science into applications with market potential; and a vast array of legal, financial, and managerial professionals who turn viable products into viable enterprises that provide profits to enterprises and economic returns to communities. But innovation cannot occur in a vacuum. The processes of innovation go on in a more or less supportive context that has a profound influence on outcomes. Collaboration between science and practice cannot be fully understood without taking this context into account.

The region is an ideal context for analyzing the dynamics of collaboration between science and practice. It is a geographically delimited area that can contain the diverse actors that are potential participants in the innovation process. In spite of its being a complex system, the region is accessible to the interested observer or researcher who wishes to know it in some detail and to develop a mental image of it. A region is large and complex enough to make it possible to observe dynamic processes involving many actors and organizations. It is also small enough for individual actors and discrete social processes to have an impact.

CHAPTER FOCUS

This chapter looks at the region from a management perspective. However, it is not the management of the individual innovation process that is our primary concern here. Rather, we are interested in how regional environments, conditions, and resources can be managed in order to bring about innovation. The basic question is this:

> How can different actors in a region interact in order to contribute to product innovation and new value creation by facilitating, or engaging in, collaboration between science and practice?

Two types of actors have a strong interest in contributing to product innovation—the *manager* of a business seeking continued competitiveness and the *entrepreneur* who wants to start a business based on an innovation. When we refer to "practitioners," we mean both of these. How such practitioners act and the role collaboration plays in their repertoire are one focus of this chapter.

We also address the actions of scientists and the role collaboration with practitioners plays for them. When scientists act, they can do it as individuals or jointly in research teams and institutes. We address both individual and collective actors in the field of scientific research.

A third type of regional actor contributing to product innovation is the *enabler*. Enablers are actors who influence the potential for innovation to occur without necessarily being directly involved themselves. Enablers can be businesspeople and professionals who will benefit from the new customers brought to them by expanding businesses based on innovation. Politicians have a strong interest in innovations that bring prosperity and jobs to their constituency and so may assist by making investments in infrastructure. In addition, there may be voluntary associations, civic groups, philanthropists, or individual citizens who are supporting innovation and mechanisms for achieving innovation because they want to contribute to the common good.

How enablers contribute to innovation and the extent to which they promote collaboration between practice and science is of great interest. Some enablers are significant actors who may have no direct relationship to the innovation, but whose actions can nonetheless be of considerable consequence for the innovative capability and the patterns of collaboration in the region. To a large extent, the shape of a region emerges as a result of the efforts of these key actors.

A very small percentage of business firms engage in research and development. For example, in Sweden, no more than a handful of companies are responsible for the lion's share of private R&D expenditures (Granstrand, 1982). Most of their R&D activities are performed in-house. The literature on innovation management has therefore traditionally focused on how internal R&D processes in the large company should be managed and how these processes should be aligned to market needs (Tushman & Anderson, 2004). However, practice is changing fast in this area. Large companies have begun to outsource a large part of their R&D activity and look for advanced partners in innovative regions (Kling, 2006). Consequently, regions need to consider how they can make themselves more attractive as hosts for the R&D activities of firms external to the region.

A MODEL OF THE INNOVATIVE REGION

The region can be understood as a playing field for a complex collaborative game of innovation requiring many participants with many competencies (compare also the concept of the non-zero-sum game as discussed by Hertzen, 1993). Players from both practice and science with distinctive competencies and orientations need to continuously interact in order to become winners in the innovation game. The metaphor of a "collaborative game" can also elucidate the activities of enablers, since they influence the rules of the game and the amount and quality of resources that are available for the players.

Regions effective and innovative in transforming their economic base have demonstrated skill at assessing their core assets and gaps and then working collaboratively to leverage assets and fill gaps. Over the last decade, empirical research has revealed some of the key factors essential to innovation that produces growth and competitiveness (Audretsch & Thurik, 2001; Branscomb & Auerswald, 2001; Florida, 2002; Henton, Melville, & Walesh, 1997; Walshok, Furtek, Lee, & Windham, 2002). These factors include critical assets like talent, creativity, inventors, and R&D capacity; venture capital resources and entrepreneurial know-how; professional business service and workforce competencies; and formal and informal collaborative institutions and networks.

The mere presence of talent and resources in a region is not sufficient to ensure knowledge flows. The trust-building and mobilization effects, so critical to the entrepreneurial development of new products and industries, require a variety of essential social mechanisms to be in place as well as new approaches to manage these mechanisms. They can include cross-disciplinary and cross-professional activities; processes for assessing opportunity and risk; mechanisms for building community confidence in the potential of innovation, as well as the trust needed for high-risk partnerships; and finally, mechanisms to link the region to critical external resources and networks. All of these require new approaches to planning, management, and benchmarking. No one individual actor can expect to have a decisive influence on the outcome of the collaborative game. The matrix in Figure 15.1 attempts to capture the dynamic interplay of the assets on the one hand with integrative social mechanisms on the other. As described in the next section on CONNECT, it takes collaboration and shared understandings between communities of actors to have an impact on the playing field as a whole. We call this collaborative approach to reinforcing the innovative capability of the region the "shared model of management." In contrast to individual approaches to leadership and management within distinct sectors, institutional mechanisms involving peers from complementary sectors require different techniques for mobilizing and sustaining long-term collaborations.

Assets interact within a variety of mechanisms, resulting in a range of new capabilities and innovations. The matrix could be used as a map for (1) identifying and measuring the presence or absence of the diverse competencies and knowledge components of a regional system and (2) identifying and probing for the

essential catalytic and integrative mechanisms that enable the components to work, in terms of producing a high rate of startup and growth companies that generate new jobs and new wealth in a region. In this way, core capabilities and weak spots can be located. We do not imply that a region has to have an outstanding capability in every cell, but we hypothesize that a region needs to have a sufficient number of core capabilities to be successful. The question of "how much is enough" is one that will need to be answered in the course of future research through the application of this framework in a comparative analysis of successful and unsuccessful regions.

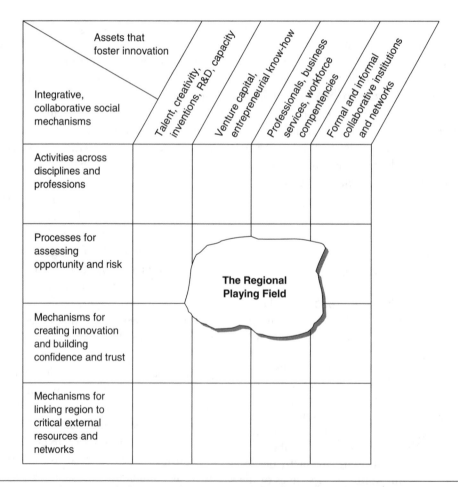

Figure 15.1   The Regional Playing Field: Location of the Shared Management Model

The matrix represents a playing field where the innovative activities and interaction and collaboration of scientists, practitioners, and other actors takes place. It is the background against which the actions of multiple essential actors can be understood.

Regional Assets

The economic system of a region contains a number of assets that are essential to the output of different products and services. A region's most important asset in today's globally competitive economy is knowledge. A region's innovation capabilities are determined by its collective fund of knowledge together with its resources for continuous knowledge production.

Regions in the United States that have done the best in terms of radical product innovations, fast-growing new businesses, growth in jobs and average wages, overall wealth creation, tax revenues, and philanthropy have one thing in common—the presence of a world-class university and/or a collection of basic research institutions peopled by the highly credentialed and creative talent that successfully wins major federal and foundation-funded research grants and contracts for their institutions. These grants and contracts fund the infrastructure of research (labs, vivariums, supercomputers); provide the intellectual talent required (professors, Ph.D. students and post-docs, technicians, lab specialists, project managers); and give rise to the output (patents, licenses, disclosures) that, in the case of the United States, has been exploited and funded by the entrepreneurial private sector in a manner that has produced enormous returns to the economy. The presence of large corporate R&D has been much less important to the recent growth in this era of global competitiveness than have R&D clusters located near major basic research institutions.

In addition to assets for research, the assets for innovation include the talent of entrepreneurs, venture capitalists, educators, lawyers, accountants, and sometimes representatives of governments or regional councils. If there are enough of these professionals available, it both leads to more diversity in specialties and creates certain competition among them, greatly benefiting the complex process of translating ideas into new products and services. These specialists also need to have the flexibility to take action rapidly enough to stay on the leading edge of the innovation curve.

Integrative Mechanisms

While universities, R&D, and high concentrations of creative, educated people are necessary, they are not sufficient to ensure that an idea, invention, or novel application actually turns into a commercially viable product or service. Even if abundant, if they are operating in "silos" in the region, they may not be productive of innovation. When mechanisms are in place to enable communication, integration, and collaboration within and between knowledge domains and professional competencies, however, a dynamic and highly productive process can be unleashed. The mechanisms that trigger this dynamic include

1. activities that create overlapping cross-disciplinary and cross-professional networks;

2. a culture of innovation characterized by a balanced approach to risk and confidence in the potential success of ventures;

3. mechanisms for locating innovation within a trusted community of competence; and

4. mechanisms for linking the region to critical external resources and networks.

A growing body of research on regional innovation points to the significance of a culture of experimentation and collaboration supported by partnerships, networks, and alliances among people, institutions, and companies. These characteristics are rarely found in less dynamic regions, even where they have good research institutions. Such a culture of collaboration and supportive webs of relationships enables the knowledge flows and collaborative activities essential to the transformation of scientific knowledge into marketable products, which become the basis for new industries and new wealth in a region (Audretsch & Thurik, 2001; Saxenian, 1994; Walshok et al., 2002; Zucker, Darby, & Brewer, 1998).

Complex and diverse regional networks continually connect people with good ideas, search relentlessly for the next innovation, and act decisively to bring innovations to life, creating economic opportunity for high-skilled workers in their regions. They address the challenge of growth by creating a competitive advantage at the regional level through the synergy of collaboration.

Innovation is a "contact sport" that requires high levels of interpersonal trust and nimble systems of communication and mobilization. Innovation requires that knowledgeable people work together, usually in close proximity to one another. It is not linear, but requires learning through trial and error. One person's ideas expand upon those of another person. A third person's feedback on a new idea helps the originator make his or her idea more marketable or practical. Collaboration makes the innovation process possible by connecting people and accelerating learning (Walshok & Vencill, 2006).

Skills and knowledge cannot be put to work for economic purposes without social networks and boundary-spanning alliances and collaborations that enable regions to become centers of innovation. Regions across the United States that have been very successful at this, such as Austin, Texas, and San Diego, California, have learned how to stimulate an entrepreneurial environment by actively connecting institutional and human resources through formal and informal innovation networks. The networks that foster collaboration leading to innovation at the regional level have included individuals with extremely diverse skills and knowledge, representing many different types of organizations.

Collaboration is a process through which partners, acting in concert, pursue a shared goal. Each partner organization begins with its own strengths, along with its own limited vision of what is possible. Success requires that each partner make a significant effort to expand its vision, explore differences constructively, recognize and combat barriers to collaboration, commit time and assets to the venture, and prioritize common purposes— sometimes at the expense of the partner's individual goals.

Regional Dynamics

The innovative assets and capabilities of a certain industry in a region take a long time to develop. An example is Oyonnax in the mountainous Jura region in France. This is a region that has shown a remarkable capability—that can be traced back to the year 650 C.E.—to make innovations in the art of producing small, nonmechanical objects (Plastics Vallée, 2006). Even if one does not want to have such a long-term perspective, it is likely that the knowledge development process, from a nascent to a full-fledged industry, spans one to two human generations, that is, 25 to 50 years. For example, a fledgling and highly experimental small computer industry emerged in California during the 1940s and became an accomplished global industry by the 1990s. One reason for the delays is that it takes time to develop the infrastructure and other subsystems that support the application of knowledge. It also takes time before users have adapted to a new product and before reliable feedback can be provided. Knowledge is usually also complex, meaning that it is composed of many subareas. All these subareas cannot be mastered by one person or one group of persons but necessitate the existence of many individual specialists or groups specialized in specific knowledge domains. Thus, the more complex an innovation is, the longer it takes to become a stable good (Dahmén, 1991).

Along with technological complexity, the time-dependent nature of knowledge has contributed to the fact that knowledge emerges in clusters. For one reason or another, a cluster starts to form around a specific type of local activity. Over time, the cluster coalesces as the knowledge of how to master that activity develops (Lundgren, 1995, p. 101). People start to produce and market differentiated goods based on that knowledge. The rivalry between various local producers and in relation to outside competitors triggers attempts to improve the products by development activities (Porter, 1990). Institutions for teaching the trade to young people come into being. Also, specialists in various aspects of management and trade in the product arena emerge.

The history of San Diego contains several examples of the dynamics out of which clusters emerge. Two examples are the now-robust clusters in biotechnology and medical devices, which can be traced back to donations for health and research by the Scripps family in the early 1900s. A cornerstone in the foundation of the region's leading position in telecommunications was laid by the San Diego congressman "Brother Bill" Kettner, whose social skills in 1912 convinced the U.S. Congress to allocate the money needed to dredge the harbor there. The improved harbor became the port of the Navy's Pacific fleet and soon thereafter Kettner was instrumental in the establishment of the North Island Naval Air Station. These military bases opened the windows initially for the expansion of naval and aerospace industries and later for a focus on missiles and satellite radio communication (Clark Duvall, 1979). There is a direct link from the military telecom industry to the case of the innovation of CDMA and the success of the Qualcomm wireless telephony company.

AN ENABLER IN THE COLLABORATIVE GAME: THE SHARED MANAGEMENT MODEL OF UCSD CONNECT

UCSD CONNECT is a program that manages the essential translational processes from science to commercial products via startup companies. It is in many ways a mini-version of the region, with its various assets, collaborative mechanisms, and rules that govern the collaborative game of innovation. The program started in 1984 in response to a scarcity of large companies that could absorb graduates and research results from the university and research institutes and a regional economic crisis that motivated local citizens to focus on science-based entrepreneurship as a driver of economic prosperity. In the absence of large companies, the growing entrepreneurial science community needed new models of collaboration in order to get the intelligence and resources embedded in business enterprises to further their research. A growing entrepreneurial business community made up of a small collection of very smart individuals and enterprises needed access to a large pipeline of good science from which to harvest the most promising developments for applications and commercialization. Providers of business service saw startups as a promising growing market.

The founders of CONNECT sought extensive consultation with university researchers, private-sector executives, and professional business service providers. Through a series of conversations and small group discussions convened by the university, these diverse but interdependent stakeholders created a mechanism for catalyzing a new approach to research/industry collaboration.

The personnel of CONNECT represent skilled enablers in the form of a small staff focused on delivering programs that draw upon the diverse talent pool in the region. The staff is accountable to a volunteer "shared management" board. The board is made up of representatives from diverse business sectors and scientific domains. CONNECT is fully funded by annual member fees from close to 1,000 companies and revenue from underwriting and fees. It sponsors more than 80 events, which bridge science and business and facilitate concrete partnerships. Twenty-two years after its inception, CONNECT is still growing.

Rules of the Shared Management Practices

The "shared management practices" as a mechanism for enabling collaboration in CONNECT grew out of what Jantsch (1980) has referred to as a "self-organizing universe." The following organizational and management principles form the rules of the collaborative game that is played out:

1. The uniqueness (competencies, cultures, standards of performance) of each of the distinctive stakeholders (science, business, services, capital, civic groups) is equally respected.

2. All stakeholders have a seat at the table and an equal say in the deliberations.

3. A common purpose and agreed outcomes have been articulated.

4. Strategies have been developed that ensure that every stakeholder has both something to gain and something to contribute in the achievement of the common goals.

5. Shared and agreed-upon metrics have been developed for evaluating outcomes from the collaboration.

The focus of the CONNECT process is the science-based startup company usually represented by the entrepreneur. In the process, the would-be entrepreneur is brought into contact with advisers representing science, business services, experienced managers, and venture capital. The collaboration between the startup and all these other sources of scientific and business knowledge helps an initially vague idea get transformed into a promising business opportunity. The transformation could be quite far-reaching so that there is little resemblance between the entrepreneur's original idea and the firm that eventually takes off. The program components of CONNECT described below form a progression of steps in the development of a science-based startup company.

Meet-the-Entrepreneur and Meet-the-Researcher Events

San Diego has academic scientists with promising ideas as well as non-research-oriented business entrepreneurs looking for new and promising technologies. Entrepreneurs and researchers often have very little understanding about the issues that the other faces or their respective modes of working. There needs to be a close connection between the two groups. CONNECT arranges two types of events to build understanding. In "Meet the Entrepreneur," encounters with successful science-based entrepreneurs provide insight into the unique challenges of starting R&D-based enterprises. In "Meet the Scientist," scientists deeply involved in research and with a good overview of some branch of the life sciences or information technology share their knowledge about what is going on, what looks promising, and what they think could develop into commercial applications.

In both types of events the would-be entrepreneurs and researchers interested in getting their ideas commercialized ask questions, speculate about ways to commercialize the ideas, and share ideas for joint undertakings. These encounters help develop a shared understanding of the scientific, technical, managerial, and business knowledge that exists in the region, in addition to building a larger community of both scientific and entrepreneurial literacy.

The Springboard Program

The Springboard is a collaborative event providing early feedback, useful contacts, and coaching on promising technology business plans to more than 60 startup companies annually. At each event, experienced individuals representing the region's many sources of knowledge offer empathic advice in a civic spirit to one specific would-be company. Before the Springboard event, CONNECT staff work with the entrepreneur or the entrepreneurial team to review their technology and business plans. In addition, the entrepreneurs are coached on effective presentation techniques. After appropriate preparation, the entrepreneurs are allowed to enter the Springboard.

The Springboard actually consists of a round table that seats 10 to 15 selected investors, corporate executives, scientists, intellectual property experts, and other providers of business services. They are all there to catapult the aspiring entrepreneurs a step further on their business trajectory by providing feedback and expressing opinions on their technology and/or business plans. For example, the entrepreneurs can get advice on applied research that is needed in order to develop the intended product. Advice on how to get private-sector financing is essential in this translational phase of business creation.

The advisers represent the region's different knowledge assets. The give-and-take between them and the entrepreneurs is an episode in an unfolding collaborative process. The concrete outcome of the episode is typically a transformed technology or business strategy for the entrepreneur presenters, built on the specific knowledge offered around the table. They also get names and coordinates of the people present and of others who can serve as sources of advice and support in the continued process of forming their business. A highly useful by-product of Springboard is that it has become instrumental in building a large community of diverse professionals in the region, who interact on a pro bono basis and get to know one another while they learn about what new enterprises, ideas, and technologies are emerging. Springboard has developed into a San Diego institution that integrates new entrants in the existing collaborative network. In addition, it develops and reinforces the existing networks and collaborative mechanisms.

The comportment of the representatives of different communities who provide input to the entrepreneur respects his or her integrity and involves a commitment not to use the information disclosed by the entrepreneur or the other participants for one's own advantage. The main benefit to the different communities comes when the firms get established, grow, and become customers to business services, suppliers to larger firms, partners in research, providers of investment opportunities, and employers of graduates.

Financial Forums

When entrepreneurs attempt to move ahead following their Springboard experience, they often find that they need business angels and other sources of capital willing to support their venture. A major initiative of

CONNECT has been to arrange financial forums twice a year. The San Diego Technology Financial Forum and the San Diego Biotechnology/Biomedical Corporate Partnership Forum attract investors from the whole country to learn more about San Diego companies. The participants represent investment funds and banks, venture capital, private equity, and larger companies that are interested in supporting future subcontractors and partners. As is the case with the Springboards, in advance of the event, CONNECT puts the entrepreneurs in contact with professionals from business services such as law, accounting, and marketing, who assist them in hammering out business proposals and making presentations that will catch the eye of capital providers.

Building Awareness and Networking

CONNECT's *Most Innovative New Products Award* is intended to ensure that the public recognize the important part played by local firms in creating innovative new products that contribute to the region's success in creating and nurturing high-tech companies and industry clusters. Committees of volunteers review over 100 nominations annually. Awards are given at an annual luncheon attended by 1,000 plus: a veritable "Who's Who" in the regional high-tech economy.

Today, San Diego has a critical mass of business service providers and local venture capitalists, who are experienced in helping scientists and who collaborate and co-venture with technology entrepreneurs. Not only provide do they technical assistance; they are also themselves sources of valuable contacts and advice. They constitute a regional resource that can help new entrepreneurs in new and emerging fields of technology. They have become an important part of San Diego's regional innovation capacity.

THREE ACTORS IN THE COLLABORATIVE GAME

The Case of an Entrepreneur: The Innovation of CDMA

CDMA—Code Division Multiple Access—is a technology utilizing a wide spectrum for mobile radio communication. It uses the spectrum in a much more effective way than the earlier-introduced and widely established competing technology, TDMA—Time Division Multiple Access. CDMA has been commonly used as the basis for the third generation of mobile telephony.

In 1948, Claude Shannon of MIT published "A Mathematical Theory of Communication." It defined information in binary terms and became a cornerstone for the future development of telecommunications. It specifies the maximum amount of information that can be carried by one channel. Shannon's theory provided crucial intellectual inspiration for the development of CDMA (Mock, 2005). In 1966, Shannon's former student, Irwin Jacobs, was recruited to the University of California, San Diego, from MIT. In 1968, Jacobs formed a firm called Linkabit, together with Andrew Viterbi, who was a professor of mathematics at USC, also recruited from MIT, and with Leonard Kleinrock, the future inventor of the Internet. Linkabit was set up to handle the professors' mainly defense-related consulting. Part of the work involved satellite radio communications.

In 1980, Linkabit was sold to M/A-COM, an East Coast communications company, and slowly the founders became the source of a large number of IT firms in the San Diego region. For his part, Jacobs, together with a team that included Viterbi and others, set up Qualcomm in 1985, focused on commercial applications of CDMA, but with no specific product yet developed. The company convinced Hughes Aircraft to sponsor the development of a system, called Mobilstar, for multiple access radio communications. In the same year, Qualcomm merged with Omnitrac to develop a system using satellite communications for tracking trucks all over the continent for the Schneider transport company. The Qualcomm team got the idea that the same principles that were applied to satellite communications could be used for the emerging mass market for cellular mobile telephony, and work on CDMA began.

In 1989, the Telecom Industry Association selected TDMA as the standard for American digital mobile telephony. Qualcomm had to engage in a long uphill struggle to convince the telecom operators that CDMA was a better solution. Some problems that many in the industry regarded as unsolvable, among them control of the strength of the signal emitted by the handsets, were solved and patented. A pivotal demonstration of the possibility of handling simultaneous communication with a large number of moving cars was arranged in New York City.

In July 1990, Qualcomm published a first version of the CDMA "de facto standard." In May 1991, South Korea contracted Qualcomm to make CDMA its standard for digital mobile communications. In this way, South Korea hoped to regain the ground its industry had lost in the telecom sector. The eventual success of Samsung supports the wisdom of this strategy. In December 1991, Qualcomm went public. In 1993, CDMA was accepted by the Telecom Industry Association as an interim standard. In 1995, CDMA was selected by several telecom operators such as PCS PrimeCO, Sprint, and Hong Kong.

In 2006, Qualcomm sales were about US$7.5 billion, out of which about $1.5 billion was spent on R&D (Qualcomm, 2006, p. 5). Qualcomm has achieved one of the most spectacular profit curves in corporate America and reported a net income of about $2.5 billion for 2006. That year about a quarter of all mobile handsets sold globally used CDMA technology. The market share for CDMA is rising fast.

The collaboration between science and practice in the Qualcomm case was a dynamic process that spanned considerable periods of time. Between the initial filing of a patent for hopping frequency transmission in 1942 (Mock, 2005) and the Telecom Association's acceptance of CDMA as a standard for mobile communications, more than 40 years passed. One main link for the collaboration between science and practice was the entrepreneur himself. As a professor, Jacobs developed scientific ideas and findings, drawing upon his earlier work at MIT, and continued in his lab at UC San Diego. His early collaboration with the defense industry was a decisive phase in the innovative process that eventually resulted in CDMA.

Perhaps the most important contribution of the University to the development process was that it brought to San Diego a scientist who put the innovation process in motion. The university also accepted that scientists collaborated with industry as consultants, and later got involved in the development of products aimed at a commercial market.

For its collaboration in the development of CDMA, the University did not simply get scientific input from Jacobs and other professors. It has also benefited from academics who, from their work on defense issues, have a broad base of knowledge of advanced satellite communication. Qualcomm employs many engineering graduates from the university. In addition, it is an important customer for continued training. The training demands from Qualcomm as well as the philanthropic gifts of the Jacobs family have made it possible for the university to greatly improve the quality of its education and the reputation of its research in the area of information and communication technology. The engineers whom the university trains make it possible for other enterprises in the telecom sector to be set up and to expand. It should also be emphasized that Qualcomm is an important philanthropic contributor to many universities. Jacobs is one of the 10 most philanthropic individuals in the entire United States. Both Jacobs (UCSD) and Viterbi (USC) have made large donations to engineering schools at UCSD and USC that now carry their respective names. Campuses such as Berkeley and MIT have received multimillion, dollar gifts as well.

The Portrait of an Entrepreneurial Scientist: Ramesh Rao

Ramesh Rao has been a professor of engineering at the University of California, San Diego, since the late 1980s, where he has built a distinguished career in research and publishing, as well as achieved membership in a variety of academies, including the National Academy of Engineering. Ramesh is also, for all intents and purposes, an entrepreneurial scientist. He has been involved in finding solutions to a series of research questions over 25 years that have broken new ground, particularly in the area of networking and networking theory. Examining important research questions long before the Internet was a household word, Rao describes his intellectual journey in terms very similar to those of pioneering entrepreneurs in industry such as Jacobs. He benefited from the seminal work of researchers such as Kleinrock and became involved in the emerging field of networks and networking as a Ph.D. student, long before it was "in."

Communications networking was not an established field when Rao was in graduate school. There were no formal courses, no journals, and no textbooks. Researchers were still formulating their own questions and drawing from a variety of disciplines. It was not a "safe" area of study if someone was looking for a secure university position. Nonetheless, it appealed to Rao because of his interest in mathematical models and his keen awareness that networks were going to be important in the future because of all the breakthroughs that were happening in basic research in the wireless communications arena. The appeal of applied math and building models that would have value to real-world problems of networking and communications is what motivated Rao.

It is interesting to note that Rao's early background may have predisposed him to openness to experimentation and the integration of diverse disciplines when trying to solve problems. His father was an industrial engineer, and Rao grew up in an educated family in an industrializing India in the 1960s and 1970s. They lived in a "frontier town" in India, which was being built from the bottom up to support India's growing industrial research, development, and manufacturing capabilities. With the move to this new community, a lot of the traditional family ties that typically locate people socially in India were severed.

People there spoke different languages and had different kinds of backgrounds and experiences. Rao describes himself and his family as having to re-create themselves in this new community and having to work with the multitude of different ethnic and social groups who lived there. "In order to fit in you had to be a good listener and learn how to connect with people whose backgrounds and values might be different than yours," Rao shared in a personal discussion. Rao suspects that he was "a kind of anthropologist" as a young person. The listening skills he developed have carried over into his academic career, giving him a certain level of comfort with open-endedness, ambiguity, and uncertainty.

In the 1980s, Ramesh was hired as a young assistant professor at UCSD as the first faculty member focused on networks, in a time when the Internet was emerging as a powerful force among academics. Its broader applications, particularly in the commercial sector, were less clear—but over the last 25 years the whole world of wireless telephony and communications networks has mushroomed. Rao has been at the leading edge of this work. He has helped develop the field, train young Ph.D's, and influence industrial engineers working in this arena. He describes it as a constantly changing, highly dynamic, unstable knowledge domain because of the rapidity with which basic research and new applications are changing the field. One needs a high tolerance for uncertainty to work in this field, according to Rao.

With initial interest and support from Qualcomm, Ramesh was a driving force behind the Center for Wireless Communications, established in the early 1990s at UCSD. He described this as a period when he had to "reach beyond his comfort zone" to involve academics from many disciplines, address questions and problems from many different arenas, and forge new kinds of partnerships with industry. At the time the Center for Wireless Communications was established, industry was still thinking in terms not of networks but rather of point-to-point communication. To begin exploring all the potential ramifications of networks in wireless telephony required physics and chemistry, as well as math. The challenge of building more robust multilayered networks required very close links to scientists from other fields and a wide range of industries interested in applications.

Rao commented that, early on, the industrial relationships were problematic and even at times seemed contradictory because of the differing expectations and returns in the two cultures. The industrial partners needed links to the rapid scientific breakthroughs occurring at the university. The academic questions that drove the faculty's interest needed to be tested in the applied communities.

Thus, there was a burgeoning of interaction, not only with the communications and cellular phone industry, but in arenas such as health and physical disabilities and the entertainment industry with video transmission. The wireless center is a lively center for university/industry collaborative research enterprise, involving a joint research agenda and millions of dollars of private and public sector funding.

Rao describes himself as a prospector for interesting opportunities. He has been looking for opportunities to demonstrate the value of networked systems to problem solutions. Thus, he attends many industrial and academic meetings "way outside" of his field. He often finds himself in conversations where there is an interest in using wireless networks to address a problem, such as in telemedicine or in environmental scanning, for which it's not clear whether they can find a solution. However, his attitude is to say to potential partners: "Let's do it. I don't know how we're going to do it, but let's find a way to do it together." It is this risk-taking orientation that has enabled him to build multiple partnerships with industry representing hundreds of thousands of dollars annually in support for his work and the center that led us to describe Rao as an "entrepreneurial scientist."

Rao describes his ability to function in this very entrepreneurial manner as a result of the distinctive culture at the UC San Diego campus. He is astounded by the intellectual and operational freedom that he continues to have after 25 years on the campus. He suggests that the campus culture, which focuses on outcomes—in his case, attraction of external investment in research, publication in internationally recognized journals, and growth in international reputation—is the reason he is able to be an entrepreneurial scientist. This entrepreneurial culture not only affects his work but also allows him to attract the kinds of graduate students and new faculty who are similarly inclined. This has produced enormous benefits for the UCSD campus in terms of research dollars and reputation, but also for the clusters of innovative wireless companies in the San Diego region, who find willing partners among the faculty.

The Case of a Research Institute: Burnham

The Burnham Institute is an independent research institute that in 2005 had a budget of more than $80 million and employed 450 scientists. It is a rather young organization, which started in 1976 under the name La Jolla Cancer Research Foundation. The founders were Bill Fishman and his wife, Lillian, both born in Canada. Bill had had a distinguished career as a world-renowned cancer scientist. Lillian had assisted him and also been the author and coauthor of scientific papers. At Bill's mandatory retirement from Tufts University of Medicine in Boston, they had decided to move to San Diego, where they were joined by their son and a handful of collaborators in order to continue their research. Lillian said that their creation grew "out of an entrepreneurial idea of scientific freedom" (Burnham Institute, 2006). The Fishmans wanted to use this freedom to understand the elusive and deadly nature of cancer by research in developmental biology in conjunction with oncology. They found that San Diego, which already housed the Salk Institute, the Scripps Research Institute, and the University of California, would provide a critical mass of research talent and offer opportunities for collaboration. As a start, Scripps offered the Fishmans 50 square meters of laboratory space for free.

In 1976, a young Finnish professor, Erkko Ruoslahti, became the scientific director of the Institute. Already frustrated with university politics in his homeland, he had welcomed the opportunity to move back to California, where he had studied and obtained his Ph.D. The Institute did not have any guaranteed funding, and Ruoslahti had to apply for research grants in order to survive. The applications resulted successfully in grants. However, they did not provide money to cover administrative overhead. Comparable research institutions use about 25% of their budget for overhead. In contrast, the new Institute launched a policy of economizing and minimizing bureaucracy, for example by demanding that the scientists write their own applications. This policy has allowed the institute not only to survive on less than 10% of nongrant financing, but also to set aside money for equipment and facilities. The strategy for attracting grants has, in the words of Ruoslahti, been to keep "an unrelenting focus on improving both science and the faculty" (interview of Erkko Ruoslahti by Bengt Stymne, March 18, 2005). Strategic plans have been devised for 10-year periods. Scientific plans target areas that will become important and where the Institute's research should expand. In this way, focal points have been established for the research. An example is a major research program on cell adhesion.

The strategy followed by the Institute has worked well. It is able to attract the best of scientists because it allows them to dedicate themselves fully to research. They are attracted also by the good facilities that the Institute has been able to build up. It organizes multidisciplinary teams of scientists and ranks among the top 10 to 20 organizations worldwide for the impact of its research. Burnham's program on apoptosis (how cancer cells are triggered to commit suicide) is probably the largest in the world. The Institute's cancer research has caused it to be designated as one of only eight basic cancer research centers in the United States by the National Cancer Institute, which is an important source of financing. Two other research centers have also been established at the Burnham Institute. One concerns neuroscience and aging, and the other, infectious and inflammatory diseases. Led today by world-renowned scientist John Reed, the Burnham Institute is also the center of gravity for a multi-institutional stem-cell research collaborative.

The Burnham Institute is one of several independent institutes in San Diego. It not only produces high-quality scientific research but also contributes to and strengthens the development of a regional cluster based on knowledge about cancer and the other two specialties, both through formal collaborative arrangements with the University of California, San Diego, and through informal social links between members of Burnham's staff and staff from the many pharmaceutical and biotech firms in the area. Discoveries of scientists from the Burnham Institute have contributed to several breakthrough innovations in the form of drugs that are now in medical use.

SUMMARY: COLLABORATION FOR INNOVATION

Only a handful of regions in the world can be described as innovative, implying high economic growth based on a sustainable capability to bring about commercially successful product innovations built on advanced knowledge. The growth in such regions is associated with the emergence of a labor market with well-paid jobs for a highly skilled labor force. This chapter has focused especially on the roles of scientists and the group of practitioners who are entrepreneurs and managers who help create this. In addition, we have pointed out that an essential part of the emerging labor market consists of jobs in the service sector, including those of a professional workforce.

Creating an Innovative Region

Many central and regional governments are trying to bring about growth, employment, and prosperity by replicating the examples of successful innovative regions. This chapter suggests that innovative regions cannot be planned or designed. They emerge over considerable time as a product of a complex interaction between the actions of scientists, practitioners, and enablers. However long the planners go on planning, they will not succeed. They must instead find ways to support the region's emergence as a continuously self-creating collaborative innovation system.

Establishing a Playing Field

We have represented the character of innovative regions as playing fields for a non-zero-sum collaborative game. The playing field contains a number of regional assets such as scientific knowledge, venture capital, business services, and elaborate social networks. The assets can be useful for the individual actor who gets involved in the social networks that facilitate their interaction. Such interactions are not entirely on the shoulders of individual actors, but rather are enabled by a number of integrative and collaborative mechanisms through which individual actors can engage and discover opportunities to become involved in collaboration with others.

One essential opportunity that recurs in the cases we have presented is a set of diverse mechanisms to attract external resources—people, capital, and strategic partners. The carriers of scientific knowledge such as Jacobs, Viterbi, Fishman, and Ruoslahti were all recruited or attracted to the region from the outside, as was the case for Farrell, the successful practitioner.

Another important type of mechanism stimulates innovation by creating confidence and trust across a diverse community of complementary talent. Other mechanisms are in place to assess opportunities and risks. The CONNECT program is an example of both of the two mechanisms. The program gives aspiring entrepreneurs opportunities to meet scientists, consultants, and venture capitalists who can assess the risk involved in the entrepreneurs' projects. In addition, the would-be entrepreneurs can get advice that will potentially improve their business ideas. In the process, entrepreneurs come to know and trust the other actors in the technology business development process, and the latter come to know and trust each other.

Scientists' Collaboration in the Game of Innovation

We now return to the chapter's initial question about how the different actors can contribute to product innovation by facilitating, or engaging in, collaboration between science and practice.

A first step for a scientist interested in participating in the collaborative game of innovation would be to move to an innovative region on his or her own initiative or by invitation. A second step would be to get immersed in the specific task that he or she has found or been assigned to with the intention of learning to master it, demonstrating competence to the larger community. The third step would be to be take part in the many occasions for meeting not just with one's own colleagues, but with people from other disciplines and occupations. In these encounters, it is important to listen to what others share about what is going on and what they are up to. It is as important to share the same things about oneself. A scientist will find that the innovative region generates many interesting options and resources. Keeping an open mind may allow the scientist to encounter various opportunities for going off on a new tack. Such opportunities involve the option of collaborating with others in an entrepreneurial venture to realize an innovation. However, scientists do not necessarily have to work directly on a project with an entrepreneur in order to collaborate. The scientist in the innovative region collaborates by being open and available to others and their ideas. In this way,

collaboration through frequent interaction and exchange across boundaries can be said to take place continuously across the region.

Practitioners' Collaboration in the Game of Innovation

Much of what applies for the scientist is also applicable to the practitioner, that is, the manager or the entrepreneur. To take part in the collaborative game, the practitioner has to be present in the region. The manager does not necessarily have to set up headquarters there, as did Farrell with ResMed. Like Pfizer, which moved part of its research activities to San Diego in order to be open to the encounters and opportunities in that region, other firms or investors can locate a component of their activities in the region.

Managers from less-innovative regions, traditional industrial firms, and even conventional MBA programs are challenged by what initially appears to be a very open-ended, even chaotic, approach to finding and developing productive collaborations. However, there is both a logic and a set of practices that can be learned and mastered. Our recommendations to individuals drawn to regions characterized by shared management settings and organizations would include these:

1. Begin with the assumption that the experience, knowledge, and networks that others have are as valuable and sometimes more valuable than your own.

2. Be sure you have a solid grounding in the processes involved in science-based start-ups and growth companies. These include the trajectory by which basic science moves into translational and applied stages followed by market testing and ultimately business plans, which, by the way, are likely to change and be adapted constantly due to unplanned-for or unanticipated technology breakthroughs, market shifts, or competitors' moves.

3. Find ways to be integrated into the community of trust and pretransactional networks that facilitate the specific science/ industry collaborations being formed almost daily.

4. Be willing to share your expertise, networks, and time in the short run for concrete outcomes and business returns in the long run.

5. Learn the language and processes of milestones, midcourse corrections, setbacks, and unplanned-for opportunities.

6. Understand how to extract from setbacks and failures what is needed to increase chances of improved performance and greater success in the future.

7. Think like a venture capitalist—only 10% of the projects invested in or managed will succeed, but their returns will more than pay for the other 90%.

How Can Enablers Contribute to the Playing Field?

The last question addressed in this summary concerns what the enabler can do to strengthen the innovative capability of a region. The model presented in Figure 15.1 suggests two types of actions: those that increase the assets and those that increase and improve the integrative and collaborative mechanisms in the region. In the 1950s, the zoning of land for research and light industry on the Torrey Pines Mesa of San Diego turned out to be an invaluable asset for the emergence of the biotech and high-tech clusters in La Jolla. The CONNECT program, the Tech Coast Angels, the San Diego Telecom Council, and other networks have strengthened the region's collaborative mechanisms. Together, these actors, aggregated in a contiguous geography, form a web of overlapping and redundant networks that is critical for the diffusion and exchange of ideas and practices that accelerate collaboration and innovation.

The thesis in this chapter is that, on the one hand, the character of the playing field for the innovative game triggers collaboration between science and practice. On the other hand, we have described the playing field as an outcome of the very actions of the participants of the game. How can we ensure that the rules of the game are such that they lead to a self-reinforcing virtuous process and not a self-destructing one? The sorts of rules and shared values underlying CONNECT's "shared management" approach influence all the emerging processes. A civic spirit of collaboration, a high appreciation of entrepreneurship, and a generosity that leads to sharing of time, experiences, relationships, and information seem to be widespread in San Diego. From wherever such values stem, they will not be sustained unless they are reflected in the daily actions of the people involved in the innovation game. In this manner, the actors become co-designers of the innovative region, and not only its beneficiaries.

IMPLICATIONS FOR MANAGEMENT RESEARCH

This chapter has dealt with the collaboration between practitioners and scientists from the life sciences and technology rather than the social sciences and management. It has dealt with regions rather than with individual organizations. We have two main reasons for this.

The first is that in today's competitive global economy, formal organizations are not the only institutions managed with innovation goals. Also, the way larger systems such as regions are socially constructed influences their capacity for innovation. Research with a management perspective on regions is still not very common. There is a tremendous opportunity also for management researchers in collaboration with practitioners, scientists, and enablers to contribute to the much-contested field of regional development.

Our second reason for an analysis of a system rather than a single organization is our desire to demonstrate, especially to policy makers, that managing a collaborative system is less a matter of finding ways to design it and more a matter of enabling the participants to help it emerge as a consequence of both their intended and, often, unintended actions.

REFERENCES

Audretsch, D. B., & Thurik, A. R. (2001). *What's new about the new economy? Sources of growth in the managed and entrepreneurial economies.* Rotterdam: Erasmus University.

Branscomb, L. M., & Auerswald, E. (2001). *Taking technical risks: How innovators, managers, and investors manage risk in high-tech innovations.* Cambridge: MIT Press.

Burnham Institute. (2006). *The Burnham Institute history.* Available from http://arthritisresearch.org/AboutTheInstitute/History/index.asp

Clark Duvall, L. (1979). William Kettner: San Diego's dynamic congressman. *Journal of San Diego History, 20*(3), 191–207.

Dahmén, E. (1991). Development blocks in industrial economics. In B. Carlsson (Ed.), *Industrial dynamics.* Norwell, MA: Kluwer.

Florida, R. (2002). *The rise of the creative class: And how it's transforming work, leisure, community and everyday life.* New York: Basic Books.

Granstrand, O. (1982). *Technology, management and markets: An investigation of R&D and innovation in industrial organizations.* London: Frances Pinter.

Henton, D., Melville, J., & Walesh, K. (1997). *Grassroots leaders for a new economy: How civic entrepreneurs are building prosperous communities.* San Fransisco: Jossey-Bass.

Hertzen, G. von. (1993). *The spirit of the game: Navigational aids for the next century.* Stockholm: Fritzes.

Jantsch, E. (1980). *The self-organizing universe: Scientific and human implications of the emerging paradigm of evolution.* Oxford, UK: Pergamon Press.

Kling, R. (2006). *Developing product development in times of brutal change.* Stockholm: Economic Research Institute, Stockholm School of Economics.

Lundgren, A. (1995). *Technological innovation and network evolution.* New York: Routledge.

Maskell, P., Eskelinen, H., Hannibalsson, I., Malmberg, A., & Vatne, E. (1996). *Competitiveness, localised learning and regional development: Specialization and prosperity in small open economies.* London: Routledge.

Mock, D. (2005). *The Qualcomm equation: How a fledging telecom company forged a new path to big profits and market dominance.* New York: AMACOM.

Plastics Vallée. (2006). La Plastics Vallée: Le plastique, votre metier dans notre vallée. Available from http://www.plasticsvallee.fr/cdcmenu_cdr.htm

Porter, M. E. (1990). *The competitive advantage of nations.* New York: Free Press.

Qualcomm. (2006). *Annual report*. San Diego: Author.

ResMed. (2004). *Annual report*. Poway, CA: Author.

ResMed. (2006). *Annual report*. Poway, CA: Author.

Saxenian, A. (1994). *Regional advantage: Culture and competition in Silicon Valley and Route 128*. Cambridge, MA: Harvard University Press.

Shannon, C. E. (1948). A mathematical theory of communication. *Bell System Technical Journal, 27*(July and October), 379–423, 623–656.

Tushman, M. L., & Anderson, P. (Eds.). (2004). *Managing strategic innovation and change: A collection of readings* (2nd ed.). New York: Oxford University Press.

Walshok, M. L., Furtek, E., Lee, C. W. B., & Windham, P. H. (2002). Building regional innovation capacity: The San Diego experience. *Industry and Higher Education, F16*(1), 27–42.

Walshok, M., & Vencill, M. (2006). Unpublished report to the U.S. Department of Labor.

Zucker, L. G., Darby, M. R., & Brewer, M. B. (1998). Intellectual human capital and the birth of U.S. biotechnology enterprises. *American Economic Review, 88*(1), 290–306.

CHAPTER 16

Collaborative Research and the Trade Unions

The Challenge of Entering Social Partnership

TONY HUZZARD

DENIS GREGORY

ABSTRACT

This chapter presents a model of collaborative research developed in a project that sought to develop a theory on trade unions and improve union practice. This involved collaboration between researchers and union practitioners at a call center and a privatized utility in the United Kingdom and the knowledge dynamics between these efforts and an international collaborative research network. By adapting the experiential learning cycle of Kolb (1984), we elaborate on a development process aimed at introducing social partnership that can be seen as a useful model for how collaborative research can be conducted from a design entailing local experimentation with managing union issues. The chapter assesses the outcomes of the project in terms, first, of changes to union policy and praxis and, second, of contribution to scientific knowledge. It appears that the two-level model could be applicable to organizational settings other than unions.

In this chapter, we aim first of all to explore the applicability of collaborative research as a way of developing theory on trade unions and improving union practice. Second, we aim to present a model for collaborative research on the management of unions. More specifically, we elaborate on a collaborative research study that has generated knowledge about what it means for unions to establish "social partnership" with employers as a means of regulating the employment relationship. We discuss projects involving collaboration between researchers and trade union practitioners at a call center and a privatized utility in the United Kingdom and show how these efforts contributed to and benefited from participation in an international collaborative research network (Huzzard, Gregory, & Scott, 2004). The case presents a development process that can be seen as a useful model for how collaborative research can be conducted from a design entailing local experimentation with managing union issues. In such a way, the model can add value to union practice and contribute to union theorizing.

Most mainstream research on unions to date has been dominated by traditional methodologies. Despite this, we show that collaborative research on and with the trade unions is in fact rather more prevalent than it would first appear from a search through much of the mainstream literature. The empirical material for our exploration of how social partnership might be introduced has been obtained from a collaborative study wherein we have been actively involved with other researchers and union practitioners. The study was designed so that experiences of applying social partnership in a specific company setting were both evaluated and influenced by a group of researchers and practitioners from different countries. In this sense, our model can be seen as an innovative two-level approach to collaborative research. In addition to elaborating and illustrating the approach, we also conclude by reflecting on its strengths and weaknesses. It appears, moreover, that there is little reason to believe that the model should not be applicable to organizational settings other than unions.

We proceed by discussing the specific nature of "management" in a union context, and review a sample of interventionist studies in the various literatures. The next sections then describe and analyze a recent project where a collaborative research methodology has been attempted. We focus in these sections in particular on the motivation behind the project, the role of the participants, the project dynamics, and the generation of knowledge through researcher and practitioner interaction throughout the course of the project. We draw on an adaptation of the experiential learning cycle of Kolb (1984) to show the path taken by the collaborative researcher as the key actor at the heart of a knowledge spiral (Nonaka, 1994). The chapter then continues assessing the outcomes of the project in terms, first, of changes to union policy and praxis and, second, of contribution to scientific knowledge. We then reflect critically on our roles as researchers both in the single-site settings and in the wider network and conclude by drawing out some general lessons on the possibilities and pitfalls of collaborative research on unions.

MANAGING AND MANAGEMENT IN A TRADE UNION SETTING

Traditionally, the notion of leadership and organizing in unions has been seen in terms of mobilizing union members, subject to democratic principles, behind a particular policy or course of action—for example, a strike or pay claim. There is evidence, however, that practitioners are now seeing that union leadership involves considerably more than this—that leadership might also involve aspects of *management*.[1] Just as the business executive is appointed by the owners of a firm, union executives are appointed by the union's principals (its members). Union leaders and business executives are both fully accountable to their principals, who have the power to dismiss them. Nevertheless, unions as organizations have a distinct managerial logic of their own in that they are dependent on a unique set of stakeholders or resources (Kochan, Katz, & McKersie, 1986) and are subject to a unique institutional logic, including a separation between administrative and representative systems (Child, Loveridge, &

Warner, 1973). This suggests that managerial knowledge for unions cannot be acquired from the mainstream in an off-the-peg fashion, but requires separate development in its own right. Yet as we point out below, the notion of applying managerial discourses or interventions in unions is ideologically contested within unions.

The apparent move to managerialism sketched out here is also problematic within the research community. As unions in their core role of representing workers are for the most part engaged in activities that are adversarial to the managers of their members, the idea that unions might also *internally* engage in management may seem somewhat contradictory. As pointed out by Dempsey (2005), the overwhelming bulk of research on unions has seen power in the unions from a critical perspective whereby it is exercised as domination by elites, as opposed to being something that is legitimate and functionally necessary to exercise in the pursuit of instrumentally rational ends (Palmer & Hardy, 2000). Given that the former view suggests political sympathy with the rank and file at the expense of union managers, it is unsurprising that the notion of "management" in a union setting has been a tricky issue for many industrial relations researchers. Many studies of union leaders or managers have thus tended to be critical in nature without any ambition of generating actionable knowledge for the union manager (see, e.g., Kelly & Heery, 1994).

Yet it is plain that unions are complex organizations requiring the application of effective management approaches to their various functions if they are to survive and prosper. The need for union leaders to be able to deliver the sorts of services that their members demand at a price they are prepared to pay is not so different from the need facing a typical CEO to meet challenges in a competitive marketplace. Neither is the need for the union leader to balance the finances of the union so different from the pressures that CEOs in both the private and public sector face in this regard. Where the union leader confronts additional management challenges is in the democratic accountability that is at the heart of both governance and policy making in trade unions. Very few either private- or public-sector organizations face the frequency of internal scrutiny and cross-checking that unions experience as "member led" organizations.

Researcher skepticism about managerialism in unions may well explain why examples of collaborative research or action research in unions do not feature strongly on mainstream research agendas. After all, interventions are likely to be sanctioned and approved by union managers or leaders and presumably aligned with their interests and not necessarily with those of union members or even union employees. A further objection is that elevating the role and practices of "management" in union settings creates inevitable tensions between administrative and representative systems (Björkman, 2005) and can arguably be seen as running counter to union cultures and traditions of political democracy.

At the end of the day, however, such skepticism is surely a matter of labeling. For some, the "management" of unions is problematic, yet the "leadership" of unions is somehow more acceptable. Perhaps, too, "governance" or "coordination" may be preferred in some quarters. In our view, however, there is little to be gained by reflecting on the appropriateness or otherwise of particular labels that try to capture the effects of what happens in unions. Rather, we see considerable merit in focusing on the light-touch view of management as described by the editors of this volume: the process of *influencing* the behavior or performance of a certain system of action (see Pasmore, Stymne, Shani, Mohrman, & Adler, Chapter 1 in this *Handbook*). Such a view is consistent with the argument of

Watson (2002) that management should be seen as a function or activity in the context of a relationship, irrespective of whether or not it is performed by those who are formally anointed with the title of "manager" in their respective organization (cf. Dempsey, 2005).

We should add, too, that managerial activities in unions are performed by many actors at many levels, including central officials in relation to regional officials, administrative managers in relation to administrative staff, local officials in relation to branch committees or even members at the workplace, chairpersons in representative systems in relation other elected members, and so on. Such a view suggests that unions are suitable sites for collaborative management research and that such research can encompass a multitude of actors and relationships that may well be interdependent. Interventions aimed at change may thus need to be of a multilevel nature such as the two-tier model suggested in this chapter. Nevertheless, in collaborative approaches the role of the researcher is never that of a politically neutral actor in a value-free reflexive space, thus rendering the notion of "research findings" decidedly problematic (Gregory, 1996).

COLLABORATIVE RESEARCH AND UNIONS: AN OVERVIEW

We can study unions as (complex) systems or sets of systems (Child et al., 1973) in their own right, or study unions as subsystems within a wider system, namely that of the employment relationship. Such an approach clearly focuses on union relationships with employers. We can also study unions in the context of their relationships with other stakeholders—for example, potential members in recruitment campaigns, regional bodies in regional development projects, and so on. Or, indeed, we can take a more macro

view and look at the industrial relations systems that are coterminous with the boundaries of the nation-state or beyond. Yet at whatever level we choose, the dominant pattern in research on unions to date, from various disciplines, is that of a distant relationship between researcher and union, with the latter as the research object. In a comprehensive review of the literature, Huzzard (2000) noted that research on unions has traditionally been overwhelmingly structuralist, with interpretive or processual studies few and far between.

The same could be said about interventionist methods such as action or collaborative research: One might be tempted to conclude from searches of industrial relations and action research journals that such work has largely passed unions by. Indeed, in Reason and Bradbury's *Handbook of Action Research* (2001) there is no explicit treatment of unions, apart from passing references to interventions in the labor movement in the United States through work on health and safety (Hall, 2001) and union training (Lewis, 2001). One might well believe, therefore, that the trend toward what Gibbons et al. (1994) have termed "Mode 2" knowledge, with researchers and practitioners collaborating to provide useful knowledge outputs for both parties, is something that hasn't happened so far as unions are concerned.

This view, however, would be mistaken. We propose in the latter part of this chapter to analyze in depth exemplar cases of contemporary collaborative research undertaken with unions in the United Kingdom. There are also other examples of such work. But before turning to these cases, it is perhaps worthwhile to discuss some of the examples of collaborative research in unions to date, much but by no means all of it constituting what one of us described some 10 years ago (Gregory, 1996) as being "concerned with attempting to elucidate and explain problems and issues located in the *realpolitik*[2] of industrial relations"(p. 167).

A sample of collaborative research in unions over the years is set out in Table 16.1. This is merely illustrative and far from exhaustive. Yet it suggests that collaborative research on unions has been broader than one might expect given the dearth of coverage in the mainstream industrial relations and HRM journals. This work tends to have two main foci—first, development activity for improving workplaces and work, and second, development activity to establish or improve relationships with key stakeholders (or resource providers). Examples of efforts from these two foci will now be discussed.

Table 16.1   Samples of Trade Unions and Collaborative Research: An Illustrative Summary

Aim of Intervention	Research Institution and Union	Targeted Key Stakeholders	Nature of Practitioner/Union Collaboration	Published Material
Development of work organization in the Norwegian Offshore Petroleum Industry (part of Norway's Value Creation 2010 program)	Work Research Institute, Oslo (Norway); various unions within the Norwegian LO Confederation	Employers, employees (union members)	Various action research initiatives aimed at introducing more participative forms of work organization	Qvale (2003)
Participatory forms of workplace development	National Institute for Working Life (Sweden); various unions	Employers, union members	Various action research initiatives aimed at introducing more participative forms of work organization	Gustavsen et al. (1996)
Organizational change at Ford Motor Company, 3M, and Yorkshire Water	Ruskin College, Oxford; TGWU, AEEU, MSF (United Kingdom)	Employers, union members	• Formulation of an employee development program (Ford) • Democratic dialogue to promote change (3M) • Formulation of alternative HRM strategy (Yorkshire Water)	Gregory (1996)
Development of market orientation methods	FENIX Centre (Stockholm School of Economics); Sif (Sweden)	Internal union actors (employees and members)	Insider action research	Björkman (2005)

(Continued)

Table 16.1 (Continued)

Aim of Intervention	Research Institution and Union	Targeted Key Stakeholders	Nature of Practitioner/Union Collaboration	Published Material
Organizing sex workers and securing union affiliation	University of East London; General Municipal and Boilermakers Union and the International Union of Sex Workers (United Kingdom)	Primarily members and potential members	Researcher was also a union activist/branch representative	Lopes (2005)
Organizing migrant workers. Addressed the issues of disadvantage faced by black and minority ethnic workers, both in the labor market and in trade unions	Queen Mary, University of London; Southern and Eastern Region TUC (United Kingdom)	Members and potential members	Researcher worked closely with union organizers, helped union members in campaigns at three different workplaces	Holgate (2005)
Occupational health and safety, work environment	Various (United States)	Union members and occupational health professionals	Action research through, e.g., employee surveys and participatory approaches to problem identification and solution	Deutsch (2005)
Trade union engagement in regional development	University of Newcastle (CURDS) and the Northern Region of the TUC (United Kingdom)	Community representatives	Participation of regional officials in various collaborative development projects; strengthening the institutional and individual capacities of unions to make effective regional policy interventions	Fitzgerald and O'Brien (2005)

IMPROVING WORK: THE SCANDINAVIAN LEGACY AND BEYOND

Without doubt, the collaborative research efforts with unions having the broadest scope have been undertaken in Scandinavia, notably Norway and Sweden. The key point of departure for much of this work was that sociotechnical systems design could be used both for democratization and for organizational effectiveness (see Kolodny & Halpern on sociotechnical design, Chapter 13 in this volume, and den Hertog & Schröder, 1989).

The period from 1966 to 1975 saw a great deal of experimentation in industrial democracy in Norway, with particular regard to work restructuring and the introduction of semiautonomous working groups. Current work is focused on the Enterprise Development 2000 program and its successor, the Value Creation 2010 program.

Action research has also been a feature of major programs on workplace development in Sweden. A number of joint efforts, supported by action research, were particularly noticeable after the enactment of codetermination legislation in 1977. This fostered a spirit in which both employers and unions agreed to take part in a series of programs supported by the state with the purpose of developing the organization of work. The focus, however, switched from rehabilitation to productivity as Sweden entered recession in the 1990s. More recently, efforts in Sweden have waned in comparison with Norway, given a withdrawal by employers from activity that is seen as overtly corporatist, and a consequent reluctance of the state to support efforts that do not enjoy bipartisan support.

In the mid-1990s rather more modest attempts by researchers at engaging with unions in action research were discernible in the United Kingdom. An example of such work was that of the Trade Union Research Unit at Ruskin College, Oxford, where interventions generally focused on the union role in workplace change and its consequences. Typical activities undertaken within action research efforts included the formulation of an employee development program (Ford), facilitating democratic dialogue to promote change (3M), and the formulation, with unions, of an alternative approach to corporate human resource management (HRM) strategy (Yorkshire Water) (Gregory, 1996).

Improving and Developing Actor Relations

More recently in Sweden, Björkman's work with Sif (formerly the Swedish Union of Clerical and Technical Employees in Industry) has sought to develop improved relations with union members (Björkman, 2005). This is an exemplary case of insider collaborative research (see Bartunek, Chapter 4 in this volume, and also Coghlan & Brannick, 2001) wherein the researcher involved was actually employed by the union. Specifically, the researcher sought to explore ideas and practices in the union in relation to methods for strategic positioning and service innovation.

Another theme that appears to feature strongly in collaborative research efforts is that of membership recruitment. For example, in her Ph.D. project, Jane Holgate focused on organizing migrant workers (Holgate, 2005). In another Ph.D. project, Ana Lopes carried out action research studying the organizing of sex workers in collaboration with the General, Municipal and Boilermakers Union in London and the International Union of Sex Workers (Lopes, 2005).

A different approach, focusing on trade union roles in regional development processes, has been reported on by Fitzgerald and O'Brien, the former a researcher at Northumbria University in the United Kingdom, the latter an official of the UK's Trade Union Congress (TUC) (Fitzgerald & O'Brien, 2005). This effort was initially triggered by the leaders of the regional trade union movement, who saw potential for a proactive role for the unions on the issue, given the entrenched labor market problems of the region, on the one hand, and the introduction of new regional institutions to tackle them, on the other. At the same time, research undertaken at the University of Newcastle's Centre for Urban and Regional Development Studies was generating awareness of some of the key issues at stake, prompting the Northern TUC to embark on new collaborative initiatives. In turn, this implied the need for new capacities in the unions internally for effective interventions to be made.

Despite the apparent plethora of collaborative research projects outlined here, little consideration has been given to how the practitioner/researcher interaction actually occurs dynamically in collaborative research projects. What scientific knowledge results from such efforts in the name of "research"? What is the nature of the contribution to practice? How does the knowledge-generation process unfold? How do researcher efforts contribute to practice, and how do practitioners contribute to science? These questions remain largely unexplored in the literatures to date; our intention in the remainder of this chapter is to elaborate on them by reporting on recent collaborative research undertaken by researchers and union practitioners working in partnership with a view to studying and implementing social partnership at the workplace.

UNIONS AND SOCIAL PARTNERSHIP: AN ILLUSTRATION OF COLLABORATIVE RESEARCH

We now turn our attention to a detailed account of the two-level collaborative research strategy introduced in the opening section of the chapter. Seen together, the interactions between these two levels, distinct yet interconnected arenas for learning, were an ongoing dynamic process of collaborative knowledge generation—what we call here "learning at home" and "learning away." What united the two arenas and provided a platform from which the dual knowledge outputs could be generated was the ambition of developing new knowledge about social partnership. Nevertheless, slightly different perspectives prevailed in the home arena compared with the away arena. At home, a joint perspective was adopted that sought to explore possibilities for mutual gains for unions and employers without privileging one side or the other, whereas "away," a clear

union perspective was explicitly adopted in the remit of the network. Although the latter aimed to draw up clear lessons on social partnership for union strategists, it nevertheless also sought to develop a language and conceptual frameworks for deepening our understanding of social partnership in a way that would be of benefit to both sides and assist the taking of each other's perspectives (Boland & Tenkasi, 1995).

The SALTSA New Trade Union Network

The international New Trade Union network was first initiated in 1998 as a research project under the aegis of the SALTSA Program.[3] The project was initiated in a context marked by two major influences. The first of these was the general international trend toward the decentralization of industrial relations. This called for the development of new or additional forms of cooperation between organized labor and capital at various levels (Ferner & Hyman, 1998; Traxler 1996). The second influence was the 1997 EU Green Paper *Partnership for a New Organisation of Work* (European Commission, 1997). Its message was that improved competitiveness and increased employment in the European Union required the social partners to develop more efficient forms of work organization through greater dialogue, participation, and cooperation at the workplace. This message, were it to be taken seriously, clearly had major implications on trade union roles, identities, and strategies, particularly in the United Kingdom, where a more adversarial mindset generally prevailed.

The notion of "social partnership," however, is conceptually troublesome, not least because of varying national and industrial relations cultures. Some practitioners argue that if unions are to exist as legitimate actors in working life they also have to "add value" to employers and that cooperation is perfectly natural where joint interests of survival and prosperity can be discerned in an increasingly competitive and globalized environment (Ackers & Payne, 1998). Others, however, inspired by Marxist positions, have been instinctively suspicious of partnership and argue that almost by definition it is an act of collusion with the adversary and must inevitably undermine the capacity of unions to perform their basic function: that of looking after members' interests (Taylor & Ramsey, 1998). As to the employers, in certain contexts, such as Sweden, trade union involvement in cooperative dialogues was natural. In others, however, such as in some firms in the United Kingdom, a mindset prevailed that sought, if not to avoid a union presence, at least to try to marginalize it. Given such misgivings, the implementation of new partnership arrangements at many workplaces in the United Kingdom would certainly be problematic. For the action researcher, therefore, the intriguing issue was how knowledge of social partnership internationally might be brought to bear in the implementation of partnership at home, in this case, the in United Kingdom?

At its inception, the project that set up the international network was unique within the SALTSA program, in that both researchers and practitioners (union activists) from a range of countries were involved (see also Barinaga, 2002). These individuals constituted a network that met twice a year for three years to exchange experiences, engage in discussion on union and industrial relations "futures," and comment critically on the emergent empirical contributions of the other participants. This generated a conceptual and empirical knowledge base that was valuable for both the practitioners and the academics in the network. At its various stages, the project included participants from Germany, the United Kingdom, the Netherlands, Ireland, Italy, Sweden, Hungary, Romania, and the

United States. The United States was included as a counterbalance to what would otherwise have been an entirely Eurocentric view of trade union futures. Moreover, it was felt necessary to have at least some reference to the many "experiments" on cooperation at a company level that have taken place in recent years in the United States.

The Learning Process and Knowledge Outcomes

As stated previously, we believe it is useful to distinguish between the knowledge-generation or learning processes at the "home" workplaces and those evident "away" in the network (Docherty, Huzzard, DeLeede, & Totterdill, 2004). Network participants learned both within the network and from it. This model of collaborative research suggests that potential experiential learning processes happen in two distinct arenas. These arenas, however, and the learning processes associated with them, are interlinked. The idea and logic of such a network is that network participants, including action researchers, undertake learning activities through interacting with others "away" within the network and take back new ideas, insights, or sources of inspiration to share with those with whom they collaborate in the "home" organization. Conceivably, this could mean contextualizing new ideas and trying out an experiment with them. Following reflection on putting such ideas into use at home, the action researcher can then take his or her experiential accounts of the experiment back into the network for further reflection.

The two interlinked processes of learning, "home" and "away," can be helpfully conceptualized by extending Kolb's well-known model of experiential learning (Kolb, 1984). In this model, individual learners engage in "concrete experience"—for example, network members engage in practices that gather information from their external environment.

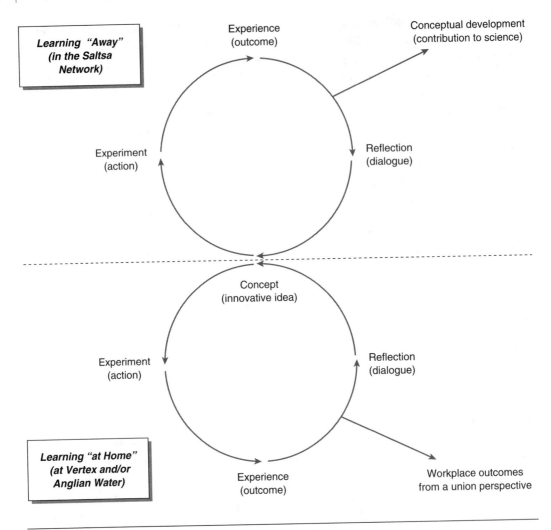

Figure 16.1 Learning Paths of the Collaborative Researcher

Concrete experience is followed by reflective observation by the individual learner. This is then followed by abstract conceptualization whereby individuals draw conclusions from experience. Finally, Kolb sees the individual as testing out his or her conclusions through experimentation; such action both tests the interpretation and generates new insights to promote further learning, thus completing a cycle. If this cycle operates both "at home" (in our study, at Anglian Water or Vertex) and "away" (in the network), we can arrive at the model set out in Figure 16.1. This is, in effect, a "figure-eight" process model that offers a useful means for analyzing the dynamics of knowledge generation associated with the collaboration between research and union practice.

The role of facilitator in the two "home" case studies involved both training in the techniques of "partnering"—in particular, joint problem solving—and action research, including the initiation of problem-solving task groups. The work and outputs from these groups were then subjected to critical scrutiny by the wider partnership forums, prior to any changes being implemented. We would describe this as learning at home. At the same time, the parties in both case studies expected the facilitator to bring experience from other organizations and to draw on a more general academic perspective to help their partnership to flourish. In this sense there was a clear attempt to integrate learning "away." Frequently, training sessions involved external comparisons, and in both cases external benchmarking visits to other, similar organizations were carried out with the explicit intention of evaluating and, where appropriate, integrating what we can call "away" knowledge.

Learning "Away": Developing Knowledge Through Collaborative Networking

The issues in focus in the international project were social partnership and its implications for trade union renewal (Huzzard et al., 2004). The specific questions the network sought to address were as follows: How do we understand social partnership? How does partnership vary across Europe and beyond? And what are the implications of partnership for union renewal? In recognizing that social partnership is ideologically contested terrain among union movements worldwide, the network sought not to take a position either embracing or debunking partnership. Rather, the network saw its role as one of evaluating social partnership experiences with a view to informing trade union practice and renewal efforts. But as stated in the previous section, the notion of social partnership was conceptually unclear and contested. To get around such difficulties, the network introduced the generic metaphors of "boxing" and "dancing" for denoting adversarial and cooperative industrial relations, respectively. As the network

unfolded, these metaphors were freely used by the practitioners not only to cut across national and ideological boundaries but also as means for opening up two rich semantic fields for animating and nuancing the network dialogue.

Having developed a specific project language around the core boxing and dancing metaphors, it then became possible to develop dialogues and conceptual frameworks to bring together the different starting points of the participants. For example, participants were asked to fill in a matrix that detailed boxing and dancing practices as well as future prospects for the main levels of industrial relations engagement in their country. In turn, the various frameworks could then be synthesized into a comparative analysis. This material consisted of two strands. First, the researchers (in some cases with practitioner assistance) each wrote book chapters detailing the storylines on strategic unionism and social partnership from their respective countries, and second, case studies were compiled and evaluated that were illustrative of aspects of the country storylines in question. The empirical material was then presented in various drafts at the network meetings. In this way, practitioners were able to act as critical discussants on the various researchers' outputs and not be restricted to the narrow dialogues of a single-site collaboration.

A further element of the network's activity was then facilitated in the form of a common evaluation tool—an audit of the case studies of social partnership practice. These audits were conducted in the network with a particular emphasis on input and comment from the practitioner participants. Each of the final case study drafts was rounded off with the audit, which could be seen as a practitioner assessment of social partnership praxis explicitly aimed at providing actionable knowledge for other practitioners.

Figure 16.2 gives a specific example of how the learning cycle operated "away" in

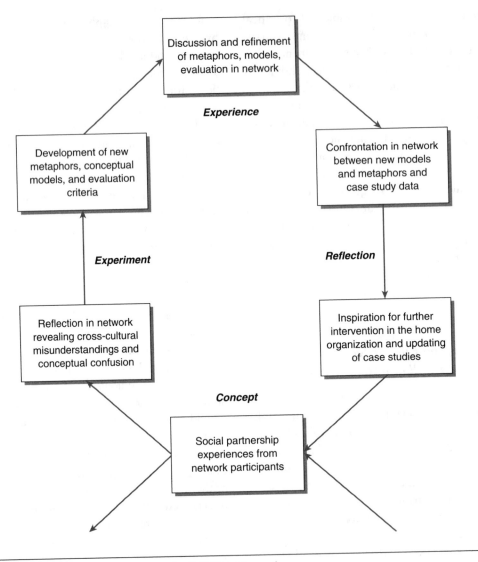

Figure 16.2   Learning "Away" in the SALTSA Network

the SALTSA network. The main knowledge generated was threefold. First, the network developed the metaphors of boxing and dancing to nuance theorizing in industrial relations. Second, a number of generalizable evaluation or audit criteria for unions on social partnership agreements and arrangements were established. Third, a number of conceptual models and analytical frameworks were developed for enhancing our understanding of social partnership.

Research Design at Anglian
Water and Vertex Data Science

It has to be said that the research design, in the sense of the formulation of a planned methodological approach designed to shed light on a given set of research objectives, was problematic for each of these case studies. The researcher in both instances was confronted with labor relations systems that were in a state of flux and with management and union agendas that were some distance apart regarding the formulation of workable solutions to the problems they faced. In effect, the research design at both Anglian and Vertex subsequently developed through four key stages, as described by Gustavsen (1992) when commenting on the Swedish LOM program, namely, (1) clustering enterprises, (2) the use of a search conference to scope the project and begin the dialogue, (3) broad base and "deep slice" projects, and (4) the building of broader networks. There was one important difference, however. The first stage clustering in the way Gustavsen describes it was modified, because we were dealing with single enterprises. However, in Anglian's case there were a number of different and widely dispersed individual workplaces that had to be clustered (i.e., represented by unions and management) in order to be properly covered by the project.

Given that trust relations were strained between the key labor relations actors in both case studies, it was of paramount importance for the facilitator (action researcher) to establish what lay behind the low level of trust and to establish his credibility with the groups involved. Accordingly, the search conference was designed to encourage a free-flowing dialogue to ascertain the extent to which the participants agreed on the scale and nature of the problems to be addressed and their underlying causality. The methodology used to facilitate the search conference followed the criteria proposed by Gustavsen and Engelstad (1986) for "democratic dialogue." These essentially aim at an open exchange of ideas in which each participant's contribution should be encouraged and taken seriously.

Learning at Home: Anglian Water

The pressures to develop a more participative approach to labor relations at Anglian Water were a direct consequence of the radical changes to the structure and ownership of

the UK water industry that took place with privatization in 1989. Following the breakup of the industry into 10 regional water companies, management in most of these companies quickly adopted corporate strategies that explicitly challenged the prevailing labor relations orthodoxies inherited from the public sector. For example, Anglian Water in the early 1990s introduced a range of initiatives including reduction in staffing levels, delayering management, promoting teamwork, and buying out long-standing nonstandard working payments such as "call–out" payments. These inevitably created uncertainty and labor relations difficulties for the four trade unions recognized by the company. The unions, it should be noted, had strongly opposed privatization on ideological grounds but had also raised fears that privatization would mean job loss and major changes in work organization. The problem that soon emerged for management was the inability of the existing industrial relations structures to deliver such changes within the timeframes they and their financial advisers desired.

Against this sort of background, the relatively high-trust labor relations that had characterized the industry when in public ownership began to decline. To deal with this, Anglian and the unions decided to adopt a more comprehensive, dialogue-based approach that, it was suggested, would enable a higher level of employee engagement to support the change process more constructively from both the employer and the union points of view.

To facilitate and promote more effective dialogue, the company proposed a consultative structure that would embrace three operational joint committees. Over and above these, there would be a joint consultative committee at the company level. The latter was formally constituted in June 1995 as the Company Council with membership comprising 5 employer's and 15 employees' representatives. In addition, one full-time official from each of the unions was also granted membership. The function of the Council was to "negotiate and consult on collective terms and conditions, to resolve any collective disputes or grievances arising from them and to address any matter that either party has a legitimate concern about."[4] Meetings were to be held quarterly or more often if the business required it, and the chair and vice chair positions would alternate annually between the two sides.

Shortly after the Company Council was set up, the secretary to the trade union side asked Ruskin College, Oxford (a college with long-standing links to the trade union movement), for help in training both union and management representatives on the Company Council. As a result, a joint training program of linked workshops was established and run over a period of six months in 1996–1997. The training was aimed at developing a range of core skills and competencies thought to be lacking in either or both sets of representatives. The central objective was to ensure that members of the Company Council were equipped to jointly identify and solve problems using a range of techniques and placing a high value on experiential knowledge.

The learning cycle that resulted is shown in Figure 16.3. A number of points are worthy of note here. First and foremost was the way in which the collective learning stabilized and then improved what had become a relatively strained and, from the management's viewpoint, "nondelivering system." The combination of more regular and more informed dialogue enabled the Company Council to assist in a number of key changes in the organization of work at Anglian. This was not without pain, because it involved both job loss and the acceptance of change that the unions found very hard to countenance—for example, outsourcing. However, some two years into the partnership dialogue, union representatives, who had experienced severe criticism from some sections of their membership, remained firmly committed to

the partnership approach as a better way to deal with difficult organizational change. There were also some important gains for both unions and management in the way that the collective bargaining process functioned. Not able to agree on an anniversary date prior to the partnership being formed, pay negotiations had become fraught and long, drawn-out affairs to the frustration of all concerned. The Company Council and the high level of information flows that surrounded it radically changed this, enabling negotiators to reach agreements on time and without undue drama.

Equally significant was the breakthrough secured by the Company Council concerning an agreement to protect the pension provision of staff who found themselves transferred to other spun-off companies. UK legislation protects most of the terms and conditions of employment of transferred employees, but it does not include pensions. The company collective agreed in effect to extend the coverage to ensure that transferred employees enjoyed the same pension rights as they would have had they remained Anglian employees. At the time this was a unique agreement in the United Kingdom.

Learning at Home: Vertex Data Science

Vertex Data Science was a company that, by contrast to Anglian Water, had been created after privatization of the United Kingdom's water and electricity supply sectors. It was set up in 1996 by United Utilities, itself a product of a merger of two privatized utilities (one from water and the other from electricity supply), to look after customer services through the operation of a number of call centers. Vertex at its inception did not formally recognize trade unions, although management acknowledged that there were union members among their staff who had transferred into Vertex from United Utilities.

It became apparent, within a year or so, that the HR strategy Vertex had devised was

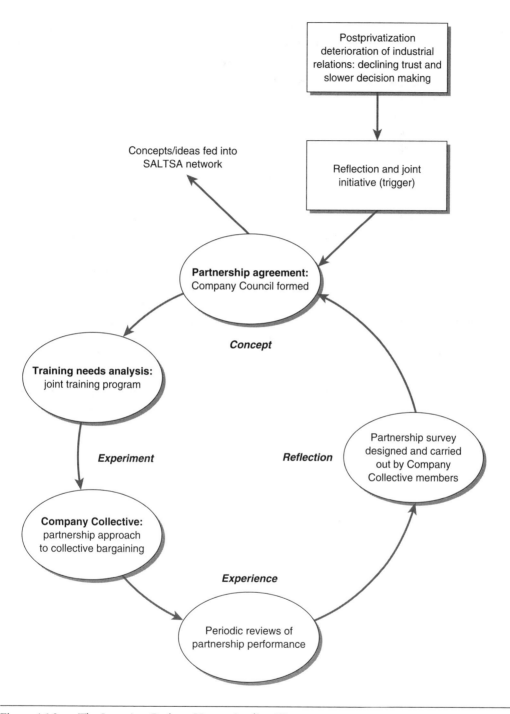

Figure 16.3 The Learning Cycle at Home: Anglian Water

running into difficulties, not the least of which were those arising from individually agreed, as opposed to collectively bargained, terms and conditions of employment. Throughout this period, the main white-collar union UNISON operated informally but constructively with key levels of HR management. As a result of this, and also inspired by the new approach to labor relations set out in the recently elected Labour Government's White Paper "Fair Deal at Work," Vertex management decided to reverse their policy and recognize UNISON for collective bargaining purposes. The management's proviso was that this would be underpinned by a partnership agreement to promote and facilitate more inclusive employee engagement and cover a wider range of strategic issues than would normally be the case with collective bargaining.

To implement and develop the partnership approach at Vertex, the agreement reached with UNISON specified that two forums be established:

1. A consultative forum of 22 elected members would consider all aspects of the business performance, business opportunities, and issues affecting staff. This forum would act as a sounding board on all matters relevant to the separately established negotiating forum.

2. A negotiating forum with 12 members (six from UNISON and six from management) was set up to review and develop changes to contractual terms and conditions of employment, including redundancy, employment transfers, and working time arrangements. In performing these functions, the forum would be expected to represent the views of all staff covered by the agreement and take into account the views of the consultative forum in reaching its conclusions.

Representation on these forums was differentiated to reflect the fact that UNISON had won support in a workplace ballot for the restoration of collective bargaining. Accordingly, the employee representatives to the negotiation forum were appointed by UNISON from within their membership. By contrast, the employee members of the consultative forum were not necessarily union members. They were elected every two years by the call center staff, although two additional seats on the consultative forum were reserved for trade union members elected from the negotiating forum. In all, the consultative forum comprised 22 members representing eight sections of the business.

Although there were a few experienced lay representatives at Vertex, it was clear that the union needed to recruit and build its local organization in order to cope with the more expansive challenge it now confronted. Moreover, it was equally plain that both management and union representatives recognized that the consultative forum would struggle to raise its profile and legitimacy against the more orthodox role and perceived influence of the negotiating forum. There was, additionally, the possibility of role confusion where some individuals sat on both forums.

In effect, both management and unions needed to explore the ramifications of what had been agreed, and both had to address the fact that neither managers nor trade union representatives locally had any real experience with a dialogue-based approach called "partnership." In these circumstances, the need for training to develop some partnering skills was compelling. Thus, shortly after the recognition agreement was signed and at the instigation of the union, contact was made with Ruskin College. It was agreed that a joint training and education program for union and management members of both forums be devised and facilitated by staff from Ruskin.

As with Anglian, the process of learning to operate as partners at Vertex began with a training needs analysis. This identified particular deficits both process knowledge (for instance, joint problem-solving techniques) and substantive knowledge (for example, methods of financial reporting and systems of corporate planning used at the companies). Building upon the experience gained at Anglian, a six-month program of joint training workshops was set up.

The process of learning (Figure 16.4) was particularly rapid at Vertex. The training workshops moved through the search-conference stage to highly specified sessions designed to plug substantive knowledge gaps, while at the same time working on key process skills such as presentation and communication. The participants redesigned the training program to move on to deep slice projects that saw three subgroups formed to come up with solutions to specific problems that had jointly been identified in the initial training workshops. These included a contentious rebalancing of the pay structure to overcome problems of recruitment and retention (a major problem area in call center operation in the United Kingdom), alterations to the shift system to ensure more effective 24/7 operations in the company's main call center, and the need to address some issues of awareness regarding the ethnic diversity of the workforce and the cultural needs that flowed from this diversity. The subgroups used the subsequent training workshops to test-run their conclusions and the proposals arising from what was in effect their action research.

In every case, the solutions that were worked out in the subgroups were subsequently put into practice with full union and management support. The value of this type of learning at Vertex was highly regarded by managers and union representatives alike. It was also recognized by the Chartered Institute of Personal Development in the United Kingdom, who in 2001 gave the partnership team at Vertex their top award that year for "people management."

The Collaborative Research Process in the Case Studies

From the outset, the training programs in the two case studies discussed here operated within the realpolitik of the workplace. Thus, participants were encouraged to use current issues and problems as the material upon which various problem-solving techniques could be tried and evaluated. In the case of Vertex, the progression from experiential learning through to deep slice projects and action research was particularly marked. At Anglian, the process and the involvement of one of the authors lasted over a longer period. This made it possible to observe the durability of the partnership process in the context of the demands for corporate restructuring that grew in intensity as the lifetime of the partnership unfolded. From an action research perspective, this yielded unusual opportunities for the author—for example, directly observing negotiations to harmonize pay and grading structures as the Vertex operation expanded. Similarly, the regular progress reviews the author facilitated at Anglian at the request of the trade unions proved a rich source of empirical evidence and provided the opportunity to monitor union opinion and support for the process.

From these reviews and from direct observation, it was possible to compare the effect that the partnership process and the learning that accompanied it had on both the trade union representatives and the managers who were involved. There were common features characterizing both case studies around the issue of trust. An improvement in trust relationships as the dialogue and learning process developed was observable. This could involve quite radical changes in perceptions, particularly as managers began to see the value of the inputs that were coming through from trade union representatives. It was linked to the more open discussions that the partnership process encouraged and the more detailed information that formed the basis for these discussions.

The trust relationship in both case studies, though, remained fragile and was easily damaged. Trade union representatives frequently felt that they were perhaps not getting the full picture, and concerns about hidden

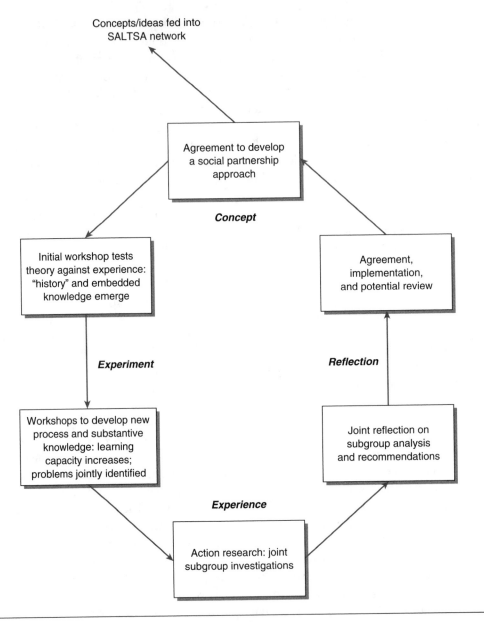

Figure 16.4   The Learning Cycle at Home (Vertex)

agendas were never far from the surface of their discussions. For their part, managers worried about the consistency of trade union support for particular decisions, fearing that individual union representatives might either renege on a decision or deliberately misreport it to their members to elicit a hostile response. Such fears are typical manifestations of low-trust relationships. With the development of the partnership process and the learning process (which in part consisted of managers and union representatives learning to trust each other), these fears tended to recede into the background, but they did not disappear altogether.

Trust was also undermined whenever either party reverted to type. Thus, when Anglian managers had to impose a highly contested change because of "orders from on high," trade union representatives on the partnership council, which itself had been struggling to deal with the change in question, immediately began to question the validity of the partnership dialogue (as, it must be said, did some of the managers who understood the damage that retreating to "command and control" would do to a dialogue that was trying to reach a consensual decision). Similarly, managers at Vertex were deeply frustrated by the union's inability to provide a united front in some difficult salary negotiations that frustrated an agreement being reached.

Linking "Home" and "Away"

The learning from the action research at company level linked in with the theoretical endeavors of the SALTSA network in a number of ways. In the first instance, it helped to support and elaborate the "boxing and dancing" metaphors that the Swedish researchers had introduced to the SALTSA network. It was evident from the earlier engagement of one of the authors at a 3M plant in South Wales and his work at Anglian that the key formulation stages in decision making, when options are being reviewed, typically would not involve either trade union representatives or the wider workforce. This gave rise to the design of a simplified 5-stage model of decision making (Box 16.1) and a "consensus curve" that attempted to depict how agreement for change at a particular organization or workplace would be achieved over time.

The consensus curve in Figure 16.5 shows how the 5-stage model creates a characteristic timeframe and potential negotiation space within which a decision can be shaped, agreed, implemented, and reviewed. Integrating the boxing and dancing metaphor neatly revealed the difference between early and late involvement of trade union representatives in the process, as shown in Figure 16.6.

Figure 16.5 postulates that managers build a consensus for a particular decision by employing an exclusive internal management dialogue in stages 1 and 2, and that when sufficient critical support has been enlisted, they involve the trade union representatives at stage 3 with a view to continuing to build

---

Box 16.1

The 5-Stage Model of Decision Making

Stage 1: Recognition of the need for change. Most likely, this would involve an internal discussion process initiated by and held with very few members of management.

Stage 2: Shaping the decision. This involves an increasing number of managers, both specialists and planners, to work out the options and evaluate which is the optimum choice.

Stage 3: Agreement. At this point, the workforce and/or their union representatives are involved to secure agreement for the change. Characteristically, at this stage the level of involvement moves beyond purely managerial inputs.

Stage 4: Implementation. The change is put into effect.

Stage 5: Evaluation and refinement. If the organization values learning, it will monitor and evaluate the impact of the change with a view to consolidating it.

consensual support and, where necessary, formal agreement for the decision. Figure 16.6 shows the difference in the consensus curve if the union involvement is limited to stage 3 (boxing) or if unions are involved earlier at stage 2 (dancing).

Depending upon the timing and the nature of the involvement, as Figure 16.6 shows, the level of support within the organization for the change can increase, stay the same, or decline. A circle, the "dance floor," is located at a much lower level on the consensus curve. This is the typical position of a company adopting a partnership approach. Partnership dialogue plays a critical role in reviewing the options and shaping the decisions necessary to make the organizational change. In contrast, collective bargaining "boxing" assumes a more adversarial approach and endgame.

Partnership enables dialogue to take place prior to management adopting its final position and is therefore less confrontational and more constructively participative (hence,

"dancing"). In theory, then, in partnership, earlier involvement will facilitate higher trust and greater consensus for the change to be achieved than would be the case under collective bargaining.

These simplified models, developed through discussion at the SALTSA network meetings, were subsequently used in the training sessions at Vertex. In this sense, they are a good example of how learning "at home" interacted with learning "away." The metaphor and the consensus curve concept were readily acknowledged among both practitioners and SALTSA colleagues to be a useful framework for understanding the differences and challenges arising where a shift from traditional bargaining to a more dialogue-based approach was contemplated.

CONCLUDING DISCUSSION

This chapter has shown that collaborative research can be a useful option for union

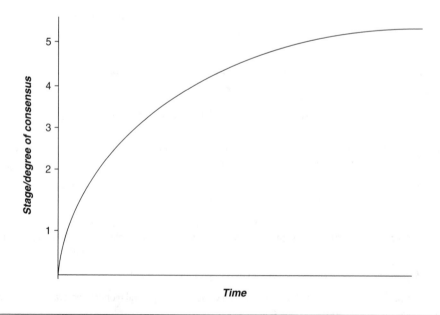

Figure 16.5   A Typical Decision-Making Consensus Curve

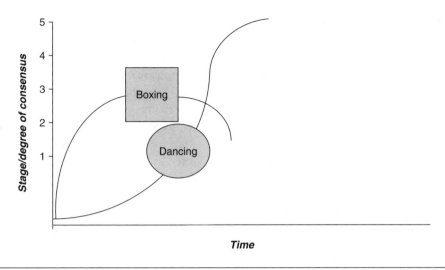

Figure 16.6. Decision Making and "Boxing and Dancing"

practitioners in their attempts to use external change agents as a means of pursuing policies. At the same time, opportunities can also present themselves to the action researcher in advancing our conceptual understanding of what are complex organizations. In particular, we have shown how these twin objectives were realized through an international collaborative research network. This network acted as a learning arena for its participants to take back ideas and concepts and introduce them as tools for dialogue in their own developmental efforts and contexts as action researchers. In practice, therefore, the knowledge dynamics of the collaborative research efforts described here provide a collaborative research model wherein the generation of Mode 1 knowledge (Gibbons et al., 1994) of conceptual development can contribute to science. It can also generate Mode 2 knowledge informing the implementation of a robust and durable solution that contributes to practice.

To sum up the work of the SALTSA network, three specific components of the collaborative effort were discernible, which can be seen together as three stages of development in an international collaborative network: forming a project language, developing conceptual frameworks, and evaluating the partnership outcomes (from a union perspective). Many of the cases were drafted from the empirical engagements with the field in which the researchers were already actively involved (including, of course, Anglian Water and Vertex), albeit as a single-site collaboration. Yet by bringing such material into the network, additional insights and reflection were possible. Accordingly, by forming a collaborative network (Gustavsen, 1998), both union researchers and union practitioners were able to generate new knowledge that would not have been available in a single-site setting.

The collaboration also showed that such networks need not just be regionally based (Fricke & Totterdill, 2004) but may offer possibilities for comparative analysis and synthesis of practitioner experiences from widely different contextual backdrops internationally. We would conclude that although many of the social partnership experiences and outcomes were indeed of a localized and context-specific nature, there is nevertheless considerable potential in collaborative networks to develop conceptual frameworks and evaluation criteria for synthesizing empirical material into a more comprehensive and coherent whole that is of interest and relevance to organizational practice. Moreover, active practitioner engagement can be said to enhance the quality of the research output in a process that we might reasonably term *practitioner triangulation* (see also Ferlie & McNulty, 1997).

The interactions described in this chapter operated at two levels: on the one hand, the research group met regularly to discuss the theoretical underpinnings and empirical evidence stemming from the development of the social dialogue process at the enterprise level across a number of EU member states (with the United States included as an external reference point). On the other hand, individual researchers from the network continued with the research and consultancy work aimed at shaping and delivering social dialogue with individual enterprises. This inevitably involved different sets of actors but also ensured that a continuous stream of new "Mode 2" knowledge was available to the wider theoretical discussions taking place within the SALTSA research group.

It should also be noted that a feature of the SALTSA group was the role of union practitioners who shared their experiences directly with the researchers and ensured that theoretical discussions and the development of the "boxing and dancing" model in particular was thoroughly tested against real-world trade union experience. In effect, a regular dialogue between theory and practice formed the basis of the SALTSA group work. The extent to which this contributed to a scientific understanding of the process of social dialogue is, perhaps, for others to judge. However, an edited book has been published (and has been generally well received by the academic community) that drew together the work of the SALTSA group (Huzzard et al., 2004). In addition, individual members have given academic papers based on the SALTSA group research to international conferences.

The contribution made by the SALTSA group to the practice of social dialogue is probably even harder to evaluate. From the perspective of the UK-based author of this chapter, it can be reported that subsequent and ongoing work with unions and managers in 17 enterprises (ranging from large to small in both the public and private sectors) shows that both the "boxing and dancing" and the 5-stage decision-making models are readily acknowledged as reflecting reality, while providing convenient frameworks for knowledge generation and transfer (Gregory, 2006). In Sweden, a translated version of the book was published by SALTSA and discussed at a seminar organized by the peak union organizations as well as in numerous union training courses.

The internal dialogue these models have stimulated at the enterprise level has helped, in most cases, to improve the process and the effectiveness of social partnership as a means of delivering higher-performance labor relations. This is a good example of how Mode 1 knowledge can support practical action. At the same time, in the United Kingdom at least, Mode 2 knowledge has sharply emphasized that where traditional notions of management prerogative and the practice of "command and control" persist, they are wholly at odds with any aspiration to move toward a knowledge-based learning organization. In this sense, "bottom-up" Mode 2 knowledge is informing a wider debate about a paradigm shift away from knowledge "possession" to knowledge "management." More than anything else, this is perhaps the measure of the contribution the SALTSA group has made at both the theoretical and practical levels.

NOTES

1. Although the terms *management* and *leadership* are often used interchangeably, certain writers have tended to distinguish them (Kotter, 1990). The former has tended to denote some notion of administrative effectiveness, whereas the latter has denoted the capacity to mobilize others to perform tasks they would otherwise be reluctant to undertake: the former indicating a context of stability, the latter indicating a context of change.

2. The concept of realpolitik is here suggested to denote that union activities in industrial relations often imply seeking pragmatic, realistic steps to maintain (fragile) relationships rather than pursuing courses of action that are strongly guided by an ideology.

3. SALTSA is the acronym for a collaboration among four Swedish actors, namely the three top union confederations, LO (the blue-collar confederation), TCO (white-collar and professionals), and SACO (professionals), together with the National Institute for Working Life, which also finances the program.

4. Presentation given by the company to the trade unions in 1995, setting out their agenda for 1996.

REFERENCES

Ackers, P., & Payne, J. (1998). British trade unions and social partnership: Rhetoric, reality and strategy. *International Journal of Human Resource Management, 9*(3), 529–550.

Barinaga, E. (2002). *Levelling vagueness: A study of cultural diversity in an international project group.* Ph.D. thesis. Stockholm: Stockholm School of Economics.

Björkman, H. (2005). *Learning from members: Tools for strategic positioning and service innovation in trade unions.* Stockholm: Stockholm School of Economics.

Boland, R. J., & Tenkasi, R. V. (1995). Perspective making and perspective taking in communities of knowing. *Organization Science, 6*(4), 350–372.

Child, J., Loveridge, R., & Warner, M. (1973). Towards an organizational study of trade unions. *Sociology, 7*(1), 71–91.

Coghlan, D., & Brannick, T. (2001). *Doing action research in your own organization.* London: Sage.

Dempsey, M. (2005). *Trade union managers: Invisible actors in trade union dramas* (Working Paper SWP 06/05). Cranfield School of Management.

den Hertog, J. F., & Schröder, P. (1989). *Social research for technological change: Lessons from national programmes in Europe and North America* (Working Paper 89-028). Maastricht, The Netherlands: MERIT.

Deutsch, S. (2005). The contributions and challenge of participatory action research. *New Solutions, 15*(1), 29–35.

Docherty, P., Huzzard, T., DeLeede, J., & Totterdill, P. (2004). *Home and away: Learning in and learning from organisational networks in Europe* (Report for EU Commission). Brussels: EU Innoflex Project.

European Commission. (1997). *Partnership for a new organisation of work* (Green Paper COM 97:128). Brussels: Author.

Ferlie, E., & McNulty, T. (1997). "Going to market": Changing patterns in the organisation and character of process research. *Scandinavian Journal of Management, 13*(4), 367–387.

Ferner, A., & Hyman, R. (Eds.). (1998). *Changing industrial relations in Europe.* Oxford, UK: Blackwell.

Fitzgerald, I., & O'Brien, P. (2005). Trade union engagement in regional development: A North East perspective. *Northern Economic Review, 33/34.* Available from http://uin.org.uk/content/view/51/1/

Fricke, W., & Totterdill, P. (Eds.). (2004). *Regional development processes as the context for action research.* Amsterdam: John Benjamin.

Gibbons, M., Limoges, C., Nowotny, H., Schwartzman, S., Scott, P., & Trow, M. (1994). *The new production of knowledge: The dynamics of science and research in contemporary societies.* London: Sage.

Gregory, D. (1996). Action research and trade unions: Some experience from the UK. *Concepts and Transformation, 1*(2/3), 165–174.

Gregory, D. (2006). Partnership, knowledge and decision-making: Some thoughts from 17 case studies. In B. Griffiths (Ed.), *Partnership at work: Studies in employee involvement.* Cardiff, UK: ACAS.

Gustavsen, B. (1992). *Social science for social action: Vol. 1. Dialogue and development: Towards organizational renewal.* Maastricht, The Netherlands: Van Gorcum.

Gustavsen, B. (1998). From experiments to network building: Trends in the use of research for reconstructing working life. *Human Relations, 51*(3), 431–448.

Gustavsen, B., & Engelstad, P. H. (1986). The design of conferences and the evolving role of democratic dialogue in changing working life. *Human Relations, 39*(2), 101–116.

Gustavsen, B., Wikman, A., Ekman-Philips, M., & Hofmaier, B. (1996). *Concept-driven development and the organization of the process of change: An evaluation of the Swedish Working Life Fund.* Amsterdam: John Benjamin.

Hall, B. L. (2001). I wish this were a poem of practices of participatory research. In P. Reason & H. Bradbury (Eds.), *Handbook of action research: Participative inquiry and practice* (pp. 171–178). London: Sage.

Holgate, J. (2005). Organising migrant workers: A case study of working conditions and unionisation at a sandwich factory in London. *Work, Employment & Society, 19*(3), 463–480.

Huzzard, T. (2000). *Labouring to learn: Union renewal in Swedish manufacturing.* Umeå, Sweden: Boréa.

Huzzard, T., Gregory, D., & Scott, R. (Eds.). (2004). *Strategic unionism and partnership: Boxing or dancing?* Basingstoke, UK: Palgrave.

Kelly, J., & Heery, E. (1994). *Working for the union: British trade union officers.* Cambridge, UK: Cambridge University Press.

Kochan, T. A., Katz, H. C., & McKersie, R. B. (1986). *The transformation of American industrial relations.* New York: Basic Books.

Kolb, D. A. (1984). *Experiential learning.* Englewood Cliffs, NJ: Prentice Hall.

Kotter, J. (1990). *A force for change: How leadership differs from management.* New York: Free Press.

Lewis, H. M. (2001). Participatory research and education for social change. In P. Reason & H. Bradbury (Eds.), *Handbook of action research: Participative inquiry and practice* (pp. 356–362). London: Sage.

Lopes, A. (2005). *Organising in the sex industry: An action research investigation.* Unpublished doctoral dissertation, University of East London.

Nonaka, I. (1994). A dynamic theory of organizational knowledge creation. *Organization Science, 5*(1), 14–37.

Palmer, I., & Hardy, C. (2000). *Thinking about management.* London: Sage.

Qvale, T. (2003). New concepts in work organization: A case from the Norwegian offshore petroleum industry. In M. Gold (Ed.), *New frontiers of democratic participation at work* (pp. 177–201). Aldershot, UK: Ashgate.

Reason, P., & Bradbury, H. (Eds.). (2001). *Handbook of action research: Participative inquiry and practice.* London: Sage.

Taylor, P., & Ramsey, H. (1998). Unions, partnership and HRM: Sleeping with the enemy? *International Journal of Employment Studies, 6*(2), 115–143.

Traxler, F. (1996). Collective bargaining and industrial change: A case of disorganization? A comparative analysis of eighteen OECD countries. *European Sociological Review, 12*(3), 271–287.

Watson, T. J. (2002). *Organizing and managing work.* London: Thomson Learning.

CHAPTER 17

Connecting Research to Value Creation by Bridging Cultural Differences Between Industry and Academia

GEORGE ROTH[1]

ABSTRACT

In the late 1990s, MIT developed a set of multiyear, multiprogram collaborative research partnerships spanning multiple disciplines with large corporations. MIT's history shows a progression in its abilities to pioneer collaborative research efforts. These alliances are analyzed to provide lessons for all collaborative research activities. A focus on value to academic and corporate participants, accompanied by efforts to recognize and bridge cultural differences, provided direction and helped to sustain the Ford-MIT Alliance.

MIT has a long tradition of working on practical problems affecting society and the economy, and in recent years it has become a leader in developing collaborative partnerships with industry. These partnerships and the research activities of our faculty have resulted in the creation of jobs, companies, and even new industries, based on new technologies. They are part of this country's innovation system—a loosely coupled alliance of industry, universities, government, and labor—that develops new knowledge and technologies, educates a highly skilled workforce to apply these new technologies, and produces the next generation of researchers to carry on the process of discovery and development. This system turns out a continuous stream of new products and services, which in turn advance our economy and improve our quality of life.[2]

The Massachusetts Institute of Technology (MIT) is an institution that is the envy of most other universities and many corporations. There are many ways in which universities are assessed—the number of students and the measures of their capabilities and success, the faculty and its share of Nobel laureates and MacArthur Fellows, as well as the articles its members have published and the prizes they have won, or perhaps the student life, size of the university's endowment, or campus facilities. While MIT is respected for many of these accomplishments, what makes it the envy of other universities and corporations is its role in economic activity and the creation of wealth. A study conducted by the BankBoston Economics Department (1997) found that if "the companies founded by MIT graduates and faculty formed an independent nation, the revenues produced by the companies would make that nation the 24th largest economy in the world. The 4,000 MIT-related companies employ 1.1 million people and have annual sales of $232 billion" (p. 2).[3]

Collaboration at Institutional Levels

Research is often thought to be an individual endeavor, or the work of a small team of collaborators. Awards for the best research, such as Nobel prizes, are given to individuals, not the institutions in which they did their work. Is there a role that institutions play in enabling great research? If so, can that role and the creation of the conditions that lead to innovative research be managed? This chapter addresses these questions by examining the conditions and practices of a new organizational form—the corporate-university alliance. These alliances create conditions at the university that link research projects to corporate sponsorship. MIT successfully initiated eight of these alliances in the late 1990s.

This chapter examines collaborative research at an interorganizational level. The title of this chapter, "Connecting Research to Value Creation by Bridging Cultural Differences Between Industry and Academia," suggests that research initiated in the university can be connected to companies, which create value, through alliances. A corporate-university alliance creates a structure and process for developing and selecting research projects and sets conditions under which projects are conducted and research results can be implemented. Interests in implementation, in turn, have implications for what research is selected and how these efforts are connected to the sponsor. This framing extends the examination of collaborative research beyond specific researchers and managers working together on individual projects to sets of projects and the interests of university administration and corporate management in a portfolio of projects. The findings from the set of MIT's alliances suggest that cultural differences need to be recognized and addressed to connect university research to corporate value.

Background and Methods

I have not only participated in collaborative research activities, but also studied, created, and managed the processes and structures through which academics and managers collaborate. My interest in the territory that lies between corporations and universities began with my own transition from corporate manager to doctoral student. As I left a decade-long career in sales and marketing management at Digital Equipment in 1987 to start an MIT Ph.D. program, I visited with my employer's director of external research. He was the liaison to MIT's Management in the 1990s program (Allen & Scott Morton, 1994). At one level, he was enthusiastic about and complimentary toward the program and people, but at another level he was full of complaints about the understanding of the MIT faculty for the "real" research questions. The schism that he embodied was perplexing, seemingly simultaneously loving and hating the program and its people. As I came to know these MIT faculty members, I found that they had similar opinions of him—a person to avoid as a pain in the ass to deal with, as well as a person to get to know who had brilliant ideas. What I realize in hindsight is that I was being exposed to the implicit differences in values and priorities of people in corporations and universities.

Another of my collaborative research activities was as the research director for the MIT Center for Organizational Learning. This center developed tools and methods that enhanced organizational learning processes by partnering with companies to apply and study their ideas in organizations (see Roth & Senge, 1996). As a project in this MIT research center involving people with backgrounds in research, journalism, and organizational consulting, I developed a learning-history methodology to capture and diffuse company initiatives (Roth, 2000, 2005). In addition to a research and management role in the MIT Center for Organizational Learning, I have also been a researcher in MIT's Management in the 1990s program, Center for Information Systems Research, Leaders for Manufacturing Program, Creating Organizations in the 21st Century Initiative, Center for Technology, Industry and Policy Development, and most recently the Lean Aerospace Initiative.

A significant shift in my engagement with collaborative research came when I accepted a position as executive director for the Ford-MIT Alliance. I felt somewhat equipped for this role based on my mid-1980s experience in developing and managing a multi-million-dollar office imaging system alliance with Eastman Kodak while at Digital Equipment Corporation. In addition to holding managerial responsibilities for the Ford-MIT Alliance, I initiated and facilitated meetings for MIT people from other alliances to share experiences and lessons learned for managing collaborative research. I also supervised several graduate students studying the collaborative

research process in these alliances. In my responsibilities for the Ford-MIT Alliance, I reported to MIT's provost, and following reorganization, to MIT's chancellor. This reporting relationship provided me with opportunities to discuss and provide suggestions on other alliances. Other insights came from my participation in a cross-institute faculty committee asked to review complaints about MIT's alliances.

MIT AS A CASE STUDY

MIT provides a rich context in which to study research relationships,[4] including the collaborative research activities that are the basis for its corporate alliances. The institutional context that enabled these alliances goes back to premises in MIT's founding philosophy. The collaborative research that is the basis for MIT's corporate alliances is best understood in the context of MIT's historical innovations and the development of a climate supporting relationships with industry and its leaders.

Corporate-University Alliances

The Ford-MIT Alliance was MIT's first broad, cross-institute alliance. It was initiated by MIT president Charles Vest and Ford CEO Alex Trotman. It took 18 months of negotiation involving over 70 MIT faculty members and even more Ford managers to come to an agreement on several broad parameters. The headlines of the October 1997 press release, "Ford, MIT Announce 5-Year, $20 Million Alliance," were based on a pledge from Ford's leaders to provide at least $3 million of new research funding and maintain Ford's current $2 million research and educational program funding at a minimum of $1 million annually.[5] This funding framework left it to the leaders at Ford and MIT to further develop the broad research areas and specific projects. Initially, they were largely technical and scientific domains. In the five years that I was in the role of the MIT Alliance's executive director, the alliance fully supported approximately 40 projects that involved over 50 faculty members and 100 students. The success of several projects and the promise of success from recently initiated projects resulted in a renewal of the alliance for a second five-year term.

My role as executive director required me to work with senior faculty and administration and put into practice ideas that would make these partnerships successful and sustainable. The Ford-MIT Alliance is not unique; it was the third multiyear, multiproject alliance, following partnerships with Amgen and Merck. These biotechnology alliances, however, added research capacity and provided support and recruitment opportunities for graduate students for the corporate partners. Subsequent partnerships with Nippon Telegraph and Telephone, Merrill Lynch, DuPont, Microsoft, and Hewlett-Packard were, like that with Ford Motor Company, more broadly based alliances (see Table 17.1).[6] The financial commitments from these eight partnerships totaled

$188 million, representing substantial pledges of funding, faculty, graduate students, and activities for both MIT and its partners.[7]

What makes an alliance with MIT attractive to corporations and governments are elements that the BankBoston economists' study (1997) said produced economic results: Success, innovation, and wealth are found in the application of science and technology to societal needs. For the United Kingdom's Chancellor of the Exchequer, this goal led to investing "£84m over five years, with £36m spent on integrated research, £20m on undergraduate student education, £20m on professional practice programmes and £8m on a national competitiveness network, the Cambridge Entrepreneurial Centre, and the administration of the CMI [Cambridge-MIT Institute]" (Kelly, 2000).

Engineering Education

The development of large multiyear, multiproject alliances built upon a series of innovations pioneered by MIT and its faculty, the very

Table 17.1 MIT's Industrial Partnerships

Year Founded	Corporation	Initial Commitment	Focus and Scope (in Terms of Fields and Departments)
1994	Amgen	$30M over 10 years	Biology
1997	Merck	$15M over 5 years	Biology
1997	Ford	$20M over 5 years	All MIT—Engineering, Product Development, and Environmental Policy & Science
1998	Nippon Telegraph and Telephone	$18M over 5 years	Artificial Intelligence & Computer Science Laboratory
1999	Merrill Lynch	$20M over 5 years	Business & Engineering (Financial Engineering)
1999	DuPont	$35M over 5 years	Chemistry, Biology, Biomedical & Materials engineering
1999	Microsoft	$25M over 5 years	All MIT—educational innovations
2000	Hewlett-Packard	$25M over 5 years	All MIT—digital libraries, software

basis of which can be seen at MIT's founding. The incorporation of the Massachusetts Institute of Technology in 1861 was the start of an experiment in scientific and technical education. Details of the educational philosophy are found in the incorporators' 1859 proposal (Commonwealth of Massachusetts, 1859), *Objects and Plan of an Institute of Technology:* "The interests of Commerce and the Arts, as well as of General Education, call for the most earnest co-operation of intelligent culture with industrial pursuits" (p. 3). MIT's motto, *"Mens et Manus,"* shown in its 1865 seal in Figure 17.1, is Latin for "mind and hand." The motto exemplifies the founding philosophy that theory is to be combined with and integral to practice. In the seal, the laborer is on the same level as the scholar. In its early days, MIT used a laboratory-based, hands-on method of education and learning for science and engineering. In the late 1800s and early 1900s, its students traveled in trucks and boats to shipyards, airstrips, mines, and factories, while at other institutions students sat and learned in classrooms.

Figure 17.1   MIT Seal

airplane navigation systems, computers, air defense systems, and the atomic bomb. Following World War II, MIT and its engineering science methods attracted significant funding. The funding brought opportunities to MIT for its faculty and the support of students. Their research is what created many successful military and commercial innovations, which in turn attracted additional funding.

Engineering Science

A second innovation that contributed to MIT's preeminence as a research university came from World War II developments. The "engineering science" approach came from scientists working with engineers in developing, testing, and producing new devices. Engineering science is an intermediate body of knowledge that connects science and technology; it is the integration of mathematics, physics, and chemistry with areas of traditional engineering such as research, design, and analysis (Channell, 1989). Scientists and their basic science research methods create an understanding of physical principles; engineering methods are applied to these understandings to develop new technologies and product applications. During World War II, engineering science rapidly produced plane-, ship-, and ground-based radar systems,

Government Funding

An important factor in university research is government funding. Prior to World War II, most support for university research came from private contributions and charitable foundations. With the application of science, technology, and engineering to the war effort, the United States government, under the orders of President Roosevelt, established the National Defense Research Committee in 1940, and it was superseded by the Office of Scientific Research and Development in 1941. These organizations coordinated the funding and research on radar and the nuclear bomb, two technologies that changed the course of world history and the outcome of World War II (Buderi, 1996).

One of the key people in the collaboration of university leaders, physicists, engineers, and military leaders in successfully providing a war-winning capabilities effort was Vannevar Bush (Bush, 1945). After earning doctorates from MIT and Harvard in 1917, Bush worked at MIT as a professor on submarine detection technologies and later became engineering dean. He went from MIT to positions of significant influence, directing government research funding for universities. In July 1945, his report "Science, the Endless Frontier" proposed that the federal government fund scientific research, arguing that the nation would reap rich dividends in the form of better healthcare, a more vigorous economy, and a stronger national defense. This proposal resulted, in 1950 under President Truman, in the creation of the National Science Foundation (NSF).

MIT was well positioned to become a major beneficiary of NSF and other government funding. This funding supported universities' research and spilled over into industry innovations. Studies of the factors contributing to industrial innovation find that "practically all of the cited academic research were supported . . . by federal funds" (Mansfield, 1995, p. 64). After World War II, the U.S. government began spending a great deal of money to support public research in military, defense, and medical technologies. The NSF has rapidly increased its expenditures, spending just over $3 million in 1952, $134 million by 1958, over $500 million in 1968, $2 billion in 1990, and $5.6 billion in 2005. In addition to providing funding, the government has passed laws to encourage industry investment in research and enable innovation. The inventions that came from government-funded research had resulted in over 30,000 patents by 1980, but, at that time, only 5% of these patents were commercially licensed. The Bayh-Dole Act, or Patent and Trademark Law Amendments Act, was enacted by the U.S. Congress in 1980.[8] It gave U.S. universities intellectual property control of inventions from government-funded research, and incentives to ensure that research was implemented.

Corporate Relations

To manage its industry relationships, MIT created and evolved various offices and programs. Following World War II, MIT's research and technology development attracted significant industry attention, and in 1948, MIT formed an Industry Liaison Program (ILP) to manage these inquiries. This office provided contacts for faculty with industry and helped develop industry research funding. ILP changed significantly in 1972. In 1969, following student antiwar protests, MIT's Instrumentation Laboratory was spun off as an independent, nonprofit research agency called the Draper Laboratory. Only public research would be done on MIT's campus. When Draper Labs, at roughly one quarter of MIT's size, became independent, MIT needed a renewed focus on industrial research support. Other changes came in the mid-1980s when the mission of the Technology Licensing Office (TLO) shifted from reactively handling patent applications to proactively commercializing MIT-developed technologies. In 1989, MIT merged corporate development, responsibility for gifts, and ILP into one office. This Office of Corporate Relations was designed to attract all types of industry funding.

MIT's reorganizations to work with industry corresponded with changes in funding. Industrial funding was 0.8% of MIT's research funding in 1930 and had risen to 6.2% in 1946. Just after World War II it climbed to 15%. Over the next two decades it declined gradually, to 3.4% in 1970. With a new focus, industry funding then began to increase, rising steadily across the next two decades: 8% in 1980, 13.9% in 1985, 15.5% in 1995, and 19.8% in 1999 (Hatakenaka, 2002, p. 99; see Figure 17.2). In 2002, industry funding provided $88 million annually, with 80% of the increase in the previous five years coming from new corporate alliances.

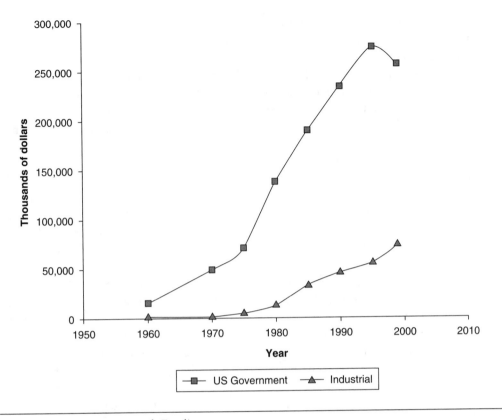

Figure 17.2 MIT's Research Funding

SOURCE: Based on the research of Sachi Hatakenaka (2002, p. 101).

The increasing government and industry funding created opportunities at MIT. In the 1950s and 1960s, MIT's faculty grew from 250 to over 1,000. Faculty charged portions of their salary to their research funding and were expected to raise over 50% of their compensation through external research support. Each faculty member also supported a number of graduate students with research funding. The faculty's relationships with industry included "outside professional activities." In 1939, MIT's policy and procedures described that it was important for faculty to serve industry through their consulting. In his memoir, former MIT president Howard Johnson describes how he consulted to both "supplement my income and build my experience," adding $6,000 to his annual $10,000 salary in 1960 (Hatakenaka, 2002, p. 117). With Boston's high cost of living, a consulting income was needed to supplement meager academic salaries. MIT's long-standing expectations for its faculty to raise research support and actively consult created an institutional climate that expected cooperative industry relationships.

Exploring New Frontiers Again

Corporate partnerships were a result of MIT's entrepreneurial spirit combined with needs created by declining government funding. In the 1990s, funding from the NSF, the National Institutes of Health (NIH), and other government sources was declining, and the trend was expected to continue.[9] MIT's

President Vest noted, "We are currently experiencing . . . a substantial rebalancing of social responsibilities among the private and public sectors, especially in the United States" (Vest, 1996, p. 1). *Pursuing the Endless Frontier* is the title of Vest's memoir (2004), which takes its "endless frontier" theme from Bush's 1945 report. Vest found that there was less trust in government and more trust in business and market efficiency; central planning had failed and been replaced by economic competition and privatization. As the U.S. administration and Congress pledged to balance the budget, federal programs were reduced or eliminated. Industry would need to address issues of common good that government had historically supported. However, while more was required from industry, global competition "caused a deeper integration of the work of corporate researchers into specific, more immediate goals of the company . . . the corporate laboratory often disappeared or was altered so as to be almost unrecognizable" (Vest, 1996, p. 3).[10]

President Vest's philosophical views on linkages among government, industry, and academia translated into actions at MIT. MIT's Center for Innovation in Product Development, cofunded by the NSF and industry, is an example. It conducted research but was guided by executives from Xerox, Ford, ITT, and other leading firms. Corporate partnerships were another example; they were based on mutually agreed-upon research developed through "intellectual synergy and sustained dialogue" (Vest, 1996, p. 9) between company leaders and MIT faculty.

Research Centers and Consortia

The basis for MIT's partnerships with industry came from its experiences, research centers, and consortia. These arrangements allow companies to access a broad range of technologies while sharing the costs of the research. The Polymer Processing Program (PPP), founded in 1973, was one of the first, if not the first, industrially sponsored research consortia at a university. The Center for Information Systems Research (CISR), founded in 1974 to conduct field-based information technology research, is among the first management school research centers. These centers have not only enabled pioneering research, but also created widely adopted research models. Other centers, such as the Laboratory for Manufacturing Productivity in 1977, the Media Lab in 1985, and the Leaders for Manufacturing program in 1987, which were innovative at the time of their founding, are today common in many universities.

High-profile programs that provide models for collaborative research activities include the Micro-electronics and Computer Technology Corporation (MCC),[11] the SEMATECH program for national competitiveness in semiconductor manufacturing,[12] and the Partnership for Next Generation Vehicles (PNGV).[13] Each of these programs provides important lessons for collaborative research. At a management level, MCC showed that the challenges for the firms that contributed their people and funding were behavioral and managerial, rather than technological (Gibson & Rogers, 1994). SEMATECH helped to contribute to a rebound in U.S. semiconductor companies' competitiveness, showing that appropriately structured consortia, where goals are aligned with industry needs, can successfully address technology policy issues. PNGV showed the importance, from the outset, of considering the proper structures and incentives for complex consortia made up of members with different interests (Roos, Field, & Neely, 1998).

Organizing for Collaborative Research

The Council on Industrial Relationships was one of four institute-wide councils appointed by the provost in April 1996 to help set MIT's future directions.[14] This council was to explore new linkages to industry. For the 20 CEOs from large corporations that the council members interviewed, universities and their relationship with them were not high priorities. These industry leaders did not think that companies would be able to offset the anticipated decreases in government funding. While industry had downsized and reorganized under competitive pressures, universities had not made similar changes. Corporations were making changes to focus their efforts with fewer organizations. They did not expect to have close relationships with many universities, perhaps only a select few. The committee's assessment of these corporations was that 35% were positively disposed, 47% were neutral, and 18% were negatively inclined toward an alliance with MIT.[15] These insights from these interviews provided the basis for strategy to more carefully pursue multiyear, alliance relationships. Those follow-on efforts, supported by MIT's president, led to the development of MIT's eight "industrial" partnerships (see Table 17.1).[16]

CORPORATE-UNIVERSITY PARTNERSHIPS

Alliances with corporations extend to other research universities. Since 1980, there has been a steady increase in industry funding for university research (National Science Board, 2000). With industry funding there has been an increasing interest in research results, and in the sponsors' abilities to leverage economic gains from them. The industry funding, although it provides resources to faculty members and university campuses, is having such an effect that Etzkowitz (1998, p. 823) describes it as part of a "second academic revolution." This second revolution adds economic development to the university's mission (the first academic revolution added research as an academic function to teaching). Establishing broad relationships creates

new opportunities for universities, but also creates cause for critique and concern. A review of concerns and how they have been addressed follows a review of the technology and knowledge transfer literature, which is the basis for many industry-funded university research projects.

Research and Knowledge Transfer

With the increased involvement of industry have come studies of university technology transfer (Powers & McDougall, 2005). These studies examine the factors such as motivation for partnering and interaction between university and industry scientists that affect outcomes. Universities and firms value different outcomes, reflecting differences in their motivations and expectations from funded research (Bloedon & Stokes, 1994; Simeral, 1994; Stewart & Gibson, 1990). These studies also find that factors within in the university's current incentives and existing practices are responsible for low success rates in the transfer of research knowledge to corporate sponsors. These factors include industry-funded research efforts developed by senior university administration in isolation from faculty members; too quickly accepting immediate corporate requests as the basis for a relationship; an aim of simply supplementing existing research with new funding; goals of using available lab-space capacity; overpromising of results; and failing to address fundamental cultural differences (Cyert & Goodman, 1997; Geisler & Rubenstein, 1989; Hesselberth, 1992; Peters & Fusfeld, 1983; Rahm, Kirkland, & Bozeman, 2000).

Cohen and Levinthal (1990) developed the term *absorptive capacity* to characterize a company's abilities to transfer and absorb externally developed knowledge. They find that the presence of internal research and development efforts better enables firms to take in external knowledge. The empirical research on utilizing absorptive capacity has utilized overall measures such as a firm's overall research spending to explain knowledge transfer. Further studies found that relative absorptive capacity (Lane & Lubatkin, 1998), which comes from similarities in the knowledge bases, organizational characteristics, and research communities, had greater explanatory power than broad spending measures. From these studies, knowledge transfer is shown to depend upon the relative characteristics of the organizations seeking to transfer and use knowledge.

Strategic Alliances

The alliance literature examines relative characteristics of organizations working together. Partners enter into alliances to create value, address new opportunities, save expenses, and work with one another because they cannot develop or maintain needed complex, specialized, and costly resources themselves (Doz & Hamel, 1998; Hagedoorn, Link, & Vonortas, 2000; Link & Bauer, 1989). Dissimilarities between partners create complexities and require capabilities for managing this kind of a relationship. Alliances are an attractive way of operating when net benefits or risk reductions from partnering are better than go-it-alone alternatives (Contractor & Lorange, 1988). While an appropriate strategic match and complementary resources are key conditions in successful alliances, the development of a learning process, rather than getting the initial conditions correct, is what makes for sustainable alliances (Doz & Hamel, 1998). Alliances that succeed go through cycles of learning, involving reevaluation and readjustment over time. Through these learning cycles, knowledgeable commitments can be made to increase the size and scope of the alliance, creating more value. Greater value justifies deeper commitments, reinforcing the learning cycle. Findings from corporate-university alliances are consistent with other alliance research (Cyert & Goodman, 1997).

Critique and Concern

While differences between corporations and universities create synergistic opportunities, these differences are also the basis for potential conflict. One potential conflict comes from varied societal expectations. Universities have nonprofit, tax-free status and receive public funding with the expectation that they will create and freely disseminate knowledge for the benefit of society. Corporations are expected to survive in contested marketplaces, where they compete for customers and investors. Corporate success depends upon developing and maintaining advantages over competitors. This need for competitive advantage becomes a basis for concern. The university's responsibility to disseminate research through publication and education can be in opposition to the corporation's desire to protect and maintain competitive advantages through funding research. Press and Washburn (2000) caution that the commercial interests that come with corporate funding "taint" the nonprofit universities' objective research. This concern broadens when corporate funding relationships might be seen to control universities' research agendas or create imbalances. Corporate funding emphasizes science, engineering, and business, threatening the loss of influence and resources in the arts and humanities.

Novartis's relationship with the University of California at Berkeley (UCB) created a flashpoint for these concerns. In November 1998, Novartis signed a $25 million agreement with Berkeley to fund basic research. This funding represented one third of the research budget of the College of Natural Resources. As part of the agreement, Berkeley granted licensing rights to state and federally funded research to Novartis and provided Novartis with two of the five seats on the committee that determined the departments' spending of its monies. Student groups protested and gathered signatures, and the school newspaper published a five-part series on growing university privatization. The Novartis-UCB alliance proceeded under a shadow of controversy. After its completion, the Berkeley faculty senate commissioned a postmortem study by Michigan State University scientists (Busch et al., 2004). They found (Lau, 2004) that the alliance

> didn't turn out as anyone expected. The company didn't try to strong-arm the scientists to pursue only commercially valuable research, as some had predicted. And participants—twenty-three faculty members in the department of plant and microbial biology, plus their research staffs and students—did not make any dramatic discoveries. The company did not license a single invention produced during the five-year period.

The negative press, campus infighting, and need to justify this relationship had, however, hurt UCB's reputation.

Although MIT has a history and culture of close collaboration with industry, MIT's alliances also raised concerns. MIT students have a tradition of protesting through "hacks," which are clever but benign public displays that challenge the perpetrators and amuse the community. The concern over growing corporate influence came on April 1, 1998, when MIT's home page declared that the university had been acquired by Disney Corporation for $6.9 billion.

In September of 2000, a few months after the start of MIT's eighth alliance with Hewlett-Packard, a faculty member published a letter in the faculty newsletter saying

that some faculty members had complained that "my arm is being twisted to get involved in a particular partnership" and that the "workload is not evenly distributed across the faculty" (McKersie, 2000). Other concerns in this letter included sponsors feeling shortchanged when faculty could not be enticed to sign up for their research interests, and departments suffering when their members were committed elsewhere.

MIT Committee on Industrial Partnerships

In April 2002, MIT's provost, chancellor, and the chair of the faculty appointed a "Committee on Industrial Partnerships." The charge[17] given to the cross-institute faculty committee was to assess the impact of the alliance funds on the students, faculty, and research staff members who had received this research support. The chair was a professor and former dean of the management school. The committee included three professors from across the Institute, the director of the office of corporate relations, and me, as the executive director of the Ford-MIT Alliance and research associate in the management school. To make its assessment, committee members reviewed all partnership agreements, talked to the MIT principal investigator for each partnership, attended department heads' meetings, discussed the topic at an open all-faculty meeting, and interviewed faculty members who had been affected by or outspoken about industrial partnerships.

The committee found many benefits and few causes for concern. Although hypothetical issues, such as faculty members' being pressured to participate, being required to undertake undesirable research, or being asked to spend excessive time in cultivating contacts, had been mentioned as concerns, most of these feared outcomes had not come to pass. No serious problems were found.[18] No faculty members were asked to undertake research they did not want to do, nor were young faculty being asked to engage in work inappropriate for building tenure cases. The only substantiated concern was that existing individual research relationships were disrupted by the new partnership arrangements; high-level company executives and senior MIT administration now regularly talked with one another.

The committee recommended that MIT "actively seek partnership opportunities to replace both completed and discontinued partnerships in order to maintain this important source of support" (Urban et al., 2003, p. 18). The committee also reported several "best practices" associated with partnerships, in the hope that they might be shared across the alliances. Their effort continued to reflect MIT's founding philosophy, "*Mens et Manus*," that theory is to be combined with practice and is integral to it.

LESSONS FROM MIT'S ALLIANCES

This chapter has examined collaborative research sponsored by managers, which is different from collaborative research on management. The two most prominent differences are that engineering and scientific research create explicit knowledge and that managing MIT's alliances relates to creating a context for research projects, rather than the details of activities within those projects. Do these differences limit the applicability of insights from MIT's alliance to collaborative management research? Several research project examples help to clarify these issues.

A technology research project tested piezoelectric materials as components in automobile suspension systems. These materials change properties, stiffness and elasticity, when activated by an electrical current. The design of a vehicle's suspension system involves making a trade-off between the stiffness required for a tight feel and good handling and the softness

required for a smooth ride and reduced vibration. Designing a suspension with materials whose properties could be altered can, in essence, provide for both tight handling and a soft ride. The electrically triggered altering of properties required material science research, and utilization of those changes in a suspension system required engineering research for a new design. This project illustrates the link of a research project to its context and application. Context comes from company people providing problem parameters, and application comes from implementing what researchers tested in their experiments. The working relationship created by the alliance provided a way for the company to specify needs as inputs to research and apply findings based on research outcomes.

Management research also has analogous needs for context and application. For example, in the process handbook project (Malone et al., 1998), researchers developed ways to capture, represent, catalogue, and retrieve specifications for innovative organizational processes. Industry managers provided a context for researchers to develop and test process handbook concepts, which those managers used to make improvements in their organizations. In applying these concepts, managers also developed innovative ways to explain and use the process handbook (Roth, 2005).

What differs in engineering and technology research is that there are different ways to protect research findings. Engineering and science research can be patented and licensed, enabling findings to be explicitly managed. Management research is more contextual, and applying principles derived in this research depends on knowing and using them appropriately. In practice, however, Agrawal and Henderson (2002) found that patenting for university faculty is a minority activity and that publication rates far outstrip patenting rates. The opportunity for what corporations want, which is competitive advantage, comes in either management or engineering research, from applying findings and innovating faster than competitors. The speed of implementation matters in a company gaining advantages from university research. Given this similarity, insights from MIT alliances apply not only to universities creating the context for collaborative relationships with company managers, but also to teams of academics and managers seeking to join research with practice.

Best Practices From MIT's Partnerships

The MIT partnership committee identified "best practice elements" from their interviews. When in place, these best practices resulted in the smoother operations of the alliance at MIT. The practices included (1) adherence to standard MIT policies, (2) transparency in governance, (3) processes to match interests and expectations of the sponsoring company with deliverables, (4) the dedication of company staff and participation by its senior management as well as the commitment of MIT faculty and staff, (5) building upon preexisting relationships of MIT faculty members with corporate managers, (6) clear corporate funding and budget allocations for partnership activities by the company, and (7) the use of fellowships to create links with MIT's students (Urban et al., 2003, pp. 14–17). What can be noted, however, in all of these "best practices" is an orientation toward maintaining MIT's status quo. These practices create minimum disruption for MIT's administration and faculty and are mechanisms that further the ways in which a corporation, through its alliance, adjusts to MIT's modus operandi. Given that the research activities were largely carried out by MIT people, this orientation and the asymmetry of adjustments are probably most effective.

An MIT-centric view of alliances permeated the partnership committee. It was beyond the charter of the committee to interview company people, and, therefore, the report noted that "based on conversations with MIT faculty and staff the consensus was that the sponsors have been satisfied with the results of their partnerships" (Urban et al., 2003, p. 13). Yet, at the time, only one of the alliances had been renewed, and only two of the remaining seven were expected to possibly go beyond their initial term. The committee's finding that the risks were minimal and the benefits great did not extend to determining companies' views of the sustainability of these alliances; that inquiry was beyond the charter of the committee. Time and effort were needed to interview the alliance company people, and conducting these interviews and collecting this data would affect that company's and MIT's politics. One view was that initial alliance agreements required such high-level contacts, made at the level of MIT's president and the corporation's CEO or VP of research, that it was very difficult for the alliances to transcend corporate executives' successions.

Sustaining Collaborative Research

No new corporate alliances have been consummated since the June 2000 agreement with Hewlett-Packard. All the alliances have run their course, with the exception of the Ford-MIT Alliance, which was renewed for a second five-year term, and the Amgen alliance, which was terminated in the seventh year of its 10-year term. The general business climate—slowed by stock market declines following the dot-com bust and 9/11 terrorist strikes—has made it financially more difficult for corporations to fund expansive research alliances. These financial conditions, top leadership changes, and new strategies at partner corporations shifted support away from their renewing their multiyear, multiprogram alliances with MIT. New government funding and corporate sponsorship for specific research have made up for the loss of broad funding from alliances. In 2004, MIT's research funding increased 12% to $531 million, with 74% of that support coming from the federal government.

MIT's history in collaborating with industry and its corporate alliance efforts illustrate efforts by its administration to create a positive collaborative research environment. MIT's historical successes and its preeminence as a research university, however, make changes difficult. The charge to the Committee on Industrial Partnerships was to address the faculty's adverse-impact concerns, which, combined with the committee's orientation for identifying "best practices," resulted in recommendations for how alliances "fit" within the current operating modes. Although senior administration were involved in establishing corporate alliances, their efforts were not fully sanctioned by the faculty. The corporate partnerships were independently developed, but in total they had a broad reach and impact. Objections toward alliances were addressed, seeking to fit them to MIT's existing operating modes.

Alliance Management

Each of MIT's corporate alliances had an executive committee led by cochairs from MIT and the corporation. The corporate cochair was a senior vice president, generally the research vice president. The MIT cochair was in senior administration, either the chancellor or provost, or dean of one of MIT's schools.[19] The other members of the executive committee were generally three or four people each on the corporate and MIT sides, active in selecting and carrying out alliance projects. For each alliance, the executive committee met once or twice a year to review results and discuss strategy.

The implementation of the executive committee's strategy for the alliance took place through an operating committee, although the form and working of the operating committees varied across alliances. Generally, these people, based on the strategy set by the executive committee, attracted involvement from MIT faculty and corporate people, then encouraged and selected proposals, and managed the financial and operating details of these projects. The MIT operating committee was cochaired by a senior faculty member, with either a previous relationship to the corporation or relevant research experience. An executive director provided support to the MIT cochair and managed the operational details. Several corporations also appointed executive directors to support their senior leaders' involvement and manage their aspects of the alliance. Three of the alliances posted their executive directors to residence at MIT. These executive directors, who reported to and were paid by their corporation, were provided office space and administrative support at MIT.

Insights From the Ford-MIT Alliance

As executive director of the Ford-MIT Alliance, it was my role to propose and manage the set of activities that enabled successful collaborative research. Success, at one level, was subjective: It depended upon the value that people placed on each of a variety of outcomes from many projects. Some of the outcomes could be directly attributed to research activities and others were indirect, such as broader benefits from the set of relationships across projects. The challenge with assessing outcomes from individual research projects and overall alliance-level relationships was that people at MIT and Ford, and in particular people at different levels in Ford, placed dissimilar values on the various activities and achievements (see the section of this chapter titled "Ensuring Value to Both Sets of Collaborators"). These values were not always hard and fast, but often a matter of perception. Perceptions can be influenced, and in creating a supportive climate for the research and other activities, identifying and communicating value to partners helped influence the perceptions of value derived from alliances and their research projects.

Managing alliance research projects involved two main areas of focus. One focus had to do with helping to identify, communicate, and select projects that were good fits between a sponsor's interests and a research team's proposal. The second focus was to help, in whatever manner possible, to make those projects that were selected as successful as possible. As already mentioned, communicating the value of these projects to the partners helped influence the perceptions of their value and success. Another opportunity to improve the research projects was to learn which initial conditions in selecting projects and what help in carrying out collaborative activities best contributed to producing valued outcomes.

It was not always clear, however, that MIT's traditional operating modes produced the best results or created the greatest value for the corporate sponsor. The corporation's time and financial commitment to an alliance suggested that it would exert influence, but imposing the corporation's requirements, which is what managers in large corporations are accustomed to doing in working with "suppliers," limited faculty members' interest in working with them. A common response from middle managers asked to work with MIT research teams was their initial efforts to renegotiate terms or project proposals. That tack led to resistance on the MIT side, which, due to lack of understanding of the context of the alliance, also led to frustration on the corporate side. Resistance and frustration are impediments to improving relationships, and relationships are essential to creating value from knowledge (Nonaka & Takeuchi, 1995). What is quickly

evident in this scenario is that both sides must have a flexibility and willingness to engage one another.

Studying While Managing the Alliance

The value and role of research can also be applied to a research alliance. My initial proposal to work with a Ph.D. student in MIT's management of technology program to study the Ford-MIT Alliance projects was not supported by Ford's codirector and research vice president. The research vice president wanted a technology focus for the alliance and would not include "management" projects. However, MIT's chancellor and alliance codirector did support this effort with other discretionary funds. At my level, the Ford executive director was supportive of the project and considered his bosses' focus to be too narrow.

The initial study on Ford alliance projects focused on the value and role of interactions for alliance project outcomes. To what extent could the success of research projects (judged by whether the project met expectations) be attributed to how these projects were initiated? In what ways did the interactions (frequency, duration, and depth) among corporate and university people in carrying out the research correlate with success? The study of an initial 13 alliance projects found that both initiation characteristics and interaction characteristics correlated with project success. Active involvement of principal investigators and top management in selecting research linked to organizational priorities and supporting frequent and deep interactions within and across projects was important in the projects that best created value (Gao & Roth, 2002a, 2003). However, capturing value from research involved efforts beyond corporate people's participation in the research project. Accordingly, whether a research project provided value depended not only on the project itself but also on people from the company having broader abilities to capture the value that the research created. The Ford manager who became Ford executive director for the MIT alliance extended the importance of interactions and bringing value from research into Ford by saying, "It doesn't matter what you pay for, what matters is what you take." His comments were based on his insight that university people are animated when talking about their own research findings to anyone who is interested, regardless of who funded it. If you were there, interacting with faculty members, you would learn about their research, its findings, and its implications.

A second study compared MIT alliance research projects with research projects contracted to other universities through Ford's university research program (URP). The URP projects involved mostly science and technology research, and a similar assessment of outcomes—the extent to which outcomes of completed projects met sponsors' expectations—was used to judge results.[20] This study found that projects conducted in the MIT alliance reported proportionally more results than URP projects, and more of the alliance projects met or exceeded sponsors' expectations. Sponsors' expectations were higher for URP projects, in part because the Ford sponsor had to support the project from the start. In the MIT alliance, projects were selected based on strategic directions set by senior managers, who then enrolled subordinates as project sponsors. These sponsors, because of how they were engaged, started with lower expectations for what would be achieved. MIT alliance projects had more Ford top management involvement than URP projects, because the MIT alliance involved regular meetings with senior Ford managers.[21] Ford's management involvement translated into support for implementing research findings, which helped the organization to better capture research value (Gao & Roth, 2002b). Simply put, the magnitude of

the MIT alliance was such that it required and justified Ford leaders' involvement, and their involvement improved the focus on, and provided more resources for, the implementation of research findings.

Senior leaders' involvement also translated into their identification with the Ford-MIT Alliance's people and projects. When the first five-year term of the alliance was in its fourth year, the Ford executives who were active in the alliance worked with other executives in their organization to make a decision regarding the continuation of the alliance.

Sustaining the Ford-MIT Alliance

A concerted effort on the part of both Ford and MIT people helped to renew the Ford-MIT Alliance. Ford's financial condition had worsened considerably since the alliance's 1997 inception.[22] Alex Trotman, the CEO who had championed the alliance, was retired. His successor, Jacque Nassar, because of the record 2002 losses, was also no longer at Ford. Bill Ford had stepped in as CEO and president to stabilize the company's financial situation. In the midst of cost-cutting efforts, Ford renewed the MIT alliance. The renewal decision, announced in October 2002, was made by three Ford vice presidents—from research, engineering, and corporate affairs. The renewal decision was not justified by the financial value Ford could attribute to gains from the research projects. Their justification included the value they saw in the processes that the alliance developed to propose, select, and carry out research projects. They had been a part of improving the functioning of the alliance, including making decisions to reduce or end some research and begin research in new areas. Ford had developed relationships between its senior leaders and MIT faculty and administration, and there were many connections, in addition to research projects, for recruiting, internships, club activities, and policy-proposing consortia, between Ford and

MIT. There was excitement for the new projects in the current research portfolio and their promise for creating future value. Enthusiasm, in short supply for Ford at the time, helped in making an affirmative decision.[23]

The executive directors of the alliance, Chris Magee for Ford and me for MIT, led efforts during the renewal discussions to collect data and develop frameworks and presentations to show the new ways in which the alliance functioned, and how it had improved and changed in its initial four years (Roth & Magee, 2002).[24] Four lessons that were learned provided important insights for collaborative research activities: (1) keeping projects fresh by enabling change, (2) establishing a high-level, benefits-based vision, (3) ensuring value to both sets of collaborators, and (4) discussing cultural differences to coordinate actions.

Keeping the Projects Fresh by Enabling Change

Little in today's world is constant except change. To stay relevant and continue to provide value, collaborative research must change in ways that reflect its partners' priorities. A prerequisite for research is sufficient stability from which to undertake in-depth investigations, making change difficult in a university context. In studies of university-industry research, one of the most difficult tasks is stopping research programs once they have been started (Jacob, Hellstroem, Adler, & Norrgen, 2000; Simeral, 1994). In contrast, at Ford, there were three different CEOs in the first four years of the alliance. To stay relevant, the alliance needed mechanisms within projects to adapt and adjust as they progressed, as well as across projects. To start new projects one must, at times, end other, ongoing projects. The requirement to manage change calls for a relationship that can rebalance the project portfolio.

The Ford-MIT Alliance began with $1 million in seed funding in 1997, and $3 million in annual funding in 1998. The rapid funding ramp enabled many initiatives, initiatives that over the course of time seemed less promising than subsequently identified alternatives. Project changes were needed, even when the project had done well, and the faculty member and his students wanted to continue after the original, often two-year, funding period had ended. Appropriately ending projects, because it involved relationships across Ford and MIT, was a delicate matter that needed to be attended to judiciously and forthrightly. Some aspects of how Ford managed these changes, to be discussed further in following sections, reflect an approach very different from one that would be taken in MIT's culture. The ability to collaboratively end existing projects and start new ones was an important capability. The Ford-MIT Alliance initiated 35 projects, averaged 17 ongoing projects at any given time, and had five projects that continued through the initial four years.[25] Stability and change, and what appeared to be a good balance of the two, were a part of the project portfolio.

Establishing a High-Level, Benefits-Based Vision

A broad partnership between MIT and Ford had the potential to create benefits at different levels. Managing the alliance required recognizing and facilitating the development and capture of these values (see Table 17.2). To capture value required identifying it and linking it to the people who would benefit. For example, MIT's efforts in the research and development of a consortium on environmental sciences linked to Ford's Corporate Affairs office. This consortium had societal benefits, more so than goals of competitive advantage. At societal levels, benefits to Ford and MIT were similar. At organizational levels, some of the benefits were valued by both Ford and MIT. For example, influencing strategies and developing complex systems design principles were areas valued by both organizations. Other organizational benefits, however, are different and reflect specific goals of Ford or MIT. For example, MIT wants its faculty to do research that gets published, while Ford wants new ideas that it can implement to improve its products and services. These goals, while they are different, can be complementary. Finally, there are individual benefits, which contribute to individuals' and groups' goals and objectives. Aligning individuals' incentives and benefits with the activities that are required of them is important to supporting and sustaining their involvement and participation.

Articulating the benefits of collaborative research helps to develop and further discussions on this important topic. The chart represented in Table 17.2 was not meant to be a definitive set of benefits, but rather a conversation starter to help people collaborating across levels of the university and corporation see a bigger picture beyond their own roles. These conversations also sparked insights that contributed to other benefits that are now listed in Table 17.2. The conversations also required guidance for understanding how various activities and outcomes had different value for collaborative partners.

Ensuring Value to Both Sets of Collaborators

Ford's main goals are to produce vehicles (recently broadened to mobility solutions) at

Table 17.2 Vision for Benefits of the Ford-MIT Alliance

Level of Benefit:	Benefit	
Societal: Industry, academia, and government levels	• Set industry standards • Model for global environmental stewardship • Educate future leaders • Transfer knowledge • Influence policy	
Organizational: Alliance, strategic, company, and university levels	• Share strategies • Shape each other's futures • Colocation • Understanding of complex system design principles • Greater credibility	
	FORD-SPECIFIC	MIT-SPECIFIC
	• Hiring • New knowledge • Innovative technology • Novel business models • Market opportunities • Competitive advantage • Improved marketplace reputation • Inventive spirit • Contribute to Ford's workforce	• Job opportunities • New research • Industry relationships • Teachable knowledge • Funding, access, and support • Understanding of real-world problems
Local/individual: Executive, manager, faculty, staff, and student levels	• Source of project support • Insight and learning • Advice • Consulting	• Funding • Access and data • Feedback • Impact • Consulting

attractive cost and performance levels. MIT's main goals are in publishing research and educating students. While Ford's and MIT's goals can be complementary, they involve different efforts and outcomes. Both sets of goals can be met through a close working relationship, with Ford helping to direct MIT people's research efforts to where they can be applied and have an impact, and MIT helping Ford people in the agile application of this research. As with any new knowledge, the advantage is ephemeral, as others often soon learn and adopt these concepts.

When looked at broadly, there are numerous activities that create and diminish the value gained from a corporate-university alliance project. We created a table to show these values, ranking them according to both positive (value-creating) and negative (value-diminishing) dimensions for Ford and MIT (see Table 17.3). Not all activities contribute directly to value, and some are more important than others. For example, Ford's research projects with MIT created a positive and congenial context for a working relationship between the two institutions. That context, and the engineers and scientists who came to MIT and met with faculty and students, created a positive climate that gave Ford advantages in recruiting MIT graduates.

Table 17.3   Balancing Values for Ford and MIT in Alliance Projects

Ford	MIT
Increasing positive value	
Competitive advantage and higher profitability	**Breakthrough research,** theory, and publications
Shareholder value and new revenue	Academic **journal article**/peer reviewed
Impact on current product or process	publication
Recruiting advantages in hiring MIT students	Academic conference **presentation**
Education, knowledge, and **technology transfer**	**Book** or book chapter
(stimulating **environment** for technical people)	Industry or trade **publications**
Convening power of university as an honest	**Faculty development**
broker on important social, economic,	**Education**/opportunities for faculty and funding
and policy issues	Education opportunities for **students,** funding,
Ability to give an idea **publicity**	and employment (hands-on work with top
Priority in **commercializing** technical	executives)
developments	Educational **materials** (real case studies)
Information transfer	**Information** on research, business, and
Inexpensive **research**	engineering issues and problems
Association with prestigious institution,	**Access**—time spent with sponsor, meeting
profession, and individuals	industry managers and technical people and
Sense of good **stewardship** and citizenship	understanding industry issues
Philanthropy and donation of time and money	**Money** and funding, prestige of link with
	successfull industrial companies
Produce good research that is **not implemented**	Funding and **time spent** that doesn't lead to
Raise expectations of Ford employees and students	publications or education
so that they leave Ford	High percentage of time spent **reacting** to
Educate and **inform competitors**	sponsors' information and meeting requests
of Ford's know-how	Good research that is not implemented because
Implement ideas at competitors	**Ford constrains** it
Increasing negative value	

The importance of Table 17.3, like the one for the vision of benefits, is that it enabled conversations about what Ford and MIT valued and the importance of each partner gaining what it valued. The goal was to provide a net sum of positive benefits for each organization along with specific benefits for each individual involved. The values table had a second important benefit in "educating" individuals at Ford and MIT about the potential impact of their actions. For example, in discussions about licensing technology developed in a project management technology project sponsored by Ford, it was important to discuss the negative implications to MIT if Ford constrained the diffusion of research to other companies, particularly if Ford was not going to itself use the idea. This point was captured in the negative value in Table 17.3 of "Good research is not implemented because Ford constrains it." In this case, an interested software company wanted to license the research. Each value point in Table 17.3 could be illustrated by additional vignettes.

Given the broad and diffuse nature of all the activities that create value, it is not always apparent where an activity would lead to a form of value, or that this value would be recognized or captured by the partner. It is also much easier in a corporate setting for people to take on tasks that produce organizational benefits than it is in a university, where individual rewards are relatively more important, and benefits need to be gained by the specific faculty member or student. Some of those organizational benefits—such as recruiting advantages, a stimulating technical environment, and publicity and association—are realized through the context that the set of projects creates.

Discussing Cultural Differences to Coordinate Actions

One of the consistent insights gained from managing the Ford-MIT Alliance is that actions and outcomes are not just valued, but interpreted, differently. We found that these differences were rooted in the basic assumptions of Ford's and MIT's organizational cultures. As part of developing and managing the relationships and projects across the alliance, we examined cultural concepts that were different for Ford and MIT people (see Table 17.4). Helping people become aware of these differences—such as the nature of priorities, concepts of time, and importance of organizational versus individual achievement—improved understanding and interaction at senior levels and within project teams. Explaining the concept of basic assumptions gave people insights into the thinking and explained the behaviors of their counterparts. It also provided an opportunity to talk about what was valued and the importance of attending not only to one's own benefit, but to those of partners. The significance of different understandings increased when the work was different—scientists working in Ford's research laboratory on emissions were more understanding of the graduate students doing emissions research in the engine laboratory at MIT than were, for example, designers in a Ford vehicles program working with graduate students developing industrial design tools. The challenge with culture differences is that when people cross cultural boundaries, the boundaries are invisible to them, and they are unaware of their impact because cultural rules inhibit confrontations about missteps.

Sustaining Collaboration by Improving Relationships

It was an important alliance activity to identify and overcome cultural differences. An alliance provides its participants with unique opportunities to work with people who have different skills, orientations, and worldviews. Being aware of these differences helps people to work together effectively. An alliance provides both partners with an

Table 17.4   Basic Assumptions in Ford's and MIT's Organizational Cultures

Ford	MIT
Follow direction provided by the organization; people create complex products and services that are only possible through the coordinated efforts of large organizations. People appreciate knowing who you work for and your agenda.	It is important to conduct novel and leading-edge work that improves personal and MIT reputation. Publication and teaching are highest priorities.
Time is what you give in working for Ford; you are expected to allocate time based on priorities of the organization and supervision.	Using time well is important; it is the most precious resource that people have. People appreciate considerate use of their time in scheduling meetings or making requests.
Working in a low-cost, conservative way is very important. Competitiveness hinges on low cost structure.	Need to have the required support; otherwise, there is little concern for cost.
The blue oval, or corporation, and Ford employee family are the reason people are working at Ford. Success depends upon contribution to the overall corporate goals, perhaps at the expense of personal gain.	At MIT, people strive for individual accomplishments; reputation is based on research accomplishments and teaching. Department is a home, as is MIT.
People relate to the team or project they are currently on, and have affiliation with people on past programs and teams (if successful).	It is important to have a good working relationship with students and other faculty; this extends to colleagues at other schools and students who have graduated.
It is important to be part of the organization and fit in. Conformity is good, as it helps everyone contribute to the overall goal. Everyone knows his or her place (and soon learns that questions asked "up" the organization are different from those asked "down" the organization).	Respect for the individual and his or her unique values and contributions, including acceptance of a wide array of personal characteristics and attributes, as long as the individual is creative and successful in classroom and research. Some people adopt what might be seen as purposefully quirky styles to differentiate and identify themselves and get what they want.
Management and supervision need to be respected and followed, leaving little room for individual overt interpretation.	Administration exists to run the place, but if they are in opposition to desired results, their direction can be altered or subverted (with discussion among colleagues) to achieve needed ends.

opportunity, because of its size, to actively manage the relationship, and to address the differences in perceptions and culture. Organizational cultures, through their survival over time, create unique ways of seeing the world and establishing their identity (Schein, 1992). Culture is visible in the symbols and their meanings that are identified with organizations. We took prominent symbols from each organization and created an icon that symbolized collaboration by joining Ford's Mustang with MIT's laborer and scholar (see Figure 17.3). This icon was used on Web sites, in communications, and in promotional items given away at large group meetings.[26]

Of the original eight alliances MIT initiated between 1995 and 2000, the Ford-MIT Alliance has been the only one that was renewed. There are many factors that have come into play in the renewal of alliances, perhaps the most significant of which was

Figure 17.3   Icon Developed as a Symbol for the Ford-MIT Alliance

that the concept and original agreement were among leaders who no longer held their positions. The attractiveness of an alliance wanes when top management levels do not directly identify with it. MIT's other alliances did not include the same level of concerted effort to articulate, test, and develop the benefit of multiple value streams through a lens of cultural differences. Many factors come into play when decisions such as to renew an alliance are addressed, and while this approach cannot take credit for renewal, or the fact that Ford was the only corporation to renew its alliance with MIT, it can be noted that these efforts did create a broader base of people with better understanding of one another for Ford and MIT. Also, the Ford-MIT Alliance provided numerous examples of "best practices" that the Committee on Industrial Partnerships proposed for other alliances (Urban et al., 2003). Although other alliances did not take a direct cultural focus, MIT's senior administration and principal investigators acknowledged that challenges in the ongoing management and renewal efforts of alliances could be characterized by an "impedance mismatch," an engineering term for an inadequate ability of one system to accommodate input from another. In MIT's other alliances the impedance mismatch was largely addressed by looking for people on the corporate side to accommodate MIT's input, or by focusing the alliance on projects linked to corporate research labs (as was the case with the Merck and Amgen alliances).

Alliances and Collaborative Management Research

The insights from MIT's alliances—keeping projects fresh by enabling change, establishing a high-level, benefits-based vision, ensuring value to both sets of collaborators, and discussing cultural assumptions to coordinate actions—apply to management research. Most people would agree that each of these insights is important, but what is so unique about them? These ideas are not difficult to conceive, but they are hard to follow through on with actions that produce these results. These insights are easy to see in engineering and technology research because the physical outcomes of this research, such as a new technology, computer system, or solution to a complex problem, are easily seen. In management research, the benefits are a by-product of the managers' involvement, presumably because the researcher and managers have collaborated in making improvements that they have then studied. In this situation, as with technology research, results will be implemented more broadly without additional effort. The need for that additional effort is clear in engineering and technology research, and the conditions created by an alliance that helps and enables that additional effort have the same implications for collaboration in management research.

Confessional Tale

It is easy to be involved in research and write up results without reflecting on how one's own involvement and research interests influenced outcomes. These confessional tales mostly go unwritten (Van Maanen, 1988). In the spirit of collaborative research and sharing my insights, I think a few words are in order. I took the role of managing this alliance to provide me with the salary support that enabled me to continue other research and academic endeavors. I relied upon and used what I knew from my own research to help make the Ford-MIT Alliance successful. My research on organizational culture, learning, and change is fairly limited in the total scheme of engineering research and management but did seem appropriate and was helpful to the task of managing collaborative research. My MIT compatriots responded well to my ideas and requests when they were framed from a research perspective. I believe that my credibility and influence with MIT's engineering faculty members were enhanced by my own research orientation. My counterparts at Ford were also largely receptive to the application of organizational research ideas, although some held firmly to how they wanted to manage MIT, and because of that, my abilities to influence them, whether by logic, research knowledge, or experience at MIT, were more limited. MIT's relationship was not that of a Ford supplier, although some Ford people seemed to act as if that were the case. Often, I found that I needed to "run interference," meaning that I needed to smooth frustration and reactions MIT people had to their treatment by particularly abrasive managers. While my view that a sensitivity to organizational culture and applying it in managing collaborative research at MIT was an effective approach, as I have outlined in this chapter, it was a lens that I brought in, and it was somewhat reinforced by my own actions and data collection. It is fortunate that the Ford-MIT Alliance was renewed, so that the tale I tell through a cultural lens is not only a compelling account, but also a success story.

I have described MIT's history and its evolution; this history is important because it embeds important cultural values and assumptions that are present in the current-day collaborative research environment. Also important to the Ford-MIT Alliance would have been a history of Ford and its evolution. Ford celebrated its 100th anniversary in 2003, and there is a rich history and culture

there that plays into the values and assumptions of its people. My explanations to Ford people about how to effectively influence MIT, based on its history and culture, resulted in people sharing their views and materials on Ford's history. Developing an understanding of Ford's history and culture helped me understand and explain to MIT people how to interact effectively with their Ford counterparts. My sensitivity to cultural issues helped me lead other people to this orientation, thereby improving overall interactions that helped to realize value from collaborative activities.

As I reflected upon my practices in MIT's alliances, I found an unexpected connection to my current organizational change research. In studies of companies that are successful at managing improvement and change across organizational boundaries, I find that they create artifacts through which they represent themselves and the others that they wish to change. An example of an artifact is a value stream map that a company and its suppliers develop to improve the flow and efficiency of the processes that connect their organizations. These artifacts become boundary objects (Carlile, 2004; Star, 1989) that are examined and altered as shared understanding is created among participants. As Mirvis (Chapter 10 in this *Handbook*) notes, various boundaries impede the exchange of knowledge in collaborative research. In managing the Ford-MIT Alliance, I realized that numerous artifacts were created and used in communicating the vision of benefits (see Table 17.2). The balance of value (see Table 17.3), and the basic assumptions of Ford's and MIT's cultures (see Table 17.4), were also boundary objects. These tables were examined and altered in discussions, and those discussions influenced and changed the collaborators in the alliances, and all this was done without resorting to formal authority.

In conclusion, it is important to note that collaboration is sustained by great outcomes. There is no substitute for the successful research that leads to both unique capabilities for the sponsor and his organization and top-level journal publications for the research team and their university. The development of relationships at senior levels between a corporation and a university enables the targeting of research efforts to areas that have promise for each. Companies know well, through their ongoing operations, where their current knowledge fails them, and can identify areas with intractable problems where they are unable to make

headway. Universities are well equipped with research methods and analytic tools, and if these capabilities are directed toward important problems, they can better contribute to knowledge advancement and societal well-being. This potential for collaborative research is what makes corporate-university alliances attractive. Directing and sustaining these alliances, however, involves confronting challenges that are beyond research or its application, but exist within the management of relationships that create a context for bridging cultural differences so as to connect university-based research efforts to value-creation processes in corporations.

NOTES

1. My work would not have been possible without the openness and support of MIT colleagues Dan Roos, Larry Bacow, Joel Moses, Phil Clay, and John Heywood. Ford managers Phil Abramowitz, Jim Anderson, Ed Krause, Chris Magee, and Steven and Kristen Schondorf also supported my research orientation in working with them.

2. From MIT's Press Office, article on MIT's alliances with industry; see http://web.mit.edu/newsoffice/nr/2000/alliance.html

3. See BankBoston Economics Department (1997), *MIT: Impact of Innovation.*

4. MIT is one of the top U.S. research universities, with historical interests in working with government and industry. In 1999, it claimed almost 4% of all the patents given to American universities and received over 1.5% of all federal funding for science and engineering at universities and colleges (Agrawal & Henderson, 2002, p. 46).

5. This strangely worded commitment of funding comes from the fact that, at the time of the signing of the alliance, Ford supported over $2 million in research and education programs at MIT. To address concerns of "cannibalization"—that managers in divisions would ask MIT professors to get their projects funded by the corporate alliance rather than their divisional funds—this clause was a part of the agreement and emphasized by Ford and MIT leaders. Thus, Ford committed to new funding of $3 million per year, and to maintain at least $1 million in the existing programs, or $4 million a year for the next five years, as part of the alliance agreement.

6. Another alliance, one with Nanovation, is not shown in the table. This partnership started in January 2000, with commitments of $95 million over six years to establish a world-class MIT center and research program for prototyping light-based photonic technologies. It ended with financial and ownership changes at Nanovation, in part due to the dot.com stock market declines in 2000.

7. MIT was also involved in educational and research alliances with the United Kingdom and Singapore, through, respectively, the Cambridge-MIT Institute (CMI) and Singapore-MIT Alliance. These educational alliances were based at national

universities and involved partnerships with these countries' governments. For example, a proponent for the Cambridge-MIT Alliance, Chancellor of the Exchequer Gordon Brown, wanted this alliance to develop and improve British industry. It was "the start of a dynamic and challenging partnership . . . [to] create entrepreneurs who can use their inspiration and perspiration to build a stronger British economy . . . [and] change the face of entrepreneurship and wealth creation in the UK" (MIT Press Release, November 10, 1999).

8. The Bayh-Dole Act addressed an important weakness in the U.S. government's patent policies. Anyone interested in government intellectual property was faced with dealing with 26 different agency policies. Efforts toward unification of government agency policies had started in 1963, led by Jerome Weisner, President Kennedy's science adviser, but these policies directed title to the agencies and not to the public. By 1980, the U.S. government had accumulated 30,000 patents. Only approximately 5% of those patents were commercially licensed. Sponsored by senators Birch Bayh of Indiana and Robert Dole of Kansas, the Bayh-Dole Act, or Patent and Trademark Law Amendments Act, gave U.S. universities intellectual property control of their inventions that resulted from federal government-funded research. This act has not been without controversy. Some in Congress argued that granting private companies the rights to publicly funded research amounted to an enormous giveaway to corporations; others pronounced the act a visionary example of industrial policy that would help America compete in the fast-moving information age. Following the Bayh-Dole Act for university-industry relations, from 1980 to 1998 industry funding for academic research expanded at an annual rate of 8.1%, reaching $1.9 billion in 1997 (many times the level of 20 years earlier). In 1978, universities produced roughly 250 patents a year (many of which were never commercialized); 20 years later, in 1998, universities generated nearly 5,000 patent applications.

9. From 1994 to 1996, the U.S. government provided roughly 75% of the research support for MIT, which amounted to $241 million, $245 million, and $242 million, respectively, for those fiscal years. Of that funding, the Department of Defense as the largest single sponsor accounted for 18% of the total. In 1995, the U.S. House of Representatives and Senate were considering a 60% reduction in this funding.

10. The implication for universities, the third partner in the system, was dual increases in responsibility—first, for better education to prepare students to work and lead in the new industrial world, and second, for greater responsibility in conducting broad, basic research. For universities to effectively respond, they would need to deemphasize narrow disciplinary approaches and pay more attention to the context in which engineering is practiced. More hands-on experience, working in teams and international environments, along with applications of new technologies in education and learning, were needed. Changes in the nature of research within industry place larger responsibility for broad, basic research with our universities, changes that require patronage from industry, which ultimately benefits. The historical investment by the federal government in higher education and research has a dual impact, funding not only the conduct of research, but also the education of graduate students who, when they graduate, transfer knowledge to industry. Observing that universities "tend to work the best and learn the most when we're actively engaged in partnerships," Vest (1996, p. 6) agrees with the Council on Competitiveness's recommendation for improved synergy among industry, universities, and the federal research apparatus.

11. MCC was launched in 1982 as a corporate-government partnership with goals to enhance the competitiveness of U.S. companies, responding to threats posed by

Japanese companies, by undertaking research on high-risk technologies—computer-aided design, packaging/interconnect, software, and advanced computer architecture. The finalist areas that competed for the location of MCC—Raleigh-Durham, North Carolina; Austin, Texas; Atlanta, Georgia; and San Diego, California—were all chosen for their research universities with strengths in microelectronics and computer sciences, along with quality-of-life factors for attracting personnel, access to airports, and state support of business (Smilor, Kozmetsky, & Gibson, 1988). However, when MCC started operations in 1984, the companies involved did not, as intended, dedicate their best staff members, it was difficult to get consensus on the projects to pursue, and technology transfer mechanisms were not initially established. The location of MCC in Austin aided the local economy. Lockheed, 3M, and Motorola established divisions in Austin. In its first decade, MCC maintained over 20 shareholder companies and increased other forms of membership. It was awarded 117 patents, licensed 182 technologies, and published 2,400 technical reports and 400 videotapes (Gibson & Rogers, 1994). However, it has not produced leapfrog technologies and has not been vital to the economic competitiveness of its member companies. MCC faced two fundamental challenges: (1) creating a centralized research environment funded by a diverse group of competitive companies to produce technical breakthroughs, and (2) successfully transferring these technologies to member companies in a timely manner. The University of Texas created an incubator to help start fledgling companies; many small companies were founded that commercialized technologies developed at MCC. The real challenges for the firms that contributed their people and funding were behavioral and managerial, rather than technological (Gibson & Rogers, 1994).

12. SEMATECH was formed in 1987 to improve the competencies of domestic chip manufacturers. In the next decade, the U.S. government provided $800 million in support. During that decade, the U.S. semiconductor industry has enjoyed a resurgence. A hands-off approach by government allowed industry to direct activities that would improve competitiveness and enable rapid changes in program directions in response to findings. With the return of health and strength to the U.S. semiconductor companies, SEMATECH board members voted in 1994 to continue without government funding. Today the organization has renamed itself International SEMATECH, recognizing the membership of international corporations and pursuing cooperative work on semiconductor manufacturing technology. The criticism of SEMATECH has been that it might not have been linked definitively to the recovery of the U.S. semiconductor industry. During that same period other industries also improved appreciably against Japanese competition. Another concern was the focus on picking technologies and promoting domestic exclusivity. Small companies that absorbed SEMATECH funding for unique and critical technologies nearly failed or were purchased by foreign companies. However, SEMATECH did illustrate that an appropriately structured consortium, where major goals are aligned with industry needs, can successfully address important national technology policy issues (Roos, Field, & Neely, 1998).

13. The Partnership for Next Generation of Vehicles (PNGV) was created in 1993 to (1) improve national competitiveness in U.S. manufacturing, (2) support fuel economy and emissions reduction research, and (3) develop vehicles with three times improvement in fuel economy over the 1994 average at comparable cost and performance levels. The social and national concerns reflected in these goals, particularly goal three, led to greater government involvement in PNGV than in SEMATECH. The funding from government flowed through the Department of Energy

(DOE), and there was great interest and pressure on industry to partner with the national labs, who are also funded by DOE. Initial efforts focused largely on working with Ford, GM, and Chrysler and largely left suppliers and universities on the sidelines. Other challenges in PNGV resulted in a set of programmatic efforts that seemed to lack an overall framework, and the National Research Council was asked to form a committee to review PNGV's progress. Political interest in reexamining the Corporate Average Fuel Economy (CAFÉ) legislation brought conditions into PNGV that had more to do with its ends than with the means by which it achieved these gains. While this consortium has brought industry and government together to discuss important technology and policy issues, it also illustrates the importance, from the outset, of considering the proper structures and incentives for complex consortia made up of members with different interests (Roos et al., 1998).

14. Other councils were educational technology, the environment, and international relationships.

15. MIT was perceived as difficult to do business with because, in part, of its high overhead rate, rigid intellectual property rules, and cumbersome contracting procedures. The main value of MIT was its basic research, since companies were generally hesitant to do basic research on their own or provide substantial funding for it. If they were to do applied research with MIT, there was concern about MIT's abilities to do this well, and that they would want people in residence to help implement research results.

16. MIT's partnerships efforts that did not succeed have not been discussed. These failures are harder to assess, in part because only those that proceeded to some stage, such as multiple meetings and discussions for how they would be organized, were visible to me. Given my limited access to these efforts, it is hard to assess, beyond informal conversation, all of what happened. The partnerships overtures that were unsuccessful did have some common elements: They did not have sufficient support in the organization, they were not funded centrally (one partnership was ready to go until the divisions learned that they, and not corporate, would have to fund the projects), or executives did not see the benefit in the extra costs of partnerships (which all provide some discretionary "gift" funds to MIT) over their current, multiple sponsored research project and consortium relationships. Some efforts, as indicated in the report of the Council on Industrial Relationships, never got started because top executives were uninterested in discussions on special relationships with MIT.

17. See "Committee chaired by Urban formed to review Institute's industrial partnerships" (2002).

18. The complete list of concerns investigated contained the following: pressure to modify policies, pressure to participate in undesirable research, diversion from teaching, elimination of funds from preexisting programs, increased demands for space, mismatch with corporate representatives, mismatch of expectations, nonpartner companies denied opportunities, excessive time spent on cultivation of relationships, and misuse of MIT's name in publicity. In only one instance did a faculty member use funding from an alliance to "buy out" teaching time. This was done, as per institute policies, with the department head's approval.

19. All of MIT's senior administrators—president, provost, chancellor, and deans—hold academic appointments. Many are MIT faculty members who take on this responsibility, or preeminent faculty attracted from other universities. Following their administrative terms, these administrators go back to faculty positions.

20. Eighty-four surveys were sent out, one each to the company counterpart and university principal investigator, on 42 projects that had been sponsored and completed within the corporation's university research program. With a 40% response rate, 28 different projects were reported on.

21. The Ford-MIT Alliance had four meetings annually that involved senior leaders from Ford and MIT. Two of these were face-to-face meetings and the other two were videoconference meetings. The face-to-face meetings originally alternated between Cambridge and Dearborn venues. Later, as senior leaders found more value hearing multiple presentations on their supported and other research, these meetings shifted to take place at MIT. Ford leaders found it convenient to charter a corporate plane to take the group to an airport near Cambridge. MIT faculty involved in the research projects continued to visit Dearborn, and their research updates were done as seminars of related projects for Ford managers, often including a vice president in the audience.

22. In 1997, Ford's stock price ranged from $30 to $37 on annual sales of $146.9 billion and profits of $4.4 billion. In 2003, the year that renewal was being discussed, the stock price ranged from $6 to $18, on annual sales of $162.6 billion and profits of $0.022 billion. In the previous year, 2002, Ford had lost $5.5 billion.

23. The renewal decision was helped by the position of the advanced development engineering vice president. His engineering organization numbered in the thousands of people, with an annual budget of several hundred million dollars, or almost an order of magnitude greater than just the research department. He could strategically justify and include the alliance funding as one of his line items.

24. Roth and Magee (2002) identified seven principles that guided their efforts in managing the alliance and selecting new research projects:

1. Engage interesting and innovative people.
2. Support personality matches.
3. Link projects to company priorities.
4. Align with existing organizational resources.
5. Look beyond costs and orient to value.
6. Gain both local and organizational benefits.
7. Seek and capture multiple value streams.

25. These 35 projects are part of the research project funding and do not include the project funded under the MIT Alliance for Global Sustainability. The seed funding from Ford for this initiative, supported at $1 million per year for the first four years, and then reduced to $750K annually, funded many research projects. The funding for this consortium also came from other corporations and foundations.

26. This icon is a combination of the Ford Mustang, one of Ford's most well-known vehicles, and the scholar and laborer in a modern version of MIT's *mens et manus* logo. Over the years, we had mouse pads and coffee cups made with this icon on them. At one meeting of MIT alumni at Ford, which took place shortly before the Christmas holiday, we made and gave out chocolates with this symbol on them.

REFERENCES

Agrawal, A., & Henderson, R. (2002). Putting patents in context: Exploring knowledge transfer from MIT. *Management Science, 48*(1), 44–60.

Allen, T., & Scott Morton, M. (1994). *Information technology and the corporation of the 1990s: Research studies.* New York: Oxford University Press.

BankBoston Economics Department. (1997). *MIT: Impact of innovation* (Special Report). Boston: Author. Available at http://web.mit.edu/newsoffice/founders/

Bloedon, R., & Stokes, D. R. (1994). Making university-industry collaborative research succeed. *Research Technology Management, 37*(2), 44–48.

Buderi, R. (1996). *The invention that changed the world.* New York: Simon & Schuster.

Busch, L., Allison, R., Harris, C., Rudy, A., Shaw, B., Ten Eyck, T., et al. (2004). *External review of the collaborative research agreement between Novartis Agricultural Discovery Institute, Inc. and the regents of the University of California.* East Lansing, MI: Institute for Food and Agricultural Standards, Michigan State University.

Bush, V. (1945). *Science: The endless frontier.* Washington, DC: United States Office of Scientific Research and Development, U.S. Government Printing Office.

Carlile, P. (2004). Integrative framework for managing knowledge across boundaries. *Organization Science, 15*(5), 555–568.

Channell, D. (1989). *The history of engineering science.* New York: Garland.

Cohen, W., & Levinthal, D. (1990). Absorptive capacity: A new perspective on learning and innovation. *Administrative Science Quarterly, 35*(1), 128–152.

Committee chaired by Urban formed to review Institute's industrial partnerships. (2002, April 24). *MIT Tech Talk Newsletter.* Cambridge: Massachusetts Institute of Technology.

Commonwealth of Massachusetts. (1859). *Objects and plan of an institute of technology; including a society of arts, a museum of arts, and a school of industrial science.* Downloaded April 12, 2007, from http://libraries.mit.edu/archives/mithistory/pdf/house260.pdf

Contractor, F. J., & Lorange, P. (1988). *Cooperative strategies in international business.* Lexington, MA: Lexington Books.

Cyert, R., & Goodman, P. (1997). Creating effective university-industry alliances: An organizational learning perspective. *Organizational Dynamics, 25*(4), 45–57.

Doz, Y., & Hamel, G. (1998). *Alliance advantage: The art of creating value through partnering.* Boston: HBS Press.

Etzkowitz, H. (1998). The norms of entrepreneurial science: Cognitive effects of the new university-industry linkages. *Research Policy, 27*(8), 823–833.

Gao, X., & Roth, G. (2002a). *Knowledge alliances: Spanning university-firm boundaries.* Manuscript submitted for publication.

Gao, X., & Roth, G. (2002b). Patterns for value creation in firm-university research. In *Report to Ford-MIT Alliance*, unpublished manuscript.

Gao, X., & Roth, G. (2003). *Factors influencing knowledge and value creation from research in a corporate-university alliance.* Manuscript submitted for publication.

Geisler, E., & Rubenstein, A. (1989). University-industry relations: A review of major issues. In A. Link & G. Tassey (Eds.), *Cooperative research and development: The industry-university-government relationship* (pp. 43–62). Boston: Kluwer Academic.

Gibson, D., & Rogers, E. (1994). *R&D collaboration on trial.* Boston: Harvard Business School Press.

Hagedoorn, J., Link, A., & Vonortas, N. (2000). Research partnerships. *Research Policy, 29*(4–5), 567–586.

Hatakenaka, S. (2002). *Flux and flexibility: A comparative institutional analysis of evolving university-industry relationships in MIT, Cambridge and Tokyo.* Unpublished doctoral dissertation, Sloan School of Management, Cambridge, MA.

Hesselberth, J. (1992). Technology transfer from academia: Prescription for success and failure. In D. Gibson & R. Smilor (Eds.), *Technology transfer in consortia and strategic alliances* (pp. 151–156). Lanham, MD: Rowman & Littlefield.

Jacob, M., Hellstroem, T., Adler, N., & Norrgen, F. (2000). From sponsorship to partnership in academy-industry relations. *R&D Management, 30*(3), 255–262.

Kelly, J. (2000, April 8). UK's top universities: Focus is on the bridge of minds. *Financial Times.*

Lane, P., & Lubatkin, M. (1998). Relative absorptive capacity and interorganizational learning. *Strategic Management Journal, 19*(5), 461–477.

Lau, E. (2004, August 1). Report: Five-year deal with Novartis hurt UC Berkeley. *Sacramento Bee.* Downloaded April 12, 2007, from http://www.sacbee.com/static/live/news/projects/biotech/archive/080104.html

Link, A., & Bauer, L. (1989). *Cooperative research in US manufacturing: Assessing policy initiatives and corporate strategies.* Lexington, MA: Lexington Books.

Malone, T., Crowston, K., Lee, J., Pentland, B., Dellarocas, C., Wyner, G., et al. (1998). Tools for inventing organizations: Toward a handbook of organizational processes. *Management Science, 45*(30), 425–443.

Mansfield, E. (1995). Academic research underlying industrial innovations: Sources, characteristics, and financing. *Review of Economics and Statistics, 77*(1), 55–65.

McKersie, R. (2000, September). The implication of mega-partnerships for MIT faculty. In *MIT faculty newsletter* Vol. XIII, No. 1.

National Science Board. (2000). *Science and engineering indicators.* Washington, DC: Author.

Nonaka, I., & Takeuchi, H. (1995). *The knowledge-creating company: How Japanese companies create the dynamics of innovation.* New York: Oxford University Press.

Peters, L., & Fusfeld, F. (1983). Current U.S. university/industry research connections. In National Science Foundation, *University-industry research relationships: Selected studies* (pp. 1–161). Washington, DC: U.S. Government Printing Office.

Powers, J., & McDougall, P. (2005). University start-up formation and technology licensing with firms that go public: A resource-based view of academic entrepreneurship. *Journal of Business Venturing, 20*(3), 291–311.

Press, E., & Washburn, J. (2000, March). The kept university. *Atlantic Monthly.*

Rahm, D., Kirkland, J., & Bozeman, B. (2000). *University-industry R&D collaborations in the United States, the United Kingdom, and Japan.* Boston: Kluwer Academic.

Roos, D., Field, F., & Neely, J. (1998). Industry consortia. In L. Branscomb & J. Keller (Eds.), *Investing in innovation: Creating a research and innovation policy that works* (pp. 400–421). Cambridge: MIT Press.

Roth, G. (2000). Constructing conversations: Lessons from learning from experience. *Organizational Development Journal, 18*(4), 69–78.

Roth, G. (2005). Creating new knowledge by crossing theory and practice boundaries. In W. Pasmore & R. Woodman (Eds.), *Research in organizational change and development* (Vol. 15, pp. 137–169). Greenwich, CT: JAI Press.

Roth, G., & Magee, C. (2002, April). Corporate-university alliances and engineering systems research: Learning from the Ford-MIT Alliance. *Proceedings of the Engineering Systems Conference.* Cambridge: MIT Sloan School.

Roth, G., & Senge, P. (1996). From theory to practice: Research territory, processes and structure at an organizational learning center. *Journal of Change Management, 9*(1), 92–106.

Schein, E. (1992). *Organizational culture and leadership* (Vol. 2). San Francisco: Jossey-Bass.

Simeral, W. (1994). The evolution of research and development policy in a corporation: A case study. In N. Bowie (Ed.), *University-business partnerships, an assessment.* Lanham, MD: Rowman & Littlefield.

Smilor, R., Kozmetsky, G., & Gibson, D. (1988). The Austin/San Antonio corridor: The dynamics of a developing technopolis. In R. Smilor, G. Kozmetsky, & D. V. Gibson (Eds.), *Creating the technopolis: Linking technology, commercialization, and economic development* (Chap. 10). Cambridge, MA: Ballinger.

Star, S. (1989). The structure of ill-structured solutions. In M. Huhns & L. Glasser (Eds.), *Readings in distributed artificial intelligence.* Menlo Park, CA: Morgan Kaufman.

Stewart, G., & Gibson, D. (1990). University and industry linkages: The Austin, Texas, study. In F. Williams & D. V. Gibson (Eds.), *Technology transfer: A communication perspective* (pp. 109–131). Newbury Park, CA: Sage.

Urban, G., Glicksman, L., Hansman, R., Koster, K., Lees, J., & Roth, G. (2003, March 11). *MIT's industrial partnerships: Report of the ad hoc committee on industrial partnership review.* Cambridge: Massachusetts Institute of Technology. Available from http://web.mit.edu/chancellor/IndlPartnerships Rpt.pdf

Van Maanen, J. (1988). *Tales of the field: On writing ethnography.* Chicago: University of Chicago Press.

Vest, C. (1996, September). Stewards of the future: The evolving roles of academia, industry and government. In *MIT report of the president for the academic year 1996–97.* Cambridge: Massachusetts Institute of Technology.

Vest, C. (2004). *Pursuing the endless frontier: Essays on MIT and the role of research universities.* Cambridge: MIT Press.

IIIC. COLLABORATIVE RESEARCH IN GOVERNMENT AND SOCIETY

CHAPTER 18

Monetary Policy and Academics

A Study of Swedish Inflation Targeting

MIKAEL APEL

LARS HEIKENSTEN

PER JANSSON

ABSTRACT

The way in which monetary policy is conducted has changed considerably in recent decades. One of the most notable differences from earlier periods is that policy now puts greater focus on keeping inflation low and stable. This chapter has two main aims. The first is to shed light on the role played by academic research in the current formulation of monetary policy. The second is to describe the interplay between scholars and practitioners during the process of reformulating monetary policy. The presentation draws on the authors' experiences of the inflation-targeting regime in Sweden.

In general terms, monetary policy can be said to be represented by a central bank's instrumental-rate decisions with a view to influencing aggregate demand and the rate of price increases in the economy. The way in which monetary policy is conducted has changed considerably in recent decades. The clearest difference from earlier periods is that policy now focuses to a greater extent on *keeping inflation low and stable*.

A consistent focus on price stability admittedly existed earlier in a few countries—for example, in Germany. A broader application of this approach began with a realignment in the United States around 1980. Later, the tendency spread to other countries, and in many cases, starting with New Zealand in 1990, it included the introduction of an *explicit numerical target* for inflation.

The results of the changes in monetary policy have been generally favorable. In addition to lower and less-variable rates of price increases, many observers consider that the revised policy has contributed to the more stable economic development in general that has prevailed in many countries in the past 10 to 20 years (see, e.g., Bernanke, 2004; Summers, 2005).

This chapter has two main aims:

- The first aim is to shed light on the role played by academic research in the current formulation of monetary policy and thereby indirectly in the favorable economic development.
- The other aim is to depict the interplay between academics and practitioners—an interplay that has facilitated, perhaps even been a prerequisite for, the transmission of research results to central banks.

The first topic has already been mapped relatively clearly, but here we strive for a picture that is more detailed than is usually the case. Less has been done on the second topic, probably because economists have traditionally not been particularly interested in the specific processes whereby research is spread to and applied in practical domains.[1] Moreover, in disciplines that do focus on such processes, monetary policy is not a matter that has attracted much attention.

We believe that an account of the interplay between academics and central banks as regards the development of monetary policy may be more widely relevant, partly because the experience that has been gained can also be pertinent in other policy fields. There is, for example, the way in which monetary policy has been delegated and "depoliticized" and how the interplay with the world of research has assisted in the development of policy and in making it more understandable and generally accepted. Other policy fields also stand to learn from the prompt way in which new research findings have been utilized to construct a basis for decisions.

This chapter refers mainly to conditions and experience in Sweden, for the simple reason that that is what is most familiar to us. But

as monetary policy in many other countries has undergone much the same change as in Sweden, what we have to say should interest those who want to take a closer look at these matters more generally.

The chapter is arranged as follows. As a background to the subsequent discussion, we present a brief retrospective survey that describes both the problems that led to the introduction of an inflation-targeting policy in Sweden in the early 1990s and economic developments since then. In the next section, various research findings are discussed that have contributed to the development of Sweden's inflation-targeting monetary policy, and an attempt is made to assess the ways in which contacts with academics have been important. Next, we describe the forms of interplay between researchers and practitioners that have facilitated the application of research findings in the practical domain. Effects in the other direction—practical policy's influence on academic research—are also considered to some extent. An appendix to the chapter reports an interview in which Lars Svensson, one of the most influential scholars in the field of monetary policy, comments on the course of events.

A RETROSPECTIVE

In the early 1990s, Sweden experienced a profound economic crisis. There were a number of specific causes, but speaking more generally, the crisis can be seen as a dramatic finale to almost two decades of problems with stabilization policy.

In the 1970s and 1980s, policy in Sweden had for various reasons tended to be unduly expansionary, and this had generated an environment that made it difficult to keep price and wage increases at a reasonable level. Thus, the policy regime with a fixed exchange rate did not serve, as had been intended, to keep inflation in line with the rate among

Sweden's main trading partners. Instead, the development of prices and wages repeatedly undermined the fixed exchange rate. These costs crises were temporarily resolved by devaluing the currency, the Swedish krona, but this did not do away with the underlying problem—the excessively rapid upward trend in domestic prices and wages.

In this way, the economy came to be characterized by "devaluation cycles" in which sudden "stops" alternated with powerful "go's." When yet another cost crisis meant that the fixed exchange rate finally had to be abandoned in November 1992—after resolute but fruitless efforts to defend the krona and break the negative trend—it was clear that fairly drastic measures were needed to put the Swedish economy on a more sound footing.

The solution was a shift in the stabilization policy regime, involving a fundamental reformulation of the tasks assigned to monetary and fiscal policy. Having previously been unduly expansionary and a factor behind the rapid inflation, fiscal policy would now be required to ensure long-term stability and sustainability in public finances. Monetary policy in turn was assigned a considerably more central role than before. With a flexible exchange rate, monetary policy's primary function would be to act more directly to keep the rate of inflation low and stable in the first place, by using the interest rate to influence aggregate demand.

Monetary policy's assignment was interpreted by the the Swedish Central bank (later on called the Riksbank in this chapter) as being to keep the annual change in the consumer price index (CPI) at 2% as of 1995. In this way, when the inflation target was announced in 1993 Sweden became one of the first countries to introduce an *inflation-targeting policy*.[2] Since then, this approach to monetary policy has become increasingly popular and is now applied by more than 20 central banks around the world (see, e.g., Berg, 2005).

Considering how the Swedish economy has developed under the inflation-targeting regime, it is hard to avoid the conclusion that this approach works well. Inflation has been low and considerably more stable than before (see Figure 18.1). Moreover, economic growth has fluctuated less and been stronger than in the 1970s and 1980s. Employment has not developed as favorably, though the situation today is better than in the mid-1990s, shortly after the crisis. Moreover, the combination of the earlier devaluation policy and an ultimately unsustainable expansion of public sector employment is commonly considered to have simply postponed the need to tackle the Swedish economy's employment problems (see, e.g., Lindbeck, 2003).

IMPORTANT CONTRIBUTIONS FROM RESEARCH

The realignment of monetary policy in Sweden can be seen as an item in a broader international process. The change to a new policy regime occurred later in Sweden than in many other countries and under more dramatic circumstances. But once it had happened, Sweden was an early starter in deciding to focus policy on an explicit inflation target as well as in moving toward a high degree of openness and clarity in policy.[3]

The following account has been structured by dividing the process of change into two phases. The first concerns changes directly connected with the regime shift—in Sweden's case, the transition from a fixed exchange rate to an inflation target and an independent central bank. The second phase concerns changes whereby the new regime has been developed in various respects. The review accordingly deals with insights and contributions from academic research that have influenced the regime shift as such and the subsequent development of the regime.

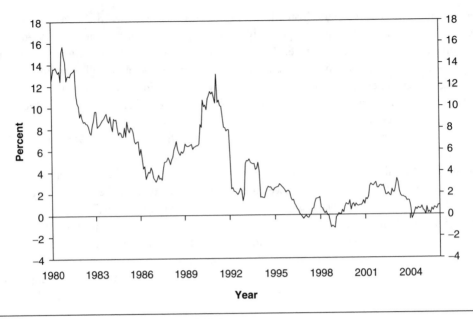

Figure 18.1   Inflation in Sweden, 1980–2005

NOTE: Inflation is measured as the 12-month change in the consumer price index (CPI).

SOURCE: Statistics Sweden.

The Regime Shift to an Inflation Target and an Independent Central Bank

Priority for Low and Stable Inflation

Academic researchers have put forward a number of theories about why inflation in many countries was so high in the 1970s and, in some cases, in the 1980s as well. A common feature of these theories is the basic premise that economic policy at the time was unduly expansionary and that a more restrictive policy would have been required to keep inflation low and stable. However, the theories differ in what they see as the reasons *why* policy was too expansionary. Simplifying somewhat, they can be said to start from the notion that the expansionary line had to do either with excessive optimism about the possibility of influencing real economic developments, that is, output and unemployment ("output optimism"), or with excessive pessimism about the possibility of controlling inflation ("inflation pessimism").[4] The research has tended to concentrate on conditions in the United States, but the hypotheses are also applicable to many other countries.

One hypothesis is that economic policy decision makers counted on the existence of a long-term trade-off between the real economy and inflation (see, e.g., Taylor, 1992). This notion stemmed from a study by Phillips (1958) on UK data over many decades. It was assumed that the negative slope of the so-called Phillips curve implied that policy makers could choose between different combinations of inflation and unemployment. It was believed that an expansionary policy could lead to lastingly higher output and employment, albeit at the price of higher inflation.[5]

However, theoretical work in the late 1960s indicated that this notion did not allow for the fact that a systematically expansionary policy would also influence inflation expectations of households and firms (see, e.g., Phelps, 1967; Friedman, 1968). One reason a rapid price rise can boost employment is that real wages fall, enabling employers to use more labor. But this effect depends on the inflation expectations of wage earners being at fault initially. In time, wage demands will be adapted to the higher rate of price increases so that real wages are restored, whereupon employment and unemployment return to their earlier levels (often referred to as natural levels), while the higher inflation persists.

Today it is generally accepted that the long-term levels of output and employment are determined by factors that monetary policy cannot influence directly, such as the rate of technological development and how well markets function. This insight has had a major impact on how the approach to monetary policy has changed in recent decades.

An alternative hypothesis as to why policy was unduly expansionary is that decision makers underestimated the role played by the level of demand in generating the higher inflation.[6] Statements by central bank representatives and politicians suggest that it was commonly believed that the high inflation was more or less exclusively due to specific nonmonetary factors such as high increases in labor costs and rising costs for oil and other raw materials. This seems to have been accompanied by the view that inflation was relatively insusceptible to changes in demand and thereby, for instance, to monetary policy. This "inflation pessimism" meant that monetary policy decision makers virtually abdicated their role as inflation fighters. Hence, the well-known statement by Milton Friedman that "inflation is always and everywhere a monetary phenomenon" was not fully acknowledged at that time.

Academic research had accordingly generated valuable insights that were already circulating when the earlier way of conducting stabilization policy failed to work in the 1970s and a search began for alternative approaches. One fundamental insight was that monetary policy is incapable of permanently influencing output and employment; another was that inflation is basically a monetary phenomenon, so monetary policy is capable of steering inflation in the somewhat longer run.

The Value of Independent Central Banks

The promotion of low and stable inflation to be monetary policy's overriding objective has been accompanied by greater central bank independence vis-à-vis the political system. Arguments for a change in this direction were provided by research into the problem of economic policy's *time inconsistency* (see Barro & Gordon, 1983; Kydland & Prescott, 1977). This research drew attention to the fact that keeping inflation down can be hard on account of difficulties in making binding commitments. The basic problem is that economic policy decision makers' motives for the short run may conflict with a long-term ambition for low inflation. It will then not be easy to convince economic agents that policy will be maintained, that is, consistent over time (hence the term, time inconsistency).

Suppose the government declares that inflation will be held at a low level in the future and that at first, economic agents believe this will be the case. Inflation expectations in the economy will then adjust to this low rate of inflation. When this has happened, however, the decision makers may be tempted to depart from the long-term ambition for low inflation. A temporary reduction of unemployment, for example, achieved by stimulating the economy and allowing inflation to move up, may be perceived as politically worthwhile, even though the benefits do not last. As inflation is low initially, moreover, the costs of a higher rate will not be considered all that serious. It is not hard to see that such a policy can be particularly tempting in certain situations, for instance in the run-up to an election.

However, as economic agents are aware that economic policy decision makers can be tempted in this way, their inflation expectations will be geared from the start to this fact rather than to the low inflation that was aimed for initially. In this situation, the best option from the government's point of view will be to implement an accommodating policy, which means that the high inflation expectations will be fulfilled. The end result is a level of inflation above the low level initially declared—an inflation bias—without this leading to higher output or employment.[7]

In line with this reasoning is the empirical fact that inflation expectations in Sweden did not stabilize until some time after the Riksbank in practical terms obtained responsibility for maintaining price stability in the early 1990s. Economic agents evidently reckoned that a central bank with a clear target for inflation would not implement the same kind of accommodating policy as before the change of regime. This is not surprising. It is, after all, rather natural that the temptation to implement an excessively expansionary policy will be resisted more readily by a central bank than by a government that continually has to make decisions under pressure from important groups in the electorate.

The influence from academic research on the decision on the Riksbank's independence is hard to gauge exactly. The change that came in the early 1990s was crucially bound up with the international context of which Sweden was a part—central bank independence was becoming the norm—together with the acute domestic crisis that restricted the freedom of action in economic policy. When the law that formally established the Riksbank's independence eventually was amended in 1999, there was a direct link to Sweden's undertakings vis-à-vis the European Union. But academic research was naturally an underlying factor in all these phases. Moreover, the problem of time inconsistency in economic policy received comparatively much attention in the Swedish debate in the early 1990s.

The Subsequent Development of the Regime

The Monetary Policy Strategy

The decision to introduce an inflation target and the Riksbank's high degree of practical independence did by no means put an end to the discussion of monetary policy. Given the assignment to an independent central bank to focus on price stability, a good deal of work remained to be done on the details of the monetary policy strategy.[8] In this context, the academic contribution mainly concerned formal analyses that helped to systematize and discipline ideas about the best way of conducting an inflation-targeting policy.

It was evident that many decision makers right from the introduction of inflation targeting realized that policy ought to be implemented in a "flexible" manner. A one-sided focus on the inflation target could entail unnecessarily large fluctuations in output and employment. Despite this insight, many central bankers have tended to be cautious in their accounts of how an inflation-targeting policy takes output and employment into consideration. The well-known American economist Stan Fischer (1996), a former deputy head of the International Monetary Fund and currently governor of Israel's central bank, put it like this:

Central bankers have a tendency to say that price stability should be the only goal of monetary policy, and to shrink from the point that monetary policy also affects output in the short run. That is not hard to understand, for explicit recognition of the powers of countercyclical monetary policy encourages political pressures to use that policy, with the attendant risk that inflation will rise. But it is also problematic and destructive of credibility to deny the obvious, as well as to undertake countercyclical policies while denying doing so. (p. 26)[9]

In the early years with the new regime, many central banks, not least the Riksbank, focused particularly strongly on inflation in their rhetoric. In the light of high and variable inflation, it was considered important to make it clear that stabilizing inflation was the priority, and to convince everyone that this was policy's overriding objective. In many cases, this rhetorical focus continued even when the inflation target started to gain credibility. This had to do in part with a concern that changing the focus too quickly could lead to policy being regarded as erratic and changeable.

To illustrate how the Riksbank has gradually modified its description of the inflation-targeting policy, statements at different times can be compared with the implications from a theoretical model for an optimal inflation-targeting policy. For the comparisons presented here, we have used a model by Lars Svensson (1997) that is simple but still serves to convey the basic principles.

At a very general level, and simplifying somewhat, Svensson's model is made up of relationships that describe how the economy functions and indicate what the central bank ought to do.[10] Monetary policy is assumed to be a matter of minimizing the following loss function:

$$L = (\pi - \pi^*)^2 + \gamma (y - y^*)^2, \qquad (1)$$

where γ measures the importance attached to stabilizing output, y, in relation to stabilizing inflation, π ($\gamma = 1$ denotes equal importance). The inflation target is represented by π^* and the long-term sustainable level of output by

y^*. The equation implies that the central bank attains perfect target fulfilment when $\pi = \pi^*$ and $y = y^*$ (i.e., when $L = 0$).[11]

In more realistic models, it is assumed that the central bank aims to minimize (1) not just over a particular period but from today and forever. The central bank then has to tackle the problem of minimizing the discounted sum of (1), summed from today to an infinite future. As future outcomes are not available, what this amounts to is that the central bank aims to minimize the *expected* discounted sum of (1). In simple terms, the optimal policy is then derived by solving this optimization problem given the other relationships that describe how the economy functions.[12]

In the model, monetary policy is assumed to be capable (via the instrumental rate) of influencing aggregate demand (y above) in the next period. The duration of a period is not self-evident but is often assumed to be one year. Changes in demand lead in turn to changes in inflation in the following period. So in this model, monetary policy is assumed to act with a time lag of two periods (years) before an interest rate adjustment has an impact on inflation. Note that the model's time lag is a consequence of how the economy functions and does *not* imply that for some reason the central bank postpones its response to deviations from the inflation target (π deviates from π^*). This means that no matter how much the central bank chooses to adjust the interest rate after a shock, it *cannot* restore inflation to the targeted level sooner than in two years' time.[13]

The assumed behavior in accordance with (1) clarifies that the central bank is not solely concerned with the development of inflation but also attaches some weight to real economic factors (as long as γ is not zero). At times, the goal of stabilizing inflation (around π^*) may conflict with the goal of stabilizing output (around y^*). If inflation suddenly increases, the central bank will want to counter this so that the discrepancy between π and π^* in equation (1) is reduced. This it does by raising the interest rate so that y falls below y^*.[14] However, the sooner the central bank wants to curb inflation (reduce the discrepancy between π and π^*), the more it has to tighten the interest rate at the cost of impairing the stability of output (an increased difference between y and y^*). It has been shown that in this situation there is an *optimal trade-off* in the sense that the central bank raises the interest rate just sufficiently for the deviation of y from y^* to relate in a particular way to the deviation of π from π^* (for details, see Svensson, 1997). Exactly how the deviation of y from y^* should relate to that of π from π^* depends on the model's parameters, of which one is the weight the central bank attaches to stabilizing output relative to stabilizing inflation (γ).

Figure 18.2 illustrates how the central bank's optimal trade-off is affected by its *stabilization policy preferences* (values of the parameter γ). The economy is in equilibrium initially, so that inflation is on the target (assumed here to be 2%). For some reason inflation then suffers a shock and jumps up to 4%. The central bank observes this and reacts with an interest rate increase. But as it

takes time (two years) for this increase to affect inflation, the latter's rate continues to be 4% for the next two years. What happens after that depends on the central bank's stabilization policy preferences. If the bank considers that variations in output are not particularly serious (γ is comparatively low, in this example 0.25), inflation returns to the target fairly quickly (which means that when the central bank observes the inflation shock, it raises the interest rate fairly markedly). On the other hand, if the central bank is more averse to real economic fluctuations (γ is higher, in this example 1.0), it takes longer for inflation to fall back because the bank raises the interest rate more cautiously so as not to generate an unduly large deviation of y from y^*.

Briefly, then, a monetary policy that is derived from the assumed behavior (1) will involve arriving at a trade-off between the goals of stabilizing inflation and output, respectively. The optimal trade-off depends on how the economy functions and on the central bank's preference for tackling deviations in

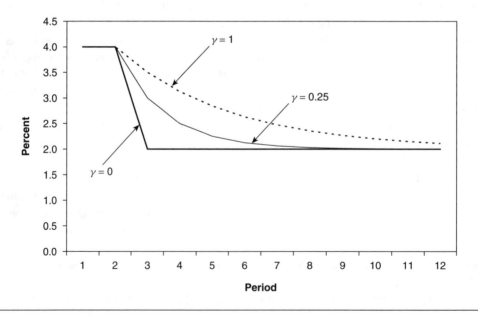

Figure 18.2 Basic Outline of Inflation's Adjustment With Alternative Stabilization Policy Preferences

SOURCE: Authors' calculations based on Svensson (1997).

inflation relative to deviations in output. In this model, it can also be shown that the shock's magnitude matters for the speed of adjustment of inflation back to target.

The model can also be used to illustrate the consequences of a monetary policy that focuses solely on keeping inflation stable. This corresponds to the case where $\gamma = 0$.[15] The thick solid curve in Figure 18.2 shows that in this case monetary policy concentrates on returning inflation to the target as quickly as possible (after exactly two years here).

How, then, do the Riksbank's descriptions of its inflation-targeting policy on various occasions tally with this model? As mentioned earlier, the bank's rhetorical focus on inflation was notably strong in the early years. The following excerpt from a speech in 1994 (Bäckström, 1994) illustrates the early emphasis:

> If inflation deviates from the target, policy has to be designed to bring it back to a level which is in keeping with the objective of price stability. The time schedule for this is governed by the substantial lag before effects of monetary measures materialize. The interval before the full effect of a change in the instrumental interest rates shows up is commonly estimated to be between one and two years. . . . [P]olicy should be constructed so that forecast inflation one to two years ahead . . . is 2%. (p. 6)

This statement can be said to imply that in the event of a deviation, inflation is to be brought back on target as soon as possible. There is no mention of circumstances that might warrant a more protracted adjustment. In the model, this corresponds to a monetary policy with the restriction that $\gamma = 0$. In this case the central bank, as indicated above, invariably aims to have inflation in line with the target as quickly as it can, and the size of the shock is of no importance.

However, it was not all that long before the argument started to shift. The following

description comes from a speech two years later (Bäckström, 1996):

> [In] the construction of monetary policy, the development of production is an implicit consideration. . . . Excessively strong growth is liable to generate rising inflation, bringing it above the inflation target. That calls for a tighter monetary policy. Conversely, weaker growth [brings] . . . inflation down below the target, which, by the same token, warrants an expansionary monetary stance. This illustrates how, with an inflation target, monetary policy serves to smooth unduly large fluctuations in economic growth. (p. 4)

In contrast to the preceding description, this underscores a need to stabilize real economic developments. However, the cited case is one where an interest rate adjustment automatically stabilizes both inflation and demand and does not require an active trade-off between these objectives. In terms of our model, one cannot tell whether $\gamma = 0$ or $\gamma > 0$, though the reference to a need of real economic stabilization does implicitly indicate that $\gamma > 0$.

One year later, the considerations behind monetary policy were formulated as follows (Heikensten, 1997):

> The inability of monetary policy to affect long-term employment, and the fact that it should focus on maintaining price stability, does not mean that its capacity to condition production and employment in the short run cannot sometimes be used for stabilizing activity. Monetary policy can contribute to an economic recovery insofar as this is feasible without jeopardizing price stability. (p. 5)

Further steps were taken in 1999, when the Riksbank's Executive Board came into being and endorsed a clarification of how

Swedish monetary policy is formulated. This clarification (Heikensten, 1999) included a specification of various situations in which it might *not* be pertinent to adjust inflation to the target as quickly as possible after a shock:

> Monetary policy acts with a substantial time lag, with the largest effect on inflation in the interval of one to two years. . . . Monetary policy is normally conducted so as to be on target . . . one to two years ahead. Departures from this general rule may be warranted for two reasons. One is that the consumer price index (CPI) can be pushed upwards or downwards in the relevant time period by one or more factors that are not considered to affect inflation more permanently. . . . The other reason for departing from the rule can be that a quick return to the target in the event of a sizeable deviation can sometimes be costly for the real economy. (pp. 8, 16)

This description of policy makes it clear that stabilizing inflation could be at odds with stabilizing real economic activity. Here, then, the ambition to stabilize the real economy is of direct importance for the formulation of monetary policy. In terms of our model, one can say that the Riksbank describes a monetary policy characterized by a *time-varying* value of γ; this parameter can "normally" be virtually zero, but a positive value can sometimes "be warranted" (when inflation changes temporarily or there are sizable shocks).[16]

In the following years, much of the discussion of monetary policy concerned the extent to which policy should be flexible and related to economic issues that were current. One such issue was how to deal with changes on the supply side of the economy that were likely to have only a transitory downward effect on inflation. Another was whether policy ought to take the development of asset prices into consideration (equity prices around the turn of the century and, later on,

house prices). Published speeches indicate that the Riksbank's view was that a flexible policy was needed, that is, there could be grounds for departing from the inflation target. The crucial reason for adopting this view involved the risks involved and how they were evaluated.[17]

The next step was taken in 2006 when the Riksbank presented a further clarification of its monetary policy strategy (Sveriges Riksbank, 2006), which it described as follows:

> Monetary policy is normally focused on achieving the inflation target within two years. . . . The two-year horizon can be interpreted as a restriction as to how much consideration can normally be given to real economic developments, a restriction which—like the specified inflation target—the Riksbank has imposed on itself to make the target of maintaining price stability credible. In certain circumstances, deviations from the inflation target can be so large that it is reasonable to allow inflation to return to the target beyond the normal two-year horizon, provided this does not undermine confidence in monetary policy. . . . The pace at which it is desirable to bring inflation back to target after a deviation depends on the disturbances the economy has been affected by. (pp. 13, 14)

A comparison with the earlier formulations about the need to consider the real economy and the principles embodied in our simple model makes two points. The first is that the Riksbank now considers that targeting inflation in the two-year perspective means per se that γ is positive. There can still be a case for varying γ over time, but its normal value is positive and there are "certain circumstances" that can call for an increased value. The other point is the explicit explanation as to why the theory's recommendations are not followed fully in practice; the Riksbank has *chosen* to adopt the two-year horizon as a "restriction" so as not to jeopardize the inflation target's credibility. This restriction does not occur in the theoretical model (where the optimal target horizon varies) for the simple reason that the model has no cause to worry about the policy's credibility (which is invariably taken for granted).

To sum up, since the inflation target was introduced in the early 1990s, the Riksbank has gradually moved toward describing its monetary policy as a trade-off between stabilizing inflation and the real economy, respectively.[18] This tendency has by no means been confined to Sweden. Virtually every country with an inflation target has followed a similar path from a strong focus on the target to a more open discussion about taking real economic developments into account.

Of course, this does not mean that inflation-targeting theory is now indistinguishable from practice. Practical applications may depart from theory for a number of reasons. A notable example is that practice does not fully apply the theoretical models' continuous trade-off between the different goals of stabilization policy. All inflation-targeting central banks still employ some kind of target horizon for the attainment of their inflation target under normal circumstances.[19] This is presumably connected with the risk that the inflation target would otherwise be perceived to be too vague and, in a worst-case scenario, perhaps no longer even fulfill its function as a "nominal anchor."

Transparency and Communication

The received wisdom in central banking then was: Say as little as possible, and say it cryptically. But attitudes toward transparency have changed dramatically since then, and central banks around the world have opened up. (Blinder, 2006, p. 12)

One aspect related to this ongoing trend toward greater openness has to do with the way central banks try to provide economic agents with information about their policy intentions. Economic theory holds that interest rates for different maturities are interconnected, so that expectations of short-term interest rates (over which a central bank exerts almost perfect direct control) are important for the prevailing levels of long-term interest rates (over which a central bank exerts no direct control). It follows that by influencing expectations about short-term rates, a central bank can also indirectly affect longer-term rates. A greater influence on the entire range of interest rates (the so-called yield curve) obviously makes monetary policy more powerful.[20] Michael Woodford (2005), a leading researcher in the field of monetary policy, has formulated this as follows:

> Insofar as the significance of current developments for future policy are clear to the private sector, markets can to a large extent "do the central bank's work for it," in that the actual changes in overnight rates required to achieve the desired changes in incentives can be much more modest when expected future rates move as well. (p. 4)

When the Riksbank started publishing numerical forecasts in the second half of the 1990s, the underlying assumption was that the instrumental rate would be unchanged in the forecast period. This approach was chosen by most of the few central banks that published forecasts at all in those days. The aim was to present forecasts and discuss potential risks in order to provide a solid basis for assessing the future path of interest rates. The fact that the bank's decision makers endorsed the forecasts gave the aim greater force.

The approach the Riksbank adopted worked satisfactorily on the whole as far as communication was concerned. The assumption of a constant instrumental rate was pedagogic in that the forecasts spoke straightforwardly about the need for monetary policy action. If inflation was forecast to rise above the target, for instance, this indicated that an increase in the instrumental rate was called for, and vice versa if the forecast was below the target.

However, the approach also posed problems that had to do with the fact that assuming a constant instrumental rate over a comparatively long period is not particularly realistic. Forecasts based on this assumption will hardly be credible at times when it is reasonable to suppose that over a longer period the instrumental rate will need to be raised or lowered. It also means, of course, that the forecasts will subsequently be difficult to evaluate.

In 2005, the Riksbank chose to base its forecasts on a more realistic assumption about future monetary policy, namely that the instrumental rate would follow market expectations. By then the inflation-targeting policy was firmly established, and similar changes had already been made by the central banks in Norway and the United Kingdom.

Besides providing better conditions for making credible forecasts, the assumption that the interest rate will follow market expectations should facilitate the central bank's communication of future monetary policy. Even if the market's expectations fail to coincide exactly with those of the central bank, by describing the extent to which this is the case the central bank can indirectly communicate information about its own expectations.[21]

Clarity about future monetary policy might be further enhanced by a central bank basing forecasts directly on its own interest rate expectations and publishing these, instead of making a detour via market expectations. This is, in fact, what the Riksbank has chosen to do from the beginning of 2007.[22] This is the approach that most academic researchers now recommend.[23] Many central bankers have been less enthusiastic to date, though they have recently become more interested in looking further into this matter.

One objection has been that with this method, central banks would "stick their necks out." It may be asked whether they are better informed about the economy than other observers. And what would the public reaction be if what actually happens were to differ markedly from the declared intention (because forecasts are uncertain and interest rate expectations are therefore revised over time)? That might be particularly serious if the deviations entailed substantial costs for economic agents. The Riksbank's view is, however, that the uncertain nature of assessments is now widely understood, as is the circumstance that new information is liable to entail appreciable changes in the conditions for monetary policy decisions.

Another difficulty in this context is that in many central banks, including the Riksbank, decisions are made by a committee (executive board). This form of decision making introduces the problem of arriving at interest rate expectations that represent the opinion of a group (as a consensus or a majority).

The development toward more openness has had to do with a combination of changes in society in general—the rapid growth of financial markets and increased attention from media, for instance—and more specific factors such as greater central bank independence in many countries and, in Sweden, the move to a flexible exchange rate. The contribution from academics has mostly been to provide an impetus by stressing the value of transparency, clarity, and making policy assessable and accountable. For the Riksbank, matters such as these were frequently on the agenda in the second half of the 1990s when policy makers met their academic advisers (see discussion of the interplay between policy makers and academics, below, for further details). Vivid discussions turned established practices inside out and demonstrated shortcomings in the methods that were being employed.

The Basis for Monetary Policy Decisions

A sound strategy and functional communication do not suffice to ensure that monetary policy contributes to a favorable macroeconomic outcome. This also calls for high quality in the analyses underlying the interest rate decisions. At the Riksbank, by far the most important part of the analytical work has been to produce forecasts of inflation as well as of factors, primarily real economic developments, that to a high degree steer inflation and can in themselves influence decisions.

In the past five years the empirical characteristics and forecasting potential of large macro models have undergone an almost revolutionary development.[24] Much progress has also been made with models that focus more directly on data regularity and have less of a basis in economic theory (time-series models). Various factors have contributed here, not least that powerful computers can perform highly advanced and time-consuming calculations, and that macro models are now constructed to a greater extent on the basis of relevant theories about the behavior of households and firms (micro foundation).[25]

Work on the assessment of macroeconomic developments has been a part of the Riksbank's activities for a long time. With a fixed exchange rate, however, there was less need of detailed forecasts. When the fixed exchange rate was abandoned and the inflation target was introduced, work on macroeconomic forecasts became essential and gained weight in the internal organization (see also next section). In recent years, the work of acquiring new and more appropriate forecasting instruments has been assigned a higher priority at the Riksbank. An entirely new macro DSGE-type model has been developed.[26] At the same time, work has been stepped up on the development and introduction of new, more modern time-series models.[27]

The empirical characteristics of the new models (macro as well as time series) are superior to those of their predecessors. Various evaluations of forecast performance show that the new models in many cases would have improved the historical forecasts made by professional forecasters, including the Riksbank (see, e.g., Adolfson, Andersson, Lindé, Villani, & Vredin, 2005). Also, the new models represent an improvement from a pedagogical point of view; the combination of good empirical characteristics and theoretical assumptions makes it possible to interpret and describe the forecasts in economic terms.

THE INTERPLAY OF ACADEMICS AND PRACTITIONERS

In the preceding section, we considered how the design of monetary policy in Sweden (and other industrialized countries) has been influenced by various contributions from research. Much of what we discussed is familiar to central bank economists and academic researchers. As noted initially, there are fewer accounts of the interplay between researchers and practitioners that has facilitated, perhaps even been a prerequisite for, the use of the insights of academics for practical purposes. That is the topic of this section. There will also be some mention of influences in the other direction, from practice to research.

First, however, it should be borne in mind that some of the most notable changes in monetary policy have not resulted primarily from an interplay between academic researchers and central bank practitioners. Compared with a business enterprise, for example, a central bank is much more bound by rules imposed by the political system. The higher priority for price stability and the increased independence of central banks are examples of more general reassessments that have required decisions by governments and elected assemblies. While insights from academic research, together with practical experience, have no doubt been important for these reforms, their impact on practice has come via the political system and political decisions rather than in a (direct) interplay with central bank practitioners.

There are, however, many other changes in monetary policy, above all in connection with the continuous development of day-to-day activities, where the consequences of this interplay have been more direct. The following account focuses on the forms of this interplay in Sweden in the period with an inflation target, that is, after the fundamental conditions for monetary policy had been established by the political system.

Three Types of Interplay

To make it easier to follow the account, we have chosen to divide the forms of interplay between research and practitioners into three types: (1) interaction, (2) formal collaboration, and (3) internalization.

Interaction denotes the interplay of academic research and practice that occurs continuously in many fields and finds expression in an exchange of influences and ideas without involving more formal contacts and forms of collaboration.

Formal collaboration refers to contacts of various kinds between academic researchers and practitioners that are established in more organized forms. As with interaction, in formal collaboration there is still a dividing line between outsider academic researchers and insider organizational practitioners.

In the third type of interplay, referred to here as *internalization,* central banks "internalize" the generation of knowledge, for instance by recruiting academic researchers to their own staff.

It should be emphasized that these types of interplay are not mutually exclusive. On the contrary, an effective practical application of research insights generated by interaction will be facilitated if a central bank has enhanced its competence through internalization, not least if, as is increasingly common, the internalization also has involved the central banks' decision makers.

Examples From the Swedish Inflation-Targeting Regime

Interaction

Through interaction, academic research gains inspiration and ideas from the practical side. Researchers then generate various types of insights and knowledge that can be used for the further development and improvement of practical activities. The process is completely informal and relies on voluntary initiatives.[28]

The theoretical foundation for targeting inflation came to a large extent from academic research, above all the emphasis that monetary policy's primary objective ought to be price stability and that central banks need to act independently of the political system. It seems, however, that the idea of focusing policy in practice on a numerical target for inflation took shape inside the central bank world.[29]

Once it had been launched, inflation-targeting policy attracted the attention of academic researchers. Right from the start, this research was very much concerned with solving practical problems. Targeting inflation was a new phenomenon, with no accepted practice to go by, so central bank practitioners were interested in what research could show.

This is clearly illustrated by the research done by Lars Svensson (discussed above). His close contacts with the Riksbank provided opportunities for discussions that benefited both parties: Svensson learned about the Riksbank's practical problems, and his formal analyses helped to systematize and discipline the Riksbank's thinking.

Research in this field has been extensive during the last 10 to 15 years, and in the new regime with a flexible exchange rate the Riksbank has been able to utilize numerous contributions. Impulses also came via contacts with other central banks that had been working with a flexible exchange rate for some time, in the beginning in particular from the Bank of Canada.

As mentioned earlier, the traffic between research and practical monetary policy was not one-way; the influence was mutual. This is illustrated in Figure 18.3, which shows the time path for the number of hits for "inflation targeting" in one of the best-known databases for scientific publications in economics. It was not until the mid-1990s, about five years after the initial introduction of inflation-targeting policy, that the subject began to attract more widespread interest in academic research. The first major international academic conference on inflation-targeting policy was held in Milan in 1994.[30] Academic interest grew rapidly, however, from the mid-1990s onward.

Formal Collaboration

The interplay of researchers and practitioners has not been confined to an informal exchange of ideas and influences. It has also found expression in various types of more established contacts, which we have chosen to call formal collaboration.

In formal collaboration, one can say that the Riksbank's primary role in the generation of knowledge has been that of a commissioner and funder, accompanied in certain cases by the provision of personnel. Obviously, this is a different, more active role compared with interaction.

An example of formal collaboration is the system of scientific advisers the Riksbank introduced in 1990, when Lars Svensson, at that time professor at the Institute for International Economic Studies at Stockholm University, was attached to the Riksbank as an adviser in scientific matters. The introduction of inflation-targeting policy, with which there was still little practical experience, accentuated the Riksbank's need for academic support (see the section below on internalization), and for that reason the

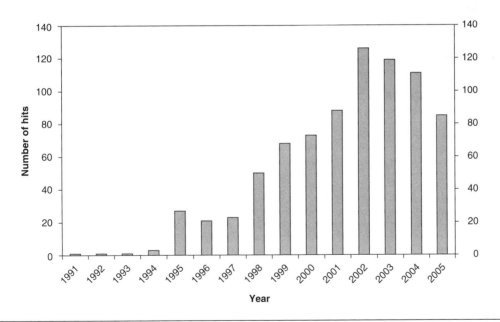

Figure 18.3   Number of Hits for "Inflation Targeting" From a Search in EconLit

NOTE: EconLit is the AEA's (American Economic Association's) electronic database for scientific publications in economics.

Riksbank has since 1993 always had four or five scientific advisers, recruited from abroad as well as in Sweden.[31]

The collaboration with scientific advisers was aided as the Riksbank adopted a more open attitude to the outside world. The publication of detailed material for decisions and an open public discussion, in speeches and other contexts, of problems confronting the bank opened up the possibility of a more detailed and in-depth dialogue with academics outside the Riksbank. The discussions with advisers broadened in the latter part of the 1990s. Besides providing support for the bank's economists, topical policy issues were discussed with the decision makers, and drafts of speeches and reports were read and commented on. The fact that a number of the senior officials had an academic background aided and stimulated the dialogue.

Another example of formal collaboration between researchers and practitioners is the set of conferences the Riksbank has arranged, often together with an academic institution. The first, Monetary Policy Rules, was held in 1998 together with the Institute for International Economic Studies at Stockholm University.[32] Since then, the Riksbank has arranged one or two conferences a year on subjects connected with monetary policy or financial economics. Examples are Inflation Targeting and Exchange Rate Fluctuations (1999), Asset Markets and Monetary Policy (2000), Central Bank Efficiency (2003), and Inflation Targeting: Implementation, Communication, and Efficiency (2005).

The conferences have regularly highlighted research that has practical applications for central banks. This is evident, for instance, from the concluding panels that have given researchers and decision makers an opportunity to discuss what the research findings have meant for policy. In this way, the conferences have promoted contacts and the dissemination of knowledge between these two worlds, elsewhere as well as in Sweden.

A third example, which in the field of monetary policy is probably closest to what is usually meant by "collaborative research," is the Riksbank's occasional commissioning of external academic researchers to examine and elucidate a specific issue. Besides financing these projects, the Riksbank has often arranged for staff economists to participate in them. However, such commissions have not been particularly common. The only notable recent example is the collaboration with external researchers the Riksbank initiated in 2005 to broaden and deepen the analysis of the exchange rate's path and determinants.[33]

Internalization

One reason external researchers have not been used more frequently to elucidate specific issues may be that the Riksbank has gradually internalized the generation of knowledge and thereby gradually increased its own ability to undertake the necessary analyses. To understand what has driven this development, it may help to look briefly at how the change to a flexible exchange rate, in November 1992, altered the conditions for monetary policy.

When the explicit target for inflation was introduced in the early 1990s, the demands on work at the Riksbank were very different from those that the fixed exchange rate had entailed. Under normal circumstances, the task of a central bank with a fixed exchange rate regime is rather simple and straightforward: The interest rate has to be set at such a level that currency inflows and outflows balance and the exchange rate is maintained.

Matters are different with a flexible exchange rate. The interest rate no longer has to defend a particular exchange rate relationship. The central bank's monetary policy can instead concentrate, as the Riksbank has done since 1993, on steering inflation directly. Trying to hold inflation at a given level is, however, difficult because of the time lag before an interest rate adjustment affects inflation. The central bank has therefore to be able to produce forecasts of how inflation and other economic factors will develop in the future. The demands on the central bank's communication are also greater—policy must be explained to the outside world clearly and pedagogically (see discussion above).

It was therefore only natural that the change to a flexible exchange rate and an inflation-targeting policy triggered a more extensive reinforcement of the Riksbank's competence in economics or, as we have chosen to put it, an internalization of the generation of the knowledge. There are various ways of illustrating this.

A separate research department was set up in the Riksbank as of 1997 with the task of "developing methods for the analysis of issues of importance for the Riksbank's activities."[34] It was underscored that, besides producing research of good international quality internally, the new department should contribute to building a bridge between academics and practitioners. In this way, relevant findings could be channelled to the bank's activities, and contacts could be established for purposes of, for example, making it easier to recruit qualified staff.[35]

The "output" from internalization can be measured by, for example, the number of articles written wholly or partly by Riksbank economists that have been accepted for publication in scientific journals. Figure 18.4 shows that in this respect, too, things have changed fairly dramatically in the past decade or so.

Another indicator of internalization is the number of Riksbank employees who have a higher academic degree. The number of economists with a Ph.D. degree working in the monetary policy department increased from three in 1991–1992 to 30 in 2005. The pattern has been much the same in the other central policy unit, the financial stability department. The level of formal academic training has also risen among the policy makers; since the new executive board was

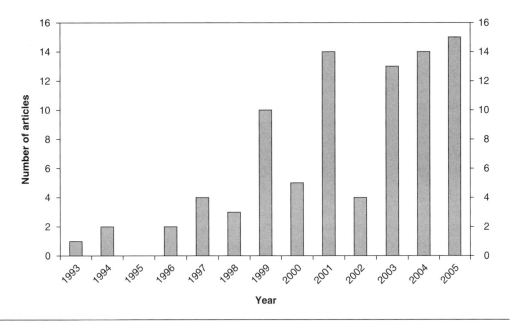

Figure 18.4 Number of Articles Authored by Riksbank Economists in Scientific Journals

introduced in 1999, at least half of the members have held a Ph.D. degree.

A similar process of internalization has been in progress in many other central banks. Just as in Sweden, it has included analytical activities (Jondeau & Pagès, 2003; St-Amant, Tkacz, Guérard-Langlois, & Morel, 2005) as well as the policy makers (Simmons, 2006).

SUMMARY AND CONCLUDING COMMENTS

The way in which monetary policy is conducted has changed in recent decades. As regards general design, two changes are particularly evident. One is that today, monetary policy in almost all countries is focused on attaining low and stable inflation. In many cases, an explicit inflation target is used to demonstrate the commitment to price stability. Another change is that a growing number of central banks have been given a high degree of independence vis-à-vis the political system. These two changes in the general design of monetary policy are so far-reaching that they can be said to have resulted in a new regime.

Just what academic research has meant for this change of regime is, of course, difficult to tell. It is clear that research has generated insights that facilitated the fundamental reassessment that has been made. For the focus on low and stable inflation, there were the insights that monetary policy is not capable of permanently affecting output and employment and that inflation is basically a monetary phenomenon. From this, it naturally followed that monetary policy's overriding objective should be price stability. For the greater independence of central banks, an important part was played by research into the problem of time inconsistency in economic policy. This research highlighted the fact that keeping inflation low can be hard because of difficulties in making

binding commitments. The problem could be greatly reduced by giving the central bank a clear mandate to conduct monetary policy independently. This type of fundamental reassessment of monetary policy naturally required political decisions and occurred more quickly in some countries than in others; but research did provide a firm foundation on which to base the new regime.

Given the new regime with independent central banks that focus on price stability, the way in which central banks work on monetary policy has also changed considerably. These changes have occurred in a number of important fields: how central banks perceive and describe their monetary policy strategy (how the interest rate is set), how they communicate with the outside world, and how they produce the analyses on which interest rate decisions are based. In all these respects, we have attempted to present a picture, from the Riksbank's perspective, of the changes that have been made and how the course of events has been influenced by research.

As regards the monetary policy strategy, the contribution from research has mainly consisted in formal analyses, whereby thoughts about the best way of conducting an inflation-targeting policy have been disciplined and systematized. The academic analyses could not be ignored, and they kept central bankers on their toes. Today there is a broad consensus, among practitioners as well as academics, that inflation-targeting policy should be conducted "flexibly" and also communicated in this way.

Research has also clearly left its mark on central banks' external communication. The observation that policy needs to be assessable and accountable has underscored the need to make communication open and clear. It is partly thanks to the impetus from research in this field that there are good grounds for believing that the trend toward increased central bank clarity and transparency will continue.

Turning, finally, to the analyses on which interest rate decisions are based, much progress has been made in recent years. Researchers have managed to develop new models with better forecasting ability and theoretical underpinning, achievements that have been facilitated not least by the growing capacity of computers. This, in turn, has made it possible both to enhance the quality of central bank analyses and to make the analytical work more effective.

These changes have proceeded against the backdrop of an interplay in various forms between practice and academic research that has served as a driving force. One of the aims of this chapter has been to describe these forms of interplay. We found it appropriate to divide the forms into three types: interaction, formal collaboration, and internalization. The forms do not fit neatly into a chronological sequence, but—simplifying somewhat—they can be said to match a pattern where central banks have moved from being an object for study and analysis by researchers (interaction), via a tendency to establish more formal links with the academic world (formal collaboration), to the internal "production" of academic research as an increasingly integrated component of the international research community (internalization). A leading monetary policy researcher, Bennett McCallum (1999), has commented on this integration as follows:

> [I]n recent years there has been a large amount of interaction between central bank and academic analysts, so that today . . . one would be hard-pressed to tell, for many research papers, whether a particular one had been written by members of one group or the other. (p. 12)

We would like to conclude with some thoughts that our survey mentions only in passing or not at all. One interesting question is *why* academic research has happened to exert so much influence in the field of monetary policy. One hypothesis is that in recent decades stabilization policy has been in what might be called a formative phase. When the Keynesian approach began to look shaky in the 1970s, a need arose to find new solutions. It was then only natural that the problem featured prominently in research and that practitioners and politicians were receptive to the insights research could provide. As we noted, academic research also played an important part in reaching the consensus that was ultimately achieved and that led to fundamental institutional changes. It is a striking fact that academics, not just in Sweden but internationally, were also engaged in questions associated with policy in the 1930s. That period, too, can be seen as a formative phase after the earlier regime had broken down.

Another explanation for the strong academic influence could have to do with the move to monetary policy independence and the clear focus on price stability. That has made it easier to depoliticize the issues and turn monetary policy into more of a technical matter. Perhaps that has made the analysis of issues more manageable than is the case in other policy fields. Moreover, the change, as in Sweden's case, from a fixed to a flexible exchange rate has called for a more elaborated analysis. Academic research has no doubt also been stimulated by the basic monetary policy issues in different countries being fairly similar.[36]

It is also of interest to consider the lessons that the developments in connection with monetary policy may have for other policy fields. In our opinion, the combination of making an institution accountable for attaining a particular objective, guaranteeing independence in the performance of the task, and evaluating goal fulfilment should be applicable to the implementation of many more public activities than is presently the case. Much of the experience that has been acquired in the central bank world as regards distinct goals, public scrutiny, and accountability should be of value in this context.

A more independent status has heightened the importance of central banks being capable of motivating what they do and pointing to distinct results. But besides being democratically important by making it easier to exact accountability, openness has played a part in how activities have been developed. Continuously scrutinized, the Riksbank and other central banks have been obliged to strive for a leading position in every aspect of their activities. This has generated a strong need both to develop activities—by recruiting competent staff and not hesitating to adopt new methods and approaches as they arise in the academic world—and to undertake them effectively. It is not least against this background that we believe that other

policy fields stand to benefit from a development that resembles what has happened in monetary policy.

APPENDIX: A VOICE FROM THE WORLD OF RESEARCH

Our picture of developments is supplemented below with an interview with Professor Lars Svensson, Princeton University, who has combined a central role in the academic research on inflation-targeting policy with close contacts with monetary policy's practical side. The interview presents a researcher's view of developments and, we hope, makes our account more "meaty."

We put four questions about matters that are considered in this chapter. The interview is reproduced in full, and we have added a couple of explanatory footnotes.

What do you consider to have been academic research's main contributions to the present design of monetary policy in Sweden (and possibly other countries)?

I have been so closely involved in these matters that it is difficult to be objective and see it all from a distance.

Academic research has been important, for example, for arriving at an appropriate framework for monetary policy decisions—the importance of central bank independence and how to avoid an inflation bias, for instance—and featured prominently in the Riksbank Commission's report as well as in the work of the Lindbeck Commission.[37]

After the move to a flexible exchange rate in November 1992, a small group of internal economists and external academics, of whom I was one, was set up to hastily produce some papers on the monetary policy alternatives that were available and could be considered for Sweden. The Riksbank published the results and hopefully they were of some importance for the decision to adopt an inflation-targeting regime.[38] The regime was announced in January 1993, and I remember how happily surprised I was that the Riksbank's

governing board was able to agree on an inflation target so quickly. I had thought it would take much longer.

For some years from 1993 onwards, I belonged to a group of external economists who regularly met and supped with the Riksbank executives. The meetings tended to involve us academic economists insisting on what an inflation-targeting regime called for, for instance producing inflation forecasts, setting the instrumental rate so that inflation a couple of years ahead would be on target, becoming more transparent, improving the Inflation Report, and gaining credibility for the policy so that inflation expectations stabilize around the target, etc. These matters are, of course, self-evident today, but I recall many heated discussions—and occasionally an irritated atmosphere—when I and my academic colleagues thought the Riksbank executives were moving too slowly and they presumably saw us as foolhardy hotheads.

A paper of mine that was published in the *European Economic Review* in 1997 began with some notes I had made after some of these frustrating evenings that made me wonder whether the Riksbank's executives really understood the implications of working with an inflation target. The paper was an attempt to explain the logic of an inflation-targeting regime, for instance that it involved setting the interest rate so that the forecast of inflation looked good in relation to the target. The paper has been frequently quoted, so hopefully it had some effect.

The credibility of the new inflation-targeting regime was extremely poor in the initial years; inflation expectations were way above the target. In the spring and summer of 1994 the bank was rather pessimistic about the chances of fulfilling the target at all—the internal forecasts pointed to inflation being far too high. It was by no means an easy time for all those concerned. In August 1994, the Riksbank bravely initiated a period of interest rate increases, raising the level in the course of twelve months by 2 percentage points to almost 9%. This produced results and helped to stabilize both inflation and inflation expectations. Starting early in 1996, the Riksbank was then able to embark on a long period of interest rate cuts, down to a level of around 4%, without losing credibility or control of inflation.

There's plenty of relevant research on the transmission mechanism, forecasting methods, Vector Auto Regression [VAR], and so on that was no doubt invaluable for the Riksbank's economists and their analyses. In recent years, the work of Chris Sims, a highly influential researcher into methods on Bayesian estimation of macro models, has had broad applications at the Riksbank and other central banks. Michael Woodford's research has also exerted a very strong influence in recent years, particularly his emphasis on monetary policy being a matter of managing expectations.

After the earlier contributions from Milton Friedman, the perhaps best-known single contribution to research on monetary policy has come from John Taylor on his famous policy rule. Personally, as you know, I'm rather skeptical about the relevance of the Taylor rule and consider that it tends to be overemphasized or misinterpreted.

Is it your impression that practical monetary policy, or the discussion around it, has influenced academic research and, if so, in what way?

Concerning my own research, a decisive part has been played by my contacts with and experience of the Riksbank in particular, but also the Reserve Bank of New Zealand, the Bank of England, the European Central Bank, Norges Bank, the Reserve Bank of Australia, and the Federal Reserve. This applies to numerous issues: how an exchange rate band works; how to estimate the credibility of a fixed exchange rate; how to estimate and interpret forward interest rates; what an optimal inflation-targeting monetary policy looks like; real stabilization as an adjunct to stabilizing inflation; how to conduct monetary policy with reference to uncertainty about the economic situation;

the transmission mechanism and future shocks; how transparent monetary policy ought to be; how to arrive at an optimal monetary policy, given that all models are incomplete, oversimplified, and uncertain; how judgments can be used in monetary policy in a systematic, disciplined way rather than arbitrarily; etc.

Many of my colleagues and friends in the academic world have evidently been very inspired by their contacts—visits, seminars, and conferences—with central banks. A lot of central banks, including the Riksbank, have world-class researchers who regularly publish research papers and scientific articles, participate as introducers and commentators at international conferences and meetings, and are fully integrated in general in the international research community, so the opportunities for contacts and inspiration are exceedingly good.

What do you consider to be the most important processes/channels/forms for collaboration through which academic research has influenced practical monetary policy?

It is hard to tell which is most important. A number of academic papers and articles have evidently had major effects on practical monetary policy. Conferences and seminars are very important for establishing contacts. Personally, I believe it is of great importance for academics to spend some time at a central bank, for instance as a visiting researcher. As I said, my own close contacts with the Riksbank over many years have had a very strong influence on the direction of my research, but hopefully also made this research more relevant for the Riksbank and therefore perhaps more useful and influential. I believe that fairly long stays at the Reserve Bank of New Zealand and the Bank of England are also examples of such an influence in both directions.

As far as I can tell, the same applies to colleagues and friends in the academic world who have regularly visited central banks or maintained contacts with them in other ways.

Could the collaboration/interaction between researchers and practitioners have functioned better/more effectively, and, if so, how could the conditions for this be improved?

As far as the Riksbank is concerned, it's hard to see how anything could have been much better. I believe it is extremely important to have, as the Riksbank does, an internal group of world-class researchers in some of the fields that are most relevant for a central bank. Such a group is needed in order to communicate with the academic world, arrange exchanges and conferences, convert relevant research findings into practical conclusions for decision makers, and transmit the bank's own research and problems to the academic world, for example.

Perhaps the guest-researcher program might be extended to include relevant but very prominent researchers for somewhat longer (from a couple of months up to a year). The New York Fed now has a special program for visiting researchers that enables a couple of senior researchers to spend up to a year on a competitive American professor's salary. The Bank of England has developed the Houblon-Norman-George grant in this direction, and the Reserve Bank of New Zealand has a similar professorial fellowship.

NOTES

1. Two exceptions that to some extent deal with this issue are Blinder (2004) and King (2005).

2. The early adopters of these policies include New Zealand (1990), Chile (where a gradual lowering of inflation began in 1990 with the aid of annual inflation targets), Canada (1991), Israel (1991), the United Kingdom (1992), and Australia (1993). An interesting point in this context is that a price-stability target for monetary policy had actually been implemented briefly in Sweden in the 1930s, when decision makers had been inspired by contacts with academics, in the first place through the work of the Swedish economist Knut Wicksell (see Berg & Jonung, 1999).

3. See Eijffinger and Geraats (2006) for a study of how transparency has been developed in central banks. The study ranks Sveriges Riksbank as one of the world's most open central banks.

4. This view is found in, for example, Bernanke (2004).

5. Another hypothesis, which to some extent can also be said to focus on "output optimism," is that inflation (in the United States) was high because the economy's underlying potential growth rate was overestimated over long periods. Monetary policy was therefore more expansionary than was intended; see, for example, Orphanides (2002). This hypothesis, unlike those outlined in the text, does not envisage that the decision makers' "model" was fundamentally wrong, simply that an error was made in the assessment of the economy's unutilized resources.

6. See Nelson (2005) for an analysis of this hypothesis about "monetary policy neglect" in the United States and the United Kingdom.

7. The problem of time inconsistency can accordingly be seen as a further explanation, in addition to those discussed above, for the high inflation. Interpreted in this way, the problem is a variant of "output optimism," though without the assumption that decision makers believe that output can be stimulated permanently.

8. We use the term *monetary policy strategy* to denote how policy is conducted by a central bank within the framework of an inflation-targeting regime.

9. See also Faust and Henderson (2004) for a similar argument.

10. Our discussion closely resembles that in Apel, Nessén, Söderström, and Vredin (1999). A more digestible and reader-friendly account of the model will be found in Svensson (1998).

11. The assumed behavior in accordance with equation (1) (or very similar variants) has a long tradition in monetary policy analyses (see, e.g., Barro & Gordon, 1983; Kydland & Prescott, 1977; Rogoff, 1985).

12. The solution for the interest rate is sometimes called a monetary policy *reaction function*. If this function, instead of being based on an explicit optimization, is just postulated, it is sometimes known as a *simple rule*. The best-known simple rule is the so-called Taylor rule (Taylor, 1993).

13. This simplified assumption is perhaps slightly unrealistic, but this is not crucial for the points of principle we want to make here. What matters is not that the time lag is exactly two years but that there is a certain interval during which a monetary policy measure has no (appreciable) impact on inflation.

14. The situation we consider here is a permanent inflation shock, so that in order to eliminate the discrepancy between π and π^*, the central bank is obliged to act.

15. In the research literature, the cases with $\gamma = 0$ and $\gamma > 0$ are sometimes respectively called "strict" and "flexible" inflation targeting (see, e.g., Svensson, 1997).

16. The clarification in 1999 meant that the Riksbank went further than most other central banks in its ambition to specify its strategy for monetary policy. One reason was that the (independent) Riksbank wanted to make it easier for the parliament to evaluate monetary policy and exact accountability.

17. See, for example, Heikensten (2000, 2001).

18. An early account of this is found in Heikensten and Vredin (1998). They write: "We believe that the greater awareness among economists and politicians that inflation-targeting policy should be 'flexible' rather than 'strict' has helped to make monetary policy and an independent central bank more acceptable. Central banks have traditionally tended to deny that in practice monetary policy decisions are to some extent influenced by other considerations than long-term price stability. An effort is made to create an impression that low inflation is their sole concern. Like Fischer [(1996)], we believe that this strategy is unwise. It is rather the case that an open discussion about trade-offs of this kind can strengthen policy's credibility" (p. 580).

19. Today, the central banks that are commonly considered to adhere most closely to the theoretical models for an optimal inflation-targeting policy are those in Norway and New Zealand. But even they do not describe monetary policy as a completely continuous trade-off between the stability of inflation and output. Like the Riksbank, for example, they both start from a certain horizon for the normal fulfilment of the inflation target (see Berg, 2005).

20. This actually applies not only to interest rates for longer maturities but also to other financial prices that are influenced by expectations, for example, exchange rates and equity prices. However, this merely underscores that by influencing expectations a central bank can render monetary policy more powerful.

21. In an interesting paper, Faust and Leeper (2005) show that drawing conclusions about a central bank's own interest rate expectations (and expectations about macroeconomic developments) is difficult if one has to rely solely on information about the bank's conditional forecasts (forecasts based, for example, on the market's interest rate expectations). As a rule, these forecasts do not provide sufficient information for conclusions about the central bank's own plans for monetary policy. That is why it is so important in such cases that the central bank convey its view on the market's expectations.

22. The Reserve Bank of New Zealand has used its own interest rate expectations for some time, and today such expectations are also used by the central banks in Norway, the Czech Republic, and Colombia (Berg, 2005).

23. See, for example, Blinder (2006), Faust and Leeper (2005), Rudebusch and Williams (2006), Svensson (2005), and Woodford (2005). Note, however, that not all scholars agree about this; for two exceptions, see Cukierman (2006) and Mishkin (2004).

24. In the research literature, these models are labelled DSGE, which stands for Dynamic Stochastic General Equilibrium; they are based to a high degree on economic theory. See Sims (2002) for a discussion of developments in this field.

25. Rebelo (2005) and Chari and Kehoe (2006) consider some of the research that has been important for achieving these micro foundations. This development can be said to stem from the well-known criticism by the American economist Robert Lucas (1976). In simple terms, he showed that unduly aggregated models (without micro foundations) were liable to produce misleading results concerning the consequences of economic policy.

26. The model and its characteristics are documented in the Riksbank's Working Paper series; see Adolfson, Andersson, Lindé, Villani, and Vredin (2005), Adolfson, Laséen, Lindé, and Villani (2005a, 2005b), and Adolfson, Lindé, and Villani (2005).

27. See the box "GDP indicators" in Sveriges Riksbank (2005a), pp. 35–39, for an account of the time-series models the Riksbank is using at present.

28. There is, of course, nothing new about this type of interplay. We have previously mentioned that in the 1930s, monetary policy in Sweden was briefly focused on price stability, partly inspired by ideas from Knut Wicksell, active some decades earlier. Contacts with academics are a traditional feature of the central bank world, though in the post-World War II era this was not generally true of the Riksbank prior to the period considered here.

29. The decisive effort to introduce an explicit inflation target for monetary policy is said to have come from far-sighted officials in New Zealand's finance ministry and central bank. Sweden's relatively short-lived experiment with a price-stability goal in the 1930s was a thing of the past and can hardly have played a part—or even been known—when New Zealand decided to target inflation some 60 years later.

30. The contributions to this conference are collected in Leiderman and Svensson (1995).

31. The Riksbank was not a pioneer in arrangements of this type. Similar solutions had already been found in Sweden in other policy fields, for instance labor market policy.

32. The conference proceedings were published in a separate issue of the *Journal of Monetary Economics* (Volume 43, No. 3, June 1999).

33. See Sveriges Riksbank (2005b), press notice.

34. See Sveriges Riksbank (2006), press notice.

35. These aims have to a large extent been achieved; see, for example, Jondeau and Pagès (2003) and St-Amant, Tkacz, Guérard-Langlois, and Morel (2005).

36. An aspect of the interplay between academics and central banks that we have not considered at any length here is the importance of international contacts. Such contacts have a time-honored tradition in the central bank world, as can be seen, for example, from the regular meetings and seminars under the auspices of the BIS and the International Monetary Fund (IMF) and from their extensive joint training programs.

37. The Riksbank Commission and the Lindbeck Commission were two public inquiries that reported (*Riksbanken och prisstabiliteten* [The Riksbank and Price Stability], SOU 1993:20 and *Nya villkor för ekonomi och politik* [New Economic and Political Conditions], SOU 1993:16, respectively) early in 1993, just after the change to a flexible exchange rate.

38. *Monetary Policy With a Flexible Exchange Rate*, Sveriges Riksbank, December 1992.

REFERENCES

Adolfson, M., Andersson, M. K., Lindé, J., Villani, M., & Vredin, A. (2005). *Modern forecasting models in action: Improving macroeconomic analyses at central banks* (Working Paper Series, No. 188). Stockholm: Sveriges Riksbank.

Adolfson, M., Laséen, S., Lindé, J., & Villani, M. (2005a). *Are constant interest rate forecasts modest interventions? Evidence from an open economy DSGE model of the Euro area* (Working Paper Series, No. 180). Stockholm: Sveriges Riksbank.

Adolfson, M., Laséen, S., Lindé, J., & Villani, M. (2005b). *Bayesian estimation of an open economy DSGE model with incomplete pass-through* (Working Paper Series, No. 179). Stockholm: Sveriges Riksbank.

Adolfson, M., Lindé, J., & Villani, M. (2005). *Forecasting performance of an open economy dynamic stochastic general equilibrium model* (Working Paper Series, No. 190). Stockholm: Sveriges Riksbank.

Apel, M., Nessén, M., Söderström, U., & Vredin, A. (1999). Different ways of conducting inflation targeting: Theory and practice. *Sveriges Riksbank Quarterly Review, 1999*(4), 13–42.

Bäckström, U. (1994, December 9). *Monetary policy and the inflation target.* Speech at the Stockholm Stock Exchange.

Bäckström, U. (1996, September 26). *Perspective on the policy of price stability.* Speech at Stora Räntedagen.

Barro, R., & Gordon, D. (1983). Rules, discretion and reputation in a model of monetary policy. *Journal of Monetary Policy, 12*(1), 101–122.

Berg, C. (2005). Experience of inflation targeting in 20 countries. *Sveriges Riksbank Economic Review, 2005*(1), 20–47.

Berg, C., & Jonung, L. (1999). Pioneering price level targeting: The Swedish experience 1931–1937. *Journal of Monetary Economics, 43*(3), 525–552.

Bernanke, B. S. (2004, February 20). *The great moderation.* Address to the Eastern Economic Association, Washington, DC.

Blinder, A. S. (2004). *The quiet revolution: Central banking goes modern.* New Haven, CT: Yale University Press.

Blinder, A. S. (2006, June). *Monetary policy today: Sixteen questions and about twelve answers.* Paper presented at the Banco de España conference "Central Banks in the 21st Century." Madrid.

Chari, V. V., & Kehoe, P. J. (2006). *Modern macroeconomics in practice: How theory is shaping policy.* Research Department Staff Report 376, Federal Reserve Bank of Minneapolis.

Cukierman, A. (2006, January). *The limits of transparency.* Paper presented at the American Economic Association meeting (session "Monetary Policy Transparency and Effectiveness"), Boston.

Eijffinger, S. C. W., & Geraats, P. M. (2006). How transparent are central banks? *European Journal of Political Economy, 22*(1), 1–21.

Faust, J., & Henderson, D. (2004). Is inflation targeting best practice monetary policy? *Federal Reserve Bank of St. Louis Review, 86*(4), 117–144.

Faust, J., & Leeper, E. M. (2005, June). *Forecasts and inflation reports: An evaluation.* Paper presented at the Sveriges Riksbank conference "Inflation Targeting: Implementation, Communication, and Effectiveness," Stockholm.

Fischer, S. (1996, August). Why are central banks pursuing long-run price stability? In *Achieving price stability* (pp. 7–34). Proceedings of symposium in Jackson Hole, WY, sponsored by the Federal Reserve Bank of Kansas City.

Friedman, M. (1968). The role of monetary policy. *American Economic Review, 58*(1), 1–17.

Heikensten, L. (1997, March 13). *Monetary policy and the economy*. Address at an event arranged by the Federation of Swedish County Councils and the Swedish Association of Local Authorities, Stockholm.

Heikensten, L. (1999). The Riksbank's inflation target: Clarification and evaluation. *Sveriges Riksbank Quarterly Review, 1999*(1), 5–17.

Heikensten, L. (2000, November 7). *Six monetary policy issues*. Address to the Umeå School of Economics, Umeå, Sweden.

Heikensten, L. (2001, May 9). *Concerning clarity and flexibility*. Address to the Centre for Business and Policy Studies (SNS), Stockholm.

Heikensten, L., & Vredin, A. (1998). Inflationsmålet och den svenska penningpolitiken: Erfarenheter och problem [The inflation target and Swedish monetary policy: Experiences and problems]. *Ekonomisk Debatt 1998*(8), 573–593.

Jondeau, E., & Pagès, H. (2003, May). *Benchmarking research in European central banks*. Paper presented at the Sveriges Riksbank conference "Central Bank Efficiency," Stockholm.

King, M. (2005, May 17). *Practice ahead of theory*. Mais Lecture, City University, London.

Kydland, F., & Prescott, E. (1977). Rules rather than discretion: The inconsistency of optimal plans. *Journal of Political Economy, 85*(3), 473–491.

Leiderman, L., & Svensson, L. E. O. (Eds.). (1995). *Inflation targets*. London: Centre for Economic Policy Research.

Lindbeck, A. (2003). Stabiliseringspolitiken i teori och praktik [Stabilization policy in theory and practice]. In M. Persson & E. Skult (Eds.), *Tillämpad makroekonomi* [Applied macroeconomics]. Stockholm: SNS Förlag.

Lucas, R. E., Jr. (1976). Econometric policy evaluation: A critique. In K. Brunner & A. H. Meltzer (Eds.), *The Phillips curve and labor markets* (pp. 19–46). Amsterdam: North-Holland.

McCallum, B. T. (1998). *Recent developments in monetary policy analysis: The roles of theory and evidence* (National Bureau of Economic Research Working Paper No. 7088). Cambridge: MIT Press.

Mishkin, F. S. (2004). *Can central bank transparency go too far?* (National Bureau of Economic Research Working Paper No. 10829). Cambridge: MIT Press.

Nelson, E. (2005). The great inflation of the seventies: What really happened? *Advances in Macroeconomics, 5*(1), Article 3.

Nya villkor för ekonomi och politik [New economic and political conditions]. SOU 1993:16. Stockholm: Allmänna Förlaget.

Orphanides, A. (2002). Monetary policy rules and the great inflation. *American Economic Review Papers and Proceedings, 92*(2), 115–120.

Phelps, E. S. (1967). Phillips curves, expectations of inflation, and optimal unemployment over time. *Economica, 34*(135), 254–281.

Phillips, A. W. (1958). The relation between unemployment and the rate of change of money wage rates in the United Kingdom, 1861–1957. *Economica, 25*(100), 283–299.

Rebelo, S. (2005). Real business cycle models: Past, present and future. *Scandinavian Journal of Economics, 107*(2), 217–238.

Riksbanken och prisstabiliteten [The Riksbank and price stability]. SOU 1993:20. Stockholm: Allmänna Förlaget.

Rogoff, K. (1985). The optimal degree of commitment to an intermediate monetary target. *Quarterly Journal of Economics, 100*(4), 1169–1189.

Rudebusch, G. D., & Williams, J. C. (2006). *Revealing the secrets of the temple: The value of publishing interest rate projections.* Unpublished manuscript, Federal Reserve Bank of San Francisco.

Simmons, B. A. (2006). *The future of central bank cooperation,* (BIS Working Paper No. 200). Basel, Switzerland: Bank for International Settlements.

Sims, C. A. (2002). The role of models and probabilities in the monetary policy process. *Brookings Papers on Economic Activity, 2,* 1–62.

St-Amant, P., Tkacz, G., Guérard-Langlois, A., & Morel, L. (2005). *Quantity, quality, and relevance: Central bank research, 1990–2003* (Working Paper 2005-37). Ottawa: Bank of Canada.

Summers, P. M. (2005). What caused the great moderation? Some cross-country evidence. *Federal Reserve Bank of Kansas City Economic Review, 2005*(3rd quarter), 5–32.

Svensson, L. E. O. (1997). Inflation forecast targeting: Implementing and monitoring inflation targets. *European Economic Review, 41*(6), 1111–1146.

Svensson, L. E. O. (1998). Inflationsmål i en öppen ekonomi: Strikt eller flexibelt? [Inflation target in an open economy: Strict or flexible?]. *Ekonomisk Debatt, 1998*(6), 431–439.

Svensson, L. E. O. (2005, October). *Optimal inflation targeting: Further developments of inflation targeting.* Paper presented at the Banco Central de Chile conference "Monetary Policy Under Inflation Targeting." Santiago.

Sveriges Riksbank. (1992, December). *Monetary policy with a flexible exchange rate.* Stockholm: Author.

Sveriges Riksbank. (1996, December 5). [Press notice]. Available from http://www .riksbank.com/upload/2606/NR43e.pdf

Sveriges Riksbank. (2005a). *Inflation Report, 2005*(3). Available from http://www .riksbank.com/pagefolders/21855/2005_3_eng.pdf

Sveriges Riksbank. (2005b, November 28). [Press notice]. Available from http://www .riksbank.com/pagefolders/23011/nr72e.pdf

Sveriges Riksbank. (2006). *Monetary policy in Sweden.* Available from http://www .riksbank.com/upload/Dokument_riksbank/Kat_publicerat/Rapporter/2007/ monetary_policy_07.pdf

Taylor, J. B. (1992). The great inflation, the great deflation, and policies for future price stability. In A. Blundell-Wignall (Ed.), *Inflation, disinflation and monetary policy* (pp. 9–34). Sydney, Australia: Ambassador Press.

Taylor, J. B. (1993). Discretion versus policy rules in practice. *Carnegie-Rochester Series on Public Policy, 39,* 195–214.

Woodford, M. (2005, June). *Central-bank communication and policy effectiveness.* Paper presented at the Sveriges Riksbank conference "Inflation Targeting: Implementation, Communication, and Effectiveness," Stockholm.

CHAPTER 19

Bridging the Academic-Practitioner Divide

A Case Study Analysis of Business School Collaboration With Industry[1,2]

DAVID KNIGHTS

CATRINA ALFEROFF

KEN STARKEY

NICK TIRATSOO

ABSTRACT

This chapter discusses industry-academic collaborative networks emanating from business schools in the United Kingdom, informed by an analysis of one such network. We set this presentation in the context of debates about business schools that are currently exercising the business and management academic community. These debates focus upon the extent of the contribution of business schools to management theory and practice.

THE RELEVANCE PROBLEM IN BUSINESS SCHOOLS

In this chapter our intent is to examine industry-academic collaborative networks primarily through a case study of a financial services network—the Financial Services Research Forum (FSRF)—in which all of the authors have been actively involved in a management and/or research capacity.[3] We examine the pitfalls and predicaments of bridging the academic-practitioner divide as part of a contribution to the debate on the role and relevance of business schools (Alferoff &

Knights, 2005; Knights, 2006; Starkey & Tiratsoo, 2007). In this debate, Pfeffer and Fong (2003) generated considerable controversy by arguing that business schools have failed to deliver both on teaching and, in terms of knowledge creation, on research, where they are simply "not very effective in the creation of business ideas" (Pfeffer & Fong, 2004, p. 1502). Influence exists, but academics learn more from business practitioners than business learns from the proliferation of academic research about business.[4] This echoes Hambrick's (1993) lament, "What if the academy really mattered?" and the various critiques of business school research for lacking relevance (Starkey & Madan, 2001).

In a similar vein, Bennis and O'Toole (2005) argue that business schools have lost their way, in part, because their research has embraced a scientific model that distances it from practice, that is, one that, makes it irrelevant. Leading business and management journals, they argue, are distinguished by their search for academic credibility and peer recognition and pay little heed to the interests of practitioners. This is problematic, considering that most business and management schools espouse a dual mission—the education of practitioners and the creation of knowledge through research. "By allowing the scientific research model to drive out all others, business schools are institutionalizing their own irrelevance. We fear that this will be a difficult problem to correct because many business professors lack enough confidence in the legitimacy of their enterprise to define their own agenda. For example, business economics journals today are practically indistinguishable from traditional economics journals. And not to be 'out-scienced,' management researchers now focus on technical issues that have the look and feel of topics studied by their peers in harder disciplines" (p. 100).

Ironically, this drive to emulate the traditional and longer-established, and therefore more reputable, social sciences occurs at a time when the nature of knowledge in other disciplines is in transition, driven by the need to more closely integrate theory and practice, discovery and application (Gibbons et al., 1994, p. 49). While not focusing attention exclusively on business, there are significant implications for the debate about business schools in the work of Gibbons et al. (see also Grey, 2001; Knights, 2004; Starkey & Madan, 2001). They propose that a distinction be made between what is termed Mode 1 academic research, which is typically seen as theoretical, disciplinary with long horizons, and peer-assessed within the community, and Mode 2 research, in which knowledge production is more closely tied to "the context of application or use" (Gibbons et al., 1994, p. 17). This new, Mode 2, practitioner-oriented form of research is transdisciplinary, problem-based, immediate, and judged by its utility in practical situations.

Huff and Huff (2001) take on board the Mode 1/2 distinctions but go on to prescribe a larger Mode 3 role for the business school. Here they propose research collaborations that are broader in scope, multidisciplinary, appealing to a wide range of stakeholders, and with a social edge as a possibility for the future. These are idealized forms, and there are probably many business schools that conduct research outside, or as hybrid constructions of, such typological formats. However, what these authors do signal is the necessity for the business school to exercise boundary-scanning operations in order to ensure the relevance of its research to the wider community and to bring about closer relationships between itself and the practitioner world.

In publicly funded higher education systems, the recent trend has been to make higher education institutions more accountable to society's needs, as interpreted by government. In the United Kingdom, this is framed by the Department of Trade and Industry in terms of developing the knowledge economy. Universities, for example, are also urged to play a significant role in regional development in terms of knowledge production and encouraging entrepreneurship. In an effort to promote industry-academic collaboration, the UK Treasury-commissioned *Lambert Review* (UK Treasury, 2003) argues that the biggest single challenge lies in boosting the demand from business, rather than in increasing the supply of products and services from universities (p. 10). The report advocates the development of forums that bring academics and businesspeople together in order to increase the chance that people with common interests and goals will find new ways to develop fruitful partnerships in terms of innovations.[5]

Aside from knowledge/technology transfer partnerships (Wright, Lockett, Tiratsoo, & Alferoff, 2005), it is possible to develop networks and forums for the pursuit of innovation, learning, and economic goals between the university and business (Boucher, Conway, & Van Der Meer, 2003). While instituting such bodies would appear to be wholly beneficial in theory, practicing managers and management researchers are often skeptical, for, as Maclean and Macintosh (2002) found in an academic-industry research collaboration on strategic transformation, "despite their common concerns . . . they remain two distinct audiences." Skepticism of this nature has plagued many attempts at academic-industry collaboration. For example, the FENIX Centre at the Stockholm School of Economics and Chalmers University of Technology met with a fairly hostile reception in their own institutions when first developing a research and doctoral program involving the secondment of business practitioners to university. At the early stages of conducting action research, FENIX failed to convince

> the host university that there was interesting learning coming from the center. The rationale of the university representatives and senior faculty was again centered on the idea that populistic research produced little or no academic value if based on a set of projects jointly defined together with

companies. In addition, the university representatives expressed their reluctance to take part in research pursuing action research methodologies, based on the basic assumption that building a truly joint collaboration with companies will take substantial time and energy and is likely to yield questionable results at best. (Adler & Norrgren, 2004, p. 60)

Industry-Academic Networks

In the context of the increased emphasis upon the need for the closer alignment of business and university, we deemed it appropriate to conduct a study of industry-academic collaborations in the United Kingdom. According to our survey of some 47 such collaborations, there appear to be around 17 business schools currently hosting academic-practitioner research networks or best-practice clubs (Alferoff & Knights, 2005). Primary empirical research was conducted in 11 of these, which represented the full range of activities relevant to the whole sample. These different forms of activities include research networks, best-practice clubs, and networks dedicated to policy or international or regional development. In this chapter, we focus in particular on one research network with which we are familiar. First, we present a brief summary of the nature of the collaborations.

Our research examined a continuum of forms of network collaboration ranging from, at one extreme, the mere dissemination of knowledge in knowledge clubs or knowledge transfer arrangements, to coproduction of knowledge at the other extreme (see Figure 19.1). While we have found very few examples of the latter, some of the networks do seek to produce new knowledge through their collaborations. Although most business-school-hosted forums and networks have knowledge generation as a primary aim, for many the transmission process would more realistically be described merely as knowledge sharing. They simply come to a common understanding or disseminate recent business school knowledge to practitioners. Achieving the stated aim of carrying out relevant "leading edge" knowledge production collaboratively is a rarity. Only a few research forums and action research roundtables have achieved this sought-after result of highly collaborative and sustained academic-practitioner relationships. We depict the different forms of network below to suggest where they lie on a knowledge-collaboration continuum.

Academics generally initiate collaborative networks to address a diverse, though not mutually exclusive, range of problems. The following were given as the reasons for establishing the different networks we investigated:

- Creating a network of fee-paying members to help secure the financial status of an existing research center (FSRF)
- Exploring, developing, or formalizing existing relationships, whether these have been a set of consultancy contacts, locations of previous research, informal contacts, or a more institutionalized arrangement relating to funded research (FSRF, Knet 1, Bankclub, Hrnet 2, Measnet, and Perfnet)
- For entrepreneurial reasons (Innovnet, Knet 1, and Knet 2)
- To develop strategic business or knowledge management tools (Knet 1, Knet 2, and Measnet)
- To improve organizational development and working practices (Hrnet 1)
- To gain credibility and reputation (FSRF, Knet 2)

- To exploit an available grant or funding opportunities for regional, national, or international social and economic development (Knet 1, Innovnet, and Socnet)
- In response to government and/or regulatory policy changes (FSRF, Innovnet, and Knet 1)

Practitioners are enrolled into networks or forums on the promise of a variety of rewards. Practitioner members of both Knet 1 and Innovnet valued the network for introducing them to ideas and practical solutions that they would not find in their own work environment. Networking itself is seen as a major benefit for practitioners, and this has been a strategic focus of some of the networks; the FSRF, for example (see below), has sought to build a group of associate members consisting of government departments, regulators, and consumer groups that have a policy connection with financial services, and this has enhanced the standing of the network with the practitioner members. Aside from the presentations by academics and thought leaders, practitioner members from three of the networks—Hrnet 1, Knet 1, and Measnet—told us that the social aspect of meeting with other members who are going through similar experiences was the most valued aspect of their membership. According to a detailed study conducted by one of the authors (Tiratsoo, 2005), the members of the FSRF take networking very seriously indeed, and in fact rate it as the prime benefit that is available to them.

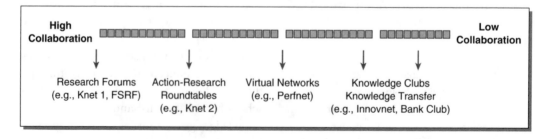

Figure 19.1   High and Low Collaboration in Knowledge Production

Networking is valuable to the firms involved for a number of reasons. For example, a manager from a large utility company values the network for

> the assurance from other companies that are on the group that their approaches are as chaotic as ours if you like. We're all sort of struggling to get the right things in place but no one can do it perfectly. You know? So it makes you sort of . . . you get the ideas, you realise you're on generally the right track, the rest of industry is broadly at the same stage of evolution and muddling along together. So it's those sorts of areas really, yeah. (Interview with Measnet, December 8, 2005)

Here the benefits of the network seem to fill an emotional need as much as a need for new knowledge generation. Consolation is drawn from the fact that all the players in the industry are struggling with a lack of clear knowledge about what to do!

The benefits of these networks for academics also vary from providing comparatively unproblematic access to research sites to providing seed corn or pilot funding for projects that could ultimately be submitted to one of the research councils, to helping teachers keep up-to-date with the latest business practices, to facilitating lucrative consultancy contracts. In the FSRF network, members were asked for research topics and interaction with them was sought both before setting up research projects and occasionally throughout. Some of the networks (e.g., Knet 1) build into their fee structure a small amount of bespoke research or consultancy for a member, which can readily be a sprat to catch a mackerel leading on to longer-term consultancy arrangements. Measnet and the FSRF are examples of networks that have been comparatively successful in using member subscriptions as seed corn funding prior to securing larger dedicated research grants. Mixing regularly with

practitioners is also seen as lending credibility when teaching MBA students, because contemporary management problems and their solutions can be brought directly into the classroom. Where consultancy work is conducted, it adds further credibility to what is being taught.

Despite the benefits, maintaining industry-academic networks is painstakingly troublesome because a diverse range of practical problems beset their continuity. First is the fact that practitioners invariably see the network as fairly marginal to their immediate and often targeted demands. Consequently, attendance at meetings is patchy and hence commitment to the activity is limited. External and internal mobility of staff in private industry, combined with limited attempts to spread network research materials and information around their respective companies, results in high membership attrition rates. The executive director of the FSRF summed up the problem as follows:

> We do continually lose people. In part it's because we're not one of those wobbling plates, we're nice to have but we're not vital. And because we've still got too much of our advocacy at too low a level, when push comes to shove and the budget when the axe goes round, we're a very you know, easy . . . you know, painless way of [trimming budgets]. So we are vulnerable but we have lessened our churn this last couple of years. (Waite, 2005, p. 7)

The problems of network continuity cannot be exclusively laid at the door of the practitioners, however, because academic support is neither wholly enthusiastic nor unreserved. Most academics prefer to focus on their scholarly publications, which rarely coincide with the less esoteric interests of business practitioners. In the United Kingdom, this is understandable because current systems of research accountability are strongly driven by the RAE (Research Assessment Exercise) in which the gold standard is publication in academic journals. At the institutional level of the university or business school, senior staff welcome the funding and status that derives from industry-academic networks, but even they are not always willing to back such activities if they involve significant opportunity costs in terms of traditional academic activity.

In what follows, we focus in more detail on one industry-university collaboration—the FSRF, a research forum established to conduct research in and on the financial services industry—not least because we have detailed personal knowledge of its genesis and development, as one of the authors created the network and three of the authors have worked with the network in an executive and research capacity (see note 1). The FSRF is also interesting because, to the best of our knowledge, it is one of the longest-standing such research collaborations in the UK business and management school context, if not the longest.

First, we explain the conceptual and theoretical lens we brought to bear on our case study.

UNDERSTANDING NETWORKS: ACTOR-NETWORK THEORY

For conceptual purposes, we found actor-network theory (ANT) a powerful aid to understanding the dynamics of business-academic networks. ANT has evolved largely as a method within the sociology of scientific knowledge designed to understand how the conditions for the development of knowledge are not simply intellectual, technical, or scientific but also, crucially, *social*. For ideas to be transformed into knowledge, they generally go through a number of not necessarily sequential stages involving a wide range of human and nonhuman actors. ANT provides an alternative model to the more common diffusion theory of knowledge development

in which "progress" is deemed to follow from the "discovery" of established facts and technical artifacts. By contrast, the model developed by ANT suggests that facts and machines are social accomplishments—humans and their nonhuman allies actively produce them through networks of translation where controversies are temporarily settled (Latour, 1987, pp. 132–133).

According to ANT, networks of human actors (people) and nonhuman actors (e.g., institutions, natural forces, technical devices, money) develop through the following four moments of translation, as described by Callon (1986, 1991):

Problematization: a moment when certain problems of a technical or social nature are defined and examined in terms of what is proposed and promoted as a means of resolving them

Interessement: the moment of persuasion where the interests of significant others can be best served by adopting the solutions offered by a new actor-network

Enrollment: a process of recruitment of both human and nonhuman actors to the network and their lock-in through taking on specific roles and responsibilities for the development of the solutions with which they have become identified

Mobilization: a moment of institutionalization in which actors and resources are mobilized to ensure that the network achieves its objectives and sustains the commitment and energy of those it has enrolled

At any one of these moments, the network can become an "obligatory passage point" where anyone seeking to solve the problem(s) that it addresses has at least to enter the network, even if only later to leave it in pursuit of an alternative. As enrollment and mobilization of people and resources proceeds, the network will reach a state of "irreversibility" when the network has become highly durable. Irreversibility is created by, for example, eradicating alternative solutions to the same problem or creating scripts that lock people in. As we shall see in our more intensive case study of the FSRF, the long-term survival of research networks depends upon a continuous cycling through the four moments of translation. Irreversibility may be the goal, but it is a prize that is hard to win and has a price to pay. In what follows we weave theory and experience in the examination of the development of the FSRF. We focus on two main issues in its development: the creation of the network and the search for network sustainability and irreversibility.

FSRF: CREATING A NETWORK

The FSRF brings together business school academics, industry practitioners, and other interested parties in order to "stimulate collaboration between management in financial services and business/management academics; . . . promote, facilitate and disseminate leading edge academic research of relevance to management; [and] . . . raise the profile of such collaboration through networking and publishing." The FSRF was founded in 1993 in a United Kingdom university (see Note 1). The vision of its founder was "to establish a regular dialogue and debate on issues of common concern" for those—academics and practitioners—active in the financial services industry. Initial funding for research from major banks, insurance companies, and mortgage companies was leveraged in what was then a novel manner by offering membership in a research network in return for an annual subscription. The unique selling point (USP), the hook for *interessement*, was the opportunity to participate in fashioning a research agenda that was

much more long-term, original, and strategic than was normal from such collaborations. Firm enrollment followed apace and soon there were 26 fee-paying members, including Barclays, Co-operative Bank, Lloyds TSB, Midland Bank, Nat West, Royal Bank of Scotland, General Accident, Royal Sun Alliance, Scottish Equitable, Britannia, Coventry, and Nationwide Building Societies.

However, defeat was almost snatched from the jaws of this victory. The FSRF met opposition from academics on the grounds that it was "selling out to industry" and that it was in effect a servant of power and capital, providing little more that a public relations activity for an industry that, even then, was enjoying comparatively poor public press. A sort of guerrilla war erupted between those claiming to occupy the academic high ground and the FSRF team committed to collaboration. For the purists, collaboration was, as in other wars, a dirty word! To cut a long story short, the founder decided to leave a university he had worked at for more than a quarter of a century and moved to Nottingham university, where the FSRF has remained since.

However, the FSRF had to go through a new phase of establishment in its second home, justifying its unique approach to research and overcoming the antipathy/animosity of those who had no time for this kind of research. What probably saved the situation was the engagement of a new actor in the role of executive director (see Note 1), a position previously held by the academic founder. Someone with senior executive experience in the financial services industry and with the academic credibility of a Ph.D. in marketing now filled this position. He had a number of pressing problems to address—in particular, the engagement of new staff in the applied kind of research projects the FSRF was commissioning and the reengagement of corporate interest in a context where a fierce focus on costs often meant that even the modest fees charged by the FSRF had to be justified in terms of contribution to the bottom line. On the academic side, the problem was, basically, to divert staff from their preoccupation with the forthcoming Research Assessment Exercise (RAE), and to convince them that there was something to be gained by conducting industry-commissioned research. This remains a perennial problem. However, enough interest was shown by tenured professors, who did not have the same career worries as junior staff, and they were the main engine of research, supplemented by contract research staff.

The FSRF's newly developed strategy was two-fold: to professionalize its operations and to strengthen its claim to a core research competence. The latter was signaled by including the word *research* in its title.[6] More difficult, though, was the struggle to align the research with the aspirations of member organizations, something the executive director realized when, while conducting a feedback exercise, he was told, "the thing is, you're not scratching where we're itching"! The FSRF started a process of subtle reorientation that, using our ANT schema, can be seen as a reshaping of the network by extension. Partly this was done by extending the reach of the network, adding to the provider membership other stakeholders drawn from the area of consumers and regulators. This led to the recruitment of the Financial Services Authority (FSA) and the Consumers' Association (CA), among others. This extended the FSRF's research reach to a broader focus upon the dynamics of interaction between provision, consumption, and regulation.

Cross-cutting research issues, such as trust, were identified and worked on. Meetings were reorganized not just as showcases for academic research, which was not always successful in holding member interest, but as windows onto a broad array of interested parties and their views on the industry, consultants, consumer groups, regulators, and industry analysts. Attendance at these meetings mushroomed. The meetings themselves were no longer located mainly in the cloisters of academia, but took place in the headquarters of leading firms in the City of London and in the corridors of power—not literally "corridors," but high-status venues in government ministries such as the Department of Work and Pensions and the Treasury in Whitehall. The latter meeting was particularly memorable, as it coincided with a demonstration on the balcony of another ministry close by of Fathers for Justice dressed as cartoon superheroes! The solemnity of the surroundings, notwithstanding the distractions outside, symbolized the coming of age of the FSRF. It was assisted by the first minister at the Treasury— the Right Honourable Boateng—giving the opening address.

The background to the FSRF's establishment and search for legitimacy is that there is no obvious space that provides a fertile ecology for the growth and survival of academic-practitioner networks, which are generally peripheral to the main research and teaching activities of the management department or business school. When it comes to publishing, aligning the interests of the business school with the interests of the practitioner-oriented network presents the academic with a dilemma that is not easy to resolve. Academics involved in the running of such networks may, in some cases, suffer from lack of opportunities, as this comment from an academic who eventually closed down another network that she had run for 10 years demonstrates:

What we haven't got is any articulation about what the middle people do, the people like me. So what's the career path? How do they evaluate it? Because, of course, some stuff, which is practice-oriented, is rubbish, just as some stuff which is blue skies is, so, what we don't have is any way of discriminating between good practice research and bad practice research and that's a problem as well. So, we just need a clear articulation and a way of measuring what it is and a way of creating career structures for people, which provides them with a feeling of value and meaning. We'd sent about four articles to AMR [Academy of Management Review] and they'd all been rejected and I just thought, "Oh, I've got to do something else now." But, it was very successful for what it was and the companies would still now say it was the most important learning event that they'd been involved in. (Research interview, June 15, 2004)

For business, these networks are, in the main, interesting, unusual, but peripheral ventures, not clearly integrated with mainstream business needs.

NETWORK SUSTAINABILITY AND IRREVERSIBILITY

In practice, networks exist in a state of uncertainty, and attempts at enrollment and mobilization of the network can be particularly precarious due to the difficulties in reconciling the interests of academic and practitioner participants. In the FSRF's case, it had the difficult task of configuring itself twice as it moved host institutions. Relationships cohered in the first instance around particular projects. However, once a project is complete, the momentum for extending the relationship into the long term around knowledge sharing and a research agenda may slowly dissipate. It requires continual regeneration of interest (*interessement*) to keep members enrolled because they will be continuously reviewing the value added by the network, especially where there is a financial cost in an annual subscription. Money serves as a significant intermediary that keeps these networks in motion and

maintains the production of knowledge, the texts (research reports, workshop materials, articles, and so on) through which it is distributed, and the communication systems that are necessary to renew enrollments and mobilize other human and nonhuman actors (Callon, 1986). Beyond the benefits for the companies involved, networks must always hold the interest of individuals.

Threats to survival come from a variety of sources: Companies fail to renew membership due to cost, changes of personnel, mergers, or a decline in interest; the network loses its sense of direction, never takes root in members' perceptions, or is insufficiently diverse, dynamic, and flexible to meet changing circumstances; inadequate support is provided by the university and business school; and so on. In short, the absence of a defined solution to a shared problem, limited interest, an insufficiently solid enrollment, and/or mobilization of human and nonhuman actors and resources may have prevented many of these networks from securing a position of irreversibility. Controversies surrounding the translations of problems into solutions through participation in the network have not been forgotten or settled so that the identities of actors are not inscribed in them. Speaking about the problems of irreversibility, Callon (1986) argues: "actors are a hybrid group—consistently threatened by dissension and internal crises—no strategy is assured of victory—irreversibility increases to the extent that it is inscribed in a bundle of inter-relationships" (p. 150).

The FSRF was struggling with the problem of reversibility on a number of fronts. Having negotiated the move between institutions, it seemed to lose momentum in its new home. Member interest was dwindling, as evidenced by a falloff of attendance at meetings, the loss of a few activist members, and a lack of academic commitment to developing its limited research program. The enrollment of new actors from government and other areas and an emphasis on more high-profile venues and more practitioner-oriented presentations were factors introduced to regenerate member interest. Recently, the FSRF has developed a trust index that will be updated on a biannual basis, and this could well have a similar effect. The ultimate weapon in seeking irreversibility could be to enroll the media more effectively to ensure a continued profile. In all of these developments, it can be seen that these innovations represent chains of "translations" that help to hold the network together and perhaps transform it into a state of "irreversibility" (Callon, 1986, 1991) in which members would find it difficult to withdraw.

The FSRF's research has continued to produce and is impressive by some measures. Its Web site currently contains about 60 reports on various facets of the financial services industry, dealing with consumer issues and provider-led topics. Some of this research has proved influential and has been quoted in government reports and in publications of the Financial Services Authority and the Organisation for Economic Co-operation and Development. The FSRF is now regularly approached for its opinion on financial services matters. However, its impact on the day-to-day activity of its members is more difficult to discern. One member found only 25% of FSRF reports valuable. Aligning the interests of academics and practitioners around the research agenda is often difficult. Practitioners, in the main, fail to be convinced of the value of "in-depth" research that takes more than a few months to complete. Indeed, practitioners sometimes wonder what academics actually do with their time. (The very word *academic* sometimes has pejorative connotations: impractical, divorced from the concerns of the "real world," irrelevant.) Academic presentations at network meetings are often seen as "too slow and cumbersome," high on data, rigor, proof, and correlations, but low on impact or usefulness. They are—the ultimate criticism—likely to fail the "chief executive test," unable to hold his or her attention for more than a brief moment. What the corporate participants want is conciseness, focused brevity, a simple message. Long reports are now reduced to three- to four-page executive briefings, but some think even these too long and want the message summed up in three or four bullet points! Too often, the academic research is seen, at best, as "interesting, must get round to reading some time," but likely to disappear deeper and deeper into the filing cabinet or cupboard. Conversely, the academics that are involved in FSRF projects find it difficult to engage the interests of practitioners or to extend their attention spans. Nonetheless, as one of the chairmen would say when introducing new members to the FSRF: "What you get from the academics may seem a bit 'off the wall,' but it is something to make you think, and certainly a refreshing change from the off-the-shelf material that is thrown at us routinely from management consultants."

Networks suffer attrition. Academics find other research activities that are less difficult to manage. According to our informants, networks tend to lose corporate members for a number of reasons: Peripheral activities fall to the knife when rationalization demands corporate cutbacks, under the threat or reality of mergers, or when perceptions of the value added by the network seem not to justify the subscription fee. Sustaining enrollment and ensuring a mix of members and activities poses a constant challenge for the organizers of these networks. Garcia (2004) observed:

> The network can be sustained for longer if the translator (an individual, a group, or an organization) becomes an "obligatory point of passage" to solve the problem presented, and for the enrolled actors to exist and develop, and solve their own problems. The

articulation of the identities of enrolled actors thus is an effect of the translator positioning her/him/itself in a certain way. (p. 8)

Identity is important. What form of identity does membership in the network offer? For some, what is available is a quality of dialogue that is in short supply elsewhere. The specifics of the research aside, what meetings offer is a chance for unusual forms of networking and the opportunity to see oneself as other stakeholders see one. The academic (here the word is positive) credibility of the events legitimizes the quality and the substance of the dialogue. The industry has a space in which it can acknowledge its problems and challenges. In the words of an FSRF corporate representative, one speaker was

> very controversial and scathing about different things, and, you know, whether you agree with it or not, it's good to be challenged. And I think that, you know, it's back to "perception is reality": If people are saying that about our industry, then we've got a perception problem. And so I think from that point of view, it does challenge you and it does make you think. And you might not agree with them, whether that's a political or personal stance, but you've got to be open to these things. (Tiratsoo, 2005, p. 9)

The role of the network here is less the explicit coproduction of knowledge through research than it is the opportunity for dialogue. Perhaps the FSRF's USP is actually its ability to promote new opportunities for dialogue through managing a complex network of stakeholders; its core competence, the production of knowledge through its network-brokering role rather than through actually conducting research.

This interpretation emphasizes the spoken rather than the written word. We do not want to give the impression that the writing of research reports is purely symbolic. Some

do read the reports and do learn from them, but not in a straightforward, linear fashion. As one senior strategy member described it, "you might take that and a bunch of other things, and you might extract a few, you know, key points out of it, and then that might go towards a formulation of a strategy." Another very active member agreed, analyzing the benefits that the Forum had brought him as follows:

> It's not necessarily going to be something . . . where I'd say "oh, actually yeah, that's going to really make a difference strategically in the next two or three years, directly." It may be taking an insight which makes you want to go off and look at something else we haven't thought about or something . . . you're saying have a look at something or my colleagues look at something or this is what we need to do, it's sometimes interesting getting a different interpretation on that. And sometimes you get into quite interesting insights. (Interview with member, February 25, 2005)

Cause and effect are difficult to disentangle, but a positive learning process seems to be taking place, and attendance at FSRF meetings, like the FSRF's reputation, continues to grow.

NETWORK DILEMMAS: MEETING THE CHALLENGE

Deliberations about the relevance of business schools have been a central focus of our research on knowledge production, brokering, and dissemination through academic-industry networks. Critics have argued that academic production often fails to be applicable, relevant, and timely and is frequently stylistically impenetrable (see also Kelemen & Bansal, 2002). As was pointed out earlier, the UK Treasury-commissioned *Lambert Review* advocated the development of forums that bring academics and businesspeople together in order to increase the chance that people with common interests and goals will find new ways to develop fruitful partnerships in terms of innovations. Our research into 11 of these business school industry-academic networks shows a very mixed bag of activities. We have argued that, at least in the case of the FSRF, the evolving relationship itself could be seen as innovative or as an attempt to promote research innovation.

The oldest networks in this study had survived for between 10 and 13 years, surviving relocation changes in administration and direction. However, organizers of these networks often found it difficult to interest and involve more junior members of the business school faculty, because of the weak link between the network and refereed publications for the RAE. These networks were, in most cases, peripheral to the main activities of the business school, and where they broke down, it was usually because of a failure of academic involvement and commitment. It became clear from our research that industry-academic networks could only survive where both human actors (members) and non-human actors (resources, reputation, media attention) were mobilized. This generally involved two strategies: (1) a constant process of recruitment of new member organizations, and (2) a reenlivening and reshuffling of existing members by the creation of new themed presentations, deepening the involvement of members by their participation in special interest groups, giving presentations at meetings or conferences, or writing papers for distribution through newsletters and by electronic means. Another way of reengaging the membership is to tie them to the network through the coproduction of knowledge, but this occurred in only three of the networks studied, and even then only intermittently.

In summary, the networks described here vary in style, scope, and mission, but insofar

as they survive it is because practitioners can see the network as at least potentially resolving some of their problems. Practitioners are aware that universities can pursue research less trammeled by the demands of short-term profits and offer insights that are comparatively independent of political or economic interests. Professors, outside the university, are viewed as an occupational group of high trustworthiness. (Willmott, 2006)! Academics, particularly—though not exclusively—in business schools, are conscious of the problems of pursuing "ivory tower" research that seems to have no connection with, or relevance to, the management practices that are their subject matter. They also are aware that strong links with business help resolve problems of research access, legitimacy, and inadequate public funding. In addition, networks are able to enroll a wide range of corporations and other bodies such as government departments, regulators, and consumer interest groups, all of which provide access to different points of view but more importantly accord the networks added legitimacy. A range of significant human actors (government ministers, for example) and nonhuman actors (prestigious venues, for example) are enrolled, thus mobilizing increased resources that begin to transform the participation into an obligatory passage point and possibly offer the prospect of network irreversibility. After 13 years of a not-untroubled history, the FSRC could be seen as being on the threshold of a possible irreversibility, but it will require the added thrust of more media publicity.

As to research, collaboration on research projects may extend as far as forming academic-practitioner steering groups and seeking to engage in the coproduction of knowledge[7] (Nowotny, Scott, & Gibbons, 2001). Only one of the networks—Policynet—actively involved practitioners in collaboration in the research process, where, after a short period of training, practitioners joined the academics in conducting research and writing up results. This is highly unusual because secondment is not a practical possibility due to the higher level of remuneration in business compared with academia. Socnet, which is still a very new venture, trawled the water for its first annual meeting in 2004 by contacting a wide range of organizations and individuals worldwide who are concerned with social enterprise, but refined the process in its second year with targeted invitations and a focus on the impact of networks on social enterprise within a given geographical area. This is the network that comes closest to prescriptions on the future role of the business school as a new knowledge space or agora (Nowotny et al., 2001; Starkey, Hatchuel, & Tempest, 2004), a space that "embraces much more than the market and much more than politics" (Starkey et al., 2004, p. 1527).

Innovnet, while deliberately aimed at regional development for the small-to-medium business sector, has been, in a way, coopted and changed by practitioner members. Increasingly, it has become a useful form of training for staff from large firms in the area and further away. Although this was not an intended outcome for the manager of the network, since it was funded through the Higher Education Fund for Innovation, it has extended resources, thus reflecting important chains of translations whereby actors can acquire new identities, different roles, and projects so that the network helps them to achieve diverse goals (Stalder, 2002). The practice has also had significant benefits for the business school as a whole in providing potential candidates for executive courses. Although networks can often survive without the direct support of their host organizations because of independent funding, it facilitates the chain of translations to have the institution fully enrolled.

As we have seen, irreversibility is a difficult end state to achieve, and we are aware of a number of industry-academic networks that have foundered on the issues we have discussed. In the political economy of business school knowledge networks, we have seen that it is no mean feat to keep practitioners or academics on board. By comparison with the scientific and technological networks primarily studied by actor-network theorists (Bijker, Hughes, & Pinch, 1987; Callon, 1986, 1991; Callon, Law, & Rip, 1986; Latour, 1987; Latour & Woolgar, 1979), where a plainly visible and usable artifact, machine, or invention is invariably the intended or actual output, business schools are at a disadvantage. Their output is much more intangible, diverse, and transient. Nonetheless, similar actor-network translations often occur where the "ability to translate (re-interpret, re-present, or re-appropriate) other's interests" (Vurdubakis, 2007, p. 431) to those of the network is realized in particular enrollments and mobilizations. While these networks may gain the status of an obligatory passage point for some participants, they are not guaranteed to become irreversible. This is probably because such irreversibility demands that there be no collective memory of the point at which alternative ways of arousing interest around particular problems, enrolling significant supporters, and mobilizing resources were available. Where disputes and controversies still remain unsettled, it is difficult for a network to become irreversible.

While not subscribing to actor-network theory, a number of studies of knowledge networks and development can be reinterpreted in the service of its premises. For example, Adler and Norrgren (2004) argue that management researchers must "leverage empirical settings to extend and innovate managerial models and theories" (p. 56) while avoiding the academic rigor rendering the research of little or no "practical relevance." At the same time, they suggest the converse whereby the interests of academic members are only sustained by ensuring that populism does not result in "research that is perceived as practical and relevant but lacks theoretical and methodological rigour" (p. 56). While this polarity is one of the major tensions within the networks that we have researched, it is not its mere description that is the problem to be resolved in knowledge networks. This can only be achieved through a process of translation where situations are defined so as to turn the network into an obligatory passage point for both practitioner and academic members, for then the result can be an easing of their enrollment alongside the various nonhuman actors (e.g., status, solutions, institutions, research materials, funding) that can be drawn upon to mobilize further allies and resources.

Building and Sustaining Academic-Practitioner Networks

As far as the future of research collaboration is concerned, much depends on what happens in universities more generally in the medium term. Beer (2001) argues that our conception of management science generally follows "the tradition of logical positivism," which is derived from "the model of natural science in ways that have maintained the separation of science and practice" (p. 60). If this model becomes even more dominant, then collaborations will be very difficult to promote and sustain. Part of the debate about the future of the business school—if indeed it has a future—is about the kind of academic entity a business school should be. The recently deceased preeminent management thinker, Peter Drucker (2001), had no doubts. For him, the business school is a professional school, like a law or medical school, whose raison d'être is to improve the profession. We have serious doubts about the business school modeling itself on the professions any more than on the scientific laboratory in the logical positivist tradition. This is because we are never likely to come even close to reaching a

public consensus about business in the way that there is broad agreement about what is, and the value of attaining, a healthy body or legal system. Consequently, business schools would not easily be able to emulate the professions to exercise the power that comes from defining the relationship and the situation between themselves and the client (Johnson, 1977). This is not to argue that business school academics cannot behave professionally in the rather looser sense of seeking to attain high standards of pedagogy, ethical practice, and levels of research competence. The kinds of networking with practitioners that we have examined can help to achieve this through the demands that are made of academics, but from which they can readily escape when teaching in the university because of their power to grant awards to their client students.

We are not entirely unsympathetic to Drucker's (2001) view that academic research is often self-indulgent intellectualism having little impact on practice, but we fear that he ultimately is subscribing to a model of knowledge production that is contradicted by actor-network theory as portrayed in our research on industry-academic networks. That is to say, despite Drucker's impact being a direct consequence of his having enrolled and mobilized supporters and resources in the form of publishers, journalists, the media, some academics, other gurus, and practitioners, he is holding on to a view that, to paraphrase the *Sun* newspaper's claim of having won the 1992 UK election for Tony Blair, it is the content "what done it." While clearly a beneficiary, as are so many other management gurus, Drucker does not want to acknowledge how his success is partly dependent on the exhibition value of his creative labor advanced through a self-conscious "management of appearances, publicity and promotion" (Lury, 1993, quoted in Adkins, 2005, p. 119). Following actor-network theory, we don't believe that this is the whole story, because performance alone cannot guarantee a positive reception. Numerous heterogeneous mobiles intervene between performance and reception, sometimes to support but often to disrupt or deflect the development of durable, orderly, and stable networks. It is partly because the academic-practitioner network is so precarious and unstable as to constitute a high-risk strategy for actors and intermediaries alike that many academics in management have chosen to remain in the comparative comfort of their ivory towers, writing more for each other than for a larger audience. We often wonder how long this state of affairs can last, and now especially with full economic costing and non-council-funded research potentially under serious threat. In the United Kingdom, the rhetoric has been mounting for creating new knowledge partnerships between the academy and business along the lines endorsed by the *Lambert Review*. In breaking the mold, could ventures like the FSRF and the other networks we have examined begin to lose their quasi-pariah status in universities? We would be, at most, very cautious in making such a suggestion, but if the choice for business schools in all but the most elite of universities is between this and becoming a teaching-only institution, the fear of being contaminated by management practice may quickly disappear.

NOTES

1. Parts of this chapter draw on Alferoff and Knights (2005) and Starkey and Tiratsoo (2007).

2. Acknowledgments: The research drawn upon in this chapter was funded by the Economic and Social Science Research Council (ESRC) program on the Evolution of Business Knowledge under Award Ref: RES-334-25-0009.

3. As we shall see later, the Financial Services Research Forum (FSRF) was set up in 1993 by David Knights in the Management School, UMIST (now Manchester Business School), but moved to Nottingham University Business School in 1997, where David and Ken Starkey as well as other staff (Chris Ennew and Steve Diacon) continue to manage its development. An executive director, Nigel Waite, was also recruited in 1999 when David moved to Keele University. Catrina Alferoff has recently worked as a contract researcher for the FSRF, and Nick Tiratsoo conducted extensive interviews with the membership as part of the ESRC project on the Dynamics of Knowledge Production in the Business School (see Note 1).

4. Indeed, this was exactly what Barley, Meyer, and Gash (1988) found when studying the relationships between academics and practitioners.

5. This may partly explain why the ESRC has found it important to become an associate member of the Financial Services Research Forum at Nottingham.

6. It has to be admitted that this also could distinguish it from a later organization that had appropriated the name Financial Services Forum due to its not having been protected by registration.

7. The FSRF had a policy of developing coproduction of knowledge, but, in practice, this was only partially successful, in that the practitioners from each company would seek to have the research pursue something that was of a burning concern for them, and this would not necessarily be of the same interest to other members of the network. On one occasion, an attempted co-management of a project on stakeholder pensions resulted in the project deviating from its research agenda, thus exceeding its budget, much to the annoyance of the network's steering committee.

REFERENCES

Adkins, L. (2005). The new economy, property and personhood. *Theory, Culture & Society, 22*(1), 111–130.

Adler, N., & Norrgren, F. (2004). Collaborative research: Strategic intents and actual practices. In N. Adler, A. B. (Rami) Shani, & A. Styhre (Eds.), *Collaborative research in organizations: Foundations for learning, change, and theoretical development.* Thousand Oaks, CA: Sage.

Alferoff, A., & Knights, D. (2005, December). *Making and mending your nets: The management of uncertainty in academic/practitioner knowledge networks.* Paper presented at the joint Advanced Institute of Management/ESRC Evolution of Business Knowledge conference on the Future of Business Schools, Warwick Business School, University of Warwick.

Barley, S. R., Meyer, G. W., & Gash, D. C. (1988). Cultures of culture: Academics, practitioners and the pragmatics of normative control. *Administrative Science Quarterly, 33,* 24–60.

Beer, M. (2001). Why management research findings are unimplementable: An action science perspective. *Reflections* (Society for Organizational Learning and the Massachusetts Institute of Technology), *2*(3), 58–63.

Bennis, W. G., & O'Toole, J. (2005). How business schools lost their way. *Harvard Business Review, 83*(5), 96–104.

Bijker, W. E., Hughes, T. P., & Pinch, T. (Eds.). (1987). *The social construction of technological systems: New directions in the sociology and history of technology.* Cambridge: MIT Press.

Boucher, G., Conway, C., & Van Der Meer, E. (2003). Tiers of engagement by universities in their region's development. *Regional Studies, 37*(9), 887–897.

Callon, M. (1986). Some elements of a sociology of translation: Domestication of the scallops and the fishermen of St Brieuc Bay. In J. Law (Ed.), *Power, action and belief.* London: Routledge and Kegan Paul.

Callon, M. (1991). Techno-economic networks and universality. In J. Law (Ed.), *Essays on power, technology and domination* (pp. 132–161). London: Routledge.

Callon, M., Law, J., & Rip, A. (Eds.). (1986). *Mapping the dynamics of science and technology.* London: Macmillan.

Castells, M. (2000). Materials for an exploratory theory of the network society. *British Journal of Sociology, 51*(1), 5–24.

Drucker, P. (2001, November–December). Taking stock. *BizEd,* pp. 13–17.

Garcia, M. (2004). *Establishing a knowledge link between university and industry in Portugal* (Working Paper No. 2004/009). Lancaster, UK: Lancaster University Management School.

Gibbons, M., Limoges, C., Nowotny, H., Schwartzman, S., Scott, P., & Trow, M. (1994). *The new production of knowledge: The dynamics of science and research in contemporary societies.* London: Sage.

Grey, C. (2001). Re-imagining relevance: A response to Starkey and Madan. *British Journal of Management, 12*(S1) [Special Issue], S27–S32.

Hambrick, D. (1993). What if the academy actually mattered? *Academy of Management Review, 19*(1), 11–16.

Huff, A. S., & Huff, J. A. (2001). Re-focusing the business school agenda. *British Journal of Management, 12*(S1) [Special Issue], S49–S54.

Johnson, T. J. (1977). *Professions and power.* London: Macmillan.

Kelemen, M., & Bansal, P. (2002). The conventions of management research and their relevance to management practice. *British Journal of Management, 13,* 97–108.

Knights, D. (2004, May). *Reflexivity, epistemology and ethics: Towards a new form of industry-academic collaboration and trans-disciplinary research.* Paper presented at the "Management as the Trans-discipline of the Second Modernity" track at the 3rd EURAM International Conference, University of St. Andrews, Scotland.

Knights, D. (2006). *Myopic rhetorics: Reflecting epistemologically and ethically on the demand for relevance in organisational and management research.* Unpublished paper available from d.knights@mngt.keele.ac.uk at the School of Economics and Management Studies, University of Keele, ST5 5BG, UK.

Knights, D., Murray, F., & Willmott, H. (1993). Networking as knowledge work: A study of strategic interorganizational development in the financial services industry. *Journal of Management Studies, 30*(6), 975–995.

Latour, B. (1987). *Science in action: How to follow scientists and engineers through society.* Milton Keynes, UK: Open University Press.

Latour, B., & Woolgar, S. (1979). *Laboratory life: The construction of scientific facts.* Princeton, NJ: Princeton University Press.

Maclean, D., & Macintosh, R. (2002). One process, two audiences: On the challenges of management research. *European Management Journal, 20*(4), 383–392.

Mintzberg, H. (2004). *Managers not MBAs.* London: Pearson Education.

Nowotny, H., Scott, P., & Gibbons, M. (2001). *Re-thinking science: Knowledge and the public in an age of uncertainty.* Cambridge, MA: Polity Press.

Pfeffer, J., & Fong, C. T. (2003). The end of business schools? Less success than meets the eye. *Academy of Management Learning & Education, 1*(1), 78–95.

Pfeffer, J., & Fong, C. T. (2004). The business school "business": Some lessons from the US experience. *Journal of Management Studies, 41*(8), 1501–1520.

Stalder, F. (2002). Failures and successes: Notes on the development of electronic cash. *The Information Society, 18*(3), 209–219.

Starkey, K., Hatchuel, A., & Tempest, S. (2004). Rethinking the business school. *Journal of Management Studies, 41*(8), 1521–1531.

Starkey, K., & Madan, P. (2001). Bridging the relevance gap: Aligning stakeholders in the future of management research. *British Journal of Management, 12*(S1) [Special Issue], S3–S26.

Starkey, K., & Tiratsoo, N. (2007). *The future of the business school.* Cambridge, MA: Cambridge University Press.

Tiratsoo, N. (2005). *The financial services research forum: "Scratching where we're itching"?* Unpublished paper, Nottingham University Business School.

UK Treasury. (2003). *Lambert review of business-university collaboration: Final report.* London: HMSO.

Vurdubakis, T. (2007). Technology. In D. Knights & H. Willmott (Eds.), *Management and organization: An introductory text* (pp. 405–438). London: Thompson Learning.

Willmott, M. (2006, June). *Trends in consumer behaviour.* Paper presented at the New Horizons in Consumer Behaviour Joint Conference organized by the Financial Services Research Forum and the ESRC, Westminster, London.

Wright, M. A., Lockett, A., Tiratsoo, N., & Alferoff, C. (2005). *Academic entrepreneurship, knowledge gaps and the role of business schools.* Unpublished paper, University of Nottingham, UK.

CHAPTER 20

Improving the Management of Ignorance and Uncertainty

A Case Illustrating Integration in Collaboration

GABRIELE BAMMER

THE GOOLABRI GROUP[1]

ABSTRACT

We are 23 researchers and practitioners who collaborated to accelerate the process of developing a multidimensional approach to ignorance and uncertainty. We focus on the integrative aspects of this partnership, presenting and then employing a framework to systematically describe integration: (1) integration *for what and for whom?* (2) integration *of what?* (3) what was the *context* in which the integration occurred? (4) integration *by whom?* (5) *how* was the integration undertaken? and (6) was the integration *successful?* This framework of six questions is widely applicable and brings to the surface aspects of collaboration that are usually hidden. We conclude by exploring (a) how to advance collaborative activity in developing multidimensional approaches to ignorance and uncertainty; (b) the use of this type of collaborative activity as a prototype for the development of the new specialization of integration and implementation sciences; and (c) how to improve the ability to measure the success of collaborations.

For complex issues and problems, how we manage what we do not know and what we are uncertain about is at least as important as how we put knowledge to good use. Yet methods for dealing with ignorance and uncertainty are still relatively unsophisticated. Indeed the notion that ignorance and uncertainty are also socially constructed (Smithson, 1989) will surprise many, as serious attention to these issues has long been a blind spot in both research and practice. Nevertheless, the last 60 years have seen burgeoning interest in this area within discipline and practice area silos (Smithson, 1989), but little exchange of ideas between different approaches in order to generate new knowledge and improve existing methods.

This chapter describes the first stage of a process to promote the trading of information between disciplines and practice areas aimed at accelerating the development of integrated approaches to ignorance and uncertainty (Bammer & Smithson, 2007b). Twenty-three researchers and practitioners with diverse perspectives on uncertainty participated. This chapter describes the collaborative process we engaged in, our successes, and the lessons we learned.

The element of collaboration that we focus on here is the integration of different disciplinary and practice knowledge. This complements other foci such as learning (see, e.g., Docherty & Shani, Chapter 8 in this volume), but has been much less intensively studied (Bammer, 2007). Our approach to integration is based on the development of the new specialization, integration and implementation sciences (Bammer, 2005). The specialization contributes to the tackling of complex problems by focusing on crosscutting theory and methods to aid integration of knowledge from different disciplines and from practice, as well as the implementation of research knowledge in practice. Developing multidimensional approaches to ignorance and uncertainty is one of the key areas of focus for integration and implementation sciences.

This chapter contributes to collaborative management research in two ways. First, it presents a structured way of planning and describing integration, which is central to all collaborations. The framework of six questions provided here has wide utility, and applying it brings to the surface aspects of collaboration that are usually hidden. For example, descriptions of collaborations rarely present exactly how the integration was done and who was involved. Thus, one aim of this chapter is to illustrate the importance of integration in collaboration and the utility of the proposed framework. The second contribution the chapter makes to collaborative management research is to deepen thinking about tackling ignorance and uncertainty, which is essential for effectively managing complex problems. We begin with a brief overview of integration and implementation sciences, which underpins our approach.

A BRIEF OVERVIEW OF INTEGRATION AND IMPLEMENTATION SCIENCES

The overarching goal of integration and implementation sciences is to address four interlinked questions relevant to confronting any complex issue:

1. How adequate is our knowledge for tackling this problem?

2. Is the best available knowledge being incorporated into policy and practice decisions?

3. Are good decisions being implemented?

4. Is there an effective process of monitoring policy and practice change, for making adjustments as required, and for learning from successes and failures?

In order to help address these questions, integration and implementation sciences encompasses six areas, one of which is developing multidimensional approaches to ignorance and uncertainty. The areas are the following:

Systems-based thinking. The core of systems-based thinking—an orientation to the whole issue and how the parts relate to the whole—is relatively simple. Operationalizing it is rather more challenging. There are a number of traditions that emphasize different facets, including system dynamics, which concentrates on feedback loops; soft systems practice, which concentrates on stakeholder participation; and complexity science, which emphasizes nonlinear dynamics, self-organization, and adaptability. Further, many disciplines are developing a systems orientation, including systems biology, systems engineering, and information systems, with little cross-talk between them. Integration and implementation sciences aims to develop a set of core concepts for systems-based thinking, as well as guidelines about the relative strengths of different systems methods for tackling real-world problems.

Cross-disciplinary and cross-sectoral collaboration and integration. Systems-based thinking depends on the ability to integrate—across knowledges, perspectives, geographical and temporal scales, and so on—with cross-disciplinary and cross-sectoral collaboration forming the base on which integration occurs. Integration and implementation sciences promotes six questions as a structured method for describing integration, namely (1) integration *for what and for whom?* (2) integration *of what?* (3) what was the *context* in which the integration occurred? (4) integration *by whom?* (5) *how* was the integration undertaken? and (6) was the integration *successful?* (Bammer & LWA Integration Symposium Participants, 2005). Integration and implementation sciences aims to further develop concepts and methods for enhancing these key practices.

Multidimensional approaches to ignorance and uncertainty. Our tools for understanding and managing ignorance and uncertainty are comparatively unsophisticated, especially in terms of cross-fertilizing developments between disciplines and practice areas. Integration and implementation sciences aim to enhance our understanding of (a) the nature of uncertainty, (b) metaphors, motives, and morals associated with uncertainty, and (c) coping and managing under uncertainty, by drawing on diverse disciplinary and practice approaches.

Research support for decision making. Research support for decision making involves (a) understanding decision making processes in relevant areas, such as government, business, and nonprofits, (b) appreciating what types of research are useful, and (c) developing efficient and effective forms of nexus between research and decision making.

Normative principles and processes for change. How can we decide what change to support? Integration and implementation sciences examines and draws together values-based approaches in different disciplines and practice areas and evaluates how these underpin decisions and change. The specialization also aims to enhance the development of dialogue-based processes that highlight and help resolve value clashes.

Making change effective. Integration and implementation sciences aims to draw together insights from various areas that focus on producing change, but that do not generally interact. These include advertising, counseling, managing organizational change, diffusion of innovation, health promotion, and agricultural extension.

None of these six areas has a single disciplinary or practice-based home, and no existing discipline or practice has the mandate, or the ability, to produce an effective encompassing approach to the development of theory and methods in any of the areas. This is why a new specialization is being developed. However, it is important to point out that the new specialization is also still emerging and developing a solid institutional base.

Although integrated investigation of the six areas outlined above through a new specialization still only has a fragile institutional home, there are developments in many disciplines and practices that are relevant to each of the six areas. For some areas, there are independent, parallel discovery processes, which lead to wasteful duplication of effort. For others, new traditions are being developed that cannot communicate with each other.

Two examples provide useful illustrations here. First, in terms of duplication of effort, the application of research results to developing policy is a major concern in almost all disciplines and also of considerable interest to policy makers and other practitioners. There are many parallel developments investigating how to improve research application or "translation," which independently cover the same terrain. Thus, researchers and practitioners in public health will be unaware of very similar developments in environmental science or sociology or defense studies.

The second example, of parallel developments that cannot communicate with each other, comes from ignorance and uncertainty itself. Here, very different traditions have arisen in different disciplines and practices, and there is no clear way of bringing them together. Thus, for example, statistics has built a whole field of endeavor based around the concept of probability. This has little relevance to how historians deal with ignorance and uncertainty, which focuses on how to draw reliable conclusions from too little (and, in the case of recent history, too much) information and how to deal with topics that society deems to be taboo, such as critical investigation of events important for national pride (Curthoys, 2007). The value of an integrated approach in this case is to have the full array of relevant concepts and methods available when dealing with complex problems, rather than being limited to approaches from single, or a small number of, disciplines and practices.

The collaborative project described here is aimed at this problem of developing an integrated approach to ignorance and uncertainty, which is central to the development of integration and implementation sciences (area 3 in the above list). Further, cross-sectoral and cross-disciplinary collaboration and integration are also key to integration and implementation sciences (area 2). As well as describing the collaboration in detail, we use the six questions for integration in collaborations outlined in area 2 above as a way to systematically describe the partnership process.

WHAT WERE WE AIMING TO ACHIEVE AND WHO WERE THE INTENDED BENEFICIARIES?

Addressing the first generic question, "integration for what and for whom," makes clear the aims of the collaboration and who is intended to benefit. As already outlined, we sought to accelerate a process of developing a richer appreciation of ignorance and uncertainty, which cannot be accomplished in any one discipline or practice area. We also aimed to provide legitimacy for thinking about ignorance and uncertainty in a cross-disciplinary and cross-sectoral manner. Our ultimate objective is to promote the development of more sophisticated methods for managing ignorance and uncertainty. Specifically, we aim to enhance considerations of ignorance and uncertainty when complex issues or problems are addressed and, in the long term, to provide one or more frameworks that will make this process of considering multiple perspectives on ignorance and uncertainty more efficient. The intention is to be of broad benefit to decision makers and researchers across the board, especially as dealing with ignorance and uncertainty is highly relevant in organizations.

WHICH PERSPECTIVES ON IGNORANCE AND UNCERTAINTY WERE INCLUDED?

"Integration of what" addresses the different elements that the collaboration aims to synthesize. In our case, the "what" was different perspectives on uncertainty, each represented by a different person. We realized we could not practically include every important perspective on ignorance and uncertainty, but we did aim for maximum diversity among the invited participants. The areas of interest and affiliations of the participants are listed in Table 20.1.

The focus of the first round of activity was a two-day symposium (held in April 2005), where the participants met face-to-face, but there was also considerable preparatory and post-symposium activity, as described below. Three of us were involved in the bulk of the planning (Gabriele Bammer, Michael Smithson, and Stephen Dovers). We chose topics and participants in an iterative process. As well as a wide spread of topic areas, we went beyond people we knew or even knew of, so that both we and the other participants would be introduced to a large number of new people and perspectives. We were aiming at around 25 participants to allow significant interaction. Practicalities also constrained the number of participants, as we had chosen a symposium venue (Goolabri Country Resort) about 20 minutes by car from Canberra, which could accommodate a maximum of 26 people.

By and large, the choice of topics and participants was idiosyncratic. There were obvious areas we wanted to cover, such as statistics and physics (the only discipline with an uncertainty principle), but otherwise we let our imaginations roam. We aimed for participants who were senior in their fields and paid conscious attention to gender balance. We decided against inviting overseas participants.

This was partly because of cost, as we did not have funding for a truly international meeting, and having a small number of international participants tends to set them apart (and to some extent above) the rest. Besides, we had plenty of talented people to choose from close at hand. For example, the Australian National University, where we are employed and from which many of our participants were drawn, ranks in the top 50 in the world.

Although we were aiming for diverse perspectives, we decided on ethnic homogeneity. We thought there would be enough to deal with in trying to integrate multiple topics and that ethnic diversity was an important area for future work. We also wanted to avoid tokenism, which might result from including only one or two people representing particular cultural interests. Indeed, we consciously dealt with trying to ensure that no particular topics were isolated by planning for clusters of participants. Therefore we had clusters from science, social science, and arts/humanities. There was a cluster of nonacademic practitioners, as well as a cluster of people we asked to focus on a problem, rather than a discipline or practice area.

Of course, not everyone we approached was interested or available, and some areas we wanted to include, particularly psychiatry, business, the media, regulation, education, information science, engineering, and ethics, had to be dropped when we ran out of time to chase leads. In the end, 13 of the participants were known by one or more of the organizers, and seven were approached "cold." Of these, two were people we knew of, two were recommended by people we knew, and three were people we searched out and took a chance on. While we deliberately aimed for clusters, as outlined above, we tried to avoid clusters who already knew each other. Apart from the organizers, most participants knew zero, one, or two other people. We ended up with a small group who

Table 20.1   Participants, Areas of Interest, and Affiliations

Area	Participant	Affiliation
Art and art history	Professor Sasha Grishin	Art History, The Australian National University
Complex adaptive systems	Dr. Pascal Perez	Research School of Pacific and Asian Studies, The Australian National University
Disease outbreaks	Professor Aileen Plant	Centre for International Health, Curtin University of Technology
Economics	Professor John Quiggin*	School of Economics, University of Queensland
Emergency management	Professor John Handmer	Centre for Risk and Community Safety, Royal Melbourne Institute of Technology
Environmental law	Ms. Judith Jones	National Europe Centre and Faculty of Law, The Australian National University
Environmental science	Dr. Stephen Dovers,* Adjunct Professor Paul Perkins, and Professor Ian White (plus additional paper coauthors)	Centre for Resource and Environmental Studies, The Australian National University
Futures and strategic planning	Ms. Kate Delaney	Delaney and Associates Pty Ltd, Deakin ACT
History	Professor Ann Curthoys	School of Social Sciences, The Australian National University
Illicit drugs	Associate Professor Alison Ritter	Turning Point Alcohol and Drug Centre
Integration	Dr. Gabriele Bammer	National Centre for Epidemiology and Population Health, The Australian National University
Jazz	Mr. John Mackey	School of Music, The Australian National University
Philosophy of probability	Professor Alan Hájek	Philosophy Program, Research School of Social Sciences, The Australian National University
Physics	Professor Stephen Buckman	Atomic and Molecular Physics Laboratories, Research School of Physical Sciences and Engineering, The Australian National University
Politics	Adjunct Professor Michael Moore	(former member of the Australian Capital Territory Legislative Assembly) MooreConnections Pty Ltd, Reid ACT
Psychology	Dr. Michael Smithson	School of Psychology, The Australian National University
Public health policy	Ms. Liz Furler	Beaumont SA
Religion	Professor Stephen Pickard	St Mark's National Theological Centre
Security and intelligence	Mr. Steve Longford	The Distillery, Dickson ACT
Statistics	Ms. Robyn Attewell	Covance Pty Ltd, Braddon ACT
Terrorism and law enforcement	Dr. Michael McFadden (plus additional paper coauthors)	Performance and Planning, Australian Federal Police

*Unable to attend the symposium.

worked on environmental issues who knew each other, but they did not form a clique. Indeed, the organizers had not worked together before either.

This collaboration also challenges the assumption that partners need to know each other for the requisite trust to be established. In our case, seniority and a high level of expertise were key factors in allowing this group of strangers to work. Participants soon figured out that they were in a group that "knew their stuff" and that they could trust the expertise that others demonstrated, even though they could not judge it themselves. Of course, some people were much more uncomfortable in this situation than others and were more reserved in their contributions as a consequence. But, on the whole, people entered into the spirit of the event wholeheartedly and with an open mind, and this generated a high level of energy and excitement.

Because it is relatively unusual to take a chance on complete strangers, it is worth describing this process. There were three particular areas we decided we wanted represented—jazz, because it involves dealing with uncertainty in the moment during improvisation; religion, because we felt that some discussion of faith was important; and intelligence, because current affairs at the time were subjecting military intelligence to a lot of scrutiny. Jazz was the easiest. The Australian National University has a School of Music with a jazz studies program. At the time, the headship was shared, and the one who answered the phone first (John Mackey) was keen to participate. Religion was more challenging and involved a good deal of Web surfing to find someone suitable (Stephen Pickard). We had little idea about how to find someone in the intelligence community, as we wanted a practitioner, not an academic, for this slot. During a trip, one of us (GB) spied someone at the airport carrying a conference satchel from a meeting of intelligence analysts. By good fortune, they were seated together on the plane, and that person recommended Steve Longford.

There were two final ingredients in the mix of participants. One was Michael Smithson's expertise in thinking about ignorance and uncertainty and the paradigms used to deal with them (see his seminal 1989 book, *Ignorance and Uncertainty: Emerging Paradigms*). He points out, for example, that the current reemergence of thinking and research about uncertainty and ignorance is the greatest creative effort in the field since 1660, when probability theory emerged. This reemergence has also seen a shift from efforts to eliminate or absorb uncertainty to coping with and managing it. The second ingredient, mentioned earlier, was my own interest in developing integration and implementation sciences, which provided the stimulus and funding for the project.

As this description of our collaboration shows, it is important to be clear about what the collaboration is seeking to integrate when choosing the participants. Partnerships with aims different from ours would be integrating different elements and would choose participants accordingly.

WHAT WAS THE CONTEXT IN WHICH THIS PROJECT WAS CONDUCTED?

The "context" for integration involves the political or other action circumstances that led to the project and that may be influential during its life. For this collaboration, two of the key contextual elements—the development of integration and implementation sciences and the relative lack of sophistication in our understanding about ignorance and uncertainty—have been described above. The other relevant contextual factor was the project funding that made the event possible, obtained as part of a larger program of activity called the Drug Policy Modelling Project (now Program). This sought (and indeed continues to seek) a "big picture" approach to Australian illicit drugs research to inform policy (Ritter, Bammer, Hamilton, Mazerolle, & the DPMP Team, in press). The integration and implementation sciences perspective has infused the Drug Policy Modelling Program, as demonstrated in a focus on integrated content areas (law enforcement, treatment, harm reduction, and prevention); using systems-based methods; decision support and policy processes; and, most pertinent here, exploring approaches to ignorance and uncertainty. Because dealing with ignorance and uncertainty is critical to how research informs policy, the project described here was initiated. We were fortunate to have philanthropic funding from the Colonial Foundation Trust, which encouraged us to be exploratory and take risks, as well as to lay the foundations for an ongoing program of work.

The ignorance and uncertainty project sought to specifically accommodate the interests of the Drug Policy Modelling Project by having illicit drugs as one of the three problem areas under consideration and inviting the director of the Drug Policy Modelling Project, Alison Ritter, to participate on that topic. Another member of the project team, Pascal Perez, was invited to participate representing complex adaptive systems.

Once the ignorance and uncertainty project was under way we attracted a small amount of additional funding from The Australian National University's National Institute of Social Sciences and Law. We also hosted a post-symposium public lecture as part of the 2005 ANU-Toyota Public Lecture Series. Steve Longford and Aileen Plant spoke on "Confronting Uncertainty: Intelligence, Epidemics and Decision Making."

As we have outlined, contextual factors shape collaborations both directly and subtly. In the case described here, funding gave the project legitimacy, allowed us to be imaginative in who was invited, and enabled us to implement our desire to have a problem-based focus. In terms of a general process to guide

planning and description of collaborations, reflecting on context is illuminating.

HOW DID WE SET ABOUT INTEGRATING PERSPECTIVES AND WHO DID THE INTEGRATION?

In this section, two of the generic questions— "integration by whom" and "how was the integration undertaken"—are dealt with together. Consideration of who does the integration highlights that even though integration is central to research partnerships, the process of synthesis need not be collaborative. It can be undertaken by an individual, usually the research leader, or by the whole group or a subgroup. The methods used for integrating are of central importance to research collaborations, but, surprisingly, have been poorly researched, and there is no definitive account of methodologies. Some starting points have been identified, including risk-benefit analyses, modeling, and deliberative approaches among stakeholders (Klein, 1990; Rossini & Porter, 1979).

We used a number of integrative techniques, with varying degrees of success. We assess success in the next section. The techniques we used were embedded in the overall process, which involved the production and reading of papers before the symposium, activities at the symposium, and finally post-symposium work. Within that context, we first encouraged participants to develop their own integrations. Second, we sought to start the process of developing an overarching framework. Third, we sought to develop a range of group projects that would take the integrative work further.

Encouraging Participants to Develop Their Own Integrations

The "price of admission" for each participant to the two-day symposium was a paper about uncertainty in their area of expertise, which was due one month before the symposium. In addition, each participant was allocated two papers by other participants to read and comment on for the symposium itself. We aimed for the two papers to be outside the readers' comfort zones, and they could comment on more papers if they wished. In this way, we set out to encourage participants to start integrating the work of others into their own.

Participants were diligent about producing their pre-symposium papers, which were excellent, by and large. They were also assiduous with their assigned reading, which was a time-consuming stretch for some of them. The first day of the symposium and part of the morning of the second day were given over to 15-minute presentations by each participant of how they had integrated the reading, followed by a 5-minute discussion. The readings undertaken are presented in Table 20.2. An additional aspect of this element of integration was that participants refined their papers after the symposium, incorporating comments from other participants and new learning.

Developing an Overarching Framework

On the second day of the symposium, we attempted to initiate a discussion that would pull the contributions together. We started with potential framework elements based on Smithson's work (see Smithson, 1989, 2007). However, although the majority of participants indicated they wanted such a discussion (see the next section), when we attempted it a number balked at our approach, leading us to abandon it and initiate a post-symposium activity in its place.

The process we engaged in instead was that Michael Smithson and I took the lead in integrating the papers and symposium discussion into existing knowledge as a post-symposium activity. One of the things we had agreed to at the symposium was to seek to have the papers published as a book. Michael Smithson and I took on the editorial role, writing introductory chapters, including one on the state of knowledge, which Michael wrote based on his 1989 book (Smithson, 2007). This was divided into three sections:

1. The nature of uncertainty

2. Metaphors, motives, and morals

3. Coping and managing under uncertainty

We used each of these as the topic for a draft integrative chapter. This process is still in train and the next step is to solicit input on each chapter from the other participants in the collaboration, a task we are about to embark on. We plan to do this through individual and small group discussion.

Developing Projects to Take the Integrative Work Further

After the individual presentations, we devoted the rest of the second day of the symposium to developing projects that would take the integrative work forward. We started with a list of topics the organizers had developed, and invited additions. We then asked participants to indicate which projects they were interested in working on and allocated four one-hour slots to plenary or small-group work, based on the topics that had the most interest.

The majority, if not all, of the participants indicated that they were interested in two projects. One was to develop a book out of our contributions, which had been flagged as a potential outcome when the symposium was first organized. We spent an hour systematically discussing the strengths and weaknesses of each chapter. The second project everyone opted to discuss, ironically, was the development of an overarching framework, described above. We were not able to take in hand all the topics nominated, but dealt with some in small group discussions.

Table 20.2   Assigned Reading for the Symposium

Participant	Assigned Reading	
Robyn Attewell (Statistics)	Curthoys (History)	Jones (Environmental law)
Gabriele Bammer (Integration)	Smithson (Psychology)	Quiggin (Economics)
Stephen Buckman (Physics)	Furler (Public health policy)	Mackey (Jazz)
Ann Curthoys (History)	Bammer (Integration)	Plant (Disease outbreaks)
Kate Delaney (Futures and strategic planning)	Grishin (Art and art history)	Ritter (Illicit drugs)
Liz Furler (Public health policy)	Buckman (Physics)	Pickard (Religion)
Sasha Grishin (Art and art history)	Attewell (Statistics)	Moore (Politics)
Al Hájek (Philosophy of probability)	White and Perkins (Environment)	McFadden (Terrorism and law enforcement)
John Handmer (Emergency management)	Pickard (Religion)	Smithson (Psychology)
Judith Jones (Environmental law)	Buckman (Physics)	Moore (Politics)
Steve Longford (Security and intelligence)	Grishin (Art and art history)	Perez (Complex adaptive systems)
John Mackey (Jazz)	Delaney (Futures and strategic planning)	Handmer (Emergency management)
Michael McFadden (Terrorism and law enforcement)	Delaney (Futures and strategic planning)	Quiggin (Economics)
Michael Moore (Politics)	Attewell (Statistics)	White and Perkins (Environmental science)
Pascal Perez (Complex adaptive systems)	Curthoys (History)	Mackey (Jazz)
Paul Perkins (Environmental science)	Hájek (Philosophy of probability)	Ritter (Illicit drugs)
Stephen Pickard (Religion)	Bammer (Integration)	Handmer (Emergency management)
Aileen Plant (Disease outbreaks)	Jones (Environmental law)	Perez (Complex adaptive systems)
John Quiggin (Economics)	Furler (Public health policy)	Longford (Security and intelligence)
Alison Ritter (Illicit drugs)	Longford (Security and intelligence)	Grishin (Art and art history)
Mike Smithson (Psychology)	White and Perkins (Environmental science)	Mackey (Jazz)
Ian White (Environmental science)	Hájek (Philosophy of probability)	Plant (Disease outbreaks)

In the first breakout session, participants could choose between developing a short course to teach an integrated approach to ignorance and uncertainty (led by Stephen Buckman) or discussing the intersections between spirituality, creativity, and disaster management (led by Stephen Pickard and Sasha Grishin). The second breakout session offered the choice between discussing different perspectives on the illicit drugs problem, especially intelligence and law enforcement (led by Alison Ritter), adaptive learning (led by Ian White and Paul Perkins), and a reconstituted small group on an overarching framework (led by Michael Smithson). There was not enough time to discuss other topics that had been raised, particularly the role of institutions and legal and regulatory instruments in dealing with uncertainty (sponsored by Pascal Perez), or to hold a broader discussion via a World Café or Futures Salon (sponsored by Michael Moore and Kate Delaney). Several people were intrigued by John Mackey's demonstration of improvisation on the saxophone and requested a practical session, which also fell victim to the time restrictions. Other potential projects, such as a journal article and a presentation in the popular media, depended on progress toward the development of an overarching framework, so were left in limbo.

Our approach to integration was obviously very particular to our task and circumstances. Other collaborations will tackle integration in different ways. The framework encourages making the integrative processes explicit. This allows us not only to reflect on our own experiences but also to learn from the experiences of others.

HOW SUCCESSFUL WAS THE INTEGRATION?

Evaluating the success of the integration requires assessment of both process and outcomes. However, the benchmarks for either dimension are not clear. At this stage, we do not have a good gauge of reasonable expectations for measures of success in collaborations. This will be returned to in the conclusion. First we provide an analysis of what happened in each of the integrative activities, in terms of not only the process but also the knowledge created.

Encouraging Participants to Develop Their Own Integrations

As indicated above, we aimed to allocate readings outside participants' comfort zones, and almost everyone made an unprompted comment that indicated this had been achieved; the comments below come from transcripts of the recorded proceedings. For example, Aileen Plant opened her remarks with the following:

> I felt completely out of my depth, and it reminded me that every now and again I get a letter addressed to Alien Planet—and that's what I felt like.

Stephen Buckman commented:

> What happened when I read all these wonderful articles, of course, was it brought to my attention that outside the hard sciences uncertainty really has a human face and it's driven by other imperatives—social, political, and financial. That's not to say that as a human being those things don't impact on my everyday life as well, but as a scientist, really, uncertainty for me is very well prescribed, whereas I think for most others in the room it probably isn't and that may be a point of contrast and comparison.

Most of the syntheses were imaginative and stimulating. For example, Sasha Grishin bounced off Robyn Attewell's (2007) citation of H. G. Wells ("statistical thinking will one day be as necessary for efficient citizenship as the ability to read and write") to use the range of Wells's work to draw insights from his two assigned papers on statistics (Robyn Attewell) and politics (Michael Moore). Wells's vision of utopia was particularly apposite, and Grishin concluded,

> For there to be a utopia, uncertainty had to be overcome, not only in the gathering of statistical data and the operation of politics, but uncertainty had to be overcome in human nature itself.

Liz Furler found strong parallels between her policy-making experiences and religious intolerance. She concluded that promoting uncertainty and the fear that accompanies it, as well as not giving people tools to manage them, leads to a rise in fundamentalism, seeing political and religious fundamentalism as "partners in crime as we look around the world today."

A small number of participants did not attempt to comment on their readings, which others remarked on with disappointment and some irritation on the end-of-symposium feedback sheets.

Nevertheless, at the end of Day 1 there was palpable high energy and excitement. Steve Longford provided the following assessment from his intelligence frame:

> For me, this has been really good for discovery. I've got to look at some other things. From an intelligence perspective we have discovery, and discovery is either closed or open, so we've sort of got across both here very quickly and very rapidly. So the way that you've actually set this whole thing out has been a very clever way to get around closed discovery because you've actually got people to comment on other people's work.

In terms of outcomes, most people again reported that their thinking had been enriched, and a small number reported profound new insights. Steve Longford again:

What I realized, and I hadn't thought about it this way before, was that uncertainty is actually a cognitive state, and that we don't have uncertainty outside of that cognitive state.

He recognized that "there are other things that we can do to reduce uncertainty that have nothing to do with the facts." Seeing a strong link between uncertainty and control had two consequences—first that increasing control would reduce uncertainty, and second that accepting uncertainty robs it of its power.

Judith Jones was another who saw her discipline in a new light:

> ... there is a heavy reliance or even blind unquestioning consumption of other disciplines by law to assist in the legal process.

She talked about the uses of psychology in jury deliberations, the relationship with policy formulation, where "broad aspirational policy goals ... then get converted into quite broadly stated legal rules that are open to very flexible interpretation," the role of economics in regulatory design, and the use of science and statistics in proof of causation and probabilities.

> As a consequence, when lawyers think about uncertainty they default to those disciplines' treatment of uncertainty. . . . Since there are so many disciplines that are relevant to law . . . and in such a variety of ways, the task of systematically addressing uncertainty is . . . quite overwhelming and perhaps it isn't a wonder that no one has attempted it within law.

Useful one-on-one conversations also emerged during the discussion of the papers or informally during the symposium. Ann Curthoys (history) and Steve Longford talked about how the way knowledge gaps were handled in each of their fields was critical—they could be made explicit or papered over. In the latter case, the appreciation that there was a gap could be lost forever. Alan Hájek (philosophy) and Michael Smithson realized that by putting their heads together they might be able to resolve a paradox in decision theory (this has resulted in ongoing work). Alison Ritter (illicit drugs) and Michael McFadden (terrorism and law enforcement) had a productive discussion about law enforcement data and its potential uses in informing drug policy.

Overall, then, we were successful in exposing individual participants to new (to them) perspectives about ignorance and uncertainty through both the pre-symposium assigned readings and the symposium interactions. For many, this provided new (to the field) insights into their own disciplines or practice areas. There were also a small number of new linkages between disparate areas, which through ongoing activity may lead to the creation of new knowledge.

Developing an Overarching Framework

As outlined above, our first attempt to do this was a group discussion. While some of the participants were keen to engage, others resisted and we decided to move on to other topics. A number of factors are likely to have contributed to the failure of this integrative method at the symposium. We deliberately, and probably mistakenly, did not allow for any general group discussion, and some of the participants reacted adversely to this. In particular, some of the practitioner participants saw this attempt at integration as an academic exercise that did not contribute to their interests. But they were not the only opponents. We had shifted from a bottom-up integration to one that was somewhat top-down, without adequately preparing the ground. We had not really signaled either that a body of knowledge to build on existed, or that this

was Michael Smithson's area of expertise. Indeed, Michael's participation to that point had been to represent the area of psychology. This was also a "battle" between inductive and deductive thinkers. Inexperienced facilitation and group meeting dynamics were probably also contributors—after a "high" on Day 1, there is often a slump on Day 2, along with a reaction against the organizers.

It is still too early to fully assess our replacement attempt at integration because the process is not yet complete. Michael Smithson and I were able to undertake the task we had set ourselves in writing three integrative chapters dealing with (1) the nature of uncertainty, (2) metaphors, motives and morals, and (3) coping and managing under uncertainty (Bammer & Smithson, 2007a; Smithson & Bammer, 2007a, 2007b). The chapters built on the insights in Smithson (1989, 2007). In our view, the combination of the individual chapters plus the integrative chapters provides a much better appreciation of the diversity of approaches to ignorance and uncertainty than any existing work. At the symposium, Michael Smithson made the following comment:

[In 25 years researching this field] I have never seen a collection that has the breadth for one thing, in terms of the variety of disciplines covered, but more importantly that has the breadth in terms of the concepts and the variety of different takes on uncertainty that was covered. I think we have something unique here . . . I think we've got a very unusual and unprecedented opportunity to put some things together about uncertainty from an amazing wide variety of perspectives. And a collection of people who clearly are able to articulate these perspectives and to listen to each other. I think that's really crucial. I think it's extremely rare to get an assembly of people with the variety of perspectives we've got who can or will listen to each other. . . . [W]e really have something genuinely new here and we have a great opportunity here.

Overall, our attempt to lead a group integration process did not work, but we were able to build on the group's learning in post-symposium writing. Forthcoming publication of this work will demonstrate whether or not it was successful. Although no really new knowledge was developed, the integrative work demonstrated that some concepts Smithson (1989) had described were robust against a larger range of perspectives on ignorance and uncertainty than previously shown. Further, the integrative work also showed that other ideas, such as a taxonomy of ignorance and uncertainty, need considerable further development to encompass all the perspectives at the symposium.

Developing Projects to Take the Integrative Work Further

Although there was considerable enthusiasm at the time, none of the other projects has progressed yet. Some may be revitalized when the book is completed. Overall, the publication of the book will be the first successful post-symposium activity and is likely to provide a stimulus for further activity, with either the same participants or new ones.

The point of assessing the success of our collaboration is to highlight that neither the process nor the content of partnerships are routinely evaluated. In order to improve collaborations, effective strategies for evaluation must be developed and implemented and the results made public, so that everyone can learn from the lessons drawn.

CONCLUSIONS

Three topics are dealt with in these conclusions: advancing collaborative activity to develop multidimensional approaches to ignorance and uncertainty; using this type of collaborative activity as a prototype for the development of integration and implementation

sciences; and improving our ability to measure the success of collaborations.

Collaborative Activity to Develop Multidimensional Approaches to Ignorance and Uncertainty

We conducted a successful first step in accelerating the production of multidimensional approaches to ignorance and uncertainty, but we still have a long journey ahead of us. We found that considerable enthusiasm can be generated for trading perspectives. A key result from this is that discipline and practice experts learn from others to improve their own fields. Indeed, Steve Longford reported back that he had incorporated his insights into his organization's approach. But we do not expect to see a huge impact from one activity alone. The main reason we spent time at the symposium examining a range of projects to take the integrative work further was to provide opportunities for cross-fertilization to continue, but to date this has not been particularly successful. Again, it may be unrealistic to expect much to arise from a single meeting. Further thought and action are needed to move forward on achieving this important goal.

The second key goal is to improve consideration of ignorance and uncertainty when complex problems and issues are addressed and to make this process efficient by developing one or more overarching frameworks. The experience at the symposium suggests that there may be a significant dilemma here. Development of overarching frameworks requires building on a considerable body of existing knowledge, which a small number of researchers, Michael Smithson being a notable example, have started to attempt to pull together. But there seems to be an incompatibility between the processes needed to trade information and those needed to build frameworks. The success of trading frameworks depends on equality (and seniority) of the participants. The success of contributing to an overarching framework depends on recognizing the greater expertise of one group member. The experience of the symposium has helped us recognize and articulate this potential dilemma, which is a crucial first step in finding a way to possibly overcome it.

The current collaborative group still has joint work to do in finishing the production of the book and will be invited to continue to work together, most probably on developing a course and a popular articulation of our work. The continuation of the Drug Policy Modelling Program also provides a context for ongoing work. We anticipate that perspectives missing from the current collaboration will also be incorporated in the future.

Cross-Disciplinary and Cross-Sectoral Collaborative Activity in Ignorance and Uncertainty as a Prototype for the Development of Integration and Implementation Sciences

The first major step in the development of each of the six primary areas of integration and implementation sciences is to bring together knowledge that is currently being independently developed in discipline and/or practice silos. This chapter describes the beginnings of such a process for the area of ignorance and uncertainty. A significant challenge for that process in the development of other areas of integration and implementation sciences has been described in the previous section, namely the unresolved tension between processes requiring equal standing among participants and processes requiring some participants to have more advanced knowledge.

A further question concerns the collaborative processes that would be most suitable for synthesis when the developments in discipline and practice silos have largely run in parallel, so that there is considerable overlap. In this case one would be bringing together synthesizers within different areas, so that the participants are more likely to have equal standing, and someone with significantly advanced knowledge would not be required. The challenge here might be that it would take time to get past the areas of overlap to more interesting differences that would provide opportunities for learning.

Certainly an important area for integration and implementation sciences is to bring together learnings about collaboration (as in this volume; see especially Holmstrand, Härnsten, & Löwstedt, Chapter 9, and Docherty & Shani, Chapter 8) to use the best processes in the development of the specialization.

Improving the Ability to Measure the Success of Collaborations

The collaboration we describe here has focused particularly on integration of knowledge. The project has been ongoing for more than 18 months and has involved several activities: the preparation and reading of perspectives by participants, an intense two-day engagement through a symposium, and a concentrated effort to synthesize the written perspectives and discussion by a two-person partnership. We have described the process of integration in detail, using a framework we believe is generally applicable to a wide range of collaborations. Our experience has also provided some reflections on measuring the success of collaboration, which we now conclude with. This complements the work of others (see in this volume, for example, Bradbury, Chapter 28; Pasmore, Woodman, & Simmons, Chapter 27).

There are no metrics for measuring collaboration success. As a rule of thumb, one would not expect everyone to rate the collaboration highly or to participate in every aspect of the collaboration. But what is an acceptable rate of dissent—5%, 10%, 50%? Because there is no standard way of reporting on collaborations and no attempt to gather standard data about collaborations, making progress here is difficult.

While such metrics are important, alone they are too narrow as measures of success. One might also argue that avoiding significant negative outcomes should also rate. For example, in the symposium described here the fact that no one shouted anyone else down, or rejected their ideas out of hand, can be considered a success. Although we did this intuitively, it is likely that bringing together people who did not know each other and who were of similar status contributed to this positive outcome. Hostile intellectual battles often have discipline or practice power dynamics behind them and play out between senior gatekeepers and/or ambitious mid-careers. Our choice of participants largely avoided these dynamics.

Another measure of success is level of engagement, moving beyond polite listening to identification and discussion of disagreements. In such a process, sparks might well fly from time to time. On this criterion, the symposium described here was moderately successful.

Processes where nothing goes wrong are relatively uncommon, so that another measure of success is whether and how successfully problems are recovered from and turned into learning experiences. When the symposium participants balked at the proposed process for developing an overarching framework, we moved on, but provided a small group space for those who did want to work together in the fashion we had envisaged.

The time at which success is measured can also be crucial. At this stage, none of the proposed follow-up activities, other than producing the book, have gone ahead. After the book has been published, this might change, and the assessment of success would change accordingly.

Finally, it is also difficult to assess what a realistic outcome relative to effort is. This brings us back to the problem of lack of benchmarks. Intuitively, it seems reasonable that a single symposium, for example, would not produce many outcomes in terms of discipline or practice change. On the other hand, we have little guidance for realistically assessing what such change would require. Have we started with the right people? The right questions? The right process?

Collaboration is key to tackling the complex problems that confront us as a society, but we still have a great deal to learn about how to work together most effectively. This is a challenge that the current volume addresses and that integration and implementation sciences will strive to learn from and build on.

NOTE

1. The Goolabri Group consists of Robyn Attewell, Stephen Buckman, Ann Curthoys, Kate Delaney, Stephen Dovers, Liz Furler, Sasha Grishin, Alan Hájek, John Handmer, Judith Jones, Steve Longford, John Mackey, Michael McFadden, Michael Moore, Paul Perkins, Pascal Perez, Stephen Pickard, Aileen Plant, John Quiggin, Alison Ritter, Michael Smithson, and Ian White, as well as Gabriele Bammer. We note, with great sadness, that Aileen Plant unexpectedly passed away in March 2007.

REFERENCES

Attewell, R. (2007). Statistics. In G. Bammer & M. Smithson (Eds.), *Uncertainty: Unifying diversity*. London: Earthscan.

Bammer, G. (2005). Integration and implementation sciences: Building a new specialization. *Ecology and Society, 10*(2), 6 [Electronic version]. Available from http://www.ecologyandsociety.org/vol10/iss2/art6/. See also www.anu.edu.au/iisn

Bammer, G. (2007). *Enhancing research collaboration: Three key management and policy challenges.* Manuscript submitted for publication.

Bammer, G., & LWA Integration Symposium Participants. (2005). Guiding principles for integration in natural resource management (NRM) as a contribution to sustainability. In G. Bammer., A. Curtis, C. Mobbs, R. Lane, & S. Dovers (Eds.), Australian Case Studies of Integration in Natural Resource Management (NRM) [Supplementary issue]. *Australasian Journal of Environmental Management, 12,* 5–7.

Bammer, G., & Smithson, M. (2007a). Towards an integrated view of uncertainty: I. The nature of uncertainty. In G. Bammer & M. Smithson (Eds.), *Uncertainty: Unifying diversity.* Unpublished manuscript.

Bammer, G., & Smithson, M. (Eds.). (2007b). *Uncertainty: Unifying diversity.* Unpublished manuscript.

Curthoys, A. (2007). History. In G. Bammer & M. Smithson (Eds.), *Uncertainty: Unifying diversity.* Unpublished manuscript.

Klein, J. T. (1990). *Interdisciplinarity: History, theory and practice.* Detroit, MI: Wayne State University Press.

Ritter, A., Bammer, G., Hamilton, M., Mazerolle, L., & the DPMP Team. (in press). Effective drug policy: A new approach demonstrated in the Drug Policy Modelling Program. *Drug and Alcohol Review.*

Rossini, F. A., & Porter, A. L. (1979). Frameworks for integrating interdisciplinary research. *Research Policy, 8*(1), 70–79.

Smithson, M. (1989). *Ignorance and uncertainty: Emerging paradigms.* New York: Springer Verlag.

Smithson, M. (2007). The many faces and masks of uncertainty. In G. Bammer & M. Smithson (Eds.), *Uncertainty: Unifying diversity.* Unpublished manuscript.

Smithson, M., & Bammer, G. (2007a). Towards an integrated view of uncertainty: II. Metaphors, motives and morals. In G. Bammer & M. Smithson (Eds.), *Uncertainty: Unifying diversity.* Unpublished manuscript.

Smithson, M., & Bammer, G. (2007b). Towards an integrated view of uncertainty: III. Coping and managing under uncertainty. In G. Bammer & M. Smithson (Eds.), *Uncertainty: Unifying diversity.* Unpublished manuscript.

Part IV

THE MULTIPLE VOICES
IN COLLABORATIVE
RESEARCH

R ecords of collaborative research projects often are written up by academics and describe the collaborative process and the learning that occurred during the program. However, the descriptions usually do not give direct voice to the various collaborators who participate in the process. Throughout this handbook, several of the authors chose to integrate the voices of the collaborators into the description, analysis, and/or discussion of the collaborative projects. In this section of the *Handbook*, we specifically asked the authors to capture and share the various voices of participants. As you will read in the first four chapters of this section, the authors did capture the voices and shared the voices in varying ways, ranging from formal interviews to including quotes from other papers where the participants had described their experience or their learning. In one case (ARC Research Team, Chapter 22), multiple voices are heard because different participants authored different sections and stated their views of the collaboration. One chapter captured the voices via in-depth interviews of the two key actors by two of the *Handbook* editors (Stebbins & Valenzuela, Chapter 23). In another case, the four coauthors interviewed one another (Mohrman, Mohrman, Cohen, & Winby, Chapter 24). And in yet another chapter, the managers of the system integrator organization who had participated as co-researchers were invited by the academic authors to reflect in writing about the experience, and those reflections were integrated into the chapter (Coghlan & Coughlan, Chapter 21).

The importance of understanding each collaborative management research project through the voices of diverse participants stems from the theory underlying collaborative management research. It is often ideologically touted as a way to foster organizational democracy, to empower many stakeholders to participate in the learning process, and to help shape the unfolding of their social system. A pragmatic case can also be made based on the theoretical view of organizations as social artifacts (Simon, 2001). Organizations are designed by human beings to achieve their purposes in complex ecosystems (Hannan & Freeman, 1977). Complex systems are composed of many agents and populations of agents, each of whom are trying to secure the resources to achieve their purposes through adaptive strategies that entail complex mixtures of competitive and collaborative behavior (Axelrod & Cohen, 1999; Holland, 1995). In the collaborations described below, individual agents include academics, consultants, managers, employees, and leaders of community agencies. Collective agents include research centers, universities, agencies, firms, departments, and divisions. The design and performance of the complex system are influenced by the relationships between the agents who compose it. A collaborative research project aimed at changing the performance capabilities of a system must thus be understood through the eyes of the participants.

At any point in time, the behavior in a complex system is governed by a set of "rules"— implicit or explicit, formal or informal (Axelrod & Cohen, 1999). These are embodied in routines, frameworks, principles, and incentives, and in the patterns of behavior that are self-reinforcing in the system. Changing the behavior in the system, the resulting distribution of resources to and interdependencies between different agents and populations, and system performance therefore requires the governing rules to be changed. It has been argued that complex activities are inevitably self-organizing (Fukuyama, 1999)—that they cannot be fully externally or hierarchically controlled. The impact of organizational design changes or initiatives that are imposed hierarchically, for example, depends on the adaptive behaviors of various agents in the organization as they respond to them. Relevant agents and populations of agents exist at multiple social levels, including individuals, various groupings of individuals, and collectives such as departments, institutions, and organizations—and each will pursue strategies aimed at accomplishing their purposes. Within one of the collective agents in a system, such as a department within the organization that is being changed, individual agents will respond differently as they pursue their individual purposes. As important, they will have different perspectives and attitudes toward collaborative research projects and different views of what occurs during the discovery or change process.

Social order in a complex system such as an organization or a work network arises and evolves from a combination of top-down and bottom-up forces. Collaborative research is an approach to changing the social order by combining knowledge that is dispersed through the system in new ways, and by introducing and creating new knowledge to guide change. Multiple sources of knowledge provide the "requisite variety" (Ashby, 1956) to address the problems of interest and the ability to address new challenges (Monge & Contractor, 2003, pp. 95–97). In a collaborative research setting, for example, the knowledge of the different populations and agents engaged in practice is extended by and combined with the knowledge of external researchers, and vice versa.

Through collaborative research that brings together the knowledge of many contributors, new knowledge can be created that alters the routines, frameworks, principles, and incentives that shape the adaptive behavior of the agents in the population, and that result in changed performance. Knowledge can disseminate among populations within the organization and outside it through various methods of diffusion, including imitation and the carrying of knowledge by people who move between populations. In that way, the knowledge gained through inquiry and development in one system can contribute to advancing the understanding of organizing and managing in general, and knowledge from one system can be useful input into the inquiry and development in other social systems. The ideal of collaborative research is that knowledge advances through two interrelated cycles of research: (1) the ongoing inquiry,

Table IV.1 The Multiple Voices in the Collaborative Research Chapters: A Comparative Preview

	Chapter 21	*Chapter 22*	*Chapter 23*	*Chapter 24*
	CO-IMPROVE (Coghlan and Coughlan)	ARC (ARC Research Team)	KP (Stebbins and Valenzuela)	HP/CEO (Mohrman, Mohrman, Cohen, and Winby)
Collaboration locus	Multiple EU regions	Multiple communities in Israel's northern region	Multiple units within Kaiser Permanente Pharmacy Operations Division	Multiple business units, multiple levels within the Hewlett-Packard Corporation
Topic(s) of collaboration	The discovery of models and learning mechanisms to improve supply chain performance	The discovery of models and approaches to initiate community-wide development projects in a complex multi-ethnic region	Wide range of topics over 30 years of collaborative research projects	The discovery of effective team models for complex knowledge-based work
Scope of collaboration	Complex, multilevel, cross-national network	Complex, multilevel, regional network	Communication forums as microcosm of the complex multilevel network	Three knowledge communities of practice that formed a community of inquiry
Key actors in the community of inquiry	* academics from four European universities with different disciplinary backgrounds * senior managers from three companies in different European countries	* academics * practitioners * research center within a regional university * managers from seven communities	* manager * academic consultant	* study teams and management teams from nine business units * internal consultant/ researchers * researchers from CEO (Center for Effective Organizations) within a university
Voices in the chapter	* managers * university researchers	* community leaders * university researchers * university administrators	* manager * employee * academic consultant	* internal consultant/ researcher * university researchers

experimentation, and learning of organizational participants who generate increasingly effective approaches for practice that are then shared with other organizations; and (2) programmatic research whereby academic researchers collaborate with multiple organizations, evolve knowledge, test its boundaries, and disseminate results.

Although different participants assume different roles in the collaboration (see Bartunek, Chapter 4 in this volume), collaborative research depends fundamentally on giving voice to multiple perspectives and incorporating the knowledge from several populations into the process of inquiry and research. One duality is the intermingling in the research of the processes that the organization is undergoing to self-develop (generate organizational knowledge as embedded in new practices) with the research that contributes to scholarly or broadly held knowledge that is accessible beyond the organization itself. Other dynamics include the interplay between various individuals and populations within the organization or across organizational networks, each of whom bring their own set of purposes.

In sum, each party to the collaboration arrives with goals and preferences, differing interests and foci, and different knowledge. The chapters in this cluster, as seen below, illustrate how the different actors that represent diverse individual agents, collective agents, or communities of practice form a community of inquiry in which different voices are shared and new meaning is created (see Coghlan & Shani, Chapter 29 in this volume). This section enriches our understanding of collaborative research by giving voice to multiple perspectives and by raising some of the challenges of and methodologies for establishing a collaboration that addresses these various purposes and builds on these various sources of knowledge.

A high-level overview of the chapters in this section is summarized in Table IV.1 on page 443. The table provides a synopsis of the section along five dimensions: the locus of the collaboration; the topic(s) of the collaboration; the scope of the collaboration; the collaborators; and the voices in the chapter.

REFERENCES

Ashby, W. R. (1956). *An introduction to cybernetics.* New York: Wiley.

Axelrod, R., & Cohen, M. D. (1999). *Harnessing complexity: Organizational implications of a scientific frontier.* New York: The Free Press.

Fukuyama, F. (1999). *The great disruption: Human nature and the reconstitution of social order.* New York: Free Press.

Hannan, M. T., & Freeman, M. (1977). The population ecology of organizations. *American Journal of Sociology, 82*(5), 929–964.

Holland, J. H. (1995). *Hidden order: How adaptation builds complexity.* Reading, MA: Helix Books.

Monge, P. R., & Contractor, N. S. (2003). *Theories of communication networks.* Oxford, UK: Oxford University Press.

Simon, H. (2001). *The sciences of the artificial* (3rd ed.). Cambridge: MIT Press.

Collaborative Research in and by an Interorganizational Network

DAVID COGHLAN

PAUL COUGHLAN

ABSTRACT

This exemplar chapter explores collaborative research in and by an interorganizational network. It describes and reflects on the process by which and the setting within which managers and academics collaborated as researchers across boundaries—including disciplinary and institutional boundaries, as well as those between academia and industry—to develop learning in collaborative improvement in the supply chain. The particular empirical setting explored was that defined by the CO-IMPROVE project, from which two cases are presented. A distinctive element of this exemplar chapter is the inclusion of the voices of participating managers as they reflect on their experiences. The chapter concludes that collaborative research in and by an interorganizational network is both possible and relevant. Three particular insights on collaborative research are presented: linking theory, practice, and collaboration; capturing difference while sustaining the collaboration; and managing quality.

This exemplar chapter explores collaborative management research in and by an interorganizational network. It describes and reflects on the process by which and the setting within which managers and academics collaborated as researchers across boundaries—including disciplinary and institutional boundaries, as well as those between academia and industry—to develop learning in collaborative improvement in the supply chain. The particular empirical setting explored was that defined by the CO-IMPROVE project. The objectives of this European Union-funded project included the facilitation of collaborative improvement of operations practice and performance in the extended manufacturing enterprise through collaborative action learning among both managers and academics.

Increasingly, competition is moving from interfirm rivalry to that between supply chains and networks (Ring & Van de Ven, 1992). In the field of manufacturing, such collaboration between firms may develop into an Extended Manufacturing Enterprise (EME), a chain or network comprising all the relevant functions of the partners. EME competitiveness depends upon how fit the partner firms are as innovative and knowledge-creative players within dynamic, complex, integrated networks. While developments in information and communication technology have facilitated process improvement both within organizations and between organizations, EMEs need a well-developed collaborative learning capability, supported by information and communication technology, to bridge geographical and time barriers. Active collaboration between the firms involved is required in order to create and maximize synergy among the capabilities of the firms involved, while allowing each individual partner to realize its own strategic goals. Collaboration requires a capacity to learn, not only at the levels of individuals or companies, but also at the interorganizational level (Coghlan & Rashford, 2006; Knight & Pye, 2004; Lane, 2001). The CO-IMPROVE project aimed at studying and reflecting on the issues and processes that would emerge and that would inform the development of understanding of collaborative improvement in the performance of EMEs as the members were interacting.

CO-IMPROVE

CO-IMPROVE was a European Union (EU)-funded project that ran from March 2001 to February 2004. The objectives of CO-IMPROVE were to develop a business model to support the design, implementation, and ongoing development of collaborative

improvement between partners in Extended Manufacturing Enterprises (EMEs), supported by a Web-based software system and action learning-based implementation guidelines. Industrial partners comprised three EMEs, one each centered in Italy, the Netherlands, and Denmark. Each EME was led by a system integrator and included three of its more significant suppliers. Academic partners comprised Aalborg University (Denmark), Politecnico di Milano (Italy), the University of Dublin (Ireland), and the University of Twente (the Netherlands). The work of the academic partners with the EMEs was facilitated by two IT companies—an ICT developer from Sweden and a subcontractor from Greece—specializing in the development of enterprise resource planning applications for industry.

The project extended over a three-year period and was broken down into eight discrete work packages. These work packages constituted the sequential stages of the project: investigating requirements, design, operation, revision, and validation. The action learning work package was the largest individual work component and constituted the operation stage. Starting 15 months into the project and extending over 15 months, the outcomes were planned to be fourfold:

1. Improved collaboration within EMEs

2. A new theory of supply chain management in EMEs

3. Implementation guidelines for collaborative improvement in EMEs

4. Contribution to theory of interorganizational action learning and action research

The project explored the premise of consistency, regularity, and balance suggested by the concept of collaboration, focusing in particular on the learning required to enhance collaborative improvement of the performance of EMEs.

Before understanding the notion of collaborative improvement, we need to define its antecedent, continuous improvement, as "an organization-wide process of focused and sustained incremental innovation" (Bessant & Caffyn, 1997). Continuous improvement addresses making changes in deliverables, operating procedures, and mechanisms on an intraorganizational, incremental basis (Lillrank et al., 1998). A related concept is that of collaborative improvement, which may be defined (Cagliano, Caniato, Corso, & Spina, 2002) as

> a purposeful inter-company interactive process that focuses on continuous incremental innovation, aimed at enhancing the EME overall operational performance. It is simultaneously concerned with bringing about change in the EME, developing the EME's capabilities, and generating actionable knowledge. Finally, it is an evolving systematic change process that is undertaken in a spirit of collaboration and learning. (p. 134)

In contrast to continuous improvement, in collaborative improvement the focus is on the intercompany context.

In the same vein, just as the field of organizational learning can encompass learning *in* organizations and learning *by* organizations (Popper & Lipshitz, 1998), similarly network learning can encompass learning *in* networks and learning *by* networks (Knight, 2002; Knight & Pye, 2004). Critical to both organizational learning and network learning is the development of learning mechanisms (Shani & Docherty, 2003; Docherty & Shani, Chapter 8 in this *Handbook*). CO-IMPROVE focused on a specific kind of intercompany context, the EME that is focused on supply chain management. As noted earlier, the EME is a form of network organization. Looking to achieve network learning in the three EMEs through action

learning, CO-IMPROVE adopted a collaborative management research approach with the expectation of improving the performance and, eventually, the service delivered to customers (Lane, 2001) and the development of actionable knowledge. The action learning approach was utilized with a view to developing a learning approach in the actual experience of the EME, which could become a learning mechanism for EMEs.

In sum, the CO-IMPROVE project was a large-scale collaborative management research project. It took place in a complex interorganizational setting. It was characterized particularly by discrete borders and boundaries. The borders were those country borders between the nine countries participating in the project. The boundaries were those organizational boundaries between buyers and suppliers with previous commercial and collaborative histories, between the four academic institutions involved, between the various academic participants, and between the business and academic participants.

METHODOLOGY

CO-IMPROVE was a research project and so committed itself to scientific rigor in the study of the project. It was undertaken through an action research and action learning approach where the academics and company managers both managed the project and studied it at the same time (Coghlan & Coughlan, 2006). Underpinning the project were two rationales: a rationale for action and a rationale for research. Evaluation of the outcomes of the project was related to these two rationales.

Action research and action learning have distinguished respective pedigrees. Both belong to the family of action-oriented forms of inquiry that constitute collaborative management research (see also McGuire, Palus, & Torbert, Chapter 6 in this *Handbook*).

Action learning has its roots in the pioneering work of Reg Revans and has developed to be a major force in management development and organizational learning. Action research has many roots, including the work on changing organizations through organization development that grew out of the life and work of Kurt Lewin and the emancipatory work for social change. While action research and action learning have many values in common, they differ in their primary focus: For action learning, the focus is on management learning and organizational improvement and learning; for action research, the focus is on research and the generation of actionable knowledge. Correspondingly, while the key steps in both action research and action learning have similarities, they differ in the degree to which action research demands reflection toward theory. In CO-IMPROVE, the practical tasks of improving EME operational performance were undertaken through action learning, while the overall research agenda was aimed at generating

- A new theory of supply chain management in EMEs
- Implementation guidelines for collaborative improvement in EMEs
- Contributions to a theory of interorganizational action learning and action research

The Action Research Approach. Action research provided a parallel emphasis on the generation of actionable knowledge in the interorganizational setting. The CO-IMPROVE project was undertaken through an action research approach wherein the researchers were both managing the project and studying it at the same time (Greenwood & Levin, 1998; Coghlan & Brannick, 2005). The collaborative research in CO-IMPROVE worked across several levels (Coghlan, Coughlan, & Brennan, 2004), as illustrated in Figure 21.1.

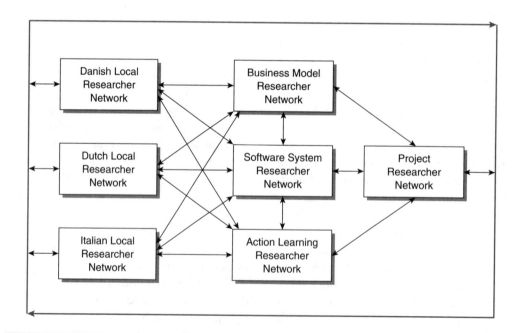

Figure 21.1   Researcher Networks

SOURCE: Adapted from Coghlan, Coughlan, and Brennan (2004).

Table 21.1   Action Researcher Key Tasks

Researcher Network	Key Tasks
Local researcher network in each country	• Gather, document, and make sense of data from their company network for the duration of the action learning process. • Review the feedback generated from assessments of practice and performance in their company network. • Develop and outline the process used to set and communicate objectives for the change initiative to management in the company network and consider the degree of conditionality in their buy-in. • Develop and outline the plan for transitional steps from project stage to stage so as to minimize possible deterioration of company performance, company motivation, and quality of research data. • Resolve issues that might arise.
Work package researcher network	• Gather, document, and make sense of data from the three company networks for the duration of the action learning process. • Develop position papers on the development, application process, usefulness, and usability of the business model, the software system, and the action learning approach. • Develop and outline the plan for transitional steps from project stage to stage so as to minimize possible deterioration of company performance, company motivation, and quality of research data. • Resolve issues that might arise.
Project researcher network	• Write position papers on the development, application process, usefulness, and usability of the business model, the software system, and the action learning approach.

There were three researcher network levels: the local researcher network in each country, the work package researcher network, and the project researcher network. The key tasks they carried out are described in Table 21.1.

The local researcher network in each country. Academics from Aalborg University, Politecnico di Milano, and the University of Twente facilitated their "local" company network and, as such, constituted local researcher networks. Each company network meeting (i.e., the action learning meetings between system integrators and suppliers) was preceded and followed by a local researcher meeting, which engaged in the action research cycle of diagnosing, planning action, taking action, and evaluating action with respect to the implementation of and research on the three themes—the business model, the software system, and the action learning process. The effectiveness of these local researcher meetings depended upon the development by the academics of a confidence in the new language and terminology of the individual company settings. Such development facilitated communication and sensemaking and, as important, signaled to the companies the commitment of the researchers to active collaboration.

The work package researcher network. The ongoing development and application of the business model, the software system, and the action learning process were each the responsibility of the institutions who led the work packages dealing with these three respective elements. Each represented a work package researcher network. The researcher network for each work package met at each partner meeting and engaged in the action research cycle of diagnosing, planning action, taking action, and evaluating action with respect to the implementation of and research on the three themes in the three company networks.

The project researcher network. The project researcher network encompassed the entire project, both academics and managers of the system integrator organizations. The concerns of this researcher network were broader than project management. They engaged also in the action research cycle. The project researcher network met three times over a five-month period prior to the start of the change initiatives within the companies. In the first two meetings, the authors led workshops on action research and action learning in order to achieve within the network a common understanding of the action learning and action research imperatives. The third meeting focused on detailed preparation of the assignments for each company network and preparation of the tracking of

what would go on within each company learning network. Together, these three meetings prepared the academics and the managers for the planned collaborative research. In particular, it helped to develop a confidence among all in the new language of the network in order to make best use of the privileged access granted. Thereafter, the network met at partner meetings where all local and work package researcher networks presented reports on the progress of their action research across the three company networks, and on progress in the development of the business model, the software system, and the action learning process. Because this group was both managing the project and studying it concurrently, meetings comprised both progress reports on the development of the elements of the project and theoretical formulations underpinning diagnosis of events. Vigorous and heated discussions on the application of appropriate theory and underlying methodological assumptions were common.

The action research approach adopted was based on Coghlan and Brannick's (2005) action research cycle comprising a pre-step, a set of main steps, and a meta-step:

1. *The pre-step:* The action research cycle unfolds in real time and begins with an understanding of the context of the project. In CO-IMPROVE, this was done through the initial conceptualization of the project and submission to the European Commission to study the issues and processes that would emerge and that would inform the development of understanding of collaborative improvement in the performance of EMEs.

2. *The four main steps:*
   i. *Diagnosing.* Diagnosing involves naming what the issues are, however provisionally, as a working theme, on the basis of which action will be planned and taken. It seeks to move from manifestation of issues to understanding

their underlying causes and is integral to the research process. In CO-IMPROVE, learning in action in the EME was adopted as the working theme. Behind this theme was an understanding among the researchers that EME competitiveness depended upon the development of a collaborative learning capability to bridge geographical and time barriers. Active collaboration between the firms involved would be required in order to create and maximize synergy among the capabilities of the firms involved, while allowing each individual partner to realize its own strategic goals. Grasping insights into this complex process through engagement in cycles of action and reflection was ongoing and critical.

ii. *Planning action.* Planning action follows from the analysis of the context and purpose of the project, the framing of the issue, and the diagnosis, and is consistent with them. It may be that this action planning focuses on a first step or a series of first steps. In CO-IMPROVE, plans to engage in cycles of action and reflection were made in collaboration with relevant key members of the three interorganizational networks.

iii. *Taking action.* Implementing the planned action involves making the desired changes and following through on the plans in collaboration with relevant key members of the organization. In CO-IMPROVE, the action learning process was enacted taking in the six distinct interactive components identified by Marquardt (1999, 2004), described in the next section.

iv. *Evaluating action.* Evaluation involves reflecting on the outcomes of the action, both intended and unintended, a review of the process in order that the next cycle of planning and action may benefit from the experience of the cycle completed. In CO-IMPROVE, review of how the action learning process was implemented was undertaken routinely and consistently, with a particular focus on how both the rationale for action and the rationale for research underpinning the project were being maintained.

3. *The meta-step:* While the action researchers are engaging in the action research cycles, they need to be continually inquiring into each of the four main steps, asking how these steps are being conducted and how they are consistent with each other, and, so, shaping how the subsequent steps are conducted. It is the dynamic of this reflection on reflection that incorporates the learning process of the action research cycle and enables action research to be more than everyday problem solving. Hence it is learning about learning, in other words, meta-learning. In CO-IMPROVE, the academics drew on Coghlan and Brannick (2005) to guide reflection on content, process, and premise:

– The *content* of what was diagnosed, planned, acted on, and evaluated was studied and evaluated.

– The *process* of how diagnosis was undertaken, how action planning flowed from that diagnosis and was conducted, how actions followed and were an implementation of the stated plans, and how evaluation was conducted were critical foci for inquiry.

– *Premise* reflection was inquiry into the unstated and often nonconscious underlying assumptions which governed attitudes and behavior.

The collaborative research methodology in CO-IMPROVE was enacted around cycles of action and reflection. Each company network submitted progress reports in advance of partner meetings, which were discussed and reflected on at the meetings; next steps were planned and then implemented in the next cycle of action. The data gathered, documented, and reflected on by the researchers were fed to the various teams, who kept an overall watching brief of the progress of their area of responsibility. Academics wrote reflection papers that aired assumptions and inferences and were tested in meetings of both academics and system integrator managers. In this way, there was continuous exposure of the events across the entire project, and their interpretation was made open to public reflection and analysis, which then led to further action. An example of this was a constant reflection on the slow progress of the introduction and use of the software system across the three networks. The content of the academics' reflection notes were fed back to the partner group overseeing the development and application of the technology, and acted as a driving force for the work of that group and the initiatives it took across the project.

The Action Learning Approach. Active collaboration between the firms involved was required in order to create and to maximize synergy among the capabilities of the firms involved while allowing each individual partner to realize its own strategic goals. Action learning is an approach to the development of people in organizations that takes the task as the vehicle for learning (Pedler, 1996; Dilworth & Willis, 2003). It reverses the traditional learning process wherein one learns something first and then applies it. Revans (1998), the founder of action learning, expressed it terms of a formula, $L = P + Q$. L stands for learning, P for programmed learning (e.g., current knowledge in use, already known, what is in books), and Q for questioning insight. It seeks to enable managers to learn by bringing real organizational problems that do not appear to have clear solutions to a group learning setting with other managers. Here, participants meet on equal terms in groups to report to one another and to discuss their problems and progress.

In CO-IMPROVE, the action learning groups were interorganizational in composition, comprising senior managers from the system integrators and from their supplier companies. The action learning approach adopted was based on Marquardt's six distinct interactive components (Marquardt, 1999, 2004):

1. *A problem.* Real, complex organizational issues that touch on different parts of the organization and that are not amenable to expert solutions are selected and worked on. In CO-IMPROVE, the problem to be confronted was a business issue: the enhancement of the EME operational performance.

2. *The group.* Participants meet on equal terms to report to one another and to discuss their problem and progress. The group typically comprises six to eight members who care about the problem, know something about it, and have the power to implement solutions. In CO-IMPROVE, the group comprised three interorganizational networks, each made up of a system integrator and their suppliers, manned by senior staff with knowledge and power to implement collaborative improvement. These staff recognized and appreciated that collaborative improvement was of strategic importance to their businesses.

3. *The questioning and reflective process.* Based on Revans's (1998) formula for action learning noted earlier, in CO-IMPROVE, new ideas were presented by participating managers at network meetings, at which actions undertaken were reported on and reviewed and plans for new actions were considered.

4. *The commitment to taking action.* Action learning is based on the premise that no real learning takes place unless and until action is taken. Implementation, rather than recommendations to others, is central. In CO-IMPROVE, the networks recognized that enhancing supply chain management through collaborative improvement was of strategic importance to their businesses. They engaged their own staff, who had the scope and capability to take the necessary action.

5. *The commitment to learning.* Action learning aims at going beyond merely solving immediate problems. An increase in the knowledge and capacity to better adapt to change is more important. The networks recognized the cyclical nature of the learning process and maintained the time and space to reflect on and codify the emerging insights for subsequent application.

6. *The facilitator.* Action learning groups benefit from having a facilitator: that is, one who plays a variety of roles for the group—coordinator, catalyst, observer, climate setter, communication enabler, and learning coach, among many others. Members of the academic partner institutions acted as learning coaches and kept the networks focused on learning—for example, through framing conceptually the emerging insights presented at network meetings or generating minutes and notes of those meetings for subsequent review and discussion.

With the action research and action learning approaches introduced, the two cases following develop the background to the reflective voices of the managers. The cases are similarly structured and describe both context and initiatives undertaken.

CASE A

Context

System Integrator A (SIA) operated in a capital equipment industry competing in both the military and civil markets. The company employed over 1,500 people and had grown by 20% over the previous two years. The industry is characterized by low-volume, high-value products with a life cycle of up to 30 years in the military sector and up to 15 years in the civil sector. Strict quality requirements are reflected in a need to certify and trace each component part, each piece of raw material, and each operation performed. Consequently, only certified suppliers can be employed,

making the management of the supply base complex. Entry into the civil market in the 1980s required a change in the company strategy, with a move from vertical integration to choosing a different network of suppliers for each program. As a consequence, purchasing had grown over 100% in the past five years, indicating the increasing importance of supplier relationships for the company.

SIA selected five suppliers to participate in the CO-IMPROVE project. The suppliers were large and small, more or less dependent on SIA for significant proportions of their turnover, and, in one case, in direct competition with SIA. Common, however, was a previous collaborative history and a willingness to engage in CO-IMPROVE. On a dyadic basis, all suppliers engaged in at least two change initiatives in collaboration with SIA. Through participation in regular meetings of the company network, all companies had the opportunity to present outcomes of their initiatives for constructive questioning and reflection.

Collaborative Initiatives

The collaboration of Supplier 1 with SIA illustrates the process, the issues addressed, and the outcomes. Supplier 1 is a specialist in high-technology metalwork parts, design, and engineering, starting from 3D models provided by customers. The set of activities performed depends on the requirements of the customer. Products are usually prototypes or small series of mechanical parts with high technological content. SIA accounted for 45% of its total turnover. The relationship with SIA was considered strong, stable, and strategic, with dedicated investments in design and process technology and equipment.

Working with SIA, Supplier 1 developed two collaborative improvement cycles during the CO-IMPROVE project, summarized in Table 21.2. Details of each improvement cycle have been presented elsewhere (Coghlan & Coughlan, 2005). The first cycle related to

Table 21.2 Case A: Collaborative Improvement Initiatives and Their Outcomes

Relationship	Collaborative Improvement Initiative	Operational Outcome	Learning Outcome
SIA – Supplier 1	**First cycle:** Reduction of delays	Delays on the specific part considered for the pilot initiative were reduced by 75%. An improvement proposal relating to order management was developed.	Analysis of the causes of the delays.
	Second cycle: Management of personnel qualifications	Database was extended to include information about process, process steps, and the types of qualifications and certifications needed for different product programs.	It was hoped that this database could be rolled out to larger suppliers if successful.

SOURCE: Adapted from Coghlan and Coughlan (2005).

reduction of delays; the second related to management of personnel qualifications.

First Cycle: Reduction of Delays

Disrespect for delivery times regarding materials, drawings, and documents was seen as a major cause of delays. The initiative was concerned with mapping the overall order process and monitoring times and dates in order to identify possible causes for delay. Supplier 1 was responsible for ensuring that all documents and parts were received on time. SIA felt that the supplier needed to be more proactive and recommended more frequent and more direct lines of communication. It was agreed to monitor all orders for three months in order to identify all the delivery dates of the parts and the dispatch date of documents, materials, and drawings. The activity steps were as follows:

- Analyze the causes of the delays noticed and then meet to discuss these causes.

- Develop an improvement proposal relating to order management, including implementing the new order management system, and analyzing the improvement activity and its results.

As a result of this activity, delays on the specific part considered for the pilot initiative were reduced by 75%.

Second Cycle: Management of Personnel Qualifications

For certain product programs, staff involved needed specific qualifications and certification. The goal was to create a database detailing the staff and processes in both SIA and Supplier 1, including the qualifications necessary for performing welding, surface treatment, and chemical treatment tasks. Data were to include a list of the people involved, medical checks necessary, nature and duration of qualifications, validity and expiration of qualifications, and a list of applicable product programs for this database. This database would allow SIA and Supplier 1 to access current data and to plan with greater visibility of employee status. The activity steps were as follows:

- Define the data needed and identify the data fields.
- Create the database.
- Upload the data.

This task took approximately one month to complete. SIA and Supplier 1 began to use the database and to monitor and evaluate its use. On the basis of this evaluation, the database was extended to include information about process, process steps, and the types of qualifications and certifications needed for different product programs. It was hoped that this database could be rolled out to larger suppliers if successful.

CASE B

Context

SIB, a specialist company, manufactured and assembled motion control systems for niche markets in the automotive and truck industry. The competitive structure of the automotive and truck industry had some clear characteristics:

- Hierarchy in the market
- Strong distinction between part suppliers and system suppliers
- Economies of scale
- Focus on competitive pricing and quality products

Within the automotive and truck industry, the order-winning criterion was price, whereas quality, delivery, and technology were qualifiers. Therefore, companies within these industries needed to constantly monitor the cost structure (throughout the supply chain) in order to remain competitive. There was a

strategic significance of collaborative supply relationships. It was essential therefore for SIB to look for long-term, highly involved, and dedicated partners who fully supported the processes of SIB. As such, SIB needed suppliers who applied Continuous Improvement (CI) with a strong focus on quality, cost, and delivery. A close collaboration with a limited number of suppliers was needed to guarantee maximum use of suppliers' knowledge in order to increase efficiency and reduce time to markets.

For the CO-IMPROVE project, SIB engaged with three of its suppliers. The suppliers that were involved represented different types of relationships with SIB in terms of trust, (relative) power, willingness to share information and communicate openly, mutual understanding, and sense of direction. Furthermore, the three suppliers produced and delivered different products to SIB and, as such, were not direct competitors of each other. As such, information could pass freely and openly among the companies within the client system. All companies expressed the intention to communicate and share information openly in order to learn from each other.

Collaborative Initiatives

SIB collaborated with three suppliers. Details of each improvement cycle have been presented elsewhere (Middel, Coghlan, Coughlan, Brennan, & McNichols, 2006). An overview of the collaborative improvement initiatives and the operational and learning outcomes is presented in Table 21.3.

The collaboration of Supplier 1 with SIB illustrates the process, the issues addressed, and the outcomes. Supplier 1 delivered pump components to SIB. Over the preceding four years, a quality problem had persisted with one component part, and many improvement attempts had proven unsuccessful. The component quality problem had severe knock-on effects for the motion control systems

Table 21.3   Case B: Collaborative Improvement Initiatives and Their Outcomes

Relationship	Collaborative Improvement Initiative	Operational Outcome	Learning Outcome
SIB – Supplier 1	Redesign of a product that caused severe problems during malfunction in the system of the SI	Cost reduction and increase of the quality of the product. The supplier was able to reduce internal scrap rate from 33% to 5%.	Increased awareness of the need to communicate and share information more regularly. Closer collaboration is necessary to overcome problems.
SIB – Supplier 1	Proposal to produce an existing aluminum product of SIB in plastic	Expected outcomes are 50% cost reduction for SIB and increase in sales for the supplier.	The inducement for improvement is not always a practical problem, but can also be more creative and proactive.
SIB – Supplier 2	Cleanliness of products	Increase in sales from SIB to supplier. Reduction in reject rate by SIB.	Need for project planning. Importance of information sharing between the companies.
SIB – Supplier 3	Information and communication on specifications of products	N.A.	Increased information exchange and awareness of need for improving communication.
SIB – Supplier 3	Analyze and evaluate a change in tooling concept by the supplier	N.A.	Increased insight in organizational structure and communication flows on both sides.

SOURCE: Adapted from Middel et al. (2006).

assembled by SIB: Component failures resulted in system collapses and component melting. The supplier was not able to optimize their manufacturing processes technically. The internal scrap rate was as high as 33%. As a result, extra quality checks and costs of failure raised the possibility of claims for large financial reimbursements by SIB. The improvement initiative took place over a period of 15 months through a cycle of 12 joint workshops. These workshops involved Supplier 1, SIB, and the other suppliers in processes of diagnosing, fact-finding, implementation, and evaluation of the improvement actions. Initially, there was no mutual understanding of the concept of collaborative improvement, which had a negative effect on the level of openness between the companies: The suppliers had the impression that this was another way of implementing cost reduction and quality programs. SIB paid particular attention to creating a shared vision and a sense of direction. In the event, the regular meetings developed a momentum within the initiatives. For Supplier 1, the outcome, a new internal scrap rate of 5%, received the approval of SIB.

REFLECTIVE VOICES

The presentation of the two case studies could stop at this point. In CO-IMPROVE, content issues of collaborative improvement, process issues of enacting action learning in the context of the EME, and the challenges to the underlying assumptions guiding the research were the focus of the learning about learning, that is, the research into EME learning in action. Reflective voices were raised and heard at the different levels with a focus on both action learning and action research. At partner meetings, both researchers and managers participated equally. The researchers' voices were captured most succinctly in published papers, such as those noted in the References section of this chapter. An additional voice was that of the managers of the system integrators, who were both actors in the action and researchers in the inquiry. In this chapter, we highlight this particular voice as a means of articulating the development of a research-based understanding of collaborative improvement in the performance of EMEs as the members were interacting.

In a subsequent interaction with two managers from among the system integrators, their voices provided additional reflective insights from this collaborative management research initiative into learning by the networked organizations. The outcomes presented here are distinguished by the voice taken—that of the managers from two of the industrial partners: Manager A from Case A and Manager B from Case B. Manager A was the senior purchasing manager at System Integrator A (SIA), with responsibility for supply relationships with an extensive network of suppliers spread across Europe and beyond. Manager B was the chief operations manager at System Integrator B (SIB), with responsibility for all aspects of the running operation, including the supply base.

The authors approached each manager with a request to reflect on the recently completed CO-IMPROVE project. The managers were well known to the authors and had worked and interacted with the authors throughout the project. As actors in the action and researchers in the inquiry, they were intimately familiar with the research process undertaken and with the underlying concepts. This familiarity came not just from their "hands-on" involvement in the practice, but also from their active participation in researcher network meetings at all levels.

The authors provided each manager with a set of prompts that invited them to consolidate and to document their reflections under a number of headings:

- Starting point
- Evolution of relationships
- Collaborative process
- Outcomes and longer-term organization changes

This consolidation was facilitated by the earlier continuous exposure of events across the entire project, where their interpretation was made open to public reflection and analysis that then led to further action. In their consolidations, the managers provided written accounts of what motivated their organizations to participate in CO-IMPROVE and of what they achieved and learned. In addition, one of the managers drew from a detailed account of the research process and outcomes that he had written in a company magazine.

Starting Point

For the companies, the starting point had a number of features: motivation and prior experience of collaborative research. Both companies were motivated to participate in the project. In each case, they had a prior research-based relationship with the "local" researcher network in their respective countries. These existing relationships predisposed them positively to accept invitations to participate in the related, but different, project that became CO-IMPROVE. As noted by Manager B,

> We were working with the local university on several quality development areas. Through this work, we were asked to be a part of the CO-IMPROVE project and we accepted the invitation. Starting into CO-IMPROVE, our expectation was of quicker and better responses at the development stage, fewer quality and delivery alerts, and quicker and more effective problem solving.

As CO-IMPROVE developed for SIB, quality improvement featured as a central part of the initiatives undertaken.

Prior familiarity with collaborative research also helped to define the starting point. As noted by Manager A,

> My first "official" exposure to collaborative research was during the CO-IMPROVE project, when we started talking and discussing this way of working. I was not unaware of the idea and, before CO-IMPROVE, I had previous "unofficial and unstructured" information on collaborative research from my earlier working life.

Evolution of Relationships

A number of kinds of relationships developed as CO-IMPROVE evolved. There was the relationship between the academics and the managers, that between the SIs and their suppliers, and, finally, the relationship between practice and theory. These relationships developed in tandem. Talking about the relationship between theory and practice, Manager A noted,

> The relationship started during the early (project researcher) network meetings and developed as I engaged with the readings circulated. At first, it seemed to me to be much too "academic" and theoretical.

Later on, however, having experienced our own "real" case and having discussed and shared information with the other industrial and academic partners, it became more interesting, understandable, and "real life." I started understanding better the theory behind the facts and started managing better the related activities.

Manager B reflected on the evolving relationship between SIB and their suppliers:

> The relationship within the CO-IMPROVE project itself developed, as you know, by regular meetings, which were OK. In fact, getting our suppliers involved was at first quite easy; the suppliers were enthusiastic at the beginning! But when resources were required and actions had to be completed, the suppliers backed off. As the "motivator," we worked to get the suppliers back on board.

Collaborative Process

Collaboration was not new to the companies and their suppliers. However, collaboration focused on action, improvement, learning, and research was a different challenge. Manager A charted the development of his understanding:

> Having deeply discussed in detail and having described together a model of how collaboration can work, how it arises, how it grows, and how it yields a profit, I started understanding the mechanism and how I could have a more profitable approach to collaboration. Knowing the model helped in improving the working of collaboration: defining and assessing collaboration status, key factors, and enablers.
>
> These project dynamics helped us to build a deeper knowledge of collaboration between us (as System Integrator) and our suppliers, and to manage better our respective roles and people. As a result, we developed a culture and a work atmosphere aimed at improving

our collaborative capabilities and this collaborative mood spread all over the EME. Of course, we also came to understand what hampers collaboration.

Manager B saw the collaborative process from a different perspective:

Our industry is rather unique in world business: There is a very specific culture with a sharp focus on quality and delivery driven by the top tier suppliers. In this context, developing the collaboration characteristic of CO-IMPROVE into our business had to be done "top down" in order to create the environment (or playground): First, we had to learn to play the piano before we could start to improvise or even compose the music.

Outcomes and Longer-Term Organization Changes

Many outcomes came from CO-IMPROVE. At the end of the project, Manager A wrote,

I believe that this project permitted a deeper reciprocal knowledge with our suppliers, a serious assessment of our relationships, and the access for good to a truly new way of working. Moreover, we gained acquaintance with some useful operational tools, easy to use again in the future, we spread across a common analytical methodology and problem-solving mindset through "action learning." We obtained quick results of concrete issues by creating an environment where people could learn through their practical experiences, improve their way of interacting with others, and enhance their reciprocal knowledge and ability to work in teams.

For his part, Manager B was more operational and somewhat more sanguine:

All the projects undertaken were related to quality problems in the supply chain.

However, they were not effective because there was still a barrier between ourselves (as the customer) and the supplier. Those barriers were hard to overcome: Spreading the project within our company and the supplier turned out to be difficult and, in some cases, required a lot of pressure from me as the leader. By introducing regular meetings, some progress was made. However, the overall collaborative process did not stick and, today, it is not "lived as a standard." Some elements, like early supplier involvement and quick follow-up of corrections on delivery and quality, have improved.

Manager A also evaluated the outcomes for his company on a different basis—knowledge exchange:

As managers, we learned from our interaction with the academics. Of course, small barriers emerged from the different "languages" of practice and theory, the more tactical approach of managers versus the more theoretical approach of academics, and from the different knowledge levels of academics and managers. Yet, defining and practicing a formal assessment and organizing information, knowledge, and theory did represent progress. I really think that without the methodology and organization of academics this learning would have not been achieved without much more effort and time.

EMERGENT INSIGHTS AND FINDINGS ON COLLABORATIVE MANAGEMENT RESEARCH

This exemplar chapter has explored collaborative management research in and by an interorganizational network. It has described and reflected on the process by which and the setting within which managers and academics collaborated as researchers across boundaries—including disciplinary and institutional boundaries, as well as those between academia and industry—to develop learning in collaborative improvement in the supply chain. CO-IMPROVE and the cases presented have been the sources of many findings and insights on collaborative research. Three merit specific mention: linking theory, practice, and collaboration; capturing difference while sustaining the collaboration; and managing quality.

Linking Theory, Practice, and Collaboration

Collaborative management research in and by an interorganizational network has the potential to generate actionable knowledge. The challenge is not just to engage in the action, but also to maintain the interest and patience of the researchers to contribute to knowledge. In CO-IMPROVE, the academics' push to generate theory was matched by the managers' concern with measurable operational outcomes. While focusing on contributions to (academic) knowledge, all participants in the collaborative research initiative had to keep in mind also the need for reinforcement of the companies' decisions to collaborate and the intercompany sensitivities characteristic of a competitive supply chain.

Capturing Differences While Sustaining the Collaboration

A challenge in collaborative research is to capture difference between related situations and contexts while maintaining the rationale for collaboration. The collaborative research undertaken in CO-IMPROVE was "fine grained" enough to surface differences and yet broad enough to achieve positive, if not equally sustainable, outcomes for both groups of companies. Although they participated in the same overall project, the managers were not of "one voice." The differences, evident in the evolution of relationships, collaborative process, and

outcomes, are explainable in terms of differences in their respective industries.

Capturing such difference required that the companies in the network supported the work of their managers as researchers engaged in rethinking their workplaces and intercompany relationships. The managers could have been just participants in meetings where they were taught how to collaborate, identified improvement opportunities, and carried out improvement initiatives. They were, however, researchers. For the managers to act as researchers required that they develop confidence in a new language and process—that of research—in order to translate their access to and experience of interorganizational relationships into actionable knowledge. For the academics to be able to engage in collaborative research with the managers and with the other researchers required that they develop a confidence in the new languages, not just of the individual company settings, but also of the network, in order to make best use of the privileged access granted.

Managing Quality

Quality in collaborative management research is discussed in this *Handbook* by Coghlan and Shani (Chapter 29), Bradbury (Chapter 28), and Pasmore, Woodman, and Simmons (Chapter 27). Coghlan and Shani articulate four dimensions. First, the research topic must be a real-life issue, relevant to both practitioners and academics and of practical and theoretical value. Second, the collaborative process must engage the practitioners and academics, insiders and outsiders, in social interaction that is genuinely participative and collaborative and that acknowledges, builds on, and actualizes the perspectives, interests, and strengths that each party brings to the process. Third, the process must be reflective, whereby the community of inquiry engages in cycles of action and reflection, supported by rigorous data-gathering methods, collaborative analysis and joint meaning construction, and agreed action as the project is conceived, enacted, and evaluated. Fourth, the outcomes must be workable and sustainable and encourage further scientific experimentation, and the theory must be understood to be actionable, transportable, and adaptable to other settings.

In CO-IMPROVE, commitment to the vision of a long-term, mutually beneficial relationship inherent in the concept of collaboration was often difficult for some companies to align with the realities of the marketplace in which they were operating. This difficulty could have led to a superficial treatment of issues based upon a nominal engagement in the action. However, the way the researcher network recorded events, articulated and discussed interpretations and assumptions, enacted cycles of action and reflection, and tested reflections in subsequent action ensured methodological rigor.

In addition, the collaborative nature of the cycles of action and reflection evident at the partner meetings enabled joint planning and implementation of actions.

Collaborative management research in and by an interorganizational network is both possible and relevant. The networked form of organization continues to grow and to provide opportunities for new research. In this chapter, we have described and reflected on the process by which managers and academics collaborated as researchers in the CO-IMPROVE project to facilitate and learn about collaborative improvement of operations practice and performance in the extended manufacturing enterprise. CO-IMPROVE was not the first such collaborative research initiative undertaken by the researchers, nor will it be the last. However, the combination of the emergent insights presented in this chapter and the other contributions to this *Handbook* advances the practice, process, and promise from further initiatives.

REFERENCES

Adler, N., Shani, A. B. (Rami), & Styhre, A. (2004). *Collaborative research in organizations*. Thousand Oaks, CA: Sage.

Bessant, J., & Caffyn, S. (1997). High involvement innovation through continuous improvement. *International Journal of Technology Management, 14*(1), 7–28.

Cagliano, R., Caniato, F., Corso, M., & Spina, G. (2002). Fostering collaborative improvement in extended manufacturing enterprises: A preliminary theory. In R. Smeds (Ed.), *Continuous innovation in business processes and networks* (pp. 131–143). Espoo, Finland: Helsinki University of Technology.

Coghlan, D., & Brannick, T. (2005). *Doing action research in your own organization* (2nd ed.). London: Sage.

Coghlan, D., & Coughlan, P. (2002). Developing organizational learning capabilities through interorganizational action learning. In M. A. Rahim, R. T. Golembiewski, & K. D. MacKenzie (Eds.), *Current topics in management* (*Vol. 7*, pp. 33–46). New Brunswick, NJ: Transaction.

Coghlan, D., & Coughlan, P. (2005). Collaborative research across borders and boundaries: Action research insights from the CO-IMPROVE project. In R. Woodman & W. Pasmore (Eds.), *Research in organizational change and development* (*Vol. 15*, pp. 277–297). Oxford, UK: Elsevier.

Coghlan, D., & Coughlan, P. (2006). Designing and implementing collaborative improvement in the extended manufacturing enterprise: Action learning and action research (ALAR) in CO-IMPROVE. *The Learning Organization, 13*(2), 152–165.

Coghlan, D., Coughlan, P., & Brennan, L. (2004). Organizing for research and action: Implementing action researcher networks. *Systemic Practice and Action Research, 17*(1), 37–49.

Coghlan, D., & Rashford, N. S. (2006). *Organizational change and strategy: An interlevel dynamics approach.* London: Routledge.

Dilworth, L., & Willis, V. (2003). *Action learning: Images and pathways.* Malabar, FL: Krieger.

Greenwood, D., & Levin, M. (1998). *Introduction to action research.* San Francisco: Jossey-Bass.

Knight, L. (2002). Network learning: Exploring learning by interorganizational networks. *Human Relations, 55*(4), 427–454.

Knight, L., & Pye, A. (2004). Exploring the relationship between network change and network learning. *Management Learning, 55*(4), 473–491.

Lane, C. (2001). Organizational learning in supplier networks. In M. Diekes, A. Berthoin Antal, J. Child, & I. Nonaka (Eds.), *Handbook of organizational knowledge and learning* (pp. 699–714). Oxford, UK: Oxford University Press.

Lillrank, P., Shani, A. B. (Rami), Kolodny, H., Stymne, B., Figuera, J. R., & Liu, M. (1998). Learning from successes of continuous improvement change programs: An international comparative study. In R. W. Woodman & W. Pasmore (Eds.), *Research in organizational change and development* (Vol. 11, pp. 47–71). Greenwich, CT: JAI Press.

Marquardt, M. (1999). *Action learning in action.* Palo Alto, CA: Davies-Black.

Marquardt, M. (2004). *Optimizing the power of action learning.* Palo Alto, CA: Davies-Black.

Middel, R., Coghlan, D., Coughlan, P., Brennan, L., & McNichols, T. (2006). Action research in collaborative improvement. *International Journal of Technology Management, 33*(1), 67–91.

Pedler, M. (1996). *Action learning for managers.* London: Lemos and Crane.

Popper, M., & Lipshitz, R. (1998). Organizational learning mechanisms. *Journal of Applied Behavioral Science, 34*(2), 144–160.

Revans, R. (1998). *ABC of action learning.* London: Lemos and Crane.

Ring, P. S., & Van de Ven, A. (1992). Structuring cooperative relationships between organizations. *Strategic Management Journal, 13,* 483–498.

Shani, A. B. (Rami), & Docherty, P. (2003). *Learning by design.* Oxford, UK: Blackwell.

CHAPTER 22

Building Partnership

Critical Reflections on the Action Research Center (ARC)

THE ARC RESEARCH TEAM[1]

ABSTRACT

This chapter is a reflective inquiry into the process of building partnership between academia and the community. It is based on an account of the Action Research Center (ARC), an attempt to build partnership between a college on Israel's northern periphery and the surrounding Jewish and Arab communities. The goals of ARC and the meaning of partnership were themselves research questions investigated through ongoing action and reflection and are addressed in this chapter.

This chapter is an inquiry into the building of partnership between academia and the community based on an account of the Action Research Center (ARC) at the Max Stern Academic College of Emek Yezreel (Jezreel Valley). Situated on Israel's northern periphery, the College serves a highly diverse range of communities: Jewish development towns, with veteran and immigrant populations; Israel's two largest Arab cities, with both Muslim and Christian populations; a variety of Jewish cooperatives (*kibbutzim* and *moshavim*); and residential communities. The Jewish and Arab-Palestinian populations are themselves very diverse. They live in close proximity, interacting amidst inequality, tensions, and latent conflict between and within groups. The majority of people in the region experience low socioeconomic status and exclusion from the economic and cultural resources that concentrate in Israel's geographic center.

ARC began as an attempt to build partnership between the College and the surrounding communities for the purpose of mutual development. As will be seen in the following account, the meaning of partnership between academia and the community—and how to create it—were not taken for granted. Rather, *the goals of ARC and the meaning of partnership were themselves regarded as research questions to be studied and answered through ongoing action and reflection.* We do not claim to have answered these questions, but rather provide insights into issues and themes that have been salient in these initial stages.

A METHODOLOGICAL NOTE

This chapter attempts to address those questions on the basis of systematic reflection on and analysis of ARC from the time it was initiated, in January 2004, through March 2006, when the initial drafts of this chapter were written. It was researched and written by a team of seven people, all of whom have been involved in ARC in some capacity. Although each one of us brought different theoretical and methodological perspectives and approaches to the work, we attempted to carry out the inquiry and writing process as action research, which can be defined as a "participatory, democratic process concerned with developing practical knowing in the pursuit of worthwhile human purposes . . . [that] bring[s] together action and reflection, theory and practice . . . in the pursuit of practical solutions to problems of pressing concern to people and more generally to the flourishing of individual persons and their communities" (Reason & Bradbury, 2001, p. 1). Because ARC is itself a kind of living research question, it is difficult to make a clear distinction between the "action" and the "research." From the very beginning, ARC involved attempts to engage uncertainty and develop knowledge through action and reflection on action.

Our research drew on a number of data sources. We depended mainly on typed protocols that were made of almost all ARC meetings from the very inception of the process. We drew on correspondence, discussion papers, and proposals that were generated and collected all along the way. In addition,

we interviewed three participants from the College, all members of the steering committee, and one from the community. These individuals were chosen because of two common features: (1) They lacked prior knowledge and experience in action research and expressed eagerness to learn about and implement it, and (2) They expressed varying degrees of dissatisfaction or disillusionment with ARC. The community member discontinued her involvement in ARC about the time of the interview. Finally, we used our thoughts and feelings as important data in this reflective research.

Another important source for this chapter was the Action Evaluation/C3 process employed by ARC as a formal method for defining goals and action planning. This method, which will be described as part of our account of ARC, is a systematic, data-based, and participatory inquiry method for involving multiple stakeholders in goal setting. The name "C3" is a play on words intended to refer to "seeing" program goals through three lenses of identity: individual, group, and intergroup (Friedman, Rothman, & Withers, 2006; Rothman & Friedman, 2002).

The research team began as three people who informally took responsibility to oversee the collection and management of ARC data in March 2005. Subsequently, three more people joined this team and focused our research on this chapter. In early 2006, it became clear that not all ARC Steering Committee members knew of this research, and some felt excluded. Therefore, the team invited all ARC participants to join, which led to the participation of the seventh team member. Team members met periodically to discuss their analyses of the data. These meetings opened up many avenues of inquiry and issues for critical reflection, but there was difficulty converging on a single focus and an analytical approach. Therefore, we decided that members of the team would write separate mini-papers and then try to combine them into a single document.

We produced five separate papers (in Hebrew). These papers were discussed by members of the research team, commented on, and revised accordingly. Finally, these documents were translated and linked to form the current chapter, composed of five parts: an account of the creation of the Action Research Center (January 2004 to March 2005), a brief discussion of the developmental tasks faced by ARC, an analysis of the partnership in terms of identity and relationship structure, a description of the politics of academic writing, and an analysis of the power of crisis in building partnership. During, and because of, the process of writing and review, our views of ARC as well as our interpretations of past events continued to develop and change. It has been a challenge to keep our focus true to the first two years and to minimize historical revisionism based on what we know now.

Each of the five parts speaks in a different voice and offers a different perspective, depending on the original authors' theoretical, methodological, and personal orientations. In their review of the first version of this chapter, the book editors commented that "the five parts provide a rich data set. Yet, the challenge is to provide a synopsis or an overview of the whole." In revising the chapter, we preserved the differences that reflect, at least in part, the realities of building partnership during this period. The conclusion, to which all of us contributed, provides a composite map that attempts to give an overview of our experiences without imposing a single interpretation of them.

AN ACCOUNT OF CREATING THE ACTION RESEARCH CENTER[2]

The following account begins with the birth of the idea of ARC in January 2004, and ends in March 2005, when formal goals were set and a formal structure was established. It is based mainly on protocols and other documentary evidence. It is intended to be as descriptive as possible and to give voice to the participants as they actually expressed themselves. It then describes in brief the projects that have begun to emerge from ARC as of this writing. Throughout this chapter we use people's real first names and often speak in the first person. In order to distinguish between academics and community people we follow each name with "/A" or "/C" respectively.

The idea. In January 2004, three faculty members—Victor/A, Helena/A, and Michal P/A—initiated a meeting to discuss the idea of initiating a "center for action research" at the College. The invitation stated the intention to "encourage and promote research projects in collaboration with different parties in the community" for the purpose of "tightening the connection between the College and its immediate environment, providing responses to important social needs, promoting research activity and collaboration among College faculty, and enriching the curriculum and student projects."[3] The 10 participants in this meeting included the three department chairpersons, five additional faculty members, an adjunct faculty member, and a teaching assistant who works in education outside of the College.[4] The aim of the discussion was to "begin a process of developing both the concept of a center and a team bringing it into fruition."

Participants proposed a variety of goals for the center: "supporting local initiatives" (Moishik/A); "creating partnerships among faculty and between faculty and the community and students" (Helena/A); "providing a concrete answer to the need for reflection [by] focusing the action research on what we do" (Shaike/A); "to develop knowledge . . . there has to be learning among the faculty . . . personal development" (Michal P/A). Shaike/A warned against attempts to "control research" and suggested that the center be like a "club" in which people learn together. On the other hand, Moshe/A advocated a "guiding hand . . . [and] focusing on something central . . . which everyone would research from their own perspectives and interests . . . and . . . then integrate them."

The participants also pointed to potential problems. Helena/A, for example, said that "there is no history of collaboration among faculty members," and Dalit/A said "just putting together a faculty seminar is almost impossible." Yoni/A expressed concern about "an emphasis on the applied pushing out a wider, intellectual focus" and supported the idea of a club in which people can "deliberate." Shaike/A said that involving students in projects would "require formulating formal principles," and Dalit/A cautioned against "using students as cheap labor for research."

Some of the participants also said that they did not know enough about action research. Dalit/A suggested learning together by conducting a pilot project of importance to everyone. Victor/A proposed carrying out a joint "learning process" and volunteered to take responsibility for the next steps, together with Helena/A and Michal P/A. After the meeting, they disseminated a protocol[5] asking faculty to invite acquaintances from the local communities who might want to take part in establishing the center.

The learning process. The next meeting, held on April 1, 2004,[6] was attended by five faculty members and one community member from the previous meeting. They were joined by two teaching assistants (Orit/A and Michal S/A); Pam/C, a mediator from a development town; Ibrahim/C, the director of Masar, an education NGO[7] in Nazareth; and Sawsan/A-C, English instructor and adviser for Arab students at the College. Victor/A gave a presentation that defined action research, which built on the definition of action research provided at the beginning of this chapter. Furthermore, he explained that action research is distinguished by

(1) research questions that emerge from the field; (2) research "with" and not "on" people; (3) cycles of action, observation, and reflection; (4) creating "actionable" knowledge; and (5) generating change.

A central theme in the ensuing discussion was criticism of normative academia and the need for paradigmatic change. Ibrahim/C said that "what is important here is a change in perception or paradigm . . . rather than extracting and disseminating knowledge, academia sometimes constitutes a barrier . . . and that needs to change." Helena/A added that "to a certain extent normative academia blocks learning and makes change difficult . . . especially by . . . preserving accepted paradigms." Participants also related to action research as a way of connecting to the field (Arik/A), as listening to others (Pam/C, Helena/A), as a process of "learning together with and from the field" (Michal P/A), and as willingness to "say that I don't know" (Pam/C).

Dalit/A, on the other hand, questioned the tendency to "denigrate accumulated knowledge that is not seen as connected to the field," saying that "the associations that help me understand the field are precisely those things that are theoretical and directly linked to the field." Later she described herself as confused, saying that she did not really understand action research. Orit/A too expressed confusion over the meaning of action research because of the "thin line between research, action, intervention, and consulting."

Moishik/C spoke of "connecting to action" and expressed his "vision" of integrating action research with teaching in order to "shatter the educational system out of a desire to improve." He wished to create a process that would provide students with the desire and the tools to do things because "they believe they can make a dream come true." Sawsan/A-C spoke about a "feeling of responsibility," asking, "Where do I want to get to? Where is my sector (the Arab sector) going to get to?"

Victor/A said that there was no need to agree, suggesting that "[we] 'not know' together and together learn and research." Afterward, Helena/A, Michal P/A, and Victor/A sent a letter[8] to the participants that suggested a "learning process" of monthly meetings (presentations and dialogue) to "formulate a concept" for the center by "a group of partners committed to promoting this issue." They expressed the importance of providing a "specific physical space within the College . . . that would constitute a kind of common 'home' for faculty and for people from the community." They also suggested turning to additional "individuals, groups, organizations, and institutions" in the community who would be "interested in tightening the connection between academia and the field."

The authors of this letter emphasize that they were not trying to dictate the process:

> What we have raised here are ideas. . . . We would be happy to hear reactions to these ideas and to hear additional and alternative ideas. . . . If the reactions are positive, we will take responsibility for organizing the monthly meetings.

They then finished the letter with a wish for success "in building the partnership and embarking on a fascinating learning journey."

At the next meeting, Ibrahim/C and Jamal/C from Masar made a presentation entitled "The Strategic Role of Action Research in Developing New Visions in Education." The meeting was attended by Moishik/C, Vera/C (a school principal from a large nearby town), and six faculty members from the previous meeting. Ibrahim and Jamal presented Masar's unique educational philosophy, which focuses on engaging difference and conflict as opportunities for inquiry, dialogue, reflection, and learning.

The subsequent discussion dealt with what the idea of an action research center meant. Victor/A began by saying that "we

need to undergo a learning process because we don't really know what we want." Ibrahim/C asked, "what did you have in mind when you began this initiative and how do you see the center?" but he did not receive a direct answer from the three initiators. "Dialogue" became a central theme in the ensuing discussion. Michal P/A said that the College needs to develop "access to the field and the ability to generate dialogue . . . as a big part of teaching." Orit/A expressed the importance of developing dialogue among faculty members and between faculty and students. Vera/C related to a connection between the College and school as a way of promoting "a dialogue among ourselves" aimed at testing "ourselves against theory and (academia) against practice." Ibrahim/C said that "thinking together interests him" and that he is interested in "being a party to change." Moshe/A said his "fantasy" was that people would "come to consult with us as action researchers." Sawsan/A-C wondered how she could "take advantage of the potential here" in learning how to deal with her new role as adviser for Arab students.

The issue of uncertainty and confusion arose again. Orit/A said she was learning many new things but still "groping in the dark about what 'action research' really means." Dalit/A said she still did not know what she wanted this group to do but suggested that "we be guinea pigs and apply something here." Michal S/A said that she needed to do action research in order to know it. Moishik/C asked whether it did not make sense to "turn our own process into action research . . . to examine the issue while doing." Toward the end of the discussion, Victor said that "learning and doing are themselves a research process" and then framed the following research question: "How can we create a situation in which there is collaboration between academia and the field?"

Sawsan/A-C suggested that one of the next meetings deal with questions about her role as Arab student adviser and how action research might help answer them. Other agenda items were discussing how the center would operate, topics for future meetings, and adding participants. It was also decided that these monthly meetings would continue in the same format until there was a need for change and that protocols would be sent to all of the participants so that they could respond and comment.

Based on these discussions, Helena/A, Michal/A, and Victor/A wrote an initial proposal for the "Action Research Center"[9] and submitted it to the college president, Professor Aliza Shenar, who had been informed of the initiative from the beginning. The proposal included a description of the process and a list of the 20 participants so far.[10] It also defined five tentative goals and a rationale for establishing the Action Research Center at the College. The proposal also included an action plan and a $7,500 budget for the 2004–2005 academic year. The president expressed support for ARC and a willingness to help the Center raise funds.[11]

The next monthly meeting involved an urban planner who had used action research to involve citizens in city planning. The month after that, there was a meeting with an expert on the use of action research in conflict resolution.[12] In the third meeting, Sawsan/A-C presented her role as Arab student adviser. This was the most highly attended of all the meetings so far, involving over 20 participants, including many new people from both the College and the community.[13] Sawsan began on a personal note, asking "Why me? Which Sawsan do I want to be in this project?" and then described her role and what she had done so far.

Shaike/A criticized the fact that Sawsan's role had been determined in a top-down manner by the administration and suggested that "we free ourselves from the hierarchy ... and construct the process through the principles of action research." Hawla/A described the "barrier of shame" that prevents Arab students from participating in class. Kamel/C disagreed, saying that Arab students are ambitious and the real need is to increase the number of Arab students in the College. Helena/A reframed the problem as "difficulty giving voice" and argued that we should not ignore the "political" aspect.

Merav/C said that the "special needs of Arab students need to be defined." Beruria/A argued that Arab students shouldn't be singled out and that the need is to find a "point of connection" between Arab and Jewish students. Jamal/C said that we need "to look at how the College relates to Arab students" in order to understand their behavior. Dalit/A added that the College is a "Jewish institution in a Jewish state ... and the Arab students' problems are different from those of the Jewish students." Reuven/A said that "it all depended upon the teachers," and Daniela/A added that "the *faculty* need[ed] an adviser."

Kamel/C called for "integration" rather than "divide and conquer." Hawla/A said that the College did not want integration—otherwise it would aim for equal numbers of Arab and Jewish students. Michal P/A disagreed because "22% Arab students reflected the proportion in the general population."

Aharon/A said that "Sawsan wasn't conducting action research, she was doing a job ... but she tried to make it action research and I would be happy to have another meeting." Sagit/C suggested that "this forum could provide an open academic look at the issues Sawsan raised" and that the "justification for academia is to improve people's lives." Arik/A pointed out that "in this forum we have dealt with issues that are usually taken for granted ... it has forced me to stop and think." Victor/A said that "no one has a ready solution for this issue ... and the only way to learn is through doing." Dalit/A suggested making this issue as ARC's first project. Helena/A pointed out that some of the differences that arose were linked to the different academic disciplines and suggested "looking into our own professional and cultural identities." Kamel/C said that the discussion itself was an indication that there is awareness of the problem and that this "was the first step." There was interest in making this issue a pilot project for ARC, but Sawsan/A resigned her position in order to enter a doctoral program in the United States, and the idea was tabled.[14]

Formal goal setting through "Action Evaluation/C3." In December 2004, the three faculty members who had initiated the process suggested conducting a formal, collaborative process for setting goals and developing an organizational structure for ARC. They sent an invitation to all the people who had attended or expressed an interest in attending ARC meetings.[15] They also recommended using an action research method for goal setting called "Action Evaluation/C3" (AE/C3). AE/C3 provided a framework for enabling all interested stakeholders to participate in this process. Dr. Jay Rothman, who had developed AE/C3 and lived in the United States, was invited to facilitate the process, which was conducted in English.[16]

The method required first defining specific stakeholder groups. There were many possible ways of grouping the stakeholders in the Action Research Center (e.g., by community, profession, academic specialty, ethnicity). For practical purposes, the organizers (Helena/A, Michal/A, and Victor/A) defined the two stakeholder groups used so far: College faculty and community people. Twenty-two people responded to the invitation: 11 faculty members and 11 people from the community. All of these participants filled out a Web-based questionnaire that included the three following questions:

What is your definition of "success" for an "Action Research Center"? In other words, what are your goals for such a Center?

Why are those goals important to you personally? Why do you feel passionately about them?

How would you go about trying to achieve those goals? What concrete steps would you suggest taking?

The data from each stakeholder group were then analyzed separately by Jay, who grouped the individual goals into categories, yielding one set of goals expressed by faculty and one expressed by community members.

Jay then met with each stakeholder group separately in a four-hour "feedback" meeting that followed a set process.[17] Each participant was given a printout of her or his individual data (responses to the three questions) and was asked to sum up her or his "Why?" response in one word (which Jay called a "passion point") and to tell a story that illustrates their personal "why."[18] The following excerpts, taken from the written questionnaires and the discussion, illustrate some of the "why" data of both groups:

- It's very personal. The home I grew up in was a Jewish home in a New England town. My mother was a social worker who created community projects for people who were left out of institutions. My father was an antique dealer. We had a house that was open to all kinds of people. Passover was one night for the family and other people—Jewish, non-Jewish. We once had a murderer for dinner. On Christmas we worked in soup kitchens. My sister is a rabbi who works with people with AIDS. My father would go out in the middle of the night to get a prostitute out of jail. I have two adopted children. It's in my blood. In my work I get a lot of personal pleasure from seeing someone do something they couldn't do before.
- There are a lot of organizations in the community that generate important knowledge that might positively impact the evolution of societies and humanity. However, academia is usually perceived as the only authorized source of knowledge. Within such a one-way relationship, a lot of knowledge is lost and academia, as a system, loses the ability to learn and change.

- You don't just talk the talk, you also walk the walk. For me the College and this area are home. I'm looking for the combination between my theorizing and my doing something that matters. . . . Writing is the beginning of a dialogue; if it doesn't get to anybody, then it's fruitless.
- As a minority group, Arabs find it hard to make the official institution embrace their needs. Through my work in the Arab Center for Applied Social Research, we try to conduct research and surveys that explore Arab society and give answers to problems the society faces. Partnership with the college could help us achieve these goals.
- Activism is what fulfills me. I have a dual identity: Israeli and Moroccan. I was born in this area and part of my identity comes from belonging to a lower social class. I feel a need to give to the areas that are economically weaker and ethnically oriental.
- Having influence is something very strong in my soul and I cannot stay passive. The big challenge for me is to translate my opinions, ways of thinking, beliefs, professional experience, and education into a tool that can change things in our lives here and now. I used to be a journalist. We could make a lot of noise but had very little influence on the outcomes. What I have learned in my work with experimental schools is that you can be part of a team that develops new knowledge in the field—knowledge you cannot find in academia. But we need tools.
- Research should have a purpose. It should speak for people that cannot speak for themselves. It is one way to face and solve problems and create justice. We see injustice for the Arabs in work and school opportunities, salaries, investments. We cannot even compare the Jewish and Arab schools. I believe that improving access to quality education is something the Action Research Center can contribute to.
- My first professional experience as an organizational consultant was in a big communications firm. . . . I discovered that at the university they don't actually teach you how to be a researcher in the real world and how to deal with resistance.

- *I'm a fanatic about reflection. . . .*
- *I'm here for a community of practice.*

Following the "why?" discussion, Jay presented his analysis, done prior to the sessions, of the aggregated individual goals of all stakeholder group members (i.e., their answers to the "what?" question). He first tested his analysis with the participants to ensure that it was complete and captured the meanings that they intended to express. He then facilitated a discussion in which the group members deliberated and crafted a consensual list of goals. This stage in the process yielded the following two sets of goals:

Community Group

1. The Action Research Center will provide the community and the College with tools in order to develop programs that will enhance the quality of life. (Passion points: meaning, influence, accomplishment)

2. ARC will be an incubator for joint community and College initiatives. (Passion points: alternatives)

3. ARC is a new partnership between the community and the College to address social issues and cultivate mutual knowledge. (Passion points: knowing, impact)

4. ARC will become an agent of community empowerment. (Passion points: inclusion, justice, responsibility)

Faculty Group

1. ARC will be a learning partnership that serves both the College and local communities and institutions as they explore, assess, and engage local problems. (Passion points: contribute, knowledge, fellowship, conflict, sharing perspective, belonging, needs)

2. ARC will provide YVC faculty and students with action research tools to improve learning and community-oriented research and practice. (Passion points:

community, unlearning, reflection, energy, fulfillment, satisfaction)

3. ARC will contribute to YVC becoming a unique institution leading in a path not taken. (Passion points: curiosity, excellence, spring, activism, inclusion, novelty)

The next stage in the process was a "merge session," held on February 18, 2005, in which participants from both stakeholder groups, college and community, met together in order to come to consensus about their shared goals. Seven community members and 10 faculty, all of whom had participated in the previous sessions, participated in the merge process. After about two hours of discussion, the group agreed on four goals that would guide ARC from this time forward (see the goals in Figure 22.1).

After the merge session, Jay composed an initial action plan, which combined the shared goals, the data generated in response to the "why" question, and the "how" responses from the questionnaires.[19] Victor/A transformed this action plan into a "map" entitled "The Action Research Center: An Initial 'Theory' for Building College-Community Partnership" (see Figure 22.1). This map attempted to integrate and concretize the collective thinking of the participants that resulted from the AE/C3 process of data collection and collaborative analysis. It was meant to be comprehensive but also concise enough to enable participants to see their collective thinking about building partnerships on a single page.

This map represented a "program theory" (Chen, 1990) reflecting the emerging organization's "espoused theory of action" (Argyris & Schön, 1996; Friedman, 2001; Lipshitz, Friedman, & Popper, 2006) for answering this question: How can we create true partnership between academia and the community? It is a causal theory that can be understood as a complex set of hypotheses or propositional (if-then) statements of the following form: Given these initial conditions, if we carry out the following action strategies, then the following results (goals) ought to occur. In this initial form, it was meant to be prescriptive—guiding action—rather than explanatory. As an "espoused" theory, it reflected participants' intentions or vision, but still needed to be tested through action.

On March 18, 2005, there was a meeting to "complete the AE/C3 process, to prepare an action plan, and to decide on a structure for leading the Center into the next stage."[20] Five community members and seven faculty participated in this meeting, which was self-facilitated (Jay had returned to the United States). Victor/A began the meeting by presenting the map and raising some of the still unresolved issues regarding the goals, which led to the following interchange:[21]

Susan/C: Here we see again the gap between academia and "doing." I want there to be "doing" because, if there isn't "doing," the Center has no reason to exist.

Dalit/A: I don't want there to be just "doing," but rather focus on learning. That's what interests me. Everyone has his or her own project and I think that the substance of the Center is learning.

Ibrahim/C: This group is a group that learns through action and through a process.

This part of the discussion ended with agreement to accept the goals as stated so that the group could move to action.

Participants agreed that ARC's organizational structure should emerge through a learning process involving action and reflection. It was decided to set up an initial steering committee that would oversee ARC's activities. Three community members and four college faculty volunteered to participate in the steering committee. Victor/A

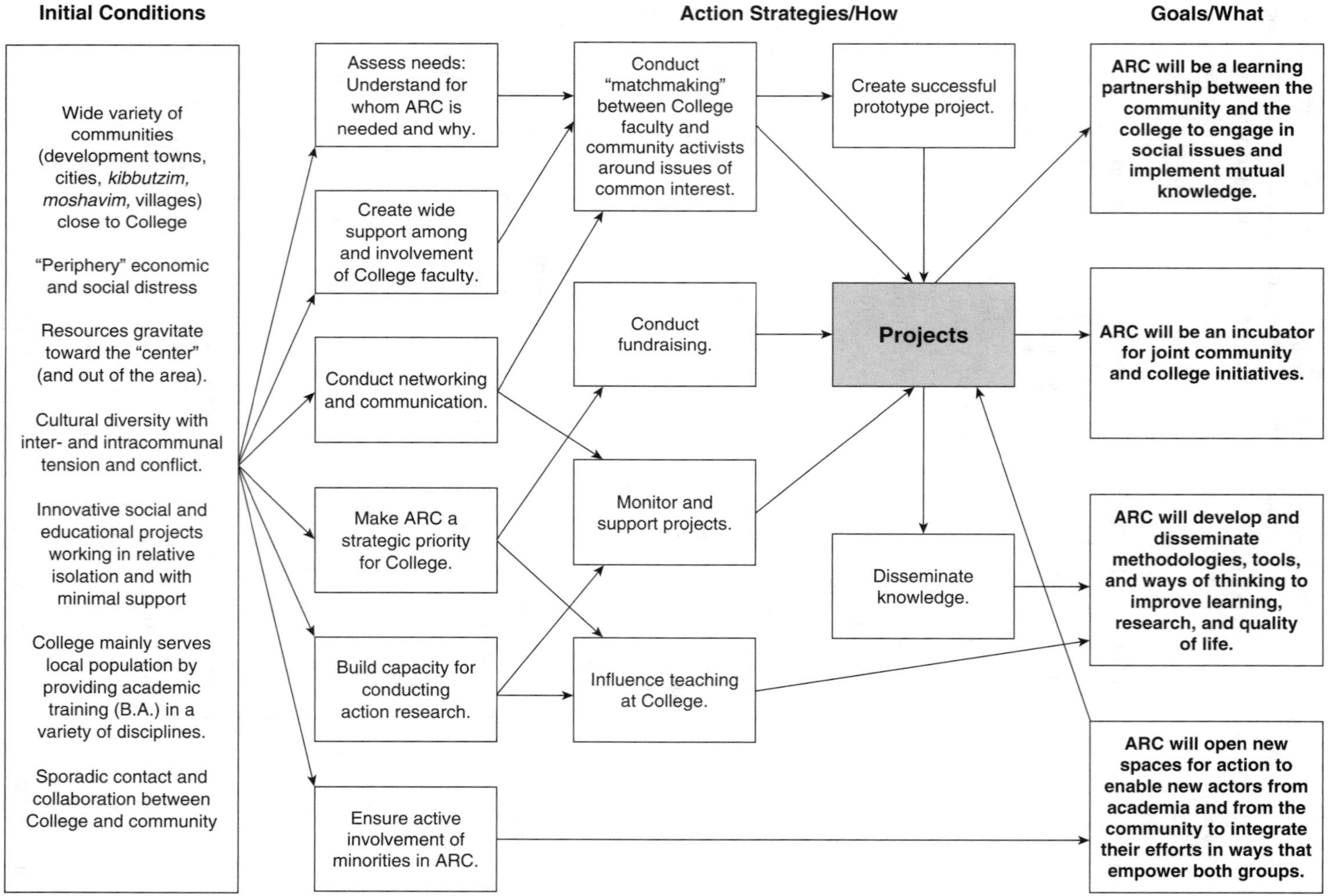

Figure 22.1 The Action Research Center: An Initial "Espoused Theory" for Building College-Community Partnership (March 2005)

volunteered to serve as chairperson. It was also decided that people who were not at this particular meeting would be invited to join as well. Finally, individuals volunteered to coordinate projects, fundraising, communications and networking, administration, and documentation of the process.

Another question was whether to focus efforts on a central pilot project or to support a wide range of initiatives. Dalit/A expressed concern that "if we define a central product it might not interest some of us." Victor/A added that "we should deal with a wide range of projects so as not to become . . . closed . . . or put ourselves in the position of selecting projects." Irit/C pointed to the need to "set very well-defined criteria [for] who we are serving and . . . what we want to focus on." Ibrahim/C said "we need to determine a rationale and concrete activities . . . with balance that will contribute to both academia and the community." Finally, Michal P/A stressed the importance of "directing ourselves towards something that we can succeed with." There was no decision on this issue, but it was decided to invite all members of ARC to submit proposals for projects.

In summing up the meeting, the participants said the following:

Michal P/A: We are setting off on a path with something concrete and that is meaningful. Even though there is some ambiguity, there is also a feeling of accomplishment.

Helena/A: I have a feeling that a learning group is forming. There is the beginning of progress and a willingness to collaborate.

Irit: I have a good feeling from the process because there is a lot of room for thinking but also commitment to progress and outputs.

Naama/C: I feel uncomfortable because I haven't taken a task onto myself. I will present a project proposal. The ability of people here really encourages me.

Ibrahim/C: I enjoy this process and feel curious.

Sagit/C: There is a group of people who are committed to doing something and that is encouraging.

Victor/A: It was a difficult process, but I enjoyed it. We are passing into a new stage and are entering a period of being "suspended in air." There is a great deal of complexity and unsolved questions—but that is exactly what learning is about.

Amid/C: I feel that we have made progress even though there is still ambiguity about the next step.

Orit/A: I am happy that we have moved to the action stage. I want to begin a project but I know that I don't yet have the tools I need.

Michal P/A: Uncertainty is a good thing. Slow, but good progress.

Epilogue

The foregoing account described in detail the birth of ARC as a formal organization, which led to actions aimed at achieving the espoused goals. It is beyond the scope of this chapter to describe everything that happened, but we will specify some of the important outcomes as of March 2006, when this chapter was first written.

A group of faculty, including members of the steering committee, initiated a relationship with Nebras, a civil society NGO in Um El-Fahum, Israel's second-largest Arab city (a 20-minute drive from the College). Through a series of meetings and field visits, they decided to focus on two issues for action research: (1) increasing the number of young people, and especially women, who enter higher education, and (2) a community public health project in cooperation with the Department of Healthcare Management.[22]

A second project was initiated by a local activist from Timrat, a Jewish residential community about 20 minutes from the College, for the purpose of building the community's capacity to "take responsibility and to build itself" by "generating knowledge . . . learning lessons from experience . . . and integrating that knowledge into future planning."[23] With the help of College faculty, this activist created a core group of about 25 community members that underwent a process of goal setting,[24] action planning,[25] and implementation.

In February 2006, ARC submitted a proposal for a grant to the European Union for the purpose of funding an "incubator for integrative social entrepreneurship in a divided society." The incubator integrated concepts of social entrepreneurship, social inclusion, and intergroup conflict resolution.[26] The proposal was not successful, but members of the Steering Committee decided to move ahead with creating the incubator using the College's extension program as a platform. ARC successfully applied to receive Fulbright Fellow Dr. Jay Rothman to conduct capacity building in conflict resolution and action research during the 2006–2007 academic year.

The steering committee grew to 10 members (six academic and four community, with one cochairperson from each group) and set a formal rule that decisions can only be made by consensus and require a quorum of at least five members, including one from each group and one cochair. The steering committee also developed and authorized a detailed strategic plan to achieve the goals set in the Action Evaluation/C3 process.[27] ARC was provided with a fully equipped office space by the College, but still had no funding.

DEVELOPMENTAL TASKS FACED BY THE ACTION RESEARCH CENTER[28]

The notion that all dynamic systems go through a life cycle containing predictable periods of stability and change has been applied conceptually to the study of individuals (Erikson, 1959; Levinson, 1978 for men and 1996 for women), families (Carter & McGoldrick, 1989), and organizations (Gersick, 1991). Common to all of these descriptions is the identification of a series of phase-specific developmental tasks that must be well negotiated in order to function optimally in each phase, and periods of transition during which the system shifts from one stage in its evolution to another.

Developmental tasks of a system are usually latent—the people involved experience them without always being able to identify them or their effects on ongoing events. The dawning of a need to respond to a developmental task is more often than not expressed in a crisis or conflict that arises as a result of a disequilibrium created by changes that took place beyond the awareness of those involved. The timely identification of these tasks (in the course of reflection in and on action) can form the basis for early and constructive responses to dynamics that could otherwise escalate destructively.

It might be useful to look at the first phase of the development of the Action Research Center through the lens of this life cycle perspective. More specifically, is it possible, on the basis of an analysis of the Center's first phase, to identify developmental tasks that faced the initiators of the Center as they attempted to create the something different that they intuited and envisioned? Explicating the conflicts and crises encountered by the

Center through the prism of developmental tasks, and particularly exploring the strategies that made possible the positive resolution of the developmental tasks, could be a first step in crafting actionable knowledge that could benefit other organizations struggling to create similar organizational structures, processes, and outcomes.

The developmental tasks identified in the course of joint reflection upon the development of the Center all seem to have been related to identity and self-definition within the Center's chosen social field. The Center's early phases required the emergent and ongoing development of answers to basic questions of identity. These questions were negotiated in the course of action and reflection on action, leading to tensions, conflicts, and ultimately to answers and decisions.

The following questions were implicitly or explicitly addressed by participants in the Center's development: What is our identity in our own eyes? Who are we? Who are we not? What developmental directions are we setting for ourselves? What do we do and what do we not do? How do we make decisions about who we are and what we do? Who are important others in our environment and where do we locate ourselves in relation to them? How do we wish to be perceived by others? How will we present ourselves? What is the significance of "belonging" to the Center? What are the entitlements and obligations that go along with membership? Are there different levels of membership? What is the nature of relationships among ourselves and between us and other stakeholders?

The following sections provide preliminary explorations and answers to some of these questions.

THE SUBSTANCE AND PROCESS OF BUILDING PARTNERSHIP[29]

One of the primary goals of ARC is creating useful mutual knowledge through building partnerships among individuals and groups in the College, in the community, and between the College and people in the community. Thus, it is extremely important to understand the substance of the partnerships that ARC is interested in developing and to carefully examine the process through which these partnerships are built. ARC itself serves as a case study through which we will attempt to learn about the characteristics of partnerships among people and the process through which they are shaped.

Partnership is fundamentally a relationship based on cooperation, which has been defined by Deutsch (2000) as positive interdependence; that is, a situation in which the parties to a particular relationship are bound together such that in achieving its own goals each party enables the other party to achieve its goals. In analyzing the system of relationships that constitute ARC, we draw on the organizational conflict literature to distinguish between the "overt" and the "hidden" levels (Kolb & Bartunek, 1992; Putnam, 2001). The overt sphere refers to open, observable behaviors and usually encapsulates formal and rational actions, whereas the hidden sphere encompasses the informal, behind-the-scenes, and often irrational dimensions of group/organizational members' activities, such as gossiping, emotional expressions and outbursts, and behavior that may be discordant with the formal roles assumed by group members.

Our understanding of the processes of building partnership in ARC draws on the conceptual framework developed by Dean Tjosvold (1994) for the development of the team organization. According to Tjosvold, building an organization on principles of cooperation requires developing a shared vision and direction, commitment to realizing shared goals and interests, and a feeling of empowerment. These elements should lead parties to work together while exploring various action strategies, engaging in ongoing reflection, and learning from experience. In addition, Tjosvold (1994) emphasizes that partnership forms through a gradual transformation process and, if built properly, it should lead to dramatic changes. Therefore, it is important to integrate the espoused values of cooperation with authentic and consistent action (Argyris & Schön, 1996). In other words, it is important to "walk the talk."

What is the substance of the partnership that ARC wishes to develop? Drawing on a typology of dimensions for analyzing partnership (Rosner & Getz, 1996), we focus our analysis on two dimensions: (1) the identity of the partners, and (2) relationships among the partners.

The first dimension, identity, contains the following elements:

- The main goal of creating knowledge that is shared by both sides.
- The basic principle of providing every participant with opportunities to contribute and to receive (social exchange).
- The impetus for contributing to the partnership through solidifying ARC's identity and each participant's own identity, in line with ARC's goals (see Figure 22.1).

The second dimension, the normative basis of relationships, also contains a number of elements:

- Power relations: voluntary partnership among stakeholders
- The means of exchange: information, knowledge, trust
- The basis for mutual relationships: interdependence; formal and informal social connections founded on personal acquaintance
- Decision making: degree and type of participation
- Ownership rights of knowledge and limits to cooperation (limits on choice of partners)
- Who stays in partnership and who exits from it

Table 22.1 presents examples of events that occurred in the establishment of ARC's identity and the normative basis of relationships. The table categorizes these events on both the overt and hidden levels of the system of relationships as reflected in the protocols and the interview data (especially useful for the hidden level).

To conclude, from the table it might seem as though there has been some erosion of participation, but the truth is that both the structure and operation processes have changed. The current structure and operation reflect a star design: namely, a nucleus that functions as a steering committee, while the other participants operate in various projects that are loosely coupled with ARC and reflect the arms of the star.

The table also points to gaps between the overt and hidden levels in both dimensions of the model of partnership: identity and relationships. These gaps can be interpreted as an expression of the gradual transition that takes place in the process of building a partnership. In the course of building partnership, ARC has experienced difficulties characteristic of building shared identity in a new organization and of a unique collaborative model of relationships. These transitions involve feelings of ambiguity and uncertainty, especially around questions of the complexity of multiple identities held by partners to ARC, the limits to partnership, and the explicit and implicit social contract between the partners: academia-academia, community-community, and community-academia.

THE POLITICS OF ACADEMIC WRITING[30]

This reflection came about as a response to questions and doubts that arose about partnership and transparency in the process of inviting members of the Action Research Center to collaborate in research about ARC. So far, these questions have come up twice: once in a steering committee meeting and

Table 22.1 A Two-Dimensional Model of Partnership: Identity and the Relationship Structure

Hidden	Overt	Dimension	Identity
Use of a single action research method with no discussion of the need for another method. Relying mainly on the knowledge of one person. Conducting informal dialogue among participants. Forming new partnerships for creating knowledge.	Learning from activities in ARC (analyzing our processes, lectures from members and guests, special workshops for members), from work with communities (e.g., Um El Fahum, Timrat), from lectures in conferences that present the work of ARC, and from project proposals to potential funders.	Knowledge creation	
In practice, participants from the College were mainly those with professional and social connections with the initiators of the idea of ARC.	Inviting all members of the College faculty to participate in ARC. In the community group, only those people who were in the social network of the academic participants were invited.	Opportunities	
Making connections with influential and knowledgeable people. Personal gains—publication, social intimacy, making new acquaintances.	To contribute to academia and to the community. To work according to a different model of collaboration among people in academia and between academia and the community. To open additional fields of research and knowledge. To collaborate according to the strategic plan.	Impetus for Contributing	
A feeling that the informal division of labor does not reflect "true" partnership since the two teaching assistants do most of the documentation and are responsible for the e-mail and the office. Using ARC for gaining the support of and/or influencing people in their other roles.	A framework in which academics with different ranks and different roles interact on an egalitarian basis. A framework that includes community people from different levels of management and different organizations. Including community people based on personal acquaintances of the academic participants.	Power relations	**The normative basis of relationships**
A feeling that there are decisions that were made by the initiators of the ideas of ARC, ie., by a small minority with power.	By consensus	Decision making	

(Continued)

Table 22.1 (Continued)

Hidden	Overt	Dimension
Concern about expressing reservations or dissatisfaction, especially among lower-ranking participants. A feeling among some participants about being excluded from certain projects. A feeling of those with knowledge that they have the right to exercise more influence. A sense that the input of participants at different academic levels has different weight.		
A feeling that some of the information does not reach everyone. For example, not everyone knew about the intention to write this chapter.	Transparency and free flow of information; information should reach all participants in ARC.	Means of exchange of information
Questions about ownership (e.g., "If I invested so much, shouldn't I have ownership over the intellectual property?" "If I do not want to work with specific people, do I have the right to exclude them from a project?")	All the outputs that are generated by ARC are open to the use of everyone, including the findings of each joint research project and the resulting written products.	The limits of partnership
The questions that arose in this context were mostly in informal contexts: Why did so many people exit? Has the process been too slow? Do people in the community have expectations that we in academia cannot meet? What expectations do the academics have of the community people?	From 11 of the College participants in the AE/C3 process, two who fully participated and one who partially participated have ceased their active involvement. Eight remained. Of the 11 community members, two who fully participated and six who partially participated in the AE/C3 have ceased their active involvement. Three have remained.	Who has stayed with the partnership and who has left it?

once in a meeting with Rami Shani, one of the editors of this book.[31] The main questions that arose in both discussions were these: How do we form partnerships in research? Should we set rules for determining who can participate in writing articles about ARC? How do we determine the ordering of the authors' names on a publication?

An analysis of these events provides the basis for addressing a broader research question about the politics of academic writing and how it can be managed differently. The goal of this reflection is to examine certain processes that took place in ARC's attempt to practice transparency, develop true partnership, and create a different kind of research organization.

Organizational politics (Samuel, 2002) is a subject that has fascinated many researchers from a wide range of fields. There are different levels of organizational politics: interpersonal politics, intergroup politics, and interorganizational politics. Even though politics does not necessarily imply something negative, frank and public discussions of organizational politics are rare because politics is often perceived as the "dark side" of organization. In general, interpersonal politics focuses on organizational roles that provide individuals with the resources and power that enable them to bestow favors and status upon others. In the academic world, the number of publications and the order of appearance of authors in publications represent important political issues because they constitute the basis for recognition, evaluation, and promotion.

ARC has placed an emphasis on implementing processes based on values of participation and democracy. It has attempted to create an organization that does not enact the "political games" typical in organizations in general and especially academic institutions. An analysis of the protocols[32] reveals that these values are deeply held and extremely important to ARC members, who espouse a desire to promote and realize them

in their actual behavior. One of the goals of ARC is to carry on its affairs differently than is accepted in established organizations and to make decisions differently than is done in many organizations.

Nevertheless, it appears that ARC has not succeeded in applying the values of transparency, democracy, and participation in determining participation in writing and in the ordering of names. For example, in the process that led to the writing of this chapter, a research team came together in a random process. There was no open call to ARC members to join the research team. Some Steering Committee members who were not on the team felt excluded when they heard about the research.

Another example was the ordering of the names of the authors on a research presentation. The ordering of the names was determined without any participation by those who shared in the writing. Those who did not participate in this decision were disappointed and somewhat bitter because participants were ordered in terms of academic status and the lower status partners, including ourselves, felt excluded.

In response to this incident, we sent an e-mail in which we asked, "As a continuation of our discussion about participation, according to what criteria was the order of authors determined?"[33] We (Orit and Michal S) did not receive a single response, which only heightened our feelings of disappointment. We intended to bring this issue before the Steering Committee, but that meeting was canceled, so we discussed our feelings with Victor/A. In our informal conversation (without a protocol), we raised this question: "Are we unintentionally perpetuating the power positions and academic status from which ARC is supposedly trying to free itself?"

It is important to point out that even those who hold relatively low academic status contributed to perpetuating the established order. Evidence for this can be seen in the draft of another research proposal that was written but not submitted. This draft was written by a teaching assistant, who ordered the authors' names according to academic rank and placed all of the community members last. This example raises the question of how a different order of names would have been received and whether it would have been considered presumptuous. Moreover, it demonstrates that institutional practices and ways of thinking are deeply embedded within us, whether we like it or not, and it is very difficult to free ourselves from them.

These incidents raise a number of questions that ARC needs to address: Who "owns" the knowledge and who holds the copyright over this intellectual property? Is it possible to establish an entity that frees itself from bonds of status and ownership over resources within the context of the hierarchical and competitive academic world? What are the criteria for determining who can participate in the research? How can the contribution of each partner to the writing be determined? Are documentation and data collection less important than analysis? Is coming up with an idea more important than developing and refining it? Should the order of authors be determined by the order of joining the research? Should the time invested in the research and writing determine the order of names? Perhaps random methods should be used? Does the issue of gratitude constitute a consideration in the ordering of authors?

Some of these questions were addressed in the writing of this chapter. The participants discussed how the names should appear on the paper. Because we agreed that this chapter was truly the expression of a team process, we decided to cite the team, which represented ARC, as the author and to name the individual authors in a footnote according to alphabetical order, without titles, and without specific reference to the extent of their contribution to data collection and writing. At first we left each section anonymous, but

in the revision process, we decided to name the person who wrote the initial draft of that section because in some cases we spoke about ourselves in the first person. These decisions were only meant to apply to this particular chapter and do not necessarily apply to future publications, when the questions will have to be discussed again.

THE POWER OF "CRISIS" IN BUILDING PARTNERSHIP[34]

I was invited by Victor/A, one of the leading initiators of ARC, and joined at the second meeting, which took place on April 1, 2004. The active "participants" in ARC changed over time. Some participants dropped out and others joined in, until a core group of "partners" was formed.[35]

In the discussion that took place on April 1, 2004, it was already clear that a focus on action research would constitute part of the unique identity of the center. This approach was led by the main initiators: Michal P/A, Helena/A, and Victor/A. For example, Michal P/A strongly advocated this view, saying that "the idea of action research is not going up to the 'Ivory Tower' but learning together with and from the field." In the same discussion, Helena/A suggested the importance of action research as a unique tool that belongs to another paradigm that enables discourse, change, and progress: "That's the basis for and the interesting thing in action research—first you must listen to others though not necessarily agree . . . to a certain extent normative academic [discourse] blocks learning processes and makes change difficult. That's mainly because it encourages and preserves the accepted paradigm."[36] Approximately a year and a half later, there was an open discussion in a Steering Committee meeting, which also included some non-Steering Committee members, about the strategic plan, and then it was determined unequivocally that ARC is a center for participatory action research.[37]

The participants decided to carry out a process of learning about action research, but never explicitly discussed the paradigms themselves. The changes that have taken place in ARC can be interpreted as meaning that a process of evolution is taking place and has been shaped by the interactions among the various partners through the discussions. Yet in meetings where new actions and knowledge emerged through reflecting on our evolutionary process, the discussions show that we often underestimated and/or misunderstood our actions and our cumulative outputs, which shape the evaluation process of ARC. Through an analysis of our collaborative actions in ARC, I will try to investigate the interplay between these paradigms.

Our understanding of an organization's evolutionary dynamics is influenced by the fundamental assumptions upon which the analysis of this process is based (e.g., De Wit & Meyer, 1994; Doll, 1993; Kuhn, 1970; Stacey, 2000). These assumptions are reflected in two different paradigms of thought. One, which we call the "dominant" paradigm, has been dominant for a few hundred years and sees evolution as a linear causal process. The second, relatively newer, paradigm sees evolution as a process shaped by nonlinear, noncausal, and nonessential interactions. Some claim that the former paradigm represents the "modernist" orientation and the latter a "postmodernist" (Doll, 1993) one. Others, especially complexity theorists, call the first an "orthodox," as opposed to a "radical," approach (Stacey, 2000). Naming these paradigms, however, runs the danger of creating a classification that limits discussion to a particular niche. Therefore, it is more interesting to specifically define the characteristics that distinguish between the two paradigms than to simply name them.

Theories identified with the dominant paradigm focus on the macro level of interactions between groups and entities (for example, organizations with organizations or groups of people with groups of people). The newer paradigm refocuses attention on interactions among individuals that form and are formed by the whole group. It considers description at the micro level as no less important, or even more important, than description at the macro level in shaping the evolutionary process (Stacey, 2000).

The differences between these two paradigms can be examined through events that took place in ARC and focused on the relationship between partnership and participatory research—two critical concepts of ARC. According to the definition given by Ian Hughes (2004), participatory action research involves participation by stakeholders, each of whom can contribute different knowledge, experience, skills, needs, and desires. They participate in inquiry, learning, and doing for the purpose of generating social change that improves their lives. Hughes clearly states that the meaning of participation is "participation in decision making." Participant stakeholders use dialogue in order to deal with different issues for the purpose of understanding their substance and for determining the processes required for dealing with these issues. Hughes emphasizes that this does not mean that each individual must have the same input because, as mentioned above, each participant is different.

At the macro level of description and definition, participatory research exists in ARC. For example, the strategic plan and the decision-making norm were produced through participation and consensus. Nevertheless, in a subsequent meeting Michal P/A said in anger and frustration that "there are people who are strong and people who only look strong on the outside."[38] She was pointing openly to the fact that, even though ARC's strategic plan (and other outputs) were developed through discussions in which all the partners participated, this agreement among partners did not necessarily stem from the unequivocal agreement of every single individual. Rather, agreement was a product of the interaction between the different partners, and, in this case, Michal P/A pointed out key differences in personality.

Michal P/A's comment came in response to Victors/A's statement that "I don't want to create a world in which people do not say what they want. If people want something, they should say so." Victor/A's intention was that he, as a leader of the process, was not blocking anyone's participation, but his reaction ignored Michal P/A's critical point that the interaction between people may be influenced by personality. A person's charisma, for example, can influence the final outcome of an interaction. However, the crisis generated by Michal P/A's angry reaction in this meeting and in the previous meeting with Rami Shani[39] surfaced conflicts that stem from differences between individuals.

This crisis provided an opportunity to change the rules of the game and influence the process of evolution. Michal P/A's claim created a reaction in Victor/A, who was perceived as leading the processes within the center and appeared to assume responsibility for the crisis that was created. His reaction pointed to change in the future: "I cannot be held responsible for what I do not know." In other words, from that moment, not just Victor/A but all those present knew something about Michal P/A, and this awareness would influence interactions with her in future discussions, thus influencing the structure of partnership. At the same time, Victor's statement expressed the expectation that people would be more open about their concerns so that they could be addressed.

Another crisis highlights the critical role of interaction in the micro level in defining the concept of partnership. About two years after the beginning of ARC, in the final discussions on this chapter, Orit/A, a teaching assistant, expressed her feelings of "exclusion" that stemmed from her being of a lower academic status and lacking professional experience. She pointed out that

"Michal P/A says that 'we include Orit/A and Michal S/A.' But in what way? As true partners? I don't think so." She claimed that it was *obvious* that Helena/A, being a senior faculty member in the department where they taught, and Ibrahim/C, being an experienced organizational manager, would not write the protocols. In the same discussion, Helena/A pointed out that "in one of the first protocols the issue of power relations came up," meaning that it emerged very early on. However, at that time we did not use it for the purpose of learning. This current discussion surfaced, once again, fundamental assumptions about factors such as partnership, equality, and dialogue that, according to Hughes's (2004) definition, shape good participatory action research.

The first two crises were between individuals from the academic group (Victor, Michal P, Orit, and Michal S). The third crisis involved a discussion between two participants from the community, Naama/C and myself. I was not very "tolerant" in my questioning of a project that Naama/C was proposing.[40] Helena/A, Michal/A, and Victor/A voiced dissatisfaction with my tone that "blocked" the process of dialogue. The situation generated discomfort in me and led to an external and internal conflict. In this case the discomfort (internal conflict) led me to write a personal response paper in which I claimed that their response stemmed mainly from a hidden fear that this style of talking would lead partners/stakeholders from the community to abandon ARC and it would fall apart (external conflict). At the time I asked what they meant by a "blocking" style of talking and whom it would block. And, in fact, in the next Steering Committee meeting Victor admitted "I was deeply afraid that people would flee . . ."[41]

These crises point to a lack of harmony between the macro and the micro in managing ARC that was generated from the very outset. It has been particularly salient in our relationship to the concept of "partnership"—the central concept of ARC as well as participatory action research—as discerned in Helena/A's statement in the very first meeting that "this is the way to focus on partnerships . . . partnerships are central."[42] The concept of partnership in ARC, throughout its history, has always referred to a relationship between two blocks or groups, usually referred to as "the community" and "academia," that have been defined at the macro level as fundamentally distinct. This distinction received clear expression in three out of four of ARC's goals. However, all the crises that I described above took place among people from the same group—that is, between academics and between community people. Victor summed this up in one discussion by saying that "we spoke at the beginning about partnership between academia and the community, but in fact we are focusing on academia."[43] This probably shows that the evolution process was defined by the interactions at the micro level and that the definitions we were using at the macro level may have been irrelevant.

Despite declarations on the part of partners about the importance of interactions at the micro level for building the identity and uniqueness of ARC, all of us, myself included, behaved according to the rules of the dominant paradigm. Although I strongly espouse a different approach, the dominant paradigm was inside of me and driving many of my actions. Throughout our long collaborative discussions and meetings, the issue of the interpersonal context and interactions at the micro level were pushed to the side to the extent that they did not even gain expression in the goals of ARC or in the strategic plan that was approved by all of the Steering Committee members. Rather, during the past year, most Steering Committee discussions focused on macro-level issues such as the relationship between ARC and the College, funding, and so on.

These examples highlight the gap between the espoused paradigm and the daily life experience in ARC that shapes the evolutionary process. This gap creates frustration and the feeling that we are stumbling. As Helena/A put it,

There were some mishaps in building the partnership. We are constantly "negotiating reality" and there are many things here that do not go smoothly and suddenly we see that even though we want true partnership that is exactly where we stumble.

However, these conflicts stem from exactly the same differences between the stakeholders that Hughes (2004) described as the source of new knowledge and change. The power of participatory action research, as defined by Hughes, stems from the interactions in which conflicts emerge and are used in order to create new knowledge. Kuhn (1970) defined *paradigm* as the "values, beliefs, and standards that determine approaches to problems, methods, and techniques" (p. 175) and stressed the difficulty of managing actions in a world of the dominant paradigm and of creating new approaches. In my opinion, the dialogue in ARC throughout the conflicts illustrates how we can really learn from the field and from our experience in order to change values, beliefs, and standards of the dominant paradigm, as well as our approach to problems, methods, and action strategies. If we truly wish to learn from our actions and experience, we need to continue to make an effort to refocus our attention on the micro level in order to see beyond the dominant paradigm.

CONCLUSION

The foregoing account and analysis covered two stages in the development of the Action Research Center. The first stage, which was described in detail in the first section of the chapter, began in early 2004 with the initiation of the idea of creating a formal framework for strengthening relations between the College and the surrounding communities. It involved a "learning process" in which members of the College faculty and the surrounding communities came together regularly to explore the idea of action research and its role in developing the relationship between academia and the community. The learning process led to the emergence of a vision of creating "true partnership" between academia and the community. This stage culminated with the Action Evaluation/C3 process that translated this vision into four explicit goals, an initial organizational structure (the Steering Committee), and an espoused organizational theory of action for realizing the vision (see Figure 22.1).

The second stage involved actions intended to put this theory into practice from March 2005 through April 2006. This stage was the main focus of analysis in the next four sections of the chapter, which provides a basis for mapping ARC's "theory-in-use" (Argyris & Schön, 1996); that is, the theory of action that can be inferred from actual practice (see Figure 22.2). During this stage, the participants in ARC encountered questions, especially about identity and the nature of relationships, that emerged through their interactions. These questions, which usually reflected perceived gaps between the espoused theory and the theory-in-use, formed as feelings of discomfort, frustrations, disappointments, and fears. Eventually, participants surfaced many of these feelings and the gaps became observable. They were discussed in open dialogue, the goal of which was learning and change. It is probably premature to talk about this stage as having come to an end, at least in terms of the time period dealt with in this analysis.

The difficulties that the partners experience in ARC, as an entrepreneurial venture, can be seen as reflecting progress toward building an organization founded on collaboration and teamwork. Tjosvold (1994) sees building partnership as an ongoing cycle of shaping a vision that inspires partners, developing cohesiveness in parallel with innovation and development, probing and testing multiple— and occasionally contradictory—perceptions, active engagement with the lack of agreement, building commitment, reflection, and

continuous learning that leads to a new vision and another cycle. Exposing gaps between espoused theories and theories-in-use and the ability to reflect upon them can be considered a successful outcome, promoting knowledge production and partnership building. At any given moment in the process, it was often difficult to see progress that becomes visible when reflecting over the process as a whole. This difference can be compared to the relationship between a still picture and an animation; only when the still pictures are "run" can the progress be seen.

The differences that influenced our ways of perceiving and acting also influenced our approaches to reflection and analysis. Even though all participants openly expressed a desire and openness to learn new things together, differences in professional socialization and identities leaked throughout various discussions. Personal, social, and professional identities affected the way reality was grasped, but partners in ARC were not fully aware of such phenomena. Each individual or several individuals together wished to have an impact via their particular outlooks, professional creeds, and values. This contrasting motivation to cooperate and yet not lose one's unique identity could be depicted as "flexible rigidity."

Flexible rigidity is manifested in the way this chapter has taken shape as a form of action research. The first part ("An Account of Creating the Action Research Center") began with an account of events—what people did or said—without using an explicit set of theoretical constructs to name, frame, or explain these events. It ended, however, with the formulation of ARC's initial espoused theory of action (Figure 22.1), which represented a kind of hypothetical answer to the research question: What is true partnership and how can it be formed?

The second and third sections ("Developmental Tasks Faced by the Action Research Center" and "The Substance and Process of Building Partnership") approached reflection and analysis from a deductive

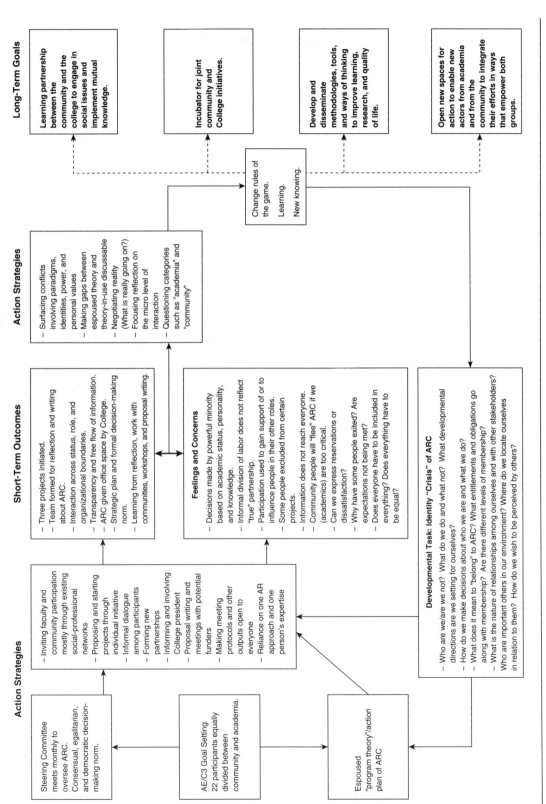

Figure 22.2 The Action Research Center's "Theory-in-Use" for Building College-Community Partnership (March 2006)

perspective. The second section framed the story of ARC in terms of the natural developmental crisis of identity formation. The third section drew on established sociological and psychological theory to set forth a conceptual framework for analyzing partnership in terms of identity and relationships. In contrast to the first section, it focused attention on hidden as well as the overt aspects of behavior.

The fourth and fifth sections ("The Politics of Academic Writing" and "The Power of 'Crisis' in Building Partnership") combined an inductive and deductive approach, both identifying specific conflicts and then attributing them to politics or a gap between paradigms. These analyses also demonstrated how conflicts provided opportunities for discovery, learning, and growth.

The different approaches converged, at least partially, in the contrast between ARC's espoused organizational theory (Figure 22.1) and its theory-in-use (Figure 22.2). The espoused theory was expressed mainly at the macro level in abstract terms, whereas theory-in-use reflected the micro level of interpersonal interactions. The espoused theory of action became an active part of the ARC's life. Making it explicit at the outset provided the basis for comparison with the implicit theory-in-use that emerged in actual practice. The hope is that ongoing testing and reflection will lead to the production of actionable knowledge about building partnerships between academia and the community (Argyris, 1993, pp. 2–3).

ARC did not blur the differences in identity but, rather, sharpened them. The power of participatory action research as defined by Hughes (2004) is exactly the fact that we, as partners, can talk about the meaning of partnership as it unfolds. This process requires that participants be aware of and recognize the need for continuous dialogue and unending negotiation of reality (Friedman & Berthoin Antal, 2004). Both processes are extremely demanding, but essential for reaching agreed-upon definitions of the substance of "true" partnership—if such a state actually exists.

NOTES

1. Ibrahim Abu Elhaija, Helena Syna Desevillia, Victor J. Friedman, Michal Palgi, Michal Shamir, Orit Shamir, and Israel Sykes.

2. The initial draft of this section was written by Victor J. Friedman.

3. Invitation, January 23, 2004, signed by Helena and Victor.

4. Protocol, March 1, 2004.

5. Protocol, March 22, 2004. This protocol does not specify to whom it was sent, but my recollection is that it was sent to additional faculty and to community members.

6. Protocol, April 1, 2004.

7. Masar Institute for Education, which is dedicated to developing new visions of education at the local, national, regional, and global level. Its flagship program is an experimental school, now in its seventh year, the first of its kind in the Arab sector in Israel and, perhaps, in the Arab world.

8. The letter itself is undated, but the Word file was created on April 4, 2004.

9. Proposal for Creating an Action Research Center at the Emek Yezreel College, June 24, 2004.

10. This list included all of the people who had participated in meetings so far, plus individuals who had not attended but had expressed interest in participating.

11. These are personal recollections from informal meetings with the president, before and after submitting the proposal. There are no written protocols from these meetings.

12. Protocol, August 9, 2004

13. Protocol, November 23, 2004.

14. Proposal for Creating an Action Research Center at the Emek Yezreel College, June 24, 2004.

15. Invitation to participate in an Action Evaluation, December 27, 2004.

16. Jay was a close friend and colleague of Victor/A, who had been involved in developing AE/C3.

17. The community group involved 10 of the 11 respondents (Protocol, Community Group "Why" Discussion, February 15, 2005). The faculty group also involved 10 of the 11 respondents (Protocol, Faculty Group "Why" Discussion, February 17, 2005).

18. Participants could also read their "why" data or simply expound upon them. Talking about the "why" before the "what" (the goals themselves) is counterintuitive, but it is meant to prepare the ground for reaching consensus (Friedman, Rothman, & Withers, 2006).

19. Action Research Center Project Action Plan, March 6, 2005.

20. Protocol, March 18, 2005.

21. Protocol, March 18, 2005.

22. From "An Invitation to a Meeting—Dec. 19, 2005" and from "Addendum to Steering Committee Agenda—December 27, 2005."

23. Meeting summary, November 17, 2005.

24. Using Action Evaluation/C3

25. Summary document of the Timrat Action Evaluation "Whither Timrat: What? Why? How?"

26. ARC Newsletter, March 2006.

27. Steering Committee Protocol, January 24, 2006.

28. The initial draft of this section was written by Israel Sykes.

29. The initial draft of this section was written by Helena Desevillia and Michal Palgi.

30. The initial draft of this section was written by Michal Shamir and Orit Shamir.

31. Protocols, March 7, 2006, and March 10, 2006.

32. See, for example, the Steering Committee protocols of November 4, 2005 (the first Steering Committee meeting), December 31, 2005, and February 21, 2006.

33. E-mail on March 18, 2006.

34. The initial draft of this section was written by Ibrahim Abu Elhaija.

35. My distinction between "participants" and "partners" is intentional and needs to be addressed, but that is beyond the scope of this chapter.

36. This statement includes a declaration about identity and uniqueness that stems from adopting action research and criticizing the existing paradigm, something we will expand upon later.

37. See the final version of the Strategic Plan, January 24, 2006.

38. Protocol, Steering Committee, March 28, 2006.

39. Protocol, March 10, 2006.

40. Protocol, April 19, 2005.

41. Protocol, June 2, 2005.

42. Protocol, March 1, 2004.

43. Protocol, March 28, 2006.

REFERENCES

Argyris, C. (1993). *Knowledge for action: A guide to overcoming barriers to organizational change.* San Francisco: Jossey-Bass.

Argyris, C., & Schön, D. A. (1996). *Organizational learning II: Theory, method, and practice.* Reading, MA: Addison-Wesley.

Carter, B., & McGoldrick, M. (1989). *The changing family life cycle: A framework for family therapy* (2nd ed.). Needham Heights, MA: Allyn & Bacon.

Chen, H. T. (1990). *Theory-driven evaluations.* Newbury Park, CA: Sage.

Deutsch, M. (2000). Cooperation and competition. In M. Deutsch & P. T. Coleman (Eds.), *The handbook of conflict resolution: Theory and practice* (pp. 21–40). San Francisco: Jossey-Bass.

De Wit, B., & Meyer, R. (1994). *Strategy: Process, content, context.* Los Angeles: West.

Doll, W. (1993). *Post modernism perspectives on education* [original in Hebrew]. Tel Aviv, Israel: Sifriat Poalim.

Erikson, E. H. (1959). *Identity and the life cycle.* New York: International Universities Press.

Friedman, V. (2001). Action science: Creating communities of inquiry in communities of practice. In P. Reason & H. Bradbury (Eds.), *Handbook of action research: Participative inquiry and practice* (pp. 159–170). London: Sage.

Friedman, V., & Berthoin Antal, A. (2004). Negotiating reality: An action science approach to intercultural competence. *Management Learning, 36*(1), 67–84.

Friedman, V., Rothman, J., & Withers, W. (2006). The power of "why": Engaging the goal paradox in program evaluation. *American Journal of Evaluation, 27*(2), 1–18.

Gersick, C. J. G. (1991). Revolutionary change theories: A multilevel exploration of the punctuated equilibrium paradigm. *Academy of Management Review, 16*(1), 10–36.

Hughes, I. (2004). Introduction. In *Action Research Electronic Reader.* Available from http://www.scu.edu.au/schools/gcm/ar/arr/arow/default.html

Kolb, D. M., & Bartunek, J. (1992). *Hidden conflict in organizations: Uncovering behind-the-scenes disputes.* Newbury Park, CA: Sage.

Kuhn, T. (1970). *The structure of scientific revolutions* (2nd ed.). Chicago: University of Chicago Press.

Levinson, D. J. (1978). *The seasons of a man's life.* New York: Basic Books.

Levinson, D. J. (1996). *The seasons of a woman's life.* New York: Knopf.

Lipshitz, R., Friedman, V., & Popper, M. (2006). *The demystification of organizational learning.* Thousand Oaks, CA: Sage.

Putnam, L. (2001). The language of opposition: Challenges in organizational dispute resolution. In W. F. Eadie & P. E. Nelson (Eds.), *The language of conflict and resolution* (pp. 10–21). Thousands Oaks, CA: Sage.

Reason, P., & Bradbury, H. (2001). *Handbook of action research: Participative inquiry and practice.* London: Sage.

Rosner, M., & Getz, S. (1996). *The kibbutz in the era of changes* [original in Hebrew]. Tel Aviv: Hakibbutz Hamehuhad.

Rothman, J., & Friedman, V. (2002). Action evaluation for conflict management in organizations and projects. In J. Davies & E. Kaufman (Eds.), *Second track diplomacy: Concepts and techniques for conflict transformation* (pp. 285–298). Boulder, CO: Rowman & Littlefield.

Samuel, Y. (2002). *The political game: Power and influence in organizations* [original in Hebrew]. Haifa, Israel: University of Haifa and Zamor Bitan.

Stacey, R. (2000). *Strategic management & organisational dynamics: The challenge of complexity* (3rd ed.). Englewood Cliffs, NJ: Prentice Hall.

Tjosvold, D. (1994). *Team organization: An enduring competitive advantage.* New York: John Wiley & Sons.

CHAPTER 23

Collaborative Research in Pharmacy Operations

The Kaiser Permanente Experience

MICHAEL W. STEBBINS

JUDY L. VALENZUELA

ABSTRACT

The chapter begins with a brief review of the changing U.S. healthcare industry context, and Kaiser Permanente's history of using collaborative management research to improve the working climate. With this background, attention shifts to Kaiser's Communication Forum, a learning mechanism that has been in place for over 30 years. Cognitive, structural, and procedural aspects of the learning mechanism are explored, and the chapter features interviews with some of the key forum players. The interviews provide rich data on internal and external researcher roles, forum processes, and the knowledge produced. Implications for the forum as a learning mechanism are explored in discussion and conclusion sections.

The role of learning mechanisms in collaborative management research is a relatively new topic, and little can be found about them, particularly in the healthcare sector. During the past few decades, there has been pressure worldwide to contain costs in healthcare organizations and respond to the changing needs of increasingly sophisticated customers. Within the U.S. context, there are daily newspaper reports about lack of insurance coverage (over 46 million people do not have healthcare insurance), publicly funded hospitals cannot handle demands from the poor, and many of the insured face obstacles in getting access to care. People have more information about their medical conditions, are aware of technology advances and the latest treatment options, and seek the best care available. It is widely observed that public expectations combined with demographic changes and skyrocketing healthcare costs have produced a crisis in healthcare.

The emerging crisis has led some organizations to participate in collaborative research programs to improve healthcare systems. This chapter explores collaboration between an external consultant/researcher (the first author) and a senior manager/internal researcher (the second author) within the Kaiser Permanente Medical Care Program (KPMCP). Most of the empirical setting concerns Kaiser's pharmacy operations division and its Communications Forum (CF). The history of collaboration on this program spans more than 34 years. The story of collaboration has been partially explained elsewhere, in the literature on long-term action research (Stebbins, Hawley, & Rose, 1982; Stebbins & Snow, 1982), vertical linking (Hawley, 1984), learning mechanisms (Stebbins & Shani, 1988), and collaborative management research (Stebbins & Valenzuela, 2004).

The chapter describes an approach to research in which insiders and outsiders jointly examine the setting and jointly author accounts of events in the setting (Bartunek & Louis, 1996). It begins with background information on KPMCP as a complex healthcare system, followed by a description of two action research programs that set the stage for creation of the CF. We then cover the CF as a learning mechanism, the separate and joint roles of the internal and external players, and the knowledge produced.

The heart of this chapter comprises two recorded interview sessions involving internal and external actors working within the Pharmacy Operations component of the KPMCP. The interviews were conducted by two of the editors of this *Handbook*, Rami Shani and Susan Mohrman. The interviewees are Judy Valenzuela, Pharmacy Services Leader, Orange County Service Area, KPMCP; Valerie Marocco, Pharmacy Operations, KPMCP; and Michael Stebbins, Emeritus Professor of Management at California Polytechnic State University.

METHODOLOGY

The methodology for this chapter relies on three sources of data: archives related to the CF; prior publications featuring content analysis of CF topics, processes, and outcomes; and finally, taped in-person interviews and telephone interviews with the actors cited above. In the case of the archives, the authors reviewed extensive written summaries for every quarterly regional CF meeting going back 30 years. These archives come to life within this manuscript via journal notes, reflections, and discussions recorded in prior publications as well as through interviews recorded during the months of May and June 2006. The first interview is gleaned from a three-hour session attended by Rami Shani, Susan Mohrman, Judy Valenzuela, and Michael Stebbins. Audio tapes and a written transcript of this session provided by Susan Mohrman formed the foundation of this interview report. The second interview report was conducted by Susan Mohrman, who also generated a written transcript of telephone discussions with Valerie Marocco and Michael Stebbins.

THE KAISER PERMANENTE MEDICAL CARE PROGRAM AND PHARMACY OPERATIONS

KPMCP is one of the oldest and largest health maintenance organizations (HMOs) in the United States. The nonprofit health plan component of KPMCP serves the healthcare needs of members in nine states and Washington, D.C., and it owns and operates Kaiser Foundation Hospitals along with diverse support units. Within Southern California, the health plan is structured as a group-model HMO. It contracts with the Southern California Permanente Medical Group (hereafter called "the medical group") to provide healthcare services to three million members. Historically, the Southern California region has been dominant in creation of innovative change initiatives that have been extended to other Kaiser regions, and the health plan's Pharmacy Operations division has often been the first to try new programs. The pharmacy division is composed of California-wide strategy and operations central offices, a major central refill facility, a mail-order pharmacy, warehouse facilities, staff services units, and diverse medical center inpatient and outpatient pharmacies. The outpatient part of the organization dispenses 20 million prescriptions a year, and the inpatient pharmacies perform wide-ranging functions that support hospitalized patients. Pharmacists, technicians, pharmacy assistants (clerks, cashiers), and diverse support staff work in locations throughout Southern California. The pharmacy organization's facilities mirror KPMCP medical facilities; there are big inpatient and outpatient pharmacies at all major medical centers as well as eight to ten general and specialty pharmacies within area medical centers and satellite outpatient clinics.

EARLY EXAMPLES OF COLLABORATIVE MANAGEMENT RESEARCH AT KPMCP

The first organizational studies of KPMCP occurred in 1973 through a research contract between Texas Christian University's (TCU's) Institute of Behavioral Research (IBR) and Kaiser's health plan organization (Jones & James, 1976). At that time, one of IBR's research tracks focused on theory building around the meaning of organizational climate and measurement of climate (James, Hartman, Stebbins, & Jones, 1977). The research contract with Kaiser was one of many conducted by Saul Sells, Larry James, Alan Hartman, and Allen Jones that explicitly aimed to benefit both science and practice. Larry James and Michael Stebbins formed a temporary inside/outside research team that adapted TCU climate instruments to the Kaiser health-care setting. At that time, Michael Stebbins was employed by Kaiser as the Southern Region's manager of action research programs, and he held this position until 1978. The IBR study, funded by Kaiser and the Office of Naval Research, covered all managers and management support employees in Southern California. It produced a body of data that formed the scientific basis for a comprehensive survey feedback program. This program touched every segment of the KPMCP organization in Southern California (Stebbins et al., 1982; Stebbins & Snow, 1982). Additional data mining on the academic side led to several doctoral dissertations, technical reports, and journal articles published by IBR staff (for example, James & Jones, 1974, 1976). The strong scientific basis for the climate improvement program along with the introduction of organization development consultants to the organization created an excellent foundation for future collaborative management research.

Internal publicity and fanfare connected with the climate study directly led to follow-up programs within physician and pharmacy components of KPMCP. The pharmacy division was particularly aggressive, and managers and consultants created an entirely new action research program called TACT (Stebbins et al., 1982; Stebbins & Valenzuela, 2004). TACT was an attempt to heal soured relationships between employees and management that stemmed from the devastating strike of 1975–1976. During the strike, pharmacists and other pharmacy employees manned picket lines around Kaiser medical facilities in Southern California. The situation was particularly volatile when employees returned to work in January 1976. The union had "lost" the confrontation with KPMCP, having received little or no gains, and employees were bitter about being on the street during the Thanksgiving and Christmas holidays. Reflecting on the strike, both management representatives and union employees viewed the battle as a "lose-lose" situation.

The TACT program was a partnership involving consultants, a few pharmacy managers, and a large number of union employees. The action research design called for extensive training in group sensing methods for forty "opinion leaders" drawn from all segments of the pharmacy organization. The opinion leaders then designed and implemented methods to reach people on a peer basis. For example, pharmacists conducted half-day group sensing sessions attended by peer pharmacists at each medical center. The process eventually involved 90% of the organization's employees in identifying issues and ideas for change. While an analysis of TACT processes and payoffs is beyond the scope of this chapter, it can be noted that the program directly produced one lasting outcome: a learning mechanism called the Communications Forum (Stebbins & Shani, 1988).

THE COMMUNICATIONS FORUM

The Pharmacy Communications Forum (CF) can best be understood through a review of the literature on organizational capabilities (see Docherty & Shani, Chapter 8 in this volume), learning mechanisms (Shani & Docherty, 2003; Docherty & Shani, Chapter 8 in this volume), insider/outsider team research (Bartunek & Louis, 1996; Bartunek, Chapter 4 in this volume), and clinical inquiry (Schein, 2001). At the outset, the CF was formed as a

microcosm of the pharmacy organization to create a new capability centered on democratic dialogue. Representative pharmacists, clerks, warehouse personnel, supervisors, and other pharmacy employees were to tackle problems not solved by the hierarchy. The theory was that, with support from a top management representative and an outside researcher, an elected set of representatives could organize themselves to address a broad range of issues. The CF would not replace the pharmacy management hierarchy, but it would be a parallel mechanism to promote creativity, communications, and problem-solving. The initial charge from management and the TACT action team was to

- discuss and investigate ways and means by which employees may better serve the needs of customers;
- keep informal and candid lines of communication open among all personnel across levels, pharmacies, and other organizational boundaries;
- serve as a forum for the expression of opinions in all matters affecting pharmacy operations; and
- propose ways and means by which the effectiveness and morale of the pharmacy organization can be maintained and improved.

The first forum meetings had the benefit of strong management and TACT program attention. Both the TACT steering body and the initial CF leadership group were composed of union activists and managers with reputations as change leaders. It should be noted that many of today's top pharmacy leaders, including the CEO, were members of both the TACT steering body and the initial CF group. These key actors took their roles seriously and began to address the task at hand. The first quarterly meetings featured attention to forum constitutions and guidelines, structural matters such as the formation of a network of regional and area (local) forums, and management/employee conflict resolution around specific issues uncovered by forum members. This work continued for several years (see Stebbins & Valenzuela, 2004, for a detailed look at CF phases) and led to organization-wide change initiatives focused on quality of services and improved facilities. Beginning in 1982, there was a shift in emphasis to local innovation and cross-fertilization within the forum network via forum-to-forum contacts. This was a renaissance of sorts, with grassroots invention of diverse programs to support employees, customers, and community organizations. The latest phase of forum growth, from 1997 to the present, has seen the pendulum shift back to an organization-wide and somewhat top-down focus. The forums are now aligned more closely with the management hierarchy. The stimulus for this phase has been economic crisis and other pressures from the environment. In order to reduce costs and improve services, the pharmacy management team has initiated wave after wave of reforms. Accordingly, current regional CF activities are mainly centered on communicating the rationale for changes initiated by management and providing two-way dialogue on intended and unintended consequences of the change programs. Examples of these dynamics are provided in the interviews below.

THE COMMUNICATIONS FORUM AND ORGANIZATIONAL CAPABILITY

By design, the network of forums created a new capability for pharmacy operations. By creating parallel learning mechanisms (Bushe & Shani, 1991) at each medical center as well as for the Southern California region, the pharmacy organization formalized a process for ongoing dialogue and change across locations and management levels. The forums continue to study and act on problems that the formal organization has not discovered or addressed (Zand, 1974). Currently, they also

improve dialogue and reflection on matters related to survival, company strategy, changed policies and procedures, and diverse change initiatives (Stebbins & Valenzuela, 2004). They are especially good at providing an early notice of unintended consequences of system-wide change initiatives for customers and employees.

The literature suggests that capabilities can be examined from four perspectives. The "resource-based" approach describes the business enterprise as a collection of resources, including those that offer unique sources of advantage that are difficult to imitate (Burgelman, 1994). The "dynamic capabilities" approach argues that competitive leadership depends on the firm having the ability to change its capabilities over time, especially in a rapidly changing technological environment (Teece, Pisano, & Schuen, 1997). The knowledge-based view of the firm claims that knowledge is a key competitive resource and stresses the importance of transforming old capabilities into new ones by recombining existing knowledge (Kogut & Kulatilaka, 2001) and by integrating knowledge from outside the organization (Cohen & Levinthal, 1990). Finally, the organizational learning approach claims that learning mechanisms are at the core of developing new capabilities (Shani & Docherty, 2003; Docherty & Shani, Chapter 8 in this volume). While the capability that Kaiser has developed would seem to be nestled under both the dynamic capabilities and organizational learning approaches, for the purpose of this chapter we will focus on the organizational learning approach.

THE COMMUNICATIONS FORUM AND ORGANIZATIONAL LEARNING

The CF is a collaborative learning mechanism, and to understand it, one must consider the context, the actors, the type of collaboration, and the learning and knowledge produced. Learning mechanisms are planned, proactive features that enable and encourage organizational learning (Popper & Lipshitz, 1998). An assumption is that the capability to learn can be designed rather than left to evolve through the normal activities of the organization. Literature on learning mechanisms identifies three foci: cognitive, structural, and procedural (Shani & Docherty, in press). All three mechanisms have been addressed in development of the forum network and are discussed below.

COGNITIVE LEARNING MECHANISMS

Cultural or cognitive mechanisms are the bearers of language, concepts, symbols, theories, frameworks, and values for thinking, reasoning, and understanding developed in creating new organizational capabilities. Cognitive mechanisms are management's main means for creating an understanding among all employees of the rationale for change. In the case of the Kaiser communications forum, the original TACT program recommendations for creation of forums and the initial constitutions for regional and local forums provide the values and reasoning for a new type of dialogue. The TACT group hoped to build dialogue and the capability for organizational learning. It can be argued that the CF closely follows Gustavsen's (1992) criteria for democratic dialogue:

- Dialogue is based on a principle of give-and-take, not one-way communication.
- All participants have the same status in the dialogue arenas.
- Work experience is the point of departure for participation.
- It must be possible for all participants to gain an understanding of topics under discussion.
- The dialogue should be able to integrate a growing degree of disagreement.

- The dialogue should continuously generate decisions that provide a platform for action.

As will be shown in the interviews below, the forums are recognized as an alternative to hierarchy and provide both a spiritual and a substantive channel for new dialogue, learning, and action.

STRUCTURAL LEARNING MECHANISMS

Structural mechanisms are organizational, physical, technical, and work system infrastructures that encourage practice-based learning. These mechanisms support discourse and the sensemaking entailed as individuals and groups learn from experience (Weick, 1995; Raelin, 2000). Structural mechanisms include creation of new communication channels; the establishment of lateral structures to enable learning of new practices across various core organizational units; changes in roles and teams; formal and informal forums for joint exploration and debate; and networks for mutual learning. In some cases they also include learning-specific structures such as parallel learning structures. In the case of the KPMCP communications forum, parallel learning structures have been created to maximize two-way communication between employees and members of the hierarchy, as well as to facilitate transfer of innovations across local forums and geographic locations. Knowledge and perspectives are also combined when representatives of local forums identify common themes and trends. This provides a coherent picture of what is occurring in the field as services are provided to patients. Striking examples of this occur in the interviews below, including employee reaction to the recent productivity improvement program. Similarly, pharmacy operations staff experts provide early information on changes such as information technology enhancements that will affect field operations, and the rationale for change is shared. Forums emphasize face-to-face exchange supplemented by e-mail, access to company Web databases, and the sharing of company documents.

PROCEDURAL MECHANISMS

Procedural mechanisms concern the rules, routines, methods, and tools that can be institutionalized within the organization to promote and support learning (Pavlovsky, Forslin, & Reinhardt, 2001). In the forum case, mechanisms have included instruction in facilitation methods, group sensing technology, team-building simulations, and other methods and tools that are shared across levels and locations. Learning tools are often shared first at the regional forum meetings and then shared at the next level. However, they have also been designed locally and then shared laterally or vertically within the forum network (see, for example, the method for employees' evaluation of their supervisors). These different methods have been successfully applied to allow participants to systematically learn from each other's experience through reflection and the encoding of new knowledge in new practice routines.

Use of the Shani and Docherty (in press) framework on cognitive, structural, and procedural learning mechanisms provides new insights into the forum network as it has developed over time. Past publications about the forum focused primarily on the forum as a structural learning mechanism and its evolution from a parallel learning structure (and experiment in workplace democracy) toward an integrated learning mechanism (Stebbins, Shani, Moon, & Bowles, 1998) that resembles typical company departments. The inclusion of cognitive and procedural perspectives allows one to see that key elements have survived intact for over 30 years while the structural learning mechanism has changed. For example, any topic, whether comfortable or uncomfortable for management, can be placed on the agenda, and employees have an active voice and strong collective impact beyond their involvement in normal hierarchical channels. Also, by monitoring discussions at the different forums within the network, one can test whether information is being accurately communicated through normal hierarchical channels.

ACTOR ROLES AND RELATIONSHIPS IN DIFFERENT FORUM PHASES

During the first phase of CF growth, Michael Stebbins's role was to work with management to broadly support startup activities and to meet with elected CF officers to discuss the issues and set the agenda for quarterly forum meetings. At the outset, the CF chairperson and other leaders were mainly nonmanagement employees. However, there was always a management presence at the forum through a top-level pharmacy leader, and while titles of managers have changed over the years, one top-team operations executive has always been a member of the forum. Judy Valenzuela is currently the top-team member, and she is one of seven operations executives in Southern California. She has served on the forum for the past 16 years.

In the early years, the consultant/researcher's task was to ensure that all issues were on the table, and to facilitate relevant collection of data between meetings so that discussions would be fact-based. During the all-day meetings, he actively facilitated discussion, often using intergroup conflict interventions to polarize different subgroups and legitimize different perspectives. Meetings were held offsite to promote a sense of equality and neutrality. During the middle years (1982–1996), the consultant/researcher and forum leadership roles changed in several ways. Michael

Stebbins left Kaiser to become a management professor at Cal Poly. Also, in the early 1980s, Stebbins, the CEO, and the top management member of the regional CF met with local pharmacy leaders to encourage their involvement in forum activities and to ensure that the combined local/regional network of forums would thrive. Active interventions by the consultant/researcher and upper managers helped demonstrate how local forums could build relationships and at the same time meet managerial needs. During regional forum meetings, the consultant/researcher relied on educational interventions, facilitation, process consulting, clinical inquiry, and periodic survey feedback interventions (Schein, 2001) to build CF member capabilities to operate the forums (see the Marocco and Valenzuela interviews below for examples of this emphasis on individual learning). The CEO's management representative on the forum gradually began to assume roles and activities related to gathering data to be shared at quarterly meetings. The management role shifted toward that of an internal researcher, and the external researcher became less involved in working with members of the management and staff groups. Currently, the internal researcher's role involves liaison with pharmacy operations staff groups, as well as following through on action items between meetings.

By 1997, the regional meeting agenda had shifted toward KPMCP's difficulties in the highly competitive healthcare marketplace, and the internal researcher had the burden of explaining business problems and the company's planned response. Both insider and outsider (I/O) researchers now play roles in sensing issues and facilitating discussions about the wide-ranging pharmacy change initiatives and the changing competitive context.

As noted in the interviews below, the internal researcher's role also includes liaison with union leaders. Under the recently developed Labor Management Partnership (LMP; see interviews below), Judy Valenzuela has been able to bring LMP players and topics into the normal CF network activities rather than create what would essentially be a whole new learning mechanism for the pharmacy organization. In contrast, the rest of KPMCP has been slow to comprehend how genuine union/management collaboration can be integrated into normal planning and operations processes.

THE EXTERNAL RESEARCHER ROLE IN CLINICAL INQUIRY

When academic researchers and consultants have established records of long-term engagement with clients, they have the opportunity to play multiple roles and to pursue diverse interventions (see Schein, 2001; Stebbins et al., 1982; Stebbins & Valenzuela, 2004; Werr & Greiner, Chapter 5 in this volume). Given mutual collaboration and trust, there is a continuing opportunity to address problems that the formal organization has not solved (Zand, 1974). Under clinical inquiry (Schein, 2001), the client and researcher are both highly involved in data gathering and problem solving. The search for relevant data is a joint quest. In the pharmacy organization case, the I/O researchers and the regional forum members all influence the agenda, learning activities, and types of data gathering. Specifically, members are polled regarding topics to be discussed and regarding the type of training and information that will be most helpful to them in operating local forums and performing their daily work. The various interventions produce insights on the part of both the forum members and the I/O researchers. This closely follows the distinguishing features of I/O research, in that members of the research team differ in physical and psychological connectedness to the organizational setting and the questions being examined. Also, the I/O team members work jointly in all phases of research design (Bartunek & Louis, 1996). I/O team members share authority for decisions about the content of the story told and knowledge to be shared. A recent example shows how I/O collaboration in data gathering led to action and organizational learning. During the latter stages of Kaiser's performance improvement program (PIP), where best practices were installed at every outpatient location within the pharmacy organization, discussions about PIP issues dominated local and regional CF meetings. The I/O researcher team relied on group sensing and written survey methods to gather data on staffing and work problems directly attributable to PIP. Triangulating interviews with numeric data (see Werr & Greiner, Chapter 5 in this volume) helped make a strong case for change. This data was used in feedback/discussion meetings at the forum and later, in management meetings. In brief, management formally recognized PIP consequences in the form of employee stress and perceptions of declining quality of work life. Additional verification through the annual pharmacy-wide "people pulse" survey led the top management team to increase hiring, improve staffing, and initiate training that would allow PIP productivity levels to be sustained. Both the internal researcher and the external researcher played roles in communicating the research findings within Kaiser and recognizing the improvements put in place. The organization realized the importance of balanced attention to multiple outcomes including employee satisfaction. Other examples of data gathering that led to individual and organizational learnings within the pharmacy organization are documented in the interview section and in literature on learning mechanisms (Stebbins & Valenzuela, 2004), change processes, and sustainable work systems (Stebbins & Valenzuela, in press).

THE ACADEMIC RESEARCH KNOWLEDGE PRODUCED AT KPMCP

It is easier to document individual and organizational learnings and lasting changes from the forum network at Kaiser than to specify academic knowledge created through collaboration at Kaiser. During the 1970s and 1980s, academic research contributions took the form of theory building and measurement of psychological climate (James et al., 1977), recognition of the value of vertical linking processes (Hawley, 1984), and theory building around structural learning mechanisms (Stebbins & Shani, 1988). During the 1990s and the current decade, most contributions have centered on the communications forum as a learning mechanism, as well as on the potential value of structural learning mechanisms in other healthcare and nonhealthcare settings (see, for example, Stebbins et al., 1998). Current research also includes an investigation of Kaiser's drug utilization change initiatives, to explore the collaboration between pharmacy staff and medical providers that promotes balanced outcomes—health outcomes, member satisfaction, provider satisfaction, and lower costs (Stebbins & Valenzuela, in press). In terms of collaborative management research, the record of scholarly research within the pharmacy organization is small but significant.

INTERVIEWS

The collaborative research model used at Kaiser closely follows clinical inquiry (Schein, 2001) and process consulting. The subject matter mainly comes from the work environment as the organization seeks to solve problems connected with growth and survival. The I/O researchers use group sensing to stay aware of emerging issues as identified internally, and, as noted in the interviews below, initiate discussion of outside management and marketplace trends. Together, the I/O researchers create methods to understand the issues on a deeper level and to provide CF members with learning opportunities. As will be shown in the interviews below, forum members are often deeply affected by the processes used and the quality of dialogue that takes place during meetings at all levels. In particular, the reader is urged to examine interviewee perceptions that they have personally grown over the years, that the CF network has created positive programs that last to this day, and that overall, the organization has a new capability through institutionalization of this learning mechanism.

Part One: Rami Shani and Susan Mohrman Interview Judy Valenzuela and Michael Stebbins

Rami: Few mechanisms documented in the management literature, such as the communications forum, have lasted 30 years. What explains this?

Judy: It is due in part to the nature of the pharmacy organization within Kaiser. We're an organization with a lot of history and we haven't had significant employee or management turnover. People have enjoyed the challenge, growth, and opportunity and have stayed here. We've had some top leaders who believe in collaboration and mentoring and the expectation has been passed down that the CF has value.

The CF stemmed from work stoppages, and there was a lot of animosity between management and staff. Mike and other organization effectiveness [OE] consultants worked with managers to start the TACT program. At the time, I was a pharmacist and brand new employee and simply wanted to get back to work after the long strike.

But other employees felt that pharmacy leaders were not dealing with issues that were highly important. They felt that information was filtered or not disclosed.

It is interesting to me that because of that painful history and because of the forum and other programs, pharmacy is a different place compared to the rest of the company on how to treat people and the need for teamwork.

Recently Kaiser as an organization has formed a labor management partnership [LMP] with the unions, and the partnership is now doing what we did with TACT 30 years ago.

A problem, though, is that some people don't have a history of working with the forum. We have added a central refill pharmacy, a mail-order pharmacy, a drug warehouse, diverse specialized clinics, and other facilities, and people at these units work in totally different environments. They don't interface with patients like we do in the other 80% of the pharmacy organization.

Rami: What impact did growth have on the forum structure?

Judy: There is a Southern California regional forum and we assume that every major hospital and clinic area has a local forum. The local forums have representatives from different hospitals and clinics in the geographic area. At the area or local forum we have some entities not represented in the meetings, but they hear about forum activities. The regional forum has minutes and action items that must be followed up on and they are posted and communicated to all through staff meetings. The same occurs for the local forums.

Rami: It started as a representative body and has evolved to create a different configuration. What are the issues connected with this?

Judy: When it started, the pharmacists were in the same union as the rest of the staff. About 20 years ago, the pharmacists formed their own professional guild, and the relationship between pharmacist and management totally changed. At the outset every area sent one pharmacist and one assistant to the meetings. Today, we can't do this as we are too short-staffed. Twenty years ago pharmacists composed 34% of the total staff. Due to automation, the hiring of technicians, and a nationwide shortage of pharmacists, the ratio is 26%. It is typical to have up to 10% pharmacist vacancies.

Mike: Other changes led to different representation. The company has moved to sell over-the-counter [OTC] drugs on a much larger scale. So a lot of the work involves OTC sales, locating drugs filled by the central refill pharmacy, inventory topics, and the like. The employees who do this work are well represented at the forum meetings to address hot issues such as patient waiting times, seasonal drug promotions, progress with drug conversions, and other outpatient service problems. I'm just realizing now that the forums *are* representative in the sense of outpatient operations.

Sue: How is the Labor Management Partnership involved in this?

Judy: It is a good way for us to invite labor to communicate with staff. I invite my LMP partner (a Kaiser employee who works full-time for the partnership) and the union business agent to the forum meetings.

The CF provides exposure to diverse people, and the opportunity to share goals, company strategy, and the challenges to be faced. Communication of that engages people to be part of something other than their daily tasks. It forces learning.

I view the CF as a management tool. Other managers don't see it that way, but I do. You would be surprised at the very big issues that I hear about firsthand such as system outages and technology changes that affect everyone, including patients. We get early warning and can prepare locally. At the regional meetings we often hear things from regional office groups for the first time, and then I can take this back to my managers and staff. It works the other way too, as we hear from the areas about issues in the field so that regional groups can make adjustments.

Mike: Judy is a champion for the forums throughout Southern California. Part of her approach is to build capabilities at the next management level. When Judy is gone, her managers can step in, as they know the CF model and its value.

Judy: Since the CF is 30 years in the making, many of the founders are retiring. A few of the local forums are floundering, and I have to pull out the constitution and written guidelines, and then coach managers at other areas to pass on the knowledge.

Mike: One thing that rings true for managers is that the forum is part of the communication around every major change initiative.

Judy: All initiatives are communicated through multiple channels, including the regional and local forums.

Sue: What is the CF role?

Mike: Pete Solyom felt that you can't overdo communications. It has a unique role to play in uncovering unanticipated problems in the change programs. If you listen only to management and those responsible for change initiatives, then everything is going well. But at the forums you find that is not true. An example is PIP (a massive productivity improvement effort). When we surveyed people at regional and local forums, employees felt that PIP improved things for patients but had negative consequences for jobs. They felt quality of work life fell.

Judy: PIP was a good thing, but there were many flaws. PIP leaders expected managers to be out there, driving the work done by teams. I feel they need to be leaders instead. It hurt us and managers and employees were exhausted. People at the forums ensure that communications about this do not stop with the immediate managers. A room full of people saying the same things is much more powerful, and you have to listen and adjust.

Mike: It helps if people who are responsible for these programs are in the meetings. The value of this upward communication cannot be ignored. Managers have degrees of freedom.

Judy: I can influence and I can correct. This brings credibility. This approach has been adopted by our service area in Orange County, too. The top medical group leader and administrators now have their own type of forums.

There have been major changes since I joined the regional forum. At the beginning, we had very difficult people who challenged us constantly. Over time, even the "burr in the saddle" people calmed down and became collaborative. We have matured as a company, and are not so upset when challenged. People are more adept and cordial in their handling of messages and give feedback in a way that you can handle it. This comes from forum work, our services culture and training, and continual emphasis on handling difficult encounters with patients.

Rami: Can the forum be used as a body to study practices that develop, in a systematic and scientific way?

Mike: In the early days, learning activities were orchestrated by the forum. But people were doing this part-time, and the forum was not an operating group. Instead, the pharmacy preferred to pull a cross-section of employees to work on change programs and to assign a "shepherd" from the management team to study things and to lead the effort. Most recently, this has taken the form of researching best practices.

Sue: It sounds like you [Judy] feel the organization has matured and learned to get people involved, get feedback, and work together across all the locations and stakeholders. What roles have Mike and other actors played?

Judy: Mike helped at startup establishing the framework and processes. As an

OE person, he asked the difficult questions and challenged us to deal with the issues and to establish ways to deal with what was an ugly time in our history. He has been the constant person to facilitate meetings. He helps us organize the agenda and bring up the issues we would rather push aside. Employee representation changes a lot at the meetings. We both welcome the new people. I'm the person who handles logistics and follow-up with upper management and staff groups, or my peers who need to get behind changes.

It is important to have a disinterested party, because otherwise you run the risk of operating just like you would in a staff meeting back home. He also brings learning activities, exercises, and tools that help us to be more effective. We can then take these back to our own forums. I use many of them with my own management team.

Mike: I use the forum to bring in things I'm intrigued with, for my own learning. I have freedom to pursue things that go beyond the pharmacy world.

Sue: What is going on in the larger Kaiser context?

Judy: The forum has been a model for building partnerships, collaboration, and communications. It allows staff to be more involved in understanding the business, what changes are afoot, and where we will enlist their support. We have a long-time leader in Al Carver, who succeeded Pete Solyom. Al is ethical and down-to-earth. He has helped us weather shifts in structure to a California-wide organization and creation of central services. He emphasizes a balance among quality, service, and affordability. His leadership, his consistency, and his values are important to us. He has helped build a management structure that over the years has allowed us to grow and is a model for the rest of Kaiser. While we are preoccupied with outpatient care issues, we also run hospital-based pharmacy units, work alongside physicians on clinical pharmacy issues, have the world's leading drug information center, address appropriate medication use, and have other lines of work.

Mike: There are many services that started out as change initiatives and then were institutionalized. For example, drug utilization changes initially involved informal cooperation, and now they are highly developed capabilities. Cooperation between pharmacists and physicians on these types of programs is extraordinary.

Judy: There are two drug utilization programs, addressing different needs. The Drug Utilization Action Team [DUAT] is physician run—we asked them to lead the charge and put them on hook to do it. The program saves costs overall and improves quality of care. Patients get the best drugs whether or not they cost less.

DUAT is only one of many ongoing initiatives where improvement teams are changing the ways that pharmacies operate. Programs expand and contract based on needs. There are so many venues. We have peer group meetings for all levels of management; they meet quarterly. I meet with the top team, hold regular meetings of my management team, and also have yearly off-site retreats.

Sue: You and Mike have written together. What kinds of audiences are you interested in reaching and what kind of knowledge are you creating?

Mike: The audience is informed practitioners. If we write about the forum, it's something any organization can do. The articles have been about learning mechanisms. I'm an academic, but also in the practitioner world. Writing involves the same kind of bridging between theory and practice that we do at the forum.

Judy: I am a practitioner and have a harder time with the theoretical. I'm a pharmacist by training. I see, touch, and do. The people coming to the forums are technicians, people doing data input, and customer contact people who have little or no college. They really enjoy and get a lot out of the exercises. I don't know if they have captured the translation from theory to actual, but what really matters is that they understand the actual.

Mike: I've always wanted a coauthor from the inside in my research. I'm currently working on another article involving another pharmacy employee who has a wonderful understanding of what goes on with DUAT action teams. I don't understand the pharmacy at a deep level, but we can put something together because she has the technical expertise and I look at management.

Sue: What's your role in the research and what comes out of collaboration?

Judy: I would not do this without a partnership. I've mostly coauthored with Mike on general management issues—not issues of pharmacy management. When I work with Mike I see why the ideas and collaboration are effective. Writing is a totally different venue for me from my normal life; to be able to touch on management theory and see things in a way that it can be passed on so others can use it. To be honest, Mike has done most of the work. I've just participated in it.

Part Two: Susan Mohrman Interviews Valerie Marocco and Michael Stebbins

(Valerie Marocco recently became a member of the pharmacy's corporate compliance unit, was one of the founding members of the regional CF, and has held a variety of pharmacy clinical assistant positions in the field.)

Sue: The forum has involved 30 years of collaboration. What is good collaboration?

Valerie: I am fortunate to have been here for 34 years. I really did get to learn in the process. I am an example of someone who did not have a managerial title, but was privy enough to be part of it and to learn along the way. When I first came, the Forum was starting. I represented the Fontana area. There was little communication then and we had little tribes—different groups in different geographic settings. We could tell each other what was happening in our area and find out if we were doing similar things. This led to problem-solving opportunities. We had minutes and shared them back home. I would go back and we began to try a mini-forum at our area and to develop the concept there. As the regional representative I was the starting person locally, too. I mimicked what was happening at the forum. We had seven pharmacies and had a non-management person from each pharmacy attend. I would facilitate. We also had a manager assigned to help us. The important thing was to give the field a voice and to make sure that it was heard. The idea was to get away from hierarchy. We had unions and I was a union employee. Since a collaborative partnership had not evolved, we had the more limiting feeling of allegiance to the union. Now with the partnership, we're more equal and it has worked out better. Back then we thought that if one of us took back the idea there was a better chance of it being heard than if a manager took it back. I never felt that the forum was an empty gesture. It gave the field a voice.

Sue: Could you provide some examples of where the organization learned and did something different?

Valerie: We developed Pharmacy Week out of the forum. In October of each year, the professional associations for pharmacies started to recognize pharmacies for a week for the kind of work they did. The forum was instrumental in sharing that. One area did it. They came to the regional forum and said we're going to recognize our employees and have activities for patients. Then, all the areas started the program and it became something we did throughout Southern California. In Fontana we would make presentations to

the different hospital and clinic floors, and gave out gifts such as IV bottles with jelly beans.

This established the regional representative as an ongoing link, not just on a quarterly basis. We started to call each other and find out how people were doing different things on a wide variety of topics.

Mike: At the quarterly meetings, they would find out what was hot in the local pharmacies and were also able to anticipate problems and come to the meetings with solutions.

Valerie: We had an opportunity. When you were in the field, you didn't know where "pharmacy operations" was, or what they did. You just got memos. There was no face or a sense of what was coming in the future. That's where the communications started to evolve. Representatives from pharmacy operations would come to forum meetings, for example Pete Solyom or Al Carver would come in and give us a sense of what was happening with their groups. We felt we were hearing what was coming down the pike and that we could judge face-to-face sincerity. We would report that back. If there was a mood of gloom or excitement about change, we could take that back and tell people about the person who gave us the information that made it sound more valid.

Locally, we met once a month and instead of people coming to one location in the Fontana area, we rotated meetings through different pharmacies so we could see the pharmacy in action. It started to snowball. When computers came in we started to do "short codes" and shared them throughout the service area, and we would identify problems such as getting a specific drug. Newsletters evolved and we posted minutes in all pharmacies.

Our local forum would sponsor community and social programs. We had a Christmas party for employees and fund-raising drives to support families and schools in the community. The big CF started to break down into smaller ones at the area level and then to individual pharmacies. Communications went both ways.

Now that I'm in operations, I'm bringing information to the regional forum. When you come, you are getting the field view of things. You feel in touch.

When we started, we were trying to see what would work for us. Michael would remind us of our purpose, and that was not to just moan about what was going wrong, but to be active in solutions. We listed problems that management didn't feel were there. Michael would facilitate to help us to be productive. We needed to establish ourselves as a valid tool and to be credible.

We are now dealing with problems that are far more complex because of the nature of the business. The CF is a front line of communication with employees. We're approaching solutions at a depth that is more important. People now know that they have a voice and are important.

The fact that Judy is a facilitator and top leader helps greatly. She is very credible. You can go to her and she will try to fix it and get back to you with answers.

Sue: What is Mike's role?

Valerie: When you mention his name in the organization, he is well thought of and credible. People feel he has contributed to the organization structure and how we share information. I got to learn new things. What does organization structure mean? Before, I was sort of a gutter dog— just do what you have to do. The people at the top have their way and disseminate things down and the front line just has to figure out how to do that. Michael taught us and developed us and gave us some tools without making us feel that we didn't know how things work— allowing us exposure to a level without feeling that we were on opposite sides. Sometimes I can't express myself well, but I know how I feel. Michael would help us lead in a productive way. He taught us the importance of voicing our opinions and how to go back. He gave us tools. I got to go back and facilitate at a local level, which I never would have thought I could have done. We would go back to our areas and use it. Even those who replaced us could learn to do it, and it became a natural way for things to happen. I never felt intimidated to voice my opinion because I felt I was speaking for the group.

Mike: We had to relearn how to run meetings as focus became more and more on the pharmacy operations departments and operational complexities. Judy and I saw it drift toward a top-down information flow, without the vital bottom-up input. So we recently changed the agenda to begin bottom-up with voice from the Areas. When operations people come, Judy and I have to make sure people don't just present; there has to be dialogue.

Valerie: When I first came to the forum you would listen to management, but then it reversed to be that they came to listen to us because we were bringing something of value. We had information they didn't have. This was a reality check.

Sue: Has the organization had learnings from the forum?

Valerie: The forum keeps alive the thought that managers have to think about what they say and how they say it if they want field support. Management tends to just shoot out information. But now they know that if they don't try it in the field first, they are going to have to reckon with it.

Other parts of pharmacy are using forum ideas and processes. When the core management group has a special issue to resolve, they will form a special group to address it and bring it back to the core group. People are ready to give feedback to management. We now have an annual "People Pulse" survey where employees are surveyed about the pharmacy environment, and management sets annual goals based on the data. This is a report card on how employees feel about the organization and management.

Mike: Relationship building with local managers has always been a big

thing. A manager at one location used the forum to develop a way of giving annual appraisals of immediate supervisors. Employee appraisal of supervisory performance became part of the supervisors' annual evaluations. This was shared across the areas.

Valerie: Management started coming to forum meetings to gauge interest in different things. It took guts. This allowed the field to participate in decisions. From a practical standpoint, management had to recruit from the field. If you felt that going over to management was the dark side, that wouldn't be good. Through the forum and other programs, we learned that there was not a division between management and employee interests, we inverted the pyramid. This was a paradigm shift. We used to talk about how we would get new employees and they wouldn't know anything. So we jointly realized that training and orientation had to happen sooner. Through the forums you could find out what they needed to learn.

Out of the forums, managers learned that decisions can't be made only at one level and you need to create different avenues for communication. This was a strong learning, and it has lasted. Now we have different ways of doing it. But the forum still has a role. Open communication has allowed us to be better at what we are doing and dealing with many of these changes. This is particularly true on business objectives versus healthcare issues. It has helped to manage change.

I feel really privileged. In fact, if I had to pick something that really helped me grow—I really feel that in the way I go about my job and try to get information out, being part of the forum has provided me with a base to understand how to do things well. Many, many people have used the forum. You have the feeling that you always have a route to bring it somewhere other than to your manager. You have a forum, you have a voice.

It takes a person to hold this together. We are lucky. Before, I would not have known what a flip chart was. It meant nothing to a person in the field, and you would never see ideas on paper. We could track our progress. That tool is something we all use now. We can all see it and make sure it's right. Michael developed us on how to communicate our thoughts and made us accountable for that. I'm really happy to be part of the forum. I'm just so proud that after all my years I'm still one of the original people.

DISCUSSION

On reflection, it appears that the forum network has evolved to be a learning mechanism that is more of a management tool than an experiment in democratic dialogue. As the pharmacy organization has grown, many other changes (addition of management levels, managerial and employee training, building a service culture) along with the forum network have combined to create a team-oriented work culture. The activism spawned by the 1970 psychological climate has subsided,

and there are fewer burning issues. Ironically, despite the addition of managers, there is a lower sense of hierarchy and employees expect to be involved in work changes whether or not there is an active forum or formal LMP mechanism. It remains to be seen whether the new LMP arrangement envelops the forum as the main vehicle for employee/management dialogue, or whether LMP initiatives will continue to be orchestrated through the forum learning mechanism. The degree of institutionalization of the forum as a learning mechanism would seem to support the latter argument.

A question inadequately addressed in the interviews is whether the forum can be used to study issues and practices in a formal and scientific way. At the local level, forums seem to invent various work, relationship-building, and community service improvement programs that respond to local needs, or at least the needs and interests of local forum members. Information about the programs is shared at quarterly regional meetings, but in recent years there have been fewer efforts to systematically grow the programs at other locations or to study program processes and outcomes. In contrast, top-down, company-wide change programs are carefully organized and actively managed to ensure action at every location. Also, these programs have scorecards with multiple performance measures for each type of pharmacy. The company-wide change initiatives continue to dominate attention and problem solving at both local and regional forum meetings, and they currently have the most potential for systematic research studies and contributions to the management research community. Importantly, these initiatives rely on very different learning mechanisms that can also be studied. The answer to the research question posed would seem to be that the door is open for future research, but that the forum itself will not be the vehicle for collaborative management research.

CONCLUSION

Over the years, the I/O researchers within pharmacy operations have achieved a balanced partnership in the service of acquiring and applying knowledge to issues of both theoretical and practical interest (Pasmore, 2004). Reason and Bradbury (2001) argue that any participatory form of inquiry, well grounded in the everyday concerns of people, will necessarily be worthwhile. Academic and pharmacy operations partners work together to design the communications forum network as a learning mechanism, and to consider the best ways to gather information that will address company problems and the changing environment. While most member/participants in the forum are oblivious to the fact of academic research products, they are well aware of learnings that come from sharing top-down and bottom-up perspectives (Hawley, 1984), such as differences on whether a particular policy and procedure change will be good for patients or for employees. They are also aware that organizational knowledge is created by pooling disparate information from the different area forums and pharmacies. Also, the forums systematically uncover problems that management has not discovered. Research publications on the forums provide many documented examples of model building and change programs created locally or regionally and then disseminated throughout the Southern California forum network and larger KPMCP organization (Stebbins & Valenzuela, 2004). Programs continue to include community, educational, and social service projects, programs to recognize and support pharmacy employees and their families, and programs that serve the needs of Kaiser health plan members and customers.

At the individual level, managers and members of the forum rely on procedural learning mechanisms that build personal skills of use in both work and nonwork settings. As noted in the interviews, much of the credit for long-term forum success rests with a supportive leadership and active teaming between the I/O researchers. From the outset, pharmacy division CEOs have periodically attended regional forum meetings and have appointed a key line manager (who serves as internal researcher) to help facilitate, gather data, and ensure sound linkages with regional support office and peer management groups. When the internal researcher participates in data gathering and data analysis, she sees opportunities that the consultant/researcher does not see. Together, they produce sensemaking of the setting and knowledge to be gleaned from it (Bartunek & Louis, 1996), including new organizational knowledge.

Theory on I/O team research and participatory action research (PAR; Whyte, 1991) is advanced by this chapter. Publications on both the PAR and I/O approaches mainly concern temporary collaborative efforts designed to produce new knowledge that contributes both to practical solutions to immediate problems and to general knowledge (Elden & Chisholm, 1993). In the case at hand, the I/O team research partnership is long-standing and vital to development of the forum network as a new capability. As noted within the interviews, both the internal researcher and external researcher are viewed as champions for the forums (Stebbins & Valenzuela, 2004) and are highly involved in making them work. The long-term I/O relationship helps build a climate of mutual trust and respect that supports democratic dialogue. Trust and comfort with the I/O researchers undoubtedly supports a brand of questioning that is emancipating for employees and supports self-direction for both individuals and the wider forum community. The long-term I/O relationship also supports a long-term development perspective on learning mechanisms, research topics, and the value of academic contributions.

In the pharmacy case, a spirit of support, collaboration, and positive response continues to prevail within the forum network, and this is due in part to a strong and positive management team and to the activities of the internal researcher. Additionally, the external researcher is able to help set the research agenda and to provide support through clinical inquiry and other approaches (Schein, 2001). The longer-term outlook for collaboration and systematic research includes forthcoming publications on topics such as drug utilization management in healthcare organizations, sustainable work systems, and innovative change processes. Accordingly, the Kaiser Pharmacy organization continues to be a positive example for collaborative management research within KPMCP and for other outside organizations.

REFERENCES

Adler, N., Shani, A. B. (Rami), & Styhre, A. (2004). *Collaborative research in organizations: Foundations for learning, change, and theoretical development.* London: Sage.

Bartunek, J. M., & Louis, M. R. (1996). *Insider/outsider team research.* Thousand Oaks, CA: Sage.

Burgelman, R. (1994). Fading memories: A process theory of strategic business exit in dynamic environments. *Administrative Science Quarterly, 39*(1), 24–56.

Bushe, G. R., & Shani, A. B. (Rami). (1991). *Parallel learning structures: Creating innovations in bureaucracies.* Reading, MA: Addison-Wesley.

Cohen, W. M., & Levinthal, D. A. (1990). Absorptive capacity: A new perspective on learning and participation. *Administrative Science Quarterly, 35*(1), 128–152.

Elden, M., & Chisholm, R. (1993). Emerging varieties of action research: Introduction to the special issue. *Human Relations, 46*(2), 121–142.

Gustavsen, B. (1992). *Dialogue and development.* Stockholm: Swedish Center for Working Life.

Hawley, J. A. (1984). Vertical linking in organizations. *Organizational Dynamics, 12*(3), 68–80.

Jones, A. P., & James, L. R. (1976). *Psychological and organizational climate: Dimensions and relationships* (Technical Report 76-4). Fort Worth: Institute of Behavioral Research, Texas Christian University.

James, L. R., Hartman, A., Stebbins, M. W., & Jones, A. P. (1977). Relationships between psychological climate and a VIE model for work motivation. *Personnel Psychology, 30*(2), 229–254.

James, L. R., & Jones, A. P. (1974). Organizational climate: A review of theory and research. *Psychological Bulletin, 81*(12), 1096–1112.

James, L. R., & Jones, A. P. (1976). Organizational structure: A review of structural dimensions and their conceptual relationships with attitudes and behavior. *Organizational Behavior and Human Performance, 16*(1), 74–113.

Kogut, B., & Kulatilaka, N. (2001). Capabilities as real options. *Organization Science, 12*(4), 744–758.

Pasmore, W. A. (2004). Academic commentary on Part II. In N. Adler, A. B. (Rami) Shani, & A. Styhre (Eds.), *Collaborative research in organizations: Foundations for learning, change, and theoretical development* (pp. 167–169). Thousand Oaks, CA: Sage.

Pavlovsky, P., Forslin, J., & Reinhardt, R. (2001). Practices and tools in organizational learning. In M. Dierkes, A. Berthoin Antal, J. Child, & I. Nonaka (Eds.), *Handbook of organizational learning and knowledge* (pp. 775–793). Oxford, UK: Oxford University Press.

Popper, M., &Lipshitz, R. (1998). Organizational learning mechanisms: A structural and cultural approach to organizational learning. *Journal of Applied Behavioral Science, 34*(2), 161–179.

Raelin, J. A. (2000). *Work-based learning: The new frontier of management development.* Reading, MA: Addison-Wesley.

Reason, P., & Bradbury, H. (2001). *Handbook of action research: Participative inquiry and practice.* London: Sage.

Schein, E. H. (2001). Clinical inquiry research. In P. Reason & H. Bradbury (Eds.), *Handbook of action research: Participative inquiry and practice* (pp. 228–237). London: Sage.

Shani, A. B. (Rami), & Docherty, P. (2003). *Learning by design: Building sustainable organizations.* Malden, MA: Blackwell.

Shani, A. B. (Rami), & Docherty, P. (in press). Learning by design: Key mechanisms in organization development. In T. Cummings (Ed.), *Handbook of organizational change and development.* Thousand Oaks, CA: Sage.

Shani, A. B. (Rami), Sena, J., & Stebbins, M. W. (2000). Knowledge work teams and groupware technology: Lessons from Seagate. *Journal of Knowledge Management, 4*(2), 111–124.

Stebbins, M. W., Freed, T., Shani, A. B. (Rami), & Doerr, K. (2006). The limits of reflexive design in a secrecy-based organization. In D. Boud, P. Cressey, & P. Docherty (Eds.), *Productive reflection at work* (pp. 80–92). London: Routledge.

Stebbins, M. W., Hawley, J., & Rose, A. (1982). Long term action research: The most effective way to improve complex health care organizations. In N. Margulies & J. Adams (Eds.), *Organization development in health care organizations* (pp. 105–136). Reading, MA: Addison-Wesley.

Stebbins, M. W., & Shani, A. B. (Rami). (1988). Communication forum interventions: A longitudinal case study. *Leadership and Organization Development Journal, 9*(5), 3–10.

Stebbins, M. W., Shani, A. B. (Rami), & Docherty, P. (2006). Reflection during a crisis turnaround: Management use of learning mechanisms. In D. Boud, P. Cressey, & P. Docherty (Eds.), *Productive reflection at work* (pp. 106–119). London: Routledge.

Stebbins, M., Shani, A. B. (Rami), Moon, W., & Bowles, D. (1998). Business process reengineering at Blue Shield of California: The integration of multiple change initiatives. *Journal of Organization Change Management, 11*(3), 216–232.

Stebbins, M. W., & Snow, C. C. (1982). Processes and payoffs of programmatic action research. *Journal of Applied Behavioral Science, 18*(1), 69–86.

Stebbins, M. W., & Valenzuela, J. L. (2004). Structural learning mechanisms in collaborative research. In N. Adler, A. B. (Rami) Shani, & A. Styhre (Eds.), *Collaborative research in organizations: Foundations for learning, change, and theoretical development* (pp. 149–166). Thousand Oaks, CA: Sage.

Stebbins, M. W., & Valenzuela, J. (in press). Change processes for sustainable innovation. In P. Docherty, M. Kira, & A. B. (Rami) Shani (Eds.), *Creating sustainable work systems: Emerging perspectives and practices* (2nd ed.). London: Routledge.

Teece, D., Pisano, G., & Schuen, A. (1997). Dynamic capabilities and strategic management. *Strategic Management Journal, 18*(7), 509–530.

Weick, K. E. (1995). *Sensemaking in organizations.* Thousand Oaks, CA: Sage.

Whyte, W. F. (1991). *Participatory action research.* Thousand Oaks, CA: Sage.

Zand, D. (1974). Collateral organization: A new change strategy. *Journal of Applied Behavioral Science, 10*(1), 63–89.

CHAPTER 24

The Collaborative Learning Cycle

Advancing Theory and Building Practical Design Frameworks Through Collaboration

SUSAN ALBERS MOHRMAN

ALLAN M. MOHRMAN JR.

SUSAN G. COHEN[1]

STU WINBY

ABSTRACT

We describe a program of collaborative research investigating the design of team-based organizations in nine divisions of Hewlett-Packard (HP). This study was an intersection of the knowledge-generating work of three communities of practice. It was part of an ongoing stream of collaborative research carried out by researchers at the Center for Effective Organizations at the University of Southern California, and the first step in a series of collaborations with companies to investigate teaming in knowledge-work settings. It was also part of a stream of research, consultation, and management knowledge asset production by the Factory of the Future group[2] at HP, an internal group that worked collaboratively with many business units at HP to carry out action research, and to generate knowledge useful throughout the corporation. The third community of practice consisted of the members of HP engaged in leading and carrying out the development of new products, who were dealing with intense competitive pressures and who were establishing teams to improve this process. We describe the collaboration, its antecedents, and the two streams of knowledge production that grew out of this collaboration. The chapter will include the individual voices of the authors.

Two critical challenges for collaborative organizational design research are (1) to build the capacity for ongoing learning and redesign as an organizational capability that is not dependent on continuing collaboration between the academic researchers and company participants; and (2) to generate knowledge that is accessible and usable beyond the participating company—both to advance academic knowledge and to stimulate broader practitioner application. If these two challenges are not addressed, the learning from the collaboration is limited to its participants. Practice may be changed in a limited and perhaps temporary manner, but the ongoing ability to enhance and disseminate the learning through application in different settings and at different points in time by different participants will be limited. In this chapter we argue that the value of collaborative research depends on the encoding of the knowledge that is generated, not only by embedding it in changed practice and the internal capabilities of the collaborating organization, but also in frameworks and models that become accessible to and integrated in the practices of internal and external change agents and academics.

Our argument emerges from the careful study of a particularly instructive case example from a research collaboration in 1991–1992 between an internal corporate organizational strategy and design consulting group at Hewlett-Packard (HP) and an academic team based at the University of Southern California's Center for Effective Organizations (CEO). This collaboration focused on the grounded discovery of effective team models for complex knowledge work in new product development (NPD). There were other critically important research collaborators—NPD groups and management teams from nine business units—each of which was interested in participating in the study by providing its data as well as participating in interpreting it, and

applying the findings in the context of their particular business issues. The project was designed as a multiple-business-unit investigation and was guided by and designed to advance organizational theory and provide a foundation for enhanced organization design capabilities, as well as to enhance practice. We employed traditional data-gathering and -analysis approaches, including conducting and systematically coding and analyzing an extensive set of interviews from each site. Internal and external researchers were involved in crafting the research questions and methodologies, collecting the data, and coding the interviews and interpreting the findings and their implications. Both internal and external researchers were also involved in working with the extended group of collaborators and the local study teams from each division, including collaboratively reflecting on the meaning of the findings and their implications, and crafting action plans.

This chapter, written by both internal and external researchers, will describe the research collaboration and the learning that resulted. Its main focus will be to understand this collaboration from the perspective of both the company and academic partners. In particular, we will describe how this collaboration, which began in 1990 (and continues to ripple into the next century), brought together three streams of ongoing learning and knowledge creation processes, the first being the ongoing generation of and embedding of knowledge in the practice of the HP internal research collaborators; the second being a similar focus for the external academic researchers; and the third being the ongoing learning through experience and self-design that characterizes any work system (Weick, 2003) and thus that was present in the various divisional settings where the research was conducted.

In keeping with the intent of this section, the chapter will incorporate the "voices" of participants from the academic setting and from the internal consulting group that part-nered with the academics to orchestrate the research. The voices will include comments made when the authors were interviewed about this collaboration, and quotes from other write-ups where they have described collaborative research from their perspec-tives. The major focus will be on the institu-tional identities and relationships that defined the collaboration in the context of the missions and purposes of the internal and external collaborators.

THE COLLABORATORS AND THE CONTEXT FOR COLLABORATION

This collaboration began with the identifica-tion of a problem that brought together mul-tiple participants, all of whom had an interest in solving it. Problem-focused research pro-vides a natural home for and evokes a need for collaboration that brings together multi-ple perspectives, including those of theory and practice. In part, this is because problems represent anomalies and present a need to step outside of the daily reality that is driven by implicit theories, and to try to achieve a detachment that enables the search for new understandings that can guide action (Argyris, 1996; Schön, 1983; Weick, 2003). "It is in the moment of interruption that the-ory relates most clearly to practice and prac-tice most readily accommodates the abstract categories of theory" (Weick, 2003, p. 469). Problem-focused research also calls for col-laborative approaches because the most important problems are often not readily resolvable within the current community of practice and furthermore call for the combi-nation of knowledge from multiple perspec-tives, expertises, and disciplines (Mohrman, Mohrman, Lawler, & Ledford, 1999; Mohrman, Galbraith, & Monge, 2006; Stokes, 1997).

This section will describe the presenting problem, and how and why members of two institutional settings came together with a common interest to solve it.

THE PROBLEM

By the 1990s, globalization had come front and center as a source of economic and mar-ket challenges facing U.S. companies. The rapid progression of technological develop-ment and the resulting criticality of innova-tion capabilities in companies that compete on technology were challenging companies to operate in a different way. The array of strategic and tactical organizational responses included initiatives to (1) increase companies' capability to focus on and link to the cus-tomer, often bringing employees out of their development labs and back offices and into direct contact with the customers; and (2) develop the capacity for speed in the devel-opment of innovative products and services, bringing together multiple functions to work in an integrated fashion rather than in sequential steps.

It was becoming clear that achieving rapid product innovation and increased alignment with the customer and market demanded new ways of organizing, and more generally that design of new organizational approaches goes hand in hand with the ability to develop new organizational capabilities (Mohrman, Mohrman, & Tenkasi, 1997). In particular, hierarchical, siloed organizations were prov-ing too slow, and the segmentation of knowl-edge into functional and disciplinary groups was preventing the integration of perspectives required for responsiveness and innovation. Organizations were looking for ways to increase integration across the organization, often by implementing various kinds of teams that brought members of various functions together to develop and deliver innovative and responsive products and services.

Sociotechnically designed teams (Pasmore, 1988) had already been used successfully on the factory floor, and there was now a groundswell of attempts to move this organizing approach into white-collar and knowledge- worker settings. But organizations were having difficulty importing the models and frameworks developed for comparatively routine production technologies into highly uncertain, dispersed, and interdependent knowledge work settings. A confusing array of white-collar teams were being tried in many companies, with many configurations and purposes. Some of the principles from factory floor studies of teams did not seem to fit complex knowledge work. For example, the assumption that employees would experience meaningfulness, growth, and motivation from being in a team where the members were empowered and trained to make decisions and work with little supervision did not seem to hold up in knowledge-work settings. Early knowledge teams yielded a great deal of employee dissatisfaction because of the increased complexity and mounting coordination demands of working interdependently with other team members, particularly in settings where it is difficult to create teams that are self-contained and self-directing because of strong interdependencies with other teams.

THE COLLABORATORS AND THEIR PURPOSES

HP was one of the many corporations that were facing this problem of how to achieve the level of integration among the various disciplines and functions required to rapidly generate innovative and responsive products and services. Consultants in its Factory of the Future group had been working with the manufacturing function using the principles and design approaches from the sociotechnical systems (STS) tradition to design high-performing plants. They were increasingly faced with requests to design high-performance approaches to the development of products.

The Center for Effective Organizations (CEO) at the University of Southern California is a research center that is sponsored by corporations interested in access to its organizational and management research findings, and that look to CEO for thought partnership and research collaborations. CEO had been engaging in collaborative research to study high-performing systems, teams, human resource systems, and other elements of organizational effectiveness. Several of its researchers, including three of the authors of this chapter, had come to the conclusion that finding design solutions for complex knowledge work was an important focus for organization theory and management research.

HP was one of the companies that sponsored the research of CEO. Stu Winby, the director of the Factory of the Future group, had been tracking and using CEO's research results. In an earlier job, he had partnered with CEO in a study of the application of high-involvement management approaches in American corporations. After attending a CEO interest group meeting on the topic of knowledge-work teaming, in which companies and CEO researchers came together to discuss this emerging area of concern, Winby initiated a research partnership with the other authors of this chapter. He realized that the relevance of his group to HP's businesses was dependent on staying abreast of leading-edge thinking and generating new organizational approaches to address dynamic business requirements and to enable high performance throughout the corporation. He intended to make R&D an integral part of the activities of his consulting group. It would be focused on developing innovative organizational approaches to address complex business challenges.

Winby's purpose and the purpose of the CEO researchers aligned well: understanding teaming in knowledge settings and generating appropriate organizational models were central to solving pressing business concerns. These focuses were also a natural extension of STS approaches as well as of the other academic approaches to understanding teams, such as those found in the work of Richard Hackman and the literature focusing on high-involvement and high-commitment management (Lawler, 1986). These streams of knowledge were foundational both to Winby's applied work at HP and to the organizational effectiveness research at CEO. In addition, we all had a background using the process tools of organization development in previous change settings. As recounted by Susan Cohen,

> We found ourselves collaborating with internals who came from the same academic heritage as we did, and who understood the competing and complementary nature of generating knowledge for theory and for practice. It turned out to be the most rewarding collaboration of my career at CEO.

CEO's mission had set the tone for the collaborative research approach that was by now its hallmark. Its mission is to conduct research that generates new knowledge that is (1) useful to and used by the participating organizations; (2) useful and accessible to the broader organizational community; and (3) academically useful and valued. The latter two elements would happen through practitioner and academic publications, respectively. The first would grow out of the collaborative approach and research methodologies, which had come to be based on the following pillars:

1. Build on past knowledge: bring knowledge of theory and practice to the collaboration.

2. Be driven by the problem-specific needs and realities of the participating organizations.

3. Build a collaborative research team with study participants and incorporate the interests and needs of all parties to the collaboration.

4. Carry out related studies in multiple organizational settings in order to discover what dynamics and findings can be generalized and to discover the boundary conditions for applicability of the knowledge.

5. Ensure that business outcomes, customer outcomes, and employee outcomes are addressed.

6. Use multimethod research designs that meet the standards of diverse communities of practice regarding legitimacy, validity, and usefulness of the findings. Worked out collaboratively, the methodological approaches include qualitative as well as quantitative methods, academically rigorous and practically accepted methods, and methods that match the phenomena of study.

The commitment to doing useful research has resulted in many of CEO's studies focusing on topic areas with an eye to how organizations can be created or changed by design in order to address specific problems—not stopping with discovering, describing, and explaining. As described by Allan Mohrman, one of its founders and a member of the research team for this collaboration,

> Collaboration is not just some kind of cooptation strategy, although it's easy enough to find aspects that can be interpreted that way. I view it as *the* research method that yields knowledge about the social dimensions of organizational science, and especially of the design sciences. It feels to me the most real, valid, useful, and interesting approach. All other methods, qualitative and quantitative, cross-sectional and longitudinal, can have a place in collaborative research.

CEO's collaborative research generally includes traditional social science methods to develop theory grounded in the phenomena of interest as well as methods for the analytical description and measurement of phenomena in terms of the variable constructs and their relationships contained in the theory. But in order to promote the application of the knowledge, CEO has also focused on developing methods for the synthetic use of the knowledge gained through research through design processes to create the desired phenomena in situ, and in so doing, test and elaborate the theory through action learning. Such design processes are inherently collaborative, as new designs are socially constructed by the participants in the setting, using the sources of knowledge available to them, including their own experience, and acting on their own goals and preferences (Buchanan, 2004). Here the methodologies are those of action research (Eden & Huxham, 1996; Elden & Chisholm, 1993; Reason & Bradbury, 2001) and of organizational design (Galbraith, 1994; Mohrman & Cummings, 1989; Romme, 2003; Romme & Endenburg, 2006; van Aken, 2004, 2005).

Again, the purposes of the HP and CEO collaborators were aligned. All were concerned with building on existing organizational knowledge and with conducting research aimed at providing participants with a knowledge foundation upon which innovative organizational approaches could be designed to address important organizational problems. All were concerned with the processes by which social systems could create knowledge and apply it. All came with deep-seated beliefs that both the creation of knowledge and the design of social systems to apply, test, and enhance knowledge are best done in situ, through collaboration among internal and external participants who bring knowledge of theory and practice, as well as their aspirations and goals for the collaboration. In Stu Winby's words,

> In many ways, the SCS [Strategic Change Services] mission was similar to the USC-CEO mission in having action research as the core and base of all its operations.

Sharing a similar mission from external and internal perspectives made the outcomes all the more robust.

THE COLLABORATION

This research collaboration started in 1991 and lasted for one year. It should be noted, however, that this was only the first of several collaborative research projects over 12 years that were carried out by CEO researchers and this HP group. The stream of collaboration that was established will be described in the next sections. Here, we will present a brief description of the collaborative research project as it unfolded, starting with the joint definition of the objectives and the research design, and continuing to address the development of the research instruments, the collection of data, the analysis and interpretation of the data and the initial knowledge-creation process, the action research components, and the development of a model of knowledge-work teaming and intervention tools and processes.

Definition of the Study

The four members of the Factory of the Future team and four CEO researchers constituted ourselves as the study team. We exchanged and iterated documents and had several teleconferences in which the members described their goals for the study and shared ideas about how these might be accomplished. We then spent a day together, agreeing on purposes and on a high-level research design. The purposes were to learn from the nascent product development teaming efforts in the corporation about

- the nature of knowledge-work teaming;
- how knowledge-work teaming differs from factory-floor teaming;
- what design features influence the effectiveness of teams in accomplishing business, customer, and employee outcomes; and

- how existing models of team systems and existing intervention models need to change to reflect the knowledge that is developed in the first three areas.

At least one HP member of the study group was uncomfortable with the study because he felt that there was a possibility that the CEO team would develop knowledge for academic publication at the expense of the need to develop practical, actionable knowledge in a form that the Factory of the Future group could use to enhance the capacity of HP businesses to address their business concerns. The study team discussed this potential pitfall and agreed among themselves that all would strive to ensure that the study met the needs of all parties. It was agreed that this issue needed to be discussable throughout the collaboration. According to Susan Cohen,

> It was our mutual passion about the subject, combined with the fact that we had all spent a lot of time working with and studying dysfunctional teams, that allowed us to transcend some very natural differences in orientation within the team. We were a knowledge team studying knowledge teams, and we confronted all the challenges in our own work. Ironically, this allowed us to realize how important it is to learn about team effectiveness.

We agreed that although the research was based on some well-tested models of teams and of sociotechnical design principles, the application of teams in knowledge settings created a new context for teaming that was apparently rendering some or much of the knowledge of past practice of questionable use. We decided to use a grounded research methodology (Glaser & Strauss, 1967) to study up to 10 of HP's then-44 divisions that were already trying to build and use product development teams to increase speed, customer/market fit, and the financial return

of their new product development processes. Grounded research methodologies are particularly useful for exploratory research as they use data-gathering and -analysis techniques that enable exploration of questions and dynamics that cannot be anticipated from current theory, while discovering through the study of multiple sequential cases which themes and dynamics are core and common, and which are context-specific. The study can proceed until the extraction of new theoretical concepts has stopped and the categories can be considered to be saturated. To assure variability, HP divisions were chosen to represent the mix of types of product technologies and teaming approaches that were present. Within each participating division, the interviews focused on four teams, including two relatively successful and two struggling ones, again in order to promote variability in the sample and to make it more likely that we would encounter the range of phenomena at work.

Nested within the overall CEO/HP collaboration were a series of local collaborations that brought in participants from each participating division. This brought the knowledge from the third community of practice—the managers and functional contributors who were engaged in new product development—into the research collaboration. This approach builds on our shared belief that research that leads to actionable knowledge is best conducted in collaboration with the participants, and that the test of the knowledge in practice happens through a design process in which the new design is socially constructed. A study team was set up in each participating division to provide input into the micro design of the study at the local level and articulate local goals and questions for the study. This team also became involved in the interpretation of the data patterns that emerged from the study, and in articulating its implications and developing action plans for the division. The study teams at the local level minimally included the general manager and the technical manager, and often the marketing and manufacturing managers. In addition, a local human resources consultant and/or organizational effectiveness consultant was a member of the study team and worked closely with the CEO and Factory of the Future members to execute the study.

DEVELOPMENT OF THE RESEARCH INSTRUMENTS

The collaborative research team decided to use interviews and the examination of archival data about the teams and their performance as the two major data-gathering approaches. The interview questions were structured to reflect what is known about teams in general and anecdotal beliefs and theoretical predictions about what is unique about knowledge settings. The questions were designed to be sufficiently open-ended to discover and pursue new and unanticipated themes that emerged. The data from each site would be coded, and hypotheses would be formed about the critical features and dynamics relating to effectiveness. Data gathering in the next site would confirm or disconfirm these hypotheses, and the new theoretical constructs would be discovered. It was agreed that the initial interview protocols would be reviewed after the completion of data gathering at each site in order to gradually increase focus on the theoretical issues and design features that were emerging.

The initial interview protocol was drafted by the CEO members of the collaborative research team, but it went through several iterations as input was given by the HP members. Changes to the protocols as the study proceeded through the sites were also made by agreement among all in the team. In practice, the team came to trust each other and to accept each other's competencies and

roles, and much of the refinement of focus and steps taken to address roadblocks that were arising occurred through informal exchange and consultation rather than through formal all-member meetings.

DATA COLLECTION

The participating teams from the division and the schema to guide the selection of interviewees were determined at the first meeting of each division-level study team. Local goals for the study and their particular questions of interest were also discussed. Minimally, the division-level functional managers, the team leaders, and a cross-functional sample of team members from each of the four teams from the division were interviewed in order to provide a variety of perspectives about the teams. At least one CEO interviewer was present to conduct all interviews. HP research team members co-conducted about half of them, subject to the constraints of their other commitments. Interviewees were told that the records of their interview comments would be maintained at USC, but that they would be accessible to the Factory of the Future team members as well to allow for joint interpretation of the data. It was promised that no one else from the corporation would have access to raw data or to comments of particular respondents and/or teams.

DATA ANALYSIS, INTERPRETATION, AND INITIAL KNOWLEDGE CREATION

As the data collection progressed, the researchers followed a cycle consisting of (1) an array of interviews in a single division; (2) the researchers as individuals writing up their interviews and other data; (3) researchers, again independently, analyzing the data to identify important theoretical concepts and relationships that they tentatively coded and (4) all researchers who conducted interviews in the division meeting together to compare their coding and working to establish a consensual set of concepts and models that captured the findings in that setting and integrated them with the models from earlier cycles. At several points, the CEO researchers presented the state of the modeling to members of the Factory of the Future department as a whole, and this led to a discussion to interpret the findings to date, to modify and/or enrich the model, and to evaluate and further refine the state of knowledge and its potential application. A packet of findings and themes was prepared that would be shared with the local divisional study team. This cycle continued until nine divisions had been studied and the collaborative research team decided that the conceptual categories had been saturated and that the theoretical model was complete.

KNOWLEDGE SHARING, FURTHER INTERPRETATION, INTERVENTION

As data collection and conceptualization regarding each division were completed, the study team in the setting would plan a knowledge-sharing and initial self-design intervention in the division, based on the particular findings grounded in that setting integrated with knowledge gained elsewhere and the model that was emerging. For each site, the data that were returned were diagnostic and could be used to jump-start their local action research and self-design processes. The first step was to share the findings in a discussion that invited interpretations, discussion of the importance of the findings, and the determination of implications by members of the division. The size of the data feedback and interpretation meetings differed. In some divisions, this discussion included only study team members. In other divisions, a much broader set of divisional members was included. The last step of the session was preliminary identification of the action implications of the results of the study. At this point, the formal involvement of the CEO researchers in the division study team ended, and the continuing action research and design activities became a collaboration between the members of the division and their Factory of the Future consultants. The intensity of the follow-up action research AR/design activities varied across the participating divisions. Several divisions went through a highly participative redesign process and ended up with significant modifications to the team-based structures of the division and/or the contextual features that were facilitating or inhibiting team effectiveness.

MODEL CREATION

As the grounded research unfolded, both the CEO and the HP members of the collaborative research team continually incorporated the knowledge from each new site into their emerging grounded theoretical and design-oriented models of team-based organization. CEO members were focusing on a generalizable, theory-based model that could be tested and further elaborated in subsequent research collaborations with other companies. The ultimate goal for CEO members was to create a robust theory and model of knowledge teams that could become part of the academic and practitioner literature, and a design model for knowledge teams that could be employed by many organizations. The goal for the Factory of the Future members was to create a grounded, substantive model to guide team transitions and redesigns at HP, to test the model through the various interventions, and to "productize" the model and the design intervention process so that it could diffuse throughout the organization.

The models of the HP and CEO members were of course variants of the same knowledge base that was created through the collaboration and in particular through collaborative interpretation of the data patterns. Members understood the results through the lens of their roles, values, and goals and encoded the resulting knowledge in formats conducive to their purposes and to contributing to the intended trajectory of their professional activities. The next section will examine these two trajectories and how they came together synergistically during this and subsequent collaborations.

TWO PARTIALLY OVERLAPPING KNOWLEDGE GENERATION TRAJECTORIES

Although CEO and HP would engage in two more research collaborations during the next decade, the collaborators from each had their own mission defined in the context of the purpose of the separate institutions in which they were embedded: the university and the corporation. Their activities converged at points in time when both were interested in pursuing common problem-focused research as part of their independent missions. Synergy was enabled by the common problem, and collaborative research was the modality that enabled the members of both institutions to jointly craft a project that allowed both to pursue the knowledge they needed. The work of both groups was fueled by the same environmental forces and changes, and both groups attended to the same unfolding organizational and competitive dynamics that were reshaping organizations around the world, and to the academic and practitioner knowledge that was being generated in universities and research groups globally. Throughout, the Factory of the Future group (renamed the Strategic Change Services [SCS] Division to reflect their

broader focus) and CEO remained loosely coupled through the sponsor relationship and mutual interest, despite the fact that the two groups had independent trajectories, defined by their mission and constituencies. These two trajectories are illustrated in Figure 24.1. We will describe these in order to get a sense of how the knowledge created through the Knowledge Work Teams collaboration became embedded in practice at HP and in the academic literature and in ongoing work in both communities of practice.

PURSUING A RESEARCH PROGRAM: THE CEO TRAJECTORY

The collaboration with HP built on earlier work at CEO and laid the foundation for ongoing work. This collaboration was the first in a series of studies with eight companies examining knowledge work teams. Susan Cohen, Susan Mohrman, and Allan Mohrman had each been pursuing individual and periodically overlapping field and action research programs examining, respectively, high-involvement organizations, performance improvement methodologies and change interventions, and performance management and development. It had become evident that teaming was essential both as an involvement strategy and as a design to foster high performance, and that the way performance is managed in an organization changes fundamentally in a team-based organization, where control and integration happen laterally. We decided to initiate a CEO programmatic focus on knowledge-work teams and initiated the interest group meeting that led to the HP collaboration and to subsequent collaborations with nine other companies.

For the CEO-HP team, collaboration enabled the exploration of the phenomenon of knowledge-work teaming, and the grounded research approach enabled the generation of

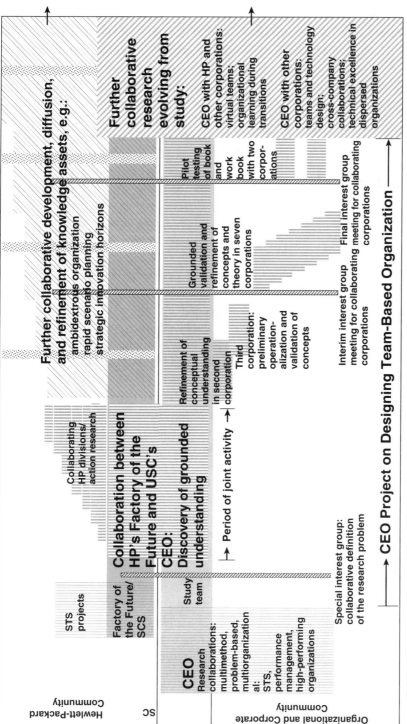

Figure 24.1   Schematic Representation of the Trajectories of Activities at HP and CEO Before, During, and After the Collaboration

theory and foundational design models—models that were, in part, tested through the action research of the participating divisions. Subsequent collaborations that were part of this research program included the following:

1. The replication of the exploratory HP study in a second corporation that had a very different business model and employed different technologies. Through this second collaborative study, we elaborated the theory and models to be able to address the different interdependencies in a setting where the products being developed are large electromechanical systems and the "team" can be hundreds of people working through highly interdependent subteams.

2. The development of a survey instrument to measure the theoretical constructs, and its field testing in a third corporation that employed teams to develop consumer food products.

3. The application of the survey instrument to confirm the team model in seven diverse company settings, as well as to test its usefulness as a diagnostic survey.

4. Close collaboration with two of the companies that participated in these earlier research collaborations (in Step 3 above) as we generated a book that captured the findings from the research study (Mohrman, Cohen, & Mohrman, 1995). The book was aimed at our dual constituencies of academics and business organizations, and the companies who participated in the study had a keen interest in making sure the book was practically understandable and usable.

5. Close collaboration with two companies in the development of a design workbook (Mohrman & Mohrman, 1997) that could serve as a tool for design teams in organizations that are creating a team-based design. Two companies served as beta sites for the use of the initial versions of the workbook, and organizational effectiveness professionals and line managers provided rich feedback and suggestions based on their use of the materials to redesign organizations.

This was one of the first programmatic thrusts where we were able to move through the various stages of knowledge creation starting with the identification of the problem, which in this case was caused by the anomaly that although the increased use of teams was clearly appropriate given the changing environment, existing team approaches were not working. Nevertheless, the use of teams for lateral integration of knowledge work was fundamentally changing the dynamics in organizations in a way that was neither understood nor controllable. After collaborations to test the theoretical and design framework that came from the initial work in partnership with HP, we worked with other collaborative partners so we could replicate and then test the model, and finally move to its "packaging" in articles aimed at the academic community; a book aimed at the dual constituency of academics, professionals, and organizations; and a workbook aimed at diffusion of the knowledge into practice in corporations.

By 1995, the CEO team had worked intensely together for six years. Through our experiences in 10 companies, each of us subsequently became interested in related relevant phenomena that emerged from the team study as important and yet inadequately understood, and we pursued them in subsequent collaborative research programs. These can be seen in Figure 24.1. Susan Cohen's work went in three directions. First, she and our colleague Don Mankin collaborated with a number of companies to examine the use of teams in defining and implementing new technology (Mankin, Cohen, & Bikson, 1996). Second, she and our colleague Cristina Gibson collaborated with multiple companies to examine virtual teams (Gibson & Cohen, 2003) and to explore whether there are new theoretical constructs and design features critical to their functioning. Third, she and Don Mankin examined complex intercompany collaborations working with three corporations (Mankin & Cohen, 2004). The seeds of interest in each of these topics were planted during the HP collaboration, where it became clear that these were important challenges to companies, and that teams were central design mechanisms in each of them.

Mohrman and Mohrman likewise pursued two additional research programs that stemmed directly from the awareness of further research needs made evident during the HP collaboration. The first was the collaboration with 10 companies and CEO colleague Ram Tenkasi to explore the change and learning challenges that are confronted as an organization moves from the design principles of hierarchy and individual jobs to lateral organization and teams (Tenkasi, Mohrman, & Mohrman, 1998). We were especially interested in understanding the phenomena underlying the nature and degree of organizational learning during such transitions. The second was a collaboration with nine companies and colleagues David Finegold and Jan Klein to examine more broadly the organization design challenges faced by technical firms as they try to maintain cutting-edge technical capability while facing pressures for speed, cost, and customer responsiveness in a global economy (Mohrman, Mohrman, & Finegold, 2003; Mohrman, Klein, & Finegold, 2003).

Although in these subsequent collaborations we only sporadically were able to achieve the extent of full alignment and deep collaboration that was present in the initial collaboration with HP, we continued the practice of defining and executing the study collaboratively in a joint research team and continued to operate in an action research model aimed at creating useful knowledge. In all cases, we attempted to work closely with internal consultants/change agents because we had learned from the HP experience the value of such partners:

During the first decade of CEO's existence we had believed that making research useful demanded that we stay with it all the way, through the process of actualizing the knowledge in some sort of organization redesign. Just delivering a report, no matter how "actionable" and valuable it might seem, rarely resulted in substantive change. This study with HP was pivotal for me because we were able to scale back on our hands-on involvement with redesign and change, since Stu's group was assuming that role. This was great because that was time-consuming and we were biting off a lot in our multicompany teams study. It allowed me to look across the settings and observe what kind of knowledge helps an organization redesign itself. All of our studies were topically focused but also examined organization design or redesign. This meta-level focus on how organizations redesign themselves became, for me, the major focus. (Allan Mohrman)

In subsequent studies, data gathering continued to serve two purposes: the surfacing and testing of theory, and providing diagnostic data as input into an action research cycle in the organization—a cycle that often led to redesign. The collaboration included joint interpretation and collaboration in action planning. Several of the multiple-company studies were longitudinal in nature, allowing us to examine the dynamics and impacts of change over time. This led to a permutation of our approach so that in some cases members of the research team worked closely as participant collaborators in the internal AR process in the company, while others focused more on the longitudinal data-gathering and -analysis components of the research.

The mixed success in achieving collaboration and effective action research led us at CEO to become interested in what features of the collaboration itself led to application and change in the company. According to Susan Mohrman,

Only in a few instances did companies have internal groups like HP's SCS group, who had achieved a position in the company where they could leverage the value of research across multiple business units. In other companies, we often collaborated with line managers, some of whom were highly engaged in the collaborative action research and others who were unable to keep a focus and dedicate the time required to derive benefit from being part of the study.

To gain some insight into how collaborative research influenced subsequent organizational change, we did a retrospective study of the 10 companies that had participated in the research on the learning challenges during transition. We wanted to see what differed between settings that effected change and those that did not (Mohrman, Gibson, & Mohrman, 2001). We found that the two conditions that led to application of the results of the research were whether the company-based collaborators actively participated in the interpretation of the data and felt comfortable that they understood the implications, and whether these results drove collaborative redesign activities. Simply having meetings and talking about the results and agreeing to changes didn't achieve the results unless there was a systematic design process to underpin new ways of operating.

> As a result of this finding, we have changed how we approach the collaboration. We have started to emphasize the importance of collaboration during the interpretation and action planning stages, and have tried to reduce the amount of time demanded of line managers in the up-front framing and data-gathering parts of the research—aiming instead to get a solid understanding of the problems they are trying to address. (Sue Mohrman)

The original mission of CEO, to do research useful to theory and practice (Lawler, Mohrman, Mohrman, Cummings, & Ledford, 1985; Lawler et al., 1999), set the frame for this research trajectory and for our ultimate need to study what makes research useful to both the practitioners and the academics who collaborate. We try to craft studies that focus on the descriptive and explanatory aspects of a problem and associated phenomena, while also examining practice, and particularly how change in practice affects outcomes for the business and its people. We generally also have been collaborators, to differing extents, in the self-designing processes of the organization. HP participated in two more collaborative research programs with CEO, the virtual teams study and the study of learning during transitions in organizational design. In general, we found that about half of the companies in any particular study would experience useful enough positive outcomes to become interested in the follow-on study. Typically, as we got to know more and more about a company, and vice versa, the collaborative relationship grew, and it became easier to craft the study to meet the needs of all parties. Yet the continual inflow of new companies and departure of others kept variety in the collaborating companies and in the business contexts that were included, as well as ensuring that there were companies with long-standing and others with newly formed relationships with the researchers from CEO.

CREATING KNOWLEDGE TO GUIDE PRACTICE: THE HP TRAJECTORY

This collaborative management research project was one of the earliest that the Factory of the Future unit at HP carried out to catalyze learning and organizational innovation. This early project built a collaborative inquiry system to learn about and generate organizational innovations to deal with a particular business challenge—achieving quicker and more innovative new product development.

But it also provided a learning laboratory for investigating how external and internal researchers can partner to carry out theory-based and practice-based research that yields knowledge to inform the management of the firm. It resulted in a strategy and design for the SCS unit to enhance its value to the firm.

The substantive knowledge generated through the teaming collaboration was built into the organization in a number of ways. Each site study team, in collaboration with the Factory of the Future group and the CEO researchers, identified areas of focus and design approaches to improve the functioning of their new product development teams. As this collaboration unfolded and as the follow-on design activities were completed and impact was assessed in many of the sites, the HP researchers, sometimes working with the CEO researchers, used the findings from these local AR projects to hone their substantive models as well as their design intervention model. They produced models that were disseminated and became available to guide line managers and organizational effectiveness professionals leading and working with many HP units moving toward team-based designs. According to Winby,

> What we discovered about ways of organizing and the artifacts we developed were helpful to people in conceptualizing what they were about. Years later, I saw the models out on managers' desks. People don't understand the impact because it's all tacit. We formalized all that into a model that could be used in consulting, not just by our group, but by many others in the organization.

The newly named Strategic Change Services group was using this project to hone its approach to contributing value to HP, including finding ways to disseminate the learnings from the project more broadly in HP. The goal was to package and disseminate the knowledge so that others, including

the HR community and other change-oriented groups, could provide the consultation required for many more local units to utilize the knowledge. But the HP team was aware from experience that successful design innovations do not diffuse easily. A series of "Work Innovation Network" (WIN) meetings were sponsored, in which line managers and various other groups came together to hear about case studies, to talk with each other about what was required and what would lead to improvements in the model, and to have participants leave with both contacts and awareness of how they could utilize this knowledge locally. According to Winby,

> We all read Dick Walton's work that pointed out that you do a new plant startup that is highly successful but never diffuses anywhere else in the company. We hired a person who started working on diffusion approaches and we developed a model for diffusing work innovations. The principle was to develop a pull system rather than rely on pushing the innovation out. Get the line managers to present their results at our Work Innovation Model, which became the distribution and marketing arm of the model. We would do the work with the customer and measure the results and, even if it was a failure, we presented at the WIN meeting—the general manager and another manager from the division and one of our group would stand up and present what happened. It was videotaped and shared beyond even the attendees. People from other businesses would come up and say, "Can I do that? Can I send someone to your business to learn?" This often provided next-generation projects so that the learning could be extended to new areas.

Both the organizational models and the consulting approaches were continually improved by the group, as they shared what they learned in subsequent collaborations with many organizational divisions. From the SCS group's point of view, however, a major learning from the CEO-HP team research collaboration was about how to play a knowledge-creating role in the company, by sponsoring collaborative studies with academics, generating knowledge, and finding ways to expand the knowledge and the awareness, proficiency, and utilization in the company. They began to see themselves as an internal organizational R&D unit. Again, according to Winby,

> The teams study confirmed the value of collaborating with academics. I had this internal group called Factory of the Future chartered with developing new knowledge in management and organization space in manufacturing. CEO was doing similar things for the world. We had a common purpose where internal and external could get together with a common charter. CEO wins because [it gets] access to a rich database and some internal resources and we have access to world-class research scientists and methodologies and external knowledge. This study established a culture— both within our team and outside, we got branded. Our charter was cutting-edge new stuff solving tough knotty problems, which was exactly what I wanted to do. From this study we learned about product development, but also about how to add value to the company and about AR [action research] and how to do research. It all came together.

Perhaps the most critical learning that came out of the study for both HP and CEO was what was required to sustain a complex and multifaceted collaborative research project. The importance of taking seriously each other's missions and adopting them as one's own was paramount. Again, as put by Stu Winby,

> Our AR was all collaborative—cocreation from the very beginning. We would sit down and jointly define the objectives and

methodologies and work jointly with the client. This became a basic principle in our group: High-involvement research with true collaboration. Not just cooperation—true collaboration. My interests expanded to their interests and not just self-interests. We needed everyone to win.

Subsequent to the teams' collaboration with CEO, the SCS group embarked on other R&D projects in which they collaborated with various academic researchers to investigate other management and organizational challenges. Figure 24.1 shows how the trajectory of issues that were investigated by CEO overlaps at various points where additional research collaborations with HP were carried out. Other HP collaborations were carried out with other academics. For example, a collaboration with Michael Tushman from Columbia University dealt with an issue that had been identified during the USC teams study. One division had talked about its difficulty pursuing an innovative and potentially disruptive technology while housing a steady stream of product innovations building on its existing, mature, and highly successful product technology. As recounted by Winby,

> I read an article from Tushman and Anderson about the Ambidextrous Organization. Tushman and I spent a day talking about this concept and we went to Greeley and we collaboratively designed one. He got a Harvard case writer and they wrote a case and we created a model for HP that was subsequently tested in other divisions.

The group began to conceptualize the products of their collaborative research with academics as the creation of "knowledge assets" for the corporation. These included the development of a rapid scenario planning tool, a strategic innovation horizons tool, and a tool for the design of virtual teams. As described by Kaplan and Winby (1999), and subsequently by Kaplan (2000),

Knowledge assets are essentially sanctioned organizational practices for innovating new products, strategies, business models, and other processes at will. To remain competitive, companies must continually review the processes they use to define what, and then how, they deliver value to customers. *By developing superior processes for solving the same problems faced by competitors, you can consistently find better solutions faster, which results in competitive advantage.* (Kaplan & Winby, 1999, p. 4)

Further, they saw the knowledge assets as underpinning organizational capabilities:

The long view of competitive advantage suggests that the capability for innovation and change should reside *within* the organization. These capabilities represent the "knowledge assets" of the organization—the intellectual properties that guide the continuous process of creating and recreating value for customers. Knowledge assets

provide success-factor blueprints for launching and managing activities critical to the long-term success of the enterprise. (p. 3)

Kaplan and Winby lay out at a high level a five-step process whereby the company derives value through collaborating with external researchers to create knowledge assets and to embed their application in the company. Their description of this five-step process is reprinted in Box 24.1. Figure 24.2 shows the knowledge asset delivery model that was developed by the SCS group. It illustrates the point at which the external expertise is combined with the internal capabilities in the form of collaborative research. This research begins a cycle of R&D action research projects with sites in the firm that are confronting cutting-edge issues. Through these action research projects, knowledge is enhanced and the application is refined and becomes a knowledge asset of the firm.

In order to assure business relevance and achieve impact, projects were established

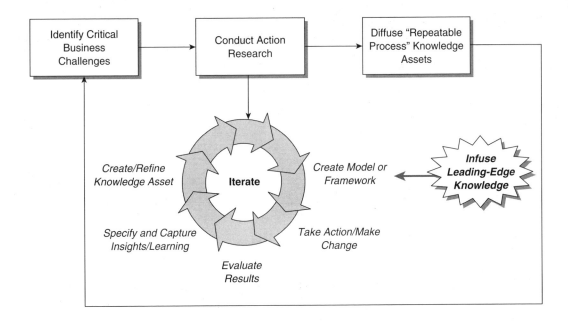

Figure 24.2   HP's Knowledge Asset Value Delivery Model

SOURCE: From *Knowledge Asset Innovation at Hewlett-Packard*, by S. Kaplan and S. Winby (1999, p. 8). Internal working paper.

through a system of MOUs (memorandums of understanding) with the participating divisions. Projects were scoped in advance, areas of targeted improvement were identified, roles and collaborative approaches were clarified, and targets were created for the improvement of financial and other outcomes. The concept underlying this collaborative R&D work is that it should be funded through the business improvements it achieves. Winby and others in the group believe that, given the business pressures, the divisions of HP would not engage in collaborative organizational R&D work unless they felt comfortable that the focus would be on performance benefits, and unless they believed that the benefits of the research collaboration would be greater than the costs. For this reason, the same rigorous targeting, measurement, and assessment processes that guided the corporation's business activities were adapted to this organizational R&D function.

The Strategic Change Services unit established an R&D Solutions Lab. Thus, there was an evolution from the initial action research on product development teams with USC-CEO in the early 1990s to a formalized management science R&D lab. SCS received 100% of its funding direct from its internal customers, and the R&D lab was its innovation capability to bring new products and services to its market (the divisions of the firm), improve margins on its pricing, and of course provide differentiation from external firms who bid on similar projects. This capability lasted eleven years, five years as a formal lab, and was eventually closed down when the central corporate capability was restructured due to a new CEO and reorganization. (Stu Winby)

Collaborative research with external academics and Action Research remained the SCS unit's core knowledge generation approaches throughout this period. They conceptualized it as consisting of five steps, which are shown in Box 24.1.

Box 24.1

Collaborative Management Research in Context:
The Steps Used by HP's Strategic Change Services Group
to Create and Disseminate Knowledge Assets

- *Identify critical business problems.* The value that a knowledge asset provides to the company correlates to the type of problem it solves and the impact of the solution. Problems that span multiple divisions and represent significant threats or opportunities are the best candidates to be solved by knowledge assets. The most powerful knowledge assets are those that address problems the industry faces as a whole, to which no apparent solution has yet been found.
- *Conduct action research.* Once a critical business problem is identified, one must conduct action research (Argyris & Schön, 1989) to find the solution. Action research is the process of solving a problem while concurrently researching, developing, and documenting the way in which the solution is reached. By documenting the best practices for solving the problem again, the organization gains new intellectual property that enables a new capability. Action research is a technique for learning from the problem-solving activity itself and, in the process, creating knowledge assets that help the organization address future business problems on its own.
- *Capture leading-edge knowledge.* Knowledge assets that incorporate the know-how of leading experts are different from canned solutions based on outdated assumptions, theories, and models. When organizations employ cutting-edge academic research or interact with industry experts, breakthrough knowledge assets often emerge. The best solutions result when action researchers harness and synthesize the latest content knowledge, translating theoretical insight into practical application.

- *Refine through iteration.* Although critical issues must be addressed, the first attempt to solve the problem is unlikely to be as successful as the second, third, or fourth. New knowledge assets need patience, perseverance, and iteration. The first attempt at solving the critical business problem should be seen as a learning experience that enables the second attempt to succeed. It is rare to achieve a final solution and capture the knowledge that allows for repeated success the first time out. Successful action research usually requires iteration, with the second or third engagement resulting in the final knowledge asset.
- *Diffuse know-how across the organization.* Competitive advantage rarely results from solving a problem once. The organization must address the problem through repeated application of the knowledge asset. To do this, knowledge assets must be diffused throughout the company, for everyone to adopt and use. The term "knowledge management" relates to managing knowledge assets—making explicit and managing the often unconscious activities and processes of the organization—and doing so in a way that makes one group's template for success accessible to all.

SOURCE: From *Knowledge Asset Innovation at Hewlett-Packard*, by S. Kaplan and S. Winby, 1999, pp. 6–7. Internal Working Paper.

CONCLUSION

The collaboration between the HP Factory of the Future group (soon renamed the Strategic Change Services division) and CEO was, in our view, a highly successful collaborative management research project that set in motion action research leading to the redesign of the teaming approaches in a number of the nine participating divisions. Three knowledge communities came together in this research: the academic community at CEO; the internal change agent community in HP; and the technical new product development community that became involved in each division.

This collaboration had some very important features that we believe contributed to the generation of knowledge for practice and theory. The internal change agents at HP and the academic researchers at CEO shared an intellectual heritage, were familiar with each other's methodologies and substantive expertise, shared a commitment to collaboration, and were focused on doing research to solve the same problem. The research focused on a problem of high interest to both our academic and practitioner communities, providing an alignment of purpose and a commitment to ensuring that the knowledge gained would be of value for all three collaborating communities. In a

real sense, the emerging R&D mission of the HP consultants and the commitment of CEO to do research useful for theory and practice were fully aligned. Additionally, the fact that the Factory of the Future/SCS consultants were highly skilled at collaborative action research and were highly respected within the organization meant that divisions asked them to work with them through the full cycle, including the self-design/action research processes required for the divisions to redesign based on the knowledge gained from the study. This greatly enhanced the application and testing and extension of the knowledge in practice.

A critical decision by the HP group was that it would judge its outcomes by the standards of the business: return on investment, goal accomplishment, market share, and other business indicators. This did not mean that it abandoned concern for the participants or that the research was crafted without concern for employees and their aspirations. The research team—both HP and CEO—were deeply steeped in the sociotechnical framework that emphasized the importance of addressing both the social and the technical systems and outcomes in designing an organization. By ensuring that each project had specific business goals and that business benefits were measured, potential conflict between business, technical, and social design concerns was incorporated into the work and overtly addressed, as the action research was conducted with a shared commitment to all three outcomes.

Clearly, this project benefited from internal company resources and expertise that are not present in many organizations. Yet it provides a model for the infrastructure and describes a process for collaborative research that contributes to both practice and theory. From this study, we learned a great deal of substantive knowledge about the design of team-based knowledge work. The CEO group engaged in substantive collaborations with other firms to enhance the applicability of the model and work toward a generally usable set of knowledge products. The HP group used this collaboration as a laboratory to learn how to do management R&D within the company, and based its organizational and process model for adding value to the firm on the learnings from this study.

NOTES

1. We dedicate this account to Susan Cohen, who passed away during its writing. Susan was the quintessential collaborator; she was enjoyable to work with, tended to the soul of the team, was talented and conscientious, brought humor to the most tense of situations, and gave of herself unselfishly. It is fitting that her academic legacy pertains to the effective functioning of teams of all kinds. We are happy that we all stumbled into this extremely gratifying collaboration and became lifelong friends.

2. At the end of the collaboration described in this chapter, the name of the HP Factory of the Future group was changed to the Strategic Change Services (SCS) Division. It will be referred to by both names in this chapter, depending on the time, frame being referenced.

REFERENCES

Argyris, C. (1996). Actionable knowledge: Design causality in the service of consequential theory. *Journal of Applied Behavioral Science, 32*(4), 390–406.

Buchanan, R. (2004). Management and design: Interaction pathways in organizational life. In R. Boland & F. Collopy (Eds.), *Managing as designing* (pp. 55–63). Palo Alto, CA: Stanford University Press.

Eden, C., & Huxham, C. (1996). Action research for the study of organizations. In S. Clegg, C. Hardy, & W. R. Nords (Eds.), *Handbook of organizational studies* (pp. 526–542). Thousand Oaks, CA: Sage.

Elden, M., & Chisholm, R. F. (1993). Features of emerging action research. *Human Relations, 46*(2), 121–142.

Galbraith, J. R. (1994). *Competing with the lateral, flexible, organization*. Reading, MA: Addison-Wesley.

Gibson, S. B., & Cohen, S. G. (2003). *Virtual teams that work: Creating conditions for virtual team effectiveness*. San Francisco: Jossey-Bass.

Glaser, G. B., & Strauss, A. L. (1967). *The discovery of grounded theory*. Hawthorne, NY: Aldine.

Kaplan, S. (2000). Innovating professional services. *Consulting to Management, 11*(1), 30–34.

Kaplan, S., & Winby, S. (1999). *Knowledge asset innovation at Hewlett-Packard.* Hewlett-Packard Internal Working Paper.

Lawler, E. E., III. (1986). *High-involvement management: Participative strategies for improving organizational performance.* San Francisco: Jossey-Bass.

Lawler, E. E., III, Mohrman, A. M., Jr., Mohrman, S. A., Cummings, T. G., & Ledford, G. E. (Eds.). (1985). *Doing research that is useful for theory and practice.* San Francisco: Jossey-Bass.

Lawler, E. E., III, Mohrman, A. M., Jr., Mohrman, S. A., Ledford, G. E., Cummings, T. G., & Associates. (1999). *Doing research that is useful for theory and practice* (2nd ed.). Lanham, MD: Lexington Press.

Mankin, D., & Cohen, S. G. (2004). *Business without boundaries: An action framework for collaborating across time, distance, organization and culture.* San Francisco: Jossey-Bass.

Mankin, D., Cohen, S. G., & Bikson, T. K. (1996). *Teams & technology: Fulfilling the promise of the new organization.* Cambridge, MA: Harvard Business School Press.

Mohrman, A. M., Jr., Mohrman, S. A., Lawler, E. E., III, & Ledford, G. E. (1999). Introduction to the new edition. In E. E. Lawler III, A. M. Mohrman Jr., S. A. Mohrman, G. E. Ledford, T. G. Cummings, & Associates (Eds.), *Doing research that is useful for theory and practice* (2nd ed., pp. ix–xlix). Lanham, MD: Lexington Press.

Mohrman, S. A., Cohen, S. G., & Mohrman, A. M., Jr. (1995). *Designing team-based organizations.* San Francisco: Jossey-Bass.

Mohrman, S. A., & Cummings, T. G. (1989). *Self-designing organizations: Learning how to create high performance.* Reading, MA: Addison-Wesley.

Mohrman, S. A., Galbraith, J. R., & Monge, P. (2006). Network attributes impacting the generation and flow of knowledge within and from the basic science community. In J. Hage & M. Meeus (Eds.), *Innovation, science, and industrial change: A research handbook.* London: Oxford University Press.

Mohrman, S. A., Gibson, C. B., & Mohrman, A. M., Jr. (2001). Doing research that is useful to practice. *Academy of Management Journal, 44*(2), 347–375.

Mohrman, S. A., Klein, J. A., & Finegold, D. (2003). Managing the global new product development network: A sense-making perspective. In C. Gibson & S. Cohen (Eds.), *Virtual teams that work: Creating conditions for virtual team effectiveness* (pp. 37–58). San Francisco: Jossey-Bass.

Mohrman, S. A., & Mohrman, A. M., Jr. (1997). *Designing and leading team-based organizations: A workbook for organizational self-design.* San Francisco: Jossey-Bass.

Mohrman, S. A., Mohrman, A. M., Jr., & Finegold, D. (2003). An empirical model of the organization knowledge system in new product development firms. *Journal of Engineering and Technology Management, 20*(1–2), 7–38.

Mohrman, S. A., Mohrman, A. M., Jr., & Tenkasi, R. (1997). The discipline of organization design. In C. Cooper & S. Jackson (Eds.), *Creating tomorrow's organizations* (pp. 191–206). Chichester: John Wiley & Sons.

Pasmore, W. (1988). *Designing effective organizations: The socio-technical perspective.* New York: Wiley.

Reason, P., & Bradbury, H. (2001). *Handbook of action research: Participative inquiry and practice.* London: Sage.

Romme, A. G. L. (2003). Making a difference: Organization as design. *Organization Science, 14*(5), 559–573.

Romme, A. G. L., & Endenburg, G. (2006). Construction principles and design rules in the case of circular design. *Organization Science, 17*(2), 287–297.

Schön, D. A. (1983). *The reflective practitioner: How professionals think in action.* San Francisco: Jossey-Bass.

Stokes, D. E. (1997). *Pasteur's quadrant: Basic science and technological innovation.* Washington, DC: Brookings Institution Press.

Tenkasi, R. V., Mohrman, S. A., & Mohrman, A. M., Jr. (1998). Accelerating learning during transition. In S. A. Mohrman, J. R. Galbraith, E. E. Lawler III, & Associates (Eds.), *Tomorrow's organization: Crafting winning capabilities in a dynamic world* (pp. 330–361). San Francisco: Jossey-Bass.

van Aken, J. E. (2004). Management research based on the paradigm of the design sciences: The quest for field-tested and grounded technological rules. *Journal of Management Studies, 41*(2), 219–246.

van Aken, J. E. (2005). Management research as a design science: Articulating the research products of Mode 2 knowledge production in management. *British Journal of Management, 16*(1), 19–36.

Weick, K. (2003). Theory and practice in the real world. In H. Tsoukas & C. Knudsen (Eds.), *The Oxford handbook of organization theory: Meta-theoretical perspectives* (pp. 453–475). New York: Oxford University Press.

CHAPTER 25

The Multiple Voices of Collaboration

A Critical Reflection

SUSAN ALBERS MOHRMAN

A. B. (RAMI) SHANI

ABSTRACT

Collaborative management research aimed at changing the dynamics and performance of a system must pay careful attention to the voices of the participants. The voices of the varied collaborators are rarely heard in reported research. This chapter builds on the four earlier chapters in this section. Reflecting across the varied cases in which the voices of the collaborative management research actors were shared and explored, we have identified and now briefly explore four issues: alignment and purpose as the basis for true collaboration; the institutional and resource context of collaboration; mechanisms that enable learning in collaborative relationships; and the convergence of the languages of practice and theory.

Collaborative management research projects involve true partnership that centers on research, inquiry, and action between different actors, agents, or communities. At the core of productive collaborative management research projects, one can find distinctly high-quality relationships that serve as the engine for the discovery and action-planning processes. Paradoxically, most of the written projects that can be found in the literature are written by the academic partners. The authors of chapters in this section attempted to magnify the multiple voices in the collaborative management research projects. We started this project with a belief that the multiple voices should be captured in order to shed light on both the process and outcomes of collaborative management research projects.

The more we got into the voices and their meanings, the more we began to see the critical role that multiple voices play in the collaborative management research process. The starting point of the project is often one where the gap in the mutual understanding and commitment to partnership between the academics and the practitioners is wide, and as time goes on the gap seems to decrease. Furthermore, we have noticed that these research collaborations start by aligning purpose, build on the institutional contexts and the resources they provide, and continue with the adoption or design of learning mechanisms; finally, shared language begins to emerge. The capacity for effective collaboration is shaped as the actors gradually build this collaborative infrastructure. Figure 25.1 captures these elements of the infrastructure that both constrain and are fashioned by the participants. Below, we further explore these elements that we have identified from reading these chapters and from our own work in the field.

THE BASIS FOR TRUE COLLABORATION: ALIGNMENT OF PURPOSE AMONG DISPARATE ACTORS

The voices in these collaborations can be heard through the filter of Deutsch's (2000) definition that a partnership is a relationship based on cooperation that entails positive interdependence in which each party, in achieving its own goals, contributes to the other parties' goals and achievements. This definition fits with the notion that a complex system is composed of agents, each pursuing its own purposes, as described in the lead-in to this section—and that true collaboration is only possible if agents accept each other's purposes as well as their own. This idea is captured in Stu Winby's comments (Mohrman, Mohrman, Cohen, & Winby, Chapter 24 in this volume) about Hewlett-Packard's (HP's) collaborations aimed at finding new organizational approaches to solving pressing business problems: "[A] basic principle in our group is to achieve high involvement research with true collaboration. Not just cooperation—true collaboration. My interests expanded to their interests and not just self-interests. We needed everyone to win" (p. 526).

Building a true collaboration requires developing a shared vision and purpose, commitment to shared goals, and empowerment

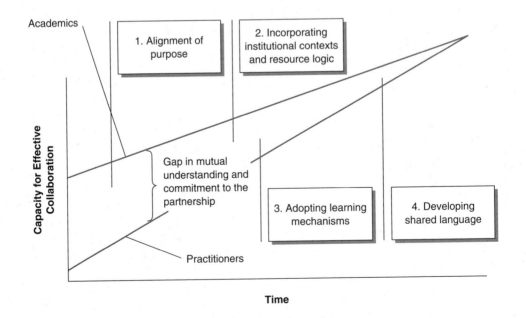

Figure 25.1 Capacity for Effective Collaboration in Collaborative Management Research: Developing the Infrastructure for Partnership

of participants (Tjosvold, 1994). True collaboration may develop gradually, as in the case of the Action Research Center (ARC), a fledgling center dedicated to the creation of a partnership between a college in northern Israel and its surrounding community "for mutual development" (ARC Research Team, Chapter 22 in this volume). Participants spent two years exploring the meaning of partnership and how to create it—a period during which collaboration around purpose was quite difficult to attain. Both the ARC project and the CO-IMPROVE project described by Coghlan and Coughlan (Chapter 21 in this volume) involve complex multistakeholder collaborations in which learning how to collaborate was a stated purpose of the collaboration.

Alternatively, collaborative research may develop very quickly if different parties find that they are at least temporarily aligned in purpose, norms, and understandings. This was the case with the recurring HP-CEO [Center for Effective Organizations] collaborations, in which all parties came together because of an intense interest in learning about a particular kind of organizational design. Both the internal consulting group and the external academics had had extensive experience with collaboration in sociotechnical systems (STS) projects and more generally with collaborative action research, and they already knew how to collaborate. The 30-year collaboration between Mike Stebbins and the Kaiser Permanente Pharmacy Operations Group was also characterized by a rapid startup (see Stebbins & Valenzuela, Chapter 23 in this volume). It began as a contract between Kaiser Permanente and a group of researchers at Texas Christian University's Institute of Behavioral Research to develop a climate survey. From the company's point of view, the purpose was to gather data and learn how to rebuild a positive climate that had been shattered by a prolonged strike. That was a pressing need for the company and its pharmacists, and it provided an opportunity for the academic researchers to pursue their

interests and advance the theory and literature about organizational climate. Communication forums were created to consider and act on the climate data, and these became an ongoing laboratory to learn about and advance the practice of using parallel structures as organizational learning mechanisms.

These four projects illustrate the usefulness of understanding collaborative research in the context of the multiple streams of activity of various agents that overlap for some period of time. Collaboration can last as long as it is instrumental to the agents in achieving their purposes, and it has to be understood in the context of the full set of goals and interests. Collaborative research is an intervention into multiple activity systems. The young researchers associated with ARC, for example, expressed concern about career advancement and competency building. Community-based participants were concerned with particular areas of social advancement for their institution and/or for the region as a whole. These interests may have converged into an overarching goal or mission for ARC or in a specific collaborative action research project, but this mission is not independent of the agendas of individual agents.

Similarly, Mike Stebbins, the researcher/ consultant at Kaiser Permanente, saw the collaboration as a way to continually study and improve the understanding in the academic and practitioner literatures of parallel organizational learning mechanisms and to test new ways to make them more effective. The managers from the organization understood the communication forums as a way for management and employees to work together to accomplish the tasks and goals of the pharmacy; yet Judy Valenzuela, the anager/leader of the communication forums, was mindful of and interested in the research and dissemination activities spearheaded by Mike Stebbins. The employee participants saw the collaboration as a way to be heard and have opportunities for development; yet they were fully aware of the functionality of the forums in providing mechanisms for management to introduce change into the organization. Over time, the function of the communication forums changed as the work changed, the climate for collaboration was established, and the environment for health-care changed. The communication forum was in one sense a naturally occurring organizational experiment—an ongoing intervention into a work system in which the research element catalyzed reflection and inquiry that impacted both the evolution of practice and theory.

Given the multiple streams of activity and purposes that converge in the collaboration, the establishment of aligned purposes and shared objectives for the collaboration is a critical enabler. Interest in a shared problem provided the impetus for alignment. The CO-IMPROVE project had clearly articulated outcomes and objectives, including the use of action research and action inquiry approaches as a methodology to yield knowledge about how to effectively build collaborative Extended Manufacturing Enterprises (EMEs). This purpose temporarily brought together a complex network of academic and company participants and yielded knowledge about various aspects of EMEs, including infrastructural elements such as IT connections and process elements such as collaborative learning. This project can be contrasted with ARC, where the purpose was very high level and aspirational—and where two years later the participants were still focusing on collaboration and democracy as their primary objective while searching for shared objectives to catalyze action research and for an institutional modus operandi that addressed and empowered the complex array of agents. Interestingly, the "crises" that the authors describe as fostering the evolution of the collaboration often reflected tensions within a common population of agents—most specifically among the various academics—who,

despite belonging to the same population, were each seeking resources such as status and influence even as they worked to establish a nonhierarchical social system. This underscores the importance of understanding agents at all levels—not simply the various groups that are included in the collaboration, but also the individuals within them. At every level, there is a complex mixture of competition and cooperation in pursuit of resources and goals.

THE INSTITUTIONAL CONTEXT FOR COLLABORATION: RESOURCES AS A DEFINING FEATURE

The institutional context defines the availability and distribution of resources, which in turn constrain or enable various approaches to collaborative research. As the ARC authors point out, dealing with the tension between the macro (institutional) needs to develop a viable center to house and catalyze collaborative action research and the micro (individual) needs that are driven by personal values and ambitions became a primary focus. In the early stages, institution building took precedence over research, and in fact became the early research focus. At the core of this institution building was a shared espoused value around democracy, but in the voices one can hear the tension about who has access to what resources, such as publication rights and order of authorship, in a situation where resources were not plentiful. One can hear in the voices that individuals were searching for a reason to participate in this nascent institution—a reason that fit with their unique constellations of interests and purposes. The CO-IMPROVE project, on the other hand, received resources from the EU that allowed the academic researchers to pursue their interests and provided an incentive to companies to collaborate. Part of the project plan was the creation of a temporary "institution" to house an elaborate research design and network that, had it not been funded by the EU, would probably never have been formed. This institutional structure defined roles and relationships, as well as enabling many activities that may not have been possible without the influx of resources and the planning of the academic researchers. The importance of resources was made very clear in the words of one of the participating managers: "Getting our suppliers involved was at first quite easy; the suppliers were enthusiastic at the beginning! But when resources were required and actions had to be completed, the suppliers backed off" (Coghlan & Coughlan, Chapter 21 in this volume, p. 528). When these participants had to supply their own resources, their active participation waned.

The HP-CEO collaboration involved two existing organizational entities that had both been built specifically to conduct collaborative research; it was, like CO-IMPROVE, a partnership for a specific purpose and at a specific point in time. Resources to fund the research were provided by the HP divisions that housed the action research, based on the expectation that the improvements to performance would much more than cover the costs. That all parties knew and agreed with this logic for the provision of resources enabled a much closer alignment of interests, and the ultimate practical goal of increasing performance of the participating units became a shared goal for all three populations of collaborators: the external researchers, the internal consultant researchers, and the nine participating divisions. Finally, the Kaiser Permanente relationship grew out of a more traditional consulting relationship in which the consultant/academic was hired to provide facilitation and consultative services, but had an accepted agenda of generating knowledge about the parallel learning mechanism he was hired to facilitate. One can hear

from the interviews that from the viewpoint of the company participants, the consultant academic was facilitating and teaching, while he reports being deeply interested in understanding the limits and elements of collaborative learning in a parallel structure and having a strong value on influencing practice: "I'm an academic but also in the practitioner world" (Stebbins & Valenzuela, Chapter 23 in this volume, p. 504).

COLLABORATION: THE VOICES AROUND LEARNING MECHANISMS

Collaborative management research learning mechanisms emerged within each of the four projects as critical discovery and learning engines. The very nature of collaboration between actors, agents, or communities of practice seems to necessitate the formation of structures and processes that can both house and facilitate the scientific discovery process and learning. The communication forums of the Kaiser Permanente Pharmacy Operations organization were created as mechanisms for discovery and learning and evolved to be a part of the organization that has lasted for the past 34 years. The study teams that were created to house the collaborative management research between CEO and HP were a necessary infrastructure for the activities of learning and research. The creation of a regional center at an Israeli college housed the formative activities involved in giving birth to a community of inquiry. Coughlan and Coghlan report on an elaborate and elegantly linked temporary network of research and learning forums in multiple EU regions, involving four universities and three companies, linked together by various collaborative research streams.

The voices reflect the essence of the mechanisms. In the Kaiser Permanente case, "The communication forum (CF) has been a model for building partnerships, collaboration, and communications. It allowed us to gain new insights into the business. It also allows staff to be more involved in understanding the business" (Stebbins & Valenzuela, Chapter 23 in this volume, p. 499). At HP, "The teams study confirmed the value of collaborating with academics. I had this internal group called Factory of the Future charted with developing new knowledge in management and organization space in manufacturing. CEO was doing similar things for the world. We had common purpose where internal and external could get together with a common charter" (Mohrman et al., Chapter 24 in this volume, p. 526).

THE CONVERGENCE OF THE LANGUAGE AND KNOWLEDGE OF PRACTICE AND THEORY

The interplay between the worldview and language of research and practice is present in all of the projects. The challenge for the outside researchers is to bring existing knowledge, including frameworks and models, to bear on the practice and personal objectives of the participants, and in so doing to test and elaborate existing theory. This often involves a gradual and almost tacit incorporation by the practitioners of these frameworks. This is explicitly described by the company participants in the CO-IMPROVE project:

The relationship started during the early (project researcher) network meetings and developed as I engaged with the readings circulated. At first, it seemed to me to be much too "academic" and theoretical. Later on, however, having experienced our own "real" case and having discussed and shared information with the other industrial and academic partners, it became more interesting, understandable, and "real life." I started understanding better the theory

behind the facts and started managing better the related activities. . . . Knowing the model helped in improving the working of collaboration: defining and assessing collaboration status, key factors, and enablers.

These project dynamics helped us to build a deeper knowledge of collaboration between us (as System Integrator) and our suppliers, and to manage better our respective roles and people. (Coghlan & Coughlan, Chapter 21 in this volume, p. 458).

Kaiser Permanente participants described a similar phenomenon as they described the contribution of the outside researcher: "He taught us the importance of voicing our opinions and how to go back. He gave us tools" (Chapter 23, p. 504). At HP, "What we discovered about ways of organizing and the artifacts we developed were helpful to people in conceptualizing what they were about. Years later, I saw the models out on managers' desks" (Chapter 24, p. 525).

Although the external researchers brought knowledge and frameworks and catalyzed the development of new knowledge in the research process, collaborative research depends fundamentally on joining the knowledge of practice and theory. This was evident in the HP-CEO collaboration, where all stages of the research process were formulated and conducted collaboratively, and where the emergent models of knowledge-work teaming were drawn from previously existing scholarly models and knowledge about teams combined with knowledge of practice gained from in-depth interviews with a broad assortment of HP employees who described their work and the challenges they faced working in teams. The knowledge-generating process also occurred through the action research in which the divisions learned through experimentation, first translating the models into their particular setting and then designing and trying out the approaches defined in the models, which would then be improved and iterated based on multiple action research cases. The importance of knowledge combination was pointed out by Stu Winby, whose HP group collaborated with academics despite the fact that the internals were all cutting-edge design consultants:

> We had a common purpose where internal and external could get together with a common charter. CEO wins because [it gets] access to a rich database and some internal resources and we have access to world-class research scientists and methodologies and external knowledge. (Chapter 24, p. 526)

Even in the process of writing up the learning from the Kaiser Pharmacy collaboration, Stebbins reports an intentional combination of the practitioner and academic perspectives:

> I've always wanted a coauthor from the inside in my research. I'm currently working on another article involving another pharmacy employee who has a wonderful understanding of what goes on with DUAT [Drug Utilization] action teams. I don't understand the pharmacy at a deep level, but we can put something together because she has the technical expertise and I look at management. (Chapter 23, p. 502)

Much of Stebbins's writing is aimed at practitioner audiences. He emphasizes that the knowledge gained from collaboration is often tightly intertwined with the knowledge of practice.

An important element of successful collaborative management research is the systematic evaluation of the impact of the application of the new knowledge on the desired outcomes of the system (see Pasmore, Woodman, & Simmons, Chapter 27 in this volume). This may be the single most important bridge between theory and practice, as it

tests whether the knowledge applied—the intervention—has the intended impact on the complex system in which it is generated. In the words of Bradbury (Chapter 28 in this volume), this is the test of whether collaborative research has generated "actionable" knowledge, and it is no less than the ultimate test of the quality of the research. This evaluation is both practically and theoretically important and relates closely to the rigor with which the research is conducted and the resulting validity of the findings. Researchers tend to equate quality with the rigor of the research process, which is in fact one of the competencies they bring to the collaboration. This is explicitly captured by Coghlan and Coughlan (Chapter 21 in this volume):

> The way the researcher network recorded events, articulated and discussed interpretations and assumptions, enacted cycles of action and reflection, and tested reflections in subsequent action ensured methodological rigor. In addition, the collaborative nature of the cycles of action and reflection evident at the partner meetings enabled joint planning and implementation of actions. (p. 461)

On the other hand, the participating managers assessed the value of the research based on system capabilities and performance outcomes. As described by one of the CO-IMPROVE managers,

> All the projects undertaken [as part of this research] were related to quality problems in the supply chain. However, they were not effective because there was still a barrier between ourselves (as the customer) and the supplier. Those barriers were hard to overcome: Spreading the project within our company and the supplier turned out to be difficult and, in some cases, required a lot of pressure from me as the leader. By introducing regular meetings, some

progress was made. However, the overall collaborative process did not stick and, today, it is not "lived as a standard." Some elements, like early supplier involvement and quick follow-up of corrections on delivery and quality, have improved. (Chapter 21, p. 459)

The following "voice," also from a CO-IMPROVE manager, illustrates the close relationship between the formal methodologies and assessment procedures provided by the academic researchers and the ability of the organization to use the learning to improve performance:

As managers, we learned from our interaction with the academics. Of course, small barriers emerged from the different "languages" of practice and theory, the more tactical approach of managers versus the more theoretical approach of academics, and from the different knowledge levels of academics and managers. Yet, defining and practicing a formal assessment and organizing information, knowledge, and theory did represent progress. I really think that without the methodology and organization of academics, this learning would have not been achieved without much more effort and time. (Chapter 21, p. 459)

PARTING THOUGHTS

We see in the voices of the individual participants their particular perspectives and purposes, as well as the purposes of the institutions and communities of which they are members. In these projects, we see multiple parties who have found a common focus that provides motivation for true collaboration, or we see a collective trying to define that uniting purpose. Collaboration must be established that fits with individuals and institutions that have their own interests, resource needs, and trajectories in the system, but who find common interests that lead, at least temporarily, to alignment in a partnership. The quality of the partnerships between the different actors is dependent to a high degree on the nature of the designed structural arrangements and processes. The collaborative management research mechanism must incorporate the knowledge of each party and that party's criteria for success. In collaborative research, a primary challenge is to attend to the intersection of those concerned with theory and practice; with the combination of knowledge and the development of language and frameworks that addresses both worlds; and with the development of criteria that address the performance needs of each. Such is the challenge of collaboration as well as its definition.

REFERENCES

Deutsch, M. (2000). Cooperation and competition. In M. Deutsch & P. T. Coleman (Eds.), *The handbook of conflict resolution: Theory and practice* (pp. 21–40). San Francisco: Jossey-Bass.

Tjosvold, D. (1994). *Team organization: An enduring competitive advantage.* New York: John Wiley & Sons.

Part V

ENABLERS, CHALLENGES, AND SKILLS

The final section in this *Handbook* deals with the art and science of conducting collaborative management research. Given the youth of the collaborative management research paradigm, it is perhaps not surprising that the authors of contributions in this section point to many opportunities to improve the quality of efforts that are being undertaken. Although there is much to improve, there are also suggestions here that should help to address at least some of the shortcomings in our current approaches to this important work.

As collaborative management research is a relatively recent addition to available methodologies for conducting research into the effectiveness of managerial and organizational arrangements, one might ask why it hasn't simply incorporated insights from earlier efforts in the social sciences to improve rigor and relevance. Certainly, there is a substantial body of work on social science research methods, much of it dealing with issues of validity, reliability, and transference from the laboratory to the real world. Previous work has also offered a broad spectrum of methodologies for data collection, ranging from the less precise, such as case studies, to the more precise, including surveys and quasi-experimental studies (see Campbell & Stanley, 1966, for an overview of the strengths and weaknesses of various methods). Despite this foundation, many of the issues addressed in earlier attempts to improve upon our methods for collecting data seem to have reappeared in the coming of age of collaborative management research. We see in this *Handbook* a tendency toward the weakest of Campbell and Stanley's designs: the single case study, and often without pre- and postmeasures. In a number of cases, researchers have resorted to measures of satisfaction with the process rather than ascertaining whether the intervention affected the system outcomes of interest to the participants. Even "actionability" as described by Bradbury in this section is not systematically reported by a number of our contributors: Did the system engaged in the collaborative research make any changes? Did they result in accomplishing the shared purposes or the separate purposes of the various participants? Rather, there is a tendency to resort to describing the process through which people collaborated. Why?

CHALLENGES

In answering this question, we can safely rule out ignorance of the literature concerning social science research methods on the part of those academics engaged in collaborative management research. We know many of these individuals personally and are confident in the quality of their training in research methods. We can also rule out laziness or shoddy workmanship for much the same reason; we know the published track record of these individuals and the quality of work they have produced using alternative methodologies. We are forced to conclude that there is something inherently challenging about conducting collaborative management research, especially with regard to undertaking research that meets the highest standards of rigor and generalizability. As we examine the previous chapters in this *Handbook* and the chapters that make up this section, we begin to understand the nature of these unique challenges as well as some potential remedies. Table V.1 presents some contrasts between experimental laboratory research (which some would say offers the highest level of control and rigor of the available social science methodologies) with some of the characteristics of collaborative management research noted by our contributors.

Any research, to be of value, must produce observations that are useful and true in the sense that they can at least roughly predict the direction and significance of the influence of one variable upon another. Collaborative management research is no different, but it lacks the precision of prediction that a tightly controlled laboratory experiment allows. As Pasmore, Woodman, and Simmons (Chapter 27) and Adler and Beer (Chapter 26) acknowledge, it is difficult for collaborative management researchers to impose the same degree of control as is common in classic experimental science. Still, collaborative management researchers must endeavor to produce "truth" about whether and why taking particular actions and influencing particular dynamics and parameters of the system lead to desired outcomes. Such truth is more likely to follow the application of rigorous scientific procedures for creating quasi-experimental studies, even if the studies occur in different systems over time. Our contributors warn that it is a mistake to try to draw generalizable conclusions from single experiments that take place in complex organizational settings. Designing rigorous research is made more difficult in collaborative management research by the fact that the focus of the inquiry only emerges over time through the collaboration of the parties involved. As several of the contributors in this section point out, allowing the topic of inquiry to be developed jointly is critical to the success of collaborative management research because it increases the likelihood that commitment to application will follow (Adler & Beer, Chapter 26; Bradbury, Chapter 28; Coghlan & Shani, Chapter 29; Mohrman, Pasmore, Shani, Stymne, & Adler, Chapter 30). Application, in turn, allows an assessment of the workability or "actionability" (Bradbury) of the outcomes of the research. The topic of research is not the only thing that may be left for co-design; in several of the studies in this volume, the research methods were also evolved through dialogue. Depending upon the circumstances, this approach can add

Table V.1   Comparison Between Methodological Features of Laboratory and Collaborative Management Research

Methodological Feature	Laboratory Research	Collaborative Management Research	Contributions in This Section
Experimental control	Random subjects exposed to treatment, compared with nonexposed control group; double-blind procedures can further enhance experimenter influence.	Nonrandom subjects; no control group; full experimenter knowledge of treatment and intended outcomes.	Pasmore, Woodman, & Simmons; Adler & Beer
Identification of research framework	Causal framework and specific hypotheses known up front.	Focus of research, methods, and application are emergent and co-defined.	Coghlan & Shani; Mohrman, Mohrman, Cohen, & Winby; Pasmore et al.; Bradbury; Adler & Beer
Reliability	Experiments can be repeated multiple times under essentially the same conditions; the effects of precise treatments can be duplicated.	One-time study. Once conducted, changed conditions make repeating the same experiment impossible; only general frameworks and approaches are generalizable.	Pasmore et al.; Adler & Beer; Mohrman et al.
Contextual influence	All variables except those of interest are controlled in the experiment.	Contextual influences are not controlled and may influence observed outcomes to a significant degree; communities of interest are involved and must have aligned interests in order to achieve optimal results. Treatment takes place over time in real-world setting. "Subjects" frequently change roles or leave.	Coghlan & Shani; Pasmore et al.; Adler & Beer; Mohrman et al.

(Continued)

Table V.1 (Continued)

Methodological Feature	Laboratory Research	Collaborative Management Research	Contributions in This Section
Experimenter skills	Not relevant as long as careful protocols are followed.	Degree of skill of experimenter in a number of areas (e.g., relationship building, shaping organizational change interventions, stakeholder management) has direct influence on success of experiment.	Mohrman et al., Pasmore et al.; Bradbury
Quality of co-inquiry with subjects	Not relevant; there is no co-inquiry with subjects.	Critical to obtaining insights and producing deep commitment to change based on knowledge generated.	Coghlan & Shani; Pasmore et al.; Adler & Beer; Mohrman et al.; Bradbury
Measurement	Measures that allow ratio scaling and precise significance testing.	Indirect measures that are influenced by extraneous events and multiple variables.	Adler & Beer

to the sense of partnership as well as making certain that the methods really do fit the problem under study (Bradbury, Chapter 28; Pasmore et al., Chapter 27).

Whereas laboratory experiments are easily repeated, studies in organizations always change the system, making it impossible to "start over again" as if nothing had happened. As pointed out by Adler and Beer and by Pasmore et al., repeated studies in different parts of the same system or across different systems afford us some degree of comfort that the results from single experiments are replicable and that the conclusions drawn are therefore reliable.

While the laboratory researcher endeavors to shut out the influence of the world on his or her experiment, collaborative management researchers have no choice but to operate in settings where the world constantly impinges on the plans, priorities, and behaviors of those involved (Adler & Beer; Coghlan & Shani; Pasmore et al.). Collaborative researchers must develop interventions and insights that are robust enough to withstand these forces, and be adaptable in their approaches to inquiry and change as the systems they work with evolve in unexpected ways. As Mohrman et al. point out, developing the highest skills in collaboration between academics and practitioners may be one of the most important and lasting effects of collaborative management research in an organization. Companies that are able to do this, as in the example of Hewlett-Packard provided earlier in this volume, are better positioned to learn and go on learning from their association with academics and to find ways to make their learning relevant and applicable to organizational issues.

Bradbury, Mohrman et al., Adler and Beer, and Pasmore et al. note that unlike in experimental research, relationships are critical to the ability to carry out rigorous collaborative management research. Especially where there is no preexisting relationship of trust between the researcher and subjects in an experiment, the skills of the parties involved in collaborative management research make a difference in the quality of research that is performed and the results obtained. Adler and Beer call for better training for collaborative management researchers and more self-monitoring by members of the collaborative management community. Mohrman et al., Coghlan and Shani, and Pasmore et al. point out that collaborative management research may best be carried out by teams of researchers, each of whom may bring different skills to the project. Beyond the content knowledge of the organizational sciences and of social science research methodology, important skills to develop include mutually defining the research agenda, applying multiple methods of research as appropriate, formulating change interventions based on the findings of the research, and helping insiders disseminate findings.

All of the contributors in this section emphasize the importance of involving managerial partners in analyzing and interpreting data and drawing conclusions from collaborative management research. In most laboratory experiments, no interaction takes place after the experiment between the experimenter and subjects, because the experimenter is simply not interested in the subjects' reasons for behaving as they did in the experiment. It is enough to note that the treatment did or did not produce the intended effects upon behavior. In collaborative management research, co-development of conclusions is important precisely because academics and practitioners bring different backgrounds, perspectives, and interests to the table. As we argued earlier in this *Handbook*, the strength of collaborative management research is in the combination of knowledge from theory and practice. As these different perspectives are explored, the depth and richness of understanding by both parties increases. Learning by both is more likely to take place when there is collaboration in interpreting results, and application issues are more likely to be surfaced, explored, and addressed.

Finally, Adler and Beer note that traditional research values precision, whereas in collaborative management research, precision is not always possible. Equal amounts of effort and resources expended against the same objectives in one system may produce different outcomes than in another. This is due to the influence of the context on outcomes, as discussed earlier. Despite the difficulties involved, measuring the outcomes of collaborative management research is important and may, as Adler and Beer note, influence the speed with which collaborative management research efforts gain notice and spread.

ENABLERS

While challenges certainly exist, the contributors in this section offer enablers that should make the conduct of collaborative management research easier and more influential over time. Bradbury notes that instilling reflection into the practice of action research can greatly increase the quality of collaborative efforts. She describes the process of completing learning histories, which are elaborate documents that capture the experiences and insights of parties involved. While advocating the use of multiple methods in conducting action research, Bradbury's description of the learning history approach sounds to us like a technique that every collaborative management researcher should consider.

Coghlan and Shani note that there are communities of interest involved in collaborative management research efforts, not just an academic and a practitioner working side by side. By paying attention to the evolution of the larger community of interest, the collaborative management researcher can gain support and alignment that is indispensable in carrying out large, complex, and long-term efforts.

Adler and Beer discuss two institutions that have been created to support collaborative management research, the FENIX program in Europe and the TruePoint managerial consultancy in the United States. In comparing the two, it was clear to the authors that the FENIX program produced better scientific results, but the TruePoint program had more success in developing interventions that led to organizational transformation. Both institutions have a rich history and remarkable track record that speak to the importance of obtaining longer-term system support for conducting high-quality collaborative management research.

In the final chapter of the *Handbook*, the editors synthesize the insights from the chapters in the book and from the many discussions and debates that we had while pulling the volume together and jointly interpreting and reflecting on our journey. We raise the question of when intervention and collective inquiry really are research, and when they are consulting—a set of activities, perhaps based on sound content and process expertise, designed to help a particular system learn and evolve. We also offer some core standards for collaborative management research.

The chapters that make up this section are thoughtful reflections on the current state of the art of collaborative management research. They are realistic in their appraisal of the strengths and weaknesses of methods in use, but also suggest helpful remedies for many of the issues that are identified. Reading them will certainly cause anyone involved in collaborative management research efforts to more thoughtfully consider opportunities to improve his or her skills in crafting high-quality studies.

REFERENCE

Campbell, D. T., & Stanley, J. C. (1966). *Experimental and quasi-experimental designs for research*. Chicago: Rand McNally.

CHAPTER 26

Collaborative R&D in Management

*The Practical Experience of FENIX and
TruePoint in Bridging the Divide Between
Scientific and Managerial Goals*

Niclas Adler

Michael Beer

ABSTRACT

This chapter will describe the work of two different centers for collaborative management research, TruePoint in the United States and FENIX in Europe, over the past 15 years. Each of the centers, using different methods, has endeavored to create competencies among professionals in undertaking more systematic R&D on approaches to management in companies. It will be argued in the chapter that R&D in management should become a functional process in complex organizations, enabling the discovery, validation, and legitimization of new management approaches while simultaneously contributing to academic research that meets international standards. The chapter concludes with an exploration of what the next-generation R&D in management in organizations might look like and elaborates on the competencies necessary, both within organizations and among external management researchers, to pursue and fully gain from these efforts.

R&D AND INNOVATIONS IN MANAGEMENT FOR SUSTAINABLE COMPETITIVENESS

Despite the fact that most managers would agree with research findings that indicate that organizational performance is affected by different approaches to management (Collins, 2002; Miles & Snow, 1978), most organizations do not conduct research into their own management practices. Managerial systems, composed of such elements as visions and goals, strategies, organizational design, general managerial teams, cross-functional teams, project teams, incentive schemes, and the overall governing logic of the firm, all affect a firm's effectiveness in significant ways. These elements influence the ways the firm makes decisions about everything from technical R&D projects to how to allocate resources. In effect, management's most important product development task is their own organization and their own management. If designed and pursued properly, the organization will produce superior products and services. However, it is rare that organizations have any planned effort to gain a deeper understanding of the sources of their effectiveness or ineffectiveness (Beer & Eisenstat, 2000), to experiment with new ways of organizing and managing, or to codify and diffuse new models of management that emerge from these efforts (Birkinshaw & Mol, 2006). This is true despite the fact that some companies have successfully improved their competitiveness by using such systematic management and R&D efforts. Consider the 40% improvement in productivity achieved by Procter & Gamble across its entire manufacturing system in the 1970s from a planned R&D initiative, in collaboration with academic scholar-consultants to research and develop a new model for organizing and managing their manufacturing plants. The company achieved so much value from this R&D that they refused inquiries into the new management model. On the other hand, a firm's R&D efforts in core technologies such as composite materials, communication algorithms, and cell molecular biology are readily accepted as a part of doing business. New hypotheses are continuously generated, positioned into the existing knowledge base, developed, and tested in systematic experiments—with a clear conviction that these efforts will enhance competitiveness.

In this chapter, we argue that it is just as important to conduct R&D in management in organizations as it is to conduct R&D in car safety, new drugs, or new telecommunications equipment technologies. Nevertheless, few companies have developed and institutionalized R&D processes and models that enable the necessary collaboration of managers with internal or external scholar-consultants. There are far too few management R&D departments staffed by sophisticated management scholar-consultants whose role is to work with managers to diagnose their organization's effectiveness and then develop and implement new models of management. Despite the fact that it is widely acknowledged that organizations are complex systems, we see a lack of explicit initiatives that could provide knowledge and techniques to design, develop, and optimize managerial work and managerial processes. The lack of a tradition and experience in management R&D leads to a depiction of the managerial work in organizations as, on one hand, stochastic, fragmented, irrational, and hard to understand (Carlsson, 1951; Mintzberg, 1973; Tengblad, 2002) and, on the other, as too structured, rigid, and based on simple routines (Bass, 1990).

Management has often failed to embrace the inevitable ambidextrous and paradoxical nature of organizations (Tushman & O'Reilly, 1996). Hence, managers are often influenced by managerial fads and solutions but fail to see their drawbacks or understand whether these solutions will fit into their own organizational context (Beer, Eisenstat, & Spector, 1990). Management is described as being captured by perceived expectations from multiple stakeholders, benchmarking out of context, and naive images of what management should be (Birkinshaw & Mol, 2006). The use of general planning tools, focused on the hierarchical breakdown of tasks, functional specialization, and minimized deviations from plans, is described as having stifled innovation and blocked the exploration of novel management approaches (Adler, 1999). Managers are often set in their comfort zones. The limited use of the vast empirical data from the daily life of any organization, coupled with limited collective reflection on alternative approaches to management that could be adopted, differentiates the treatment of management from other R&D efforts in organizations.

We argue that one important explanation of why management is treated differently than other areas is that such treatment is partly a function of the dominant model of research on management in universities and business schools. Management research is fragmented, retrospective, and focused on narrow problems that ignore the systemic nature of organizations and the fundamentally important question of how to change them. Consequently, research outcomes are perceived to be of limited guidance to managers—and many authors argue that a relevance gap exists (e.g., Starkey & Madan, 2001; Starkey & Tempest, 2005; Tranfield & Starkey, 1998). The question of how to change organizations to incorporate research findings has been ignored by academics and is sometimes resisted by managers. The divide between the "scientific" goals of academics and the "practical" goals of managers has not been bridged effectively.

The new demands on and emerging challenges for management increase the need for R&D in management and for a more evidence-based development of new management models, approaches, and concepts (Pfeffer & Sutton, 2006) and motivate continued exploration of collaborative management research approaches and their sustainability. More knowledge-based workforces, more distributed ownership, and increasing needs to bridge different types of national, cultural, functional, organizational, and sectoral boundaries, together with emerging paradigm shifts in core technologies in a number of major industries and governmental sectors, contribute to that need, as does the emerging evidence that fundamental assumptions for managing—such as a

hierarchical breakdown of tasks to cope with complexity, functional specialization to be effective, and the use of plans and minimized deviations from them to cope with uncertainty—do not fit with many of the contemporary challenges that managers face.

Using the experiences from FENIX and TruePoint, we describe and evaluate two approaches to R&D in management. Both of these research centers enabled evidence-based inquiry and innovation because they attended to both the tradition of management research and practice-driven management and organization development. We believe such efforts demand new competencies and new processes for both managers and management researchers. Moreover, to be influential and sustainable, the types of approaches we evaluate demand new boundary-spanning initiatives and institutions to compensate for limitations in the incentive systems and governing logics in the world of management and academia. To understand the strengths and weaknesses of any collaborative R&D process, including the two presented in this chapter, requires a clear articulation of the goals of scientific inquiry and the goals of managers who may potentially collaborate in such an endeavor. After all, a collaborative process must find ways to meet both sets of goals. We now turn to the divide that must be bridged if collaborative R&D in management is to take place.

GOALS OF MANAGEMENT RESEARCHERS AND MANAGERS

As Van de Ven and Johnson (2005) have argued, higher investment in R&D requires engagement and collaboration between practitioners and scholars in developing a research strategy that incorporates each party's interests and goals. In effect, the research strategy must be a synthesis of inevitably different but equally valid perspectives. Though the goals may not always be clear to the actors involved, collaborative R&D strategies like the two presented in this chapter cannot be objectively evaluated unless the criteria for evaluation are clear. This is particularly important because, as we shall show, there are contradictions within and between the goals each side brings to the research design question.

Goals of Scientific Inquiry: Below, we list the dominant criteria by which social scientists judge the quality of explanations or theories about observed phenomena (Thorngate, 1974). These are likely to influence, explicitly or implicitly, the choice of a research strategy by scientists.

• *Veritas:* Scientists and researchers are supposed to seek the truth, but social scientists, at least, are not supposed to directly influence the actors they study. Researchers want their explanations to reveal all of the variables or forces that affect outcomes of interest, but do not take on the responsibility of taking action or even developing actionable theories. Data from which conclusions are reached are therefore supposed to be based on valid observations, which represent what is really going on but avoid becoming part of or even influencing what happens. To guard against bias in the analyses, normal research methods distance the researcher from the research objects (and/or subjects). Unfortunately, this distance prevents researchers and managers from engaging in an active and productive dialogue and collaboration. Managers do not stimulate collective and public conversation about the purpose of the research and its relevance to the goals of the organization nor do they engage in dialogue with the researchers about the possible findings and their implications. Unless such a dialogue takes place, neither managers nor researchers will be able to learn about tensions and conflicts in the organization or leadership values and assumptions that have created these. And

these contextual factors will ultimately prevent change in the problem situations being investigated. Consider a researcher whose obsession with "objective" survey research prevents him or her and a key executive in an organization from learning about and confronting the political forces in that organization, which in turn ultimately prevents management from making any changes suggested by the research (Beer, 1982). This suggests that there may be great potential for researchers to develop research methods that engage managers and their staff in dialogue and collaboration that reveal the whole truth about the organization as a system.

• *Precision:* Scientists are supposed to strive for explanations that predict precisely what will happen under certain conditions specified by the theory. The assumption is that the more exact the prediction of the amount of change in B resulting from changes in A, the higher the precision. In addition, it is generally believed by management scholars that predictive validity increases with more precise measurements. Researchers have therefore gravitated to quantitative methods such as surveys and the use of existing archival data. Where possible, they attempt to predict quantitative performance outcomes. The effect of this rush to precision is that management researchers often define the domain of their research more and more narrowly—fewer variables are included in the research, in order to make precision possible. In their striving to increase precision, researchers may run the risk of seriously decreasing relevance—and hence also their ability to engage in collaboration with managers. This suggests that if they are to collaborate with managers in the study of complex real-world problems, collaborative management researchers must find new ways to search for scientific precision.

• *Generality:* Scientists prefer to develop explanations that apply to many different situations. For management researchers, this means predictions that apply across situations such as companies, industries, cultures, and so on. This increases the researcher's stature in the scientific and practitioner community, because his or her explanation is more widely acknowledged and employed. The researcher's expert and social power increase. While generality may be important to scientists, managers are generally less concerned about generality, though some managers regard findings as more robust and are more likely to act when the findings have been substantiated in other settings. Most managers, however, want a solution to their unique problems in order to improve performance. The desire for generality by researchers leads them to employ measures of variables developed by others researching the same domain. This may preclude grounding their measures and their theory in the complexity of the unique situation. Together, this suggests that collaborative management research—and its formulation and measures—must of necessity be primarily grounded in the phenomena experienced by the organization, even at the risk of sacrificing generalizability.

- *Simplicity:* Parsimonious explanations—those that employ fewer factors and are linear—are preferred to more complex multidimensional and nonlinear explanations. These simple explanations are judged to be more elegant and are naturally easier to understand and manipulate. Simplicity is antagonistic to the goal of generality, however. To reduce an explanation's complexity, researchers must inevitably narrow the focus of the inquiry. It is unlikely that a simple and elegant explanation can successfully guide managerial action in complex multilevel and multifaceted organizations. Researchers' efforts to create a simple and elegant theory undercut the development of a rich and grounded clinical explanation of what is happening in a single organization, and are therefore less useful in practice. The applied researcher may have to settle for a complex multilevel

explanation of the phenomenon being studied, one that does not fit neatly into the traditional academic journal article that requires short, focused discussions with airtight measures and causal hypotheses.

The ideal goal of science, to develop explanations that reveal the truth and are also precise, simple, and general, may even be unreachable due to the inner contradictions of these four goals. Thorngate (1974) states that it is "impossible for an explanation of social behavior to be simultaneously general, simple and accurate [valid]" (p. 126). For example, research methods that produce simple and precise explanations may also fail to reveal the unvarnished truth about what is really going on in the organization. The truth about why managers behave as they do is likely to be heavily defended by them. They may not fully understand—or want to reveal—their motives. It is also unlikely that precise methods, such as surveys, actually reveal what respondents do not fully understand or are unable to articulate.

Hence, the goals of scientific inquiry, and the dominant approach to try to reach them, conflict with management's goals for the inquiry. We now turn to a discussion of these goals.

Practitioner Goals: Managers typically enter a collaborative research enterprise with an interest in solving important organizational or management problems that have a direct impact on value creation for investors, customers, or employees, though some managers may also have a secondary goal of contributing to knowledge for the greater good. The following are specific criteria that explicitly or implicitly influence the goals and expectations managers bring to a collaborative research activity.

- *Relevance:* Practitioners are interested in research that yields an understanding of the relevant and salient problems they are faced with. This suggests that collaborative management research needs to focus on problems as opposed to extant theories or models of interest to academics. This is not to say that existing academic theories should not inform how practical problem-centered research is conceived, or that the significance of problem-centered research for theories should not be explored and developed. To ensure relevance, managers and academics must engage in a discussion of their mutual interests. A negotiation of a research design that serves the interests of both must take place (Van de Ven & Johnson, 2005), and some "red and hot issues" need to be pinpointed (Adler & Shani, 2001). And, if both parties are to learn from the research, both must be involved in a discussion of the data, something that places demands on managers and researchers that they may not be used to meeting, or may not even be motivated to meet.

• *Change:* When practitioners engage an academic researcher in a collaborative inquiry, they want to make a difference in the affairs of their enterprise and its outcomes. They most often seek improvements in management practice and in value created for investors, customers, and employees. But even though an urgent problem may motivate managers to enter a collaborative inquiry, this does not ensure that they will be motivated to confront their own role in the problem, even when the data clearly point to it. Indeed, managers' own needs for distance from the "subject" can cause them to collude with scientists, who seek distance for their own purposes. Collaborative research must therefore be designed to be an effective intervention into the affairs and daily challenges that management faces. This intervention must make it difficult for managers and employees to avoid the truth and deny findings. Such interventions can also serve the goals of scientific inquiry by enabling

management researchers to learn about "hidden data" (assumptions, perceptions, and mental models) that they might otherwise not discover. Such a research intervention increases the chances of managers being able to lead change successfully because opinion leaders at lower levels in the organization will appreciate this degree of honesty and become less cynical about management's motives, and consequently more committed. On the other hand, given that they may lose control, experience findings as painful, or be required to dedicate more time and commitment, management may not embrace such an intervention easily. Also blocking the design of such research methods is a lack on the part of academics of the inclination or intervention skills to manage an action learning process.

• *Learning:* Significant organizational and management problems are not defined and resolved with an initial, one-time definition of a new management model. Rather, the full nature of the problem and its causes, even after careful study, is revealed over time as managers and consultants take action to solve the problem. This action reveals the assumptions, skills, and motivations of managers and employees. Equally important, the context within which the problem is situated is revealed. Moreover, solutions that managers may design after a first round of research may have unintended consequences. In effect, change in human affairs is a process of successive approximation. For this reason, research that has the practical goal of solving problems must be longitudinal (Adler & Shani, 2001; Van de Ven & Johnson, 2005). It must enable managers to learn about unintended consequences of their solutions and alter them over time to deal with those problems. Such an iterative process of solution design, action, data collection, and redesign also deepens managers' and researchers' understanding of the underlying logic of the solution. Truth is revealed over time, Churchman and Mitroff (1995) argue.

Therefore, it is in the practitioner's and researcher's interests to design research that enables organizational and managerial learning. The truth, however, is that promotional processes in academia do not reward this type of open-ended and long-term commitment to research, thus increasing the likelihood that researcher and manager collaborate to contain the timeframe and scope of the research.

- *Low Cost:* Managers are most often very busy and generally overcommitted. It is not surprising, therefore, that they want fast, economical, and painless solutions to problems. The pain they are trying to avoid may often be that of confronting the truth about the effectiveness of the organization and their leadership of it, and the demands on their time and emotional engagement that the truth inevitably makes. Practitioners are fully aware that research into their affairs may challenge their managerial practices, and this may cause many to eschew inquiry. Their desire to avoid or severely limit the cost of research is an additional force for collusion with scientists, whose natural inclination is also to avoid engagement. The desire to minimize investment in research is particularly problematic given that failures in leading change come about because leaders are distanced from business and organizational problems, delegate change to staff groups or lower levels, and do not create the sense of urgency needed to change organizational behavior (Beer et al., 1990; Greiner, 1967; Kotter, 1996).

As with scientists, the goals of practitioners conflict with one another. The desire for quick and painless solutions to problems, at a low cost, is contradicted by the goals of change and learning, which require engagement and continuous involvement. The desire to make a contribution to knowledge and society, though a worthy motive, can also lead to a lack of engagement. The role of collaborating with the academic researcher is delegated to a staff group and/or lower-level line managers. This makes it likely that top management may not learn about their leadership and the cultural context it has created. Unless practitioners are made aware of these contradictions in their motives regarding management research, they will gravitate to the least-costly and most-painless research design.

There are also contradictions between the goals of the scientist and the manager. For example, the scientist's goal of revealing truth directly opposes the manager's natural inclination to avoid the truth—at least, if the truth should happen to involve underperformance of the manager. The scientist's goal of accuracy and simplicity can easily lead to a research design that is not relevant, one that defines the problem on the basis of what can be measured accurately and precisely. The scientists' desire to fit their research into an existing theoretical paradigm—to develop or contribute to an explanation that applies to a variety of situations—leads to a research design that may be too abstract and ungrounded to permit meaningful learning and change. The challenge is to design research that represents the best integration of scientific and practical goals.

The tendency to collude in a practically impotent research design may actually be a bigger barrier to collaborative research than the opposing interests of scientists and practitioners. This suggests that intervention-minded scholar-consultants are potentially important members of a collaborative research design, bringing with them the scientific as well as the change and learning perspectives to the collaboration.

It is important to note that different collaborative management research approaches contribute to different facets of the research enterprise. Some, typically those that serve the goals of *veritas*, relevance, and change, are better suited to the discovery and development of a new model of management. Methods that are typically associated with the positivistic research tradition—those methods that are more precise and distanced from the phenomena—are better suited to the validation and legitimization of theories and models. They enable building theory that gives universal value to the model and enable linking the model to general theory. Linking the model to a general theory, according to scientific standards, means following clear rules: separating science from managerial ideology and critical evaluation and helping to go beyond the illusion of universality of models. Here, we agree with David and Hatchuel's argument (Chapter 2 in this volume) that it is meaningful to analytically separate the discovery stage from the validation stage but to organizationally integrate the two stages. As we describe the experience of FENIX and TruePoint, the reader will want to evaluate these approaches against both objectives.

Is joint publication of findings by the scholar-consultant and manager an essential quality of collaborative R&D? We argue that it is not. Though it is nice when they do, it is simply not realistic to expect most managers to invest in joint publications. What does seem important to us, however, is that managers and scholars maintain an open, honest, and data-driven discussion of the research findings—those that pertain to understanding the organization and their implications for action, as well as those that reflect on the efficacy of participants' efforts to lead change—to develop a new model of management and apply it effectively. It is also important that managers become more educated about knowledge in the field of management science that serves as an important theoretical context for diagnosis and action. A halfway step that managers are more likely to participate in, and that may be used to assess their engagement in expanding knowledge in the field and their own intellectual horizons, is participation in symposia at professional meetings. Thus, in our evaluation of the two case studies below, we do not make

joint publication a criterion for evaluating contribution to science and practice, though we do evaluate the extent to which both parties come to have the same understanding of organizational diagnosis, and their success in leading change toward a new management innovation.

R&D IN MANAGEMENT AS A STRATEGIC FUNCTION

If R&D in management is to play a major role in enabling firms to achieve competitive advantage through systematic and systemic management research, it must institutionalize the management research and development process. Just as R&D regarding a firm's core technology requires a differentiated function with dedicated human and financial resources connected to the firm's other value-creating activities, so, too, does R&D in management. We argue that a differentiated management research and development department staffed with internal scholar-consultants connected to key managers and the world of academic management research is required. And such an organizational research and development function must develop collaborative research methods and strategies that bridge the divide between scientific inquiry—necessary to attract first-rate researchers and academic collaborators—and the managerial goals of real change and improvements in human and business outcomes. And if R&D in management is to be institutionalized, these methods must enable sustained R&D.

We now turn to a discussion of two collaborative management research efforts that we have helped shape and lead over a number of years. Each effort attempts to deal with the trade-offs between the goals of science and practice in different ways. The first is an academically based collaborative research strategy implemented by the FENIX

Centre for Innovations in Management. FENIX is based on two principal foundations: a multidisciplinary research program engaging senior researchers and managers in collaborative projects, and a doctoral program for high-potential managers enrolled by their companies and engaged as resources in the research program. FENIX was founded by researchers at Chalmers University of Technology and the Stockholm School of Economics in Sweden and l'École des Mines de Paris in France, and is sponsored by the Swedish government and several major corporations in Sweden, Denmark, and France.

The second effort was developed by two academics at the Harvard Business School, one of whom had founded and led an internal organizational research and development effort at Corning, Inc., from 1965 to 1975. Action research conducted by these two academics was later incorporated into the practices of TruePoint (formerly the Center for Organizational Fitness), a research-based consultancy. TruePoint employs a management research method that doubles as a powerful intervention into the life of the organization, called the Strategic Fitness Process. Its design requires scholar-consultants and managers to jointly develop the focus of the inquiry—typically the fit or alignment of the organization with management's intended strategic direction—and to engage in diagnosis and planned change collaboratively.

THE FENIX CENTRE FOR INNOVATIONS IN MANAGEMENT

FENIX and its preceding centers, the Gothenburg Centre for Work Science and the Centre for Research on Organizational Renewal, reflect 15 years of experience in changing the way management research is organized and funded and interacts with stakeholders outside of the research community. Based on positive experiences from a series of collaborative research projects, top management in four major Swedish companies and a new, governmental foundation for research and development invested 14 million euros in a six-year research and Ph.D. program. The initial stakeholders agreed on six goals for FENIX: (1) to move from working cross-functionally in research projects toward building a transdisciplinary, colocated research program in management, (2) to intensify collaboration with managers and specialists in the whole research process to increase relevance of research, (3) to renew theoretical contributions through developing much closer collaboration with practice and to develop new research methods, (4) to develop new methodologies that not only compensate for the differences between collaborative and other research approaches but also leverage close collaboration to strengthen the research process, (5) to deliver scientific training for company employees, and (6) to actively analyze the experiment to influence management research approaches at the participating universities. The theoretical work was intended to contribute by providing well-founded guidance to knowledge creation and to constructively reveal or criticize inefficient actions. The original idea was that collaborative methods for producing knowledge and training managers in collaborative research methodologies would contribute to building sustainable relationships between the collaborating partners (as described by, among others, Harvey, Pettigrew, & Ferlie, 2002, and MacLean, MacIntosh, & Grant, 2002). The original intent was also that joint research that takes both the idiosyncrasies of firms and generic models into account would open up possibilities for breakthroughs in knowledge and practice.

Since its formation in 1997, activities in FENIX have included different models for collaboration, such as the following:

Collaborative research studies and research projects on major management challenges.

Issue-driven workshops to speedily generate and test alternative management models and approaches to address real and specific management challenges.

Management reviews supporting organizational learning, diffusion, and sustainability.

Research-based training of leaders and managers integrated with organizational development and research.

Ph.D. candidates among active managers and executives to build an in-house tradition, capacity, and competence to handle R&D in management work and participation in international research programs.

Academic Ph.D. candidates who will be trained in collaborative management research.

The intention has been for collaborative research projects to be based on the active and collegial participation of managers and specialists in research projects on *red and hot issues,* that is, issues of vital importance for the survival or well-being of the organization (Adler, 1999; Adler & Shani, 2001). The collaborative research projects were to be vehicles for more reflective experimentation and relatively systematic action learning. However, of the more than 50 projects pursued, less than 20 succeeded in actively engaging managers outside the group of executive Ph.D. students to take an active part in more than the formulation of the research focus and in the discussion of the emerging research findings. And in only a few participating organizations did the collaborative research projects lead to an expanded use of these approaches to cope with management challenges. The most commonly stated reasons for this were time limitations, competing priorities, and no legitimate tradition to engage in endeavors of this type. In the successful projects, the senior researchers succeeded in clarifying the

expectations of active engagement, in depicting the actual process, and in showing how it fit with the contemporary corporate agenda. This enabled a different prioritization, a different type of engagement, and a different experience, and most often led to a long-term collaboration in a series of projects with an overlap of an engaged core team of managers.

The learning from other contexts and joint research and development with colleagues in other companies has been supported by (senior) management researchers. The issue-driven workshops have been organized as follows: The input has been red and hot issues such as *how we should cope with succession planning for key managerial roles.* The output has been elaborated and tested solutions on an issue such as *how succession planning could become a strategic tool for business and organizational renewal.* Once agreed on as a focus of a workshop, the theoretical and empirical background and relevant parallel examples are investigated by the participating managers and management researchers. Intermediate models are jointly created from investigations and workshops. An experiment is designed, the concept may be implemented in a part of the organization, the most relevant indicators of success are defined, a process for evaluating the experiment is agreed upon, and action is taken. The workshop is then used to analyze and interpret results from the action and then redesign the new model, and to revisit assumptions. Most of the workshops led to the definition of important research topics, and many of the participating managers reported that they really enjoyed and appreciated the reflections and learning generated in the workshops. Some of the workshops also led to the formation of collaborative research projects. However, few of the workshops generated a directly useful action agenda for the participating managers, and few of the engaged organizations or managers adopted a continuous use of such workshops to address their emerging challenges.

The executive Ph.D. candidates were all recruited from the partner companies, with the formulated goal of developing future leaders able to see relevant patterns in complexity and to capture important opportunities in uncertainty. The candidates were expected to become colleagues in collaborative management research projects (on a half-time basis) in their own and other organizations, and to take an active role in building a tradition, a capacity, and a competence to pursue R&D in management in their companies. On average, 20 qualified applicants were considered for each candidate position, and the candidates were selected collaboratively by company executives and the faculty at FENIX. (For a more extensive description of the executive Ph.D. program, see Hart, Kylén, Norrgren, & Stymne, 2004). Many of the candidates made a successful shift from a traditional managerial position to a combined role as researcher-consultant and, in some cases, also to a top management position. Many of the candidates also succeeded in establishing research activities on contemporary and future management challenges in their organizations. However, few of the candidates succeeded in engaging large numbers of colleagues in their work and the collaborative research projects, and few of the candidates succeeded in influencing the tradition of how to cope with management challenges in their organizations in a sustainable way.

Were Practitioner Goals Achieved? We conclude that the FENIX experience in large part did not meet managers' hopes that user-friendly methods would be found to develop new patterns for management work. Moreover, while most individual research projects were perceived to generate important management learning, they most often failed to generate real action and, in some cases, also failed to guide action. The most important positive outcomes stated from management's point of view include (1) the development of 18 executive Ph.D. candidates who took on important managerial roles in the companies; (2) the legitimization of long-term and strategic R&D in management; (3) the development of management concepts based on research; and (4) more systematic and evidence-based learning between contexts within and between companies.

The FENIX experience has clearly shown that collaboration necessitates a significant effort from both the engaged companies and the engaged academic institutions. On the engaged companies' part, it is imperative that senior management be convinced of the importance of moving out of the "comfort zone," as illustrated in Figure 26.1. The FENIX experience makes it clear that any new initiative or concept that threatens the dominant management approaches or assumptions held by the key managers seldom leaves the conference room or enjoys the benefits of being elaborated on, tested, or experimented with.

The FENIX experience has also clearly shown that even when deliberately sought, it is hard to seek and explore ideas and concepts that challenge the dominant approaches and the assumptions held by key actors in the company and in the industry and to bring this exploration into action. It has proven difficult both for individual executive Ph.D. candidates and for teams of candidates and senior researchers to influence the participating organizations and managers outside the more noncommittal workshops or conversations on emerging research findings. There are numerous examples from the FENIX experience of important conversations and syntheses that were highly appreciated and acknowledged as valuable in addressing contemporary challenges but that never really came to influence decisions and actions in the participating organizations.

However, it has been shown to be equally imperative that the participating academic

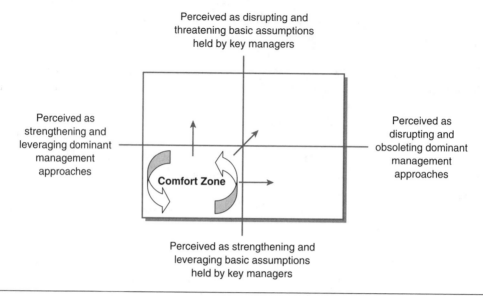

Perceived as disrupting and
threatening basic assumptions
held by key managers

Perceived as
strengthening and
leveraging dominant
management
approaches

Perceived as
disrupting and
obsoleting dominant
management
approaches

Comfort Zone

Perceived as strengthening and
leveraging basic assumptions
held by key managers

Figure 26.1   Managers' Unwillingness to Leave Their Comfort Zone

researcher also move out of his or her comfort zone and engage in collaborative activities that may threaten dominant research approaches and basic assumptions in the research community. Doing this, and motivating junior researchers in particular, necessitates that the engaged academic institutions develop sustainable ways to compensate for the lack of incentives and support for developing the necessary skills to truly engage in collaborative research efforts that produce research of international standards, research that can guide action, and research that will lead to action.

Were Scientific Goals Achieved? The set of collaborative initiatives within the FENIX experiences clearly met the goals of science. The use of triangulations and experiments to test and validate hypotheses—in a way that traditional academic research would not—has added value to validation and enabled an extensive research output.

The FENIX experiment has thus far resulted in the formation of a boundary-spanning research organization and an international research network. Twenty leaders

from the four major companies have been recruited to pursue an executive Ph.D. program; 18 of them graduated before or at the expected time despite their half-time commitment to their corporate jobs. Another 13 traditional academic Ph.D. students have also graduated, having contributed to joint research endeavors in several projects.

A faculty of 12 senior researchers at the three universities has been at the center of the FENIX research organization, and another four senior researchers from the United States and the United Kingdom have been connected to the research for many years. An additional 34 senior researchers have been involved in the various research projects or in the supervision of Ph.D. students. Forty-one research projects have been jointly designed by academics and practitioners, and more than 100 managers and specialists in the companies have actually worked in the research projects. The original budget for the six-year period increased by 65% after five years due to new external funding. The number of publications has been rising steadily and totals over 250 for the past five years. FENIX has joined forces with U.S., French, German, and

U.K. researchers and research groups in methodological development in management research and is now discussing an expansion of the experiment with two European universities.

The sixth initial goal, to actively influence university research and education, has, however, been the most difficult to achieve. Only incremental and limited changes, such as educational and pedagogic methods in Ph.D. programs and the launch of derivative approaches and products such as new master's programs for managers, can be noted.

THE TRUEPOINT STRATEGIC FITNESS PROCESS

The Strategic Fitness Process (SFP) employed by TruePoint in over 200 organizations in approximately 35 corporations was first developed in 1990 in response to a request by Ray Gilmartin, then CEO of Becton Dickinson (BD), a global medical technology company (Beer & Eisenstat, 2000, 2004). Senior management at BD, most of whom had previously been strategy consultants at leading strategy consulting firms, were experiencing difficulties in implementing corporate and business unit strategies. Though the company was not in trouble, it was judged by Wall Street analysts to be a "hold" and not a "buy." They invited some scholar-consultants to help to find a way for BD to become a company capable of implementing strategy.

A guided action learning process was developed, in which senior teams at the corporate and business unit level would collaborate with a task force of eight appointed key people and with scholar-consultants. The SFP process is intended to enable management and scholar-consultants to co-investigate the effectiveness of the organization and develop new models of organizing and managing based on data gathered by the process. The questions

motivating the research are these: "Does management's strategic intent, a two-page statement that the senior team develops, make sense?" and "What are the organization's strengths and what are the barriers to strategy implementation?" Is SFP research or merely another OD intervention? If our premise that joint publication is not a realistic goal or criterion for collaborative research (see above) is accepted, the answer to this last question is "research," as we shall show below.

The motivation to engage in the process is senior management's concern about the organization's effectiveness and performance. The intervention was designed to enable truth to speak to power. This was enabled by a design that provides employees and the task force that reports findings to senior management psychological and career/employment security. Whereas management research conducted by academics is often ignored, the truth about the organization delivered by the organization's own key people, selected by management for their credibility, creates a mandate for change. The scholar-consultants participate with managers as partners in a conversation about the data from which a diagnosis and an action plan emerge. The fact that the senior team is itself involved in the diagnosis and in developing solutions builds commitment and rapid change.

In effect, the senior team is presented with a verbal "case" about their business and organization and is then asked to analyze the case and fashion a change plan that is responsive to the diagnosis. The role of the scholar-consultants is to bring to the conversation, analysis, and action plan extant frameworks, research, and theories in the field of management. The fact that SFP is designed to collect macro and micro issues (leadership and top team effectiveness, as well as organization-level issues such as strategy and structure) would make it difficult, if not impossible, thought the architects of the process, for senior teams to dodge a commitment to change their leadership and management patterns. In virtually all situations, an action for change in the leader's and senior team's role and behavior was developed, and immediate changes were made. In a few cases, the action plan for change was allowed to atrophy. These conditions now define the boundary conditions for successful implementation of SFP and constitute important research findings about organizational change.

SFP becomes an accepted management research process that matters and that managers and employees want to continue because SFP requires senior teams to communicate with the larger organization about the changes in organizing and managing they are planning and how these are linked to the feedback they have received. Moreover, to sustain the action learning process, senior management meets with the task force quarterly to obtain further feedback about progress. Finally,

management that recycles SFP yearly is in effect creating a sustainable R&D in management process. Key steps in the process are listed below and shown in Figure 26.2.

1. *The senior team meets for one day to develop a two-page statement of strategic and organizational direction* and at that meeting selects a task force of eight high-potential people one to two levels down from them who are credible and whom they will believe when they report findings from the inquiry.

2. *The task force meets for one day to prepare to collect data.* The CEO or general manager discusses the statement with the task force. The task force selects approximately 100 people from all parts of the organization and key outsiders to be interviewed. They receive training and practice in interviewing.

3. *Task force members go into the field to conduct confidential interviews* with

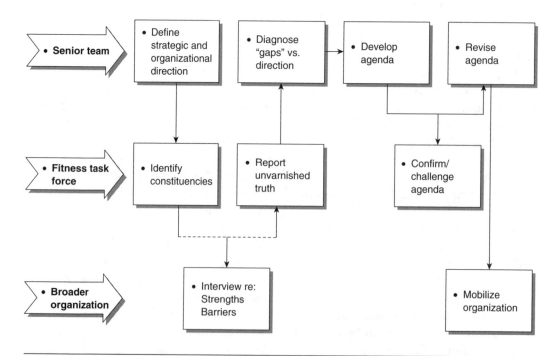

Figure 26.2   The Strategic Fitness Process: A Platform for Collaborative R&D in Management That Matters

people outside their own function or subunit. They employ an unstructured interview around two key questions: "Does the strategic direction make sense?" and "What are the barriers to implementing the strategic direction and what are the strengths that support implementation?" The consultants interview the senior team using the same questions plus a question about the top team and leaders' effectiveness. Using a rigorous process of analysis, themes for feedback are developed by task force members in an additional day of analysis after the field interviews have been completed.

4. *Findings are fed back by the task force on the first day of a three-day fitness meeting.* When the task force discusses the themes as a group in front of the senior team, a rich multidimensional picture of the system is revealed. By speaking as a group, under ground rules of engagement, the task force reports the unvarnished truth and the senior team, taking notes, is able to capture the essence of their organization.

5. *On the second day of the fitness meeting, the top team develops a diagnosis* of the organization after completing an overnight assignment. The consultants facilitate by helping the senior team frame the right questions.

6. *On the third day of the fitness meeting, the top team develops an action plan* for redesign of the organization and their leadership consistent with the diagnosis. The consultants provide heuristics that help the senior team to make choices.

7. *Critique of the action plan by the task force* occurs in a one-day meeting in which they are briefed about the action plan and meet alone to give their feedback.

8. *Concerns* about the adequacy of the senior team's diagnosis and action plans *lead to negotiated changes.*

9. *The top team and the task force meet with the 100 interviewed* to present what was learned and actions planned. Small group

sessions stimulate further discussion. Following the meeting, implementation of the change plan begins.

Were Practitioner Goals Achieved? Because SFP is designed for senior teams to research their own organization, most practitioner goals were met in the applications we researched. The research is perceived by senior teams as highly relevant. An analysis of task force findings across 12 organizations supports this claim. It revealed a syndrome of six fundamental management barriers to effectiveness. And our research shows that these barriers are reduced and transformed into strengths as a result of SFP in most situations (Beer & Eisenstat, 2000). Of course, these are situations where the leader has chosen to engage in a collaborative management research process because of pressing effectiveness problems.

With regard to the power of this collaborative research method to create organization change and learning, a meta-analysis of 12 organizations that undertook SFP showed that in eight of the 12, long-term change and learning occurred in organizational and managerial effectiveness as well as performance, while, in the remaining four, less change, of less long-term consequence, occurred (Beer, Eisenstat, & Foote, 2002). The capacity for long-term learning occurred when senior teams integrated SFP into their annual strategic planning process. Successive applications of the process provided new revelations about the organization and the change process itself. Many of these revelations required changes in managerial behavior that would not have been discovered by normal science research methods. SFP motivated change in management behavior precisely because the organization's own employees collected the data and fed it back themselves, and managers felt they had no choice but to respond to findings or lose their credibility and legitimacy as leaders.

SFP is not perceived by managers as a low-cost research process, however. The senior team has to spend seven days in a series of meetings and follow up with communication to the organization. There were also emotional costs. The unvarnished truth disconfirms management's assumptions and theory of management. Managers find this stressful. One senior team member reported going back to his room and considering resigning. One senior team submitted letters of resignation to the CEO to be exercised by him if, in a year, things had not changed. One general manager reported that the day he received feedback from his task force was easily the worst day of his career in the company. Of course, managers who were willing to bear these costs were also able to lead frame-breaking changes.

Were Scientific Goals Achieved? SFP achieves the goal of *veritas*. It is far better than most management research designs in surfacing the "deep grammar" of the organization. Because SFP enables truth to speak to power about things that matter, senior teams are motivated to make sense of their experience, and the conversations in which scholar-consultants participate reveal insights that more positivistic methods do not enable. Collaborative inquiry through SFP does not, however, meet the precision goals of positivistic research methods. SFP reveals "big boulders" that are in the way of effectiveness, not precise findings that enable scaling of the phenomena. This enables new insights and theory development as well as the opportunity to test and experiment with new models of management. Rigorous meta-analysis of multiple organizations that have undergone SFP has enabled generalization of the knowledge gained. A theory of organizational effectiveness has emerged from the research (Beer & Eisenstat, 2000). Findings from SFP have also yielded knowledge and publications in the following areas, though none were joint publications:

- The role of governance and learning processes similar to SFP in overcoming organizational silence and spurring change
- The leadership and cultural conditions necessary for truth-telling, action learning processes to be chosen as the preferred intervention and later institutionalized
- The role of organizational learning processes in organization design
- The role of organizational learning processes in strategic management

In addition, research into the effectiveness of SFP has led to the development of principles of organizational learning and a social technology that applies these principles.

We conclude that SFP effectively integrates the goals of scientific inquiry and management, though it is not well-suited to a focused and precise inquiry into a specific domain or to the test of a theory. It also enables management to sustain R&D in management if it fits the process into its strategic management process. Diffusion of the SFP process and knowledge throughout the larger corporation was, however, limited, except in instances where top management made efforts to institutionalize the process and had or developed consulting resources in HR or an organization development department.

We argued earlier that joint publications are not a defining criterion for judging the success of collaboration research, but that open and honest conversations about findings at various states of the collaborative action learning process are. Though there was variability in this outcome across the many organizations where SFP was applied, in many, this objective was achieved. First and foremost, when SFP is recycled—which it was not in at least half of the applications—both scholar and manager are conducting longitudinal research that is revealing. In nearly 30 organizations, either teaching cases or research cases were written about the organization and its progress. These data were shared with executives in many, but far from all, situations. Why? Because case writing or other data gathered by scholars independently of the SFP process—a double-loop research process, if you will—was not always contracted for at the start of the project. This was a function of the unpredictable availability of resources. When this independent research was conducted by scholars, however, it led to open and honest conversations about findings, though that outcome would have been of higher quality had this more scholarly research been contracted for at the start of the project and received more consistent support in the form of resources. A positive example is illustrated in a corporation in which the results from a 12-research-case meta-analysis were fed back to the CEO and his key people. The response of the CEO led to revelations about him and his assumptions regarding leadership and management and their implications for the SFP intervention and organizational effectiveness not previously revealed. These findings led to a continuous dialogue with the CEO over several years of involvement. What was learned found its way into an academic publication. In sum, the TruePoint collaborative research model met the co-investigatory goal of honest dialogue about findings and increased shared understanding of the phenomena in many, but far from all, cases. It was far more than simply an OD intervention. However, with better contracting and more scholarly resources, the full potential of the TruePoint model for collaborative practical and scholarly collaborative research may be achievable.

DISCUSSION

Collaborative management approaches can make contributions to both the discovery of new management models and their validation and legitimization by building theory that gives universal value to the model and linking the model to general theory. We agree with David and Hatchuel's argument (Chapter 2 in this volume) that it is meaningful to analytically separate the discovery stage from the validation stage but to organizationally integrate the two stages. Such an approach is also followed in the example of collaborative research at Hewlett-Packard (HP) described by Mohrman et al. (Chapter 24 in this volume).

The FENIX model seems to have served the goals of legitimization and perhaps validation better than TruePoint's model of collaborative inquiry. That is because it incorporated more positivistic scientific inquiry methods. Problems are more specifically defined in advance, and therefore models, theories, and measures extant in the academic context can be incorporated into the definition and measurement of phenomena. On the other hand, the FENIX approach did not generally lead to fundamental change in the organizations where it was applied. Though there was considerable collaboration between researchers and managers, it tended to be several levels below the top. The definition of the research problem and process tended to leave out contextual political, managerial, and cultural issues that had to be engaged in order for fundamental changes to occur. Moreover, there was not commitment to or process for truth to speak to power.

The TruePoint model, on the other hand, did not focus research on specific problems such as product development or employee turnover, or frame the research using existing academically based theories or measures. However, it was more effective than the FENIX effort in achieving frame-breaking changes with measurable improvements in overall business performance. Why? Because by insisting that senior teams define the purpose, goals, and strategy, confront data directly, analyze that data, and then develop a new model of management themselves, senior management was intellectually and emotionally involved. Having opened Pandora's box, managers quickly understood that they had to respond to the feedback and take action or risk their legitimacy as leaders. The task force's involvement in critiquing senior management's action plan also made it difficult for managers to introduce a new model of management without also addressing the leadership and cultural context. On several occasions, managers were confronted if their action plan did not match the data and diagnosis. The FENIX model seems to make most sense in bringing a specific management concept to an intermediate model within a certain context and also in informing general theory (as depicted in Figure 26.3), while the TruePoint model has its primary strength in helping leaders to understand their organizations and to make

collective sense of and implement new approaches into the organizations.

In summary, it appears that TruePoint's SFP is better than the FENIX model at achieving the scientific goals of *veritas*, developing overarching theories of effectiveness, and stimulating new models of management in practice, but less effective in focused and precise inquiry. The FENIX model, on the other hand, is better at meeting the goals of academic scientific inquiry, providing a platform for academics to combine collaborative research activities with a scientific career, and building an R&D capacity within the partner organizations through the executive Ph.D's, but less effective at surfacing the truth and stimulating change in the political, cultural, and managerial context.

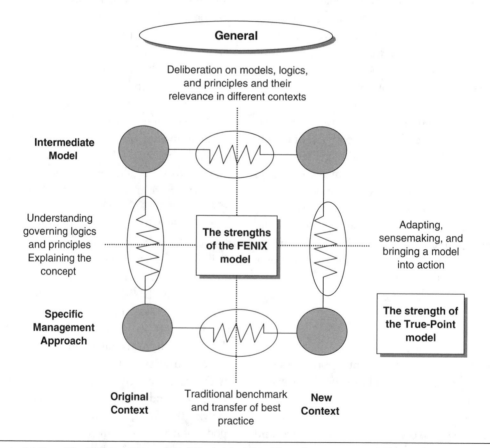

Figure 26.3   The Primary Strengths of Each Model in Transforming Knowledge and Practice Between Contexts

What about sustainability of these collaborative management research models? The FENIX executive Ph.D. program and collaborative research projects that have now spanned approximately a decade have proved to be a powerful model for embedding the motivation and skills to engage in management research in high-potential managers. This powerful model required government funding. It is not clear yet whether companies are willing to fund this on their own, a requirement for sustainability. Moreover, it is too early to know whether the tradition of management research instilled by FENIX in its executive Ph.D's can survive without a differentiated management R&D function staffed by internal scholar-consultants, now that FENIX no longer has the funds to support studies with university-based academics. Time will also tell whether FENIX graduates will want to leave their executive role and migrate into consulting or academia. This would defeat the sustainability objectives.

TruePoint's model has been institutionalized in some, but not all, of the organizations where it was applied. In most of these cases, senior teams in the unit where it was applied continued to employ SFP when they had support from a committed and skilled human resource or organization development specialist and when the process was integrated into the strategic planning process. Interestingly, with the exception of two organizations, TruePoint's scholar-consultants were not asked to remain involved, despite the fact that the process is designed to enable scholar-consultants to add value through participation in the key three-day fitness meeting where data is fed back and analyzed and changes are planned. This suggests that most managers did not fully appreciate the value that the scholar-consultants offered in the first iteration of the process. Thus far, it has also proven to be complex to combine the TruePoint model with a traditional scientific career for the scholar-consultants. Moreover,

wider diffusion of SFP as a standardized collaborative management research method did not occur except in a few corporations where the CEO himself or herself saw its value and was willing to make the investment. We conclude that, in most instances, R&D in management did not become functionally integrated into the life of the larger corporation.

CONCLUSIONS

The discussion above leads us to conclude that the objective of creating a sustainable capability for R&D in management within organizations requires an integration of the FENIX and TruePoint collaborative research models. The time-tested operating principles underlying the SFP (Beer & Eisenstat, 2004) constitute an essential platform for inquiry into the dynamics of the whole organizational system and its multifaceted and interrelated strengths and weaknesses. It can yield the outlines of an empirically based and fundamentally different model of management, and it can motivate managers to lead change toward that new model. It can compensate for the failed transfer of best practices to bring experiences and learning from the use of a specific management approach in a certain setting to a new management approach in a new setting, through an intermediate model level as illustrated in Figure 26.3. In addition, longitudinal research on the overall efficacy of the new model and the context required to support it can add to our broader understanding of effective approaches to management. At the same time, SFP processes would yield more insights and further refinement of new models if the FENIX task force study groups or laboratories were later commissioned to study aspects of the new model in more depth. Such studies would enable an organization to focus the lens of collaborative inquiry on a number of critical aspects of the new organizing model so that it could be refined and enriched. That did happen in one organization, where a task force was commissioned to study and make recommendations for a new order fulfillment process that SFP identified as necessary. Such second-order inquiries, linked to an SFP-like process, are more likely to lead to change than similar collaborative research efforts that are not linked to a strategic change agenda. Because scholar-consultants can inform these management studies with theories and measures extant in the academic literature, they are more likely to yield findings that inform existing management theories and models. Researchers concerned about publication in academic journals are also more likely to participate in these second-order studies.

A committed HR executive is an essential element in the sustainability of SFP, but is better at managing the process than at helping managers frame the diagnosis and action plan from a knowledge base of management research and theory. Consequently, the two-tiered collaborative management research model we recommend requires a differentiated management R&D function staffed by scholar-consultants. In the 1960s and 1970s, companies such as AT&T, GE, Corning, and IBM, among others, established such differentiated management R&D functions staffed by academically trained researchers, who then developed consulting skills (Dowling, 1975). Multiple innovations in organizing and managing their businesses emerged. These R&D departments gave focus to the company's management R&D efforts and forced a dialogue about the human and financial resources required for organizational transformation. HP's Strategic Change Services Division described in this volume (Mohrman et al., Chapter 24) played this role at HP during the 1990s. Some corporations support doctoral education for managers who become interested in management research and consulting. If more academic institutions were to develop the type of executive doctoral program created by FENIX, they would significantly aid in the development of usable knowledge and training of the cadre of sophisticated management consumers of collaborative research and scholar-consultants required by the management R&D function we are proposing.

REFERENCES

Adler, N. (1999). *Managing complexity in product development: Three approaches.* Ph.D. dissertation, EFI, Stockholm School of Economics.

Adler, N., & Shani, A. B. (Rami). (2001). In search of an alternative framework for the creation of actionable knowledge: Table-tennis research at Ericsson. In R. W. Woodman & W. A. Pasmore (Eds.), *Research in organizational change and development* (Vol. 13, pp. 43–79). Oxford, UK: Elsevier Science.

Bass, B. M. (1990). *Bass and Stogdill's handbook of leadership: Theory, research and managerial applications.* New York: Free Press.

Beer, M. (1982). Research and implementation: A case study. In M. D. Hakel, M. Sorcher, M. Beer, & J. L. Moses (Eds.), *Making it happen: Designing research with implementation in mind* (pp. 156–157). Beverly Hills, CA: Sage.

Beer, M., & Eisenstat, R. (2000). The silent killers of strategy implementation and learning. *Sloan Management Review, 41*(4), 29–40.

Beer, M., & Eisenstat, R. (2004). How to have an honest conversation about your strategy. *Harvard Business Review, 82*(2), 82–89.

Beer, M., Eisenstat, R., & Foote, N. (2002). *A meta analysis of SFP.* Unpublished manuscript.

Beer, M., Eisenstat, R., & Spector, B. (1990). *The critical path to corporate renewal.* Boston: Harvard Business School Press.

Birkinshaw, J., & Mol, M. (2006). How management innovation happens. *MIT Sloan Management Review, 47*(4), 81–88.

Carlsson, S. (1951). *Executive behavior.* Stockholm: Strombergs.

Churchman, C. W., & Mitroff, I. (1995). *On the fundamental importance of ethical management: Why management is the most important of all human activities.* Unpublished manuscript.

Collins, J. (2002). *Good to great.* New York: Harper Business.

Dowling, W. F. (1975). To move an organization: The Corning approach to organization development. *Organizational Dynamics, 3*(4), 16–34.

Eisenstat, R., & Beer, M. (1998). *The Strategic Fitness Process manual.* Unpublished manuscript, TruePoint Partners.

Greiner, L. (1967). Patterns of organizational change. *Harvard Business Review, 45,* 119–130. May–June.

Hart, H., Kylén, S., Norrgren, F., & Stymne, B. (2004). Collaborative research through an executive PhD program. In N. Adler, A. B. (Rami) Shani, & A. Styhre (Eds.), *Collaborative research in organizations: Enabling learning, change and theory development* (pp. 101–116). Thousand Oaks, CA: Sage.

Harvey, J., Pettigrew, A., & Ferlie, E. (2002). The determinants of research group performance: Towards Mode 2? *Journal of Management Studies, 39*(6), 747–774.

Kotter, J. (1996). *Leading change.* Boston: Harvard Business School Press.

MacLean, D., MacIntosh, R., & Grant, S. (2002). Mode 2 management research. *British Journal of Management, 13*(3), 189–207.

Miles, R. E., & Snow, C. C. (1978). *Organizational strategy, structure and processes.* New York: McGraw-Hill.

Mintzberg, H. (1973). *The nature of managerial work.* New York: Harper & Row.

Pfeffer, J., & Sutton, R. I. (2006). *Hard facts, dangerous half truths and total nonsense: Profiting from evidence-based management.* Boston: Harvard Business School Press.

Starkey, K., & Madan, P. (2001). Bridging the relevance gap: Aligning stakeholders in the future of management research. *British Journal of Management, 12*(S1) [Special Issue], S3–S26.

Starkey, K., & Tempest, S. (2005). The future of the business school: Knowledge challenges and opportunities. *Human Relations, 58*(1), 61–82.

Tengblad, S. (2002). Time and space in managerial work. *Scandinavian Journal of Management, 19*(4), 85–101.

Thorngate, W. (1974). Possible limits on a science of social behavior. In L. H. Strickland, F. E. Aboud, & K. J. Gergen (Eds.), *Social psychology in transition* (pp. 121–139). New York: Plenum Press.

Tranfield, D., & Starkey, K. (1998). The nature, social organization and promotion of management research: Towards policy. *British Journal of Management, 9*(4), 341–353.

Tushman, M., & O'Reilly, C. (1996). Ambidextrous organizations: Managing evolutionary and revolutionary change. *California Management Review, 38*(4), 8–30.

Van de Ven, A. H., & Johnson, P. E. (2005). Knowledge for theory and practice. *Academy of Management Review, 31*(4), 802–821.

CHAPTER 27

Toward a More Rigorous, Reflective, and Relevant Science of Collaborative Management Research

William A. Pasmore

Richard W. Woodman

Aneika L. Simmons

ABSTRACT

Beginning with its roots in the early 1900s, collaborative management research has evolved in the sophistication of its methods and the scope of its concerns. Three areas in which it hasn't evolved sufficiently, we argue, are in its degree of rigor, its ability to build upon past research, and its relevance to mainstream efforts at improving organizational effectiveness. We develop the concepts of rigor, reflection, and relevance as they pertain to this type of research, and then address the key steps to be taken to elevate the level of practice in the field.

Collaborative management research, the subject of this *Handbook*, is not a new invention, although it continues to be rediscovered by new generations of managers and researchers who bring fresh perspectives to the practice.[1] In our view, collaborative management research dates back at least to the time and motion studies of Frederick Taylor shortly after the turn of the last century. Others might mark the true beginning of efforts to understand human behavior in the workplace with the famous Hawthorne studies conducted by Harvard researchers in collaboration with AT&T in the 1930s. Still later, researchers from the Tavistock Institute in London explored ways to enhance the productivity of British coal mines, Lewin and his colleagues undertook their classic studies on groups, and Blake and Mouton worked with companies in the United States to develop the concepts behind the managerial grid.[2] Thereafter, the field of collaborative management research exploded, with intensified interaction between companies and scholars examining issues ranging from the causes of turnover and stress to the optimal design of jobs and organizations.

Most of what we know about collaborative management research in the early years is based upon the reports of scholars who were incented to write about their insights either as a requirement of their academic positions or as a way to support their growing institutes or consulting practices. Certainly, there were books by executives as well, including the works of Sloan, Barnard, Rockefeller, and McGregor, that remain as classics today. However, it is not clear that these executives worked in close collaboration with academics, so we can't put their works forward as representative of the joint efforts of both communities.

Recent interest in collaborative management research has focused on making the contributions of academics and managers more balanced, in every sense and in every phase of the research effort. History demonstrates that managers have been thinking about how to improve their organizations for at least as long as academics, and are in fact quite good at drawing on their experiences to publish insights on the topic. What isn't as clear is how often the efforts of managers and academics have been aligned, or how often efforts at collaboration in management research have been attempted without success. It is probably safe to conclude from the vast majority of what has been published in academic journals over the past 50 years that independent research by academics has far outweighed collaborative research, even including cases where collaboration occurred at a minimal level in the form of organizations granting access to scholars wishing to collect data from employees. Studies involving moderate to high levels of collaboration between researchers and managers over an extended period of time still make up a tiny minority of what gets published in our journals today. The vast majority of executives are unaware of the journals in which these articles are published and are not likely to be influenced by the findings. In some respects, this state of affairs is rather peculiar, given that organizational studies represent an applied science devoted to both understanding organizations in a theoretical sense and helping them become more effective. Much of the research and writing on organizational science is done in business schools (certainly not all of it), further emphasizing the applied nature of research in the area. Despite this applied focus, there is a huge relevance gap between organizational research and management practice (Rynes, Bartunek, & Daft, 2001). Collaborative management research could be used to bridge this gap (cf. Amabile et al., 2001; Bartunek & Louis, 1992).

The reasons for this state of affairs, from the researcher's point of view, are well known:

- Building effective collaborative relationships with managers takes time and effort and makes the entire process of conducting research much more complicated and expensive.
- Sometimes, researchers are interested in exposing issues or problems with the ways managers are leading, which managers would prefer remain hidden. We must recognize that the actors in collaborative management research may not have identical agendas (cf. Woodman, Bingham, & Yuan, in press).
- Companies frequently wish to safeguard insights from research as sources of competitive advantage, making the task of disseminating knowledge more difficult; without permission to publish, the incentives for undertaking collaborative research decline dramatically.

- Managers don't understand the requirements for scientific rigor in research (Woodman et al., in press), making it difficult to conduct studies in ways that don't benefit the company directly and immediately (using control groups that are not exposed to interventions, for example); this leads to lower publication rates and more ridicule from the traditional research community that controls the majority of the journals in the field.

From the manager's point of view, the following reasons apply:

- Researchers come to the table with an agenda, a specific set of questions they are interested in answering, which may be of little or no interest to the company.
- Researchers are interested in publishing their findings, not in sticking around to make certain that the insights they gained are put to good use.
- Researchers ask the company to bear the costs and disruption of conducting the research, without clear guarantees regarding the usefulness of the work.
- Researchers have been known to publish unflattering reports concerning the companies or leaders they study, exposing those companies or leaders to risk in the eyes of concerned stakeholders.

Considering these issues, it's amazing that collaborative management research takes place at all. The fact that it does points to how critical the problems are that companies need to solve and how important it is for academics to get "inside" the ways companies work in order to fully understand the reasons for the otherwise inexplicable sets of decisions that leaders make. In the long run, the benefits of collaboration outweigh the difficulties and risks. The question therefore is not "Should researchers and managers collaborate in research?" but rather "What is required to make collaborative management research more valuable to the parties involved and,

ultimately, to the beneficiaries of their joint efforts?" In our review of the current state of the field, based in part on the contributions we have received as editors of the Elsevier series *Research in Organizational Change and Development* over the past 19 years, we have come to the conclusion that the answer to the latter question is to make collaborative efforts more rigorous, reflective, and relevant. Let us define what we mean by each term.

RIGOR IN COLLABORATIVE MANAGEMENT RESEARCH

Scientists have not always agreed on standards for research design and data analysis. Campbell and Stanley (1966), and later Cook, Campbell, and Perracchio (1990), set out a series of principles for designing real-world research experiments under less than the ideal "laboratory" circumstances that continue to be the standard by which submissions to many journals and doctoral theses in the field of management research are judged. Despite familiarity with these principles among the vast majority of researchers in the field, we continue to see submissions that ignore even some of the most basic stipulations put forth by Campbell and Stanley. Here are some recommendations for improving the rigor of collaborative management research.

Data-Driven

On the one hand, there are many researchers who simply lack influence over the sources of their data. These researchers describe what they observe, read, or are told, but do not have "control" over the design of an "experiment" or "quasi-experiment." Even if managers are collaborating in providing these researchers with background data, the reports take the form of case studies rather than quasi-experiments, limiting their generalizability and therefore attractiveness for publication. In other instances, researchers simply don't seem to care about rigor, when steps could easily be taken to improve the objectivity of their observations. Imagine where we would be today if the Hawthorne researchers hadn't bothered to turn the lights back down to verify their hypothesis that lighting and productivity were related!

Multiple Methodologies

Rigor, in our view, does not mean that researchers must employ experimental research designs and methodologies. Today, more researchers are applying alternative scientific methodologies that do not fit the experimental mode. Using ethnographic, anthropological, or grounded research methods, these researchers gather data by rigorous observation (e.g., Glaser & Strauss, 1967; Lincoln & Guba, 1985; Strauss & Corbin, 1998; Yin, 2003). Underlying these methodologies is the belief that "intervention" in an organization by the researcher or manager would change the natural dynamics that are under study. Because the fruits of their labors are captured in the form of their own interpretations of the behaviors they observe, fellow scientists applying traditional standards sometimes cry foul at the subjective nature of these methodologies. In the view of these more conservative critics, two researchers conducting observations and drawing inferences from them could arrive at entirely different explanations and conclusions. These same critics contend that while such studies make interesting reading, they are not defensible from a scientific standpoint.

In our view, the problem is not that scientists produce case studies or interpretive works instead of conducting experiments to test hypotheses. Case studies and interpretive works are valuable because they supply the rich understanding of organizations that allow us to fashion more appropriate, interesting, and potentially useful hypotheses to test. The problem is that the same researchers who do case studies or interpretive research rarely follow up their efforts with more rigorous hypothesis testing to prove the validity of their assertions (Woodman et al., in press). Furthermore, scientists rarely build on one another's work, so no one else tests the hypotheses either. No methodology is perfect for conducting research in an organizational setting; each has its flaws and drawbacks. Multiple methodologies are required to provide a truly rigorous explanation of behaviors (cf., Lawler, Mohrman, Mohrman, Ledford, & Cummings, 1985; Woodman, 1989).

The issue of rigor is not only the concern of scientists; rather, managers and scientists must be co-evaluators of research quality. It is clear that managers have concerns about rigor as well, in the form of justifying their time and expenditures in conducting collaborative research. Scientists who have done little more than pilfer data with no concern for their application to improving the effectiveness of the organizations involved have done a great disservice to their managerial colleagues as well as to future generations of researchers who need to establish trust with their managerial counterparts. To executives, rigorous studies that demonstrate the link between practices and performance are valuable because they justify significant expenditures on training, work redesign, process reengineering, executive development, and other improvement methodologies. Forward-thinking managers recognize that unsubstantiated investments are not likely to be continued, and that long-term commitments are often required to produce results. Some of the best collaborative research has been the result of collaboration between scholars and managers who want objective scientific verification that their theories and practices are beneficial (e.g., Adler & Shani, 2001; Amabile et al., 2001).

Reliability Across Settings

The effort required to mount and execute a collaborative management study in a single organization is significant. That may be why we see so few studies that test the same hypothesis or program in multiple settings. As we know from Campbell and Stanley, extraneous variables can influence the effects we observe in a single experimental setting. A charismatic leader may be able to pull off a difficult reorganization that improves bottom-line performance, while a more ordinary executive would fail under the same circumstances, for example. Before we accept reorganization as an antidote to performance problems, we need to understand how robust the intervention is, and what factors might temper its impact. Such understanding can only be achieved via replication in different settings, where extraneous variables are studied and their effects noted.

Co-evaluation

Scientists can also augment rigor by subjecting their data and conclusions to objective review and interpretation. Here, the spirit of collaborative research should extend not only to managerial counterparts, but also to other scientists. As an example of how different things can look from a managerial perspective, recall that the T-group movement was born because scientists allowed their "subjects"—in this case group participants— to listen to their debriefing of group dynamics. The scientists' interpretations of behavior were quite different than the explanations offered by the participants themselves. If the scientists hadn't been interested in listening to what the participants had to say, not only would our knowledge of groups not have advanced; we probably would have been misled. Today, scientists are quick to point out why employees or managers do what they do; but how often do they risk asking employees or managers to confirm their explanations?

Even if subjects are not queried, there is no excuse for not reaching out to a professional colleague to review one's preliminary analysis and findings. The journals provide editors who perform this function, of course, but only very late in the process. The decision to accept or reject an article for publication is usually made long after a study has been concluded. As editors ourselves, we often find ourselves asking authors to collect additional data that would require reopening contact with a system. Sometimes, this is simply impossible, as the conditions that supported collaboration or data collection no longer exist. The best time to enhance rigor is during a study, not afterward.

Causality

The subject of causality is well understood among researchers and is certainly tied to our notions of scientific rigor (Kerlinger & Lee, 2000). Two events that happen to occur in roughly the same timeframe are not necessarily related. A new leader may take over an organization, proclaim an aspiring vision, and then see performance begin to improve. The link between the leader's vision and performance improvement cannot be drawn simply because one followed the other in time. Experimental or quasi-experimental methods must be employed to prove that a valid link between the two exists. We do no favors to executives by reaching erroneous conclusions. Especially as scientists, we owe executives the truth that can only be obtained through rigorous testing of popular theories and assumptions.

Underlying Mechanisms

If we find, through rigorous experimentation, that vision and performance are indeed related, we should go further to make certain that we understand the underlying mechanisms that support the relationship. By digging deeper to understand how things really work, we may find that visions that specify clear behaviors and goals are more effective in producing performance effects than broad aspirational statements, for example. As researchers, applying more rigor to our studies will help leaders understand what it really takes for them to succeed.

Publishable

Finally, we should note that efforts to publish the results of collaborative management research do usually invoke certain safeguards as far as rigor is concerned. Good journals and reviewers will require that authors describe their methodology in detail, publish their data, and clarify their assumptions. To our earlier point regarding co-evaluation, only so much can be done to improve the rigor of research reporting after the research is concluded. Nevertheless, meeting professional standards for publication requires that authors pass a hurdle that at some level protects us all from being influenced by shoddy work or false assumptions.

In sum, we define rigor with regard to collaborative management research in both scientific and practical terms. For our purposes here, *rigor is upholding the standards of scientific proof in assessing the impact of leadership, management practices, or organizational arrangements on organizational performance.* Collaborative management research that fails to meet this dual standard falls short of what is required to sustain future efforts to improve organizational performance in a way that relies upon joint efforts between organizations and academia. Table 27.1 summarizes our views concerning

Table 27.1   Elements of Rigorous Collaborative Management Research

Data-driven	Well supported by objective sources of data, preferably both qualitative and quantitative, that tie behaviors or practices to organizational performance.
Multiple methodologies	A combination of experimental and unobtrusive methodologies provides the most rigorous explanation for behaviors in natural settings.
Reliability across settings	Test-retest studies in different organizations are especially valuable in confirming the generalizability of results.
Co-evaluation	The immediate collaborative interpretation of data to determine findings. Scientists aren't immune to bias in their observations; using independent co-researchers or even managers to review data and conclusions supports rigor.
Causality	Using experimental or quasi-experimental methods, the existence and directionality of the link between independent and dependent variables should be established.
Underlying mechanisms	In addition to verifying that certain behaviors or practices are related to organizational performance, it is often important to understand why the link exists, as in understanding that lung cancer is the mechanism underlying the link between smoking and mortality rates.
Publishable	Academic standards for publication do help scientists conform to practices that support rigor, such as describing the methodology used to conduct the research in detail, making data public, and subjecting their analysis to objective reviewers.

the elements of rigorous collaborative research.

While this definition is strict (some might argue too strict), the good news, in our view, is that once researchers adopt this definition, achieving the dual standard is not much more difficult than achieving less rigorous research. While more work will go into planning the research on the front end to make certain the dual outcomes are achieved, conducting the research itself and implementing its findings may actually become simpler if both parties see the benefit of more rigor. Researchers will be motivated by the reward of more noteworthy and publishable findings, while managers should find the enhanced attention to the bottom line attractive. We next turn our focus to the issue of reflection in collaborative management research, which can help mitigate single-study issues with regard to rigor.

MORE REFLECTIVE COLLABORATIVE MANAGEMENT RESEARCH

To understand the importance of reflection in collaborative management research, think for a moment about advances that have been achieved in medical research in the same time-frame as collaborative management research. In the past 100 years, medical researchers eliminated smallpox, cured polio, made major advances in fighting cancer, improved survival rates at birth, pioneered new organ transplant techniques, developed joint replacement therapies, and made a host of other major breakthroughs. Would we in management research claim a comparable level of achievement? There are many explanations for why the advances in management research have been fewer and less significant, but one of them, we believe, has to do with how little the work of one management researcher builds on that of another, or alternatively, how little attention we pay to what happens over time in the

organizations we study. Here are some suggestions for making collaborative management research more reflective.

Referential

Researchers are trained early on in their careers to be aware of the work of others in the field and to give credit for ideas to those who invented them. This is more than professional courtesy; understanding the work of others in the field helps one to avoid reinventing the wheel, allows one to build upon the foundations laid by others, and alerts one to truly unique findings that deserve more careful attention and explanation. As Kuhn (1970) points out in *The Structure of Scientific Revolutions,* scientific advancement is not the work of one person, but of many. True revolutions in science occur when a study casts doubt on accepted theory, leading to additional studies that confirm the new view of the world. Such breakthroughs are rare, but always interesting and highly prized. To make such a breakthrough, however, one needs to be aware of accepted theory and research. Paradoxically, in order for collaborative management research to produce interesting breakthroughs in how we think about organizing or leading, we need to build more reflection into our practice.

As editors, we frequently find ourselves reminding young authors especially of classic works in the field, or even of recently published papers relevant to their topic. The quality of research in our field will improve greatly by simply having scientists read more, be more aware of each other's contributions, and build more upon one another's efforts. In addition to moving things forward more rapidly, greater knowledge of others' work will aid authors in detecting patterns that lie hidden in single studies but become evident as broader samples of studies are reviewed.

For example, a single collaborative study into the effects of introducing a quality initiative in an organization may produce disappointing results as measured by only a slight reduction in the number of defects observed. The collaborators could be puzzled by this result unless they compare the situation and conditions of the intervention to similar interventions in other companies to determine what the key differences might have been. Had the collaborators simply published their results without referencing other studies, we would know little more than that the intervention apparently failed; but with the additional step of comparing their own intervention to others, we learn much more about why the failure may have occurred. Armed with that information, new hypotheses can be formulated that shape more effective interventions in the future (e.g., Barnes, Pashby, & Gibbons, 2002; Beard, Woodman, & Moesel, 1998; Holweg, Disney, Holmstrom, & Smaros, 2005; Sommer, 1983).

Historical Impact

Another step that collaborative researchers can take to improve the reflective quality of their contributions is simply to monitor results over longer periods of time than is customarily the case. Because speed to press is important for a number of reasons, we rarely see studies that measure the impact of an intervention for more than three to six months. We believe that a whole series of interesting articles could be written about the longer-term impacts of interventions by simply returning to the sites of previous studies and analyzing what has occurred in the intervening years. Three-, five-, and 10-year follow-ups would produce truly valuable insights into the transitory and permanent effects of interventions in organizations. Pettigrew, Woodman, and Cameron (2001), among many others, have argued that change processes cannot be adequately captured by cross-sectional, one-time assessments; rather, the field needs more longitudinal work in order to advance.

Co-interpretation

What we think is important at the time of an intervention is frequently not what is important at all in the long run. By working with our collaborative partners over time, we can come to understand the valuable perspective that time adds to our explanations of why things occurred as they did. When we discussed enhancing the rigor of our studies, we advocated co-evaluation, which involved collaboration in reviewing data and reaching conclusions about the impact of an intervention. Co-interpretation is the same idea, just extended out over time. A good example of co-interpretation is provided by the CO-IMPROVE project—a nine-country action research project funded by the European Union that involved company networks of managers and research networks of academics. The researchers were both managing the project and studying it at the same time, according to Coghlan and Coughlan (2005). In their words, "The way the researcher network recorded events, *articulated and discussed interpretations and assumptions* [italics added], enacted cycles of action and reflection and tested reflections in subsequent action ensured methodological rigour" (p. 292).

Community of Practice

The concept of community of practice takes these ideas one step further (see Coghlan & Shani, Chapter 29 in this volume). Dialogue among scholars and practitioners with similar interests enhances the sharing of knowledge and the development of new theories. As studies are conducted in different settings, using different methodologies, or testing different approaches to intervention, there is much to be gained by pausing to reflect jointly on what is being learned. The appreciative inquiry community and the work redesign/sociotechnical systems/large group intervention community are two examples of active virtual gatherings that are collaborative in nature and involve both scholars and practitioners. If Lewin was correct in his assertion that nothing is as practical as a good theory, then communities of practice should be excellent places for practitioners to discuss putting theories to the test. In light of what is discussed, new theories and forms of practice should evolve more rapidly than in the absence of such a community. Collaborative researchers are beginning to formulate communities of practice. The FENIX program at the Stockholm School of Economics has brought scholars and practitioners from around the globe together for live events and virtual discussions (see Adler & Beer, Chapter 26 in this volume). This book may represent the nascent beginning of another community, with membership that overlaps with that of the FENIX group. If the publication of this volume makes it easier for collaborative researchers to know and reference each other's work, it will have served a valuable purpose.

Collection

Publications such as this volume do serve a valuable reflective function in their own right. While individual studies are the foundation for all advancements in our application of theory, collections of studies often allow us to see patterns that might not be visible in a single study. These patterns allow us to formulate new theories, address common challenges, see gaps in our understanding of phenomena, and compare and contrast results across settings.

Repeated Application

Finally, repeated applications over time in different settings add both rigor and reflection to our work as collaborative researchers. Through repeated application, combined with reflection, we learn how to fine-tune interventions, account for discrepancies in

results across settings, and understand how the context of an intervention affects its outcomes. Medical researchers would never support the widespread distribution of a new drug based on success in a single patient or even a single panel study. Multiple, repeated studies on different groups over time, investigating doses, demographics, interactions with other medications, and so forth are required before a drug is allowed to be widely prescribed. As scientists, we need to learn to build upon our own and others' work so that we can be more confident in the medicine we are recommending to leaders of organizations.

In sum, we define reflection in collaborative management research as the process of jointly and collectively creating new insights and theories by referring to the related work of others and the investigation of intervention effects over time. Table 27.2 summarizes our views on the elements of reflective collaborative management research. Next, we turn our attention to the topic of relevance in collaborative management research.

MORE RELEVANT COLLABORATIVE MANAGEMENT RESEARCH

If collaborative research is to demonstrate its full potential value in terms of being mutually beneficial in the current business environment, researchers must become much more concerned about improving organizational performance than they are today. In their review of needed research in the organizational change and development field, Pettigrew et al. (2001) argued that insufficient attention has been paid to connecting change interventions with performance outcomes. Few studies done under the banner of collaborative management research that we have seen would provide enough return to pay for themselves, let alone make a significant difference to the bottom line.

Table 27.2   Elements of Reflective Collaborative Management Research

Referential	Built on past research and theory; recognizing and building upon the contributions of others; adding weight to current conclusions through the pattern of previous findings.
Historical impact	Observing the long-term impact of interventions; following through on the effects of previous efforts; understanding what did and what didn't endure.
Co-interpretation	The collaborative reflection on events and outcomes over time to assess impact and formulate theory; coauthoring accounts to ensure balanced representation in historical interpretations.
Community of practice	Dialogue among groups of scholars and practitioners with similar interests leading to repeated experiments using different methodologies in different settings, and ultimately to joint reflection leading to the formulation of new theories.
Collection	Publishing collections of studies on similar topics with the intention of reflecting on consistencies and inconsistencies or patterns that advance understanding of the dynamics involved; meta-analysis of results.
Repeated application	Learning about underlying mechanisms from repeated application of an intervention or methodology in different organizational settings; using collaborative approaches to bring together networks of practitioners and researchers to derive deeper understanding from comparing results achieved in different settings.

ROI

Companies today cannot afford to squander time or resources looking for answers that promise marginal improvements in performance. Most companies in competitive global markets have been forced to adopt strategies that include both cutting costs aggressively and finding ways to grow the top line at rates that exceed the cost of capital. Neither of these tasks is easy, and both demand whatever attention managers can give to them in addition to running the day-to-day business. Taking additional time and resources to invest in collaborative management research only makes sense if there is a high enough return to offset the costs involved. Moreover, because of short-term financial pressures, such returns will need to be realized in months rather than years. Researchers who understand the harsh realities of corporate existence in the 21st century will design their studies with greater relevance when it comes to improving organizational performance

quickly and significantly. Because we are discussing collaborative management research, rather than simply action research, it shouldn't come as a surprise that we place return on investment (ROI) at the top of our list of elements relating to the relevance of this research. If our practitioner partners cannot explain "what's in it for me" in terms that are compelling from a business perspective, the collaboration will be short-lived, the research will be less interesting, and its impact will not be as large.

Practical

We continue along this vein by suggesting that good collaborative management research should be practical, meaning that the effort to conduct the research should not impose a severe financial burden upon the company or take forever to conduct. In an age of increased attention to quarterly results and the bottom line, we need to think about parsing out our inquiries to show greater short-term value at less initial cost. It's not that we should avoid complex opportunities that involve spending more money or time, but only that we should find the right setting in which to conduct our research. The setting should drive the practicality of the inquiry; small organizations don't have large budgets or the capability of dedicating many people to work part-time or full-time as assistants to the researcher. Larger organizations are better off financially but still impose rigid controls and standards on what efforts will be funded. It's probably a good idea to collaborate in building a business plan for the research as well as an experimental design (cf. Mohrman, Mohrman, Cohen, & Winby, Chapter 24 in this volume).

Codetermined

If our research is to be viewed as important by executives, they should be involved in codetermining the goals of the research as well as how it is carried out (Mohrman, Gibson, & Mohrman, 2001). This is probably the single most defining characteristic of collaborative management research and should therefore need little explanation here. Yet time and again we continue to receive manuscripts for studies that are proclaimed to be collaborative on topics that it is simply hard to believe are of interest to any executive. What collaboration there was in the eyes of the researchers was probably not experienced as true collaboration by the managers in these studies. To have the greatest impact and longevity, our work should be aligned with the most important goals of the enterprise and measured by the metrics that the organization deems most important to its success. When both parties are working the same agenda, the quality and impact of collaboration are remarkably superior.

Re-applicable

Achieving success in one demonstration or in addressing a single issue is good; creating ideas and approaches that are re-applicable is better. When we learned that groups are capable of making better decisions than individuals if they are facilitated properly, for example, we didn't just celebrate success in the laboratory. That knowledge has been reapplied to groups in corporations, government, and nongovernmental organizations; it has been applied to work teams and to boards of directors; and it has been applied in countries around the world (Barner, 2006; Ellis, Bell, Ployhart, Hollenbeck, & Ilgen, 2005; Mathieu, Heffner, Goodwin, Salas, & Cannon-Bowers, 2000; Offermann & Spiros, 2001). Researchers are building on the theories developed in small groups as they conduct large group interventions and even as they work with virtual decision-making groups on the Internet (e.g., Jarman, 2005). We urge authors to consider the implications of their work beyond the immediate application they describe; it surprises us how difficult an exercise this apparently can be for even some of our more thoughtful colleagues.

Teachable

From an organizational standpoint, it's important that the insights gained from collaborative management research be teachable and transferable to others. Usually, studies are conducted in departments or single locations of large companies. If the results of the studies are interesting and worthwhile, there will naturally be an interest in applying the results elsewhere. Beyond the originating organization, others in the community of practice will want to adapt the approach to their own use. Both internal and external application require that the approach be teachable to others with no more than a reasonable investment in training. Some interventions are designed to be conducted only by the person who invented them, or only by those whom the inventor "certifies" as competent through some long and expensive process. For ideas to be useful and gather momentum, the roadblock of single ownership and the requirement for extreme amounts of training need to be eliminated. We sometimes refuse to publish articles in *Research in Organizational Change and Development* that are clearly self-serving attempts by the authors to advertise their expertise rather than share their knowledge with others.

Face Valid

Face validity is an important consideration in the dissemination and application of research findings. The ideas have to make sense to the layman and must be neither too simplistic nor too complicated to address the issues or opportunities involved. Elaborate theories with complicated multistep interventions to address what appear to be simple issues don't make sense to the average manager. Neither do one-size-fits-all solutions to complicated problems that managers have studied and tried to address for years. Collaboration is a vital step in avoiding over-complicating or oversimplifying the solutions that our research suggests.

Interesting

It is important that we endeavor to make our research more readable and interesting. Much of what we see in first-draft papers isn't written for popular consumption. We understand the need to impress our academic colleagues and to meet standards for research rigor in what we write. But we also strongly advocate that at least part of every manuscript pertaining to interventions that are intended to improve organizations be readable by the average executive with no research training. It's also a valuable exercise to see if we can describe our study and findings in words that our families would understand. If we can clarify why our findings are novel or our approach is better than what others are doing currently, so much the better.

True Significance

A related issue here is that we overreport inconsequential findings. We think that one of the reasons management research is not given the attention it deserves by executives is that each of our studies is portrayed as the most important study of its kind ever undertaken. Eventually, the noise of our self-adulation drowns out the credibility of our message. By setting a higher standard for what we publish and report, we could expect greater attention to be given to our most important findings. In a way, this is what makes the *New England Journal of Medicine* such a great journal; when a study makes it into that journal, the public knows that it is important and relevant.

Specific

Finally, the relevance of any research is enhanced when its application to a specific setting of interest can be demonstrated. By repeating studies in different industries, types of organizations, geographies, or conditions we can broaden the number of people who will find the research of interest (Adler & Shani, 2001; Pettigrew et al., 2001).

In sum, we define relevant collaborative management research as research that (a) is practical and addresses important organizational issues, (b) is useable by competent organizational members, and (c) has clear implications for organizational performance. Table 27.3 summarizes our views concerning the elements of relevant collaborative research.

SUMMARY: RIGOROUS, REFLECTIVE, AND RELEVANT RESEARCH

We have laid out a few of the elements of rigorous, reflective, and relevant research for consideration by collaborative management

Table 27.3 Elements of Relevant Collaborative Management Research

ROI	The approach has demonstrated returns that make the collaborative effort worthwhile.
Practical	The interventions and studies can be supported economically and carried out in a straightforward fashion within a reasonable timeframe.
Codetermined	The research goals, design, and ultimate impact are jointly conceived and aligned with the issues that leaders and other stakeholders care the most about.
Re-applicable	The approach is generalizable to a broader array of organizations or settings; the theories have relevance to a broader set of issues governed by similar dynamics.
Teachable	The method or approach can be taught to others in a reasonable amount of time and eventually carried out by the average person with the proper training and guidance.
Face valid	The approach is sensible and appropriate, taken at face value, for addressing the issue; it is neither too simple nor too complex.
Interesting	The approach promises a new solution to a long-standing issue; the approach is simpler, cheaper, more effective or has some other performance-related quality that makes it more attractive than the current approach.
True significance	The importance of results is not inflated.
Specific	The approach has demonstrated relevance to a specific situation, industry, type of organization, or geography.

researchers in the hope that by doing so, we can enhance the quality of the work that these researchers are doing and, ultimately, the advancement of the field. We have noted that a community of practice accelerates the sharing of ideas and the pace of learning in an area, and we hope that this chapter and volume contribute to the evolution of a community of practice for collaborative management research.

What remains to be said is perhaps obvious, but we will say it anyway. There is a great deal of work to be done to elevate the standards of practice in the field of collaborative management research. Much of what we read today falls short of meeting standards we would like to see in terms of rigor, reflection, or relevance. One reason for this is simply that collaborative management research is still an emerging field; we have a lot to learn about doing it, and a long way to go before it is widely accepted and embraced, particularly

by executives. Another reason, we believe, is that we aren't pushing ourselves hard enough to do the things that are within our grasp to do. None of the suggestions we have made in this chapter are unreasonable, at least in our view, especially if they are built into the design of research efforts on the front end. Most involve a little extra time and effort, but not a lot of expense or difficulty.

The consequence of continuing to fall short of the quality mark on these three dimensions of rigor, reflection, and relevance is that the field will advance more slowly or not at all. The "social capital" of the field with executives is already limited and further strained by experiences many have had of difficulties in collaborating on studies with academics. The rewards executives experience for collaborating with us can and should be worth the price they have to pay, and it's our responsibility to pay attention to their perspective and needs to ensure that the rewards are sufficient to engender positive regard for our practice. In most cases, there is no one to hold us accountable to this standard other than ourselves. As members of an emerging community of practice, we should take responsibility for our common future by adding to the stock of positive social capital in the way we do our work.

Finally, we want to make the point that we see no trade-offs among achieving rigor, reflection, and relevance in our work. Often, when a triad of concepts is presented, theorists like to play each dimension off the others to understand why achieving one point of the triangle takes one farther away from the other two. We don't see that being the case here; in fact, we find the three concepts overlapping and reinforcing one another. Greater rigor adds to relevance; greater reflection leads to rigor; greater relevance provides more incentive for reflection; and so forth. One shouldn't have to concentrate on meeting one of these standards at the expense of the others.

As exciting as the field of collaborative management research is today, we imagine a future in which the findings of our studies are even more rigorous, reflective, and relevant than they are today. In that future, we see the solutions to many long-standing challenges facing executives and managers, and the emergence of even more exciting questions to be addressed by researchers.

NOTES

1. We are using the term *collaborative management research* in a manner consistent with the definition provided by Pasmore, Stymne, Shani, Mohrman, and Adler, Chapter 1 in this volume.

2. For good overviews of these historical developments, see Burnes, in press; Cummings and Worley, 2005, pp. 6–12; French and Bell, 1999, pp. 32–54.

REFERENCES

Adler, N., & Shani, A. B. (Rami). (2001). In search of an alternative framework for the creation of actionable knowledge: Table-tennis research at Ericsson. In R. W. Woodman & W. A. Pasmore (Eds.), *Research in organizational change and development* (Vol. 13, pp. 43–79). Oxford, UK: Elsevier Science.

Amabile, T. M., Patterson, C., Mueller, J., Wojcik, T., Odomirok, P. W., Marsh, M., et al. (2001). Academic-practitioner collaboration in management research: A case of cross-profession collaboration. *Academy of Management Journal, 44*(2), 418–431.

Barner, R. (2006). Managing complex team interventions. *Team Performance Management, 12*(1/2), 44–54.

Barnes, T., Pashby, I., & Gibbons, A. (2002). Effective university-industry interaction: A multi-case evaluation of collaborative R&D projects. *European Management Journal, 20*(June), 272–285.

Bartunek, J. M., & Louis, M. R. (1992). Insider/outsider research teams: Collaboration across diverse perspectives. *Journal of Management Inquiry, 1*(6), 101–110.

Beard, J. W., Woodman, R. W., & Moesel, D. (1998). Using behavioral modification to change attendance patterns in the high-performance, high-commitment environment. In R. W. Woodman & W. A. Pasmore (Eds.), *Research in organizational change and development* (Vol. 11, pp. 183–234). Stamford, CT: JAI Press.

Boud, D., Cressey, P., & Docherty, P. (Eds.). (2006). *Productive reflection at work.* London: Routledge.

Burnes, B. (in press). Kurt Lewin and the Harwood studies: The foundations of OD. *Journal of Applied Behavioral Science.*

Campbell, D. T., & Stanley, J. C. (1966). *Experimental and quasi-experimental designs for research.* Chicago: Rand McNally.

Coghlan, D., & Coughlan, P. (2005). Collaborative research across borders and boundaries: Action research insights from the CO-IMPROVE project. In R. W. Woodman & W. A. Pasmore (Eds.), *Research in organizational change and development* (Vol. 15, pp. 272–295). Oxford, UK: Elsevier.

Cook, T. D., Campbell, D. T., & Perracchio, L. (1990). Quasi experimentation. In M. D. Dunnette & L. M. Hough (Eds.), *Handbook of industrial & organizational psychology* (Vol. 1, 2nd ed., pp. 491–576). Palo Alto, CA: Consulting Psychologists Press.

Cummings, T. G., & Worley, C. G. (2005). *Organization development and change* (8th ed.). Mason, OH: South-Western.

Ellis, A. P. J., Bell, B. S., Ployhart, R. E., Hollenbeck, J. R., & Ilgen, D. R. (2005). An evaluation of generic teamwork skills training with action teams: Effects on cognitive and skill-based outcomes. *Personnel Psychology, 58*(3), 641–672.

French, W. L., & Bell, C. H. (1999). *Organization development: Behavioral science interventions for organization improvement* (6th ed.). Upper Saddle River, NJ: Prentice-Hall.

Glaser, B. G., & Strauss, A. L. (1967). *The discovery of grounded theory: Strategies for qualitative research.* New York: Aldine de Gruyter.

Holweg, M., Disney, S., Holmstrom, J., & Smaros, J. (2005). Supply chain collaboration: Making sense of the strategy continuum. *European Management Journal, 23*(April), 170–181.

Jarman, R. (2005). When success isn't everything: Case studies of two virtual teams. *Group Decision and Negotiation, 14*(4), 333–354.

Kerlinger, F. N., & Lee, H. B. (2000). *Foundations of behavioral research* (4th ed.). Fort Worth, TX: Holt, Rinehart and Winston.

Kuhn, T. S. (1970). *The structure of scientific revolutions.* Chicago: University of Chicago Press.

Lawler, E. E., Mohrman, A. M., Jr., Mohrman, S. A., Ledford, G. E., & Cummings, T. G. (1985). *Doing research that is useful for theory and practice.* San Francisco: Jossey-Bass.

Lincoln, Y. S., & Guba, E. G. (1985). *Naturalistic inquiry.* Beverly Hills, CA: Sage.

Mathieu, J. E., Heffner, T. S., Goodwin, G. F., Salas, E., & Cannon-Bowers, J. A. (2000). The influence of shared mental models on team process and performance. *Journal of Applied Psychology, 85*(2), 273–284.

Mohrman, S. A., Gibson, C. B., & Mohrman, A. M., Jr. (2001). Doing research that is useful to practice: A model and empirical exploration. *Academy of Management Journal, 44*(2), 357–375.

Offermann, L. R., & Spiros, R. K. (2001). The science and practice of team development: Improving the link. *Academy of Management Journal, 44*(2), 376–392.

Pettigrew, A. M., Woodman, R. W., & Cameron, K. S. (2001). Studying organizational change and development: Challenges for future research. *Academy of Management Journal, 44*(4), 607–713.

Rynes, S. L., Bartunek, J. M., & Daft, R. L. (2001). Across the great divide: Knowledge creation and transfer between practitioners and academics. *Academy of Management Journal, 44*(2), 340–355.

Sommer, R. (1983). Action research is formative: Research at the Saskatchewan hospital, 1957–61. *Journal of Applied Behavioral Science, 19*(12), 427–438.

Strauss, A. L., & Corbin, J. M. (1998). *Basics of qualitative research: Techniques and procedures for developing grounded theory* (2nd ed.). Thousand Oaks, CA: Sage.

Woodman, R. W. (1989). Evaluation research on organizational change: Arguments for a "combined paradigm" approach. In R. W. Woodman & W. A. Pasmore (Eds.), *Research in organizational change and development* (Vol. 3, pp. 161–180). Greenwich, CT: JAI Press.

Woodman, R. W., Bingham, J. B., & Yuan, F. (in press). Assessing organization development and change interventions. In T. G. Cummings (Ed.), *Handbook of organization development and change.* Thousand Oaks, CA: Sage.

Yin, R. K. (2003). *Case study research: Design and methods* (Vol. 5, 3rd ed.). Thousand Oaks, CA: Sage.

CHAPTER 28

Quality and "Actionability"

What Action Researchers Offer From the Tradition of Pragmatism

Hilary Bradbury

ABSTRACT

Actionability refers to people's ability to use knowledge to produce the actions they want. This chapter offers a framework informed by pragmatist thinking and practice for working toward actionability, while simultaneously holding a concern for quality, or rigor and vigor. Because action researchers, who often work within the qualitative paradigm, have been at the forefront of rethinking quality to include actionability, examples are drawn especially from the work of action researchers around the world. Action researchers generate knowledge to be shared with both their client systems and other scholar-practitioners, thus contributing both to scholarship and to practice. Better appreciation for generating action in a context of inquiry is particularly timely as we move away from the duality of knowing and doing that has plagued conventional social science since Descartes.

The current revival of pragmatism (Dickstein, 1999) offers an opportunity to think anew about quality in social science, especially with regard to how we might once again integrate concern for actionability into our work. Actionability refers to people's ability to use knowledge to produce the actions they want. As Argyris (1996) has noted, concern for actionability is usually lacking in organizational science as a result of the pursuit of conventional notions of validity. This chapter emerges from the world of action research practice. Action research is an umbrella term for varied practices that, as the term suggests, include cycles of reflection on experience that lead to desired experiments and action. In this chapter, the conceptualization of actionability, a central concern for action researchers, is informed by action-research-based planning (Friedmann, 1987), community medicine (Mendenhall & Doherty, 2003), social work

(Baldwin, 2001; Chiu, 2003), feminist activism (Lennie, Hatcher, & Morgan, 2003; Maguire, 2001), nursing (Barrett, 2001), business (Kristiansen & Blouch-Poulsen, 2004; Pasmore, 2001; Senge & Scharmer, 2001), sustainability (Bradbury & Waage, 2005), education (Zeichner, 2001), and majority world—also referred to as developing world—perspectives and institutional collaborations (e.g., Brown, Bammer, Batliwala, & Kunreuther, 2003; Hughes & Yuan, 2005; Pimbert & Wakeford, 2003).

This chapter proceeds by first describing conventional validity/quality criteria in their social-historical context, followed by a review of pragmatist philosophy, which informs concepts of quality related to actionability. The contribution of the chapter then lies in offering a parsimonious framework for conceptualizing quality as actionability, which is illustrated by an action research practice called the "learning history," chosen because it draws on practices familiar to qualitative researchers.

THE HISTORICAL CONTEXT OF CONVENTIONAL VALIDITY CRITERIA

In 17th-century England, King Charles II sponsored the formation of the Royal Society of London. Its quiet beginnings belied the profound effects that have since spread over centuries and continents. Membership in the Royal Society was limited to male aristocrats and landed gentry for whom "credit" (credibility) of knowledge was based on the honor of its members. All were independently wealthy and agreed to use of the principles outlined by Sir Francis Bacon and informed by the scientific methods of Galileo, Kepler, and others. Thus, the Royal Society embodied notions in Bacon's writings of an academy that would interpret nature. Within a century, sister academies had developed across Western Europe. The historian Stephen Shapin (1999) explains how the gap between theory and practice was institutionalized in these academies. Importantly, the knowledge creation of nonaristocrats (and all women) was considered to lack "credit" because, unlike aristocrats, whose technical knowledge was now developing rapidly, women and the less privileged were seen to be compromised by their financial dependence on others and thus could not be "disinterested." As action researcher Tom Wakeford points out (Pimbert & Wakeford, 2003), the academies thus put into effect an abstract knowledge system at the expense of "contextualized know-how" and simply discounted other competing knowledge systems, despite their longevity and usefulness (e.g., Micronesian navigational systems, indigenous calendars, "women's ways of knowing"). Theories that were deemed to have credit or quality were proven in the quiet chambers of the Academy, in front of its members. Proofs were empirical, hence the Society motto: "*nullus in verba*" (nothing [proved] by words). Largely centered on the laws of physics, the experiments that were deemed valid, according to the review of Society peers (hence peer review), were not ones that dealt much with the complex dynamics of social systems. Moreover, concern for experimentation was eclipsed by insistence on explanation and prediction with the help of mathematical models, which became the ideal after Newton. Unlike others less financially independent, these male aristocrats had no need to use their knowledge to provide for their needs. Successful Society members gained in social-academic rank and not in financial standing. Many of these key characteristics continue in the standards by which current academia decides which work is credible and which lacks quality. Slowly and surely, the very parameters of what constituted knowledge shrank. As Chandler and Torbert (2003) argue persuasively, knowledge became circumscribed to those facts about the past that could be modeled mathematically. Moreover, in a sense best described by Foucault's theory of power (stated simply: Something is really powerful when you don't even permit that an alternative exists), this quietist and aristocratic orientation to knowledge came to be the last word on what might be considered "quality" in inquiry. The privileging of this account of knowledge was further encased within the historical movement of post-Cartesian duality, which separates and hierarchically privileges thinking as superior to doing. This nexus of vestigial privileged power and Truth has since been assaulted—some might say overturned entirely, at least in the social sciences—by the onslaught of postmodernism in the aftermath of the linguistic turn. And it is within this contested context that action research makes its contribution, suggesting also the importance of the turn to action.

ACTION RESEARCH

The intent of action researchers is to have knowledge develop intersubjectively in a context of practice that engages relevant stakeholders. The result is that theory is grounded and better practice is accomplished. The material-empirical standard ("*nullus in verba*") has been therefore particularly inimical to the work of action researchers. In an often-cited definition, action research is described (Reason & Bradbury, 2001) as

> a participatory process concerned with developing practical knowing in the pursuit of worthwhile human purposes. . . . It seeks to bring together action and reflection, theory and practice, in participation with others, in the pursuit of practical solutions to issues of pressing concern to people. (p. 1)

Examples of action research practices have changed the world in great and small ways. In the business world, the "balanced scorecard" (Kaplan & Norton, 2005), the impact of which has reverberated widely, was first developed as an action research

project over a number of years by professors based in the Harvard Business School. Their work began as an effort to work closely with students and clients as they grappled with the need to account differently in the midst of organizational change. Their work brought multiple stakeholder perspectives more directly into the financial decision making of the company, thereby facilitating and enriching feedback mechanisms. New theory of accounting and practice have ensued and garnered significant support in contemporary companies.

In development work, the action research of Mohammed Yunus, founder of the Grameen Bank and originator of the practice of microlending, has recently earned a Nobel Prize. A recent report (Brown, 2002) from Harvard's Hauser Center, also an action research center, describes the work: "Yunus tested the hypothesis that accountability to peers might replace collateral as an incentive for poor borrowers to repay small loans, and helped create the practice innovations for a microcredit movement that now serves millions of borrowers around the world" (p. 32). This neat account, neat in the sense that it portrays quite nontraditional research in the familiar language of "hypothesis testing," suggests an orientation to research that is aimed at improving participants' lives. We have learned that Yunus's work resulted from his personal experience. Returning after completing a doctorate in the United States, he was distraught by the poverty and helplessness in his native Bangladesh. He discovered that just a few dollars could change compatriots' lives, but sought a sustainable solution. Rethinking the rules of how new enterprises are financed, Yunus went on to develop microlending. In so doing, he changed our theory of why loans are repaid and has profoundly influenced the lending practices of global bodies such as the World Bank, as well as the borrowing practices of those who had been heretofore left out of the economy altogether, especially the groups of women who originally participated and honed the practice. Though quite different, these examples both suggest core, ideal elements of action research. Action research is grounded in lived experience, it responds to a real need that people have, and it is developed in partnership with these people—as exemplified by the students/clients and the poor compatriots above. It addresses significant needs and develops new ways of seeing/interpreting the world (i.e., theory) and working with (rather than simply studying) people, thereby using methods that are appropriate to the audience and participants at hand. Finally, action research seeks to develop needed structures to allow for follow-up or institutionalization of new practices in its wake.

ACTION RESEARCH AND QUALITATIVE INQUIRY

Action researchers design their projects overall in ways that can at first appear to be indistinguishable from qualitative designs that are also field-based, longitudinal, and engaged. Qualitative researchers on the whole, however, seem to hold to the separation between academic researchers and their participants. There is often not the primary purpose of actionability but of producing academic writing. Multiple qualitative research methods, however, may be used by both (e.g., interviewing, focus groups, social network data gathering) and combined as deemed appropriate, given the aims of people involved. In the course of inquiry, action researchers might also include network analysis and surveys (or other quantitative anchors), depending on how best to accomplish the outcomes deemed necessary by those involved in the research.

Action research, qualitative—especially constructivist—approaches to inquiry, and critical theory overlap significantly, sometimes to the point of being inseparable (Lincoln, 2001). Each research paradigm seeks to empower research subjects to influence decision making

for their own aspirations. They can share a mandate for social justice and accept considerable rupture among traditional divisions of objectivity and subjectivity.

Key differences between action research and nonaction (or curiosity-driven rather than need-driven) qualitative work also lie in the way in which researchers from each paradigm work with others. In action research, the distinction between researchers and subjects may become quite blurred—indeed, that is often the goal for some action researchers—in the course of what is usually a lengthy, collaborative relationship. Additionally, there is a different relative emphasis on the importance of action and its relationship to conceptual insight. These key differences allow for action research to offer an alternative to the trenchant gap between traditional research and its application (Wells, 2000). Most efforts to describe the gap (e.g., Kirk, 1979), perhaps ironically, continually reestablish it, by underscoring the disconnect between research and application. Research has traditionally been assumed to occur in a different domain from application, and practice is left to "practitioners," who, by definition, are not researchers. Strategies for enhancing appropriate use of research stress the importance of new institutional emphasis on forging closer bonds between the fragmented spheres of knowledge generation and knowledge application. As action research is research *with,* rather than *on,* practitioners—who in many instances become co-researchers themselves—in effect, action research bypasses the tradiitional, constructed separation between research and application. Action research is therefore not a form of translational or applied research; instead, it is an integrative research in which action is informed by reflective practice. Table 28.1 contrasts primary foci among qualitative, quantitative, and action research approaches during the research process. Needless to say, researchers vary as to how many of these modes they

Table 28.1   Primary Foci at Different Stages of the Research

	Qualitative	*Action Research*	*Quantitative*
Research design	What is interesting?	What is useful?	What can be proven?
Data-gathering method	Participation-observation	Insider/outsider team development	Noncontamination
Data analysis	Textual	Participatory	Statistical
Validation	Interrater reliability	Dialogue and application meetings	External validity
Quality	Credibility	Actionability	Validity
Audience	Fellow academics	Insider audience and wider stakeholders in context, and scholarly practitioner audience	Fellow academics

encompass. Torbert suggests (Rooke & Torbert, 2001) that the more competent a researcher becomes with developing her own as well as generating others' inquiry skills, or action logics, the more successful she can be in bridging inquiry and action. In other words, there may well be a developmental component to the work of transitioning from curiosity-based to action-oriented inquiry.

GROUNDING ACTIONABILITY IN PRAGMATIST PHILOSOPHY

For action research to be deemed "good," or worth the time and trouble expended, it must contribute to desired or positive action. This approach to judging action research is based on a philosophy of practice. It builds upon the concept of "actionability" as the core of quality in action research. Actionability distinguishes between people knowing about something and their being able to produce that which they desire by using their knowledge. For example, contrast a conventional approach to diabetes management that informs people to limit their high-glycemic intake and increase exercise. An action

research approach does not simply supply information on best practices; instead, in this case, it is designed to bring diabetics together, usually with their family and support system, offering a chance to reflect on the instances in which eating habits are not conducive to goals, and through that, facilitating the development of coping strategies (Mendenhall & Doherty, 2003). We may say that the more actionable an action research project is, the more it has succeeded in helping people systematically meet their goals for sustained desired practice. Simultaneously, new theories of practice are developed. Needless to say, any one simple example of action research may contain some but not all ideal action research components. Bradbury and Reason have suggested (2001) that the primary criterion for what constitutes quality in action research must first and foremost connect with the goal that the co-inquirers hold. One might therefore say that the primary "rule" in approaching quality within the practice of action research is to be aware of the choices one is making and their consequences for actionability.

Actionability, however, does not get much attention in conventional research, which is more often judged on its validity through rigorous, usually quantitative, methods focused greatly on internal validity. As noted at the start, society has not always judged its research in this way. The classical Greeks—who have had great influence on how we think and what we study today—operated with holistic notions of *praxis*, *phronesis* and *poiesis*.[1] Praxis, a term we have taken into our philosophical lexicon, joins reflection with an ability to produce desired outcomes. It lies at the heart of endeavors such as experiential learning (Kolb, 1984) or action science (Argyris, Putnam, & Smith, 1987). Praxis is judged by the quality of the links created between experimentation with new ideas and their generation and conceptualization. The pragmatic tradition—a philosophy that Americans are credited with impressing upon the world—similarly works with notions of praxis as it equates truth with what truth can accomplish, rather than an abstract conception of truth.

Action research is a way of working in the arena of social science that is fully consistent with, and in many instances is, the direct result of a philosophically pragmatic orientation (cf. Lewin, 1951). As such, it's helpful to review the fundamentals of pragmatism to articulate afresh the fundamentals of action research, even as it expresses itself in a myriad of practices.

Axiomatic to pragmatism is that inquiry starts with lived experience in response to a need and that the treatment of truth claims is contingent and contextual.

William James is credited with first using the term in a lecture in 1898 and writes in *Pragmatism* (James, 1908/1978) that he builds on his previous ideas of "radical empiricism." By this, he insists that truth is always partial and liable to modification in accord with experience. James is a systems thinker insisting that "radical empiricism takes conjunctive relations at their face value, holding them to be as real as the terms united by them." He is not a materialist (an

important contrast to empiricists of the Academy's tradition); indeed, one of his most popular books is about the varieties of religious experience, which embraces the mystical—the sine qua non of nonmaterial inquiry. His pragmatism followed the main lines of pragmatist methods as conceived by Peirce (Copleston, 1966/1994, p. 334). In essence, James and Peirce offer us an account of truth in which truth does not seek verification outside itself. In this, they depart from rationalists of the Academy and any intellectualists by stressing that truth is what works intersubjectively to offer satisfaction.[2]

Dewey (1938) also took experience (rather than abstraction of ideas) as the starting point of knowledge for action. He emphasized creative intelligence and added experimentation more fully to pragmatist thinking. He writes,

> [Conventional] empiricism is conceived of as being tied up with what has been given. But experience is in its vital form experimental, an effort to change the given; it is characterized by projection, by reaching forward into the unknown; connection with a future is its salient trait. (p. 8)

Working after Darwin and Freud in the historical moment of Joyce, Picasso, and Einstein, the original pragmatists held a dynamic view of history and life. Dewey speaks often of effecting change in the physical and cultural environment, compelled by human needs. He depreciates general theory and is sharply opposed to developing a body of unchanging timeless truths, instead preferring partial theory for the purpose of affecting desired change. Dewey envisioned communities of inquiry proceeding experimentally but not claiming to uncover timeless truths. This scientific method—much as Thomas Kuhn would later describe—offers an opportunity for the union of thought and practice. Dewey summarized that "the hypothesis that works is the true one." This builds on James's (in)famous pronouncement that concepts and theories must be made to yield "cash value." Nonetheless, the point is that the truth of an idea is a process in which the idea is found to be useful to a community of inquiry. Self, truth, and reality are constituted through social interaction (indeed, Richard Rorty, America's premier pragmatist philosopher, calls the pragmatists early postmodernists; see Reason, 2002). Validity claims reside in the process of their validation among people, for pragmatism is always contextual. Certainly, the pragmatic is not to be conflated with the expedient, for the process of transforming a problematic situation is more than merely achieving a purely personal end.

Given the fact that many of us have probably been pragmatizing all our lives, it may help to suggest who is not a pragmatist. Certainly, fundamentalists could not accept the contingent view of truth inherent in pragmatism. This may include scientific fundamentalists who have, as Rorty (1996) wrote, "their own metaphysical assumptions; far from being provisional and experimental conventional science has become another quest for certainty having adopted a faith in an objective order of truth" (p. 21). On the more progressive side, pragmatism is rejected as utopian and naive by those who have given up hope in the progress of enlightened planned change in light of the horrors of the 20th century and beyond. Pragmatism is not a unitary philosophy; it is instead a large and growing camp of divergent thinkers. For example, Habermas—perhaps the world's leading philosopher, who also refers to himself as "a good pragmatist"—is frequently criticized by fellow pragmatists for his notions of undistorted communication as the paradigm for social democracy.[3] Nonetheless, common in these otherwise divergent works are the premises that a practical outcome, in response to human need, is central to our actions; that reflection is integrally intertwined with action; and that the bridge between action and reflection involves social interaction for active experimentation. Moreover, the reality of relations and concern for the relational component of inquiry that leads to action are central.

Action research draws on the three overlapping strands of the pragmatic tradition: the primacy of the practical,[4] as articulated by James's notion of "cash value"; creative learning and experimentation, as articulated by Dewey; and the tradition of social justice, as articulated by Habermas (1984). These three strands lead, in turn, to varieties of action research practices (Bradbury, 2004) that may appear to the outsider to be otherwise quite unrelated. For example, Schein's action research with corporate leaders, called "clinical research" (2001) or "process consultation" (1999), shows a direct lineage to James's notions of the primacy of the practical. Large dialogue networks that have involved as many as 40,000 businesspeople in Scandinavia in a quest for improved work life show a direct lineage to the concern for social justice via dialogue, best articulated by Habermasian action researchers (e.g., Kemmis, 2001). Learning-oriented organizational change that involves large networks of business leaders, researchers, and consultants (e.g., Senge & Scharmer, 2001) hearkens back directly to Dewey. Shared among these is a recognition that the holism of action research dictates a need to integrate reflection and action (Argyris & Schön, 1996; Freire, 1992; Kolb, 1984; Senge, 1990), informed especially by the belief that dialogue and conversation allow for better thinking together (Bohm, 1996; Isaacs, 1999; Rorty, 1999). Indeed, conversation has been suggested as the most appropriate mode both for integrating action and reflection (Baker, Jensen, & Kolb, 1998; Ford & Ford, 1995) and inquiring into, and possibly transforming, the values from which one is operating (Nielsen, 1996; Torbert, 2001). Table 28.2

Table 28.2   Dimensions of the Pragmatic Tradition in Action Research

Fundamentals of Pragmatism	Dimensions of Actionability	Action Research Example
Practical outcome in response to human need	Practical value	• Identifying and enjoining key stakeholders • Participants inform research questions
The reality of relations and context	Social interaction	• Sharing ownership • Insider/outsider team formation • Meeting design • Conversation
Reflection integrally intertwined with action	Action/reflection cycles	• Appropriate methods (many shared with qualitative paradigm but made actionable)
Active experimentation	Active experimentation	• Validation • Dissemination • Designing infrastructure

lists the core principles of the pragmatic tradition and their manifestation in action research as dimensions of actionability.

QUALITY: DIMENSIONS OF ACTIONABILITY

Generally, qualitative scientists have fallen into two camps: those who question the use of even having standards of validity/quality (e.g., Kvale, 1989), and those who offer a replacement set of standards (e.g., Lather, 1993). Though quite sympathetic to Kvale and others, I take a more pragmatic approach to the question of what constitutes quality in action research and qualitative work more generally. After all, standards are inherently political; to avoid the question is to lose the argument; to engage the question is—in time—to help unseat the hegemonic aura of conventional validity that is an obstacle to our imagining alternatives more suitable to our goals. Lincoln (1995), in calling for a profusion of validities that emerge from the context of a given study, began a shift in the

discourse about the *nature* of criteriology (i.e., what they are) to their *function*. Joining with such scholars as Haraway (1984), Wolcott (1990), and Schwandt (1996), Lather has continued this trajectory as "a rehearsal for a new social imaginary out from under scientism" (1997, p. 2).

Clarifying choice points for quality should, on the one hand, help those of us interested in avoiding practice that is poorly articulated and, on the other hand, prevent our borrowing uncritically from traditional, yet inappropriate, quality standards. We need our concern for quality to move from "policing" (Bradbury & Reason, 2001) to stimulating dialogue (Gergen, 1994) that gradually generates communities of inquiry within communities of practice in each research site. Figure 28.1 offers a graphic representation of the four dimensions of quality as actionability.

Dimension One: Practical Value

Our experience usually focuses our attention on specific areas of need for change. Practical value supposes that people prioritize

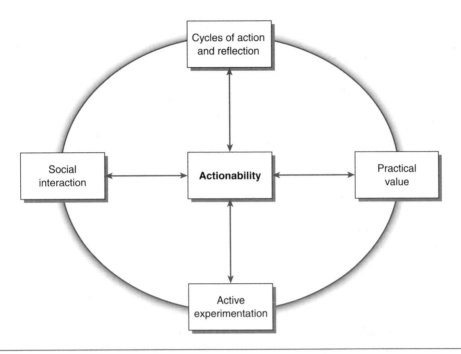

Figure 28.1   The Consequences of Actionability

the causes deemed worthy of their efforts. We may say that perceived need is the best departure point for successful action research. The primary questions that are raised by the dimension of practical value are "what is needed" and "by whom." Research questions need to be articulated with participants in the research in a process of co-scoping. In the organizational world, this means that research proposals need to be "owned" by salient stakeholders inside an organization. For this reason, action researcher Edgar Schein suggests (Schein, 2001) that organizational action researchers wait to be "invited" in, which attests to the importance of junior action researchers starting out to develop a network of colleagues that will allow access to organizational decision makers at all levels of an organization where co-scoping of projects can occur. A helpful practice at the early stage is to develop a map of the system that the action research project will work within; this can then be refined to focus on areas of most leverage for change.

It is critical to think from the start about creating an insider/outsider team (Bartunek & Louis, 1996) with salient stakeholders. This helps ensure that working toward practical value remains central to the effort. Connected to this is the need to understand from the start who are the salient stakeholders in the research. While not all stakeholders can or should be included directly, awareness of social and political groupings inside the organization best informs the creation of a robust insider/outsider team. For some stakeholders, it will be enough simply to be recognized as part of a change (especially if they have felt ignored); for others, much more effort must be expended to enable people to feel that they too are a part of the whole. From the start of the research, questions are asked with an insider and outsider audience in mind. Colleagues in this volume have much to share on this issue—see especially Bartunek (Chapter 4).

Dimension Two: Social Interaction

Human relations are as core to action as people are to plans. Though this may seem obvious when stated, many strategists who develop strategies for change independent from implementation plans for change overlook this relationship (Pettigrew, Thomas, & Whittington, 2002). Participation, for action researchers, is the vehicle by which stakeholders become co-designers as well as implementers of desired changes, which in turn leads to the development of new theory. Lewin's (1951) famous statement that "nothing is more practical than a good theory" emerges in a context of being able to check regularly with practitioners. The dimension of participation started with an initial crucial step of identifying salient stakeholders (as described above) and continues with subsequently mobilizing those who can best help develop the work (sometimes "best help" means offering insider criticism). This in turn leads to continuously clarifying the aims and goals of the action research project. Joining particular stakeholders to the action research can best proceed when there is clarity about why some and not others are to be involved. Schein suggests (Schein, 2001) the articulation of emergent hypotheses to help determine choices to be made. For example, action researchers such as Checkland, in the field of system mapping, or Sterman, in the field of system dynamics, develop system diagrams to aid in discussion of hypotheses they are developing. However it's done, action researchers proceed in inquiry, seeking validation or disconfirmation from stakeholders.

It is important not to assume that stakeholders are willing to or can easily be involved with the action research. Power structures inside an organization may make it hard for some to show themselves, while stretched resources may make it hard for others to find time. The action researchers therefore need to be reflexive about designing for participation. As the research is "with"

and not "on" participants, any evidence during the course of a project that insiders are not participating must be taken seriously. For example, meetings in which outsider researchers dominate (even if they are speaking about participation!) send a message that insiders are not partners. On the positive side, the more dialogue is engendered, the better the chances of a thriving project.

Dimension Three: Cycles of Reflection and Action

Action research is an experimental mode of learning among stakeholders. Learning requires the transformation of experience through reflection for action (Kolb, 1984). Thus, the question of specific methods to be used by action researchers is often a question of how to modify methods so that reflection by stakeholders informs desired praxis.

Adequate methods are important for bringing in rich information. Generally, participation will decrease if a method is understood to offer merely "scholarly" insight. For example, an action researcher was invited to help with a group of social scientists using network analysis techniques to study business leaders' support of interorganizational collaboration. The invitation was issued after business leaders responded poorly (response rate 22%) to the social scientists' invitation to participate in a network survey considered crucial for understanding the network. The action researcher asked the business leaders about the low response rate and learned that it was due to business leaders' hesitance in sharing their political networks when they did not see a sufficient payoff for doing so. An alternative "action network study" was designed by the action researcher with input from the businesspeople. It would use the previous network surveys but invite all who participated to view the results of the network study, in a way that preserved anonymity. The network diagram was shared in a dissemination meeting focusing on the identification of breakdown in communications within the current network structure. The network diagram provoked a lot of conversation, with particular interest in understanding the patterns of ties among certain groups. Reviewing the diagram together both validated its veracity and provoked actionability as practitioners began to think together about how to change the network structure to better meet the groups' goals of communicating across all groups. As this case illustrates, the issue of adequate methods is one of generating data while simultaneously meeting the needs of those providing that data through cycles of action and reflection. The point here is how the method is used rather than what the method is. Many action research practices have developed as a result of modifying conventional methods, while others have been developed specifically by groups of insiders and outsiders to meet their needs, such as the learning history that is discussed below to make the dimensions of quality more concrete. Getting the research method right, while often the primary preoccupation of a conventional researcher, is but one concern for the action researcher. Generally, as Argyris has noted, the action researcher needs to have competence in a wider range of skills, both scientific and interpersonal, than is required of conventional researchers.

Dimension Four: Active Experimentation

Validation/disconfirmation is required to complete the action research cycle. Results of the action research need to be brought back to the insider audience so that they can say "yes, that's true" or "I see it differently." Moreover, the conversation engendered by the learning history is the goal of the learning history. Given our desire to be right with our findings, it is particularly important to craft validation efforts so as to maximize the chance of hearing otherwise. Any signs of disconnect with stakeholders are best surfaced and discussed to avoid defensive routines (Argyris, 1990) and to support the openness to productive conversation that the learning history seeks to inspire.

BUILDING INFRASTRUCTURE: "DESIGNING THE FUTURE"

The concept of infrastructure implies developing a robust capability that continues to be available in the future. The best time to think about infrastructure is when the stakeholders and purpose are determined. It is particularly important to enlist those with authority to make change as early in the process as possible. Such people might ask, What do we need to do in order to institutionalize our learning? At the final, discussion stage of the findings, the conversation needs to turn to what will support people in taking their insights into action. For example, managers might need to use or change reward structures to reinforce new practices. Tracking impact—especially where qualitative and quantitative reports can be obtained—is particularly effective in providing people a sense of progress, which, in turn, creates the feedback that helps reinforce a virtuous learning cycle. There is, however, a difference between a robust capability that continues to be available and a robust capability for continual learning that needs also to be in place for the virtuous learning cycle to emerge and continue. The former must be held in mind from the early stages; the latter is emergent and, at this point in time, very much occupies the author's thoughts as a challenge yet to be fully embraced by action researchers.

Generally speaking, the questions suggested by Argyris (1996) are a good guide to the kinds of conversations that need to be accomplished toward the later stages of an action research process:

1. How do the stakeholders know they are producing the actions that they intended?

2. How do they know that the actions they have produced are having the intended effect?

3. How do they know that the answers they are providing to the first two questions are not wrong?

4. To what extent are they acting in accordance with these questions in ways that permit and encourage other individuals (or larger social units) to answer the same questions?

The latter, especially, allows us to contribute to the scholarly stock of knowledge.

Action Research and Representation

Appropriate representation of the work of the project—the findings—increases actionability and therefore deserves more attention than it receives in conventional research methods. Representation must be culturally synchronous with the action research stakeholders. We see this most starkly in nonliterate cultures where theater is used to share new health practices. However, in literate contexts, it is also important that accountants be given numbers, that schoolchildren be given cartoons, and so on, so that the data is accessible. Appropriately constructed representations (pictures or texts) offer communities of inquiry a concrete platform for focused conversation (Carlile, 1998; Nonaka & Takeuchi, 1995) from which praxis may evolve.

We now turn to one of a myriad of action research practices, the *learning history,* to briefly make concrete the dimensions laid out so far.

ACTIONABILITY EXEMPLIFIED: LEARNING HISTORY

A learning history (Bradbury & Mainemelis, 2001; Kleiner & Roth, 1997; Roth &

Bradbury, 2007) is useful to scholarly practitioners in their work of evaluating organizational efforts. Its purpose is to capture learning from an innovating group and transfer their "new knowledge" to other groups in their own organization and others. This is done by convening salient stakeholders of an organization to reflect together on their past so that they are enabled to create the future they want, and allowing others interested in their work to learn from their efforts. The collective reflection is facilitated by the co-design, development, and use of a "shared narrative" based on interviews with the stakeholders.

A learning history is a product as well as a process. It is a process that assesses a change initiative through (1) developing the capability of the people in the organization to evaluate their accomplishments in the service of (2) creating materials to (3) diffuse their learning to other interested parties. In combining these three elements, participants create a cycle of organizational-level feedback. The emphasis of the learning history process is on reflecting, capturing, analyzing and distilling, writing, and using participant narrative and other data about participants' change efforts. Others that later use the learning history create their own experience as they read and talk about the document. In conversing with one another about learning and change, a group reading a learning history creates a shared understanding that guides its future efforts.

Learning histories are typically 50 to 100 pages long, providing a retrospective account of significant events in an organization's recent past. Content comes from the people who initiated, implemented, and participated in the original efforts, as well as nonparticipants affected by the change. Learning histories have been conducted by many different individuals and teams in several dozen settings, with these projects resulting in manuscripts presently available as company documents, working papers (see http://www.sol-ne.org/res/wp/index.html), scholarly articles, dissertations (Bradbury,

1998; Bradbury & Mainemelis, 2001), and books (Roth & Kleiner, 1999).

The learning history originators (Roth & Bradbury, 2007) suggest generic stages of a learning history in which the various dimensions of quality and actionability are active. These are as follows:

1. A planning stage delineates the range and scope of the document as well as the audience seeking to learn from the organization's experience. The noticeable results of the improvement effort are initially specified in the planning stage. Crucially, insiders are included in the planning process to help develop their skills in planning and conducting assessments for learning. This stage is especially geared toward ensuring practical value throughout the process, which may last around a year.

2. There are a series of retrospective, reflective conversational interviews with participants in a learning effort—taking pains to gather perspectives from every significant point of view. In this, the tasks of action research may be apportioned according to skills in inquiry and implementation. The interviewing process itself develops the skill for reflective conversation that provides benefits for the organization. This particular method (interviewing) is altered slightly from a method of extracting information to being part of the process of inviting reflection for action. The same concerns for piloting and sampling that are present for qualitative researchers are present here.

3. A small group of internal staff members and outsider learning historians "distills" the raw material (from reflective conversation interviews, documents, observations, and so on) into a coherent set of themes with relevance for those seeking to learn from the effort. This analytic effort, based on techniques of qualitative data analysis and the development of grounded theory, builds the capacity of the inside/outside learning history team for assessing and making sense of improvement efforts.

4. A small group of key managers, participants in the original effort, and others interested in learning from their efforts, attend a disconfirmation and validation workshop after reading the learning history draft. This workshop allows those who participated in the improvement effort to reflect on and review for accuracy the material and their presentation in the learning history.

5. The learning history document is used to focus dissemination workshops in which people throughout the company consider what has been learned, how to judge success, and, crucially, how to move forward in other initiatives. The learning history surfaces and presents data, but it does not develop the skills needed to organizationally process controversy. The learning historians should work as a team to strike a balance in the document with interesting, but not overwhelming, findings and develop the skills to talk about difficult issues. The skills that people learn in discussing a learning history are skills that they can later apply in conversations about new, immediate organizational challenges.

The learning history exemplifies the dimensions of quality that action researchers find important, in that it is aimed at generating practical as well as conceptual insights and contributions to the scholarly stock of knowledge, it emerges from partnership, it uses rigorous methods of validation/disconfirmation, and it aims for actionability by creating a product and developing infrastructure to allow the insights to spread after the learning history process is complete.

CONCLUSION

Since there is considerable scholarship about the nature of quality both in action research (see especially Bradbury & Reason, 2001) and more broadly in critical, constructionist, and qualitative inquiry, it's increasingly important that action researchers explicitly connect their own judgments as to how to craft a work of quality to discussions in the current literature.

It is unrealistic to assume that one piece of action research can "score" on all quality dimensions equally. It might be that in one inquiry what is most important is to create new forms of emancipatory dialogue, while in another it is to carefully check how claims to effective practice match descriptions of the external world. One might expect a Ph.D. thesis using action research to pay particular attention to issues of methodological rigor— for example, the sampling should be adequate by standards of the field. For action researchers, this is merely one of a handful of quality criteria, but for a Ph.D. student it may be preeminent—at least until the hurdle of the defense has been taken successfully. Additionally, she or he needs to show a concentrated effort to validate findings and reflect on the possibility of generalizability. A community development effort might get greater payoff from involving large numbers of participants and working in an emergent process. In a participative inquiry, which has emerged in its fullest sense as research not *with* people but *by* people, responsibility for exploring these issues will rest with the action research participants as a whole. As a rule, one may say that to the degree the level of desired system impact is removed from the leadership team, participative co-design is limited to those stakeholders who can carry the work into the larger system.

Actionability will likely seem familiar at first; nonetheless, it's not that easily built into our research practices. It seems familiar because it is pragmatic (we respond to a need), and most of us have been pragmatizing all our lives. Yet it is not easily practiced, because it requires multiple competencies— one must be part scientist, part matchmaker, part executive—not to mention the broad skill set required: interpersonal skills, meeting design, artistic representation, project management. For many, this may suggest that a multiskilled team is advisable (Werr & Greiner, Chapter 5 in this volume). Indeed, it's interesting to note at this point in history that research funded by government agencies increasingly demands such collaborations as well as more attention to implementation.

Today action research flourishes particularly in think tanks, consulting and planning agencies, and academic institutions with research centers or practitioner funding. Action researchers are also to be found inside the institutions they are seeking to change. These scholarly practitioners are called upon to unify oppositional approaches that include the integration of theory and practice, action and reflection, empirical analysis and normative vision, critique and affirmation, explanation and action, and vision and current reality. In a culture, especially academic culture, that more readily replaces "and" with "or," this will always be a challenge (Friedmann, 1987). As the will to practical results will likely never fade, however, the question is simply whether conventional social science can keep open a place for dialogue with this holistic, dialogical science. A richer understanding of quality, along with a richer practice that leads to research of consequence in which actionability is considered central, can be accomplished.

NOTES

1. See especially the work of classics scholar and action researcher Olav Eikeland (e.g., 2001).

2. The concern for intersubjectivity helps avoid solipsism.

3. His critics claim that such views are naive because all human communication is distorted by its very nature. Habermas responds that the critics hold a self-defeating point of view that won't lead to much positive action.

4. The term is from action researcher John Heron (1996).

REFERENCES

Argyris, C. (1996). Actionable knowledge: Design causality in the service of consequential theory. *Journal of Applied Behavioral Science, 32*(4), 390–407.

Argyris, C., Putnam, R., & Smith, D. M. (1987). *Action science: Concepts, methods, and skills for research and intervention.* San Francisco: Jossey-Bass.

Argyris, C., & Schön, D. (1996). *Organizational learning II: Method and practice.* Reading, MA: Addison-Wesley.

Baker, A. C., Jensen, P. J., & Kolb, D. A. (1998). *Conversation as experiential learning* (Working Paper 98-4 [4a]). Cleveland, OH: Case Western Reserve University, Weatherhead School of Management, Department of Organization Behavior.

Baldwin, M. (2001). Working together, learning together: Inquiry in the development of complex practice by teams of social workers. In P. Reason & H. Bradbury (Eds.), *Handbook of action research: Participative inquiry and practice* (pp. 287–293). London: Sage.

Barrett, P. (2001). The early mothering project: What happened when the words "action research" came to life for a group of midwives. In P. Reason & H. Bradbury (Eds.), *Handbook of action research: Participative inquiry and practice* (pp. 294–300). London: Sage.

Bartunek, J., & Louis, M. (1996). *Insider/outsider team research.* Thousand Oaks, CA: Sage.

Bohm, D. (1996). *On dialogue* (Lee Nichol, Ed.). London: Routledge.

Bradbury, H. (1998). *Learning with the Natural Step: Cooperative ecological inquiry through cases, theory and practice for sustainable development.* Unpublished doctoral dissertation. (UMI No. 9901365)

Bradbury, H. (2004, November). *Varieties of action research.* Keynote address, Conference on Action Research, Aalborg University, Denmark.

Bradbury, H., & Mainemelis, C. (2001). Learning history and organizational praxis. *Journal of Management Inquiry, 10*(4), 340–357.

Bradbury, H., & Reason, P. (2001). Conclusion. In P. Reason & H. Bradbury (Eds.), *Handbook of action research: Participative inquiry and practice.* London: Sage.

Bradbury, H., & Waage, S. (2005). Introduction to Special Edition. *Action Research, 3*(2), 131–134.

Brown, D. L. (Ed.). (2002). *Practice-research engagement and civil society in a globalizing society.* Cambridge, MA: Harvard University/The Hauser Center.

Brown, D. L., Bammer, G., Batliwala, S., & Kunreuther, F. (2003). Framing practice-research engagement for democratizing knowledge. *Action Research, 1*(1), 81–102.

Carlile, P. (1998). *From transfer to transformation: Working through knowledge boundaries in product development* (Working paper). Cambridge, MA: MIT, Sloan School of Management.

Chandler, D., & Torbert, W. R. (2003). Transforming inquiry and action: Interweaving flavors of action research. *Action Research, 1*(2), 133–152.

Chiu, L. (2003). Transformational potential of focus group practice in participatory action research. *Action Research, 1*(2), 165–183.

Copleston, F. (1994). *A history of philosophy: Vol. 8. Modern philosophy: Empiricism, idealism and pragmatism.* New York: Doubleday Press. (Original work published 1966)

Dewey, J. (1938). *Experience and education.* New York: Macmillan.

Dickstein, M. (Ed.). (1999). *The revival of pragmatism: New essays on social thought, law and culture.* Durham, NC: Duke University Press.

Eikeland, O. (2001). Action research as the hidden curriculum of the Western tradition. In P. Reason & H. Bradbury (Eds.), *Handbook of action research: Participative inquiry and practice* (pp. 145–156). London: Sage.

Ford, J., & Ford, L. (1995). The role of conversation in producing intentional change in organizations. *Academy of Management Review, 20*(3), 541–570.

Freire, P. (1992). *Pedagogy of the oppressed.* New York: Continuum.

Friedmann, J. (1987). *Planning in the public domain: From knowledge to action.* Princeton, NJ: Princeton University Press.

Gergen, K. J. (1994). *Toward transformation in social knowledge.* London: Sage.

Gustavsen, B. (2001). Theory and practice: The mediating discourse. In P. Reason & H. Bradbury (Eds.), *Handbook of action research: Participative inquiry and practice* (Chapter 1). London: Sage.

Habermas, J. (1971). *Knowledge and human interests* (J. Shapiro, Trans.). Boston: Beacon Press.

Habermas, J. (1984). *The theory of communicative action* (T. McCarthy, Trans.). Boston: Beacon Press.

Haraway, D. (1984). Situated knowledges: The science question in feminism and the privilege of partial perspective. *Feminist Studies, 14*(3), 575–599.

Heron, J. (1996). The primacy of the practical. *Qualitative Inquiry, 2*(1) [Special issue].

Hughes, I., & Yuan, L. (2005). The status of action research in the People's Republic of China. *Action Research, 3*(4), 383–403.

Isaacs, W. (1999). *Dialogue and the art of thinking together.* New York: Currency/Doubleday.

James, W. (1978). *Pragmatism and the meaning of truth.* Cambridge, MA: Harvard University Press. (Original work published 1908)

Kaplan, R. S., & Norton, D. P. (2005). The balanced scorecard: Measures that drive performance. *Harvard Business Review, 83*(7), 172–186.

Kemmis, S. (2001). Exploring the relevance of critical theory for action research: Emancipatory action research in the footsteps of Juergen Habermas. In P. Reason & H. Bradbury (Eds.), *Handbook of action research: Participative inquiry and practice* (Chapter 8). London: Sage.

Kirk, S. (1979). Understanding research utilization in social work. In A. Rubin & R. Rosenblatt (Eds.), *Sourcebook on research utilization.* New York: Council on Research Utilization.

Kleiner, A., & Roth, G. (1997). How to make experience your company's best teacher. *Harvard Business Review, 75*(September–October), 172–177.

Kolb, D. A. (1984). *Experiential learning: Experience as the source of learning and development.* Englewood Cliffs, NJ: Prentice Hall.

Kristiansen, M., & Blouch-Poulsen, J. (2004). Self referentiality as a power mechanism: Toward dialogic action research. *Action Research, 2*(4), 371–388.

Kvale, S. (1989). To validate is to question. In S. Kvale (Ed.), *Issues of validity in qualitative research* (pp. 73–92). Sweden: Studentlitteratur.

Lather, P. (1993). Fertile obsession: Validity after poststructuralism. *Sociological Quarterly, 34*(4), 673–693.

Lather, P. (1997). Validity as an incitement to discourse: Qualitative research and the crisis of legitimation. In V. Richardson (Ed.), *Handbook of research on teaching* (4th ed.). Washington, DC: American Education Research Association.

Lennie, J., Hatcher, C., & Morgan, W. (2003). Feminist discourses of empowerment in an action research project involving rural women and communication technologies. *Action Research, 1*(1), 57–80.

Lewin, K. (1951). *Field theory in social science.* New York: Harper.

Lincoln, Y. (1995). Emerging criteria for quality in qualitative and interpretive research. *Qualitative Inquiry, 1*(3), 275–289.

Lincoln, Y. (2001). Engaging sympathies: Relationships between action research and social constructivism. In P. Reason & H. Bradbury (Eds.), *Handbook of Action Research: Participative inquiry and practice* (Chapter 11). London: Sage.

Maguire, P. (2001). Uneven ground: Feminisms and action research. In P. Reason & H. Bradbury (Eds.), *Handbook of action research: Participative inquiry and practice* (pp. 59–69). London: Sage.

Mendenhall, T., & Doherty, W. (2003). Partners in diabetes: A collaborative, democratic initiative in primary care. *Families, Systems & Health, 21,* 329–335.

Mohammed Yunus and the Grameen Bank. (1999, September). *Scientific American.*

Nielsen, R. P. (1996). *The politics of ethics.* New York: Oxford University Press.

Nonaka, I., & Takeuchi, H. (1995). *The knowledge creating company.* New York: Oxford University Press.

Pasmore, W. (2001). Action research in the workplace: The socio-technical perspective. In P. Reason & H. Bradbury (Eds.), *Handbook of action research: Participative inquiry and practice* (pp. 38–47). London: Sage.

Pettigrew, A., Thomas, H., & Whittington, R. (2002). *Handbook of strategy and management.* Thousand Oaks, CA: Sage.

Pimbert, M., & Wakeford, T. (2003). Prajateerpu, power and knowledge: The politics of participatory action research in development. *Action Research, 1*(2), 184–207.

Reason, P. (2002). Interview with Richard Rorty. *Action Research, 1*(2).

Reason, P., & Bradbury, H. (Eds.). (2001). *Handbook of action research: Participative inquiry and practice.* London: Sage.

Rooke, D., & Torbert, W. R. (2005, April). Seven transformations of leadership. *Harvard Business Review.*

Rorty, R. (1996). Does academic freedom have philosophical presuppositions? In L. Menand (Ed.), *The future of academic freedom.* Chicago: University of Chicago Press.

Rorty, R. (1999). *Philosophy and social hope.* London: Penguin Books.

Roth, G., & Bradbury, H. (2007). Learning history: An action research practice. In P. Reason & H. Bradbury (Eds.), *Handbook of action research* (2nd ed.). London: Sage.

Roth, G., & Kleiner, A. (1999). *Car launch: The human side of managing change.* London: Oxford University Press.

Schein, E. (1999). *Process consultation revisited: Building the helping relationship.* Reading, MA: Addison Wesley Longman.

Schein, E. (2001). Clinical inquiry/research. In P. Reason & H. Bradbury (Eds.), *Handbook of action research: Participative inquiry and practice* (Chapter 21). London: Sage.

Schwandt, T. (1996). Farewell to criteriology. *Qualitative Inquiry, 2*(1) [Special issue], 41–56.

Senge, P. M. (1990). *The fifth discipline.* New York: Currency/Doubleday.

Senge, P. M., & Scharmer, O. (2001). Community action researcher: Learning as a community of practitioners, consultants and researchers. In P. Reason & H. Bradbury (Eds.), *Handbook of action research: Participative inquiry and practice* (pp. 238–250). London: Sage.

Shapin, S. (1999). Rarely pure and never simple: Talking about truth. *Configurations, 7*(1), 1–14.

Torbert, W. R. (2001). The practice of action inquiry. In P. Reason & H. Bradbury (Eds.), *Handbook of Action Research: Participative inquiry and practice.* London: Sage.

Wells, K. (2000). Use of research in mental health practice and policy. In Drotar (Ed.), *Handbook of research in pediatric and clinical child psychology.* New York: Kluwer Academic/Plenum.

Wolcott, H. (1990). On seeking—and rejecting—validity in qualitative research. In E. Eisner & A. Peshkin (Eds.), *Qualitative inquiry in education: The continuing debate* (pp. 121–152). New York: Teachers College Press.

Zeichner, K. (2001). Educational action research. In P. Reason & H. Bradbury (Eds.), *Handbook of action research: Participative inquiry and practice* (pp. 273–284). London: Sage.

CHAPTER 29

Collaborative Management Research Through Communities of Inquiry

Challenges and Skills

David Coghlan

A. B. (Rami) Shani

ABSTRACT

Communities of inquiry, whereby distinct communities of practice (i.e., managers and researchers) form a community of inquiry, are an important way of engaging in collaborative management research. At the same time, the collaborative management research process influences the development of the community of inquiry. The interplay between collaborative management research and the community of inquiry has received little attention in the emerging body of knowledge. Following a brief discussion of the basic notions of community of inquiry, this chapter explores the dynamic interface between collaborative management research and the creation and development of a community of inquiry. Next, it focuses on the complex dynamics and challenges of a community of inquiry by using a framework that enables us to work with task and relational issues in terms of content, process, and culture. Finally, it explores the notion of quality in a community of inquiry.

A review of the literature on collaborative management research, including the contributions to this volume, points to a lack of awareness on the part of participants of the importance of paying attention to how the simultaneous evolution of the research task and the relationships in the community of inquiry affect the outcomes of collaborative research efforts. Just setting out with an intention to collaborate in conducting research is not enough to assure high-quality outcomes for either science or the organization (see Pasmore, Woodman, & Simmons, Chapter 27 in this volume). We believe strongly that it is the responsibility of researchers, and not their managerial collaborators, to develop and bring the right set of skills to the table. Without a greater understanding of what these skills are, or how they affect the outcomes of collaborative management research, it is unlikely that the quality of collaborative research efforts will improve.

The starting point for this chapter lies in the notion that collaborative management research activities trigger the development of a community of inquiry as a way of engaging in this form of research. Such a community integrates a variety of communities of practice, such as communities of managers, researchers, disciplines, functions, and organic units or subunits within and outside a system. The quality of a community of inquiry has a great deal to do with its effectiveness in producing practical and scientific outcomes. To date, little research has been conducted on the factors that affect the formation of vibrant communities of inquiry, although the chapters in this volume will certainly add to our understanding of this topic. To research a community of inquiry requires a holistic understanding of its key elements and complex dynamics and a heightened awareness of the skills that are required to first define the task and relationship factors involved in collaborative inquiry and then examine how these factors affect the quality of research efforts. The chapter is organized in three sections: The first introduces the notion of communities of inquiry and discusses how collaborative management research facilitates the creation of a community of inquiry out of the engagement of communities of practice; the second focuses on the dynamics and challenges of a community of inquiry through a framework that enables us to work with task and relational issues in terms of content, process, and culture; and the third section explores notions of quality in a community of inquiry.

FROM COMMUNITIES OF PRACTICE TO A COMMUNITY OF INQUIRY

The notion of communities as a business construct is relatively new. Recently, communities of practice have become key components in the organization development, change, and learning literature (e.g., Brown & Duguid, 1991; Wenger, 1998; Wenger, McDermott, & Snyder, 2002). A community of practice is a group of individuals in an organization who share an interest in generating new understanding, knowledge, and action about a topic. Its foundations are in practitioner inquiry (Wenger, 1998). A primary activity of the community of practice is learning, connections, and generating new ideas. It provides the arena for people with shared interests to interact and gain new insights. Communities of practice share a few distinct features: collaboration, narration, social construction, mutual engagement, joint enterprise, and shared repertoire (Brown & Duguid, 1991; Wenger, 1998). Most view mutual engagement and collaboration among individuals as the primary requisite for the development of a community. As individuals engage in the actions of their projects, they collaborate with others. In the course of the project, individuals may face unexpected circumstances that the organization's formal procedures do not address or cover. As they attempt to sort the issue out, it is through collaboration and narration that the members of a community of practice negotiate meaning and joint enterprise. Wenger (1998) argues that as the community negotiates its enterprise, relations of mutual accountability to the community arise as well as the development of a common identity. In addition, the community develops a shared repertoire of both tacit and explicit means of communicating and working, enabling the community to perform its practice in a satisfying manner (Teigland, 2003). In collaborative management research, members of different communities of practice come together and form a community of inquiry in order to address the particular issues posed by the shared research project. In this *Handbook* we are calling this community of inquiry a collaborative management research community (CMRC).

Collaborative management research has been defined in this *Handbook* as an emergent and systemic inquiry process, embedded in a true partnership between researchers and members of living systems for the purpose of generating actionable scientific knowledge. At the most basic level, it attempts to refine the relationship between academic researchers and organizational or interorganizational actors from research "on" or "for" to research "with." In doing so, it integrates knowledge creation with problem solving and "inquiry from the inside" with "inquiry from the outside." As such, collaborative management research is viewed as partnership among a variety of individuals forming a "community of inquiry" within spheres of practice. Shani, David, and Willson (2004) emphasize the qualitative elements in this definition: true partnership between insiders and outsiders encompassing the dynamics and equality of integrated collaboration; emergent and systematic inquiry through systematic and reflective inquiry; and the generation of actionable scientific knowledge—knowledge that is both scientific and actionable. Huxham and Vangen (2001) report how practitioners approach collaborative research in terms of problems and issues that ought to make it work better, and so they generate wish lists and prescriptive "must do" lists. When these lists are analyzed, they reflect deeper, less straightforward themes. Collaborative management research is typically constructed out of the interactions between practitioners' and scholars' perceptions of key challenges and out of key issues that emerge from the themes when issues are explored and analyzed. As

some chapters in this *Handbook* illustrate (Huzzard & Gregory, Chapter 16; Kolodny & Halpern, Chapter 13; Olascoaga & Kur, Chapter 12), negotiating collaborative management research tasks within the community is a complex endeavor that requires distinct sets of skills.

Collaborative management research is built on a partnership between different stakeholders, namely insider organizational or interorganizational practitioners and outsider academic researchers (Adler, Shani, & Styhre, 2004; Amabile et al., 2001; Bartunek, Chapter 4 in this volume; Bartunek & Louis, 1996; Huxham & Vangen, 2001; Louis & Bartunek, 1992; Lowstedt & Stjernberg, 2006; Rynes, Bartunek, & Daft, 2001). Insiders and outsiders may be practitioners and/or academics who bring their perspective on action and theory generation to the community of inquiry.

As this *Handbook* well illustrates, collaborative management research takes place in multiple settings. Kolodny and Halpern (Chapter 13 in this volume) extend collaborative management research to include managers and external consultants. The ARC Research Team (Chapter 22 in this volume) describe the collaborative process between academics in a college and the local community as they build a partnership by creating an Action Research Center (ARC) in order to learn together, initiate projects to stimulate mutual development, and generate new knowledge. Bammer and the Goolabri Group (Chapter 20) brought a group of colleagues together to engage in cross-sectoral and cross-disciplinary work in a new specialization called integration and implementation sciences, to develop an integrated approach to confronting the ways in which ignorance and uncertainty inhibit tackling complex issues. Huzzard and Gregory (Chapter 16) describe efforts to build social partnership between management and trade unions. Mirvis (Chapter 10) describes three different forums of interorganizational collaborative management research between multiple companies with distinct common interests and multiple researchers with different research agendas. He illustrates how common research-and-practice interests are defined, combined, and realized in complex collaborative interorganizational relationships. In each of these examples, the CMRC took a slightly different form, was composed of individuals representing different interest groups, and formulated different ways of working on issues of importance to the community. The success of these efforts depended in part upon the insights gained from the research that was conducted, but also in part upon the ability of the players involved to construct and maintain a viable CMRC.

From a design perspective, one must establish the structures and processes that facilitate the development and direction of a collaborative management research community (see Docherty & Shani, Chapter 8 in this volume). Designing a CMRC is a challenge for the designers. As shown in Table 29.1, many choices are available. Designers need to investigate the degree of fit between the cultural context, the research content, and the scientific discovery process. As the chapters in this *Handbook* demonstrate, in practice, CMRCs have been designed and managed in various ways. Yet in most collaborative management research projects, some form of community of inquiry is designed—in which insiders and outsiders are involved to varied degrees—that results in significant organizational insight for action and new scientific management knowledge.

Any community has task and relational issues, which affect what is done (content), how it is done (process), and how people feel about what is being done (culture). Table 29.1 provides a framework for making necessary distinctions between content, process, and culture challenges within task and relational issues (Coghlan & Rashford, 2006). Content refers to *what* is done, while process refers to *how* it is done. Task issues refer to the project itself, its practicality and relevance to theory and practice; whereas relational issues refer to the quality of collaboration. Content and process apply to both task and relational issues. Yet what we see and hear is not the whole picture. Much of what goes on in CMRCs is grounded in collective assumptions that are hidden and reflect the emerging and evolving culture of the community (Schein, 2004). Academics and practitioners, insiders and outsiders belong to different communities of practice, and as they interact through their representatives in research teams, the dynamics of intergroup distortion and power plays will have negative effects on how the community functions unless they are surfaced and managed. Within the insider/outsider, academic/practitioner groupings, individual members may belong to different occupational cultures and hold different perspectives and tacit knowledge on what constitutes knowledge, for example. Unless these different views of knowledge are reconciled, the joint effort will not produce outputs that satisfy the needs of one or both parties, diminishing their interest in future collaboration with other members of the community. The six-cell framework in Table 29.1 provides a comprehensive mechanism for distinguishing the different elements of a CMRC and thereby enabling clearer assessment of those elements and providing the basis for designing interventions to remediate problems or build improvement.

The implications for the design of collaborative management research are that insiders and outsiders, academics and practitioners are responsible for both the task and relational dynamics in the community of inquiry. Theme selection, methods of data collection, ways of data generation, frameworks of data

Table 29.1   Creating a Collaborative Management Research Community: Tasks and Relational Issues

	Task	*Relational Issues*
Content	• Project identification and selection • Project relevance and intended contributions to theory and practice • Design for quality and sustainability • Knowledge base of project • Organizational action • Task conflict	• Quality of participation • Insider/outsider roles • Academic/practitioner roles • Role clarity
Process	• Research project design • Data collection • Data generation • Data interpretation • Organizational action • Cycles of action and reflection • Quality and rigor of the scientific discovery process • How theory is extrapolated	• Role negotiation • Collaborative engagement in cycles of action and reflection • Dialogue and conversation • Conflict • Power • Intergroup dynamics
Culture	• Assumptions within each community of practice about the nature of the issue and the nature of scientific knowledge	• Assumptions within each community of practice about its own and the other communities' views of research and the scientific discovery process • Assumptions within each community of practice of its own and the other communities' views of organizational action

interpretation, data sensemaking, and design and implementation of organizational action constitute critical task content and process issues that must be explored and agreed upon. For example, Coghlan and Coughlan (Chapter 21 in this volume) report that the CO-IMPROVE project practitioners' concerns to improve supplier relationship in order to enhance competitiveness were combined with the researchers' interest in researching collaborative improvement in the supply chain (the content) through action learning (the process). The study also illustrated how both academics and managers participated in cycles of action and reflection in which organizational actions were evaluated and theoretical constructs were articulated. Relational issues refer to how the academics and managers worked together. Thus, the study addressed simultaneously both the task and relational challenges. As this example shows, the quality of relationships will affect the overall effectiveness of the community of inquiry. Future research should investigate the effects of a variety of relationship variables on the effectiveness of collaborative inquiry tasks. These variables should include the cultural differences between actors from different spheres of practice, the percentage of time spent on task versus relationship issues, the development and application of norms of behavior intended to guide the partnership, and the ability of the parties to resolve outstanding issues or conflicts in a way that strengthens the ongoing partnership. As these and other variables are researched, we will be able to provide more helpful advice to improve the productivity of collaborative management research.

THE DYNAMICS OF A COLLABORATIVE MANAGEMENT RESEARCH COMMUNITY

The context within which collaborative management research takes place is likely to influence how the collaborative effort unfolds (Shani & Pasmore, 1985). By context we mean the structure and dynamics of the setting within which the research takes place. As this *Handbook* aptly illustrates, a community of inquiry faces significant practical and scientific challenges. For example, access to the research site has to be negotiated and representation and participation of the multiple and different formal and informal organizational groupings clarified. Furthermore, following the creation of the community of inquiry, the dynamics within the community itself must be carefully managed. Differences must be acknowledged and managed so that intellectual shifts in direction may both occur and be accepted and respected. Mohrman and colleagues (Chapter 24 in this volume) recall that on the initial planning day, one of the practitioners in their study group expressed discomfort with the study because he felt there was a possibility that the academic team would develop knowledge for academic publication at the expense of the need to develop practical, actionable knowledge in a form that the business could use to enhance its capacity to address its business concerns. The study team discussed this potential pitfall and agreed among themselves that all would work to ensure that the study met the needs of all parties.

The collaboration extends to the writing and dissemination stages. Writing should not be left to the outsider academic partner, nor should the presentation of findings to senior management be left to the insider. The emergent nature of the community of inquiry has an impact on content and process dynamics. For example, at times the practice of collaboration shifts the dynamics of power and the different actors need to work it out, as illustrated by the ARC Research Team (Chapter 22 in this volume), who discuss how joint publishing became a political issue within the collaborative process.

Task Issues in a Community of Inquiry

Task content refers to what the collaborative management research topic is and what the organizational outcomes are intended to be. It is grounded in and flows from the context and involves defining what is to be researched. Deciding the task content also involves determining whether the research will draw on an existing knowledge base or seek to generate entirely new approaches to solving organizational problems. For Coghlan and Coughlan (Chapter 21), the task content was collaborative improvement in the supply chain, in which area there is an existing extensive literature, and its contribution aimed at the application of action learning to this interorganizational setting. While it might seem that the definition of research questions and organizational outcomes is a straightforward matter, creating alignment among the spheres of practice in collaborative inquiry efforts is often more difficult in practice than the parties imagine at the outset. This *Handbook* provides many examples of content topics: finding design solutions for complex knowledge work (Mohrman et al., Chapter 24), collaborative improvement in the supply chain (Coghlan & Coughlan, Chapter 21), university-industry partnership (Roth, Chapter 17), understanding manager-consultant collaboration in sociotechnical systems design (Kolodny & Halpern, Chapter 13), integrated and implementation sciences in addressing complex problems (Bammer & the Goolabri Group, Chapter 20), local community and community college collaboration (ARC Research Team, Chapter 22), and management and trade union partnership (Huzzard & Gregory, Chapter 16), to select some examples. As Bartunek (Chapter 4) points out, conflict about defining the task and what it entails may be productive.

The act of addressing the task process in a community of inquiry involves deciding how the project is selected and designed, how data are collected, generated, and interpreted, how organizational actions are taken and evaluated, and how theory is extrapolated. For Bammer and her colleagues (Chapter 20), a symposium involving cross-sectoral and cross-disciplinary perspectives and expertise was organized. Task definition within a community of inquiry was then undertaken in a reflective mode, through enacting cycles of action and reflection. Coghlan and Coughlan (Chapter 21) explain that the way the researcher network recorded events, articulated and discussed interpretations and assumptions, enacted cycles of action and reflection, and tested reflections in subsequent action ensured methodological rigor. Mohrman and colleagues (Chapter 24) provide similar details of how in their research project they gathered, analyzed, and interpreted data, shared it, and enacted cycles of knowledge creation. Whatever methods are used, the processes of capturing data and events, reflecting on them, and moving to new actions are critical to quality and rigor, as we will discuss later in this chapter.

The collaborative process within a community of inquiry needs to acknowledge the nature of the tasks and task culture that exist within different communities of practice. The task culture is embedded within a set of basic assumptions that have formed within each community of practice around critical issues in dealing with the task at hand. For example, as a practitioner, "Manager A" in

Coghlan and Coughlan (Chapter 21) reflected how in the early stages of the project he found the material too academic and theoretical, and then later as he engaged with the project it became more interesting, understandable, and "real life." In this case, the manager and his community of practice had to become aware of the academic community of practice, and the academics had to become aware of the perspectives of the managers. The researchers' assumptions about the nature of knowledge and of research had to be shared and explored alongside the practitioners' needs for practical outcomes in order that they could continue to work together on the project.

Relational Issues in a Community of Inquiry

Partnership relationships within communities of inquiry do not happen automatically; they have to be designed and nurtured. Working relationships have to be built and all actors need to be explicit about their respective goals. The questions that drive the inquiry and action need to be developed together. The design of data collection processes and the design and implementation of action need to draw on all sets of expertise. Similarly, the analysis and interpretation of data need to be done by the community of inquiry. In short, all stages of the research require collaborative action that draws on the perspectives and skills of all actors, insiders and outsiders, academics and practitioners. The ARC Research Team note (Chapter 22) that while on the macro level of collaboration, a nice picture of the evolution of the partnership may seem evident, on the micro level, crisis and conflicts are everywhere. Bammer and colleagues (Chapter 20) allude to several difficulties that emerged in their group as the symposium proceeded, but note that as its participants did not shout one another down or reject ideas out of hand, the symposium can be considered a success from a relational standpoint.

A knowledge base of collaborative management research is that of the content and process of collaboration itself, which we have termed *relational* in Table 29.1. As this chapter and Bartunek's (Chapter 4) in particular illustrate, there is a growing literature and knowledge base about the different actors in a community of inquiry: (1) insiders as they engage in the research, (2) outsiders as they work to enable the insiders to perceive, understand, and act upon the events relevant to the research project, (3) practitioners and their perspectives and issues, and (4) academics and their perspectives and issues. In addition, there are the collaborative dynamics themselves, which involve genuine partnership, acknowledging the different perspectives and skills that each participant brings to the project and the relationships between them. This *Handbook* as a whole addresses these five issues and provides pointers to the knowledge base that helps us understand these complex dynamics. Relational culture points to how practitioners' practical orientation views academics' theoretical orientation and vice versa. Unless these are surfaced through the cycles of action and reflection and through the quality of dialogue and conversation between the actors in the community of inquiry, the issues remain hidden and can impede collaboration. Here, as Bartunek points out, the intergroup dynamics between the representatives of different communities of practice need to be such that intergroup trust, power equalization, and willingness within a community of inquiry can be named and dealt with.

We need to understand the perspectives of different actors—insiders, outsiders, practitioners, and academics. Hart, Kylen, Norrgren, and Stymne (2004) describe insiders as managers who "act to control and influence the actions of others to obtain certain ends" and outsiders as "actors who

produce explicit theories and models explaining how the world of managers hangs together" (p. 101). In this *Handbook*, Stebbins and Valenzuela (Chapter 23) and Coghlan and Coughlan (Chapter 21) provide examples of outside researchers who collaborated with inside managers and how the collaboration between the two contributed to both the outcomes of action of the respective projects and scientific knowledge from the research. As Bartunek (Chapter 4) reports, there has been a loosening of boundaries; researchers and practitioners may be insiders or outsiders, and the categories of insider and outsider are socially constructed and inseparable from other constructed identities.

The issues that insiders face when they engage in collaborative research in their own organizational systems are important to note. These issues identify the challenges that the insider community of practice confronts in its exercise of collaborative management research and that the outsiders may need to be sensitive to and work on with the insiders. The challenges are preunderstanding, role duality, and organizational politics (Coghlan, 2001; Coghlan & Brannick, 2005). The preunderstanding challenge is to have both closeness to the data and distance from it. This is particularly relevant in relation to organizational culture, where insiders' familiarity with the hidden shared assumptions that govern behavior is tacit and out of consciousness (Schein, 2004). The second challenge facing insiders in collaborative research centers on role duality. When insiders augment their normal organizational membership roles with the multiple roles in the community of inquiry, they are likely to encounter role conflict and find themselves caught between loyalty tugs, behavioral claims, and identification dilemmas. Throughout the collaborative research project, insiders are confronted with managing organizational politics. They have to maintain their credibility as effective drivers of inquiry and change and as astute political players. Addressing this set of challenges seems to require an ongoing assessment of the power and interests of relevant stakeholders in relation to different aspects of the project.

Within a community of inquiry, outsiders are external to the system being studied. They have a temporary relationship to the setting and have an impartial perspective, and if they are academics they learn through scientific observation, analysis, and intervention through collaboration with insiders. Interestingly, Cohen (in Mohrman et al., Chapter 24 in this *Handbook*) noted that she found that the insider practitioners were from the same academic heritage as the outsider academics and that they understood the competing and complementary nature of generating knowledge for theory and for practice. For her, this turned out to be the most rewarding collaboration of her career. If the outsiders are practitioners, they learn through observation and interaction with the insiders. Outsiders carry the responsibility of helping insiders create some distance from what they are close to, and if they are academics, the responsibility of educating insiders about the scientific discovery process. In short, they do not have the in-depth or experiential knowledge of the system that insiders have. Accordingly, they require skills at working with insiders to draw on and develop insiders' preunderstanding through the scientific discovery process, or skills to help the insiders move beyond their current understanding of the situation.

The dynamics in the CMRC are complex. While insiders may think they know the answers to questions they do not actually know, outsiders know that they do not know. Outsiders work with the insiders in supporting and confronting ways of thinking and action that are embedded in the insiders' patterns of interpreting events, in their relationships with other parts of the system, and in managerial behavior. Accordingly, an important dynamic in the collaboration between insiders who may be blind to what they don't actually know and the outsiders who try to clarify between knowledge and inference is the dynamic that enables them to learn to distinguish between them. In his contribution to this volume, Stebbins (Stebbins & Valenzuela, Chapter 23) reports that feedback he received as an outsider revealed that the insiders appreciated how he was constant, asked difficult questions, helped the managers communicate and listen, provided tools, organized meetings, and brought learning to the fore. As one of the insiders in this case, Valenzuela provided logistics, a different perspective and alternative ways to interpret the data, new insights, and follow-up.

Researchers, especially those who work in an action and collaborative mode, require skills in working collaboratively with others in a face-to-face mode. This mode is sometimes referred to as second-person skills (McGuire, Palus, & Torbert, Chapter 6 in this volume; Reason & Torbert, 2001). These skills include the ability to listen, to inquire, and to distinguish inferences and attributions in order to build and maintain the community of inquiry. Schein's work on clinical inquiry and process consultation, in which he identifies three skill sets—pure inquiry exploratory-diagnostic inquiry—and confrontive inquiry, provides a useful typology for developing skills that are required in collaborative management research (Schein, 1995, 2001; Coghlan & Shani, 2007). Actors within the community of inquiry—insiders, outsiders, academics, and practitioners—can all use the skill sets from their own perspective. Outsiders strive to help insiders see what is happening, understand why, and develop and implement action. Drawing on the typology of different forms of inquiry enables outsiders to draw out from insiders what they do not know and confront the limits of insiders' preunderstanding, and to explore the issues emerging from insiders' tensions between dual roles and their knowledge and ability to play the political games as required to survive and thrive. Insiders can use the typology to draw out of outsiders what they are thinking and what are intending. Similarly, academics can use it with practitioners and practitioners with academics.

In summary, how task and relational issues are handled in collaborative management research is at the core of determining how effective such efforts are. While the skills required to negotiate these issues are sometimes shared by the parties involved, more often it appears to be the case that the outsider will need to bring such skills to the table. More research on the development and application of these skills by outsider researchers is needed to understand how to improve the effectiveness of communities of inquiry.

The Challenge of Collaborative Management Research Communities

In the preceding pages, we have outlined the many challenges that confront those taking part in collaborative research into management issues. Our interest, however, is specifically in the community of inquiry that is created and evolves in such efforts. In contrast to the majority of writing on this topic, even in this volume, we are concerned with the entire community of inquiry and its evolution over time, rather than with a single researcher interacting with a single practitioner. A frequent notion of action research or collaborative inquiry is that of two individuals coming together to collaborate in producing knowledge; but in fact, this is never really the case. While there may be a primary individual representing scholarly interests in the project and a manager who represents the organization, both parties are representatives of larger systems that have

their own dynamics, momentum, interests, and concerns that must be considered and managed throughout a collaborative research effort. As key actors in either system enter or leave the collaboration, or shift roles within their respective organizations, the delicate negotiations that were conducted to create the original CMRC may need to be reopened to take new views and interests into account. Especially in longitudinal research, the evolving dynamics in the community probably have as much to do with shifts in membership or the priorities of the parties as they do with what is being learned.

Unless we understand that communities are more than individual actors, and that unique processes that transcend those of a simple two-person partnership are required to maintain the vibrancy of a community, many collaborative management research efforts will fail. Our call in this chapter is for our colleagues to undertake research on CMRCs that will shed light on the dynamics that must be managed at the community level, and not just in the partnership between one researcher and one manager. All of the many challenges outlined above in the literature must be managed at the community level as the community evolves over time. At present, we lack an understanding of how communities should be engaged in managing these issues in order to produce optimal results. This is research that needs to be undertaken.

QUALITY IN COLLABORATIVE MANAGEMENT RESEARCH COMMUNITIES

All research traditions postulate how research must be conducted to achieve high standards of rigor. Accordingly, within each research tradition, there are expressions of standards that are set with regard to validity, reliability, rigor, and quality. Because this

Handbook aims to address both practitioner and academic communities, it is vital that the quality dimensions of collaborative management research be articulated.

Bradbury (Chapter 28 in this *Handbook*) offers four dimensions around which the quality of collaborative management research may be based: practical value, social interaction, cycles of action and reflection, and active experimentation. Pasmore et al. (Chapter 27) talk about collaborative management research being rigorous, reflective and relevant. Levin (2003) suggests four criteria for judging the quality of action research: participation, real-life issues, joint meaning construction, and workable solutions.

Drawing on these authors, we suggest a framework of four dimensions for assessing the quality of CMRCs (Table 29.2).

1. The research topic must be a real-life issue, relevant to all members of the collaborative management research community.

2. The collaborative process must engage the community of inquiry in social interaction that is genuinely participative and collaborative and that acknowledges, builds on, and actualizes the perspectives, interests, and strengths that each party brings to the process.

3. The process must be reflective; the CMRC engages in cycles of action and reflection, supported by rigorous data-gathering methods, collaborative analysis and joint meaning construction, and agreed action, as the project is conceived, enacted, and evaluated.

4. The outcomes must be workable and sustainable and must encourage further

Table 29.2   Quality in a Collaborative Management Research Community: A Checklist for Action

Real-life issue studied	• Is this a real-life issue, relevant to both practitioners and academics and of practical and theoretical value? • Is the collaborative research guided by a simultaneous concern for real-life practical outcomes and the advancement of scientific knowledge?
Quality of collaborative process	• With regard to participation, how well does the collaborative research reflect partnership between insiders and outsiders, academics and practitioners?
Reflective process	• Is the process governed by a constant and iterative reflection? • Is the process of interpreting events, articulating meaning, and generating understanding a collaborative process between the insiders and outsiders, academics and practitioners?
Workable outcomes and actionable knowledge	• Does the collaborative research engage in significant work and sustainable change? • Is the knowledge generated actionable, and does it add to the scientific body of knowledge?

scientific experimentation, and the theory must be understood to be actionable and transportable and adaptable to other settings.

There are several questions that should be answered to test the quality of work performed by a community of inquiry. With regard to real-life issues, is the research guided by a concern for real-life practical outcomes and is it governed by systematic reflection as part of the process of organizational change? With regard to participation and true partnership, how well does the research reflect partnership between insiders and outsiders, academics and practitioners? With regard to joint meaning construction, is the process of interpreting events, articulating meaning, and generating understanding a collaborative process between the insiders and outsiders, academics and practitioners? Finally, with regard to workable solutions, does the collaborative management research engage in significant work and sustainable change?

CONCLUSIONS

Our understanding of organization and management issues is constrained by the dynamic nature of the organization under inquiry as well as by our ability to create a collective sensemaking of it. Scientific discoveries occur when we conceive the workplace in a new way (Stymne, 2006). Collaborative management research, involving insiders and outsiders, practitioners and academics, brings the values of theory and practice together in such a new way. Communities of practice tend to evolve within an organization and between organizations, where complex issues are subjected to practical analysis and combined with scientific inquiry that seeks to build on the practical knowing in order to generate deeper and broader understanding.

Our argument has been that attention to task and relational issues in collaborative management research efforts is central to making such efforts effective. The preferred position is that these issues are best shared by all the parties involved, though we acknowledge that some parties are more likely to exercise some roles more readily than others—writing by the scholars, as one example. More research is needed on the development and application of these skills by the different parties so as to understand how to improve the effectiveness of communities of inquiry.

A community of inquiry that is formed by discrete communities of practice involving insiders and outsiders, practitioners and academics in multiple configurations engages in collaborative management research. In this chapter, communities of inquiry are presented as a way of engaging in collaborative management research. We have suggested that little is known about managing the dynamics of collaboration at the community level over time and that more research is required to provide insights that will improve the current state of our practice. This chapter has also drawn together an integrating framework, with distinct components of content, process, and culture that pertain to task and relational issues in understanding and managing a community of inquiry. The framework provides a comprehensive way of thinking about the design of a community of inquiry. The designer is challenged to reflect on the many choices that are available and to search for the fit between the cultural context, the research content, and the scientific discovery process. Finally, this chapter provides a window into the issues of quality within the collaborative management research community and provides a synthesis that aims to help readers of this *Handbook* bring together the theory and accounts of the many varieties of collaborative management research that occur in the preceding pages.

REFERENCES

Adler, N., Shani, A. B. (Rami), & Styhre, A. (2004). *Collaborative research in organizations*. Thousand Oaks, CA: Sage.

Amabile, T., Patterson, C., Mueller, J., Wojcik, T., Odomirok, P., March, M., et al. (2001). Academic-practitioner collaboration in management research: A case of cross-profession collaboration. *Academy of Management Journal, 44*(2), 418–431.

Bartunek, J. M., & Louis, M. R. (1996). *Insider/outsider team research*. Thousand Oaks, CA: Sage.

Brown, J. S., & Duguid, P. (1991). Organizational learning and communities of practice: Toward a unified view of working, learning and innovation. *Organization Science, 2*(1), 40–56.

Coghlan, D. (2001). Insider action research projects: Implications for practising managers. *Management Learning, 32*, 49–60.

Coghlan, D., & Brannick, T. (2005). *Doing action research in your own organization* (2nd ed.). London: Sage.

Coghlan, D., & Rashford, N. S. (2006). *Organizational change and strategy: An interlevel dynamics approach*. New York: Routledge.

Coghlan, D., & Shani, A. B. (Rami). (2007). Insider action research: The dynamics of developing new capabilities. In P. Reason & H. Bradbury (Eds.), *The Sage handbook of action research* (2nd ed.). London: Sage.

Evered, M., & Louis, M. R. (1981). Alternative perspectives in the organizational sciences: "Inquiry from the inside" and "inquiry from the outside." *Academy of Management Review, 6*, 385–395.

Friedman, V. (2001). Action science: Creating communities of inquiry in communities of practice. In P. Reason & H. Bradbury (Eds.), *Handbook of action research: Participative inquiry and practice* (pp. 159–170). London: Sage.

Hart, H., Kylen, S. F., Norrgren, F., & Stymne, B. (2004). Collaborative research through an executive Ph.D. program. In N. Adler, A. B. (Rami) Shani, & A. Styhre (Eds.), *Collaborative research in organizations* (pp. 101–116). Thousand Oaks, CA: Sage.

Huxham, C., & Vangen, S. (2001). What makes practitioners tick? Understanding collaboration practice and practicing collaboration understanding. In J. Genefke & F. McDonald (Eds.), *Effective collaboration: Managing the obstacles to success* (pp. 1–16). London: Palgrave.

Levin, M. (2003). Action research and the research community. *Concepts and Transformation, 8*(3), 275–280.

Louis, M. R., & Bartunek, J. M. (1992). Insider/outsider research teams: Collaboration across diverse perspectives. *Journal of Management Inquiry, 1*(2), 101–110.

Lowstedt, J., & Stjernberg, T. (2006). *Producing management knowledge: Research as practice*. New York: Routledge.

Reason, P., & Torbert, W. R. (2001). The action turn: Towards a transformational social science. *Concepts and Transformation, 6*(1), 1–37.

Rynes, S., Bartunek, J., & Daft, R. (2001). Across the great divide: Knowledge creation and transfer between practitioners and academics. *Academy of Management Journal, 44*(2), 340–355.

Schein, E. H. (1995). Process consultation, action research and clinical inquiry: Are they the same? *Journal of Managerial Psychology, 10*(6), 14–19.

Schein, E. H. (1999). *Process consultation revisited: Building the helping relationship.* Reading, MA: Addison-Wesley.

Schein, E. H. (2001). Clinical inquiry/research. In P. Reason & H. Bradbury (Eds.), *Handbook of action research: Participative inquiry and practice* (pp. 228–237). London: Sage.

Schein, E. H. (2004). *Organizational culture and leadership* (3rd ed.). San Francisco: Jossey-Bass.

Shani, A. B. (Rami), David, A., & Willson, C. (2004). Collaborative research: Alternative roadmaps. In N. Adler, A. B. (Rami) Shani, & A. Styhre (Eds.), *Collaborative research in organizations* (pp. 83–100). Thousand Oaks, CA: Sage.

Shani, A. B. (Rami), & Pasmore, W. A. (1985). Organization inquiry: Towards a new model of the action research process. In D. D. Warrick (Ed.), *Contemporary organization development: Current thinking and applications* (pp. 438–448). Glenview, IL: Scott, Foresman.

Stymne, B. (2006). The innovative research enterprise. In J. Lowstedt & T. Stjernberg (Eds.), *Producing management knowledge: Research as practice* (pp. 261–274). New York: Routledge.

Teigland, R. (2003). *Knowledge networking: Structure and performance in networks of practice.* Stockholm: Gotab.

Wenger, E. (1998). *Communities of practice: Learning, meaning, and identity.* Cambridge, UK: Cambridge University Press.

Wenger, E., McDermott, R., & Snyder, W. (2002). *Cultivating communities of practice.* Boston: Harvard Business School Press.

CHAPTER 30

Toward Building a Collaborative Research Community

Susan Albers Mohrman

William A. Pasmore

A. B. (Rami) Shani

Bengt Stymne

Niclas Adler

We arrive at the end of our journey in a very different place than we began, which is one measure of a successful trip. In undertaking the creation of this volume, we expected to learn a great deal about the current state of the art in collaborative management research, and we have. We were also prepared to be impressed by the thoughtful and dedicated efforts of our colleagues, and we are. What we didn't anticipate, and where we turn our attention now, is how difficult it would be to define the parameters of collaborative management research. Without alignment at a fundamental level concerning what constitutes collaborative management research and a shared vision for the role it can play in advancing practice and theory, it is difficult to sustain the healthy dialogue that is necessary among members of a community of interest for the continuing evolution of this methodology.

We can now, with the benefit of the views of our contributors here, do a better job of defining what it is that we know, and get a better sense of the range of activities that are offered as collaborative management research. The book has presented many examples and a variety of approaches, in many cases employing sophisticated intervention and learning approaches to address important managerial and organizational issues as well as to challenge dominant approaches and frameworks. We are able to get a sense of what their impact has been, and of their potential. We are also more able to see into the dark spaces where progress may have stalled and where additional work is necessary to illuminate the path to further progress. The rich material in this book can be used to reflect on what truly constitutes collaborative management research. In our opinion, at least, this has the feel of making headway.

It is clear from many of the chapters that enacting collaborative management research in a complex setting is a challenging task, although one with great potential to improve both the knowledge and the practice of managing and organizing. It is also clear that collaborative management research brings an exciting potential to address major boundary-spanning challenges that necessitate joint efforts by different groups of stakeholders driven by different governing logics. If, despite the many difficulties that have been recounted in this volume, there is still as large an appetite for undertaking this kind of work as there appears to be, there must truly be something of great value here. In this final chapter, we hope to make clear what we have gained from efforts to date as well as the many challenges and exciting opportunities that lie ahead.

DEFINITIONAL ISSUES

We start with our definition that collaborative management research involves collaboration between scholars and practitioners to yield knowledge to inform practice and the theoretical understandings that pertain to the academic field of management and organization studies. The approaches and examples described in this volume are quite diverse, and indeed, appear to constitute a tool chest that can be used to yield knowledge about different kinds of systems, different levels of analysis, and different theoretical foci, as well as to deal with the very different practice foci of a wide variety of actors. We describe the following three approaches not as a

typology, but to give a sense for the range of activity.

One approach offered by contributors here is the assembling of networks of practitioners and academics to share perspectives about and collaboratively investigate a particular realm of concern with a hoped-for emergent set of actions that can also serve as a focus for learning and knowledge generation. Examples include the networks/learning forums described by Mirvis (Chapter 10), which focused on sustainability, branding, or corporate citizenship; bringing together various academic fields and policy makers to address issues of ignorance and uncertainty in policy realms (Bammer & the Goolabri Group, Chapter 20), and assembling an international gathering of trade unionists to learn about and hopefully develop a strategy for forging social partnerships (Huzzard & Gregory, Chapter 16).

A second approach involves the convening of stakeholders to address a particular system's needs for development through setting up a highly participative inquiry process that may include action research. The learning process and action taking of the participants in the system are the major focus. The researchers, while bringing useful frameworks and theories to the action system, may be focused on advancing knowledge of how collaboration and learning occurs. Examples from the book include Olascoaga and Kur's piece on strategic alignment (Chapter 12); the work of the ARC Research Team (Chapter 22) to establish regional university-community partnerships; Stebbins and Valenzuela's focus on communication forums (Chapter 23); McGuire, Palus, and Torbert's example of developmental action inquiry (DAI; Chapter 6); and Docherty and Shani's treatment of learning mechanisms (Chapter 8).

A third approach entails targeted collaborative research in which the academic researchers and the practitioners set out to research a problem where their interests intersect, and where the shared purpose is to create knowledge of new organizational/ managerial approaches. The examples include Hatchuel and David's collaboration with Renault (Chapter 7) to discover new organizational forms for the innovative organization; the MIT/corporate technology research collaborations described by Roth (Chapter 17); and the collaboration between Hewlett-Packard (HP) and the University of Southern California (USC) described by Mohrman et al. (Chapter 24) that was aimed at creating an empirically grounded model for new product development teams. The Coghlan and Coughlan piece (Chapter 21) on the complex network of collaborative research structures formed to yield knowledge and improve practice in extended manufacturing enterprises is another example.

This has also been the intended focus of the work of TruePoint and FENIX, reported by Adler and Beer (Chapter 26). These authors argue that internal management R&D departments in organizations, such as the one at HP described by Stu Winby (Mohrman et al., Chapter 24), are required in order to pursue and sustain these activities.

Clearly, these three approaches are not mutually exclusive. The Coghlan and Coughlan work (Chapter 21), for example, included highly focused collaborative research teams doing research and creating knowledge about particular aspects of extended manufacturing enterprises, and it included regional learning networks in which companies came together in learning forums to share best practices and find ways to apply the new knowledge. Roth (Chapter 17) explores the cultural issues enabling or inhibiting technology collaborations at MIT, in a setting where collaborative research was the core task process of the social systems he studied. In addition, Roth facilitated the Ford/MIT collaboration in an action research approach involving the building of a learning forum to overcome cultural barriers to effective

collaboration. In fact, this set of chapters provides evidence of and makes an argument for the versatility that is required to carry out truly collaborative research—attending to the structural, process, and cultural aspects of the collaboration (Coghlan & Shani, Chapter 29), as well as to practical and theoretical knowledge-generating activities. It also supports the argument made by Pasmore, Woodman, and Simmons (Chapter 27) that if collaborative research is to be successful in changing system performance and generating knowledge outcomes, a team of researchers may be required.

Some defining features of collaborative management research seem to be held in common by most of the authors. Most describe the integration of the knowledge of diverse stakeholders in the process of yielding new management/organizational approaches and also deal in some way with the need to achieve collaboration between these actors. Almost all include a model of learning in practice, with most aspiring to action research to either yield or test knowledge in practice. In most cases, these scholars engage with the world of practice in an effort to yield knowledge useful for both theory and action.

Our contributors differ in their depiction of what is being learned, for what purposes, and through what methodologies. A core difference is most starkly captured in the discussion by Hatchuel and David (Chapter 7) comparing action research to their advocated approach, intervention research in management (IRM). In their view, action research primarily aims "to implement an impact-seeking intervention in organizations that face complex problems" (p. 146) and involves learning through constructive dialogue and reflexivity among all concerned members of the targeted system. According to Hatchuel and David, the belief system underlying action research is that "pursuing humanistic values in organizations in the long run constitutes a major factor of organizational motivation and performance" (p. 147). They contrast this approach with the intent of IRM to conduct research that yields new models of organizing and working that, through systematic development and testing, become "legitimized and validated *outside the organization* by a widely referenced set of academic and professional supports" (p. 148).

IRM is inherently collaborative, in that the hosting organization or system works collaboratively with the academic researchers to provide the access and data required to generate and test such models. But the academic researchers are not concerned with ensuring that the new models that are established become embedded in practice—the action domain of establishing a model in use is seen as the purview of the system itself. This division of focus was also seen in the HP/USC collaboration, in which systematic research into new models for knowledge teams was the collaborative focus between the academics, internal consultants, and the product divisions, but the action research component was carried out by the internal consultants working in a highly participative manner with interested divisions to determine the implications of the new models for their own practices.

Underlying this differentiation in purpose and methodologies are differences of values, intent, and epistemology. Yet these may not be as stark as they at first glance seem. Whereas Hatchuel and David (Chapter 7) and Mohrman et al. (Chapter 24) may be searching for generalizable or new models of management and organization, they both, we believe, would subscribe to a social view and a practice-based understanding of how knowledge such as management models is generated and embodied. Neither would disagree that the ultimate disposition of this knowledge in the form of actual practices within an organization will emanate from social processes in the organization, which can be informed, but not prescribed, by management models. Mohrman et al. would explicitly include an action research phase in their research, based on the notion that the ultimate test of the validity of management knowledge is in practice, and that this goes beyond but includes the need for learning and tailoring to occur in situ. Such tests would no doubt also be part of the legitimation and validation that Hatchuel and David would recommend.

It is thus possible to adhere to the belief that knowledge is socially constructed and that collaboration between people with different perspectives and knowledge bases is required to generate effective management models, without believing that democratizing the workplace and providing voice are necessarily the ultimate aims of the research collaboration. This can be true even if one also values participation and democratic principles of interaction. Yet other researchers who contributed to the book (e.g., the ARC Research Team, Chapter 22; Holmstrand, Härnsten, and Löwstedt, Chapter 9) adhere to a strong values-driven practice of collaborative research that strives to create democratic systems as the, or one of the, explicit objectives of the research. This may be based on a strongly held epistemology that holds that knowledge is not ever generalizable, but rather is created by each community as it reflects, plans, enacts, and learns. It may also be based on a strongly held pragmatic philosophy (see Bradbury, Chapter 28) that judges the outcome of action research by the impact of the research on action.

It should be noted that the chapters in this volume show that differences in these beliefs and values may also lead to a different focus of collaborative research. At one end of the continuum is collaborative research strongly aimed at generating models and solutions, while at the other end is research aimed at understanding how to set up and embed the collaborative learning process required for humanistic ends and collaboration in the solving of problems. Of course, many of the chapters in the book incorporate a mixture of these purposes, while tending to lean one way or the other. The pieces by Walshok and Stymne (Chapter 15) and Roth (Chapter 17) are clear examples of this mixture—where the authors are interested in the conditions that enable collaborative research, but the parties engaging in the collaborative research are focused almost completely on scientific outcomes. Olascoaga and Kur, in their work on strategic alignment (Chapter 12), and Coghlan and Coughlan, in their work on extended manufacturing systems (Chapter 21), exhibit a similar dual focus on achieving participative cultures and on learning about a particular organizational capability.

Many questions about the defining characteristics of collaborative research are raised by this interesting and unavoidable juxtaposition of the search for content knowledge about how to lead or design an effective organization with the search for knowledge about how to build a collaboration that includes the various actors or agents who are relevant to the generation of such knowledge. When is the bringing of knowledge about process and content to a system that wants to participatively address problems or redesign itself consulting and not research? Does a case study of such a process constitute research, or is it simply a description of the application of known knowledge, albeit with an increase over time in the ability to address nuances and address local complexities and conditions? Does collaborative management research require that the academics and practitioners jointly pursue generalizable and locally effective knowledge (as in the case of the HP/USC or the Renault examples), or can the scholar-practitioner be seen by the organization as a consultant, and "slip in" the research activities, as described by Tenkasi and Hay (Chapter 3) in their treatment of the role of the insider scholar-practitioner. What are the basic standards for research? For example, is it necessary that collaborators in research take into account (if only to go in a different direction) what is already known and models that already exist, rather than reinventing knowledge? Does research have to aim at extending rather than reapplying that knowledge—or even at addressing anomalies that bring previous knowledge into question and require the invention or discovery of new modes of managing and organizing? Is it research if a group of participants are learning from each other and from their own experience but not bringing in expertise and knowledge from the outside? Or is that an example of learning in practice, but not of research?

We do not believe that it is possible to answer these questions definitively at this early stage in the treatment of collaborative research, although we will take a stab later in the chapter at addressing the standards for collaborative research that we believe should guide the unfolding of this methodology.

WHAT WE NOW KNOW ABOUT COLLABORATIVE MANAGEMENT RESEARCH

We have learned much about collaborative management research through our collaborative work with the many authors of the different chapters as well as through the ongoing dialogue and debate among the editors over a two-year period. Listed below are seven of these conclusions.

1. Conditions for undertaking collaborative management research are seldom optimal.

2. The best way to maintain and enhance collaboration is to work collaboratively.

3. Opportunities for using collaborative management research to enhance organizations and systems are much broader than we imagined.

4. If methods are hammers, opportunities may look like nails—but fitting the tool to the opportunity is a critical part of responsible action research.

5. Researchers and managers live different experiences, but the greatest progress occurs when their dreams align naturally.

6. Developing the capacity to conduct collaborative management research may be the only way to address the growing knowledge-relevancy gap.

7. Sustainability of the collaborative management research paradigm will depend on the ethics and behaviors of members of the community.

We now briefly discuss each of these conclusions.

1. Conditions for undertaking collaborative management research are seldom optimal.

As described by a number of contributors to this volume (Adler & Beer; Bartunek; Coghlan & Shani; Knights, Alferoff, Starkey, & Tiratsoo; Pasmore & Woodman; Roth; and Werr & Greiner, among others), the preconditions for undertaking successful collaborative research are seldom ideal for supporting the kinds of joint effort required to produce the highest quality outcomes for all parties. In a number of cases represented in the book, the nature of collaboration is not of the depth and duration that we would wish for under optimal conditions. "Full collaboration" would entail the following:

- An up-front discussion and agreement between the researchers and practitioners of the objectives of the research effort, including the clear benefits to be gained by all parties.
- Agreement on the overall approach to the research and a discussion of available methods for involving participants in the research and for the collection of data.
- Agreement on the specific hypotheses to be investigated, the problem to be solved or

opportunities to be captured, and the knowledge outcomes desired.
- Agreement on the intervention or change to be introduced, including scope, timing, method, level of involvement, roles, and communications.
- Involvement by all parties in determining the data collection approaches and, to the extent possible, in collecting the data.
- Mutual interpretation of results, drawing conclusions based on the perspective of various actors involved in the system as well as external researchers.
- Support for the implementation of new processes, procedures, or arrangements that return value to the system for the effort expended.
- Joint participation in the dissemination of knowledge internally and externally, whether through meetings, speeches, publications, or the creation of materials.

Few efforts conform to these ideal parameters. In practice, researchers are sometimes satisfied to simply gain access to systems where they can collect data, and managers may be interested in answers but not necessarily in spending a great deal of time or effort as collaborators in research undertakings. When collaboration is less than ideal, research can still be conducted and insights gained, but the overall value of the work is likely to be less in terms of its impact on either the system or its contributions to the body of knowledge. If too many corners are cut, or the difficulties associated with collaborative management research become too pricklish to easily surmount, potential collaborators on both sides will begin to question the value of the approach and may decline opportunities to engage in future efforts.

2. The best way to maintain and enhance collaboration is to work collaboratively.

Although the above may sound like a tautology, the fact that the need for greater collaboration is mentioned so many times by the contributors to this volume means that the statement is not as obvious as it seems. In fact, one of the core messages of several of our contributors (ARC Research Team; Bartunek; Coghlan & Shani; McGuire et al.; Pasmore, Woodman, & Simmons; Roth) is that improving our ability to collaborate between management and academia may be the single most important step we can take to enhance the overall quality and value of our joint efforts. If we think of collaborative management research as a process that begins with the discovery of common interests and ends with knowledge dissemination or reapplication, rather than simply the collection and feedback of data in an organization or system, the importance of collaboration in this approach to research becomes more evident.

In traditional research, deep collaboration is not required because the goal is the collection and analysis of data, not its application to practice. Traditional research may not even require the consent of those studied for data collection, as in the case of research based on published financial data or public documents. Since one goal in collaborative management research is to see new insights applied to enhance organizational performance, it is obvious that the work will not be complete until both the researcher and the practitioner concur that there is something of value to be applied in practice. Indeed, it can be said that what is learned through research is not truly knowledge until it has been tested in practice. Knowing that this is the end goal changes the relationship between the researcher and the practitioner from the beginning. Although many of the same data collection and analysis techniques may be used in both, a completely different mindset is required to engage in collaborative research as compared with traditional research, and it is one that is not easily adopted or carried out. As McGuire et al. point out, a certain amount of introspection and development may be required on the part of individuals before they are capable of becoming effective collaborators in learning.

Other authors (for example, Tenkasi & Hay; Mirvis; Roth; and Mohrman et al.) stress the importance of bridging the language and culture of practice and theory, and discuss the importance of scholar-practitioner hybrid roles and of boundary artifacts to connect the different worlds. Werr and Greiner suggest that closer collaboration between consultants and academics can help bridge the gap and increase relevance to practice, consultancies, and academic knowledge. At a minimum, this work has raised our awareness of the important challenges that must be overcome to achieve a level of collaboration that supports truly excellent joint efforts at learning how to build more effective organizational systems. While even more attention must be paid to the issues surrounding the formation and evolution of productive collaborative relationships, we hope that readers will no longer make the mistake of underestimating the difficulty involved in developing the mindset and skills that are required for this kind of work.

3. Opportunities for using collaborative management research to enhance organizations and systems are much broader than we imagined.

Our initial focus on organizations in the for-profit sector was immediately challenged by our contributors. Several submitted manuscripts that carried the application of collaborative management research into realms we had not anticipated. Tandon and Farrell (Chapter 14) addressed gender differences in the management of not-for-profit organizations in India. Walshok and Stymne (Chapter 15) examined the effect of innovative regions on this kind of research, while Huzzard and Gregory (Chapter 16) explored applications of these methods with trade unions and Apel, Heikensten, and Jansson (Chapter 18) discussed how the collaboration between academics and central bankers has affected the Swedish economy. The ARC Research Team (Chapter 22) discussed collaboration to increase connectedness between a university and its surrounding community, and to find ways to increase the economic base and opportunity for the diverse population in the region.

What is clear now is that the applicability of methods addressed in this volume is not limited to a particular venue. The variety of organizations and systems that can benefit from collaborative management research is limited only by our imagination and the willingness of those involved to lend their knowledge, time, and attention to efforts to understand and improve the way their systems work. While there will always be unique considerations to be addressed in conducting research in for-profit corporate settings, the challenges these considerations pose are no greater and the benefits no more important than those that present themselves in not-for-profits, networks, and governmental settings.

As the challenges that affect our future spill over borders and regions, we are forced to adopt a more global perspective. Companies are becoming more global, and some of the most pressing issues they face have to do with how to operate effectively in many countries and cultures without losing coherency of purpose or incurring coordination costs that are excessive. Societies are more porous, so that work and populations move back and forth across former barriers with greater regularity. Electronic communications, television coverage, and higher levels of literacy have created more global awareness and more careful international observation of practices that were once known only to dictators and their victims. Conflicts that arise in one part of the world draw in others and affect international trade. Natural catastrophes bring in volunteers and aid from all corners of the world.

Many of these issues are amenable to collaborative management research, provided that we can gain the right footholds. The contributions here demonstrate that even complex and far-flung systems are open to study and improvement. We are truly limited only by the stature of our dreams.

4. If methods are hammers, opportunities may look like nails—but fitting the tool to the opportunity is a critical part of responsible action research.

We seem to have created a system in our profession that rewards individuals for inventing and promoting methodologies that can be named by acronyms. We have fallen prey to this convention ourselves at times, referring to collaborative management research as CMR. Elsewhere in this volume, the reader will have been exposed to DAI, EME, IRM, DSA, STS, and ARC, among others. The desire to innovate is strong, as is the need to differentiate one's innovations from those of others. The price we pay, of course, is that it is difficult to speak with one another, let alone understand how we might work more closely together in advancing the discipline. At best, we are working at an exciting moment in the evolution of the field, where we are pointed sharply upward on the innovation "S" curve. At worst, we are competing for legitimacy, fame, and fortune, and confusing the hell out of our potential partners in the process.

There are, of course, more than enough settings crying out for the generation of knowledge to guide practice in the turbulent world we live in. There are plenty of organizations and systems in need of new approaches and far too few members of this small community to service all of them. But from examples given in this volume (by Knights et al., Roth, Bammer, Coghlan & Coughlan, and others) we know that to date there is not a broad understanding of how to reliably carry out this research in a manner that keeps the parties engaged and that results in knowledge products. Success requires tremendous skills, patience, and relationship building. It also requires that all parties come to value the generation of management knowledge through collaborative research. The building of a community of inquiry (Coghlan & Shani, Chapter 29) requires a deep understanding of the elements of successful collaboration. Obviously, increasing the frequency with which collaborative research is successfully conducted and advancing the knowledge of how to do it successfully to meet the outcomes of the various actors should be a primary goal. This type of work is recognized by very few managers at this point and is suspect to many academics—and the plethora of individual approaches and obscure terminology cannot help. Yet the imagined opportunity to become the next Google or eBay brand in collaborative management research by being associated with some special method is difficult for us to resist.

While the differences in language and approaches may slow the overall rate of progress in the field, we are even more deeply concerned about how our choices of method ultimately affect our collective track record. It stands to reason that if different approaches to collaborative management research exist, they have definable strengths and weaknesses when compared with other approaches. It also stands to reason that opportunities to work with systems come in different shapes and sizes. Putting these two thoughts together, we hypothesize that certain methods are better suited to particular organizational settings or issues than others. If we all bring the full deck of approaches with us to these opportunities and choose from the best among them, there is no issue; but if each of us arrives at every opportunity with only one tool, we grow concerned. Since the field is still fragile and evolving, we would prefer to see our collective attention placed on making certain that our collaborators' needs are met rather than to have the majority of our attention go to improving our individual approach or reputation.

Again, we draw the comparison with medical research and suggest that one of the reasons that patients have faith in physicians is that doctors do a reasonable job of self-monitoring when it comes to introducing new treatments to patients. Patients who are "impatient" can choose to see individuals who offer treatment outside the established system; but when they do so, we hope they are aware of the risks they are taking. In our profession, we are less organized and less likely to self-police.

While we are very pleased with the efforts of our contributors to advance the state of the art, we are nevertheless concerned that without some shared knowledge and vocabulary, collaborative management research could devolve into each individual's favorite method. Currently, management collaborators have no way of knowing whether the methods applied are "approved" by the scientific community. Since very few managers will ever work with more than one academic partner, it is unlikely that they will become familiar with the range of methods that are available and be assisted in choosing the one that is best for them. It is our responsibility to educate ourselves and our partners in this regard, and to advise them to adopt the methods that are most likely to create value, given their circumstances. It is also our hope that this will bring both our scientific community and our organizations to a better place.

5. Researchers and managers live different experiences, but the greatest progress occurs when their dreams align naturally.

The history of collaborative management research tells us that one of the most successful "schools" of this kind of work is that of sociotechnical systems thinking and practice. As noted by Kolodny and Halpern (Chapter 13), from its inception there was a happy coincidence of shared values and concerns between academic thought leaders and practitioners in the sociotechnical school. The school began its efforts utilizing techniques that are very much in keeping with the principles outlined by the most forward-thinking contributors to this volume. Objectives of the research were framed jointly, methods were discussed and shaped by mutual input, interventions were carried out with the full participation of both parties, and the knowledge disseminated frequently included the names of both the academics and the practitioners.

More than simply discovering that everything old is new again, our contributors are looking at what made the old so good through a new pair of lenses. Werr and Greiner (Chapter 5) remind us that collaborative management research started even earlier than the sociotechnical school, with the work of Frederick Taylor, followed by the Hawthorne studies. Tenkasi and Hay (Chapter 3) take us back even further, to the teachings of Aristotle, who believed as strongly as Lewin in the practical value of good theory.

By examining these roots, we discover that behind the history are individuals with a commitment to learning in a collaborative environment, often with partners who bring practical concerns and day-to-day needs to the table. Whether it was producing more coal or oil, finding ways to engage members of communities in their community's development, or discovering how to span the gulf between universities and consumers of knowledge, the best of the early exemplars and cases here have a number of things in common:

- The researchers and practitioners shared common values regarding collaboration and participation as a means of building commitment to change. They trusted that people in systems were capable of learning, understanding the operation of their organization or system, and making good choices about how to improve them. Although the academics brought expertise, they did not function as "experts" in the sense of giving preformulated advice or answers; they were, in the vernacular of organization development, "process-oriented"—they paid attention to how things were done, including how their knowledge and frameworks were shared, and were less concerned about the specific answers that were created by participants to the challenges they faced.

- There was a desire on the part of both parties to contribute broadly to knowledge rather than simply fix a problem. In the best exemplars, academics and practitioners could easily have exchanged roles, and in some sense they did from time to time. Often, joint publications resulted from these collaborative efforts.

- Both parties were highly driven to invent improvements in how organizations or systems operate. These were not individuals who cherished the status quo. They were the restless dreamers who believed deeply that change was not only possible, but beneficial. In almost every instance, there was also a humanist bent to their dreams; they wanted systems to be better places for people to work and live, not just more efficient or profitable.

We can't say with certainty that collaborative management research is possible between parties who do not share values like those above, but we have our doubts. Based on what we have seen in the cases presented and reviewed here, we would assert that the greater alignment there is on the values outlined above, the more likely it is that collaborative management research will take root and produce results of true value to both the organization and the scientific community.

6. Developing the capacity to conduct collaborative management research may be the only way to address the growing knowledge-relevancy gap.

Several of our authors (Knights et al.; Roth; Werr & Greiner) note that the gap between the interests of academic researchers and practitioners appears to be growing, as members of the academy are rewarded for producing journal publications that often deal with questions of concern only to fellow academics rather than being rewarded for working to improve management practice. In their first contribution to the volume, David and Hatchuel (Chapter 2) explore the issues and tensions involved in moving back and forth from universal theory to actionable knowledge, and in their second (Hatchuel & David, Chapter 7), they remind us that some of the greatest innovations in management have been driven by the actions of managers instead of academics. Bartunek points out how the roles of academics must "stretch" toward management in insider/outsider research, and she, like Mirvis, Roth, Tenkasi and Hay, and Werr and Greiner describe the gap that has to be overcome between the perspectives of academics and practitioners, if relevancy is to be achieved.

In fact, much of the collaborative research reported in this volume has been carried out by academics located in centers or research institutes set up specifically to enable research that is connected to practice. The institutional setting and the reward criteria appear to be important enablers, as does the orientation of the researchers toward the theory-practice "divide." The ARC Research Team report on their study of their own efforts to build such a center to conduct action research to have a positive impact on the economy and society of a region in northern Israel. They stress how difficult the journey has been for those caught between the expectations of the academic community and their personal desires to make a difference in their society. Mohrman et al. depict the ongoing research trajectories that have been carried out as part of the programmatic collaborative work of the Center for Effective Organizations at USC—a center that has cultivated collaborative research relationships with a number of companies for the past 28 years. In the particular collaboration they describe, their partner, Hewlett-Packard, had established an internal management R&D group to partner with academics to generate

knowledge and produce knowledge assets. This kind of firm-based management R&D capability is advocated by Adler & Beer from their more than 15 years of experience of running two centers devoted to collaborative management research. Such a group provides the mirror to the academic research center, and a natural point of linkage between academics and practitioners who have a mission to develop rigorous knowledge that can inform practice.

Docherty and Shani argue generally for more permanent mechanisms for encouraging collaboration between academics and managers, and Holmstrand et al. offer the Swedish research circle approach as evidence that under the right conditions, sustainable collaborative research models can develop in a society. Although desirable, building a stable institution based on collaborations that are relevant to practitioners as well as academics is not easy. Knights et al. and Roth examined university-industry research networks and found that very few have achieved long-term viability, in large part because the evaluation criteria for faculty work against the provision of value to collaborating companies. Companies find that they do not derive the value they had hoped for in part because the academics have such a different focus. Stebbins and Valenzuela discuss a long-term collaborative effort in the pharmaceutical operations department of a hospital system—a relationship where the academic is also oriented to the company's valued outcomes because he is also providing consulting services. This provides substantiation that consultants are a natural bridge between the academic and practitioner participants in collaborative research—individuals with a foot in both camps, because their professional practice demands both the continual advancement of their own formal knowledge and the ability to advance practice through the application of that knowledge. Tenkasi and Hay have found that the ability of internal scholar-practitioners, often members of internal consulting groups, to carry out research depends on their simultaneously delivering consulting services. George Roth concludes from his study of collaborative company/academic research at MIT that collaborations are sustained through the achievement of results. The value that collaborating practitioners seek is the generation of knowledge that results in enhanced practice.

In their own way, each of the contributions in the book points to progress that was made in improving management practice that would have been unlikely to occur had there not been a close association between academics and practitioners. In none of these instances could it be imagined that the events described would have taken place if managers in the systems involved had been left on their own to extract knowledge from journal publications. Nor is it likely that the work of the academic researchers would have been so well informed about the issues facing members of these systems that the theories and publications that resulted could be readily reapplied in other systems challenged by similar circumstances. This deep understanding of the systems being studied is, we believe, an important part of learning the boundaries of the knowledge that is created. We conclude, with acknowledged bias, that the only effective way to rapidly close the knowledge-relevancy gap is through closer collaboration between the academic and management communities, as evidenced in the contributions in this volume.

7. Sustainability of the collaborative management research paradigm will depend on the ethics and behaviors of members of the community.

Bartunek points out the emergence of institutional review boards in many academic settings, which require researchers to obtain informed consent from their research subjects. She points out that in interventional research, it is often difficult to know what people are consenting to, although ideally the course of action is jointly determined. She also points out that ensuring "safety" for participants who are being asked to speak and contribute to that course of action is an essential element of ethical outsider intervention. These issues underscore the importance of academic researchers nurturing effective relationships with their practitioner partners and putting their interests first. The interests of various institutional settings and the model for resourcing the collaboration can also raise potential ethical issues. Both Roth and Knights et al. point out that universities struggle with their independence when they accept funding from industry sources, and this is certainly indicative of the larger issue of maintaining "objectivity" in conducting research in organizational settings when managers expect returns on their investments of time and money. Werr and Greiner also discuss the tensions that arise among researchers, consultants, and managers as the three parties attempt to find ways to work together that achieve their joint and separate goals.

Ethical issues such as those described above inevitably hover over the context of collaborative management research. As pointed out by Mohrman and Shani in the "voices" section of this *Handbook*, research collaborations, like any other social system, are populated by various "agents"—individuals and collectives each working to achieve their own purposes through the collaboration. That their goals are partially aligned around the research collaboration does not mean that the temptations to derive personal benefit at the expense of the other collaborators goes away. Certainly, to achieve sustainability, issues of mutual benefit need to be addressed, and finding the right solution to balance the interests of each party is not always straightforward. It is our view, again, that widespread utilization of collaborative research methodologies will not occur if academic researchers do not become aware of these potential pitfalls and develop codes of behavior that unequivocally protect the participants at the research site and guard against their exploitation.

We believe strongly in the power of collaborative management research to bridge the knowledge-relevancy gap between academia and managers. We are also aware that managers are suspicious of the value that researchers bring, having experienced directly or heard through others stories about researchers who disrupted operations to gain data without returning any immediate value. Frankly, we marvel at times at the willingness of some managers to allow their organizations to be the subjects of case studies that are used to teach students the "wrong way" to do things, or to open their doors to researchers simply for the sake of advancing knowledge without any expectation of direct benefit in return. Researchers anxious to publish may use whatever relationships they have to gain access to systems they wish to study, and perhaps because, at times, personal friendships are involved, less attention may be paid to making certain that there is resulting benefit to both parties.

Simply sending a copy of the research results or a published article or case study to the manager is not, in our view, enough to compensate for their willingness to allow researchers access to their world. For sustained collaboration on increasingly interesting and important topics of concern to both academics and managers, we need to ensure that real value is returned or at least offered. Real value must be defined by our partners; we must ask them the question of what they expect or need to receive that would make the collaboration worthwhile and encourage them to repeat the experience in the future. Over time, if we do this correctly, the depth and breadth of the issues we are able to explore will grow, as will the importance of

our findings and the value of those findings to our collaborators. If, on the other hand, we leave our partners with the impression that they have been duped in the name of science, we should not expect collaborative management research to flourish.

Since we share a common reputation, it is important for us to self-regulate and to call ethical violations on the part of our colleagues to their attention. In the future, we would like to see violations of collaborative ethics treated in the same way that we treat data falsification or unsafe human subject experiments today; at a minimum, we should refuse to publish work based on data obtained without value to the system from which it was obtained.

Of course, there are many other ethical issues that are involved in the conduct of research in organizations, including those that have been addressed by the research and consulting communities elsewhere, such as making certain that we aren't harming workers when we help managers make their systems more efficient, or ensuring that as we collect data, specific individuals aren't identified as "the problem" in our analyses. Space doesn't allow us to go into a full discussion of these issues here, so we simply repeat our call for our colleagues to be aware of their decisions and avoid situations that would bring discredit to the academy and the evolving community of interest in collaborative research.

STANDARDS FOR COLLABORATIVE MANAGEMENT RESEARCH

This volume has opened the door to a debate of the standards for and even the definition of collaborative management research. And yet, it would seem to be in the interest of advancing the methodology and its legitimacy to offer a first stab at setting such standards. These standards stem in part from the definitional statements that we provided in the introductory chapter.

1. Collaborative research efforts include the active involvement of managers and researchers in the framing of the research agenda, the selection and pursuit of methods, and the development of (implications for) action.

2. "Collective inquiry," the joint pursuit of answers to questions of mutual interest through dialogue, experimentation, the review of knowledge, or other means, is necessary but not sufficient for a learning and development collaboration to be called collaborative research.

3. Collaborative research is characterized by dual and intermingled processes of (a) self-development of the organization or system that is adopting new structures and processes, and (b) systematic knowledge production processes as researchers contribute to a broader body of knowledge that is accessible beyond the organization itself. Creating forums for collective inquiry is a common approach to ensure that these two processes are learning from each other.

4. Inputs into the research process include relevant existing knowledge from theory and from practice, including knowledge about the substantive issues facing the system and methodological knowledge about how to conduct research and how to establish collaborations. Collaborative management research, like other forms of research, builds on and expands beyond, and in some cases purposefully departs from, existing knowledge and practice.

5. Collaborative management research involves the exchange and recombination of knowledge from multiple sources, including both theory and practice. This requires the ability to translate knowledge across different communities of practice.

6. Collaborative management research has a clearly defined knowledge-generation process that adheres to research standards appropriate to the research methodology being employed.

7. The quality standards for collaborative management research include actionability (as defined by Bradbury, Chapter 28 in this volume).

8. Collaborative management research must be evaluated in relationship to the intended outcomes of the collaboration, including the impact of the collaboration on the host system and whether the knowledge that is produced is disseminated more broadly than within the participating system.

It is not our intent to denigrate action research or other collaborations that do not adhere to these standards; certainly there is a tremendous need for consultants and action researchers to work as collaborators with systems that need to develop their capabilities and to apply known knowledge and innovative techniques for this purpose. But we do not believe that all collaborative inquiry and action research constitutes collaborative management research. Certainly, collaborative processes of collective inquiry and learning are highly valuable, and a case can be made that they should be routinized within a complex system in order for the system to perform optimally in achieving its objectives (Docherty & Shani, Chapter 8). Nevertheless, it is our intent to lay out what we believe to be the requirements for knowledge generation through research in a collaborative mode that contributes to theory and practice.

CHALLENGES AND OPPORTUNITIES THAT LIE AHEAD IN BUILDING A COLLABORATIVE MANAGEMENT RESEARCH COMMUNITY

To build a larger and more vibrant community of interest that will propel us forward, a number of things need to happen. First, we need to understand exactly what the field is about; we need a cogent statement of the epistemology of collaborative management research that helps us understand what's in and what's out, so that we can come together where we hold common interests. Second, we need to create a compendium of methodologies that can be applied by more than one person in a variety of settings, and provide the means by which our colleagues can become more proficient in implementing them. Third, we need to communicate the value of this work more broadly among both academic and managerial audiences. Fourth, we need to develop a more stable base for funding sustained partnerships, and fifth, create the infrastructure that is needed to support the workings of the community, including learning processes so that individuals can become skilled at the building of a collaborative inquiry community (Coghlan & Shani, Chapter 29). Sixth, we need to create the necessary legitimacy and incentives both for junior researchers entering our field and for managers, to allow resources to be allocated in this direction. Finally, we need to conduct research that pushes the boundaries of our imagination, so that all involved are drawn to the possibilities that collaborative management research presents.

1. Confronting the epistemological and methodological differences that have prevented traditional management research from being carried out in a collaborative manner, and defining a set of epistemologies for collaborative management research.

Understanding the organization and other complex systems as artifacts (Simon, 1996) that are socially constructed through the actions of their agents leads to the conclusion that they cannot be fully understood independently of the knowledge, goals, purposes, interests, and preferences of the people who construct and continually enact them (Axelrod & Cohen, 1999; Holland, 1995). Such a perspective may be anathema to a "positivistic" social scientist who is seeking objective truth. On the other hand, most of the data-gathering, analytic, and pattern recognition techniques of traditional social scientists, including learning through experimentation, can be applied within the context of a research collaboration. Detecting patterns of behavior and their contribution to outcomes requires systematic research processes, whether within a collaborative setting or not. Many collaborating parties share the interest of academics in using exploration and discovery techniques that allow them to both challenge and transcend the assumptions that are built into their unique experiences and shared practice. We believe that the collaborative management research community must get beyond its tendency to label some research as traditional and therefore not valid. We believe that it is possible to do research *with* rather than *on* members of the system being studied and still conform to systematic knowledge-producing processes. We also believe that knowledge is produced and consumed by communities (departments, organizations, communities, networks) and that it is therefore not necessary to achieve randomness in order to generate knowledge. It is, however, necessary to test the boundary conditions of insights from one system through programs of research that are conducted in multiple settings.

2. Creating a shared set of methodologies.

To overcome the confusion created by the idiosyncratic alphabet soup of methodologies that is rapidly emerging, we need a compendium of methodologies for conducting collaborative management research that presents each methodology succinctly and compares and contrasts it with others. Like Campbell and Stanley's invaluable guide to quasi-experimental research, we need a methodological primer that helps us understand the strengths and weaknesses of each approach and how to use a variety of methods to strengthen our designs for research and the pursuit of knowledge.

This guide should begin at the beginning, with a discussion of the ways in which collaborative relationships are formed, directions agreed on, and solid partnerships built. It should cover the variety of methods available to partners for generating and validating data and also address the ways in which the implementation of findings from the research can be strengthened. Finally, it should address opportunities for enhancing the dissemination of knowledge in written, electronic, and oral forms.

One element of a shared set of methodologies might be the creation of road maps for the conduct of collaborative management research—varieties of paths that researchers may follow in establishing the foundation for research collaborations. We have seen in this volume that a variety of paths have been followed and developed, including intentional network development (e.g., Coghlan & Coughlan, Mirvis), consultation where the researcher is paid to provide value to the system and observes or measures the impact of change (Stebbins et al.; Tenkasi & Hay), institutional relationships that enable the examination of fundamental issues (Hatchuel & David; Adler & Beer; Mohrman et al.), and interventionist research, in which the academic researcher learns from collaborating in system self-development activities (Holmstrand et al.; Kolodny & Halpern). Although the pathways are different, they are characterized, we believe, by a generic set of issues that have to be resolved and gaps between academic researchers and practitioners that have to be crossed. Mohrman and Shani have proposed that at the starting point of most successful projects, the very large gap in the mutual understanding and commitment to the partnership between the academics and the practitioners must decrease. They noted that there are four ways in which this gap is closed: (1) alignment of purpose, (2) acknowledging institutional, contextual, and resource logics in the formulation of the research, (3) designing joint learning mechanisms, and finally, (4) developing shared language. The capacity for effective collaboration improves as the actors work through these issues.

3. Communicating the value of this approach within the academy and to potential practitioner-colleagues.

To build a larger and more vibrant community, we need to expand the circle of interested participants. There are a number of ways in which this could be accomplished. We offer the following suggestions for starters:

- Introduce collaborative management research methods into research training for doctoral students in management as well as into executive education programs and even basic educational programs.
- By publishing exemplary collaborative research in which knowledge results for both practice and theory, increase its legitimacy among research funders and create understanding of how to evaluate quality.
- Create a collaborative management research interest group at the Academy of Management and European Academy of Management.
- Develop a journal devoted to collaborative management research with very clear quality control guidelines that include actionability and the generation of knowledge for both theory and practice among the criteria.
- Introduce managers who have participated in this kind of research to one another so that they can begin forming a network.
- Publish accounts of some of the most interesting exemplars in management periodicals or the popular press in addition to academic publications.
- Learn from the future search network and appreciative inquiry network; create a virtual electronic community of those interested in collaborative management research.

To do these things would support the formation of a tradition, a competence, and a capacity for pursuing collaborative management research in organizations and would support its dissemination.

4. Developing support for sustained partnerships.

It is interesting that one of the most challenging hurdles to overcome is securing continuing financial support for collaborative management research. Despite the fact that many companies and governmental organizations spend up to 10% of their total turnover on R&D endeavors and almost nothing on management research, it is still hard to motivate investments in management research. While individual scholars will continue to create their own opportunities, the press of doing the research, writing up the results, and carrying out other responsibilities makes it difficult for academics to concentrate on the fundraising, grant-writing, and community building so important to the advancement of this approach. Many of the examples of collaborative management research in this volume are one-time incidences that are unlikely to be repeated in the same system or other systems. Sustained support would allow more rapid diffusion, the creation of multiple case studies to test the limits of knowledge that is derived from one system, and more attention to implementing benefits and publishing results versus having to chase the next research opportunity.

It is not a coincidence that a number of the "academics" associated with collaborative management research work in institutes, consulting firms, or other nontraditional academic settings. These organizations provide a context that encourages and enables their members to interact with practitioners. The support for these organizations is frequently based in total or in part upon the ability of its members to establish collaborative working relationships with managers, so the skills required to do so are developed and people who can succeed at creating successful relationships are selected in while others are selected out.

Regardless of their organizational affiliation, scholars interested in collaborative management research would do well to learn the skills involved in creating effective industry or government-academic partnerships. More broadly, it would be wise for members of the collaborative management research community to make certain that leaders of government funding agencies, industry research consortiums, heads of organization development, and other professional groups are aware and knowledgeable of the approach. Creating a critical mass of participants and supporters for this kind of research, both within academic institutions and within organizations, will be important. While few countries may provide the level of support for this work offered by Sweden over the past decade, the example can be used to educate and inform others so that new funding possibilities might be created.

5. Creating the infrastructure to sustain a community of interest.

The infrastructure to sustain a global community of interest like this one usually consists of journals, conferences, a membership network, training institutions, organizations that provide employment possibilities, and a Web site for storing and exchanging information. At the moment, we have none of these in place, with the possible exception of a loose network of interested individuals. Obviously, there is much work to be done if the community is to grow and thrive. The contributors to this volume represent the nucleus of that community, but the nucleus is currently too small and too busy with other commitments to devote the amount of energy that would be required to create the elements of infrastructure outlined above. The more who join the community, the faster its development will be; as the old adage goes, many hands make light work. But perhaps even more important than gaining in numbers alone would be finding the few with the passion to step forward and organize the network, create the Web site, and do the work of building the infrastructure so that others may benefit. These are generous souls, and we hope they are out there among us.

6. Creating the necessary legitimacy and incentives both for junior researchers entering our field and for managers.

Accomplishing the first five imperatives in this list will go a long way toward creating legitimacy and changing the incentives that are at work. By building the infrastructure to create a community, and by clarifying the epistemology, methodologies, and standards, this work becomes associated with a community of practice that evolves relevant knowledge by sharing, analyzing, and making sense of experiences with collaborative management research. By disseminating learning and increasing awareness of the collaborative research processes that have generated important knowledge for the academy and for practice, the community will demonstrate value that transcends the particular collaborators in the research. Assuming that the collaborations do indeed deliver demonstrable value that is acknowledged for both practice and the academy, the legitimacy of this approach should increase in both. Generating some high visibility exemplars that can both inspire confidence and excitement and concretize the concepts of collaborative research for students and practitioners who are interested in learning how to do it is critical to the development of this methodology. This is described next.

7. Conducting groundbreaking work that enlarges our collective understanding of the tremendous possibilities that can be realized using this approach.

In the end, success sells itself, as so it shall be with collaborative management research. When studies are published in top journals because they are too compelling to be denied, recognition in scholarly circles will follow. When results achieved make organizations that participate in collaborative research vastly more effective than their competitors, or create significant improvements compared with past performance, leaders will take notice. The more audacious, innovative, wide-reaching, and visible this work is, the faster we will make progress in solidifying the future of the community. Small efforts will add to the mix, but landmark studies have been and will remain the currency of the realm when it comes to attracting attention as well as interest in further exploration.

With all that said, creating a more sustainable community of interest in collaborative management research will take hard work, despite the promise the approach affords. Many other methodologies will make claims for legitimacy and attention over the next few decades, and whether collaborative management research remains of interest will be determined not only by the efforts of those who are supportive but also by the efforts of those who would offer other solutions. We can predict with certainty that the issues facing for-profit, not-for-profit, and governmental organizations will only grow in intensity in the coming years. Solutions will be needed and sought. Collaborative management research offers tremendous potential and can play an important role in generating solutions to the difficult management challenges that are faced in today's world—providing that we do the work that needs to be done.

REFERENCES

Axelrod, R., & Cohen, M. (1999). *Harnessing complexity: Organizational implications of a scientific frontier.* New York: Free Press.

Holland, J. H. (1995). *Hidden order: How adaptation builds complexity.* Reading, MA: Helix Press.

Simon, H. A. (1996). *The science of the artificial.* Cambridge: MIT Press.

Author Index

Subject Index

About the Authors

Ibrahim Abu Elhaija is managing director of the Nazareth-based Masar Institute for Education and is a founder of its alternative school. He is a founder of the Action Research Center and a member of the ARC research team at the Max Stern Academic College of Emek Yezreel and is cochairperson of its steering committee. Since moving from the fields of marketing and hi-tech 10 years ago, he has led development of new visions in education using action research methods. He has supervised participatory action research dealing with issues such as collaborative management methods in schools, developing critical thinking through language teaching, and the use of swimming classes as a means of perceiving reality in new ways. He has been a project facilitator in the Ministry of Education's Division of Experiments and Initiatives.

Niclas Adler is a professor in business administration and dean at Jonkoping International Business School. He is the founding director of the FENIX Centre for Innovations in Management and the founding president of the Stockholm School of Entrepreneurship, and he is engaged as a researcher at the Stockholm School of Economics, the Chalmers University of Technology, l'École des Mines de Paris, the Institute for Management of Innovation and Technology, and the Sunningdale Institute in the UK. His work has been published in such scientific journals as *Human Relations*, *R&D Management*, and *European Management Review* and by Sage, Oxford University Press,

Open University Press, and Elsevier Science. In addition to his academic engagements, he is the cofounder of 14 companies, is engaged as director at TruePoint Partners, Boston, and is a board member in seven technology-based companies.

Catrina Alferoff has worked on a number of ESRC- and EU- funded projects and also carried out independent research. Most recently she has worked on the ESRC project "The Dynamics of Knowledge Production in the Business School: A Comparative Study," focusing on the topic of business school-industry collaborative networks and forums. Recent publications have been on call centers, the delivery of financial services in the home, and out-of-hours health provision.

Mikael Apel, Ph.D. (economics), is senior economist at the Division for Applied Research at the Monetary Policy Department of the Riksbank (the Swedish central bank), where he was first employed in 1994. From 2001 to 2003, he worked at the National Institute of Economic Research. He has also acted as secretary on government commissions on responsibility for exchange rate policy and on stabilization policy in the monetary union.

Gabriele Bammer is a professor at the National Centre for Epidemiology and Population Health in the College of Medicine and Health Sciences at the Australian National University and a research fellow at the Hauser Center for Nonprofit Organizations at Harvard University. She is developing a new cross-cutting specialization—integration and implementation sciences—to provide new concepts and methods to enhance knowledge by drawing on multiple disciplines and practice areas, as well as to increase the uptake of research in practice.

Jean M. Bartunek is the Robert A. and Evelyn J. Ferris Chair and professor of organization studies at Boston College. Her doctorate in social and organizational psychology is from the University of Illinois at Chicago. She is a fellow and past president of the Academy of Management and an associate editor of the *Journal of Applied Behavioral Science*. Her research focuses on organizational change, conflict, and social cognition, and on methodologies by which inside members and external researchers can collaborate to study organizations. She is coeditor with Mary Ann Hinsdale and James Keenan of *Church Ethics and Its Organizational Context: Learning From the Sex Abuse Scandal in the Catholic Church* (Rowman and Littlefield, 2006).

Michael Beer is Cahners-Rabb Professor of Business Administration, Emeritus, at the Harvard Business School, and cofounder and chairman of TruePoint Partners and the not-for-profit TruePoint Center for High Commitment and Performance. Prior to joining the Harvard faculty, Dr. Beer was director of organization research and development at Corning, Inc. His research and writing are in organization effectiveness, organizational change, and human resource management. Dr. Beer has authored or coauthored nine books and numerous articles and book chapters. He has received several awards for his writing and professional contributions and is a fellow of the Society of Industrial & Organizational Psychology and the Academy of Management.

Richard E. Boyatzis is professor in the departments of organizational behavior and psychology at Case Western Reserve University and an adjunct professor at ESADE in Barcelona. He is the author of more than 150 articles and books that include *The Competent Manager;* the international best-seller *Primal Leadership,* coauthored with Daniel Goleman and Annie McKee (published in 29 languages); and *Resonant Leadership,* coauthored with Annie McKee (published in 18 languages). Professor Boyatzis has a B.S. in aeronautics and astronautics from MIT and an M.S. and a Ph.D. in social psychology from Harvard University.

Hilary Bradbury, Ph.D., is director of sustainable business programs at the University of Southern California's Center for Sustainable Cities and an associate research professor in the College of Letters, Arts, and Sciences. She brings her expertise in action research—a community design approach—to work with businesses dealing with sustainable development. She was previously associate professor of organizational behavior at Case University's Weatherhead School of Management. She has published widely in journals including *Organization Science* and *Academy of Management Executive.* She is coeditor of the Sage journal *Action Research* and of the *Handbook of Action Research* (2001, 2007). She grew up in Ireland and lived and worked in Germany, Switzerland, and Japan. She now lives in Los Angeles with her family.

David Coghlan is at the School of Business, Trinity College, Dublin, Ireland, and is a Fellow of the College. He specializes in organization development and action research and is active in both communities internationally. He is currently on the editorial review boards of several journals, including *Action Research* and the *Journal of Applied Behavioral Science.* His recent coauthored books include *Doing Action Research in Your Own Organization* (2nd ed., Sage, 2005) and *Organizational Change and Strategy* (Routledge, 2006).

Susan G. Cohen was a senior research scientist at the Center for Effective Organizations in the Marshall School of Business at the University of Southern California. She has coauthored and/or edited books, articles, and book chapters about teams and teamwork, employee involvement and empowerment, and human resource strategies. Her most recent books are, with Don Mankin, *Business Without Boundaries: An Action Framework for Collaborating Across Time, Distance, Organization and Culture* (Jossey-Bass, 2004); and, with Don Mankin and Tora Bikson, *Teams and Technology: Fulfilling the Promise of the New Organization* (Harvard Business School Press, 1996). With Cristina Gibson, she edited *Virtual Teams That Work: Creating Conditions for Virtual Team Effectiveness* (Jossey-Bass, 2003).

Paul Coughlan has, since 1993, researched, taught, and published in the areas of operations management and product development at the University of Dublin, School of Business, Trinity College, Ireland. He holds a Ph.D. from the University of Western Ontario, Canada, and M.B.A. and B.E. degrees from University College, Cork, Ireland. He is president of the board of the European Institute for Advanced Studies in Management and a member of the board of the European Operations Management Association.

Albert David is professor of management at l'École Normale Supérieure, France. He has been collaborating with the Centre de Gestion Scientifique (l'École des Mines de Paris) for many years. He recently created M-Lab, an "R&D in management" research team. Albert David's publications are about the structure and dynamics of management innovation and the epistemology of management research.

Helena Syna Desevillia is a social-organizational psychologist by training and a faculty member at the sociology anthropology department at the Max Stern Academic College of Emek Yezreel. There, she is among the founders of the Action Research Center and serves on its steering committee. Her research focuses on interpersonal and intergroup relations in organizations, especially on intragroup dynamics, processes of cooperation versus competition, team building, and development of partnerships. She has an expertise in program evaluation of social projects and, recently, a special interest in action research. She is on the editorial board of *Conflict Resolution Quarterly*, *Negotiation and Conflict Management Research*, and the *International Journal of Conflict Management* and publishes her work in these as well as organization-related journals.

Peter Docherty, Ph.D., D.Sc., is a member of the faculty of the Institute for Management of Innovation and Technology at Chalmers University of Technology in Gothenburg, Sweden, and senior researcher at ATK Arbetsliv. He was formerly professor at the National Institute for Working Life, Stockholm. His research is mainly in the fields of learning at the individual, group, organization, and network levels and the organization and management of sustainable organizations.

Martha Farrell received an M.S.W. from Delhi School of Social Work in 1981. She is currently the director of the Society for Participatory Research in Asia's (PRIA's) Continuing and Distance Education Programme, where programs on civil society building, panchayati raj, urban governance, gender mainstreaming, and participatory development are being developed. Ms. Farrell has coauthored several books for children on environmental issues. She has also prepared learning materials and manuals on gender and other developmental issues. She is the chairperson of the Society for Participatory Research in Asia's (PRIA's) Committee for Gender Awareness and Mainstreaming. Her experience in gender issues includes conducting training programs for a range of different audiences.

Victor J. Friedman is associate professor of organizational behavior with a joint appointment in behavioral sciences and sociology-anthropology at the Max Stern Academic College of Emek Yezreel. He is a founder of the Action Research Center and is cochairperson of the Steering Committee. His life's work has been to help individuals, groups, organizations, and communities learn through "action science"—ongoing experimentation and critical reflection in everyday life. He works with educational, social service, and business organizations to promote organizational learning, social entrepreneurship, and social inclusion. He is a senior associate of the Action Evaluation Research Institute and is on the editorial board of *Action Research*. He is an author, with R. Lipshitz and M. Popper, of *The Demystification of Organizational Learning* (Sage, 2006).

Denis Gregory teaches labor relations and labor economics at Ruskin College, Oxford. He has been a consultant to the Trade Union Research Unit at Ruskin for more than 30 years, supporting many UK unions as a consultant and trainer. He is also an associate consultant to the TUC Partnership Institute.

Larry Greiner is professor of management and organization at the University of Southern California, where he currently serves as academic director of the school's Shanghai Global Executive MBA Program. Professor Greiner is the author of numerous publications on the subjects of organization growth and development, management consulting, and strategic change.

Goolabri Group is a collaborative research team that included Professor Bammer and Robyn Attewell, Stephen Buckman, Ann Curthoys, Kate Delaney, Stephen Dovers, Liz Furler, Sasha Grishin, Alan Hájek, John Handmer, Judith Jones, Steve Longford, John Mackey, Michael McFadden, Michael Moore, Paul Perkins, Pascal Perez, Stephen Pickard, Aileen Plant, John Quiggin, Alison Ritter, Michael Smithson, and Ian White.

Norman Halpern is president of Halpern Associates, Inc., a Toronto, Canada-based firm specializing in organization design. He is adjunct professor in the department of mechanical and industrial engineering at the University of Toronto.

Gunilla Härnsten, Ph.D., is professor of education at Växjö University, with a special focus on adult education and gender. Over the years, her research has become more and more participatory and inspired by feminist research. She is the author of *The Research Circle: Building Knowledge on Equal Terms* (2003).

Armand Hatchuel is professor and deputy director of the Center for Management Science at l'École des Mines de Paris and a guest professor at the FENIX Centre, Chalmers Institute, Gothenburg, Sweden. His research is on the theory and history of management and design, focusing on innovative firms, design processes, and collaborative research principles. He has published books and papers and is on the editorial boards of international journals and on national scientific boards in France and Sweden. In 1996, he was awarded a French prize for his work in management, and in 2003 he received the medal of the School of Arts and Crafts for his work on design theory. He is also columnist for management issues at the French newspaper *Le Monde*.

George W. Hay, Ph.D., is a scholar-practitioner of business research and organization development and change. He is a director of Global Consumer and Business Insight at McDonald's Corporation. His academic interests involve the creation of actionable knowledge, critical realism as a model for organization change, and executives as internal change agents.

Lars Heikensten, Ph.D. (economics), was from 1972 to 1984 a researcher and teacher at the Stockholm School of Economics. In 1985, he was appointed assistant undersecretary at the Swedish Ministry of Finance and in 1990 undersecretary for economic affairs. He became chief economist at Svenska Handelsbanken in 1992, deputy governor of the Swedish central bank responsible for monetary policy in 1995, and governor in 2003. He has held several board positions in government agencies, companies, and universities. He has also represented Sweden at the International Monetary Fund (IMF), the Bank for International Settlements (BIS), and the European Central Bank (ECB). Since 2006, he has been a member of the European Court of Auditors.

Lars Holmstrand, Ph.D., is professor of education at Växjö University. He has a broad research background in traditional educational areas. For over two decades he has also been engaged in working-life research. His main interests are research circles and democratic knowledge processes.

Anita Howard is a Ph.D. candidate in the department of organizational behavior at Weatherhead School of Management, Case Western Reserve University. Her research interests are emotional and social intelligence, leadership, intentional change, and executive coaching. She is an executive coach and organizational consultant with experience in corporate, nonprofit, and educational settings. Before coming to Weatherhead, she cofounded a management consulting company and codeveloped training models to enhance the performance of African American and nontraditional performers in secondary school, college, and professional settings. She also worked in college administration at Radcliffe College, Harvard University, and Tufts University.

Tony Huzzard is currently an associate professor at the Department of Business Administration, Lund University, and was formerly visiting research fellow at the National Institute for Working Life in Malmö. He has researched and published widely on organizational development, work organization, and industrial relations.

Per Jansson, Ph.D. (economics), is associate professor of economics at the University of Uppsala. Since 2006, he has been state secretary at the Ministry of Finance. Previously, he was deputy director at the Monetary Policy Department of the Swedish central bank, where he was first employed in 1995. From 2001 to 2003, he worked at the National Institute of Economic Research.

David Knights is professor of organizational analysis in the School of Economic and Management Studies at Keele University. He is a founding and continuing editor of the journal *Gender, Work and Organisation* and has published widely in the field of management and organization analysis. His most recent books are *Management Lives: Power and Identity in Work Organisation* (Sage, 1999) (with H. Willmott); *Organization and Innovation: Gurus Schemes and American Dreams* (Open University Press, 2003) (with D. McCabe); and (with H. Willmott) *Introducing Organizational Behaviour and Management* (Thomson Learning, 2007).

Harvey Kolodny is professor emeritus with the Rotman School of Management and the Faculty of Applied Science and Engineering at the University of Toronto. His current research, writing, and academic work are in the areas of change management, project management, and organization design.

Ed Kur teaches in the organization change doctoral program at Pepperdine University. He has published in *Training and Development, Supervisory Management, Personnel Administrator, Journal of Management Inquiry,* and *Leadership and Organization Development.* He has taught at Arizona State University, Universidad de Monterrey, and Loyola Marymount University. He has consulted nationally and internationally on team-based systems, organization change, leadership development, organization design, and strategic planning in many industries. He has worked with Motorola, SmithKline Beecham, VLSI Technology, Phelps Dodge, Boehringer Engelheim, Sundstrand, Marion Merrell Dow, American Express, Taco Bell, and Bank One. His Ph.D. is from UCLA.

Jan Löwstedt, Ph.D., is professor of business administration at Mälardalen University. He is currently conducting research on integration processes in company mergers, knowledge collaboration in and between organizations, and the management of school organizations. His most recent book is *Producing Management Knowledge* (2006, coedited with T. Stjernberg).

John McGuire's diverse work history includes senior business management positions in private and not-for-profit organizations; he is president of the McGuire Consulting Group. John is currently a senior faculty member at the Center for Creative Leadership and holds master's degrees from Harvard and Brandeis University.

Philip H. Mirvis is an organizational psychologist whose research and private practice concern large-scale organizational change and the character of the workforce and workplace. A consultant to businesses in the United States, Europe, Latin America, and Asia, he has authored eight books on his studies, including *The Cynical Americans* (social trends), *Building the Competitive Workforce* (human resource investments), and *Joining Forces* (the human side of mergers). His most recent book is a business transformation story, *To the Desert and Back.* Mirvis is currently a senior research fellow, Boston College, Center for Citizenship.

Allan M. Mohrman Jr. was a founding member of the Center for Effective Organizations (CEO) in the Marshall School of Business at the University of Southern California. His research and publications focus on performance management, organization design, team-based organizations, and research methodologies that bridge theory and practice.

Susan Albers Mohrman is senior research scientist at the Center for Effective Organizations (CEO) in the Marshall School of Business at the University of Southern California. Her research and publications focus on organizational design for lateral integration and flexibility, networks in basic science, management of knowledge and knowledge workers, organizational change and implementation, and research methodologies for bridging theory and practice. She is cofounder and a faculty director of CEO's certificate program in organization design.

Ernesto Olascoaga was the founder, in 1976, of Grupo Visión Global (GVG), a consulting firm. He specializes in strategic change management, leadership development, and organization/process redesign for collaborative work systems. As a business coach and consultant, Ernesto has helped thousands of leaders and teams in organizations from a wide range of sectors to keep focused and aligned while executing their strategies. His passion has been to blend his organizational change competencies with information technology products for achieving performance enhancement through productive participation. He has worked with General Motors, Coca-Cola, Unilever, SCA, Roche, Pizza Hut, and Pepsico International. He received his master's degree in organizational behavior from Brigham Young University and his doctorate in organizational change from Pepperdine University.

Michal Palgi is the chair of the department of sociology and anthropology at the Max Stern Academic College of Emek Yezreel and a senior researcher at the Institute for Research of the Kibbutz and the Cooperative Idea at Haifa University. She is a founder of the Action Research Center and a member of its Steering Committee. Her research, publications, and activity are in the areas of organizational democracy, organizational change, gender-based inequality, social justice, kibbutz society, organization democracy, and community development. Professor Palgi is an adviser to the Austrian-German research project ODEM (Organizational Democracy—resources of organizations for social behavior readiness conducive to democracy). She is the coeditor of the *Journal for Rural Cooperation.*

Charles J. Palus, Ph.D., is a senior faculty member in research and innovation at the Center for Creative Leadership. Palus is the author and designer of numerous publications, programs, and products related to creativity and leadership, including The Leader's Edge, the Leading Creatively program, and Visual Explorer.

William A. Pasmore (Ph.D., Purdue University) is a partner at Oliver Wyman Delta Organization & Leadership Consulting in New York. He works with CEOs and senior executives on organization change, organization design, and executive development/ succession. As a former full professor at Case Western Reserve University, he taught in the Weatherhead School of Management's programs at the Ph.D., M.B.A., and under-graduate levels and served as director of the

master's degree program in organization development. He is the author or editor of more than 20 books, including the series *Research in Organizational Change and Development* with Richard Woodman. He currently resides in Maine.

Brigette Rapisarda, ED.M., is director of training for Royal Caribbean Cruise Lines.

George Roth is a senior research associate in MIT's Sloan School of Management and Lean Aerospace Initiative program. His research examines leadership, culture, learning, and change, with a current focus on change across sets of organizations (enterprise value streams). George has been a part of many collaborative research efforts and has coauthored four books, including *The Dance of Change* and *To the Desert and Back.*

Michal Shamir is a teaching assistant at the Max Stern Academic College of Emek Yezreel, where she received her B.A. in organizational behavior and human resources from the department of sociology and anthropology. She is currently studying for a research M.A. in applied sociological research at Haifa University, specializing in the transfer and use of knowledge through social networks linking individuals in organizations. She is among the founders of the Action Research Center and a member of its Steering Committee. She teaches courses in research methods, anthropology, human services, introductory sociology, and Israeli society.

Orit Shamir is a teaching assistant at the Max Stern Academic College of Emek Yezreel, where she received her B.A. in organizational behavior and human resources from the department of sociology and anthropology. She is among the founders of the Action Research Center and a member of its Steering Committee. She is a doctoral student in sociology and anthropology at the University of Haifa, specializing in distance learning in organizations. She teaches courses in research methods, organizational theory, introductory sociology, and Israeli society.

A. B. (Rami) Shani is professor and chair of the Management Area at the Orfalea College of Business at California Polytechnic State University and a visiting adjunct professor at the FENIX Centre for Innovations in Management at the Chalmers University of Technology, Sweden. He has held visiting professorship appointments at the Stockholm School of Economics, Sweden; Politecnico di Milano, Italy; and Recanati Graduate School of Business Administration, Tel Aviv University, Ramat Aviv, Israel. He also served on the board of the Organization Development and Change division of the Academy of Management for five years and acted as chair of the division. His research and publications focus on work and organization design, organizational change and development, collaborative research methodologies, learning in and by organizations, and new product development. His most recent books include *Creating Sustainable Work Systems, Learning by Design,* and *Collaborative Research in Organizations.*

Aneika L. Simmons is an assistant professor at Sam Houston State University in Huntsville, Texas. She received her Ph.D. in management from Texas A&M University in 2006. She also has a B.B.A. from the University of Texas at Austin and an M.A. from the University of Houston. Her primary research interests are related to individual creative performance, organizational justice, and discrimination issues.

Ken Starkey is professor of management and organizational learning and head of the strategy division at Nottingham University Business School. His research interests include strategy and learning, the theory and practice of organization and organization

development, and management education. He is author of 10 books, including *How Organisations Learn* (International Thomson Press, 2004), and of over 100 articles in journals such as *Sociology, Strategic Management Journal, Academy of Management Review,* and *Organization Science.* He is former chair of the British Academy of Management Research Committee and author of a number of reports on the future of management research and management education. He is currently writing *The Future of the Business School* for Cambridge University Press.

Michael W. Stebbins, Ph.D., is emeritus professor of organization design at Cal Poly's Orfalea College of Business. His consulting and research interests include new product development, change processes, and building sustainable work systems. In retirement, his interests include travel with his wife, Margaret, gardening, and visiting his new granddaughter, Stella Buckley.

Bengt Stymne is professor emeritus of organization theory at the Stockholm School of Economics. At present he is carrying out a study of how different regions in the world succeed in encouraging their firms, entrepreneurs, and scientists to make product innovations. He was a cofounder and management director of the Scandinavian Institutes of Administrative Research and has been a managing director of the Economics Research Institute in Stockholm and of the Institute for Management of Innovation and Technology in Gothenburg, Sweden. He is a founder of the Stockholm School of Entrepreneurship and was director of research at the FENIX Centre. He has published books and articles on organization design and strategy, organizational values, industrial democracy, IT and management, and research methodology.

Israel Sykes has master's degrees in organizational behavior from Tel Aviv University and in family therapy from

Hahneman University in Philadelphia. He has worked over the years as a therapist, social entrepreneur, organizational consultant, and researcher. He is currently a freelance organizational consultant specializing in social service development and social entrepreneurship.

Rajesh Tandon is an internationally acclaimed leader and practitioner of participatory research and development. In 1982, he founded the Society for Participatory Research in Asia (PRIA), a voluntary organization providing support to grassroots initiatives in South Asia. He has a Ph.D. from Case Western Reserve University. Dr. Tandon has served on government task forces and committees and has also held key positions in national and international organizations. He has published in the areas of participatory research, participatory training, NGO-government relations, NGO management, and the role of civil society and voluntary development organizations in development. His recent publications include *Does Civil Society Matter? Governance in Contemporary India* (coeditor), Sage, 2003; *Voluntary Action, Civil Society and the State*, Mosaic Books, New Delhi, 2002; *Civil Society and Governance* (coauthor), Sanskriti, New Delhi, 2002; *Participatory Research: Revisiting the Roots* (editor), Mosaic Books, New Delhi, 2002; and *Reviving Democracy* (coauthor), Earthscan, UK, 2002.

Scott Taylor, Ph.D., is assistant professor in the Department of Organizational Behavior at Boston University.

Ramkrishnan (Ram) V. Tenkasi is professor with the Ph.D. program in Organization Development and Change at Benedictine University. His research and practice interests cover the topics of organizational knowledge, learning, innovation, and change. Multiple grants from federal agencies and private corporations have supported his research in the above areas.

Nick Tiratsoo has worked at a number of British universities and is now retired. He has published widely in the fields of British contemporary history, planning history, and business history and has edited, with Duncan Tanner and Pat Thane, *Labour's First Century* (Cambridge University Press, 2000). He is affiliated with the Business History Unit, London School of Economics.

Bill Torbert taught at Yale, SMU, and Harvard before coming to Boston College as graduate dean and later director of the Ph.D. program in Organizational Transformation. A board member of Trillium Asset Management and various academic journals, Torbert has also consulted widely in Europe, Latin America, and the United States.

Judy L. Valenzuela, Pharm. D., is pharmacy services director for Orange County in Kaiser Permanente's Southern California Region. She has more than 25 years' experience in pharmacy management and is responsible for outpatient, inpatient, ambulatory care, and drug education/utilization services for a patient population of more than 350,000 health plan members.

Mary Lindenstein Walshok, Ph.D., is associate vice chancellor for public programs at the University of California, dean of the University Extension, and adjunct professor of sociology. She has been a visiting professor at the Stockholm School of Economics and in 2004 held an international appointment at Oxford University. Walshok is responsible for UCSD's outreach programs including executive education, continuing professional education, UCSD-TV, and a variety of community and economic development initiatives. She has authored many chapters and journal articles and two books: *Blue Collar Women* and *Knowledge Without Boundaries*. The latter deals with the role of research universities in the economy. She has received many awards, including the Kellogg Foundation's Leadership Fellowship, and was recently inducted into Sweden's Royal Order of the Polar Star.

Andreas Werr is an associate professor at the Stockholm School of Economics. His research interests include different aspects of management consulting, professional service firms, and interorganizational collaboration. He has acted as supervisor in several collaborative executive Ph.D. projects.

Stu Winby is founder and managing partner of Sapience-Silicon Valley and of Innovation Point, two Silicon Valley firms specializing in strategy, organization, and innovation. He has more than 30 years of executive and management experience in organization strategy and effectiveness. As director and general manager for Hewlett-Packard's Strategic Change Organization, he innovated and introduced new management technologies to the company and the field.

Richard W. Woodman (Ph.D., Purdue University) is the Fouraker Professor of Business and Professor of Management at Texas A&M University, where he teaches organizational behavior, organizational change, organizational creativity and innovation, and research methodology. He is editor of the *Journal of Applied Behavioral Science* and coeditor of the annual series *Research in Organizational Change and Development*, published by Elsevier. His research interests focus on organizational change and organizational creativity. In a previous life, Dr. Woodman was a military intelligence officer in the U.S. Army, worked in both the petroleum and banking industries, and served for several years as vice president of a financial institution.